David Powell

The History of Wales

Comprehending the lives and succession of the princes of Wales, from Cadwalader the last king, to Lhewelyn the last prince, of British blood. With a short account of the affairs of Wales, under the kings of England.

David Powell

The History of Wales
Comprehending the lives and succession of the princes of Wales, from Cadwalader the last king, to Lhewelyn the last prince, of British blood. With a short account of the affairs of Wales, under the kings of England.

ISBN/EAN: 9783337393090

Printed in Europe, USA, Canada, Australia, Japan

Cover: Foto ©ninafisch / pixelio.de

More available books at **www.hansebooks.com**

THE HISTORY OF WALES.

Comprehending the

Lives and Succession

OF THE

PRINCES of *WALES*;

FROM

CADWALADER the laſt King, to *Lhewelyn* the laſt Prince, of *Britiſh* Blood.

WITH

A ſhort Account of the Affairs of *WALES*, under the Kings of *England*.

Written originally in *Britiſh*, by *Caradoc* of *Lhancarvan*; and formerly publiſhed in *Engliſh* by Dr. *Powel*.

Now newly augmented and improved by W. *WYNNE*, A. M. and Fellow of *Jeſus* Colledg, *Oxon*.

LONDON:

Printed by *M. Clark*, for the Author, and are to be ſold by *R. Clavell*, at the Peacock at the Weſt-End of S. *Pauls*. 1697.

TO THE

Right Revd Father in GOD,

HUMPHREY

Lord BISHOP of

B A N G O R.

My Lord,

WHEN I had finiſhed the following Book, I was not long to determin under whoſe Patronage I ſhould make it publick; your Lordſhip's Extraordinry Knowledge in all the *Britiſh* Antiquities, eſpecially that Part which relates to the *Welch*,

A 2   juſtly

DEDICATION.

juftly claiming what I now make bold to offer to your Favour. For it feems to be as Natural a Defign of a Dedication, to prefent one's Labours to the greateft Judge, as to him who is the greateft Encourager of his Writings; and if fo, my Lord, this fingle Reafon would fufficiently juftify me from any Prefumption, in fubmitting the following Papers to your Lordfhip's Protection. But where the Obligation is corroborated by an equal Engagement; and fince your Lordfhip has been pleafed to encourage and promote the Defign before it came to any Growth, I hope, I may fafely prefent now in its perfect Strength and Vigor, what you were then pleafed to receive in its Infancy.

The Hiftory of our Country, my Lord, has been fo much neglected, that there feems a very great Neceffity of reviving, what to the generality of the Kingdom, is almoft loft;

and

DEDICATION.

and there are too many, otherwise very Learned Persons, nay, some of our own Nation, who are so great Strangers to this Subject, that they are almost ignorant, that there is such a History in being. We have hopes indeed, that from your Lordship's Excelling Knowledge in the *Welch* History, and other *British* Antiquities, with those Curious Collections, you have with great Labour made towards that Matter, and from others now Travelling the same good Way; we may expect, that the World shall receive such Information relating to our Country, that they who have hitherto despised our History, will be ready to Light that Candle which they now purposely extinguish, and ignorantly undervalue. In the mean time, if by the following History, I can revive the Memories of the several Princes therein contained, which in the *English* Histories, are either totally omitted, or but partially interwoven,

DEDICATION.
woven, and render our History more generally Known, I have my Aim; and especially, since I gain the Opportunity of Acknowledging my self,

Your Lordship's

most humble Servant,

W. WYNNE.

THE

THE PREFACE.

THE *History of the* Britains, *may not improperly be distinguished into two Periods; the former comprehending the interval from* Brute *to* Cadwalader, *whilst the* Britains *are thought to have enjoyed a general Possession of the whole Island; the other containing the Memoirs and Transactions of the* Britains, *under their several Princes, after their recession to that part of the Island, since called* Wales. *The former of these has been generally accounted of late, absolutely false and unhistorical; and 'tis undoubtedly concluded that all the Passages in* Geoffrey *of* Monmouth *(the only remaining Monument of the Affairs of the antient* Britains*) which are not consonant to, and agreeable with the* Roman *Historians that speak of* Britain, *are absolutely fabulous and unsincere. The History of the Princes of* Wales, *has indeed met with better fortune, and the Author* Caradoc *of* Lhancarvan *is accounted just and authentick; so that there need no other Apology for the following Work, than that it is for the best part the genuine History of that Author. But because the History of* Wales *has no small dependance upon, and relation to the History of the antient* Britains *published by* Geoffrey, *I think it necessary*

The PREFACE.

necessary to make some general reflection, in relation to the Truth and Authority of that Copy.

And here in the first place, I must take notice of two sorts of Opinions, most widely repugnant, and as I may say, diametrically opposite to each other; and both in my opinion, equally deviating from the right apprehension of the matter in debate. The one, perfectly rejecting the whole foundation and process of Geoffrey's History, will not believe so much as one passage relating to the antient Britains, but what is delivered by Roman Writers; as if nothing remarkable could happen in Britain, but what must needs fall under their special Cognizance and Observation. The other, without any allowance to the Age when these British Affairs were transacted, (not to mention the utmost Antiquity of some part of this History, cotemporary with which, nothing is certain among the more civilized Greeks and Romans) will believe the whole Frame, and all the Circumstances of Geoffrey's History, be they never so ridiculous and extravagant. But not to insist on so bigotted an Opinion, as to think that the British History is universally true, and altogether authentick; I will confine my self to the examination of the other Extream, to see whether that History published by Geoffrey, be so absolutely fabulous as is frequently represented, and generally believed. Now they who discredit this History, either wholly attribute the Frame and Invention of it to Geoffrey, or else granting him to be a faithful Translator, assure themselves that the Copy he received was fictitious, and perfectly owing to the unwarrantable Forgeries of the fabulous Monks. So that the subject of my present enquiries, will naturally fall under these two

Disquisitions;

The PREFACE.

Difquifitions; 1. *Whether* Geoffrey *be the real Contriver and Compofer of this Hiftory? And* 2ly, *Suppofing him to be innocent of this Sufpicion, whether the Hiftory publifhed by him, be perfectly fabulous, and in all refpects a Monkifh Legend?*

1. *As to what relates to* Geoffrey, *though methinks there need no greater Argument to evidence his Innocency from fo fufpected an Impofture, as his being the Contriver of this Hiftory, than that he profeffedly owns the receipt of the* Britifh *Manufcript from* Walter, *Arch Deacon of* Oxford; *yet becaufe the Prejudice of fome Men oftentimes obfcures their Underftanding, in things otherwife very clear and open, it will be requifite to dwell fomewhat more particularly upon that Subject: or if the World be once perfwaded, that the whole Invention is owing to* Geoffrey, *and that there was no fuch Account of the* Britains *in being, before he publifhed his Hiftory; the whole feries of* Britifh *Affairs not mentioned in the Writings of the* Roman *Authors, and all that long continued Succeffion of* Britifh *Kings for fo many Ages, muft of neceffity be accounted fabulous, and a perfect Legend. But before that* Geoffrey *fhould be fo unreafonably attainted of fuch notorious Forgery, and his Hiftory be fo generally condemned; one might expect that fuch evident Proofs could be produced to evince fo abfolute a Pofition, as to render it paft all Difpute and Contradiction. For to charge any one with Infincerity, for no other reafon, than becaufe it is the common Vogue and Sentiment of the World, is in my opinion a greater Argument of Partiality and Prejudice, than of folid and judicious Reafoning.*

Now,

The PREFACE.

Now the greatest reason that I can think of, why the British *History is attributed to the invention of* Geoffrey, *is, that almost upon its first appearance in the World,* William *of* Newborough *and* Geraldus Cambrensis *exclaim against it, and seem to lay the whole Imposture to the charge of* Geoffrey. *The words of* Newborough *are these* ; At contra quidem *(speaking before of* Gildas) noſtris temporibus pro expiandis his Britonum maculis ſcriptor emerſit, ridicula de iiſdem figmenta contexens, eoſque longè ſupra virtutem Macedonum & Romanorum impudenti vanitate attollens. Gaufridus hic dictus eſt, Agnomen habens Arturi, pro eo quod fabulas de Arturo ex priſcis Britonum figmentis ſumptas, & ex proprio auctas per ſuperductum Latini ſermonis Colorem, honeſto hiſtoriæ nomine palliavit. Qui etiam majori auſu, cujuſdam Merlini divinationes fallaciſſimas, quibus utique de proprio plurimum adjecit, dum eas in Latinum transfunderet, tanquam Authenicas, & immobili veritate ſubnixas prophetias vulgavit.

From this Paſſage it is apprehended, that Newborough *thought that the* British *History was ſolely owing to the Contrivance and Invention of* Geoffrey; *whereas nothing is more evident, than that the only thing he lays to* Geoffrey's *charge, is, that he augmented, and of his own head made Additions to the Copy he received. And ſeeing that* Newborough *expreſly mentions* Geoffrey's *tranſlating into Latin, ſome antient Figments of the* Britains *concerning King* Arthur, *and unwarrantably adding to the ſame; it is manifeſtly apparent, that he never took* Geoffrey *to be the Contriver of the whole of what he publiſhed,*

The PREFACE.

lifhed, otherwife it is hardly conceivable, that such an inveterate Enemy of that Hiftory, would conceal any thing that might derogate from the Truth and Authority of it. Befides, Newborough throughout his whole Preface, wherein he endeavours to invallidate, and render the Britifh Hiftory fabulous, chiefly infifts upon the Life of King Arthur, and the Prophecies of Merlyn; not a word of Brutus and his Trojans, which, thô fince accounted as notorious a piece of Romance as any at all; it feems he had Faith to fwallow. Indeed, the Paffages in King Arthur's Life, and the Prophecies of Merlyn tending much to the fame purpofe, were too great and extravagant to be credited by him, (who by his Character of them, feems to have bore but very flender Affection towards the Welch) by reafon that they derogated much from the Fame and Valour of the Saxons; fo that I am afraid, that the Odium which Newborough bore to Geoffrey and his Hiftory, depended more upon National Honour and Reputation, than the Truth and Sincerity of Hiftory. For furely he could never be fo warmly exafperated againft a fabulous Hiftory, had he but the Candor to confult his own, unlefs there had been fome other motive to raife and foment his Paffion. As to the fcurrilous Language he cafts upon the Britifh Hiftory, and his unmannerly treatment of the Tranflator; he therein expreffes his Ignorance and Malice, rather than any Love and Regard to Truth and Ingenuity. For who but an ignorant and an unskilful Pretender, would confidently affert the Britains never had any Metropolitans or Archbifhops, and would produce this as an invincible Argument for the Falfity of the Britifh Hiftory; whereas it is notoriously

The PREFACE.

toriously manifest, that the Britains *had their Archbishops long before the arrival of* Augustine *the Monk, whom* Newborough *pretends to have been the first who underwent that Dignity in this Island. But as his Arguments against* Geoffrey's *History are weak and invalid, and his whole Preface more an Invective than a Confutation, so his Credit should be rejected and undervalued, for charging another History with falshood, when his own seems wholly interwoven with ridiculous Legends and Monkish Fictions.*

But be the occasion of Newborough's *dislike of the* British *History what it will, 'tis evident, that nothing can be concluded from the above quoted Passage, more than that* Geoffrey *made Additions to the* British *Copy he received of the Archdeacon of* Oxford. *And this is no more than what may easily and safely be granted; for the Life of King* Arthur, *and the Prophecies of* Merlyn, *the main Subjects of* Newborough's *Discontent, may probably be inserted into the History by* Geoffrey, *at least they were augmented, and several Traditions were added by him.* Bale, *assures us, that he writ the Life of King* Arthur *in a distinct Treatise; and himself owns in the Preface to his fourth Book, which comprehends the Prophecies of* Merlyn, *that upon the Request of* Alexander *Bishop of* Lincoln, *he had translated* Merlyn's *Prophecies out of* British *into* Latin, *before the* British *Copy came to his Hands. Now, when* Geoffrey *had received the Manuscript from the Archdeacon, and was engaged in translating it into* Latin, *'tis no strange matter to imagine, that as occasion required, he might amplify, and add to it, out of his former Tracts. For it is obvious to suppose, that the several things concerning* Arthur *and* Merlyn, *might be preserved*

in

The PREFACE.

in the Island of great Britain, *which were long ago obsolete among the* Britains *of* Armorica, *from whence the* British *Copy is said to have been brought over.*

But supposing that Newborough *had attributed the whole Frame of the* British *History to* Geoffrey, *which is evident he does not, his Authority cannot ballance with far more authentic Historians, such as* H. Huntington, R. Hovedon, Matthew *of* Westminster *and others, but more particularly* Matthew Paris, *who in express Terms, calls* Geoffrey, *Ad Ann.* The Faithful Translator of *the British History.* 1151. *And seeing then, that it was in those times apprehended to be an antient Manuscript, and none of* Geoffrey's *Contrivance, when the Cheat might be best discovered, and there wanted not good Inclinations to detect so notorious a Forgery; how in these latter times, it could be so luckily found out, that* Geoffrey *was the sole Inventor and Composer of the History, I cannot possibly divine.*

The other Reason, why Geoffrey *is thought to be* Camb. *the Author of the* British *History, is grounded upon* Descript. *a Passage in* Giraldus Cambrensis, *who speaking* Cap. 7. *of the Etymology of* Wales, *rejects the Denomination of it from either Duke* Wallo, *or Queen* Wendolen, licut fabulosa Galfredi Arturi mentitur Historia. *Now this is thought an invicible Argument against* Geoffrey, *and a palpable detection of his insincerity, since* Giraldus, *his own Country-man strikes at him, and accuses him of* Forgery; *whereas upon nicer examination, we may easily discover how that* Giraldus *quarrels only with the History which* Geoffrey *published, and which upon that account bore his Name. For had* Giraldus *thought it to be only a Contrivance of* Geoffrey's, *had he suspected that* Geoffrey *falsly pretended to have received an*

antient

The PREFACE.

antient British *Manuscript*, and by that means to have imposed upon the *World*; Can it be supposed that upon so plain Conviction of falshood, he would believe and give Credit to an *History*, which he was satisfied was altogether a *Fable*? But on the contrary, we find him assenting to the Story of Brutus, and the division of the *Island* betwixt his three Sons; and in short, excepting in this one place, he expresses himself to be an absolute *Votary* of the British *History*, whence 'tis evident, he apprehended Geoffrey to be no more than a faithful *Translator* of an antient British *Copy.*

I need not take notice of William of Malmsbury, because that by the best account, he is supposed to have been dead before Geoffrey published his History, and consequently he could never see it; so that this *Expression* in him, Hic est Arthurus de quo Britonum Nugæ hodieque delirant, *must likely* refer to the then present *Traditions and Accounts of* the Welch concerning King Arthur, which probably might be too great and extravagant. For 'tis certain that a traditional Account of any *Person* or *Action*, the farther it recedes from the Spring and Original, the more corrupt and imperfect it still proceeds; and like a Ball of Snow, it gathers and augments in its journey; so that it may be reasonably supposed, that the vulgar Account which the Welch in Malmsbury's time delivered of King Arthur, was too far incredible and surprising.

But since the Reasons produced for proving Geoffrey to be the Author of the British *History*, seem not to be satisfactory and evincing; let us see whether the contrary assertion can be more reasonably maintained. And first, 'tis manifest that Geoffrey could not be the total Inventor of the British *History*, by reason that several things, and some of the

Lib. I.

The PREFACE

the moſt material Paſſages therein contained, are agreeable with the Hiſtories of Gildas and Nennius, the Poetical Fragments of Talieſſyn, not to mention the Saxon Manuſcript, quoted by Mr. Wheelock, and other Authors far more antient than Geoffrey. 'Tis owned indeed Geoffrey might borrow the ground and Plat-form of his Romance from Merlyn or Talieſſyn, or rather from Nennius, in whoſe Writings there is ſome ſlight Account of the Britains being deſcended from the Trojans; but the ſuperſtructure is all his own, who living in an ignorant Age, and well knowing he could not well be diſproved, took the Liberty to make what Invention he pleaſed, and then recommended it to the World, for a true, undoubted Hiſtory. But notwithſtanding all this conceſſion, I think there is as little reaſon to attribute the Frame and Compoſition of this Hiſtory to Geoffrey, as there can be, to think him Contriver of the Ground and Plot of it. For it ſeems to me very unaccountable, that if Geoffrey was to invent and compoſe this Hiſtory, why in this account of the Tranſactions betwixt the Britains and Romans, he ſhould ſo widely diſagree with, and deviate from the Writings of the Roman Hiſtorians. For certainly, nothing could add more Authority to a Fable, than exactly to follow the ſteps of creditable Authors, in thoſe things they both had occaſion to treat of. This in all probability, would not only render that part of the Hiſtory unſuſpicious, but likewiſe Credit and Authorize the reſt, of which there was no account in Roman Authors. And this diſagreement betwixt the Britiſh Hiſtory, and the Writings of the Roman Hiſtorians, tho' frequently produced to overthrow the Authority of it, induces me to believe, not only that Geoffrey was not the Author, but likewiſe that the Manuſcript

Notes upon Bede.

The PREFACE.

Manuscript was antient, and much elder than the time, in which it was first made publick.

But besides, Geoffrey dedicates his Translation to Robert Earl of Glocester, Son to King Henry the First, which in all likelihood he would never have ventured to do, had the Original been of his own Contrivance, for fear least that the Cheat being discovered, he should be found, to put upon a Person of Eminent Quality, with whom the British History was then in great Esteem. For to him it is that Geoffrey owns the Receipt of this Manuscript from the Archdeacon of Oxford, which he affirms to be very antient, and by his Request was persuaded to translate it into the Latin Tongue. It was a very easie matter for the Earl of Glocester to find out Geoffrey's Integrity, by enquiring of the Archdeacon (who by all Accounts is reckoned his co-temporary) whether he had delivered such an antient British Copy into Geoffrey's hands, and whether the Translation justly answered the Original. These Enquiries were natural, upon the publication of any new History, which made such considerable noise and clamour in the World, and which gave such an Account of the antient Britains, as was never before thought or heard of among the English Nation. And supposing the Earl of Glocester to have omitted these Enquiries, yet it is scarce conceivable, but that in case of so open a Forgery, the Archdeacon would discover the Cheat, unless it can be thought that he was privy to, and had a hand in the Contrivance. But he was so far from detecting Geoffrey's Imposture, that he himself owns too, to have translated the British History first into Latin, and then in his latter days, to British again from the Latin, as may be still seen in the Archives of Jesus-College Library. Now if there be any heed to, or dependance upon this,

The PREFACE.

this, if it be true, that the Archdeacon did translate, and consequently allow of this History, it appears very evident to me, that Geoffrey can be in no wise the Author or Contriver of it.

But that Robert of Glocester took a fancy to Geoffrey's Translation, more upon the account that his Father had lately subdued the Welch, and therefore seemed to add to his Father's Glory, than that he did credit and believe the History, does not seem to be so true and evincing. For wherein could the publication of this History contribute to the advancement of his Father's Name? Was it because he had Conquered a People, whose Ancestors appeared by this History, to be formerly Valiant and Warlike? This was performed by others before him, and I can conceive no great addition to any Man's Fame, to Conquer a handful of People with a numerous Army, tho' their Fore-fathers had been Stout and Victorious. This is surely too slight a Pretence for the reception of the British History by the Earl of Glocester, and too weak an Argument to destroy the Truth and Authority of it. 'Tis certain, that it took exceeding well in the World at that time, nor was it opposed till after Robert's Death, when William of Newborough more out of Malice and Discontent, than any Love he bore to Truth, began to charge both the Original and Translator with insincerity. I cannot see, upon the whole, the least Reason, why the Contrivance and Invention of this History should be attributed to Geoffrey, or that the Authority of it depends any way upon him, more than the Fidelity of his Translation. I shall therefore conclude this Subject with the Character bestowed upon Geoffrey, and the History by him published, by Ponticus Virunnius, who flourished in the Year 19⁻. a Man of great Reading, and excellent Learning of his time, who did not think it lost Labour to draw an Epitome of the British History: Giraldus (says

*

be)

The PREFACE.

he) Historicus egregius & Cardinalis, magnæ vir auctoritatis apud Robertum Claudiocestriæ Ducem, Henrici Regis filium, ac patriæ suæ curiofissimus Fautor, ex summâ Philofophiâ atque Archivis, Historiam antiquissimam continuâ serie ab ipsis Trojanis collectam transtulit. Verissimas esse Britannorum Historias arguit RegumOccidentalium consuetudo; quæ erat,secum semper habere eos, qui veritate præcipua eorum gesta notarent.

2. *But supposing Geoffrey to be innocent from this suspected Imposture, and that he did no more than faithfully translate a* British *Manuscript he received of the Archdeacon; it may be farther objected, that seeing it abounds with so many unwarrantable matters of fact, and so extravagant Fables and Prodigies, it appears extreamly suspicious, and sensibly smells of a Monkish production. For how is it possible, you will say, that any Account, excepting what is found in the* Roman *Histories, could be had of the* Britains, *and that not only before, but even after their subjection to the* Romans; *since there is much reason to doubt, whether the* Britains, *as well as other unlettered Nations, had any means to convey any Knowledge to Posterity, for want of the Art of Writing? For if the Affairs and Transactions of the* Britains *were only handed down by Tradition, and they had no other way or method to preserve their Memories, then certainly all Pretences to antient Records, and consequently to this* British *Manuscript, supposed to have been translated by* Geoffrey, *must of necessity be vain and groundless.*

And thus it is supposed, that the Britains *had no Writing among them, neither before nor after the* Roman *Conquest; whence it follows, that there is no true nor certain account of any matter translated among them, but what is recorded in* Roman *Histories. But tho' this be frequently insinuated, yet I think,*

The PREFACE.

think, the contrary can with greater ease and perspicuity, be made to appear. As to the Britains *having no Writing among them, during their subjection to the* Roman Empire, *the contrary is so evident and notorious, that I conceive it lost time to go about to disprove it.* 'Tis *sufficient to lay down the Words of* Tacitus, *an Author of unshaken Reputation;* Jam verò Principum filios Vita A-liberalibus Artibus erudire, & ingenia Britanno- gric. rum studiis Gallorum anteferre, & qui modò linguam Romanorum abnuebant, eloquentiam concupiscerent. Inde etiam habitus nostri honor, & frequens toga; paulatimque discessum ad deliniamenta Vitiorum, porticus & balnea, & conviviorum elegantiam. *Now, can any one suppose, that when the* British *Youths were instructed in all the Arts and Sciences of the* Romans, *when they began to ape and imitate them in their Habits, Buildings, and other necessary fooleries, they should neglect so necessary a Qualification, as that of Writing? And can we imagine, that among so many Able and Learned Persons, as the* Britains *must in reason be, when educated in the* Roman *way, and owned to be very tractable in their Education, not one should prove so affectionate to his Country, as to note down the State and Transactions of it? Certainly, if they learnt all the Civilities and Sciences of the* Romans, *History was not so slight and trivial a subject of their Industry, as to be undervalued; and I know not where they could better employ their Skill, than in Writing the History of their Native Country. It was natural for them being once civilized, to enquire into the Origine and Antiquity of their Nation, the State and Condition of their Country before the* Roman Conquest; *and having made the best search they could, whether by oral or written Tradition into these Enquiries, they would in all reason, according to the Custom and*

* 2 *manner*

The PREFACE.

manner of the Romans, *commit all to Writing.*

But allowing the Britains *to have learnt the Art of Writing from the* Romans, *after their subjection to the Empire, yet 'tis certain they had no such thing among them, before the discovery of this Island by* Julius Cæsar, *and consequently, that all the former Part of the* British *History which precedes that Epoch, must be false and fictitious. And that this is no precarious Objection, a Passage out of* Cæsar's *Commentaries is produced to strengthen it, which in my Opinion, evidently proves the contrary. The Words of* Cæsar *are these:* Magnum ibi numerum (*speaking of the* Druids) versuum ediscere dicuntur, itaque annos nonnulli vicenos in disciplina permanent; neque fas esse existimant ea literis mandare, cum in reliquis ferè rebus, publicis privatisque rationibus, Græcis literis utuntur. *Why any one from hence should conclude, that the Superstition of those antient Philosophers the* Druids, *forbad the Britains to commit to Writing the Transactions of their Country, much more that they had no Writing at all among them, does I confess, very far exceed my comprehension.* Cæsar, *truly does intimate, that the Doctrine and Mysteries of their Religion, the* Druids *did not think fit to commit to Writing; but in all Matters besides, whether private or publick (among which, History may be reasonably accounted) they used the* Greek *Characters: for so I understand those words,* Græcis literis utuntur. *For it may not be supposed that all publick and private Affairs of the* Britains *were translated in* Greek, *when they had a different Language of their own, and which in all reason must be the common Tongue of the Country; but only that when the* Britains *had occasion to put any thing in Writing, they used the* Grecian *Character, which probably was the only Letter, they then were acquainted with. But to confirm this matter the more,* Cæsar *makes*

De Bell.
Gall. Lib.
VI.

The PREFACE.

ligious, and their Kings cruel and tyrannical. For a little before the above quoted passage, he says of Britain, Hæc erecta Cervice & mente ex quo inhabitata est, nunc Deo, interdum Civibus, nonnunquam etiam transmarinis Regibus ingrata consurgit. *And a little after,* Tacens vetustos immanium Tyrannorum annos, qui in aliis positis regionibus vulgati sunt. *Here he passes his Judgment very liberally upon the State and Condition of* Britain *from all Antiquity; and yet by and by, he confesses, that he had no guide to direct him to the Knowledge of those times he so freely censures; so that if he had not the Spirit of Divination, he may falter in his conjectures, or else he was guided by some* British Light, *of which he was not willing to own the perusal.*

But allowing that Gildas, *in composing that small Fragment of the* British History, *received no Light from any* British Record, *but was constrained to borrow out of the Writings of Foreigners; it concludes no farther, than that he had not the good Fortune to meet with* British Manuscripts, *not that there were none really remaining in* Britain. *And farther, supposing that in* Gildas *his time, there were no remains of the antient* Britains *left in this Island, but were all utterly lost; yet according to* Gildas *his own acknowledgment, and upon the* Saxons *prevailing in the Country, they might be carried over by the exuled* Britains *to* Armorica, *from whence the Archdeacon of* Oxford *is said to have brought over the* British *Copy he delivered to* Geoffrey. *But if there was no written Account of the former State of* Britain, *in the Age of* Gildas, *how comes it to pass, that any such thing should be discovered and brought to light in succeeding Ages. And not to insist upon the Authority of the* British Manuscript *translated by* Geoffrey, *we have good reason to presume, that the antient* Britains

before

The PREFACE.

before Gildas *had both Ecclesiastical and Civil Histories of their Country.*

As to the former, Bede, *whose Authority I presume, will not be questioned, expressly affirms it. For in his Preface to his* Ecclesiastical History, *he says,* A principio itaque Voluminis hujus, usque ad tempus quo Gens Anglorum fidem Christi percepit, ex priorum maximè scriptis hinc inde collectis, ea quæ prommemoramus, didiscimus. *Here* Bede *plainly declares, that in Writing a Church History of* Britain, *he extracted all his matter, before the conversion of the* Saxons *to Christianity, out of antient Authors. But who can these former Writers be? Surely they were not* Saxons, *for we read of no* Saxon *Writer before* Bede; *besides, that several things contained in this History, were translated before the Landing of the* Saxons; *and as to the Ecclesiastical part, betwixt the arrival, and the conversion of the* Saxons *to Christianity that cannot be extracted out of their Writings. For in the first place they were no Christians, and it is very unreasonable to suppose, that they would write the History of a Church, of which they were at that time very fatal and implacable Enemies; not to question whether the* Saxons *before their Conversion had any Writing or Learning at all among them. For though it be pretended, that the* Irish, *who use the same manner of Writing, borrowed their Characters from the* Saxons; *yet 'tis extremely suspitious, that these received them from the* Irish, *if not rather from the* Britains. *As to the former, it is well known, that during the Disturbances betwixt the* Britains *and* Saxons *here in* Britain, *the Incursions of the* Goths, Vandals, *and other Northern Nations into other Countries; all the Learning of these Western Parts of the World, fled into* Ireland, *which for a considerable time remained*

to

The PREFACE.

to be the Nursery of Learning and learned Men. And that the Saxons, long after their Conversion to Christianity, retired to Ireland *for this purpose, we have the Testimony of their antient and most authentick Historian; so that, I think, 'tis no Presumption to suspect, that as the Saxons borrowed their Learning from the* Irish, *they might for the same reason, receive their Characters and form of writing from them. But 'tis again to be doubted, whether both the* Saxons *and the* Irish *did not primarily derive their Characters from the* Britains: *For though the British Language be now writ in a different Character from the* Irish *and* Saxon, *yet upon antient* British *Monuments and Inscriptions, most of the Saxon Letters, different from the present* Roman *Alphabet, are plainly to be seen. Nor was this Character originally* British, *the same being used in the first Age of the* Roman *Empire, if we can lay any stress on* Julius Cesar's *Will and Testament, represented by* Mabillon. *But farther yet; if the* Irish *Character be originally* Saxon, *the* Saxons *must either bring it along with them from* Germany, *or else they must have invented it after their arrival and settlement in* Britain: *If the first, it may seem wonderful, how it came to be quite lost and forgotten in all parts of* Germany; *unless we can suppose, that it was limited only to the* Saxons, *and that they to a Man came and settled in this Island: For no body can be ignorant, that not only the* Germans, *but the* Swedes *and* Danes *too, use the* Latine *Character; which, if we suppose them to have but lately borrowed, yet in all probability, their former Letter was* Gothick *or* Runick, *to which the* Saxon *bears no great resemblance. But if it be said, that the* Saxons *invented this Character after their coming to* Britain; *I cannot well*

Bed. Hist.
Eccl.lib.3.
chap. 27.

De Re Diplo.p.345.

conceive

The PREFACE.

conceive, *why they should put themselves to such unnecessary trouble, when with far greater ease and facility they might copy and borrow from the* Britains; *unless the odium betwixt both Nations made them scorn to ape and imitate an Enemy.* But be it so, *that the* Saxons *invented this Character in* Britain; *it will follow, that they had no Letters nor Learning before they came over; and consequently, that these Authors which* Bede *mentions to have transcribed out of, could not be* Saxons.

As to the civil part of the British *History, that the Transactions of State were recorded, and that Copies thereof came to the hands of Posterity, we have the express Testimony of* Nennius, *who flourished about Three Hundred Years after* Gildas. *For in his Preface to his History of the* Britains, *he openly declares, that he compos'd his History,* Partim majorum Traditionibus, partim Scriptis, partim etiam Monumentis veterum Britanniæ Incolarum. *Here* Nennius *says, that he partly extracted his History out of the Writings of the Antient* Britains. *And what could these Writings be? Certainly, they were not the Works of* Gildas, *the only* British *Author we read of before* Nennius; *upon the account that the History of* Nennius *is much larger, and far more complete than that of* Gildas; *this latter, besides the Names of a few* British *Kings, having left nothing Historical to Posteritty; the main, it seems, of his design being to rail, and to inveigh against his Countrey, to which he had taken some Displeasure. From whence then else could* Nennius *extract the Materials of his History? Why, 'tis reasonable to suppose, that from some* British *Records, which possibly might be recovered since the time of* Gildas; *And if then, why might not more be discovered since* Nennius, *and that delivered to* Geoffrey *by the Arch-Deacon of* Oxon, *be one?*

But

The PREFACE.

But besides, That the Britains *kept Memorials of their Transactions, we may rationally gather from the Constitution and Profession of the* Bards. Diodorus Siculus *says,* Οὗτοι ἢ μετ' Ὀργάνων ταῖς λύραις ὁμοίων, ὡς μὲν ὑμνῶσιν, ὡς βλασφημοῦσι ; *The* Bards *singing to an Instrument like a Harp, repeat the Praises and Commendations of some, the Faults and Dispraises of others. And in like manner* Marcellinus ; Bardi quidem fortia virorum illustrium facta heroicis composita versibus, cum dulcibus lyræ modulis cantitarunt. *And above the rest* Lucan ;

Lib. 15.

Pharsal. lib. 1.

Vos quoque qui fortes Animas, belloque peremptas
Laudibus in longum vates emittitis ævum,
Plurima securi fudistis Carmina Bardi.

But that the Bards *did not only commit to memory the famous Deeds of their Princes and Heroes, and so recite and repeat them upon occasions ; but also that they wrote down and recorded what they repeated, we have the ample Testimony of* Giraldus Cambrensis. Hoc etiam mihi notandum videtur, quòd Bardi Cambrenses, & Cantatores seu Recitatores, genealogiam habent Prædictorum Principum in libris eorum antiquis & authenticis, sed tamen Cambricè scriptam, eandémque memoriter tenent à Roderico Magno usque ad Belinum magnum, & inde usque ad Silvium, Ascanium, & Æneam ; & ab Æneâ usque ad Adam, Generationem linealiter producunt.

Cambr. Descrip. cap. 3.

Now that the Genealogies here mentioned by Giraldus, *were not only a bare account of the several Descents and Successions of the* British Kings, *but also some Memorials of their Lives and Actions, may be easily gathered from the abovesaid Manners and Customs of the* Bards. *And seeing these* Bards *did preserve not only in Memory but in Writing too, the lineal Succession and*

The PREFACE.

and most famous Transactions of their Kings; I see no reason why the History of Geoffrey *may not, as to a great part of it, pretend to greater Authority than is generally attributed to it. And if it be objected, that the* Bards, *by a Poetical Liberty outdid the Truth of History, in the Praises of those Princes they were to celebrate; yet thus far it may reasonably be acknowledged, that the Names and Succession of the several Kings are real, and consequently that* Geoffrey *could never be the Inventer of so large a List of Nick-Names, as he is generally thought to be. For it is very probable, that the History of the* Britains *translated by* Geoffrey, *was composed partly out of these Genealogies peculiar to the* Bards, *and partly out of any other Records and Monuments of the* Britains; *both which I have shewn to have been preserved, and used among them antiently.*

But to descend to the particulars of this History, the first and most suspicious Relation, is that of the landing of Brute *with a Colony of* Trojans, *the several Crosses and Encounters he sustained in his Voyage; and then of this Island receiving its Name from him. Should we indeed reflect upon the particular Circumstances of this Story, we might upon good reason be satisfied of the Vanity and falseness of them; but therefore to conclude, that because the Building is suspicious, the Foundation consequently must be fabulous, and a perfect Contrivance; does, I think, deserve some better Examination: For if we do but reflect upon the contemporary Histories of the* Greeks *and* Romans, *those more polite and literate Nations, we may with equal pretence of Reason affirm, that there is no foundation for any matter of Fact before the* Olympiads; *or that the relation of* Æneas's *coming to* Italy, *and all that History, to the Building of* Rome, *are altogether groundless and imperti-*

The PREFACE.

impertinent, because they are intermixt with Fables and impossibilities. Livy *assures us, that all the Transactions before the Building of* Rome, *are rather owing to Poetical Fancy and Extravagancies, than to any true and certain Matter of Fact; and therefore he declin'd to give either his Assent or Dissent, to any thing related of those Times:* Quæ ante conditam condendamve Urbem, poeticis magis decora fabulis, quam incorruptis rerum gestarum monumentis traduntur, ea nec affirmare, nec refellere in animo est. *And* Plutarch *goes farther, and tells us, that the Original and Etymology of* Rome, *that famous City, so well known afterwards over all the World, could not be agreed upon among the diversity of Authors, and consequently must be very obscure and uncertain.* Τὸ μέγα τῆς Ῥωμης ὄνομα κỳ δόξη δία πάντων ἀνθρώπων Κεχωρηκὸς ἀφ' ὅτε κỳ δἰ ἦν αἰτίαν τῇ πόλει γέγονεν, ὐχ ὁμολόγηται περὶ τοῖς συγγραφεῦσιν.

Præfat.

VitaRom.

But for all their own Historians do allow that the History of those Times are fabulous and uncertain; yet there are none that question the being of Æneas, *and that the* Romans *were descended from him. The like may be urged for the History of* Brutus, *and the landing of the* Trojans *in this Island; that though many particular Circumstances are fabulous, and entirely poetical, yet it does not thence necessarily follow, that there is no manner of ground or foundation for such a Relation. Neither is it sufficient Conviction, to urge, that the very being of* Brute *is all a Fiction, by reason that the* Roman *Historians make no mention of such a Person to be the Son of* Silvius; *because, that through the whole Succession from* Æneas *to* Romulus, *the Histories of those Times take notice only of the Son that was to succeed; it being unreasonable to suppose, that all the Kings of* Latium *during that period, should be-*
get

The PREFACE.

get each of them, but one Son. And therefore, what by the obscurity of those Ages, and what by bearing regard only to the Line of Succession, many collateral Princes escaped the Cognizance of future Historians. Nor is it enough to affirm, that the History of Brute is but lately known and discovered to the World; whereas the fabulous Roman History has been recorded from Antiquity; because, that though we are not certain that the British History has been handed down to Posterity in Writing; yet we are sure, that it was an antient Tradition, long before Geoffrey's publishing of it; and one should think, that an antient National Tradition, might require a stricter Examination, than hastily to throw it aside, as fabulous and of no Consequence.

But the Question is not, Whether the British History, as related by Geoffrey, be, as to all the Circumstances of it, true and real Matter of Fact; for that, no Man, I presume, can reasonably maintain; but whether there be any ground or foundation of Truth couched under these Poetical and fabulous Narratives. Now the first thing we meet with in the British History, is, an Account of Brutus his Pedigree, how he was descended from the Trojans, and having accidentally slain his Father Silvius, how he was forced to flee into Greece, whence, after several Scuffles with Pendrasus, a petty Prince of that Country, he thought fit to retire, and to seek his Fortune by Sea. But he had not wandered long, when he met with Corinæus, with another Party of desolate Trojans, with whom having joyned his Forces, he followed the Counsel of the Oracle, and at last arrives in this Island, from him afterwards called Britain. Now as to the particular Circumstances related in the Life of Brutus, they may properly be placed in the same

Class

The PREFACE.

Class with Homer's account of the Travels of Ulysses, or Virgil's Description of Æneas his Adventure to Italy; that is to say, that they are Poetical Fictions, and perfectly consonant to the humour of that fabulous Age. But the Question in hand will be, whether there be any probability for the ground of this Story, that Brute should bring over a Colony of Trojans, and seat himself in this Island. Now what is most materially urged against it, is the Novelty of this Discourse, that none of the Roman Historians make the least mention of such a Person as Brutus; and that Cesar and Tacitus, who seem to have enquired more narrowly into the Original of the Britains, found no such Tradition in their time; otherwise in giving their opinion whence the Britains were derived, they would never have omitted such an antient National Tradition, of their being descended from the Trojans. Besides, that Gildas, who was a Britain, takes no notice of such a Tradition, which in all probability he would never have omitted, had there been such an account of their Origine in his time.

As to what is objected against the Antiquity of this Tradition, is certainly very erroneous; for 'tis so far from being first known to the World, at the publication of Geoffrey's History, that Nennius, long before that time, and Merlyn, much antienter than he, speak of the Britains being descended from Troy. Nay the Saxons themselves before Geoffrey, were not unacquainted with this Tradition, as plainly appears, from the antient Saxon Poet, mention'd by Mr. Wheelock, whom he thus translates;

Notes on Bede.

——Hæc unica Fœmina prima
Ante omnes sævit Trojani femina belli,
Hanc Britones dixere Helenam, sed Dardanus ille
Excelsus Bruti pater extitit, unde Britanni
Heroum sumpsere genus ; fortissimis idem
Hunc orbem primus regere, & dominarier ausus.

And

The PREFACE.

And again;
Infula dicta fuit Britannia nomine Bruti.

That Gildas *should make no mention of this* British *Tradition, is no great wonder, and as little to the purpose, to invallidate the Antiquity of it; for we must not regard the Intent and Purport of* Gildas's *Writing, which was not to give an account of the History and Antiquity of the* Britains, *as much as to inveigh against the Prophaneness and licentiousness of the Age; wherein his Zeal and Passion carried him so far, that he did not spare either Princes or the greatest Persons; and therefore he might well omit to give an account of the Origine of the* Britains, *seeing it was remote from, and exclusive of his purpose.* Cesar *indeed seems to have been somewhat more inquisitive about the antient State and Descent of those People he invaded; but his stay in* Britain *was so short, and his knowledg of the Country so defective, being he had no Communication with the Inland* Britains, *whom he owns himself to be the antient Inhabitants, that it can be no great wonder he should be ignorant of this Tradition: for if this curious Person had had the opportunity of a free Conversation with the* Britains, *he would in all likelyhood have left a large Discovery of their Manners and Customs, and given a more perfect Description of* Britain; *which at that time would have been a very acceptable Performance, to all the Persons of Learning and Curiosity in* Rome, *who as yet had but very shallow knowledg of this Island. Or if we suppose that he made the strictest enquiry about the state of the* Britains, *which he might probably have learnt from* Mandubratius *the Son of* Imanuentius *King of the* Trinobantes, *who, for fear of* Cassibelan, *had come over to him to* Gaul, *and sided with him during the* British *Wars, 'tis very possible he might be ignorant that the* Britains *were descended from the* Trojans, *and that to*

be

The PREFACE.

be an antient and a current Tradition among them. Tacitus was never in Britain, but from the relation of his Father in Law, Julius Agricola, and others, he made a Guess, that from the different Shapes and Colour, they were descended from different Nations; some from Germany, some from Gaul, and others from Spain; but yet, as to the Primitive Britains, those who seemed to be the antient Inhabitants of the Island, he concludes after the usual Pagan manner, Britanniam qui mortales initio coluerint, Indigenæ an Advecti, ut inter Barbaros parum compertum. *The Britains, indeed, in* Tacitus *his time, were well known to the* Romans, *and consequently these latter might have been easily instructed, as to what knowledg the* Britains *had of their Antiquity; but it does not therefore necessarily follow, that because this Historian does not mention any such Tradition, there was none really among them; because possibly he might never have heard of it; or if he did, he might have omitted inserting of it in his History: For what he has delivered relating to the Antiquity of the* Britains, *was but contingent to his purpose, the whole scope of his design being to describe the Actions of his Father in Law, during his Lieutenancy in this Island; and therefore it is not at all wonderful, that he has given but a slight and an imperfect account of what he never design'd to make a narrow inspection into. Besides, if we suppose him to have made a diligent enquiry into the matter, and to have mind to know the antient State and Origine of the* Britains; *yet since he wanted the opportunity of conversing with them, having been never in* Britain; *and none of the* Britains *that we know of, being at* Rome, *except those who from their youth were educated there, and consequently were in all probability ignorant of the Traditions of their own Country; he might very well at such a distance have been never made acquainted with such a National Tradition, which for all that, might have been current and prevailing among the* Britains

In vita Agric.

them-

The PREFACE.

themselves. As to other Roman Historians, who have writ of the Antiquity and Primitive State of Rome, *that they have made no mention of any such Person as* Brutus *the Son of* Sylvius; *I have already observed, is not of that force as to overthrow this Tradition, by reason that, from* Æneas *down to* Romulus, *there is regard only had to the Line of Succession, and those only recorded who succeeded in the Throne.*

Let us consider now, in the next place, what probable Reasons may be assigned to vindicate this supposed Trojan *Origin from an utter Fiction; and whether the History of* Brutus *have any probable dependance upon some real Foundation. And not to insist on the Antiquity of this Tradition, nor the Authority of the* British *History published by* Geoffrey, *nothing gives greater Confirmation to assert some real Foundation for this supposed Fable, than the near Alliance and Affinity betwixt the* Britains *and the* Grecians. *All Learned Men allow that the* Greek *was the antient Language of the* Trojans, *and that their Customs were not much different; and whoever will compare the Manners, Religion and Customs of the* Britains *with those of the* Grecians, *will easily discover a palpable Conformity betwixt both Nations, but more especially in the Language; in which, as Mr.* Camden *says,* Maximum est disputationis firmamentum & certissimum originis gentium argumentum. Qui enim (*as he goes on*) linguæ societate conjuncti sunt, originis etiam Communione fuisse conjunctos, homo opinor nemo inficiabitur.

I shall not, at present, trouble the Reader with a particular annumeration of that Affinity; but will refer him to Sir John Price's Defensio Historiæ Britannicæ, *and Mr.* Sheringham's *Treatise* De Gentis Anglorum Origine. *Now, since there is such demonstrable Affinity betwixt the* Britains *and the* Grecians *in all these respects; we must either suppose, with Mr.* Camden, *that they are of the same Origin, at least*

that

The PREFACE.

that a Colony of either Greeks or Trojans *came over to this Island; or else, that the* Britains *had Correspondence, Traffick and Communication with the* Grecians. *Now, that the* Grecians *had no knowledge of the* Britains *till very late, may be gather'd from hence, that even the Name of* Britain *is not so much as mentioned by any* Greek *Author before* Polybius, *who liv'd less than two hundred years before the* Roman *Invasion, and by him but just named, as betokening a very remote and distant Country, wherein indeed it was reported that there was plenty of Tin. Nay,* Britain *was so far unknown to the Eastern parts of the World, long after this, that even* Cæsar *himself, when he intended an Invasion, was perfectly ignorant of the State of the Island; and tho he made what Enquiry he could of the* British Merchants *in* Gaul, *yet for all that, as he says himself,* Neq; quanta esset Insulæ magnitudo, neq; quæ aut quantæ Nationes incolerent, neq; quem usum belli haberent, aut quibus institutis uterentur, neq; qui essent ad majorum navium idonei portus, reperire poterat: *and therefore he was forced to send* Cajus Volusenus *before him, to search into the State and Condition of the Island. Such Strangers were the* Romans *at this time to the Isle of* Britain. *And can it be supposed, that the* Grecians *had a better knowledg of it, since, in all probability, if they had had a Commerce with the* Britains, *the* Romans, *who were Masters of the Sea long before this, would have quickly discovered their Merchandizing; which if as profitable as is imagined, they were no such Enemies to Gain but they would share in the Booty. At least, had the* Grecians *had any Correspondence with the* Britains, *the* Romans *would in all probability have known it, and consequently they must needs have received better Intelligence of the Island than what they seem to have had at* Cæsar's Landing. *But* Dion Cassius *seems to put this matter out of dispute, and gives us a very plain account of what knowledge the* Greeks *and* Romans, *had*

Bell. Gall. Lib. 4.

The PREFACE.

Lib. 39.

had of this Island, which I will set down in the Latin Translation, Primis Græcorum Romanorúmq; ne esse quidem Britanniam compertum fuit, posteriores in controversiam adduxerunt, continens ea terra, an verò insula esset; multáq; de utraq; opinione conscripta sunt ab iis, qui certi quidem nil noverant (quippe qui nec vidissent, nec ab Indigenis qualis esset accepissent) sed conjecturis tantum, quantum vel otii vel studii singulis aderat uterentur. *And the antient Poet, in* Eustathius *upon* Dionysius, *reckoning up the greatest Islands of the World in his time, makes no mention of* Britain, *which shews it was not then known. And that* Britain *was the antient* Cassiterides *of the* Grecians, *from whence they received their Tin, is altogether uncertain; for* Herodotus, *making mention of those Islands of* Cassiterides, *fairly declares he knew not where they were; which cannot well be supposed, if the* Grecian *Merchants traded thither in his time; it being rational to imagin that, in treating of any Country, such a Learned Historian would endeavour to get the best intelligence he possibly could; and Learning being at the highest pitch in* Greece *at this time, 'tis very strange we had not a better account of this Island, which is supposed to be so well known to those who had a constant Trafick here. But indeed, all Authors who have mentioned these* Cassiterides *do not seem to have known where they were situated, only* Dionysius, *in his* σελήνησις, *makes them plainly to be the same with the* Hesperides, *those Islands lying in the* Atlantick Ocean, *far enough from* Britain, *concerning which the Poets have invented so many Fables.*

———— Αὐτὰρ ὑπ' ἄκρην,
Ἰερὴν ἣν ἐπέπυστι κάρην ἑῷν Εὐρωπείης,
Νῆσες δ' Ἑσπερίδας τόθι κασσιτέροιο γενέθλη,
Ἀφνειοὶ ναίουσιν ἀγαυῶν παῖδες Ἰβήρων.

But admitting the Grecians *to have been ignorant of any such Place as* Britain, *and that there never was*

The PREFACE.

was any Traffic or Communication betwixt these two Nations; yet since the Gauls spoke Greek, it is not very improbable but that the Britains might borrow from them. That the Gauls used the Greek Tongue, we have the Testimony of Cæsar; and it is very certain, that all the Grecian Learning flourished at Marseils, which was an antient and famous University, and is very much celebrated by all almost, both Greek and Latin Writers. And by this means, it may be reasonably concluded, how the British and Gaulish Druids became acquainted with the Grecian Philosophy, which being as to all the different Sects and Opinions of it, taught at Marseils, the Druids more particularly adhered to the Pythagorean, to which the Druid Philosophy bears a very near resemblance, both as to the Doctrine of the Μετεμψύχωσις, or the Transmigration of the Soul, and the rest of their Mystical Cabala, which they so superstitiously kept secret and close from the People.

But in opposition to this, it may be with greater certainty urged, that neither the Gaulish nor British Druids had any Correspondence with the Grecians, and consequently could not borrow their Philosophical Mysteries from them. For if Cæsar may be believed, The Art and Learning of the Druids was first found out in Britain, and from thence is thought to be brought into Gaul; and at this time, as he goes on, such as will attain to the perfect knowledge of that Discipline, do for the most part travel thither to learn it. Now if this be true, that the British Druids were the Inventors of this kind of Learning, and that the Gauls came over hither to be instructed in the Way and Method of it; I can see no reason, why they should have any communication with the Grecian Academy at Marseils, much less that they borrowed it from the Disciples of Pythagoras, especially since they accounted their Mysteries so Sacred, that they would communicate them to none, besides those of their own Order. Nay, it may be better questioned, whe-

Lib. VI.

The PREFACE.

ther Druidism be not much antienter than Pythagoras, and antecedent to that Æra, when the Grecians began to Philosophize. And for the same reason, that the Druids of Britain did not derive their Philosophy from Marseils, it will follow, that they could not borrow their Language; for if we suppose, which is the most we can, that the Gauls had some communication with those Grecians, and upon that account that their Language was in some measure mingled with the Greek; yet in their travel to Britain, they came not to communicate, but to borrow; and 'tis not likely that the Britains should be affected with the Language of those who came to learn of them. Besides, of all the number of Gaulish Words collected by Cambden, which agree with the British, few or none seem to be of Greek Derivation; so it is highly improbable, as far as we can see into this Matter, that the Gauls should ever communicate the Greek Tongue to the Britains. And therefore, since this difficulty cannot be removed by any other way, it is not unreasonable to suspect, that there is some real Foundation lodged in the Ruins of the Story of Brutus, and that the Truth is disfigured by the boundless accession of Poetical Invention.

I should tire the Reader, and exceed the just bounds of what I at first proposed, if I should take a particular view of the British History published by Geoffrey, and therefore I shall now only take notice of the Life of King Cadwalader, where the History of Wales begins, and where a palpable Mistake, I may call it Forgery, has been committed by one side or another. For the very same things, which the British History relate of Cadwalader, the Saxon Writers attribute to Ceadwalla King of the West Saxons, how he was driven by a Famine out of his Dominions, came afterwards to Rome, and was received by Pope Sergius, with other particulars too tedious here to relate. But that which seems to charge the Fault upon Geoffrey, or whoever else was the Author of the British History, is, that Bede an Author of established Credit,

and

The PREFACE.

and one who lived near those times, says that it was the *West* Saxon King Ceadwalla *that went to* Rome *in* Pope Sergius's *time. But then on the other side, it is hardly conceivable, supposing the* British History *a perfect Contrivance, that* Geoffrey *or any other should be so grossly over-seen, as to borrow the Transaction of a real King, and one so well known, to make up the Life of a fictitious one cotemporary with him.* Bede's *Reputation was too firm, to be shaken by an upstart History, and therefore it cannot well be supposed that the Author of the* British *History was so unwary, in case he designed a Cheat, as to let himself open to so easy a detection of Forgery. All then that can be said, is, that the agreeableness of the Names and time that these two Princes lived in, and possibly their both going to* Rome, *which was not unusual in those days, might without any design of putting upon the World, make a confusion in their Histories. But whether the Life of* Cadwalader *be a Fable, the Reader is at his own liberty to judge; it being prefixed to the History of* Wales, *not as it is more Authentick, or any way of greater certainty than the rest of* Geoffrey's *History, but only because the Author* Caradoc of Lhangarfan, *began his continuace of the* British *History with it.*

This Caradoc *of* Lhangarfan, *an Author of undoubted Integrity, was cotemporary with* Geoffrey, *who taking his rise from the place where the* British *History concluded, made a continuation of it thro' the Reigns of several of the Princes of* Wales, *till the Year* 1157. *about which time he flourished. After him, all things of moment that happened in* Wales, *were kept and recorded in the Abbies of* Conwey *in* North-Wales, *and* Ystratflur *in* South-Wales, *where the Princes and Noblemen of* Wales *were buried, as appears by the Testimony of* Gutryn Owen, *who lived in the time of* Edward IV. *and writ the most exact and perfect Copy of the same. All the most notable Occurrences being thus Registred in these Abbies, were most generally compared together every third*

* * 4 *Year,*

The PREFACE.

Year, when the Beirdh *or* Bards *belonging to these two Houses spent their ordinary Visitations, which was called* Clera. *And this continued until the Year* 1270. *a little before the Death of the last Prince* Lhewelyn, *who was slain at* Buelht. Humphrey Lloyd *Gent. who flourished in the Reign of* Henry VIII. *and one greatly skill'd in the* British *Antiquities, continued this History to the Death of Prince* Lhewelyn; *and afterwards having translated the whole into* English *Language, had designed to commit it to the Press. But his Death prevented what he purposed, and stopped the publication of this History for a long time after, until* David Powel *D. D. in the time of* Queen Elizabeth, *having met with* Humphrey Lloyd's *Translation, collected what he could out of* English *Historians, which he added by way of Annotations, and so published it in the Year* 1584. *This being the sole History of the Princes of* Wales, *and the only Edition of this History, I was moved to prepare it for another Impression, by a new modelling the Language, making the Body of the History intire, without troubling the Reader to see the same thing by way of Annotation, Dr.* Powel's *Notes being for the greatest part but a repetition of the same matter of Fact out of the* English *Historians, with what other Improvements could be made. The Additions which I made to the former History, I chiefly took out of the Notes of that late great Antiquarian Mr.* Robert Vaughan *of* Hengwrt; *by whose help also I have corrected, supplyed, and continued the Chronology. Sir* John Price's *Description of* Wales *will pretty well answer the Geographical part of this History, til we shall be able to recover and fix several of those places whose* Names *are only left to us at present, which we have great hopes, will be successfully perfected, by the unwearied Labours of my ingenious Friend Mr.* Edward Lhwyd, *in his intended Etymological Dictionary. I have added by way of Appendix, the several Records belonging to this History, and chose rather to insert the Articles of Peace betwixt Prince* Lhewelyn, *and* John Peckam *Archbishop of* Canterbury, *in the Original, with reference thereunto, than to insert all the Grievances which the* Welch *then made in the* English *Language, which do not so handsomly bear a Translation.*

A

A DESCRIPTION OF *CAMBRIA,*
Now Called
WALES:

Drawn firſt by Sir John Price *Knight, and afterward augmented and made perfect by* Humphrey Lloyd *Gentleman.*

THE Three Sons of *Brutus* having divided the whole Iſle of *Britain* into Three Parts; that part contained within the *French* Seas, with the Rivers of *Severn* (called in *Britiſh Hafren*) *Dee* and *Humber*, fell to the eldeſt Son *Locrinus*, which was after his Name called *Lhoyger*, which Name it hath in the *Britiſh* Tongue to this Day, and in *Engliſh* now it is called *England*, and is augmented Northward to the River *Tweed*. The ſecond Son *Albanactus* had all the Land Northward

from

The Description of WALES.

from *Humber* to the Sea *Orkney*, called in the *British* Tongue *Mor Werydh*, and in the Latin *Mare Caledonicum*. The third Son *Camber* had to his part, all that which remained undivided, lying within the *Spanish* and *Irish* Seas, and separated from *England*, with the Rivers *Severn* and *Dee*; and this part was after his Name called *Cambria*, and the Inhabitants thereof *Cambry*, and their Language *Camberaec*, and so are at this Day. So that they have kept the same Country and Language this 2700 and odd years, without commixtion with any other Nation, especially in *North-Wales*, as it shall hereafter appear.

And because the Name of this Country is changed, or rather mistaken by the Inhabitants of *England*, and not by them called *Cambry*, but *Wales*: I think it necessary to declare the occasion thereof, which is, that where the *Saxons* a People of *Germany* were the first that after the *Britains* inhabited and ruled the greatest part of this Isle, and drove the *Britains* to that Corner, which according to the manner of their Country they called *Wales*, and the People *Welch-men*, and the Tongue *Welch*, that is to say, Strange, or not of them understood. For at this Day the Inhabitants of the *Low Countries* call their next Neighbours Language of *Henegaw*, or other that speak *French*, *Walsh*, as a Language to them unknown. Likewise the dwellers of *Tyroll* and other the higher Countries of *Germany* do Name the *Italian* their next Neighbour a *Welch-man*, and his Language *Walsh*. And this is an evident Proof, that they which harped upon a Queen *Gwalaes*, and of a Prince *Wala* (of whom neither *British*, *Latin*, nor *English* History maketh mention) were foully deceived; and so likewise was a great Historiographer of late Days, which saith, that it was called *Wallia*, *quasi Italia*, because the rest of the *Romans* which remained in the Isle were driven thither. Neither is this any new Invention, although *Polydore Virgil* with an *Italian* brag doth glorify himself to be the first that espied it out, for divers antient Writers do alledge the same cause of the Name of *Wales*, of whom *Sylvester Gyraldus* is one, who

wrote

Cambria.

The Description of WALES.

wrote in the time of *Henry* the Second, after the Conqueſt, before 380 years paſſed; which is an evident Token, that the ſaid *Polydore* did either never ſee nor read the antient Hiſtories of this Realm, or diſſembleth the ſame to the Advancement and Praiſe of himſelf and his Country; which to the learned and indifferent Reader ſhall appear to be the only occaſion he took that work in hand, for all his Book redoundeth only to the Praiſe and Honour of the *Romans*, as well Spiritual as Temporal, and to blaſe forth their Acts and Deeds within this Realm: and upon the other part doth either openly ſlander, or elſe privily extenuate, or ſhamefully deny the martial prowefs and noble Acts, as well of *Saxons, Danes*, and *Normans*, as of the *Britains*, all Inhabiters of this Iſle. Which thing he that liſt to prove, let him read and confer *Cæſar's* Commentaries, *Cornelius Tacitus, Herodianus*, and other antient Writers, as well in *Latin* as in *Greek*, with his Work. As for the antient Writers of the *Britiſh* Hiſtory, as the *Britiſh* Chronicle, the Hiſtory of *Gildas*, *Ponticus Verunnius*, yea the Golden Work of *Matthew Paris* Monk of St. *Alban*, which wrote from *William Baſtard*, to the laſt years of *Henry* the Third; I dare well ſay he never ſaw them, they be in divers places to be had, ſo that the truth may be eaſily proved. To make an end I ſay, that he being firſt a Stranger born, and alſo ignorant as well in the Hiſtories of this Realm, as of thoſe Tongues and Languages wherein the ſame were written, could never ſet forth the true and perfect Chronicle of the ſame. But he having a good Grace, and a pleaſant Stile in the *Latin* Tongue, and finding himſelt in a Country where every Man either lacked Knowledge or Spirit to ſet forth the Hiſtory of their own Country, took this Enterpriſe in hand, to their great ſhame, and no leſs diſpraiſe, becauſe he a blind Leader ſhall draw a great Number of undiſcreet and raſh Followers, as well Geographers and Coſmographers, as Chroniclers and Hiſtoriographers, to the dark Pit of Ignorance, where I leave them at this time, remitting the Reader to the Apology of Sir *John Price*

The Description of WALES.

Price Knight, and his *British* History, written by him of purpose, against the envious Reports, and slanderous Taints of the said *Polydore*, where he shall see a great number of his Errors confuted at large. And

Wales. to return to my former matter of the Name of *Wales*, which Name to be given of late by a strange Nation may be otherwise proved: for the *Welch-men* themselves do not understand what these words *Wales* and *Welch* do signify, nor know any other Name of their Country or themselves but *Cambry*, nor of their Language but *Cambraec*, which is as much to say as *Camber*'s Language or Speech. So likewise they know not what *England* or *English* meaneth, but commonly they call the Country *Lhoyger*, the *English* Men

A Locrino. *Saison*, and the *English* Tongue *Saisonaec*. Which is
A Saxon. an evident token that this is the same Language which the *Britains* spake at the beginning; for the Works of *Merdhyn* and of *Taliessin*, who wrote above 1000 years past, are almost the same words which they use at this day, or at the least easy to be understood of every one which knoweth perfectly the *Welch* Tongue, especially in *North Wales*.

Beside this, where at this day, there do remain three remnants of the *Britains*, divided every one from other with the Seas, which are in *Wales*, *Cornwall* (called in *British Cerniw*) and little *Britain*, yet almost all the particular words of these three People are all one, although in pronunciation and Writing of the Sentences they differ somewhat, which is no marvel, seeing that the pronunciation in one Realm is often so diverse, that the one can scarce understand the other. But it is rather a wonder, that the *Welch-men* being separated from the *Cornish*, well nigh these 900 years, and the *Britains* from either of them 290 years before that, and having small Traffick or Concourse together since that time, have still kept their own *British* Tongue. They are not therefore to be credited, which deny the *Welch* to be the old *British* Tongue. And here I cannot pass over what one of these fine Chroniclers wrote of late, of the Name of *Britain*, affirming that it should be so

called

The Description of WALES.

called of *Britanie* in *France*, as the Elder of that Name. But surely he had either never seen *Ptolomy* nor *Cæsar*, nor any other antient Writer, or read them with small Judgment and Memory. For there he might have learned, that when this Land was called *Britain*, the other was called *Armorica*, and how in *Maximus*'s time, *Conan Meriadoc* was the first that gave it that Name, and inhabited it with *Britains* out of this Isle. Other derivations of these words *Britannia* and *Albion*, out of *Greek* and *Latin*, I am ashamed to rehearse; for unto such Errors do they commonly fall, that either puffed up with vain-glory of their own Wits, or pinched with despite and envy at other Men's Works, or blinded with Igorance, do go about to write and set forth any History or Chronicle. But passing over this matter until another time, I will return to the Description of *Wales*, which (as I said) was of old time compassed almost about with the *Irish* Seas, and the Rivers *Dee* and *Severn*, although afterwards the *Saxons* wan by force from the *Britains* all the plain and champion Country over the Rivers, and specially *Offa* King of *Mercia*, who made a Ditch of great breadth and depth, to be a Mear betwixt his Kingdom and *Wales*, which Ditch began at the River *Dee*, by *Baffingwerk*, between *Chester* and *Ruthlan*, and ran along the Hills sides to the *South* Sea, a little below *Bristol*, reaching above a hundred Miles in length, and is in many places to be seen at this day, bearing the Name of *Clawdh Offa*, that is to say, *Offa*'s Ditch, and the Country between it and *England* is commonly called in *Welch*, *Y Mars*, although the great part of it be now inhabited by *Welch*-men, namely in *North-Wales*, which yet keepeth the antient limits to the River *Dee*, and in some places over it. Other (as *Sylvester Giraldus*) make the River *Wy*, called in *Welch Gwy*, to be the Mear between *England* and *Wales*, on the *South* part, called *South-Wales*, who measureth the breadth of *Wales*, from *Salow* or *Willoweford*, called *Rhyd yr helig* upon *Wy*, to St. *Davids* in *Menevia* 100 Miles, and the length from *Caerlheon*

Rob. Cæ-nal. lib. 2. Per. 2.

The mears & bounds of Wales.

upon

The Description of WALES.

upon *Yse* in *Gwentland*, to *Holyhead*, called *Caergybi* in *Anglesey*, in *Welch*, called *Môn*, above 100 Miles, and these be the common Mears at this day, altho' the *Welch* Tongue is commonly used and spoken in *England*, beyond these old Mears a great way, as in *Hereford-shire*, *Glocester-shire*, and a part of *Shropshire*. And thus for the general Description of *Wales*, which afterward about the Year of Christ 870. *Rodericus Magnus*, King of *Wales*, divided into three Territories which they called Kingdoms, which remained until of late days.

These three were *Gwynedh*, in English *North-Wales*, *Debeubarth*, in English *South-Wales*, and *Powys*-Land; in every of the which he ordained a Princely Seat or Court for the Prince to remain at, most commonly; as in *Gwynedh* (which some old Writers call *Venedotia* for *Gwynethia*) *Aberffraw* in the Isle of *Môn* or *Anglesey*. In *Debeubarth*, called in *Latin* Demetia, *Caermardyn*, from whence it was afterward removed to *Dynefowr*, eight Miles thence. In *Powys*, *Pengwern*, call'd *Y Mwythic*, and in English *Shrewsbury*, from whence it was removed to *Mathrafal* in *Powys*-Land. And because this History doth as well intreat of Wars betwixt these three Provinces, as betwixt them and the *Saxons*, *Normans* and *Flemings*, I think it good to set forth the particular Description of every part by it self. And first of *North-Wales* as the chiefest part, which he gave his Eldest Son, ordaining that either of the other two should pay him yearly 200 *l*. of Tribute, as it appeareth in the Laws of *Howel Dha*, which are to be had in *Welch*, and also in *Latin*. Therefore *Gwynedh* (called *North-Wales*) had upon the *North*-side the Sea, from the River *Dee* at *Basingwerke* to *Aberdyfi*, and upon the *West* and *South-West* the River *Dyfi*, which divideth it from *South-Wales*, and in some places from *Powys*-Land. And on the *South* and *East*, it is divided from *Powys*, sometimes with Mountains, and sometimes with Rivers, till it come to the River *Dee* again. This Land was of old time divided to four parts, of which the chiefest was *Môn*, in *English* called *Anglesey*, where the Prince's chief

Aberffraw.

Dynefowr.

Mathrafal.

North-Wales.

Môn.

The Description of WALES.

chief House was at *Aberffraw*, which is an Island separated from the main Land, with an Arm of the Sea called *Mænai*, and had in it self three Cantreds or Hundreds, which were subdivided to six Comots, as Cantref *Aberffraw* to Comot *Lhion*, and Comot *Malhtraeth*, Cantref *Cemais*, to the Comots *Talibelion* and *Twr Celyn*; Cantref *Rossyr* to the Comots *Tyndaethwy* and *Mænai*. And at this day there is a fine Town in that Isle called *Bewmoris*, and a common Passage to *Ireland* at *Caergybi*, called in *English*, *Holyhead*. But here I cannot wink at that notable Error of *Polydor*, which (after his accustomed fashion) denieth this Isle to be called *Mona*, but *Anglesia*, or *Anglorum Insula*, because it is called in *English Anglesey*, and giveth this Name *Mona* to *Man*, and so hath lost the Names of both Isles: which ignorance and forgetfulness might be forgiven him, if he had not drawn a great number to this Error with him, which in their Charters do daily wrong Name these Isles, which may be easily proved. First, because the Inhabitants of the Isle do know none other Name but *Môn*; and it is called through all *Wales*, *Tir Môn*, that is to say, the Land of *Môn*, unto this day. So that neither by memory of Man, neither by any Monument in Writing in the *British* Tongue can it appear, that ever it had any other Name but *Môn*, yet there be manifest Monuments for these 1000 years. It is also grown to a Proverb through *Wales*, for the fertility of the ground, *Môn mam Gymry*, that is to say, *Môn* Mother of *Wales*.

The antient History of *Cornelius Tacitus* (which be-like Age had beaten out of *Polydor's* Head) faith, that the Souldiers of *Paulinus Suetonius*, and afterward of *Julius Agricola*, after they had passed thro' *North-Wales*, then came over against *Mona*, where they did swim over an Arm of the Sea of 200 paces, and so by force won the Isle. Now whether it is more reasonable thus to swim over 200 paces, or 20 miles? I know there is no Man that believeth *Polydor* in this point; let all Men therefore judge the rest. As for that which he faith of the great Woods, it is nothing;

The Description of WALES.

for both the *Romans*, and after when the Chriftian Faith took place in this Realm, the Chriftians did fall and root them out, for the Idolatry and abfurd Religion which was ufed there; that the King of *Man* fent for Timber to *Môn*; read the Life of *Hugh* Earl of *Chefter*, which alfo is evident by the great Beeches and other Trees found in the Earth at thefe days. His other reafon is, becaufe it is called *Anglefey* in the *Englifh* Tongue: fo is *Lhoyger* England, and *Cambry* Wales; Are thofe therefore the old Names? No furely. And what if the Inhabitants called it fo? (as they did not) had it not a Name before the *Angles* won it? Yes, I warrant you, but he had forgotten that. Now to the Name of *Man*, it was ever, or at the leaft thefe 1000 years named in Britifh *Manaw*, of which cometh the *Englifh* Name *Man*. The Inhabitants thereof call it fo, and no Nation about it did ever call it *Môn*, no nor any Writer but *Polydor*, which was too young a Godfather to name fo old a Child. For *Gildas* who wrote above 900 years paffed, whofe Writings *Polydor* never faw, but untruly Fathers upon him his own devife; *Giraldus* in his Defcription of *Ireland* to *Henry* the Second, and *Henry Huntington*, do plainly call *Man* in Latin *Bubonia*, adding thereto either *Manaw* or *Man*, for the better underftanding of the Name; Will you believe them or *Polydor*? Other Arguments there are which I will pafs over, till I have more leafure and occafion to write of this Matter.

Arfon. The fecond part of *North-Wales* was called *Arfon*, which is as much as to fay, over againft *Môn*; and had in it four Cantreds, and ten Comots.

Cantref *Aber* had in it three Comots, *Y Lhechwedh-uchaf*, *Y Lhechwedh-ifaf*, and *Nant-Conwey*.

Cantref *Arfon* had two Comots, *Twch Gwyrfai*, and *Ifgwyrfai*.

Cantref *Dunodic* had two Comots, *Ardudwy* and *Efionyth*.

Cantref *Lhyn* containeth three Comots, *Cymytmayn*, *Tinlhayn*, and *Canologion*. This is now called *Caernarvon-fhire*, as *Môn* is called *Anglefey-fhire*, and have

the

The Description of WALES.

the same division at this day. In this Shire are *Snowden*-Hills, called *Eryri*, neither in height, fertility of the Ground, Wood, Cattel, Fish and Fowl, giving place to the Famous *Alps*, and without Controversy the strongest Country within *Britain*.

Here is the Town of *Caernarvon*, called in the old time *Caersegonce*; and there is also *Conwey* called *Caergyffyn*. And the See of *Bangor*, with divers other antient Castles and Places of Memory, and was the last part of *Wales* that came under the Dominion of the Kings of *England*. It hath on the *North* the Sea and *Menai*, upon the *East* and *South East*, the River *Conwey*, which divideth it from *Denbigh shire*, altho' it now pass the River in one place by the Sea-shore. And on the *South-West* and *West*, it is separated from *Merionyth* by high Mountains and Rivers, and other Meats.

The third part of *Gwynedh* was *Merionyth* containing three Cantreds, and every Cantred three Comots. *Merionyth.*

As Cantref *Meyreon* hath three Comots, *Talybont*, *Pennal*, and *Tstumaner*.

Cantref *Arustly* had these, *Vwchcoed*, *Iscoed*, and *Gwarthrenion*.

Cantref *Penlhyn* had these, *Vwchmeloch*, *Ismeloch*, and *Micnaint*, and this keepeth the said Name till this day, but not within the same Mears, and is full of Hills and Rocks, and hath upon the *North* the Sea, notable at this day for the great resort and number of People that repair thither to take Herrings. It hath upon the *East*, *Arfon* and *Denbigh*-Land, upon the *South*, *Powys*, and upon the *West*, *Dyfi* and *Cardigan-shire*.

In this Country standeth the Town of *Harlech*, and *Tegyd*, a great Lake called *Lhyn-Tegyd* through which the River *Dee* runneth, and mingleth not with the Water of the Lake, which is three Miles long and also the *Salmons*, which are commonly taken in the River hard by the Lake, are never seen to enter the Lake. Likewise a kind of Fish called *Gwyniaid*, which are like to *Whitings*, and are full in the Lake, are never taken in the River. Not far from this Lake is a place called

* * *   *Caergay,*

The Description of WALES.

Caergay, which was the House of *Gay*, *Arthur*'s Foster-Brother. This Shire, as well as *Arfon*, is full of Cattel, Fowl and Fish, with great number of Red Deer and Roes; but there is great scarcity of Corn.

y Berfedh-wlad. The fourth part of *Gwynedh*, was called *y Berfedh-wlad*, which may be Englished, the in-land or middle Country, which contained five Cantreds and thirteen Comots, as Cantref *Rhyfoniec* had in it these Comots, *Uwchalet* and *Isalet*.

Cantref *Ystrad* had *Hiraethoc* and *Cynmeirch*:

Cantref *Rhos* these, *Uwchdulas*, *Isdulas* and *Creuthyn*, all which are in the Lordship of *Denbigh*, saving the *Creuthyn* which is in *Caernarvonshire*, wherein the Castle of *Dyganwy* did stand, which was the Earls of *Chester*, and is commonly called in the *Latin* and *English* Chronicle, *Gannoc*.

Dyffryn Clwyd. The fourth Cantref was *Dyffryn Clwyd*, which may be Englished the Valley of *Clwyd*, and now is called the Lordship of *Rhuthyn*, and hath these Comots, *Coleigion*, *Lhannerch* and *Dogveilyn*.

The fifth Cantref is *Tegengl*, and now is a part of *Flint-shire*, having these Comots, *Counsylht*, *Prestatyn*, and *Ruthlan*. And in this part is one of the fairest Vallies within this Isle, containing 18 miles in length, and 4, 5, 6, or 7 in breadth, as the Hills either draw inward together, or backward asunder, which high Hills do inclose it on the *East*, *West*, and *South* parts, and *Northward* the Sea. It is plentiful of Cattel, Fish and Fowl, Corn, Hey, Grass, and Wood, and divided along in the midst with the River *Clwyd*, to whom runneth *Clywedoc*, *Ystrat*, *Whilar*, *Elwy*, and a great number of other Rivers from the Hills. In this Valley two miles from the Sea, is the Town and

Ann 12. Castle of *Ruthlan*, where sometimes a Parliament
Edw. I. hath been kept. And two miles above it is the See of St. *Asaph*, between the Rivers *Clwyd* and *Elwy*, called in the old time the Bishop's See of *Lhan-Elwy*. Four miles thence, and two miles from the River, is situate upon a Rock the Town and Castle of *Denbigh*, where is one of the greatest Markets in the Marches of *Wales*, and one of the fairest and strongest Castles

within

The Description of WALES.

within this Realm, which being the House of *David* Brother to *Lhewelyn*, the last Prince of the *Welch-Blood*, was enlarged and strengthned by *Henry Lacy* Earl of *Lincoln*, to whom King *Edward* gave the same Lordship ; it is also the Shire-Town of that Shire. Five miles above this, is the Town of *Ruthyn* with a fair Castle, which sometimes belonged to the Lords *Gray* Earls of *Kent*. This part of *North-Wales*, hath upon the *North* the River *Dee*, and the Sea. Upon the *West*, *Arfon*, and the River *Conwey*. *South* and *East*, *Merionyth*, and the Country then called *Powys*. And these be the Mears and Bounds of *Gwynedh* or *Venedotia*, for the Name of *North Wales* containeth besides this all *Powys* at these days. So there was under the Territory of *Aberffraw* fifteen Cantreds, and in them thirty eight Comots.

The second Kingdom was *Mathrafal*, which in *Mathra-* right order was the third, as that which came to the *fal* or third Brother, yet for the better understanding of the *Powys*. History following, I have placed it here. To this Kingdom belonged the Country of *Powys*, and the Land betwixt *Wy* and *Severn*. Which part had upon the *South* and *West*, *South-Wales*, with the Rivers *Wy* and *Tywy*, and other Mears. Upon the *North*, *Gwynedh*, and upon the *East* the Marches of *England*, from *Chester* to *Wy*, a little above *Hereford* ; and therefore it was most troubled with Wars, as well of the *Saxons*, as afterwards of the *Normans*, Lords Marchers, who daily wan some part thereof, and by that means it was the first part that served the Kings of *England*, and therefore less esteemed of all the rest. This part called *Powys*, was divided again into *Powys Fadoc*, and *Powys Wenwynwyn*. *Powys Fadoc* contained in it self five Cantreds and fifteen Comots.

Cantref *Y Barwn*, which had three Comots, *Dynmael*, *Edeyrneon*, and *Glyndourdwy*, which are now in *Merionyth-shire* (saving *Dinmael* which is in *Denbighshire*.)

Cantref *Y Rhiw*, whose Comots were these, *Yal* now in *Denbigh-shire* ; *Ystratalyn* and *Hop* now in *Flintshire*. Cantref

The Description of WALES.

Cantref *Uwchnant* hath thefe Comots, *Merfforth* in *Flint-fhire*. *Maelor Gymraeg*, in Englifh *Bromfield*, now in *Denbigh-fhire*, and *Maelor Saefneg* in *Flint-fhire*.

Cantref *Trefred* containeth thefe Comots, *Croef-fain*, *Tref y Wayn*, in Englifh *Chirke*, and in *Denbigh-fhire*. *Croefofwallt*, in Englifh *Ofweftrey*, and in *Shrop-fhire*.

Cantref *Rhaiyder* with his Comots *Mochnant Ifraiyder*, *Cynlhaeth* and *Nanheudwy* all in *Chirke*-Land, and in *Denbigh-fhire*. Alfo the Lordfhip of *Whytington* now in *Shrop-fhire*, was in this part of *Powys*, which part at this day hath loft the Name of *Powys*, and is fituated in divers Shires, as it appeareth by the Difcourfe before paffed. In this part is the Caftle of *Holt* in *Bromfield*, and the Caftle of *Chirke* in *Chirke*-Land. Likewife the Lordfhip and Caftle of *Whytington*, which came by marriage to *Foulk Fitzwarren*. There is befide thefe, the Lordfhip of *Ofweftry*, of the which the *Fitzalans* have been Lords thefe 300 and odd years, and of divers other Lordfhips in thofe Marches, as *Shrarden*, the eleven Towns, *Clun* and many others, which are all now in *Shrop-fhire*.

The fecond part called *Powys Wenwynwyn*, had likewife five Cantreds, and twelve Comots.

Cantref *Y Fyrnwy* had thefe Comots, *Mochnant uwch Rayader Mechain Ifcoed* and *Lhannerch Hudol*.

Cantref *Yllyc* had thefe, *Deuthwr*, *Gorthwr Ifaf*, and *Yftrat Marchelh*.

Cantref *Lhyfwynaf* had thefe, *Caerneon*, and *Mechain Uwchcoed*.

Cantref *Cydewen* had Comot *Conan* and Comot *Hauren*.

Cantref *Conan* had *Cyfeilioc* and *Mouthwy*, which is now in *Merionyth-fhire*. Of all thefe, the three firft Cantreds do only at this day bear the Name of *Powys*, which are upon the *North*-fide of *Severn*, and are all five (faving the Comot of *Mowthwy*) in *Mongomery-fhire*.

This is a Country full of Woods, Hills, and Rivers, and hath in it thefe Towns, the *Poole*, *New-Town*, and *Machynlhaeth*.

The Description of WALES.

Machynlhaeth. Aruftly was in old time in this part, but afterwards it came to the Princes of *Gwynedh*. These Lordships came by just descent from the Princes thereof, to a Woman named *Hawys*, the Daughter of *Owen ap Gruffydh*. *Aruftly* and *Cyfeilioc* came to the Baron of *Dudley*, and afterwards it was sold to the King.

The third part belonging to *Mathrafal*, was the Land between *Wy* and *Severn*, containing four Cantreds, and thirteen Comots.

Cantref *Melienyth* hath these Comots, *Ceri, Strydh-ygre, Rhiwalalht*, and *Glyn Ieithon*.

Cantref *Elfel* hath these, *Uwchmynydh, Ifmynydh*, and *Lhechdhyfnog*.

Cantref *yClawdh* these, *Dyffryn Teyfediat, Strydhynogen*, and *Pennwelht*.

Cantref *Buelht* hath these, *Strydh y Fam, Dreulys*, and *Ifyrwon*. Of this part there is at this day some in *Montgomery-shire*, some in *Radnor-shire*, and some in *Brecknock-shire*. In this part, and in the Lordships marching to it, which altho' at the time of this division, which was in the time of the last Prince, were not in his subjection, yet to this day speak *Welch*, and are called *Wales*, and in these Comots are these Towns and Castles. *Montgomery* called in Welch *Trefaldwyn*, a pretty Town and a fair Castle. The Castle of *Clun*, called *Colunwry*, which is the Earls of *Arundel*. The Town of *Knighton*, in Welch *Trefyclawd*. The Castle of *Cymaron*. *Prefteyn* in Welch *Lhanandras*. The Town and Castle of *Radnor*, in Welch *Macfyfed*, at this day the Shire Town. The Town of *Kington* and the Castle of *Huntingdon*, called in Welch *Y Caftelh Mayn*, which were the *Bohuns* Earls of *Hereford*, and after the Dukes of *Buckingham*. Castle *Payne, Haye, Lhanfair* in *Buelht*. These Lordships with *Brecknock* and *Abergefenny*, were belonging to the *Bruces* Lords of *Brecknock*, and after came divers times, and by sundry means to the *Bohuns, Nevils*, and *Mortimers*. And so (as I have rehearsed) in this Territory or Kingdom were found fourteen Cantreds, and forty Comots. Two of these

parts,

The Defcription of WALES.

parts, which are *Powys* and *Gwynedh*, are at this day called *North-Wales*, and divided into fix Shires. *Môn* called *Anglefey*, *Caernarvon*, *Mericnyth*, *Denbigh*, *Flint*, and *Montgomery-fhire*, and are all on the *North* fide *Severn*, faving a piece of *Montgomery-fhire*.

And here I think it good to let the Reader underftand what the *Britifh* Chronicle faith of *North-Wales*, which affirmeth that three times it came by Inheritance to Women. Firft to *Stradwen*, Daughter to *Cadfan ap Conan ap Endaf*, and Wife to *Coel Godebec*; Mother to *Genaw*, *Dyfyr* and *Gwawl*. The fecond time to the fame *Gwawl* Wife to *Edeyrn ap Padarn*, and Mother to *Cunetha Wledic*; which *Cunetha* inhabiting in the North parts of *England*, about the year 540. after the Incarnation of Chrift, and hearing how the mingled Nations of *Irifh-Scots*, and *Picts*, had over-run the Sea-fhore of *Cardigan*, which was part of his Inheritance, fent his Sons thither to enjoy their Inheritance, of whom *Tibiaon* his eldeft Son died in *Man*, which Land the faid *Irifh-Scots* had won. For *Gildas* faith, that the Children of *Glam Hector*, which peopled a great part of *Ireland*, *Yfcroeth* with his People inhabited *Dalrieuda*, which is a part of *Scotland* : *Builke* with his People came to *Man*. But I think it good to put in *Gildas* words, which faith ; *Builke cum filiis fuis inhabitavit Euboniam infulam vulgo Manaw, quæ eft in meditullio maris inter Hyberniam & Britanniam* ; that is to fay, *Builke* with his Children inhabited the Ifle *Eubonia*, commonly *Manaw* (for fo it was and is named in *Britifh*) which lieth in the middle of the Sea, between *Ireland* and *Britain*. This was not called *Môna*, as *Polydor* faineth. The Children of *Bethoun* inhabited *Demetia*, which is *South-Wales*, with *Gwyr* and *Cydweli*, till they were chafed thence by the Children of *Cunetha*. Thus far *Gildas*. Therefore the Sons of *Cunetha*, being arrived in *North Wales* (as well I think being driven by the *Saxons*, as for their Inheritance) divided the Country betwixt them. And firft *Meireaon* the Son of *Tibiaon*, the Son of *Cunetha*, had Cantref *Meireaon* to his part, *Arufel ap Cunetha* had
 Cantref

The Description of WALES.

Cantref *Aruſtly*. *Caredic ap Cunetha*, had *Caerdigion*, now called *Cardigan-ſhire*. *Dunod* had Cantref *Dunodic*. *Edeyrn* had *Edeyrnion*. *Mael* had *Dymmael*. *Coel* had *Coleyon*. *Doguael* had *Dogueilyn*. *Rhyfaon* had *Rhyfonioc*, now *Denbigh*-land. *Eineon Ych* had *Caereneon* in *Powys*. *Uſſa* had *Maeſuſwalht* now *Oſweſtry*. For ſurely that they ſay commonly of *Oſwald* King of *Northumberland*, to be ſlain there, and of the Well that ſprung where his Arm was carried, is nothing ſo. For *Beda* and all other Writers teſtify that *Peanda* ſlew *Oſwald* at *Maſerfelt*, in the Kingdom of *Northumberland*, and his Body was buried in the Abby of *Bradney*, in the Province of *Lhyndeſey*. But to my former matter. Theſe Names given by the Sons of *Cunetha*, remain to this day. After this the *Iriſh-Picts* or *Scots*, which the *Britains* called *Y Gwydhyl Phictiaid*, which is to ſay, the *Iriſh-Picts*, did over-run the Iſle of *Môn*, and were driven thence by *Caſwalhon Lhawhir*, that is *Caſwalhon* with the long hand, the Son of *Eineon Yrch ap Cunedha*, who ſlew *Serigi* their King with his own hands, at *Lhan y Gwydhyl*, which is the *Iriſh* Church at *Holyhead*. This *Caſwalhon* was Father to *Maelgon Gwynedh*, whom the *Latins* call *Maglocunus*, Prince and King of *Britain*.

In his time was the Famous Clerk and great Wiſeman *Talieſſyn Ben Beirdh*, that is to ſay, the chiefeſt of the *Beirdh* or Wiſemen; for this word *Bardh* in *Cæſar*'s time, ſignified (as *Lucan* beareth Witneſs) ſuch as had knowledge of things to come, and ſo it ſignifieth at this day. This *Maelgon* had a Son called *Run* in whoſe time the *Saxons* invited *Gurmond* into *Britain* from *Ireland*, who had come thither from *Affric*, who with the *Saxons* was the utter deſtruction of the *Britains*, and ſlew all that profeſſed Chriſt, and was the firſt that drove them over *Severn*. This *Run* was Father to *Beli*, who was Father to *Iago*, (for ſo the *Britains* call *James*) who was Father to *Cadfan*, and not *Brochwel* called *Brecyfal* (as the *Engliſh* Chronicle ſaith) for this *Brechwel* called *Yſgithroc*, that is, long toothed, was choſen Leader of ſuch as met with *Adelred* alias *Ethelbertus Rex Cantiæ*, and other Angles

Maelor Gwran, Son to Cuhnedha had Maeloron, that is the two Maelors, Maelor Gymbraeg, called Br. and led Br. and Maelor Saeſneg.

* * * 4

The Description of WALES.

and *Saxons*, whom *Augustine* had moved to make War against the Christian *Britains*, and these put *Brochwel* twice to flight, not far from *Chester*, and cruelly slew a 1000 Priests and Monks of *Bangor*, with a great number of lay-Brethren of the same House, which lived by the Labour of their Hands, and were come bare-footed and woolward to crave Mercy and Peace at the *Saxons* Hands. And here you shall understand that this was not *Augustine* Bishop of *Hippona* the great Clerk, but *Augustine* the Monk, called the Apostle of *England*.

Then this *Brochwel* retired over *Dee*, hard by *Bangor*, and defended the *Saxons* the Passage, till *Cadfan* King of *North Wales*, *Meredyth* King of *South-Wales*, and *Bledrus* or *Bletius* Prince of *Cornwal*, came to succour him, and gave the *Saxons* a sore Battel, and slew of them the number of a 1066, and put the rest to flight. After the which Battel, *Cadfan* was chosen King of *Britain*, and was chief Ruler within the Isle; after whom his Son *Cadwalhon*, who was Father to *Cadwalader*, the last of the *British* Blood, that bare the Name of King of *Britain*, was King.

The third time that *North-Wales* came to a Woman, was to *Esylht* the Daughter of *Conan Tindaytbury*, the Son of *Edwal Twrch*, the Son of *Cadwaladr*. She was Wife to *Merfyn Frych*, and Mother to *Rhodric* the Great, as shall be hereafter declared. By this you may understand, that *North-Wales* hath been a great while the chiefest Seat of the last Kings of *Britain*, because it was, and is the strongest Country within this Isle, full of high Mountains, Craggy Rocks, great Woods, and deep Vallies, strait and dangerous Places, deep and swift Rivers, as *Dyfi*, which springeth in the Hills of *Merionyth*, and runneth *North-West* through *Mowthwy*, and by *Machynlaeth*, and so to the Sea at *Aberdyfi*, dividing *N.r.h* and *South-Wales* asunder. *Dee*, called in *Welch Dourdwy*, springing also on the other side of the same Hills, runneth *East* through *Penllyn*, and the Lake *Tegyd*, down to *Corwen* and *Llangollen*, between *Chirke*-Land

and

The Description of WALES.   xvii

and *Bromfield*, where it boweth *Northward* toward *Bangor* to the *Holt*, and to *Chester*, and thence *North-West* to *Flint*-Castle, and so to the Sea.

There is also *Conway*, rising likewise in *Merionyth-shire*, and dividing *Caernarvon* from *Denbigh-shire*, runneth under *Snowden* North-East, by the Town of *Aberconwey* to the Sea.

Also *Cluyd*, which rising in *Denbigh*-Land, runneth down to *Ruthyn*, and plain *North*, not far from *Denbigh* to *St. Asaph*, and so by *Ruthlan* and to the Sea. There be many other fair Rivers, of which some run to the Sea, as *Mawr* at *Traethmawr*, and *Afon y Saint* at *Caernarvon*, and other that run to *Severn*, as *Murnwy* in *Powys*, and to *Murnwy*, *Tanat*; some other to *Dee*, as *Ceirioc* betwixt the Lordships of *Chirke* and *Whittington*; *Alyn* through *Yal* and *Molds dale*, and *Hope dale*, and so to *Dee*, a little above *Chester*. And this shall suffice for the perfect Description of that which in old time was called *Grynedh* and *Powys*, and at these days the six Shires of *North-Wales*.

Now remaineth the last Kingdom of *Wales*, called *Dynefawr*, which although it was the greatest, yet was not the best, as *Giraldus* witnesseth, chiefly because it was much molested with *Flemings* and *Normans*, and also that in divers parts thereof, the Lords would not obey their Prince, as in *Gwent* and in *Morganwc*, which was their own confusion, as shall hereafter appear. This was divided into six Parts, of the which *Caredigion* was the first, and contained four Cantreds and ten Comots, as Cantref *Pentredic* had in it these Comots, *Genzurglyn*, *Perfedh* and *Creuthyn*. *Caredigion*.

Cantref *Canawl* had these, *Mefenyth*, *Anhunoc*, and *Pennarth*.

Cantref *Castelh* had these Comots, *Mabrynion* and *Caerwedroc*.

Cantref *Symwn* had these, *Gwenicnyth* and *Iscoed*; and this part is at this day called in English *Cardigan-shire*, and in Welch *Swydh-Aberterfi*. This is a Champion Country without much Wood, and hath been divers times overcome with *Flemings* and *Normans*, which builded many Castles in it, and at the last were beaten out

xviii *The Description of* **WALES**.

out of them all. It hath on the East *North-Wales*, with the River *Dyfi* and part of *Powys*, upon the South *Caermardhyn shire*, upon the West *Pembroke shire*, with the River *Teifi*, and upon the North the *Irish* Sea. In this part is the Town of *Cardigan* upon *Teifi*, not far from the Sea. The Town of *Aberystwyth* upon the River *Ystwyth*, by the Sea, and *Lhanbadarn Fairr*, which was a great Sanctuary, and a place of Religious and Learned Men in times past. And in this Shire were a great number of Castles, as the Castle of *Ystratmeyric*, of *Walter*, of *Lhanrysted*, of *Dynerth*, of the Sons of *Wyneaon*, of *Aber-Reidol*, and a great number more, with the Town of *Tregaron*, and *Lhandhewibresi*.

Dyfet. The second part was called *Dyfed*, and at this day *Pembroke-shire*, and had in it eight Cantreds, and twenty three Comots, which were these. Cantref *Emlyn* had these Comots, *Uwchcuch*, *Ifcuch* and *Lefethyr*.

Cantref *Arberth* had these, *Penrhyn ar Elays*, *Esterolef* and *Talacharn*.

Cantref *Daugledheu* had these, *Amgoed*, *Pennant* and *Efelfre*.

Cantref *Y Coed* had these, *Lhanhayaden* and *Castelh Gwys*.

Cantref *Penfro* hath these, *Coed yr haf*, *Maenor byrr*, and *Penfro*.

Cantref *Rhos* hath these, *Hulfforth Castelh Giralchmai* and *Ygarn*.

Cantref *Pubidioc* hath these, *Mynyw*, *Pencaer* and *Pebidioc*.

Cantref *Cemais* hath these, *Uwchmefer*, *Ifnefer* and *Trefdraeth*.

In this part are divers Towns and Havens at this day, as *Pembroke*, *Tenby*, in Welch *Dynbegh-y-pyfcot*, *Hereford-West*, in Welch *Hulfforth*, with the fair Haven of *Milford*, called in Welch *Aberdaugledheu*. St. *Davids* or *Menevia*, called in Welch *Mynyw*, the chiefest See in all *Wales*. Then *Fifcard* called *Abergwayn*; and *Newport*, named *Trefdraeth*; these be along the Sea-coast, or not very far off. Besides these

there

The Description of WALES.   xix

there be divers Castles, as *Cilgerran, Arberth, Gwys, Lhanhayaden,Walwyn,*and divers others. This part was won first by the *Montgomery's* Earls of *Shrewsbury,* and after given to the *Marshalls,*and so to *Valence,*and from thence were the Princes of *Wales* most troubled with the *Normans* and *Flemings,* who do remain and inhabit about *Tenby, Pembroke* and *Rhos* to this day, which can neither *Welch* nor good *English* as yet. *Dyfed* (for so will I call it hereafter) hath on the the *West* and *North* the *Irish* Sea, upon the *South* the *Spanish* Sea, and upon the *East Caermardhyn-shire,* and on the *North-East Cardigan-shire.* The third part was *Caermardhyn-shire,* having four Cantreds, *Caermar-* and fifteen Comots, as Cantref *Finioc* with the Co- *dhyn.* mots of *Harfryn, Derfedh,* and *Isgeneny.*

Cantref *Eginoc* with these, *Gwyr,* now in *Glamorgan-shire, Cydweli,* and *Carnwilhcon.*

Cantref *Bachan* with these, *Malhaen, Caeo,* and *Maenor Deilo.*

Cantref *Mawr* with these,*Cethineoc*Comot *mabElfyw,* Comot *mabUchdryd* and *Wydigada.*In this Shire are the TownsandCastles of *Caermardhyn;Dynefowr,*which was the Prince's Seat of the Country, *Newtown, Lhandeilo, Lhanymdhyfri, Emlyn, Swansey,* now in *Glamorgan-shire,* called in *Welch Abertawy* upon the Sea, the Castle of the Sons of *Uchtryd,* of *Lhanstephan,* and others. It hath upon the West *Dyfed* or *Pembroke-shire,* on the North *Cardigan-shire,* upon the South-West the Sea, and upon the South-East *Glamorgan,* and upon the East *Brecknock-shire.* This is counted the strongest part of all *South-Wales,* as that which is full of high Mountains, great Woods, and fair Rivers, especially *Tywy.* In this, and in the other two parts of *South-Wales,* were the notablest Acts that this History treateth of, atchieved and done.

The fourth called *Morganwc,* now *Glamorgan-shire, Morga-* containing four Cantreds, with fifteen Comots. As *nwc.* Cantref *Croneth,*with these Comots *Rwngneth ac Afan, Tir yr Hwndrwd,* and *Maenor Glyncgwr.*

Cantref *Pennythen* with these, *Meyscyn, Glynrhodny, Maenor Talafan,* and *Maenor Ruthyn.*

Cantref

The Description of WALES.

Cantref *Brenhinol* with thefe, *Cibowr*, *Senghennyth*, *Uwchcaeth*, and *Ifcaeth*.

Cantref *Gwentlhwg*, which is now in *Monmouth-shire*, with thefe Comots, *y Rhardh Ganol*, and *Euthaf-dylygion*. In this part are thefe Towns and Caftles, *Lhandaf* the Bifhop's See, *Caerdyffe*, called *Caerdhyf*, *Cowbridge*, called in Welch *Y bont faen*, which is as much as to fay, Stone-bridge, *Lantwyd*, *Caerffyli*, and others, and hath divers Rivers which run to the South-Sea, as *Lay*, *Taf*, *Tawy*, *Neth*, *Afan*, *Ogwr*, and *Lhy-chwr*; it hath on the South, the Sea of *Severn*, which divideth it from *Devon-fhire* and *Cornwall*; upon the Weft and North-Weft, *Caermardhyn-fhire*; upon the North-Eaft, *Brecknock-fhire*; and upon the Eaft, *Mon-mouth-fhire*. Of this you fhall read very little, for one *Ieftyn* being Chief of the Country, and having War with his Neighbours, called one *Robert Fitzhamon*, with a great number of Strangers to his fuccours, which after they had atchieved the Enterprife, liked fo well the Country, that they found occafion to fall out with *Ieftyn*, and inhabited the Country themfelves and their Heirs to this day.

The fifth part was called *Gwent* and now in *Mon-mouth fhire*, which had three Cantreds, and ten Co-mots, as Cantref *Gwent*, which hath thefe Comots, *Y mynyth*, *Ifcoed Lhefnydh*, and *Tref y grug*.

Cantref *Ifcoed* thele, *Brynbuga*, *Uwchcoed*, *y Teirtref*, and *Erging ac ewyas*, now in *Hereford-fhire*.

Cantref *Côch* was the feventh Cantred of *Morga-nwc*, which is now in *Glocefter-fhire*, and is called the Foreft of *Dean*.

In this part was the antient City of *Caerlheon* upon *Usk*, where was the Archbifhop's See of *Wales*; here are alfo divers Towns and Caftles, as *Chepftow*, *Glyn Strigul*, *Rôs*, *Tyntern* upon the River *Wy*; there is alfo *Newport*, called *y Cafteih Newydh*, *Uyfc* called *Brynbuga*, *Grofmont*, *Raglan*, *White-Caftle*, *Abergefenny*, and many others. This is a fair and a fertile Country, of which likewife the Gentlemen were never obedient to their Prince, which was the caufe of their own deftruction. It hath on the Weft *Glamorgan* and

Brecknock-fhires,

The Description of WALES.

Brecknock-shires, upon the North *Hereford-shire*, upon the East *Glocester-shire*, with the River *Wy*, and upon the South and South-East *Severn*.

Last of all cometh *Brecheinoc*, now *Brecknock-shire*, *Brecheinoc*, which hath three Cantreds, and eight Comots. As Cantref *Selef* which hath these Comots, *Selef* and *Trahayern*.

Cantref *Canol* these, *Talgarth Ystradyw* and *Brwynllys* or *Eglwys Tail*.

Cantref *Mawr* these, *Tir Raulff*, *Lhywel* and *Cerrig-Howel*. In this part is the Town of *Brecknock* upon the meeting of *Usk* and *Honddi*, and is called *Aberhonddi*, and *Hay* called *y Gelhy*, with *Talgarth*, *Buelht*, *Lhangors*; it hath West *Caermardhyn-shire*, with the River *Tywy*, upon the North *Radnor-shire* with *Wy*, upon the East *Herefordshire* and *Monmouth*, upon the South *Glamorgan*. This for the most part is full of Mountains, Woods and Rivers, especially *Buelkt*. And the Lords of this Country called *Bruces* with the *Mortimers*, most of all others Lords Marchers, sometimes by Might, but oftner by Treason, have molested and grieved the Princes of *Wales*. This Land came after the *Bruces* to the *Bohuns* Earls of *Hereford*, and so to the *Staffords* Dukes of *Buckingham*.

These six Shires being subject to the Territory of *Dynefawr* with *Radnor-shire*, which was belonging to *Mathrafal*, are now commonly called *South-Wales*, which Country is both great and large, with many fair Plains and Vallies for Corn, high Mountains and Rocks full of Pasture for Cattel; great and thick Woods, with Forrests and Parks for Red Deer and Fallow; clear and deep Rivers full of Fish, of which *Severn* is the Chiefest, which with *Wy* and *Rheidol* spring out of a high Mountain called *Pymlhymon*, in the edge of *Cardigan-shire*, and are called commonly the three Sisters. *Severn* runneth full East through *Cydewen* by the Pool, and under the Castle of *Shraden* to *Shrewsbury*, from whence it turneth Southward and runs to *Bridgenorth*, *Bewdley*, *Worcester*. *Glocester*, and so to the Sea by *Bristol*. The second Sister is *Guy*, in English *Wy*, which took her Journey South-East, by

Rayade

The Description of WALES.

Rayader Gwy to *Buelht*, where *Irwon* meeteth her, thence to *Glasbury*, and so to *Hereford* and *Monmouth*, and to the Sea of *Severn* at *Chepstow*; for so they call *Môr Hafren* the Sea which severeth *Wales* from *Somerset-shire*, *Devonshire* and *Cornwal*. The third Sister named *Rheidol*, ran Northward to the Sea being not far off, at *Aberystwyth*. There be other fair Rivers as *Usk*, which rising in a high Mountain called *y Mynydh dy* in the South part of *Brecknockshire* runneth to *Brecknock*, and so through *Monmouthshire* to the Town of *Usk*, *Caerlheon* and *Newport*, and so to the said South Sea. *Tywy* also rising not far from *Wy*, runneth South to *Lhanymdhyfri*, and thence South-West by *Lhandeilo* and *Dynefawr* to *Abergwily* and *Caermardhyn*, and so by *Lhanstephan* to the Sea.

Teifi likewise which riseth in the edge of *Caermardhyn shire*, and runneth North-West by *Emlyn*, *Cilgerran*, *Cardigan*, and so to the North Sea. In *Teifi* above all the Rivers in *Wales*, were in *Giraldus*'s time a great number of *Castors*, which may be Englished *Bevers*, and are called in Welch *Afanc*, which name only remaineth in *Wales* at this day, but what it is very few can tell. It is a Beast not much unlike an *Otter*, but that it is bigger, all hairy saving the Tail, which is like a Fish Tail, as broad as a Man's Hand. This Beast useth as well the Water as the Land, and hath very sharp Teeth, and biteth cruelly, till he perceives the Bones crack, his Stones be of great efficacy in Physick. He that will learn what strong Nests they make, which *Giraldus* calleth Castels, which they build upon the face of the Water with great Boughs which they cut with their Teeth, and how some lye upon their Backs, holding the Wood with the fore-Feet, which the other draweth with a cross stick, the which he holdeth in his Mouth to the water-side, and other particularities of their Natures, let him read *Giraldus* in his Topography of *Wales*. There be besides these a great number of Rivers, of which some run to the South, and some to the West and North Sea, as *Tywy* in *Glamorgan-shire*, *Taf* also in *Caermardhyn shire*

Κάςωρ *Greek*, Fiber, *Lat.* Beaver *English*, Afanc *British*, *Giraldus in Itiner.*

The Defcription of WALES.

dhyn fhire, which runnenh to *Cledheu,* two Rivers either called *Cledheu,* which do give *Milford* the name of *Aberdaugledheu* in *Pembroke-fhire, Arth, Aeron,* and *Tjlwyth,* in *Cardigan.* There be alfo divers Lordfhips which be added to other Shires, and were taken heretofore for parts of *Wales,* and in moſt part of them at this day the *Welch* Language is ſpoken, as *Ofweftry, Knocking, Whittington, Elfmer, Masbroke, Chirbury, Caurs, Clun,* which are now in *Shrop-fhire, Ewyas-Lacy, Ewyas-Haroald, Clifford, Winforton, Yardley, Huntingdon, Whitney, Loghardneys* in *Hereford-fhire.* Alſo this Country of *South-Wales* as all the reſt of *Britain,* was firſt inhabited by the *Britains,* which remain there to this day, ſaving that in divers places, eſpecially along the Sea-ſhore, they have been mingled with *Saxons, Normans* (which the *Welch* Hiſtory cálleth *French-men*) and *Flemings*; ſo that the Princes cf *Wales,* ſince the Conqueſt of the *Normans,* could never keep quiet poſſeſſion thereof, but what for Strangers, and what for diſloyalty of their own People, vexation and War, were for the moſt part compelled to keep themſelves in *Caermardhyn-fhire.*

THE

THE
HISTORY
OF
WALES.

WHEN the *Roman* Empire, under *Valentinian the Younger*, began to decline, and became fenfibly unable to reprefs the perpetual Incurfions of the *Goths, Huns, Vandals,* and other barbarous Invaders; it was found neceffary to abandon the remoteft Parts of that unwieldy Body, and to recal the *Roman* Forces that defended them, the better to fecure the Inward, and the Provinces moft expofed to the Depredations of the *Barbarians*. And in this Exigency of the *Roman* Affairs, *Britain*, as lying far remote from the Heart of the Empire, was deprived of the *Roman* Garrifons; which, being tranfported into *Gaul* upon more urgent Occafions, left it naked and expofed to the inveterate Cruelty of the *Scots* and *Picts*: for no fooner had they underftood of the *Romans* Departure out of *Britain*, and that the *Britains* were to expect no further Help from the Empire; but they defcend in greater Number than formerly, and with greater Courage and Expectation, being now rid of the Fear they entertained of the *Roman* Legions, who always ufed to hinder their

B   Progrefs

The History of WALES.

Progress, and to prevent their Incursions into the *Roman* Province. The *Britains* perceiving their antient and implacable Enemies to fall upon them, and finding themselves far too weak to repel their Endless Devastations; with a lamentable Narrative of their own Miseries, and the cruel Oppressions of their Enemies, they sent over to *Gaul*, imploring Aid of *Ætius* Præfect of that Province; who, being moved with the deplorable Condition of the *Britains*, dispatch'd over a Legion under the Command of *Gallio*, which unexpectedly surprising the *Picts* and *Scots*, forced them, with great Loss and Destruction, to retire over the Seas or Friths to their own Habitations. Then helping them to build a Wall of Stone cross the Land, for a Bulwark against any future Irruptions; the *Romans*, at their Departure, told them, they could not any more undertake such dangerous Expeditions for their Defence, and therefore admonished them to take Arms, and like Men vindicate their Country, their Wives, Children and Liberties from the Injuries of their barbarous Enemies.

But as soon as the *Roman* Legion was transported into *Gaul*, back return the *Picts* and *Scots*; and, having by a desperate Assault passed the Wall, pursued the *Britains* with a more dreadful and bloody Slaughter than formerly. The *Britains*, perceiving their Condition most desperate, once more send their miserable Complaints to *Ætius* in these Tragical Words; *To Ætius thrice Consul, the Groans of the* Britains : *the Barbarians drive us to the Sea, and the Sea drives us back to them*; *and so, distracted betwixt two Deaths, we are either drowned, or perish by the Sword.* But they solicite to no purpose; the *Romans* having already bid absolute farewel to *Britain*, and the Empire being cruelly oppressed by the *Goths*, and other Barbarous Nations, was not in a Condition possible to assist them. The *Britains* therefore finding themselves absolutely forsaken by the *Romans*, and conceiving it utterly impracticable to drive away the Barbarians by their own Strength; saw it urgently necessary to call in the Aid of some Foreign Nation, whose Labour in repelling their

their Enemies should be gratefully and satisfactorily Rewarded.

The Reason that the *British* Nation was at this time so weak and impotent, and so manifestly unable to withstand these barbarous Enemies, who were far inferiour as to extent of Country, and probably in number of People, may in great measure be attributed to the Ease and Quietness the *Britains* enjoy'd under the *Roman* Government. For whilst the *Roman* Legions continued in *Britain*, they ever undertook the Security and Preservation of it; so that the *Britains* heretofore were little concerned at the Incursions of the *Scots* and *Picts*, depending wholly upon the Strength and Valour of the *Romans*, insomuch, that within a while, they fell into a fit of Luxury and Effeminacy, and quickly forgot that Martial Prowness, and Military Conduct which their Ancestors so Famously excelled in. For after their intire Subjection to the *Roman* Empire, they had little or no Opportunity to Experience their Valour, excepting in some home-bred Commotions, excited by the aspiring Ambition of some *male*-contented General, which were quickly compos'd and reduced to nothing. And after the *Scots* and *Picts* grew Formidable, and durst venture to make Incursions into the *Roman* Province, the *Britains* were the least concerned in Opposing them, leaving that to the Care and Vigilancy of the *Roman* Garrisons. And this Easiness and Supinity of the *Britains*, may not be untruly attributed to the Policy of the *Roman* Constitution: For when the *Britains* were brought subject to the Empire, the first thing the *Romans* effected towards the Confirmation of their Obedience, was to take the Sword out of their Hands. They were sensible how Bold and Valorous the *Britains* naturally were, how unlike to submit their Necks to a Foreign Yoke, and therefore they found it impracticable to obtain a quiet Possession of this Province, as long as the *Britains* had Power and Opportunity to Oppose them. This Course they found very effectual, and when they had once lulled them asleep, they were not over solicitous to rouse and awaken them.

The History of WALES.

The *Britains* also might possibly be too much taken with this sedentary and unactive Life; and as long as they lived Secure under the Protection of the *Roman* Empire, they little feared their Countrey would become a Prey to any barbarous Nation. No one would have imagined that that Glorious Empire would be so soon crushed to pieces, which could not otherwise be effected, than by the insupportable pressure of its own Weight. This apprehension of the Greatness and Strength of the *Romans*, made the *Britains* probably less solicitous of enabling themselves to Defend their Countrey, not thinking they would ever forsake and relinquish the Province of *Britain*. But to their Sorrow they experienc'd the contrary, the Affairs of the Empire elsewhere requiring the Help of the *British* Legions, so that they were left exposed to the Cruelties of the *Northern* Invaders, having not as yet recovered any Power or Conduct to oppose them. For had not the *Scots* and *Picts* come on so forcibly at first, but had given time to the *Britains* to shake off that Lethargy they had for many Years been buried in, and to renew their Antient Discipline and Vigour, there had been no need of calling in the *Saxons*, seeing they would in all probability been able to Maintain their Ground against any Opposition, and likely had been in Possession of their whole Countrey to this time. But next to the Decree of Heaven, the Ruin of the *British* Nation must be attributed to its too much Luxury and Effeminacy, and to the universal Lapse of the Nobility and People, into an aversion of all Military Action and Martial Discipline. For tho' a continued Peace be in it self desirable, yet oftentimes nothing tends more to the future Ruin and Downfal of a Nation. For Peace begets in Men generally a habit of Looseness and Debauchery, is the occasion of many notorious Extravagancies and vitious Practises, which weakens their Hands, and cools their Courage and Greatness of Mind, so that in case of any open Danger, they are uncapable to Defend their Countrey, and unfit to Oppose the Common Enemy. Scarce any Kingdom or Nation was subverted, but the Ruin of it it was usher'd in by these means; witness the *Assyrian* under *Sardanapalus*, the *Persian* under *Darius*, and the *Egyptian* under *Cleopatra*; so that it was most prudently urged by a *Roman* Senator, that *Carthage* might not be demolished, lest that for want of an Enemy abroad, the Valour of the *Romans* might degenerate, and their Conduct be forgotten. Had the *Britains* had the Fortune to be continually in action, and not exchanged their Courage and Discipline for Ease and Laziness, they had had no reason to dread the Incursions of the *Scots* and *Picts*, nor any need of the Aid and Assistance of a foreign Nation; but the condition of their Affairs then required it, and Help must be had., or else their Countrey must unavoidably become a Prey to those Northern Invaders.

To prevent therefore and repel their Violence, King *Vortigern* held a Council of his Great Men and Nobles, where it was concluded to be most advantageous to the *Britains*, to invite the *Saxons* out of *Germany* to their aid, who in all probability would gladly embrace the opportunity, by reason that their own Countrey was grown too scanty for their superfluous Numbers. This Message of the *Britains*, however originally delivered, is by an antient *Saxon* Writer repeated in this manner; *Most noble Saxons, the miserable Britains, shatter'd and quite worn out by the frequent Incursions of their Enemies, upon the news of your many signal Victories, have sent us to you, humbly requesting that you would assist them at this juncture. A Land large and spacious, abounding with all manner of Necessaries, they give up entirely to your disposal. Hitherto we have lived happily under the Government and Protection of the* Romans; *next to the* Romans *we know none of greater Valour than your selves, and therefore in your Arms do now seek refuge. Let but that Courage and those Arms make us Conquerors, and we shall refuse no Service you shall please to impose.* To this Message the *Saxons* returned this short Answer: *Assure your selves, the* Saxons *will be true Friends to the* Britains, *and as such, shall be always ready both to relieve their Necessities, and to advance their Interest.*

The *Saxons* being thus happily courted to what themselves had a thousand times wish'd for, arriv'd soon after in *Britain*, in three Gallies, called in their own Language *Kiules*, under the Conduct of two Brethren *Hengist* and *Horsa*. Being honourably received by the King, and affectionately treated by the People, *their Faith* was given of both sides; the *Saxons* stipulating to defend the *Britains* Countrey, and the *Britains* to give the *Saxons* a satisfactory Reward for all the Pains and Dangers they should undergo upon their account. At first the *Saxons* shewed themselves very diligent in their Employment, and successfully repell'd the *Scots* and *Picts*; who being probably ignorant of the landing of the *Saxons*, and fearing no opposition, boldly advanc'd to the Heart of the Countrey. But when the *Saxons* became better acquainted with the Island, and happily discovered the Weakness and Inability of the *Britains*; under pretence that their Pay was not answerable to their Service and Deserts, they quarrelled with the *Britains*, and instead of supporting them according to Oath, entered into a League with their Enemies the *Scots*. Moreover, *Hengist* perceiving with whom he had to do, sent over to acquaint his Countreymen with the Beauty and Fertility of the Island, the Infirmity and Effeminacy of the Inhabitants; inviting them to be Sharers of his future Success and Expectations. To his Invitation they readily comply, and sailing over in great Numbers, they thought to take possession of that Countrey, which Fortune promised should be their own: But they must fight for it first; the *Britains* being resolved to the last to defend themselves and their Country against these treacherous Practices of the *Saxons*; and if possible, to drive them to their primitive Habitations. For when the *Britains* became sensible of the undermining aim of the *Saxons*, how they secretly endeavoured the total extirpation of the *British* Nation, they presently betook themselves to their Swords, and in a short time became signally famous for their Valour and Conduct. This the *Saxons* afterwards grievously felt, though the total recovery of *Britain* proved impracticable

The History of WALES.

practicable for want of Power; the *Saxons* having by Massacres and other treacherous means, most unmercifully lessened the Force and Number of the *Britains*. King *Vortigern* loved his Ease too well to observe their Practices; and besides, became so *foolishly enamour'd* with the Daughter of *Hengist*, which purposely was laid to intrap him, that the *Saxon* upon the strength of their Marriage began to carve for himself, and during *Vortigern*'s Reign, laid so firm a Foundation for the *Saxon* Conquest, that the succeeding *British* Kings, tho' famously valiant, could never undermine it. This Sottishness of his Father, young *Vortimer* could not at length endure; to see himself and his Country so openly and shamefully imposed upon by Strangers; and therefore he resolved to take the *British* Government upon himself, and to endeavour the universal Expulsion of the *Saxons*. With him the *British* Nobility willingly joyn, and after several famous Victories over the *Saxons*, he was unhappily poysoned by a *Saxon* Lady. After him the *Britains* bravely defended themselves against the prevailing Greatness of the *Saxons*, under these valiant Princes, *Aurelius Ambrosius, Uter Pendragon, Arthur, Constantine* II. *Aurelius Conanus, Vortiper,* and *Maelgon.* To him succeeded *Careticus*; in whose time the *Saxons* aspiring to a total Conquest of *Britain,* invited over one *Gurmundus*, a *Norwegian* Pyrate, who had lately signalized himself in *Ireland,* and obtain'd a Conquest over that Kingdom. Him they employ to march against *Careticus,* who being overcome and vanquished by him, the *Britains* were forced, some to retire beyond the Rivers *Severn* and *Dee,* some to *Cornwal,* and the rest to *Little Britain* in *France.* The *British* Affairs were now brought very low, and their Government reduced within a very narrow compass; so that the Title of the *Kings* of *Britain,* can be but superficially attributed to the succeeding Princes, *Cadwan, Cadwallan,* and *Cadwalader.*

B 4 *Cadwalade-*

Cadwalader.

Adwalader, furnamed *Bhendiged*, or the Bleſſed, was the laſt of *Britiſh* Race, that enjoyed the Title of *King of Britain*; after him, the *Welch*, who were the moſt numerous remains of the *Britains*, diſdaining to own any Subjection to the oppreſſing *Saxons*, ſet up a new Government among themſelves, and alter'd the Stile of *Britiſh* Kings, to that of Princes of *Wales*. But whilſt *Cadwalader* ruled in *Britain*, a very ſevere Famine, attended with a raging Peſtilence, which aſſuredly ſprung from the continued War, which was ſo eagerly carryed on betwixt the *Britains* and *Saxons*, happen'd in the Iſland, which occaſioned a moſt lamentable Mortality among his Subjects; inſomuch that he was compell'd, together with a great Number of his Nobility and others, to retire for Refuge to his Couſin *Alan*, King of *Lhydaw*, or *Little Britain* in *France*. There he was ſure, to meet with all Civility ſuitable to his Quality and Condition, as well, becauſe of his own near Relation and Conſanguinity to *Alan*; as upon the account that their Subjects were originally one and the ſame People: For the *Britains* of *France*, about the year of Chriſt 384. went over out of this Iſland under the Command of *Conan*, Lord of *Meriadoc*, to the aid of *Maximus* the Tyrant, againſt the Emperour *Gratianus*. For this Service *Maximus* granted to *Conan* and his Followers the Country of *Armorica*, where the *Britains* having driven out the former Inhabitants, ſeated themſelves, and erected a Kingdom, which laſted for many Years under ſeveral Kings, whoſe Names and Succeſſion are as follows:

The History of WALES.

The Catalogue of the *Armorican* Kings.

1. *Conan Meriadoc.*
2. *Gradlonus.*
3. *Salomon* I.
4. *Auldranus.*
5. *Budicus* I.
6. *Howelus Magnus.*
7. *Howelus* II.
8. *Alanus* I.
9. *Howelus* III.
10. *Gilquellus.*
11. *Salomon* II.
12. *Alanus* II.
13. *Conobertus.*
14. *Budicus* II.
15. *Theodoricus.*
16. *Ruhalbonus.*
17. *Daniel Dremroft,* i.e. *rubicunda facie.*
18. *Aregftanus.*
19. *Maconus.*
20. *Neomenius.*
21. *Harufpogius.*
22. *Salomon* III.

Alan II. then reigned in *Little Britain*, when *Cadwalader* was forced to forfake his own Dominions, and to retire beyond the Seas. He was defcended from *Rune* the Son of *Mailgon Gwyneth*, King of *Great Britain*, by a Daughter married to *Howel* the Second King of *Little Britain*. This Kingdom remained firm, till *Salomon* III. who was treacheroufly flain by his own Subjects; upon which unlucky Accident, the Kingdom was converted to an Earldom, whereof one *Alan* was the firft, a valiant and warlike Prince, who ftoutly refifted the *Normans*, and frequently vanquifhed and overcame them.

But after that *Cadwalader* had continued fome time with *Alan*, the Plague being abated in *Britain* he purpofed to return, and if poffible, to recover that part of his Kingdom which the *Saxons* were now in poffeffion of. He received frequent Intelligence of their Number and Increafe, how they fairly bid for the Conqueft of that Country, which had been governed by *Britifh* Kings for the fpace of 1827. Years. This troubled him exceedingly, and tho he had little hopes of prevailing by the Strength and Number of his Forces, yet he made the beft preparation that the Opportunity would permit, and difpatched his Fleet for the tranfportation of his Army, which

confifted

consisted partly of his own Subjects, and partly of such Succours as he received from *Alan*. Whilst he vigorously prosecuted this Design, and was ready to strike sail for Britain; his Voyage was prevented by a Message from Heaven; which counselled him to lay aside the thoughts of recovering his Kingdom, because it was already decreed above, that the *Britains* should no longer enjoy the Government of *Britain*, till the Prophesie of *Merlyn Ambrose* was fulfilled. And instead of a Voyage to *Britain*, he is ordered to take his Journey to *Rome*, where he should receive Holy Orders at the hands of Pope *Sergius*, and instead of recovering the *British* Crown, have his own Crown shaved off, and be initiated into the Order of the Monks. Whether this Vision was signified to him in a Dream, or by the impositious Illusion of some wicked Spirit; or whether it may be a phantastical Conceit of his own, being a Man of a mild and easie temper, wearied with Troubles and Miseries, is very dubious: Only this is certain, that he never returned again to *Britain*, after he had gone over to *Alan*. But *Cadwaladar* had no sooner received this Vision, but immediately he relates the whole to his Friend *Alan*, who presently consults all his prophetical Books, chiefly the famous Works of the two *Merlins*, *Ambrose* and *Silvester*: The first is said to be begotten on a Spirit, and born in the Town of *Carmarthen*, whence he received the Name of *Merlin*, and to flourish in the Reign of King *Vortigern*. The latter called *Caledonius*, from the Forest *Caledon* in *Scotland*, and *Silvester* or *Merlyn Wylht*, by reason he fell mad, and lived desolately after that he had seen a monstrous shape in the Air, prophesied in the time of King *Arthur*, and far more full and intelligible than the former. Both these were in great Reverence and Reputation among the *Britains*, and their Works very religiously preserved, and upon any considerable occasion most venerably consulted. They were of opinion, that nothing could escape their Knowledg; and that no Accident of moment or revolution could happen, which they did not foretel, and was to be

disco-

The History of WALES.

discovered in their Writings. In the consultation therefore of their Prophesies, and the Words which an Eagle is said to have spoken at the building of *Caer Septon*, now *Shaftsbury*; namely, that the *Britains* must lose the Government of *Britain* till the Bones of King *Cadwalader* were brought back from *Rome*. *Alan* found out that the time was now come, when these Prophesies were to be accomplished, and the *Britains* forced to quit their native Inheritance to Strangers and Invaders. Upon this he advised *Cadwalader* to obey the Commands, and follow the Counsel of the Vision, and to hasten his Journey for *Rome*. This he was willing to submit to, being desirous to spend the remainder of his Days in Peace and Quietness, which before he had no opportunity to enjoy. To *Rome* therefore he hastens, where he was kindly received by Pope *Sergius*; and after eight Years spent there in Piety and Devotion, he died in the Year 688. and with him the Kingdom and total Government of the *Britains* over this Island.

King *Cadwalader* is said to have been a considerable Benefactor to the Abby of *Clynnoc Vawr* in *Arvon*, upon which he bestowed the Lordship of *Grayanoc*. This place was primarily founded by S. *Beuno*, to whom it is dedicated, who was the Son of *Hywgi ap Gwynlliw ap Glywis ap Tegid ap Cadell*, a Prince or Lord of *Glewisig*, Brothers Son to S. *Cadoc ap Gwynlliw*, sometime Bishop of *Beneventum* in *Italy*. He was by the Mothers side Cosin German to *Laudatus* the first Abbot of *Enlli*, or the Island of *Bardsey*; and to *Kentigern* Bishop of *Glascow* in *Scotland*, and of *Lhaneliwey*, or S. *Asaph* in *Wales*; which last was Son to *Owen Regent* of *Scotland*, and Grandson to *Urien* King of *Cumbria*. The building of a Monastry at *Glynnoc* happened upon this occasion: *Beuno* having raised to life, as the Tradition goes, S. *Wenifryd*, who was beheaded by one *Caradoc*, a Lord in *North Wales*, upon the account that she would not yield to his unchast Desires, became in very great esteem with King *Cadvan*, who bestowed upon him certain Lands whereon to build a Monastery. *Cadwallon*

wallon also, *Cadrans* Son, gave him the Lands of *Gwareddoc*, where beginning to build a Church, a certain Woman with a Child in her Arms prevented his further progress, assuring him, that those Lands were the proper inheritance of that Child. *Beuno* was so exceedingly troubled at this, and without any more consideration on the matter, taking the Woman along with him, he went in all haste to *Caer Sevant* (called by the *Romans Segontium*, now *Carnarvon*) where King *Cadwallon* then kept his Court; when he was come before the King, he told him with a great deal of Zeal and Concern, that he had not done well to devote to God's Service what was another Man's Inheritance, and therefore demanded back of him the Golden Scepter he had given him in lieu and consideration of the said Land, which the King refusing to do, was presently excommunicated by *Beuno*, who thereupon departed and went away. But a certain person called *Gwyddeiant*, the King's Cosin-German, hearing what had happened, immediately pursued after *Beuno*; whom when he had overtaken, he bestowed upon him (for the good of his own Soul and the Kings) the Township of *Clynncovawr*, being his undoubted Inheritance; where *Beuno* built a Church, about the Year 616. about which time King *Cadvan* dyed, leaving his Son *Cadwallon* to succeed him. And not long before this time, *Eneon Bhrenin*, or *Anianus* King of the *Scots*, a considerable Prince in the North of *Britain*, leaving all his Royalty in those Parts, came to *Lhyn* in *Gwyneth*, where he built a Church, which is still called from him, *Lhan Eingan Bhrenin*; where he is said to have spent the remainder of his Days in the Fear and Service of God. He was Son to *Owen Danwyn*, the Son of *Eneon Irth*, Son to *Curedba Wledig* King of *Cambria*, and a great Prince in the North, and Cosin-German to the great *Maelgwn Gwyneth* King of *Britain*, whose Father was *Caswallon law-hîr*, the Brother of *Owen Danwyn*; and his Mother *Medif* the Daughter of *Voylda ap Talu Traws* of *Nanconwey*. This *Maelywn* died about the Year 586.

Ivor

Ivor and *Edwal Ywrch*.

WHen *Cadwalader* was departed for *Rome*, *Alan* began to reflect upon the state and condition of *Great Britain*; he imagin'd with himself that the Recovery of it was not impracticable, but that a considerable Army might regain what the *Saxons* now quietly possessed. Therefore he was resolved to try the utmost, and to send over all the Forces he was able to draw together; not doubting the Conquest of some part of *Britain*, in case the whole should prove irrecoverable. He was the more encouraged to this Expedition, by reason that the Advantage was like to be his own, and no one could challenge the Government of *Britain*, in case Fortune should deliver it to his Hands. *Cadwalader* was gone to *Rome*, and in all probability never to return; his Son *Edwal Ywrch*, or the *Roe*, was young and under the Tuition of *Alan*; so that the event of this Expedition must of necessity fall to himself, or by his Concession to his Son *Ivor*, who was to be chief in the Undertaking. Having raised a considerable Army, consisting chiefly of his own Subjects, with what remain'd of the *Britains* that came over with King *Cadwaladar*, he dispatch'd it for *Britain*, under the Command of his Son *Ivor*, and his Nephew *Ynyr*: They safely landed in the Western Parts of *Britain*, which put the *Saxons* into so great a Fright, that immediately they drew up all their Power to oppose them, and to hinder their Progress into the Country. The *Britains*, tho somewhat fatigued with their Voyage, however gave them Battel, and after a very great slaughter of the *Saxons*, possessed themselves of the Countries of *Cornwal*, *Devon*, and *Somersetshires*. This proved a fortunate beginning for the *Britains*, and gave them great hopes of farther Success in the recovery of their

Countrey;

The History of WALES.

Country; but that could not be expected without great Opposition, and several hot Engagements with the *Saxons*. This they were immediately made sensible of; for they had scarce time to breath, and to recover their Spirits after the last Battel, but *Kentwinus*, King of the *West-Saxons* marched against them with a powerful Army, consisting of *Saxons* and *Angles*. The *Britains* resolved to fight them; but whilst both Armies were in view of each other, they thought it more adviseable to cease from any Hostility, and to enter into Articles of Composition. *Ivor* seemed already satisfied with his Conquest, and willingly agreed to marry *Ethelberga*, *Kentwyn*'s Cousin, and peaceably to enjoy for his life so much as he was already in possession of. This he faithfully observed during the Reign of *Kentwyn*, and his Nephew *Cadwal*; who, after two Years, resign'd the Kingdom of the *West-Saxons* to his Cousin *Ivor*. And now *Ivor* was become unexpectedly powerful, being King as well of the *Saxons*, as *Britains* that inhabited the Western parts of the Island. He was now able to undertake somewhat considerable, and therefore began to fall foul upon his Neighbours the Kings of *Kent*, the *West-Saxons*, and *Mercia*, whom he vanquished in several Battels. But being at length tir'd with the Weight of Government, he went to *Rome*, after the Example of *Cadwalader*, and resign'd the Rule of the *Saxons* to his Cosin *Adelred*, leaving the *Britains* to the care of *Roderick Molwynoc*, the Son of *Edwal Ywrch*.

This *Ivor* founded the Abby of *Glastenbury*, called in the *British* Tongue *Ynys Avalon*; where there had been a Christian Church for several Years before, and the first that was ever erected in *Britain*. For *Joseph* of *Arimathea* being sent by *Philip* the Apostle in the days of *Arviragus, An. Chr.* 53. to preach the Gospel in *Britain*, seated himself here, and built a Church for the *British* Christians. This Church afterwards *Ivor* converted into an Abby, which she endowed with very large Possessions; being famous for the Burying-place of *Joseph* of *Arimathea*, and King *Arthur*. He bestowed also some Lands upon the Church of *Winchester*. But

The History of WALES.

But there happen'd several Casualties in his time. *Brythe*, a Subject to *Egfride* King of *Northumberland*, passed over to *Ireland*, and wasted and destroyed a great part of that Kingdom. In the Fourth Year of his Reign their happen'd a remarkable Earthquake in the Isle of *Man*, which much disturbed and annoyed the Inhabitants; and the year following it rain'd Blood both in *Britain* and in *Ireland*. This occasion'd the Butter and Milk to resemble the colour of Blood; and two Years after the Moon also appear'd all bloody. These Accidents of Nature might probably presage some Tumults and Disturbances in the Kingdom; which were very great in his time. For he was almost in perpetual Hostility with the Kings of *Kent*, *West-Sex*, and *Mercia*; which occasion'd great Bloodshed and Slaughter in *Britain*. His Journey to *Rome* put an end to all these Commotions, from whence he never did return, but ended his Days there in the practice of Piety and Religion.

Roderick Molwynoc.

THE Government of the *Britains Ivor* resign'd to *Roderick Molwinoc* the Son of *Edwal Twrch*, who began his Reign *An.* 720. But *Adelred*, King of the *West-Saxons*, was displeased that *Ivor* had not bestowed upon him his whole Kingdom; and upon that account he is resolved to trouble and plague *Roderick* and his *Britains*. He rais'd immediately a powerful Army, and with all his Forces marched to *Devonshire*, which he destroyed with Fire and Sword. From thence he proceeds to *Cornwal*, intending to make that Country sensible of the same Misery; but he came far short of his Expectation; for upon his entrance into the Country, the *Britains* opposed him, and gave him Battel, where he was vanquished, and forced to retire with all speed to his own Dominions. This
Victory

A.D. 720.

Victory the *Britains* called *Gwaeth Heilyn*, from the
A.D.721. place where this Battel was fought. The Year following, the *Britains* again obtained two notable Victories over the *Saxons*, the one at a place called *Garth Maclawch* in *North-Wales*, the other at *Pencoct* in *South-Wales*. But the Joy and Satisfaction which the *Britains* entertained of these Successes, was somewhat abated by the Death of *Belin* the Son of *Elphin*, a Man of noble Birth, and great Worth among them.

About the same time *Celredus* King of *Mercia* died, and was succeeded by *Ethelbaldus*, who being very desirous to annex that fertile and pleasant Country lying between the Rivers *Severn* and *Wye* to his Kingdom of *Mercia*, entred *Wales* with a puissant Army. He destroyed and ravaged the Country before him, to *Carno*, a Mountain lying not far from *Abergavenny*, where he was met with by the *Britains*, between whom a bloody and sore Battel was fought in the Year 728. but the Victory proved very dubitable.

A.D. 733. Not long after dyed Venerable *Bede*, who was educated and brought up in the Abby of *Wynnetham* or *Iaretre*; a Man of great Learning and extensive Knowledg; who wrote several Books, one of which entitled, *The Ecclesiastical History of the English Nation*; he dedicated to *Cleowolfe* King of *Northumberland*. The same time *Adelred* King of the *West-Saxons*, and *Ethelbald* King of *Mercia*, united their Forces, and joyntly marched to fight against the *Britains*. The *Welch* were now put to very hard Streights, and forced to oppose the numerous Armies of two powerful Kings. However, fight they must, or suffer their Country to be miserably over-run by their inveterate Enemies. Both Armies being engaged, a very dismal Battel ensued thereupon, and a very great slaughter happen'd on both sides; but the *Saxons* prevailing by the number of their Forces, obtained a very bloody Victory over the powerless *Britains*. But *Adelred*, who was shortly follow'd by *Edwyn* King of the *Picts*, did not long survive this Battel; and *Cudred* took upon him the Government of the *West-Saxons*.

The

The History of WALES.

The *Welch* found themselves unable to cope with the *Saxons*, and too weak to repress their endless Incursions; therefore they apply themselves to *Cudred* and joyned in league with him, who upon some occasion or other, was actually fallen out with *Ethelbald* King of *Mercia*. But *Ethelbald* was so proud with the success of the last Engagement, that notwithstanding the League with *Cudred*, he must needs again fall upon the *Welch*. He advanced as far as *Hereford*, where the *Britains*, by the help of *Cudred*, gave him a signal Overthrow, and caused him to repent of his rash and precipitous Expedition. But shortly after, *Cudred* and *Ethelbald* were unluckily reconciled, and made Friends together, and *Cudred* relinquishing the *Welch*, joyned his Forces to *Ethelbalds*. Hereupon ensued another Battel, in which the *Welch* being greatly overpower'd, were vanquish'd by the *Saxons*; after which Victory, *Cudred* shortly dyed. To him succeeded *Sigebert*, a Man of a loose and vicious inclination; who for his ill Behaviour in the Management of his Kingdom, was in a short time expell'd and depriv'd by his Nobility, and at last miserably slain by a rascally Swineherd. After him *Kenulph* was chosen King of the *West Saxons*, *Ann*, 750. in whose time dyed *Theodore* the Son of *Belin*, a Man of great Esteem and Reputation among the *Britains*. And about the same time, a remarkable Battel was fought between the *Britains* and the *Picts*, at a place call'd *Magedawc*; in which the *Picts* were put to a total rout, and *Dalargan* their King casually slain. But the *Britains* did not succeed so well against the *Saxons*; for *Roderic Molwynoc* was at length forced to forsake the Western Countries of *Britain*, and to claim his own Inheritance in *North Wales*. The Sons of *Bletius* or *Bledericus* Prince of *Cornwal* and *Devonshire*, who was one of them that vanquished *Adelred* and *Ethelbert* at *Bangor* on the River *Dee*; had enjoyed the Government of *North Wales* ever since *Cadfan* was chose King of *Britain*. *Roderic* therefore demanded the Government of this Country as his right, which he was now willing to accept of, seeing he was forced to quit what he had hitherto possessed.

A.D. 746.

A.D. 747.

A.D. 750.

C But

But he did long enjoy it, but dyed in a short time, leaving behind him two Sons *Conan Tindaythwy* and *Howel*; after that he had in all reigned over the *Britains* Thirty Years.

Conan Tindaythwy.

A.D. 755. Roderic *Molwynoc* being dead, his Son *Conan Tindaythwy* took upon him the Government and Principality of *Wales*, in the Year 755. He was scarce settled in his Throne, but the *Saxons* began to make In-Roads into his Country, to spoil and destroy what they conveniently could meet with. They were animated hereto by the bad Success of *Roderic*; and having forced the *Britains* out of *Cornwal* and *Devonshire*, they thought it practicable to drive them out of *Wales* too, and so to reduce the Possession of the whole Island to themselves. This was their Aim, and this they endeavour'd to put in execution; but they were met with at *Hereford*, where a severe Battel was fought between them and the *Welch*, in which *Dyfnwal* the Son of *Thecdor* a stout and valiant Soldier, was slain. And shortly afterwards dyed *Athelbert* King of *Northumberland*, and was succeeded by *Oswald*.

About the same time happened a religious Quarrel between the *Britains* and *Saxons*, concerning the observation of the Feast of *Easter*, which *Elbodius* a learned and a pious Man, endeavoured to rectifie in *Wales*, and to reduce it to the *Roman* Calculation, which the *Saxons* always observed. The *Britains* did differ from the Church of *Rome* in the celebration of this Feast; and the difference was this. The Church of *Rome* according to the order of the Council of *Nice*, always observed *Easter-day* the next *Sunday* after the 14*th.* day of the Moon; so that it never happen'd upon the 14*th.* day it self, nor passed the 21*th.* The *Britains*

The History of WALES.

Britains on the other hand, celebrated their *Easter* upon the 14th, and so forward to the 20th, which occasioned this Difference, that the *Sunday* observed as *Easter* day by the *Britains*, was but *Palm-Sunday* with the *Saxons*. Upon this account the *Saxons* did most uncharitably traduce the *Britains*, and would scarcely allow them the Name and Title of Christians. Hereupon, about the Year 660, a great Contest happen'd, managed on the one part by *Colman* and *Hylda*, who defended the Rites and Celebration of the *Britains*; and *Gilbert* and *Wilfride* on the part of the *Saxons*. *Hylda* was the Neece of *Edwine* King of *Northumberland*, educated by *Pauline* and *Aedan*. She publickly opposed *Wilfride* and other superstitious Monks; as to such Trifles and Bigotry in Religion, alledging out of *Polycrates*, the Fact of *Irenæus*, who withstood *Victor* Bishop of *Rome* upon the same account; and the custom of the Churches of *Asia* observed by S. *John* the Evangelist, *Philip* the Apostle, *Polycarpus* and *Melito*; and likewise observed in *Britain* by *Joseph* of *Arimathea*, who first preached the Gospel here.

Offa was made King of *Mercia*, and *Brichtrich* of A.D. 763, the *West-Saxons*; about which time dyed *Fermael* the Son of *Edwal* and *Cemoyd* King of the *Picts*. The *Saxons* did daily encroach upon the Lands and Territories of the *Welch* beyond the River *Severn*, but more especially towards the South part of the Country. These Enchroachments the *Welch* could not endure, and therefore were resolved to recover their own, and to drive the *Saxons* out of their Country. The *Britains* of *South-Wales*, as receiving the greatest A.D. 776. Injury and Disadvantage from the *Saxons*, presently took up Arms and entered into the Country of *Mercia*; which they ravag'd and destroyed with Fire and Sword. And shortly after, all the *Welch* joyned their Forces together, fell upon the *Saxons*, and forced them to retire beyond the *Severn*, and then returned home, with a very considerable Spoil of *English* Cattel. The *Welch* finding the Advantage of this last Incursion, and how that by these means they gauled and vexed

vexed the *Saxons*, frequently practifed the fame; and entering their Countrey by ftealth, they killed and deftroyed all before them; and driving their Cattel beyond the River, ravaged and laid wafte the whole Countrey. *Offa* King of *Mercia* not being able to endure thefe daily Incurfions and Depredations of the *Welch*, entered into a League with the reft of the *Saxon* Kings, to bend their whole Force againft the *Welch*; who having raifed a very ftrong and numerous Army, paffed the *Severn* into *Wales*. The *Welch* being far too weak to oppofe and encounter fo great an Army, quitted the even and plain Countrey, lying upon the Banks of *Severn* and *Wye*, and retired to the Mountains and Rocks, where they knew they could be moft fafe from the inveterate and revengeful Arms of the *Saxons*. But as foon as the *Saxons* decamped, being not able to effect any thing againft them in thefe ftrong and natural Fortifications, the *Welch* ftill made In-roads into their Territories, and feldom returned without fome confiderable Booty and Advantage. The *Saxons* were heartily nettled at thefe bo-peeping Ravagers, and would compliment them ftill to their Holes, but durft not purfue them further, for fear they fhould be entrapp'd by fuch as defended the Streights and Paffages into the Rocks. King *Offa* perceiving that he could effect nothing by thefe Meafures, annexed the Country about *Severn* and *Wye* to his Kingdom of *Mercia*, and planted the fame with *Saxons*. And for a farther fecurity againft the endlefs Invafions of the *Welch*, he made a deep Ditch, extending from one Sea to the other, called *Clawdh Offa*, or *Offa*'s Dike; upon which account, the Royal Seat of the Princes of *Powys* was tranflated from *Pengwern*, now *Shrewsbury*, to *Mathraval* in *Montgomeryfhire*.

*A.D.*795. While thefe things are tranfacted in the Weft, the *Danes* began to grow powerful at Sea, and durft venture to land in the North of *England*; but without doing any great hurt, being forced to betake themfelves to their Ships again. Within Six Years after, they landed again in greater numbers, and proved much

more

The History of WALES.

more terrible; they ravaged and destroyed a great part of *Linsey* and *Northumberland*, over-ran the best part of *Ireland*, and miserably wasted *Rechreyn*. At the same time a considerable Battel was fought at *Ruthlan*, between the *Saxons* and the *Welch*; wherein *Caradoc* King of *North Wales* was killed. The Government of *Wales* was as yet green, and not firmly rooted, by reason of the perpetual Quarrels and Disturbances between the *Welch* and the *Saxons*; so that the chief Person or Lord of any Country assumed to himself the Title of *King*. *Caradoc* was a Person of great Esteem and Reputation in *North Wales*, and one that did very much contribute towards the Security of the Countrey, against the Incursions of the *Saxons*. He was Son to *Gwyn*, the Son of *Colhoyn*, the Son of *Ednowen*, Son to *Blethyn*, the Son of *Blecius* or *Bledericus* Prince of *Cornwal* and *Devonshire*. *Offa* King of *Mercia* did not long survive him, and was succeeded by his Son *Egfert*, who in a short time left his Kingdom also to *Kenulphus*, a year after that *Egbertus* was created King of the *West Saxons*. About the same time dyed *Arthen* Son to *Sitsylht*, the Son of *Clydawc* King of *Cardigan*; and sometime after, *Run* King of *Dyfed*, and *Cadelh* King of *Powys*: who were followed by *Elbodius* Archbishop of *North Wales*, before whose Death happen'd a very severe Eclipse of the Sun. The Year following, the Moon was likewise eclipsed upon *Christmas-day*. These Fatalities and Eclipses did portend no Success to the *Welch* Affairs; the laying of S. *Davids* in Ashes by the *West Saxons* being followed by a general and a very grievous Murrain of Cattel, which was like to impoverish the whole Country. The following Year *Owen* the Son of *Meredith*, the Son of *Terudos*, dyed; and the Castle of *Deganwy* was ruined and destroyed by Thunder.

A.D. 808.

But these several Losses which the *Welch* sustained could not reconcile Prince *Conan* and his Brother *Howel*; but they must needs quarrel and contend with one another, when they had the greatest occasion to embrace and unite their endeavours against the common

mon Enemy. *Howel* claimed the Isle of *Anglesey*, as part of his Father's Inheritance, which *Conan* would by no means hearken to, nor consent that his Brother should take possession of it. It was the custom of *Wales*, that a Fathers Estate should be equally distributed between all his Sons; and *Howel* by virtue of this Custom, commonly called *Gavelkind*, from the word *Gafel* to hold; claimed that Island, as his Fathers Estate. This Custom of *Gavelkind* has been the occasion of the Ruin and Diminution of the Estates of all the antient Nobility in *Wales*; which being endlesly divided between the several Sons of the same Family, were at length reduced to nothing. From hence also proceeded several unnatural Wars and Disturbances between Brothers; who being either not satisfied with their Portions, or displeased with the Country they were to possess; disputed their Right by Dint of the Sword. This proved very true in this present instance; for *Howel* would not suffer himself to be cheated out of his paternal Inheritance, and therefore he would endeavour to recover it by Force of Arms. Both Armies being engaged, the victory fell to *Howel*, who immediately thereupon possessed himself of the Island, and valiantly maintained it against the Power and Strength of his Brother *Conan*.

The *Welch* being thus at variance and enmity among themselves, and striving how to destroy one another; had yet another Disaster added to their Misfortune. For the following Year they received a very considerable Loss by Thunder, which very much spoiled and annoyed the Country, and laid several Houses and Towns in Ashes. About the same time, *Gruffith* the Son of *Run* a Person of considerable Quality in *Wales*, dyed; and *Griffri* the Son of *Kyngen*, was treacherously murthered by the Practices of his Brother *Elis*.

But *Conan* could not rest satisfied with his Brother *Howels* forcible possession of the Island of *Anglesey*; and therefore he was resolved to give him another Battel, and to force him to restore and yield up the Possession

of

The History of WALES.

of that Country, which he had now violently kept in his hands. *Howel* on the other hand, being as refolutely bent to maintain his Ground, and not to deliver up a foot of what he was now upon a double refpect, *viz.* his Fathers Legacy, and his late Conqueft, Owner of; willingly met his Brother, put him to flight, and killed a great number of his Forces. *Conan* was cruelly enraged at this fhameful Overthrow, and therefore made a firm refolution, either to recover the Ifland from his Brother, or to facrifice his Life and his Crown in the Quarrel. Having drawn up all the Forces he could raife together, he marched to *Anglefey* to feek his Brother *Howel*; who being too weak to encounter and oppofe fo confiderable a Number, was compell'd to make his Efcape to the Ifle of *Man*, and to leave the Ifland of *Anglefey* to the mercy of his Brother. But *Conan* did not live long to reap the fatisfaction of this Victory, but dyed in a fhort time, leaving Iffue behind him, one onely Daughter called *Efylht*, married to a Nobleman of *Wales* named *Merfyn Frych*. He was Son to *Gwyriad* or *Uriet*, the Son of *Elidure*, who lineally defcended from *Belinus* the Brother of *Brennus* King of the *Britains*. His Mother was *Neft*, the Daughter of *Cadelh* King of *Powys*, the Son of *Brochwel Yfcithroc*; who together with *Cadfan* King of *Britain*, *Morgan* King of *Demetia*, and *Bledericus* King of *Cornwal*, gave that memorable Overthrow to *Ethelred* King of *Northumberland*, upon the River *Dee*, in the Year 617. This *Brochwel* by the Latin Writers named *Brecivallus* and *Brochmaelus*, was a very confiderable Prince in that part of *Britain*, called *Powys-land*; as alfo Earl of *Chefter*, and lived in the Town then called *Pengwern Powys*, now *Salop*; in the Houfe where fince the College of *S. Chad* ftands. He was a great Friend and a Favourer to the Monks of *Bangor*, whofe part he took againft the *Saxons* that were fet on by *Augustine* the Monk, to profecute them with Fire and Sword, becaufe they would not forfake the Cuftoms of their own Church, and conform to thofe of *Rome*.

A.D. 817.

C 4 *Merfyn*

Merfyn Frych and *Esylht*.

Onan being dead, *Merfyn Frych* and his Wife *Esylht*, who was sole Heir to *Conan*, took upon them the Government or Principality of *Wales*. This *Merfyn* was King of *Man*, and Son to *Gwyriat* and *Nest* the Daughter of *Cadelh ap Brochwel ap Elis* King of *Powys*. *Howel* being forcibly ejected out of *Anglesey* by his Brother *Conan Tindaethwy*, and escaping to the Island of *Man*, was honourably and kindly received by *Merfyn*; in return of whose Civilities *Howel* used such means afterwards that *Merfyn* married *Esylht*, the Daughter and Heir of his Brother *Conan*, (tho others say, that he died presently after his Escape to *Merfyn*.) *Howel* after that he had for about five years enjoyed the Isle of *Man*, and other Lands in the North, given him by *Merfyn* to hold under him, dyed about the year 825; after whose Death, they again returned to *Merfyn*, whose Ancestors had always held the same, under the Kings of the *Britains*; and so, upon his Marriage with *Esylht*, the Isle of *Man* was annexed to the Crown of *Wales*.

In the first year of their Reign, *Egbert*, the powerful King of the *West Saxons*, entred with a mighty Army into *Wales*, destroyed and wasted the Countrey as far as *Snowden* Hills, and seized upon the Lordship of *Rhyvonicc* in *Denbighland*. About the same time a very sore Battel was fought in *Anglesey*, between the *Saxons* and the *Welch*, called, from the place where this Fight happened, the Battel of *Lhan-*
A.D. 819. *vaes*. Fortune seemed all this while to frown upon the *Welch*, and their Affairs succeeded very ill; for shortly after that *Egbert* had advanced his Colours as far as *Snowden*, *Kenulph* King of *Mercia* wasted the Countrey of *West Wales*, over-ran and destroyed
Powis-land,

The History of WALES.

Powis-land, and greatly disturbed and incommoded the *Welch* Nation. Soon after this, *Kenulph* died, and was succeeded by *Kenelm*; and he in a short time by *Ceolwulph*, who, after two years Reign, left the Kingdom of *Mercia* to *Bernulph*.

Egbert King of the *West Saxons* was grown very strong and powerful, able to reduce all the petty Kingdoms in *Britain*, under one single Monarchy; upon the thoughts of which, he set upon *Bernulph* King of *Mercia*, and vanquished him at *Elledowne*; and afterwards brought under Subjection the Countries of *Kent* and of the *West Angles*. But the *Britains* could not be so easily subdued; for after a long and a cruel Fight at *Gavelford*, between them and the *West Saxons* of *Devonshire*, in which several thousands were slain on both sides, the Victory remained uncertain. He had better Success against *Wyhtlafe* King of *Mercia*, whose Dominions he easily added to his now increasing Monarchy; and passing *Humber*, he quickly reduced that Country to his Subjection. The *Saxon* Heptarchy was now become one Kingdom, and *Egbert* sole Monarch of all the Countries that the *Saxons* possessed in *Britain*; which Name he ordered should be changed to *England*, his People to be called *Englishmen*, and the Language *English*. A.D. 829.

They who came over out of *Germany* into this Island to aid the *Britains* against their Enemies the *Picts* and *Scots*, were partly *Saxons*, *Angles*, and *Juthes*; from the first of which came the People of *Essex*, *Sussex*, *Middlesex*, and the *West-Saxons*; from the *Angles*, the *East Angles*, the *Mercians*, and they that inhabited the North side of *Humber*; from the *Juthes*, the *Kentishmen*, and they that settled in the Isle of *Wight*. These *Germans*, after that they had drove the *Britains* beyond *Severn* and *Dee*; erected seven Kingdoms called the Heptarchy in the other part of the Island; whereof, 1. *Kent*. 2. Of the *South-Saxons* containing *Sussex* and *Surrey*. 3. The *East-Angles*, in *Norfolk*, *Suffolk*, and *Cambridgshire*. 4. The Kingdom of the *West-Saxons*, comprehending *Berkshire*, *Devonshire*, *Somersetshire* and *Cornwall*. 5. *Mercia*

5. *Mercia*, containing *Glocester, Hereford, Worcester, Shropshire, Stafford, Chefhire, Warwick, Leicester, Darby, Nottingham, Lincoln, Northampton, Oxford, Buckingham, Bedford*, and half *Hartfordshire*. 6. The *East-Saxons*, containing *Essex, Middlesex*, and the other part of *Hartford*. 7. Of the *Northumbrians*, taking in all the Country beyond *Humber*, which was divided into two parts, *Deyra* and *Bernicia*; the first from *Humber* to *Tyne*, the other from *Tyne* to the *Scottish Sea*.

Egbert King of the *West-Saxons* having feverally conquer'd thefe Kingdoms, annexed them together, and comprehended them under one Monarchy, which was called the Kingdom of *England*, 968 years after the coming of *Brute* to this Ifland; 383 Years after the landing of *Hengift*; and 149 after the Departure of *Cadwalader* to *Rome*.

Egbert having thus united under one Government thefe feveral Kingdoms, which ufed continually to moleft, and to incroach upon each others Territories; might reafonably have expected to enjoy his new Kingdom quietly, and not fear any difturbance or trouble in his Dominions. But no fooner was he eftablifhed King of *England*, but the *Danes* began to threaten new Commotions, and landed in great numbers, and in divers places of the Kingdom. *Egbert* fought feveral Battels with them, and with various Succefs: at length the *Danes* landed in *Weft-Wales*, marched forward for *Eng.and*, being joined by a great number of *Welch* and met *Egbert* upon *Hengift down*, where a fevere Battel was fought, and the *Danes* put to a total Rout. The *Welch* fuffered feverely for this; *Egbert*, being highly incens'd that the *Danes* were fupported by them, laid fiege to *Caer Lheon ar Dhyfrdwy*, or *Chefter*, the chief City of *Venedotia*, which hitherto had remained in the hands of the *Welch*; took the Town, and, among other Tokens of his Indignation, he caufed the Brazen Effigies of *Cadwalhon* King of *Britain* to be pulled down and defaced, and upon pain of Death forbad the erecting of fuch again. He iffued out alfo a Proclamation, by the

A.D. 883.

Infti-

The History of WALES.

Inſtigation of his Wife *Redburga*, who always bore an inveterate Malice to the *Welch*; commanding all that were any ways extracted from *British* Blood, to depart, with all their Effects, out of his Kingdom, within ſix Months, upon pain of death. Theſe were very ſevere and inſupportable Terms; but he did not live long to ſee them put in execution; for dying ſhortly after the Battel of *Hengeſtdown*, he was ſucceeded by Son *Ethelwulph*. This King *Ethelwulph* married his Daughter to *Berthred*, who was his tributary King of *Mercia*; by whoſe help he ſuccefsfully oppoſed the cruel Incurſions of the *Danes*, who miſerably deſtroyed the Sea-coaſts of *England*, with Fire and Sword. Theſe *Daniſh* Commotions being indifferently well appeaſed, *Berthred* King of *Mercia* ſet upon the *Welch*, between whom a remarkable Battel was fought at a place called *Kettell*; where *Merfyn Frych* King of the *Britains* was killed, leaving, to ſucceed him in the Governmet of *Wales*, his Son *Roderic Mawr*, or the Great.

Roderic the Great.

Merfyn Frych having loſt his Life, and with it his Kingdom, in the Battel of *Kettell*; his Son *Roderic*, ſurnamed the Great, without any Oppoſition or Conteſt, ſucceeded in the Principality of *Wales*. The firſt thing he effected after his Advancement to the Crown, was the dividing of *Wales* into ſeveral Provinces, which he diſtinguiſhed into theſe three; *Aberffraw*, *Dinevowr*, and *Mathraval*. *Berthred* King of *Mercia*, being animated by his late Succeſs againſt *Merfyn Frych*, purpoſed to perform the like Exploits againſt his Son *Roderic*. And having gained the Aid and Aſſiſtance, of King *Ethelwulph*, he entred *North Wales*, with a ſtrong Army, and advanced as far as *Angleſey*, which he cruelly and miſerably deſtroyed.

A.D. 843.

Roderic

Roderic met him several times, and the *Welch* did at length so gaul and torment him, that, in fine, he had little or nothing to boast of; only *Meyric*, one of the chiefest Princes among the *Britains*, was slain.

But he was soon forced to quit his Expedition against the *Welch*, and to convert his Forces another way; his own Dominions requiring their constant Residence, being severely threatned by a foreign Invasion. For the *Danes* were by this time grown so very powerful, that they over-ran a great part of *England*, fought with *Athelstan* King of *Kent*, Brother to *Ethelwulph*; and obtained so much Conquest, that whereas before they returned to their own Country when the Weather grew too cold for Action, they now took up their Winter-quarters in *England*.

A.D. 846.

The *Welch*, in the mean time, being secure from any Violence, which might otherwise be expected, from the *English*; began to quarrel and fall out amongst themselves. *Ithel* King of *Gwent* or *Wentland*, for what occasion not known, fell foul upon the Men of *Brecknock*, who were so resolute as to fight him; and the Event proved very unfortunate to *Ithel*, who was slain upon the spot. It is the Unhappiness of a Nation that is governed by several Petty States, when it is apprehensive of no Danger from an outward Enemy that it will fall at variance, and create Disturbances among it self.

Had the *Britains*, instead of falling upon one another, taken the Advantage of this opportunity, when the *Saxons* were altogether imployed in opposing and repelling the *Danes*, to increase and strengthen their Number, and to fortify their Towns; they might at least securely have possessed their own Dominions, if not extended their Government to a great part of *England*. But a sort of an Equality in Power, begat an Emulation between the several Princes, and this Emulation for the most part ended in Blows and Contention; so that instead of strengthning themselves whilst they had respite from the *English*, they rather weakened their Power by inward Differences.

Kongen

The History of WALES.

Kyngen King of *Powys* was gone to *Rome*, there to A.D. 854. end his Days peaceably and religiously, but his Death did not prove so natural as he expected, being barbarously slain, or (as some say) choaked by his own Servants. Shortly after died *Cemoyth* King of the *Picts*, and *Jonathan* Lord of *Abergeley*. It was now become Customary for Princes wearied with Government to go to *Rome*, and the Pope willingly dispensed with the Resignation of their Crowns, by reason that his Holiness seldom lost by it. King *Ethelwulph* paid very dear for his Entertainment there, made his Kingdom tributary to the Pope, and paid the *Peter*-Pence to the Church of *Rome*. The *Saxon* Genealogists bring the Pedegree of *Ethelwulph* for several Successions and Generations, up to *Adam*, as may be seen in *Matthew* of *Westminster*, who in like manner derives the Pedigree of *Offa* King of *Mercia*. This has been the Custom of most Nations, both antient and modern; and is always practised by them whose Families are any thing Antient and Honourable; so that it is a very great mistake to scoff at, and deride the *Welch* because they keep up this antient and laudable Custom.

Berthred King of *Mercia* became at length far too weak to repel the daily increasing Power of the *Danes*, who so numerously poured upon him, that at last he was forced to relinquish his Kingdom and fly to *Rome*, where in a short time he sorowfully ended his days. *Ethelwulph* shortly followed, and left his Sons. *Athelbald* King of the *West-Saxons*, and *Athelbright* King of *Kent* and the *East-Saxons*. *Ethelwulph* is reported to be so Learned and Devout, that the Church of *Winchester* elected him in his youth Bishop of that See, which Function he took upon him about seven years before he was made King. He is said also to have Conquered the Kingdom of *Demetia* or *South-Wales*, which together with the Kingdom of the *South-Saxons* he bestowed upon his Son *Alfred*, upon Condition he would bring a Thousand Men out of *Wales* to *Winchester*, to the Aid of his Brother *Ethelbert* against the *Danes*. *Athelbald* succeeding

his

his Father in the Kingdom of the *West-Saxons*, kept his Mother-in-Law the Wife of *Ethelwulph* for his Concubine, and afterwards married her in the City of *Chester*. But he did not live long to enjoy this unnatural Conjunction, but dying without Issue after that he had reigned Eight Years, left his Kingdom to his Brother *Athelbright*.

About the same time the *Danes* began again to bestir themselves and fell upon the City of *Winchester* and destroyed it, which *Athelbright* perceiving, after a long Fight forced them to quit the Land, and to betake themselves to Sea again. But the *Danes* quickly returned to the Isle of *Thanet*, where they remained for that Winter, doing much Mischief upon the Sea-Coast, and destroying all places near the shoars of *England*. The *English* were very glad that they durst venture no further, and the more, because the *Welch* began again to be troublesome, against whom an Army must be speedily dispatched, otherwise they would certainly advance to the *English* Countrey. Both Armies met at *Gweythen*, where a fierce Battel was fought, and a great Number slain on either side, but the Victory was not plainly discoverable. But the *Welch* not long after, received a considerable Loss by the Death of *Conan Nant Nifer*, a Stout and Skilful Commander, who oftentimes had Valiantly repulsed the *English* Forces, and obtained many signal Victories over them.

The *Danes* had been for some time quiet, being unable to venture upon any considerable Action, and therefore they thought it advisable to secure only what they had already won, and to expect a re-inforcement from their own Countrey. This was quickly sent them, under the Command of *Hungare* and *Hubba* who landed in *England* with a very considerable Army of *Danes*. King *Athelbright*, whether terrified with a dismal apprehension of these Invaders, or otherwise being indispoted, quickly afterwards gave up the Ghost, leaving the management of his Kingdom, together with that of his Army against the *Danes*, to his Brother *Ethelred*. The *Danes* in the mean time

got

The History of WALES.

got sure footing, and advanced as far as *York*, which they miserably destroyed, killing *Osbright* and *Elba* two Kings of *Northumberland* that opposed them. From hence they proceeded, and over-run all the Countrey as far as *Nottingham*, destroying and spoiling all before them, and then returned back to *York*. But having once tasted how sweet the Spoil of a Countrey, much more fertile than their own was, they could not rest satisfied with what they had already obtained, but must needs make a farther Progress into the Countrey, and fall upon the Kingdom of the *East-Angles*. *Edmund* King of that Countrey being not able to endure their Insolencies, endeavoured to oppose them, but in the Undertaking was unfortunately slain. And now after the same manner that the *Saxons* had formerly attained to the Conquest of *Britain*, the *Danes* proceeded to the Conquest of *England*. For the *Saxons* having found out the Sweetness of this Island, and withal, discovered the weakness and inability of the *Britains* to oppose them, brought over their Numbers by degrees, and in several Companies, by which they wearied and tired out the *British* Armies. For it is certain that nothing can conduce more to the Conquest of an Island, than the landing an Army at several Places and at several Times, which distracts the Counsels and Proceedings of the Inhabitants, and which at this time for want of sufficient Power at Sea, could not be prevented. And so the *Danes* being informed of the good Success of *Hungare* and *Hubba* in *England*, sent over another Army under the Command of *Basreck* and *Alding*, who landed in *West-Sax*, and fought five Battels with King *Ethelred* and his Brother *Alfred*, namely at *Henglefield*, *Estondown*, *Redding*, *Basing* and *Mereton*, in which two first the *English* overcame, and the three last the *Danes* got the Victory.

Soon after this *Ethelred* died, leaving his Kingdom to his Brother *Alfred*, who no sooner had taken the Government upon him but considered with himself what a heavy Burthen he was to sustain, and therefore

fore he began to enquire after the Wiseſt and Learnedeſt Men that he could hear of to be directed by them, whom he worthily Entertained, making uſe of their Advice as well in the Publick Government of the Kingdom, as in his Private Studies and Conference of Learning. He ſent for two Men famouſly Learned out of *Wales*, the one called *John de Erigena*, Surnamed *Scotus*; the other *Aſſerius*, Surnamed *Menevenſis*. De *Erigena* was born at *Menevia* or St. *Davids*, and was brought up in that College; who for the ſake of Learning having travelled to *Athens*, and beſtowed there many Years in the Study of the *Greek*, *Hebrew* and *Caldaick* Tongues, and the ſecret Myſteries of *Philoſophy*, came to *France*; where he was well accepted of by *Carolus Calvus*, or *Charles* the *Bald*, and *Ludovicus Balbus*, or *Lewis* the *Stammerer*; and there tranſlated the Works of *Dionyſius Areopagita*, De *Cœleſti Hierarchia* out of the *Greek* into the *Latin* Tongue. Being returned home to *Wales*, he was ſent for by this King *Alfred*, who was then founding and erecting the Univerſity of *Oxford*, of which *Erigena* became the firſt Profeſſor and publick Reader. But King *Alfred* bore ſo great a reſpect to Learning, that he would ſuffer none to bear any conſiderable Office in his Court but ſuch as were Learned; and withal, exhorted all Perſons to embrace Learning, and to Honour Learned Men. But tho' a Love to Learning be ſeldom reconcilable with a Warlike and a Military Life, King *Alfred* was alſo forced to regard the Diſcipline of War to defend his Kingdom againſt the increaſing Power of the *Danes*. For he was ſcarce ſettled in his Throne, but this reſtleſs and ever troubleſome People began to moleſt and deſtroy his Countrey, inſomuch that he was of neceſſity forced to oppoſe them, which he did twice upon the South-ſide of the River *Thames*, in which Engagements he ſlew of the *Danes* one King, nine Earls, together with an innumerable multitude of Inferior Souldiers. About the ſame time *Gwgan ap Meyric ap Dunwal ap Arthen ab Sitſylht* Prince of *Cardigan* died, being as ſome ſay, unfortunately drowned. But the

late

The History of WALES.

late Victories which *Alfred* had obtained over the *Danes*, did not so much weaken and dishearten them, but that in a short time they recovered their Spirits and began again to look terrible and threathing. For as soon as they could reunite their scattered Forces, they set upon and destroyed the Town of *Alclyde*, wan the City of *London* and *Redding*, over-ran all the inland Countrey, and the whole Kingdom of *Mercia*. Another Army of *Danes* at the same time proved very successful in the *North* and possessed themselves of the Countrey of *Northumberland*, which Action did not so much grieve the *English*, as trouble and vex the *Picts* and *Scots*, who were incessantly gauled, and frequently beat off by these *Danish* Troops. The next Year three of the *Danish* Captains marched from *Cambridge* towards *Warham* in *Dorset-shire*, of which Expedition King *Alfred* being informed, presently detached his Forces to oppose them, and to offer them Battle. The *Danes* were so startled at this, that they immediately desired Peace, and willingly consented forthwith to depart out of the Country, and to forswear the sight of *English* Ground. According to which Capitulation, the Horse that night marched for *Exeter*, and the Foot being shipped off, were all of them drowned at *Sandwich*. The *Danes* having thus abjured *England*, were not willing to return home empty, but thought it Prudent to bend their Course against *Wales*. They fancied that they were like to meet with no great opposition from the *Welch*, and therefore could carve for themselves according as their Fancy directed them. But having landed their Army in *Anglesey*, they quickly experienced the contrary; Prince *Roderic* opposing them, gave them two Battels, one at a place called *Bengole*, and the other at *Menegid* in *Anglesey*. At the same time another Army of *Danes* under the Command of *Halden* and *Hungare* landed in *South-Wales*, over-ran the whole Country, destroying all before them, neither sparing Churches nor Religious Houses. But they received their due Reward at the hands of the *West-Saxons*, who meeting with them on the Coasts

873.

of

of *Devonshire*, slew both *Halden* and *Hungare*, with 1200 of their Men. The same Year *Einion* Bishop of St. *Davids* died, and was the following Year succeeded by *Hubert*, who was installed in his place.

A.D. 876. The *English* being rid of their powerful and ever restless Enemies the *Danes*, began now to quarrel with the *Welch*, entring into *Anglesey* with a numerous Army, fought a fore Battel with *Roderic*, who together with his Brother (or as others say his Son) *Gwyriad*, was unhappily slain in the Field, which Battel is called by the *Welch*, *Gwaith Duw Sul y Mon*. This *Roderic* had Issue by his Wife *Anghârad*, *Anarawd*, *Cadelh* and *Merfyn*, the last of which, *Giraldus Cambrensis*, contrary to the vulgar and received Opinion, will have to be the eldest Son of *Roderic*, upon whom was bestowed the Principality of *North-Wales*. For it is unanimously granted that *Roderic* was undoubted Proprietor of all the Dominions of *Wales*, *North-Wales* descending unto him by his Mother *Esylht* the Daughter and sole Heir of *Conan Tyndaethwy*; *South-Wales* by his Wife *Anghârad* the Daugter of *Meyric ap Dyfnwal ap Arthen ap Sitsylht* King of *Cardigan*; *Powis* by *Nest* the Sister and Heir of *Congen ap Cadelh* King of *Powis* his Father's Mother. These three Dominions *Roderic* divided between his three Sons, appointing *North Wales* for his eldest Son *Anarawd*, *South Wales* to *Cadelh*, who shortly after his Father's Death, forcibly seiled upon his Brother *Merfyn's* Portion, upon whom *Roderic* had bestowed *Powis-Land*. *Wales* being thus divided between these three Princes, they were called *Y Tri Tywysoc Talaethicc*, or the three crowned Princes, by reason that each of them did wear on his Helmet a Coronet of Gold, being a broad Head-band indented upward, set and wrought with Precious Stones, which in the *British* Tongue is called *Talaeth*. To each of these Princes *Roderic* built a Royal Seat, for the Prince of *Gwyneth* or *North-Wales*, at *Aberffraw*; of *South-Wales*, at *Dinefawr*; for the Prince of *Powis*, at *Mathrafel*. *Roderic* had Issue also, besides these three, *Roderic*, *Meyric*, *Edwal* or *Tudwal*, *Gwyriad* and *Gathelic*. But

The History of WALES.

But *Roderic* having divided his Principality betwixt his eldest Sons, namely, *Aberffraw* with the fifteen Cantreds thereunto belonging to *Anarawd*; *Dinefawr* with its fifteen Cantreds extending from the mouth of the River *Dofi*, to the mouth of *Severn* to *Cadelh*; and *Powis* with fifteen Cantreds from the mouth of the River *Dee* to the Bridge over *Severn* at *Glocester* to *Merfyn*; ordained that his eldest Son *Anarawd* and his Successors should continue the payment of the antient Tribute to the Crown of *England*; and the other two, their Heirs and Successors should acknowledge his Sovereignty, and that upon any Foreign Invasion, they should mutually Aid and Protect one another. And he farther appointed, that when any Difference should arise betwixt the Princes of *Aberffraw* and *Cardigan* or *Dynefawr*, the three Princes should meet at *Bwlch y Pawl*, and the Prince of *Powys* should be Umpire. But if the Prince of *Aberffraw* and *Powys* fell at Variance, they should meet at *Dôl Rhianedd*, probably *Morva Rhianedd*, on the Bank of the River *Dee*, where the King of *Cardigan* was to adjust the Controversy; and if the Quarrel happened betwixt the Princes of *Powys* and *Cardigan*, the meeting was appointed at *Llys Wen* upon the River *Wye*, and to be decided by the Prince of *Aberffraw*. And the better to frustrate any attempt of the *English*, he ordained moreover, that all Strongholds, Castles and Cittadels should be fortified and kept in repair; that all Churches and Religious Houses should be re-edified and adorned, and that in all ages the History of *Britain*, being faithfully registred and transcribed, should be kept therein.

D 2   *Anarawd*

Anarawd.

THE *Welch* had often forrowfully felt the unnatural Effects of inward Seditions, and of being governed by several Princes, which were now unavoidably to be renewed by reason of *Roderic*'s imprudent Division of his Dominions between his three Sons. For the several Principalities being united in him, it was certainly the moſt politick means for the preservation of the Countrey from the inveterate Fury of the *Engliſh*, to compose the inward Differences which would otherwise happen, by perpetuating the whole Government of *Wales* in one Prince. For it was impoſſible effectually to oppose the Common Enemy by separate Armies, and where a different Intereſt interfered, as if the Safety of the same Countrey, and the Honor of the same Prince were unanimouſly regarded. This was the unhappineſs of the antient *Britains* when the *Romans* invaded their Countrey; domeſtick Broils and inward Diſſentions being sown among themselves, they could not agree to unite their Powers, and jointly to oppose the Common Enemy; so that *Tacitus* wisely concludes, *dum ſinguli pugnant univerſi vincuntur.* There are few Nations but have experienced the folly of being rent into several Portions, and the downfal of that great Body the *Roman* Empire, may not be abſurdly attributed to *Conſtantine*'s dividing of it between his Sons. But the *Welch* at this time preſently felt the unhappineſs of it; *Cadelh* Prince of *South-Wales* being diſſatisfied with his Portion, and deſirous to feed his Ambition with larger Territories, could not spare his Brother *Merfyn*'s Countrey, but muſt needs forcibly diſpoſſeſs him of his lawful Inheritance, and so involve the *Welch* in a Civil War.

But

The History of WALES.

But the Succession of the Princes of *Wales* proceeds in *Anarawd* the eldest Son of *Roderic*, who began his Reign over *North-Wales*, in the Year 877. At that time *Rollo* with a numerous Army of *Normans* descended into *France*, and possessed themselves of the Countrey of *Neustria*, which from them has since received the Name of *Normandy*. But the treacherous *Danes* in *England*, who had retired to the City of *Exeter*, quickly violated the Capitulation which they had lately sworn to observe, and upon that account were so warmly pursued by King *Alfred*, that they gladly delivered up Hostages for the performance of the Articles formerly agreed upon between them. But it was not their Intention to keep them long, for the next Year they again broke lose, possessed themselves of all the Countrey upon the North-side of *Thames*, and passing the River, put the *English* to flight, and made themselves Masters of *Chippenham* in *West-Sax*. But their whole Army did not succeed so well, for *Alfred* meeting with a Party of them, slew their Captain and took their Standard, which the *Danes* called *Raven*. After this he vanquished them again at *Edendown*, where after that the *Danes* had given Hostages for their peaceable behaviour; *Godrun* their Commander received the Christian Faith, and so reigned in *East-Angle*. But this opportunity seemed to threaten a great Storm upon *Wales*; for besides the Death of *Aedan* the Son of *Melht*, a Noble-man of the Countrey, the Articles of Composition between the *English* and the *Danes*, occasioned these last to join their Power with the People of *Mercia* to Fight against the *Welch*, between whom a severe Battel was fought at *Conwey*, wherein the *Welch* obtained a very signal Victory, which was called *Dial Rodri*, or the Revenge of the Death of Prince *Roderic*. The Reason why the *Mercians* were so irreconcilably enraged against the *Welch* at this time, was this. After the Death of *Roderic the Great*, the Northern *Britains* of *Stratclwyd* and *Cumberland* were mightily infested and weakened thro' the daily Incursions of the *Danes*, *Saxons* and *Scots*, insomuch

877.

A.D. 878.

insomuch that as many of them as would not submit their Necks to the Yoke were forced to quit their Countrey, and to seek for more quiet Habitations. Therefore towards the beginning of *Anarawd*'s Reign, several of them came to *Gwyneth* under the Conduct of one *Hobert*, whose distressed Condition the Prince commiserating, granted them all the Countrey betwixt *Chester* and *Conwey* to seat themselves in, in case they could drive out the *Saxons* who had lately possessed themselves of it. The *Britains* having returned their thanks to *Anarawd*, presently fell to work, and Necessity giving edge to their Valour, they easily dispossessed the *Saxons* who were not as yet warm in their Seats. For some time they continued peaceably in this part of *Wales*; but *Eadred* Duke of *Mercia*, called by the *Welch Edryd Wallthir*, not being able any longer to bear such an ignominious ejection, made great Preparations for the re-gaining of the said Countrey. But the Northern *Britains*, who had settled themselves there, having intelligence of his Design, for the better security of their Cattel and other Effects, removed them beyond the River *Conwey*. Prince *Anarawd* in the mean time was not idle, but drawing together all the Strength he could raise, encamped his Army near the Town of *Conwey* at a place called *Cymryt*, where himself and his Men having made gallant Resistance against the pressing Efforts of the *Saxons*, obtained a very compleat Victory. This Battel was by some called *Gwaeth Cymryt Conwey*, by reason that it was fought in the Township of *Cymryt* near *Conwey*. But Prince *Anarawd* would have it called *Dial Rodri*, because he had there revenged the Death of his Father *Rodri*. In this Battel *Tudwal Rodri*'s Son received a wound in the Knee, which made him be denominated *Tudwal Glôff* ever after; but for his signal Service in this Action his Brethren bestowed upon him *Uchelogoed Gwynedd*. But the *Britains* pursuing their Victory, chased the *Saxons* quite out of *Wales* into *Mercia*, where having burnt and destroyed the Borders, they returned home laden with rich Spoils, and so took possession of the Country betwixt *Chester* and

The History of WALES.

and *Conwey*, which for a long time after they peaceably enjoyed. But *Anarawd* to express his thankfulness to God for this great Victory, gave very considerable Lands and Possessions to the Collegiate Churches of *Bangor* and *Clynnoc Vawr* in *Arfon*. After this, those *Danes* that lay at *Fulhenham* near *London*, crossed the Sea to *France*, and passing to *Paris* along the River *Seyn*, spoiled the Country thereabouts, and vanquished the *French* that came against them; but in their return towards the Sea-Coast, they were met with by the *Britains* of *Armorica*, who slew the greatest part of them, and the rest confusedly endeavouring to escape to their Ships, were all drowned. One should think that the several Misfortunes the *Danes* sustained, first at *Sandwich*, then by King *Alfred*, and now in *France*, would have quite drained their Number, and utterly have rid *Britain* from so troublesome an Enemy. But like ill Weeds, the more you root them, the faster they will grow; the *Danes* were still supplied from abroad, and if an Army was vanquished here, another was sure to come in their room. This the *Welch* found too true, for not long after this famous Defeat by the *Armorican Britains*, the *Danes* not able to venture upon these, were resolved to revenge themselves upon their Friends of *Wales*, and therefore landing in *North-Wales*, they cruelly harassed and destroyed the Country. Nor is it strange to consider from whence such a wonderful Number of *Danes* and *Normans* could come. For the Kingdom of *Denmark* had under it, not only *Denmark*, which is a small Country divided by the Sea into *Infulas* and *Peninfulas*, as that which joins upon *Saxony* and *Holfatia*, called *Cymbrica Cherfonefus*, with the Islands of *Zealand* and *Finnen*, but also *Norway* and the large Country of *Sweden*, reaching to *Mufcovy*, and almost to the *North-Pole*. This Country being then scarce known to the World, did of a sudden pour out such a multitude of People, which like a sudden Storm unexpectedly over-ran all *Europe*, with a great part of the Country of *Africa*. From hence proceeded these *Danes* who annoyed *England*; And

And the *Normans*, who conquer'd *France*; both Nations being originally derived from the fame Stock. *A.D.* 850. The *Danes* had not appeared in *England* for fome time, and therefore are now refolved to take fo fure a footing, as they cannot eafily be repulfed. Two Hundred and Fifty Sail being landed at *Lymene* in *Kent*, hard by the great Foreft of *Andreflege*, they built the Caftle of *Auldre* or *Apledore*. The fame time *Hafting* with a Fleet of Eighty Sail ventured to the *Thames* mouth, and built the Caftle of *Mydlton*; having firft made an Oath to King *Alfred*, not to moleft him or any of his Subjects: But having built the Caftle of *Beamfleet*, he thought himfelf to have obtain'd fo great a Strength, that there was no neceffity of obferving the Oath lately fworn to King *Alfred*, and therefore invaded the Country round about him. . But he foon found his Miftake, and was forced to betake himfelf back to his Caftle, which was quickly pulled down upon his Head, and his Wife and two Sons taken Prifoners; who being chriftened, were again reftored to their Father. Upon this *Hafting* and his *Danes* departed from *England*, and made their way for *France*; where laying fiege to the City of *Limogu*, and defpairing of a fpeedy furrender of it, betook himfelf to his ufual way of dealing finiftroufly, and devifed this Trick to win the Town. He feigned himfelf to be dangeroufly fick, and fent to the Bifhop, and the Conful of the City, defiring of them moft earneftly, that he might be admitted to the Chriftian Faith, and be baptized before his departure out of this World. The Bifhop and Conful fufpecting no Deceit, were very glad, not only to be delivered from the prefent danger of being befieged, but alfo to win fo great a Perfon to the Congregation of Chrift. Whereupon a firm Peace being concluded betwixt both Nations, *Hafting* is baptized, the Bifhop and Conful being his Godfathers; which being ended, he was carried back by his Soldiers to his Ships, in a very infirm condition, as he outwardly pretended. About midnight he caufed himfelf with his Arms about him to be laid on a Bier, and commanded his

Soldiers

The History of WALES.

Soldiers to carry their Weapons with them under their Coats, and so to be ready when he should give them the word. The next day, all things being in a readiness, he was solemnly brought by his Soldiers with great Clamour and counterfeit Mourning, to be interr'd in the chief Church of the City; where the Bishop and Consul, accompanied with all the most honourable Members of the Town, came to honour the Funeral. But when the Bishop had made himself ready to bury the Body, and all the Citizens being in the Church, up starts *Hasting* with his Sword drawn, and killing first the Bishop and the Consul, afterwards fell in with his armed Soldiers upon the naked People, putting all to the Sword, and sparing neither Age, Sex, nor Infirmity. Having ransack'd the Town, he sent Messengers to *Charles* the *French* King, to mediate for Peace, which he easily obtain'd, together with the Town of *Chartres* towards the defraying of his Charges.

At this time *Hennith ap Bledric*, a Baron of *Wales*, died; and Two Years after, *Anarawd* Prince of *North Wales*, with a considerable number of *English*, marched against his Brother *Cadelh*, and spoiled the Countries of *Cardigan* and *Ystradgwy*. At the same time the *Danes* laid siege to the City of *Excester*; and when *Alfred* had marched to oppose them, they that continued in the Castle of *Auldre* passed over to *Essex*, and built another Castle at *Scobrith*, and from thence marched to *Budington*, seated upon the *Severn*. When *Alfred* came near to *Excester*, the *Danes* presently rais'd the Siege, and betaking themselves to their Ships, sailed towards *Wales*, and spoiled the Sea-Coast thereof, and advanced as far as *Buellt*.

But the *Danes* at *Budington* being informed that King *Alfred* marched against them, fled back to their Castle in *Essex*: So that the King was fain to alter his march, and to convert his Forces against *Leycester*; where a Party of *Danes* was so warmly besieged, that at length they were reduced to that Extremity, as to feed upon their Horses. But the Season of the Year for Action being ended, and the Extremity

A.D.891.
893.

mity of the Weather being advanced, *Alfred* was forced to raife the Siege, and to wait the next Oppor-
*A.D.*895. tunity for the recovery of the Town. But before he could appear before it again, the *Danes* fairly quitted it, and together with thofe in *Northumberland*, paffed by the North-Sea to *Merefige*, an Ifle in *Effex*. The
896. next Year they entred the *Thames*, and built a Caftle twenty Miles diftant from *London* ; upon the ftrength of which, they ventur'd to fpoil and waft the Countrey thereabouts ; but paid very dear for their Courage, being accidentally met with, they received a bloody Overthrow, having four of their Princes flain upon the Spot, and the reft very glad to make their Efcape to the Caftle. Upon this *Alfred* divided the River into three Streams, by which Stratagem the Water became fo diminifhed in the *Thames*, that the *Danifh* Ships could not return back into the Sea. When the *Danes* perceived this, and found it impracticable for them to efcape in their Ships, they left their Wives and Children and all their Effects in *Effex* ; and fo paffed by Land to *Enadbryge* upon the *Severn*, and then paffing the River, fpoiled the Countries of *Brecknock*, *Gwentland*, and *Gwentlhwg*. Some of them at the fame time paffed over to *France* ; and another Company coafting about *Devonfhire*, deftroyed the maritime Countries ; but being met with by the *En-*
897. *glifh*, loft Six of their Ships in the Difpute. The following Summer the Kingdom of *Ireland* fuffered extremely by Locufts, who confumed all the Corn and the Grafs through the whole Country; but were at length by continued Prayers and Fafting quite deftroyed. Thefe are common in *Africke*, and other hot Regions, but feldom feen in colder Climates ; and when they happen to travel fo far, they are always very peftilentious and deftructive to that Country they come to.
900. This Year *Igmond*, with a great number of *Danes*, landed in *Anglefey*, and was met with by the *Welch*, at a place call'd *Molerain*, where *Merfyn* was flain: Though others call it *Meilon*, and from the Battel fought there, *Maes Rhôs Meilon*. The fame Year
King

The History of WALES.

King *Alfred* dyed, who tranflated the antient Laws of *Dyfnwall Moelmut* King of *Britain*, and the Laws of Queen *Marfia*, out of *Brittifh* into *Englifh*, and call'd it *Marfian* Law, which was afterwards called *Weft Saxon*-Law, and obferved in part of *Mercia*, with all the Countries on the South of *Thames* : The other part of the Country having another Law call'd *Dane Lex*, both which remained to the time of *Edward* the Confeffor, who of thefe two made one Law. It is very obfervable, what is related of King *Alfred*, concerning his divifion of the Natural Day into three parts; the one he fet apart for Devotion and Study, the next for the Affairs of the Common-Wealth, and the third for his own Reft and Refrefhment.

Alfred being dead, *Edward* his eldeft Son took upon him the Crown, which fo difpleafed the ambitious Spirit of his Brother *Adelwulph*, that prefently he raifed a cruel War againft him, and flying to *Northumberland*, ftirred up the *Danes* againft his Brother *Edward*. The *Danes* were glad of the opportunity, having now a fair pretence to render themfelves Mafters of the whole Ifland; and therefore *Adelwulph* is made King, as well of the *Angles* as of the *Danes*, who by this time were grown to be one People. Marching then proudly with a very confiderable Army at his heels, he fubdued the *Eaft Saxons*, fpoiled the Country of *Mercia*; and paffing over the *Thames* at *Crickland*, deftroyed *Brythend*, and returned home with very great Booty. At the fame time *Eunetb* was flain in *Arwyftly*. But *Edward* being informed of his Brothers retreat, purfued him very eagerly; but miffing of him, over-ran and deftroyed all the Country betwixt *Oufe* and the Dike of *S. Edmund*, and then returned home with his whole Army; faving the *Kentifh* Men, who being too greedy of Plunder, rafhly tarried behind. For the *Danes* perceiving the Body of the Army to be returned, and that a fmall Party ftill continued to ravage the Country, prefently fet upon them, flue a great Number of them, and put the reft to a fhameful Flight. Nor were the

Danes

Danes only powerful in *England*, but molested and grew prevalent in *Ireland*: For this Year they entred that Kingdom, slew *Carmot* King and Bishop of all *Ireland*, a religious and a vertuous Person, the Son of *Cukeman*; and *Kyrnalt* Son of *Murgan* King of *Lagines*. The Year after dyed *Asser* Archbishop of S.*Davids*, Uncle to the famous and learned *Asser* surnamed *Menevensis*; who being Chancellour to his Uncle the Archbishop, was sent for by King *Alfred* to instruct his Children; whose Life he afterwards wrote, and was made Bishop of *Shireburn*.

Edward, to force his Brother from his Country, and to revenge the death of the *Kentishmen*, dispatch'd an Army to *Northumberland*; which having spoiled the Country, returned home: Upon which the *Danes*, to return their Kindness, destroyed a great part of *Mercia*. But within a while after, *Edward* having raised a very considerable Army, gave the *Danes* battel, overthrew them, and slue their Kings *Alden* and *Edelwulph*, with a great number of their Nobles. This added very much to his Dominions, which were the more increased and strengthned by the Addition of the Cities of *London* and *Oxford*; which upon the death of *Edelred* Duke of *Mercia*, *Edward* seized into his own hands, permitting his Wife *Esfleda* to enjoy the rest of his Dukedom.

Shortly after, *Cadelh* Prince of *South Wales* died, leaving behind him three Sons; *Howel Dha*, or the Good, who succeeded his Father in the Kingdom of *South Wales*; *Meyric* and *Clydawc*. King *Edward* having obtained so signal a Victory over the *Danes*, and rendered his Kingdom for some time quiet, began to build places of strength, which might be serviceable against a future Storm: He built a Castle at *Hartford*, betwixt the Rivers *Benefic*, *Minier*, and *Lige*; and also erected the Borrough of *Wytham* in *Essex*; and continued sometime in *Wealdyne*, to keep those Countries in awe. But in spite of all this precaution, the *Danes* of *Leycester* and *Hampton*, began the following Year to be very troublesom, slew a great number of *English* at *Hotchnorton*; and in their return homeward,

The History of WALES.

ward, destroyed the Country of *Oxford*. About the same time a considerable Fleet from *Tydwike*, under the command of *Uther* and *Rahald*, sailed by the Western Sea to *Wales*, and destroyed S. *Davids*; where was fought the Battel of *Dinarth*, and *Mayloc* the Son of *Peredur Gam* was slain. After this they entred into *Herefordshire*, where they were fought withal, and *Rahald* was slain, and the rest compell'd to forswear the King's Land, and never to return any more to *England*. King *Edward*, to prevent any future Disturbance from such open Invaders, caused a strong Army to be quartered upon the South side of *Severn*; but the *Danes*, for all he could do, enter'd twice into his Country, once at *Werd*, and then at *Portogan*; but were both times overthrown by the *English*. From thence they departed to the Isle of *Stepen*, whence they were forced by Hunger to sail to *South Wales*, intending to make a considerable Prey of that Country; but failing of their aim, they were constrained to make the best of their way for *Ireland*. But the next Year, a Party of *Danes* fought a very severe Battel with the *Kentish-men* at *Holm*; but which of them obtain'd the Victory, is not certainly reported. About the same time *Anarawd*, Prince of *North Wales*, died, leaving behind him two Sons, *Edwal Foel*, and *Elis*; and some say a third named *Meyric*.

*A.D.*911.

913.

Edwal Foel.

AFter the death of *Anarawd*, his eldest Son *Edwal Foel* took upon him the Government of *Northwales*; *Howel Dha* holding the Principality of *Southwales* and *Powis*: At what time, a terrible Comet appeared in the Heavens. The same Year the City of *Chester*, which had been destroyed by the *Danes*, was, by the procurement of *Elfleda*, new built and repaired,

The History of WALES.

repaired, as the antient Records of that City do testifie. This in the antient Copy is called *Leycester*, by an easie mistake for *Legecestria* or *Chester*, called by the *Romans*, *Legionum Cestria*. The next Summer the Men of *Dublin* cruelly destroyed the Isle of *Anglesey*; and soon after, *Clydawc* the Son of *Cadelh* was unnaturally slain by his Brother *Meyric*, about the same time that the *Danes* received a cruel overthrow by the *English*, at *Tottenhale*. But *Elfleda* did not long survive the rebuilding of the City of *Chester*; a Woman of singular Virtues, and one that greatly strengthned the Kingdom of *Mercia*, by building of Towns and Castles against the Incursions of the *Danes*; as *Strengat* and *Bruge*, by the Forrest of *Morph*, *Tamworth*, *Stafford*, *Edelburgh*, *Cherenburgh*, *Wadeburgh*, and *Runcofe*. After this, she entered with her whole Army into *Wales*, wan *Brecknock*, and took the Queen, with 33 of her Men Prisoners; which in *Welch* is called *Gwaith y Ddinas Newydh*, or the Battel of the new City. From hence she marched for *Derby*, which she took from the *Danes*, losing only four of her chief Commanders in the Action. The occasion of these two Expeditions, according to some, was this: *Huganus*, Lord of *West Wales*, perceiving King *Edward* to be unavoidably busie in the *Danish* War, gathered an Army of *Britains*, and entring into *England*, destroyed the Kings Country. Upon the News of this, *Elfleda* came to *Wales* with a great Army, fought with the *Welch* at *Brecknock*, and putting *Huganus* to flight, took his Wife and some of his Men Prisoners; whom she carried with her to *Mercia*. *Huganus* being thus defeated, fled to *Derby*, and being there kindly received, joined himself with the Kings Enemies, the *Danes*. *Elfleda* being certified of that, followed him with her Army; but in storming the Gates of the Town, had Four of her best Officers kill'd by *Huganus*. But *Gwyane* Lord of the Isle of *Ely*, her Steward, setting fire to the Gates, furiously ran upon the *Britains*, and entered the Town; upon which *Huganus* perceiving himself to be over-match'd, chose rather to fall by the Sword, than

The History of WALES.

than cowardly to yield himself to a Woman. The next Year *Efleda* laid siege to the City of *Leicester*, which was quickly surrender'd, and the *Danes* therein perfectly subdued. The Fame of these several Actions being noised abroad, her Neighbours became somewhat fearful and timorous; and the *Yorkshiremen* voluntarily did her Homage, and proffer'd their Service. She died at *Tamworth*, after Eight Years rule over *Mercia*; and lies buried at *Glocester* by S. *Peters*.

After the death of *Elfleda*, King *Edward* most ungratefully disinherited her Daughter *Alfwyen*; and entering into *Mercia*, seized all the Land into his own hands; upon pretence that she, without his knowledg, (whom her Mother had appointed her Guardian) had privily promised and contracted Marriage with *Reynald* King of the *Danes*. But this unjust and unnatural Action of King *Edwards*, might possibly bring upon him those vehement Troubles, which presently ensued upon it. For *Leofred* a *Dane*, and *Gruffydh ap Madoc* Brother in Law to the Prince of *West Wales*, came from *Ireland* with a great Army to *Snowdon*, and minding to bring all *Wales* and the Marches thereof to their subjection, over-ran and subdued all the Country to *Chester*, before King *Edward* was certified of their arrival. Whereat being sore offended, and loth to trouble his Subjects for help, vowed that himself and his Sons, with their single Forces, would be revenged upon *Leofred* and *Gruffydh*; and thereupon marching to *Chester*, forced the City from them. Then he divided his Army into two Battels, whereof he and his Son *Ethelstan* lead the first, *Edmund* and *Edred* the second; and followed them so close, that he overtook them at the Forest of *Walewode* (now *Sherwode*) where *Leofred* and *Gruffydh* set upon them so fiercely, that the King at first was in some danger; until *Athelstane* stepped in and wounded the *Dane* in the Arm in that manner, that being no longer able to hold his Spear, he was taken Prisoner, and committed to the custody of *Athelstane*. In the mean time *Edmund* and *Edred*
encountring

encountring with *Gruffydh*, flew him, and brought his Head to their Father; and *Leofreds* Head being likewife cut off, they were both fet up upon the Town of *Chefter*; and then *Edward*, together with his Sons, victoriously returned home. But King *Edward*, having built *Glademutham*, foon after this dyed at *Farandon*, and his Son *Alfred* the fame time at *Oxford*, and were both buried at *Winchefter*.

A.D. 924.

Edward being dead, his bafe Son *Athelftane*, for many excellent Virtues appearing in him, was preferred to the Crown; the worthieft Prince of the *Saxon* Blood that ever reigned. He overcame *Cudfryd* the Father of *Raynald* King of the *Danes* at *York*; and being invaded by *Hawlaf* King of *Ireland*, who with all the Power of the *Scots* and *Danes* marched againft him, gave him battel at *Brimeftbury*, and obtained a very notorious Victory; King *Hawlaf*, together with the King of the *Scots*, five Kings of the *Danes* and *Normans* being flain upon the fpot: fo that the whole Country of *England* and *Scotland* became fubject to him, which none of his Predeceffors ever attempted. Sometime after *Owen* the Son of *Gruffydh* was flain by the Men of *Cardigan*: And then *Athelftane* entring with his Army into *Wales*, forced the Princes thereof to pay a yearly Tribute of 20*l*. in Gold, 300*l*. in Silver, and 200 Head of Cattel; which notwithftanding was not obferved, as appears by the Laws of *Howel Dha*, wherein it is appointed, that the Prince of *Aberffraw* fhould pay no more to the King of *London*, than 66 *l*. Tribute; and that the Princes of *Dinefawr* and *Powis* fhould pay the like Sum to the Prince of *Aberffraw*. But King *Ethelftane* was not lefs terrible abroad, than he was awed and feared at home; the Kings of *France* and *Norway* fending him very great and coftly Prefents, to obtain his Favour, and to gain his good Will.

933.

This Year *Euneth* the Son of *Clydawc*, and *Meyric* the Son of *Cadelh* died. The fame time King *Athelftane* removed the *Britains* who lived at *Excefter* and the neighbouring Country to *Cornwal*; bounding them with the River *Cambria* (now *Tamar*); as the *Britains*

936.

The History of WALES.

tains of *Wales*, with the *Wye*. Not long after, the *A.D.* 939 noble Prince *Athelstane* dyed, to the great and inexpressible sorrow of all his Subjects, and was buried at *Malmesbury*; and succeeded by his Brother *Edmund*, not inferiour to him in Courage; but preferable by right of Nativity, being born in Wedlock. In the first Year of his reign, he gave a very considerable blow to the *Danes*; took from them the Cities of *Leycester*, *Darby*, *Stafford*, *Lincoln*, and *Nottinham*. Then *Aulafe* King of the *Danes*, finding it impracticable to withstand the force of King *Edmund*, desired peace, and withal to be initiated in the Christian Faith; which being granted him, he and all his *Danes* received Baptism, King *Edmund* standing Godfather at the Font: after which both Parties concluding a firm and a lasting Peace, *Edmund* honourably returned to *West-Sex*. The same Year dyed *Abloic* chief King of *Ireland*: And the Year following, *Cadelh* the Son of *Arthuael* a Nobleman of *Wales*, was, for what reason not discovered, imprisoned by the *English*. To revenge which Indignity, *Edwal Foel* and his Brother *Elis* gathered their Forces together, and fought against the *English* and *Danes*, but were both unhappily slain. This *Edwal Foel* had six Sons, *Meyric*, *Ievaf*, *Iago*, *Conan*, *Edwal Fychan*, and *Roderic*: And his Brother *Elis* had Issue *Conan*, and a Daughter named *Trawst*, the Mother of *Conan ap Sitsylht*, *Gruffydh ap Sitsylht*, and *Blethyn ap Confyn*, which two last were afterwards Princes of *Wales*.

Howel Dha.

*H*Owel *Dha* had been for a considerable time Prince of *South-Wales* and *Powis*; in which Government he had so justly and discreetly behaved himself, that upon the death of *Edwal Foel*, he was worthily 940.
E preferred

preferred to the Principality of *Wales*: Notwithstanding that *Edwal* had left behind him several Sons, who at first seem'd to murmure at and resent the Election of *Howel Dha*. The first thing he took care of, was to enact good and wholsom Laws for the benefit of his Country; which held in force in *Wales*, till the time of *Edward* the First, when the *Welch* received the Laws of *England*, yet not so generally, but that in some places they continued long after, and are still to' be seen in the *Welch* and *Latin* Tongue: For *Howel Dha* perceiving the Laws and Customs of his Country to have grown to great abuse, sent for the Archbishop of *Menevia*, with the rest of the Bishops and chief Clergy, to the number of 140. and all the Barons and Nobles of *Wales*, and ordered that Six of the wisest and best esteemed Persons in every Commote should be cited before him, at his Palace called *y Ty Gwyn ar Taf*, or the white House upon the River *Taf*. Thither coming himself, he remained with his Nobles, Prelates, and Subjects for all the Lent, in Prayers and Fasting, imploring the assistance and direction of Gods Holy Spirit, that he might reform the Laws and Customs of the Country of *Wales*, to the Honour of God, and the peaceable Government of his Subjects. Towards the end of Lent, he chose out of that Assembly Twelve of the wisest and gravest, and Persons of the greatest Experience, to whom he added *Blegored*, a Man of singular Learning, and one exquisitely versed in the Laws. To these he gave commission to examine the antient Laws and Customs of *Wales*, and to collect out of them what was requisite towards the Government of the Country; according to which Charge they retained those that were wholsom and profitable, expounded those that were doubtful and ambiguous, and abrogated them that were superfluous and hurtful: And so these Laws were distinguished into three sorts; The first concerned the Order and Regulation of the King's Houshold and Court; The second the Affairs of the Country and Commonwealth; and the last had regard to special Customs belonging to particular Persons and Places. All

which

The History of WALES.

which being publickly proclaimed and generally allow'd of, Prince *Howel* ordered three Copies to be written; one for his own ufe, another to be laid up at his Palace of *Aberffraw*, and the third at *Dinefawr*; fo that the three Provinces of *Wales* might have eafie recourfe to either of them, when need required. And for the better obfervation of thefe Laws, he caufed the Archbifhop of S. *Davids* to denounce Sentence of Excommunication againft all fuch of his Subjects as would not obey the fame. Within a while after, *Howel*, to omit nothing that might procure any Countenance or Authority to thefe his Laws, accompanied with *Lambert* Archbifhop of S. *Davids*, *Mordaf* Bifhop of *Bangor*, and *Chebur* of S. *Afaph*, and Thirteen of the moft prudent and learnedft Perfons in *Wales*, took a Journey to *Rome*, where the faid Laws being recited before the Pope, were by his Holinefs ratified and confirmed: After which, *Howel*, with all his Retinue, returned home to his Country. The particulars of thefe Laws are too numerous to be here inferted; only it is obfervable, that all matters of Inheritance of Land were determined and adjudged by the Prince in Perfon; or if fick, by his fpecial Deputy: And that upon view of the fame Land, citing together the Freeholders of that place, two Elders of his Council, the chief Juftice always attending in the Court, the ordinary Judge of the Country where the Land lay, and the Prieft. The Method of their proceeding was in this manner; the Prince fate in his Judicial-Seat above the reft of the Court, with an Elder on each hand, next to whom the Freeholders on both fides, who upon that account were probably called *Uchelwyr*. Below the Prince at a certain diftance, fate the chief Juftice, having the Prieft on his right hand, and the ordinary Judg of the Country concerned upon the left. The Court being thus fate, the Plaintiff with his Advocate, Champion and *Rhingylh* or Sergeant, ftood on the left fide of the Court, as did the Defendant in like manner on the right. And laftly the Witneffes on both fides appeared, and ftood at the lower end of the Hall, directly

E 2   oppo-

oppofite to the chief Juftice, to teftifie the beft of their knowledg in the matter in debate. After the taking the Depofitions of the Witneffes, and a full pleading of the Caufe in open Court, upon notice given by the Sergeant, the chief Juftice, the Prieft, and the ordinary Judg, withdrew themfelves for a while, to confult of the matter; and then *fecundum allegata & probata*, brought in their Verdict. Whereupon the Prince, after Confultation had with the Elders that fate next him, gave definitive Senrence; excepting the Caufe was fo obfcure and intricate, that the Juftice of it could not appear; and then the two Champions put an end to the Controverfie by Combate

Whilft *Howel Dha* is thus regulating the Cuftoms, and meliorating the Laws and Conftitutions of *Wales*; *Aulafe* and *Regnald* Kings of the *Danes* forcibly entered the Country of King *Edmund*, who being vexed with their inceffant Hoftility, gathered his Forces together, and (as fome fay) by the help of *Lhewelyn ap Sitfylht*, who was afterwards Prince of *Wales*, followed them to *Northumberland*; and having overcome them in a pitch'd Battel, utterly chafed them out of his Kingdom, and remained a whole Year in thofe Parts, to regulate and bring that Country to fome quiet order. But finding it impracticable to reduce the Inhabitants of *Cumberland* to any peaceable Conftitution, having fpoiled and wafted the Country, he gave it up to *Malcolme* King of *Scotland*, upon condition that he fhould fend him Succours in his Wars, whenever demanded of him. In the mean time the *Welch* had but little occafion to rejoyce; *Hubert* Bifhop of S *Davids*, *Marclois* Bifhop of *Bangor*, and *Uffa* the Son of *Lhafyr* being dead: And fhortly after the *Englifh* entering into *Wales* with a very ftrong Army, put the Country into a great confternation; but being fatisfied with the Deftruction and Spoil of *Strat Clwyd*, they returned home without doing any more Mifchief. The fame time *Conan* the Son of *Elis* was like to be treacheroufly put to death by Poyfon; and *Eierus* Bifhop of S. *Davids* dyed. The

A.D. 942.

544.

next

The History of WALES.

next Year *Edmund* King of *England* was unluckily flain upon S. *Auguftines* day; but the manner of his Death is varioufly delivered; fome fay, that difcovering a noted Thief who was out-law'd, fitting among his Guefts, being tranfported with Indignation againft fo confident a Villain, ran upon him very furioufly, who expecting nothing lefs than Death, thought to dye not unrevenged, and therefore with a fhort Dagger gave the King a mortal Wound in the Breaft. Others report, that as the King would have refcued a Servant of his from an Officer who had arrefted him, he was unwittingly and unhappily flain by the fame. But however his Death happened, he lies buried at *Glaftenbury*; in whofe place his Brother *Edred* was crowned King of *England*, who no fooner had entered upon his Government, but he made an Expedition againft *Scotland* and *Northumberland*, which being fubdued, he received Fealty and Homage by Oath of the *Scots* and *Northumbrians*, which they did not long obferve. Shortly after *Howel Dha*, after a long and peaceable Reign over *Wales*, dyed, much lamented and bewailed of all his Subjects, being a Prince of a religious and a virtuous inclination, and one that ever regarded the Welfare and Profperity of his People. He left Iffue behind him, *Owen, Run, Roderic,* and *Edwyn*, betwixt whom and the Sons of *Edwal Foel*, late Prince of *North Wales*, great Wars and Commotions arofe afterwards about the chief Rule and Government of *Wales*.

A.D. 948.

But the Sons of *Howel Dha*, as fome Writers record, were thefe. *viz. Owen*, who did not long furvive his Father, *Eineon, Meredyth, Dyfnwal,* and *Rodri*, the two laft whereof, as is conceived, were flain in the Battel fought near *Lhanrwft*, in the Year 952. by the Sons of *Edwal Foel*; *Run* Lord of *Cardigan*, who was flain before the death of his Father; *Conan y Cwn*, who poffeffed *Anglefey*; *Edwin*, who was alfo flain, as is fuppofed, in the forementioned Battel. There was alfo another Battel fought betwixt *Howel* and *Conan* ap *Edwal Foel* for the Ifle of *Anglefey*, wherein *Conan* fell; and *Gruffydh* his Son renewing the War, was likewife

E 3 over-

overcome; and so *Cyngar*, a powerful Person, being driven out of the Island, *Howel* enjoyed quiet possession thereof, and of the rest of *Gwynedh*. It is supposed that this *Howel Dha* was chosen Governour of *Wales*, during the minority of his Uncle *Anarawd*'s Sons, who, at the death of their Father, were too young to manage the Principality; which he kept till his return from *Rome*, at which time *Edwal Foel* being come of age, he resigned to him the Kingdom of *Gwynedh* or *North-Wales*, together with the Sovereignty of all *Wales*: Before which time *Howel* is styled *Brenhin Cymry oll*, that is, King of all *Wales*, as is seen in the Preface to that Body of Laws compiled by him.

Ievaf and *Iago*, the Sons of *Edwal Foel*.

After the death of *Howel Dha*, his Sons divided betwixt them the Principalities of *South-Wales* and *Powis*; laying no claim to *North-Wales*, though their Father had been a general Prince of all *Wales*. But *Ievaf* and *Iago* the Sons of *Edwal Foel*, having put by their elder Brother *Meyric*, as a Person uncapable of Government, and being dissatisfied with the Rule of *North Wales* only, imagined that the Principality of all *Wales* was their Right, as descending from the elder House; which the Sons of *Howel Dha* denyed them. Indeed, they had been wrongfully kept out of the Government of *North Wales* during the Reign of *Howel*; in whose time the recovery of their own was impracticable, by reason that for his Moderation and other good Qualities, he had attracted to himself the universal Love of all the *Welch*. But now, he being gone, they are resolved to revenge the Injury received by him upon his Sons; and upon a small

The History of WALES.

small pretence, endeavour to reduce the whole Country of *Wales* to their own subjection. *Ievaf* and *Iago* were indeed descended from the elder branch; but since *Roderic* the great conferred the Principality of *South Wales* upon his yonger Son *Cadelh*, the Father of *Howel Dha*, it was but just his Sons should enjoy what was legally descended to them by their Father: But Ambition seldom gives place to Equity; and therefore, right or wrong, *Ievaf* and *Iago* must have a touch for *South Wales*, which they enter with a great Army; and being opposed, they obtained a very opportune Victory over *Owen* and his Brethren the Sons of *Howel*, at the Hills of *Carno*. The next Year the two Brothers entred twice into *South-Wales*, destroyed and wasted *Dyfet*, and slew *Dwnwalhon* Lord of the Countrey. Shortly after which, *Roderic* the third Son of *Howel Dha* dyed. But his Brethren perceiving the Folly of standing only upon the defensive, muster'd all their Forces together, and entering *North-Wales*, marched as far as *Lhanrwst* upon the River *Conwy*; where *Ievaf* and *Iago* met them. A very cruel Battel ensued upon this, and a very great number were slain on both sides, among whom were *Anarawd* the Son of *Gwyriad*, the Son of *Roderic* the Great; and *Edwyn* the Son of *Howel Dha*. But the Victory plainly favoured the Brothers *Ievaf* and *Iago*; so that the Princes of *South-Wales* were obliged to retire to *Cardiganshire*, whither they were warmly pursued, and that Country cruelly harrass'd with Fire and Sword. The next Year *Merfyn* was unhappily drowned; and shortly after *Congelach* King of *Ireland* was slain.

A.D.950.

951.

952.

953.

The *Scots* and *Northumbrians* having lately sworn Allegiance to King *Edred*, he was scarce returned to his own Country, but *Aulafe*, with a great Army, landed in *Northumberland*, and was with much rejoycing received by the Inhabitants. But before he could secure himself in the Government, he was shamefully banished the Country; and so the *Northumbrians* elected one *Hircius*, the Son of *Harold* for their King. But to shew the Inconstancy of an unsettled Multitude, they

The History of WALES.

they soon grew weary of *Hircius*, and after Three Years space expelled him, and voluntarily submitted themselves to *Edred*, who after he had reigned eight Years, dyed, and was buried at *Winchester*. To him succeeded *Edwin* the Son of *Edmund*, a Man so immoderately given to Venery, that he forcibly married another Man's Wife; for which, and other Irregularities, his Subjects, after four Years reign, set up his Brother *Edgar*, who was crowned in his stead; with grief of which, he soon ended his days. The Summer, that same Year, proved so immoderately hot, that it caused a very dismal Plague in the following Spring, which swept away a great number of People; before which, *Gwgan* the Son of *Gwyriad* the Son of *Roderic* dyed. At this time, *Ievaf* and *Iago* forcibly managed the Government of all *Wales*, and acted according to their own good Pleasures, no one daring to confront or resist them. But for all their Power, the Sons of *Abloic* King of *Ireland*, ventured to land in *Anglesey*; and having burnt *Holyhead*, wasted the Country of *Lhyn*. Also the Sons of *Edwyn* the Son of *Colhoyn*, destroyed and ravaged all the Country to *Towyn*, where they were intercepted and slain. About the same time dyed *Meyric* the Son of *Cadfan*, *Rytherch* Bishop of S. *Davids*, and *Cadwalhon ap Owen*. Not long after, the Country of *North-Wales* was cruelly wasted by the Army of *Edgar* King of *England*; the occasion of which Invasion was the non-payment of the Tribute that the King of *Aberffraw*, by the Laws of *Howel Dha*, was obliged to pay to the King of *London*. But at length a Peace was concluded upon these Conditions, that the Prince of *North-Wales*, instead of Money, should pay to the King of *England* the Tribute of 300 Wolves yearly; which Creature was then very pernicious and destructive to *England* and *Wales*. This Tribute being duly performed for two Years, the third Year there were none to be found in any part of the Island; so that afterwards the Prince of *North-Wales* became exempt from paying any Acknowledgment to the King of *England*. The Terror apprehended from the *English*, being by these

*A.D.*958.

961.

965.

966.

The History of WALES.

these means vanished; there threatned another Cloud from *Ireland*; for the *Irish* being animated by their late Expedition, landed again in *Anglesey*; and having slain *Roderic* the Son of *Edwal Foel*, they destroyed *Aberffraw*. And this danger being over, *Ievaf* and *A.D.* 967. *Iago* who had jointly and agreeably, till now, managed the Government of *Wales* from the death of *Howel Dha*, began to quarrel and disagree among themselves; and *Iago* having forcibly laid hands upon his Brother *Ievaf*, confined him to perpetual Imprisonment. These Heats and Animosities between the two Brothers, gave occasion and opportunity to *Owen* Prince of *South Wales* to carve for himself, who presently seized to his hands the Country of *Gwyr*. And to augment the Miseries of the *Welch* at this time, *Mactus* the Son of *Harold*, with an Army of *Danes*, entered the Isle of *Anglesey*, and spoiled *Penmon*. King *Edgar* was so indulgent to these *Danes*, that he permitted them to inhabit through all *England*; insomuch that at length they became to be as numerous and as strong as the *English* themselves; and fell into such lewd courses of Debauchery, and such horrid Drinking, that very great Mischief ensued thereupon. The King to reform this immoderate Sottishness, enacted a Law, that every one should drink by measure, and so stamped a Mark upon every Vessel, how far it should be filled. But *Harold* having taken *Penmon*, made subject to himself the whole Isle of *Anglesey*, which however he did not keep long, being forced to quit the same, and to return home; as did the Fleet of King *Alfred*, which he had sent to subdue *Caerlheon* upon *Usc*. And now being rid of the *English* and *Danes*, the *Welch* begin to raise Commotions among themselves. *Ievaf* continued still in Prison, to rescue whom, his Son *Howel* raised his Power, and marched against his Uncle *Iago*, who being vanquished in fight, was forced to quit the Country, to save himself. *Howel* having won the day, took his eldest Uncle, *Meyric* the Son of *Edwal* Prisoner, and pulled out both his Eyes, clapt him in Prison, where in a woful condition he shortly dyed, leaving behind him

968.

969.

970.

971.

972.

him two Sons, *Edwal* and *Ionafal*; the firſt of which lived to be afterwards Prince of *Wales*, and to revenge upon the Poſterity of *Howel*, that unnatural Barbarity ſhewed to his Father. But though *Howel* delivered his Father from his long and tedious Impriſonment, yet he did not think fit to reſtore him to his Principality; for whether by Age or Infirmity he was incapable, *Howel* took upon him the ſole Government of *Wales*, which he kept and maintained for his lifetime, but afterwards it deſcended to his Brethren. For *Ievaf* had Iſſue beſides this *Howel*; *Meyric*, *Ievaf*, and *Cadwalhan*; all three Men of great Repute and Eſteem.

About this time dyed *Morgan Hên*, in his younger days called *Morgan Mawr*, being an Hundred Years old, having lived Fifty Years after the death of his Wife *Elen*, Daughter of *Roderic* the Great, by whom he had one Son called *Owen*. *Morgan* was a valiant and a victorious Prince, and well beloved of his Subjects; but ſometime before his death, *Owen*, the Son of Prince *Howel Dha*, laid claim to *Yſtradwy* and *Ewy*, (called the two Sleeves of *Gwent Uwchcoed*) being the Right of *Morgan*, and ſeized upon them to his own uſe. But the matter, through the mediation of the Clergy and Nobility, being by both Parties referred to the deciſion of *Edgar* King of *England*, it was by him adjudged, that the ſaid Lands did of right belong to *Morgan*, and to the Dioceſs of *Lhandaff*; and that *Owen ap Howel Dha* had wrongfully poſſeſſed himſelf of them. The Charter of the ſaid Award was made before the Archbiſhops, Biſhops, Earls and Barons of *England* and *Wales*; as may be ſeen at *Lhandaff*, in an old Manuſcript called *y Cwtta Cyfarwydd o Forgannwg*. And there is ſomewhat to the ſame purpoſe in the old Book of *Lhandaff*; only the miſtake in both is, that they make *Howel Dha* the Intruder into the ſaid Lands, who had been dead at leaſt Twenty Years before King *Edgar* began his Reign.

Howel

Howel ap Ievaf.

Howel, after that he had expelled his Uncle *Iago*, and forced him to quit his own Dominions, took upon himself the Government of *Wales*, in right of his Father, who tho alive, yet by reason of his Years, was willing to decline it. About the same time *Dwnwalhon* Prince of *Stradclwyd*, took his Journey for *Rome*; and *Edwalhon* Son of *Owen* Prince of *South-Wales* died. But the *English* received a greater Blow by the Death of King *Edgar*, who was a Prince of excellent Qualities, both warlike and religious, and one that founded several Monasteries and religious Houses, and particularly at *Bangor*.

For *Iago ap Edwal* having fled to King *Edgar*, prevailed so far with him, that he brought an Army into *North-Wales* to restore him to his Right. Being advanced as far as *Bangor*, he was honourably receiv'd by *Howel*, who, at his request, was contented his Uncle *Iago* should have a share in the Government, as he had in his Father *Ievaf*'s time. Then *Edgar* founded a new Church at *Bangor*, on the South-side of the Cathedral, which he dedicated to the Blessed Virgin *Mary*; and confirmed the antient Liberties of that See, and bestowed Lands and Gifts upon it: And then with *Howel* and *Iago* in his company, he marched towards *Chester*, where met him, by appointment, Six Kings more, viz. *Keneth* King of the *Scots*, *Malcolm* King of *Cumberland*, *Macon* King of *Man*, and *Dyfnwal*, *Sifrethus*, and *Ithel*, three *British* Kings. These Eight Princes having done Homage, and sworn Fealty to him, entred with him into his Barge, and rowed him, four of each side, from his Palace to the Church or Monastery of S. *John Baptist*, and Divine Service being ended, in like state rowed him back again, To King *Edgar* succeeded his Son *Edward*, surnamed

The History of WALES.

named the Younger; who after four Years reign, was treacherously slain through the Treason of his Stepmother *Elfrida*, to make room for her own Son *Edelred*, upon pretence of whose minority, being a Child only of Seven Years, she might have the management of the Kingdom in her own hands. But whilst the *English* were in this waving and unsettled condition, *Eineon*, the Son of *Owen* King of *South-Wales*, the second time entered the Country of *Gwyr*, and having spoiled and wasted it, returned home again. This, though an unsufferable Affront to *Howel* Prince of *North-Wales*, yet he thought it most convenient to pass by and wink at it; being then warmly engaged against the Aiders and Abettors of his Uncle *Iago*; and marching against them with a numerous Army, consisting of *Welch* and *English* pursued them to *Lhyyn* and *Kelynnoc Fawr*, the very extremity of *Wales*; where after cruel ravaging and miserable harassing of the Country about, *Iago* was at last taken Prisoner; but so generously received by *Howel*, that he granted his Uncle to enjoy his portion of the Country peaceably for his Life. But he did not deal so kindly with his Uncle *Edwal Fychan* the Son of *Edwal Foel*; who, for what pretence, not discover'd, was slain by him. It may be, that being in a manner secure of his Uncle *Iago*, he was apprehensive that *Edwal Fychan* would put in his Pretence for the Principality; and therefore he judged it convenient to remove this Obstacle in time, and to send him to seek for it in another World. For nothing can be the cause of greater Injustice and Inhumanity in Princes, than the jealousie and apprehension of Rivals and Pretenders to their Government; to prevent which, they will sacrifice any thing that is just and legal, so that the Person offending be removed out of the way. But though *Howel* had murthered his Uncle *Edwal Fychan*, yet he could not remove all Disputes and Pretences to *North Wales*: For at the same time that he was employed in this unnatural Action, *Cystenyn Dhu*, or *Constantine* the Black, Son to *Iago* then Prisoner to *Howel*, having hired an Army of *Danes*, under the command of *Godfryd*

the

A.D. 976.

979

The History of WALES.

the Son of *Harold*, marched against his Cousin *Howel*, and entring *North-Wales*, destroyed *Anglesey* and *Lhyn*. Whereupon *Howel* having drawn his Forces together, set upon them at a place called *Gwayth Hirbarth*, where the *Danes* received a very shameful overthrow, and *Constantine* the Son of *Iago* was slain. But another Army of *Danes* fared better in *England*, who having landed at, and spoiled *Southampton*, over-ran the Countries of *Devon* and *Cornwal*, burnt the Town of *Bodman*, whereby the Cathedral Church of St. *Petrokes*, with the Bishop's Palace, were laid in Ashes; by reason of which Disaster, that Bishop's See was translated to St. *Germains*, where it continued till the uniting thereof to *Crediton*. Within a while after, St. *Dunstan* Archbishop of *Canterbury* died, a Pious and Religious Person, who fore-told of very great and insupportable Calamities, the *English* should endure by the cruel Outrages of the *Danes*.

But *Godfryd* the Son of *Harold* being highly disgusted at the shameful rout he received of *Howel* in the Quarrel of *Constantine*, was resolved to recover his Credit, and to revenge himself of the *Welch*. And accordingly he landed with a powerful Army in *West-Wales*, where after that he had spoiled the Land of *Dyfed*, with the Church of St. *Davids*, he fought the famous Battle of *Lhanwanoc*. But *Harold* being forced upon this to retire and forsake the Country, the following Year Duke *Alfred* with a considerable number of *English* came to supply his room, and to conquer the *Welch*. But he received as little Advantage or Honor as *Harold* in this Expedition; for after that he had laid waste and destroyed the Town of *Brecnock*, with some part of *South-Wales*, he was shamefully vanquished, and his Army almost totally cut off by the Troops of *Eineon* the Son of *Owen* Prince of *South-Wales*, and *Howel* Prince of *North Wales*, who had joined their Forces against him. And now the *Welch* having quite disabled the *Danes* and the *English*, began to fall to their old Courses, to make use of their Prosperity and Quietness from abroad, for quarrelling and creating Disturbances at home.

981.

982.

983.

The

The Inhabitants of *Gwentland* imagined themselves very Strong and Powerful, and therefore must needs endeavour to shake off their Allegiance to their Prince, and to set up one of their own making. *Owen* Prince of *South-Wales* to pacify the rebellious Humor of these seditious and turbulent People, sent his Son *Eineon* to perswade them to Obedience. But a distracted multitude got loose, is not to be worked upon by Arguments, which *Eineon* fatally experienced, who was so far from perswading them in their Allegiance by fair means, that they presently set upon him, and thinking that they had the Bird in their fist, who was next to succeed, put him to present Death. And thus most ignobly fell this worthy Prince, who in his Father's time was the only Support of his Country, being a stout and a valiant Commander, and one famously experienced in the Art and Discipline of War. He had Issue two Sons, *Edwyn* and *Tewdor Mawr*, or *Theodor the Great*, out of whose Loins several Princes of *South-Wales* were since descended. But *Howel* Prince of *North-Wales* did not regard this Dissention and Rebellion in *South-Wales*, and therefore took opportunity to strengthen and multiply his Army, with which he marched the next Year for *England*, intending to revenge the Incursions and Invasions of the *English* upon *Wales*, and to destroy and waste their Country. But having entred into *England*, he was presently fought with, upon which, being resolved either to return Victoriously, or to die Couragiously, he fell in among them, but in the Action was slain, leaving no Issue behind him to succeed in his Principality, tho' in some antient Genealogies he is reputed to have a Son called *Conan y Cwn*.

Cadwalbon

The History of WALES.

Cadwalhon ap Ievaf.

Howel the Son of *Ievaf* had for a long time enjoyed the Principality of *North-Wales*, more by main Force and Ufurpation, than any right of Succeffion he could pretend to it. For *Ionafal* and *Edwal* the Sons of *Meyric*, the eldeft Son of *Edwal Foel*, were living, and tho' their Father had been rejected as unfit for Government, yet that was no reafon to deprive them of their Right. Indeed, *Howel* could pretend to no other Right or Title, than that his Father *Ievaf* had been Prince of *North-Wales* before him, and this he thought fufficient to maintain his Poffeffion againft the rightful Heir, who was far unable to oppofe or moleft his wrongful Ufurpation. But he being flain in this rafh Expedition againft the *Englifh*, and leaving no Iffue to fucceed him in the Crown, his Brother *Cadwalhon* thought he might rightfully take upon him the Government of *North-Wales*, feeing his Father and his Brother had without any moleftation enjoyed the fame. However to make his Title fecure, he thought fit to remove all manner of rubs which might create any Difpute concerning his right of Succeffion, and to that end, concluded it neceffary to make away his Cofins *Ionafal* and *Edwal* the lawful Heirs; the firft of which he executed accordingly, but *Edwal* being aware of his Intention privately made his efcape, and fo prevented his wicked Defign. This unnatural Dealing with his Coufins *Ionafal* and *Edwal* coft *Cadwalhon* not only his Life, but the lofs of his Principality and the utter ruin of his Father's Houfe. For he had fcarce enjoyed his Government one Year, but *Meredith* the Son of *Owen* Prince of *South-Wales* entred into *North-Wales*, flew *Cadwalhon* and his Brother *Meyric* the only remains of the Houfe of *Ievaf*, and under the

985.

pretence

pretence of Conquest, possessed himself of the whole Country. Here we may observe and admire the Wisdom of Providence, in permitting Wrong and Oppression for some time to flourish and wax great, and afterwards by secret and hidden Methods, in restoring the Posterity of the right and lawful Heir to the just and pristine Estate of his Ancestors. For after the Death of *Edwal Foel*, *Meyric* who by right of Birth was legally to succeed, was not only deprived of his just and rightful Inheritance, but had his Eyes most inhumanly put out, and being condemned to perpetual Imprisonment, for grief of being so barbarously treated, quickly ended his Days. But tho' his Brothers *Ievaf* and *Iago*, and *Howel* and *Cadwalhon* the Sons of the former successively enjoyed the Principality of *North-Wales*; yet not one died naturally or free from the Revenge of *Meyric*'s ejection. For *Ievaf* was imprison'd by his Brother *Iago*, and he with his Son *Constantine*, by *Howel* the Son of *Ievaf*, and afterwards *Howel* fell by the hands of the *English*, and his Brethren *Cadwalhon* and *Meyric* were both slain by *Meredith ap Owen*. On the other side, *Edwal ab Meyric* who was right Heir of *North-Wales* after the Death of his Brother *Ionafal*, escaped the snare intended by *Cadwalhon*; and *Meredith ap Owen* after some time leaving *North Wales* exposed to the Enemies, by reason he had enough to do to preserve *South-Wales*, *Edwal* was received of the *North-Wales* Men as their true Prince.

Meredith ap Owen.

586. Meredith having won the Field and slain *Cadwalhon* and his Brother *Meyric*, the only seeming Pretenders to the Principality of *North-Wales*, took upon himself the Rule and Government of it. But before he could be well confirmed in his Dominions, *Godfryd*
the

The History of WALES.

the Son of *Harold*, the third time entred into the Isle of *Anglesey*, and having taken *Lhyarch* the Son of *Owen* with 2000 Men Prisoners, most cruelly put out his Eyes; which so startled and struck such a Terror into Prince *Meredith*, that with the rest of his Army he forthwith made his escape and fled to *Cardigan*. This loss to the *Welch* was the same Year seconded by another, but of another sort; for there happened such a dismal and unusual Murren, that the best part of the Cattle of *Wales* perished. Neither were the *English* at this time free from Adversities and Troubles, for the *Danes* landed again in *England* with several Armies, and at *Westport* and *Witest*, gave two *English* Lords, *Godan* and *Britchbould* such a blow, that the King was forced to buy his Peace, with the payment of 10000 Pound, which was termed, *Dane Gelt*. But within a while after, King *Edelred* violated and brake the Peace himself, and prepared a great Fleet, thinking to vanquish the *Danes* at Sea: But it proved far otherwise, and much contrary to his expectation, all his Ships being either destroyed or taken, together with the Admiral, *Alfric* Earl of *Mercia*. The *Danes* being animated with this Victory, sailed up to the Mouth of the *Humber*, and landing in *Yorkshire*, spoiled and destroyed the City of *York* and *Lindsey*; but in their march through *Northumberland*, were routed and put to flight by *Godwyn* and *Fridgist*, two *English* Generals who were sent to oppose them. The same time *Anlaf* King of *Norway*, and *Swane* of *Denmark* with 94 Gallies sailed up the *Thames* and besieged *London*, which the Citizens so bravely defended, that at length the *Danes* thought best to raise and quit the Siege. But though they could effect nothing upon the City, yet the Country was at their mercy, and therefore leaving their Ships, they landed and wasted with Fire and Sword, all *Kent*, *Essex*, *Sussex*, *Surry* and *Hampshire*. Wherefore King *Edelred* instead of manly opposition in the Field, sends Ambassadors to treat about another payment; and so the *Danes* being satisfied with a great Sum of Money and Victuals, lay quiet that Winter at *Southampton*;

thampton. Upon this Compofition, *Anlaf* was invited by *Adelred*, and Royally entertained, and being difmiffed with very many rich Prefents, he promifed upon Oath to depart the Kingdom and never to moleft it any more, which he faithfully performed.

987. Whilft the *Englifh* and the *Danes* were thus for a time agreed, *Ievaf* the Son of *Edwal* having fpent for feveral Years a retired and a private Life, died: And was quickly followed by *Owen* the Son of *Howel Dha* Prince of *South-Wales*. This *Owen* had three Sons, *Eineon* who in his Father's time was flain by the Rebels of *Gwentland*, and *Lhywarch* who had his Eyes put out by *Godfryd* the Son of *Harold* the *Dane*, and Prince *Meredith*, who had already Conquered *North-Wales*, and now upon his Father's Death takes poffeffion alfo of *South-Wales*, without any regard had to *Edwyn* and *Theodore* the Sons of *Eineon* his elder Brother. But upon his advancement to his new Principality, he was like to meet with no very fmall troubles; for the *Danes* at *Hampton* quickly broke the League with King *Adelred*, and failing towards the *Weft* mightily annoyed the Coafts of *Cornwal* and *Devonfhire*, and at laft landed in *South-Wales*. Having deftroyed St. *Davids*, *Lhanbadarn*, *Lhanrhyftyd*, *Lhandydoch*, and feveral other Religious places; the Country was fo cruelly haraffed and weakened, that Prince *Meredith* was forced to compound with them, and to

988. pay a Tribute of one Peny for every Perfon within his Dominions, which in *Welch* was called *Glwmaen*, otherwife, the Tribute of the Black Army. And *Ireland* too at this time received no inconfiderable blow from the *Danes*, who flew *Elwmaen* the Son of *Abloic* King of the Country, and fo fpoiled and ravaged that Kingdom, that a great Number of the Natives perifhed by Famine.

989. The year following *Owen* the Son of *Dyfnwal*, a Man of a confiderable Note and Reputation among the *Welch* was flain; befides which nothing remarkable happened this year. But the next year *Edwyn ap Eineon*, who was right Heir to the Principality of *South-Wales*,

having

The History of WALES.

having drawn to his help a great Army of *English* 590.
and *Danes* hostibly entered into *Meredith*'s Country,
spoiled all the Land of *Cardigan, Dyfed, Gwyr, Kyd-
wely* and *St. Davids*, and received Hostages of the
Chief Persons of those Countries to own him as their
rightful Prince. To return these Outrages upon
Edwyn, Meredith destroyed the Town of *Radnor*, spoil- 991.
ed *Glamorgan*, and carried the Chiefest Men therein
Prisoners, who paying their Ransom, were set at Liberty.
But whilst *Wales* was in this tottering Condition,
and scarce any place free from Hostility; it
happily fell out, that *Meredith* and *Edwyn* were made
Friends, and the Differences composed between them,
so that the *English* and *Danes* who came in with *Edwyn*,
and who expected to fare best by these Civil Disturbances
of the *Welch* were unexpectedly cashiered
and sent home. And soon after this agreement, *Cadwallon*
the only Son of *Meredith* died, which rendered
the Composition between *Meredith* and *Edwyn*
more firm, by reason that this latter thought now,
without any Dispute to succeed *Meredith* in his Principality.
But this fell short of his aim, for *Meredith*
being very much disturbed in *South-Wales*, had
so much work upon his hands to defend that Country,
that he left *North-Wales* open and exposed to
the Common Enemy, which the *Danes* were quickly
acquainted with, and so landing in *Anglesey*, they ravaged
and laid waste the whole Island. The *North-Wales*
Men finding themselves thus forsaken by *Meredith*,
and their Country like to be over-run by the
Danes, if not timely prevented, set up *Edwal* the Son
of *Meyric*, the indisputable Heir of *North-Wales*, 992.
though long kept from it, and owned him for their
Prince. But those incessant Wars and Commotions
in *South-Wales*, occasioned a very dismal Famine and
Scarcity in the Country, of which a very considerable
number of People perished. And thus *Meredith* who
had once conquered *North Wales* and for a long
time had got possession of *South-Wales*, without any
Right or Title to either, was now obliged to relinquish
the one, and was scarce able to maintain the other.

F 2 *Edwal*

Edwal ap Meyric.

993. Edwal after a long and tedious expectation, being now joyfully received by the *North-Wales* Men for their Prince, endeavoured the first thing to defend his Subjects from the Injuries and Depredations they received from the *Danes*. And having in a measure effected that, he was accosted by another Enemy; for *Meredith* being resolved to Revenge the Indignity and Disgrace put upon him by the *North-Wales* Men, in depriving him of the Government of their Country, gathered and mustered together all his Power, intending to recover again that Principality. Being advanced as far as *Lhangwm*, *Edwal* met him, and in plain Battel routed his Army; in which Action, *Theodor* or *Tewdor Mawr*, *Meredith*'s Nephew was slain, leaving behind him two Sons, *Rhys* and *Rytherch*, and a Daughter named *Elen*. But 'tis probable that it was not *Tewdor Mawr*, but his Brother *Edwyn* that was slain in this Battel, which also seems rather to have been fought at *Hengwm* in *Ardudwy* in *Merioneth-shire*, than at *Lhangwm*, for in that place there are to this Day certain Monuments of Victory to be seen, as heaps of Stones, Tomb-Stones and Columns, which they call *Carneddi Hengwm*. *Edwal* returning home triumphantly after this Victory, thought he had now secured himself in his Government, and expected to enjoy his Dominions quietly, and without any molestation. But he had scarce recovered the Fatigue of the last Engagement, when *Swane* the Son of *Harold* having lately pillaged and wasted the *Isle of Man*, landed in *North-Wales*, whom *Edwal* endeavouring to oppose, was slain in the Encounter, leaving one Son behind him, called *Iago*.

The History of WALES.

Within a while after, the *Danes* returned again against St. *Davids*, and destroying all before them with Fire and Swords, slew *Morgeney* or *Urgeney*, Bishop of that Diocese. Prince *Meredith* being highly concerned at the Mischiefs these Barbarous People continually did to his Country, and the more, because he was not able to repel their Insolencies, out of Grief and Vexation died; having Issue one Only Daughter, named *Angharad*, who was twice Married; first to *Lhewelyn ap Sitsylht*, and after his Death to *Confyn Hirdref*, or as others think, to *Confyn ap Gweryflan*. She had Children by both Husbands, which occasioned afterwards great Disturbances and Civil Commotions in *Wales*, the Issue of both Adventures pretending a Right of Succession to the Principality of *South-Wales*.

Aedan ap Blegorad.

EDwal Prince of *North-Wales* being killed in the Battel against *Swane*, and having no other Issue than *Iago*, who was a *Minor*, and too young to take upon him the Government; and *Meredith* Prince of *South-Wales* dying without any other Issue than a Daughter, caused very heavy Quarrels and Contentions among the *Welch*, several without any colour of Right, putting in their Claims and Pretensions to the Government. In *North-Wales*, *Conan* the Son of *Howel*, and *Aedan* the Son of *Blegorad* were the chief Aspirers to that Principality; and because they could not agree who should be the Man, they fairly consented to try the matter in open Field, where *Conan* had the misfortune to be slain; and so *Aedan* was Victoriously proclaimed Prince of *North Wales*. But who this *Aedan* was descended from, or what

1003.

F 3   Colour

The History of WALES.

Colour or Pretence he could lay to this Principality, cannot be as much as guessed at, there being none of that Name to be met with in any *Welch* Records, excepting that *Blegorad* who is mentioned in the Line of *Howel Dha*, whose Estate and Quality was too mean, that his Posterity should lay any Claim to the Principality of *Wales*. But be that how it will, *Aedan* after his Victory over *Conan ap Howel*, was owned Prince by the *North-Wales* Men, over whom he bore Rule for the space of twelve Years; tho' besides his Conquest of *Conan ap Howel*, there be nothing recorded of him, excepting his being slain, together with his four Sons by *Lhewelyn ap Sitsylht*.

But whilst the *Welch* are in this inconstant and unsettled Condition, the *Scots* in *Ireland* began to grow powerful, and having destroyed the Town and Country of *Develyn*, they took *Gulfath* and *Ubiad*, two *Irish* Lords prisoners, whose Eyes they most inhumanly put out. The *Danes* also, who had lately made their Incursions into *South-Wales*, began now to molest the *English*, and having landed in the *West*, passed through the Counties of *Somerset*, *Dorset*, *Hamp-shire* and *Sussex*, destroying and burning all before them. Having advanced without any Opposition, as far as the River *Medway*, they laid Siege to *Rochester*, which the *Kentish*-men endeavouring to preserve, assembled themselves together, and gave the *Danes* Battel, but were vanquished in the Undertaking. King *Edelred* was then in *Cumberland*, where the *Danes* were more numerously planted, which Country he kept quiet and in subjection. But in the mean time another Army of *Danes* landed in the *West*, against whom the Country People of *Somerset-shire* assembling themselves, shewed their readiness to attack them, but wanting a Head to direct them, were easily put to their Heels, and the *Danes* ruled and commanded the Country at their pleasure. The King being sorely vexed at the Insolencies and restless Depredations of the *Danes*, thought convenient to strengthen himself by some powerful Affinity, and to that end, sends Ambassadors to *Richard* Duke of *Normandy*, desiring
his

The History of WALES.

his Daughter *Emma* in Marriage, and Succours to repel the *Danish* Incursions. Here it is observable, that as the *Saxons* being formerly called over as Friends and Allies to the well-meaning *Britains*, violently and wrongfully possessed themselves of the greatest part of the Island; so now the *Normans* being invited to Aid the *English* against the *Danes*, took so good a liking to the Country, that they never gave over their Design of gaining it, till at last they became Conquerors of the whole Island. The Mischief of calling in the *Normans*, tho' foretold to King *Adelred*, he was so far concerned about the present Calamities received by the *Danes*, that he was deaf to all futurities, how dangerous and mischievous soever they might prove. And therefore being puff'd up with hopes of Increase of Strength by this new Affinity, he sent private Letters to all Cities and Towns throughout his Dominions where the *Danes* were quartered, requiring them all upon St. *Brice*'s Night to Massacre the *Danes*, which was accordingly performed with much Unanimity and Secrecy. This cruel Disaster was so far from discouraging the *Danes*, that they now began to Vow the Eradication of the *English* Nation, and to Revenge that unmanly Massacre of their Country-men; to which end they landed in *Devon-shire*, and over-running the Country with Fire and Sword, spared nothing that had the least spark of Life in it. The City of *Exeter* they razed to the ground, and slew *Hugh* the *Norman*, whom the Queen had recommended to the Government of it. To prevent their further Incursions, *Almarus* Earl of *Devon* gathered a great Army out of *Hamp-shire* and *Wilt-shire*, and the Country thereabouts, and marched with a Resolution stoutly to oppose the *Danes*, who put *Almarus* to Flight and pursued him to *Wilton* and *Salisbury*, which being ransacked and plundered, they carried the Pillage thereof triumphantly to their Ships.

A. D. 1004. The next Year, *Swane*, a Prince of great repute in *Denmark*, landed upon the Coast of *Norfolk* and laid siege to *Norwich*, and wasted the Country thereabouts. But *Wolfkettel* Duke of that Country, being too weak to oppose him, thought it most convenient to make a Peace with the *Dane*; which was quickly broke; and then *Swane* marched privately to *Thetford*, which after he had spoiled and ransack'd, he return'd with his Prey to his Ships. *Wolfkettel* hearing this, privately drew up his Forces, and stoutly marched against the Enemy; but being far inferiour in number, the *Danes* got the day, and afterwards sailed to their own Country. Within Two Years after, the *Danes* returned again, bringing with them their usual Companions, the Fire, the Sword, and the Spoil and landed at *Sandwich*; which after they had burnt and pillaged, they sailed to the Isle of *Wight*, where they took up their Winter-Quarters till *Christmas*: And then coming forth thence, they over-ran, by several Parties, the Countries of *Hamshire* and *Barkshire*, as far as *Reading*, *Wallingford* and *Colsey*; devouring up, for want of other Plunder, all the Provisions and Victuals they found in the Houses, and retributed the same with Fire and Sword at their departure. In their return they met with the Army of the *West-Saxons* near *Essington*, but this consisting only of a raw and unexperienced Rabble, they easily broke through, and passing triumphantly by the Gates of *Winchester*, they got safe with great Booty to *Wight*. King *Adelred* all this while lay at his Mannor-House in *Shropshire*, much troubled and concerned at these uninterrupted Devastations of the *Danes*. But the Nobility of *England*, rather to save some than lose all they possessed, bought their Peace of the *Danes* for the Sum of 30000 *l*. during which interval, King *Adelred* rousing his drooping Spirits, ordained, that every three Hundred Hides of Land, one Hide being as much as one Plough can sufficiently till, through his Dominions, should man out a Ship, and every Eight Hides a Corslet and a Helmet; beside which the King had no inconsiderable Navy sent him from *Normandy*.

This

The History of WALES.

This Fleet when rendezvous'd at *Sandwich* seemed terrible in those days, and was the greatest that ever afore then rode upon the *British* Sea. And now, one might have thought, that all things would go well with the *English*, when of a sudden another Cloud appears; for one *Wilnot*, a Noble Man of *Sussex*, being banished by King *Adelred*, got to Sea with a small number of Ships, and practised Pyracy along the Coasts of *Britain*, and mightily annoyed all Merchants and Passengers. *Brightrych*, Brother to the traiterous *Edric* Earl of *Mercia*, thinking to advance his Reputation by some signal Exploit, promised to bring *Wilnot* dead or alive before him: To which end, he sets forth with a considerable Fleet; which meeting with a terrible Storm, was by the Tempest driven back, and wreck'd upon the shoars; so that a great number of the Ships were drowned, and the rest burnt by *Wilnot* and his Company. *Brightrych* being abashed with this unfortunate beginning, returned ingloriously by the *Thames* back to *London*; so that this great Preparation against the *Danes*, was dash'd to pieces, and came to nothing.

A. D. 1008.

The *Danes* were not ignorant of the Misfortune the *English* received by this Storm, and without any further enquiry, landed at *Sandwich*, and so passed on to *Canterbury*, which they intending to destroy, was by the Citizens bought off for 3000 *l*. Passing from thence, through *Kent*, *Sussex* and *Hampshire*, they came to *Barkshire*, where King *Edelred* at length met with them, and purposing resolutely to set upon them, was by the cunning Insinuations and subtile Arguments of traytor *Edric* dissuaded from fighting. The *Danes* being thus deliver'd from the danger which they certainly expected, passed on joyfully by the City of *London*, and with great Booty returned to their Ships. The next Year they landed again at *Ipswich*, upon *Ascension-day*, where *Wolfkettel* entertained them with a sharp Encounter; but being over-power'd by Number, he was forced to give back, and yield the day to the *Danes*. Passing from thence to *Cambridge*, they met with *Ethelstan*, King *Edelred*'s Nephew by his Sister, who

1009.

who with an Army was come to oppofe them ; but the *Danes* proving too powerful, he with many other Noblemen were flain ; among whom were Duke *Ofwyn* and the Earls *Edwyn* and *Wolfrike*. From hence they paffed through *Effex*, leaving no manner of Cruelty and Barbarity unpractifed, and returned laden with Booty to their Ships, which lay in the *Thames*. But they could not contain themfelves long in their Veffels ; and therefore fallying out, they paffed by the River fide to *Oxford*, which they ranfack'd over again ; adding to their Prey *Buckingham*, *Bedford*, *Hartford*, and *Northamptonfhire* ; and having accomplifhed that Years Cruelties, at *Chriftmas* they returned to their Ships. Yet the Prey of the Countrey from the *Trent* Southward, would not fatisfie thefe unmerciful Barbarians ; but as fo:n as the Seafon gave them leave to peep out of their Dens, they laid fiege to the City of *Canterbury*, which being deliver'd up by the Treachery of *Almarez* the Archdeacon, was condemned to Blood and Afhes, and *Alfege* the Archbifhop carried Prifoner to the *Danifh* Fleet, where he was at length moft cruelly put to death. The next Year *Swane*, King of *Denmark*, came up the *Humber*, and landed at *Gainesborow*; whither repaired to him *Uthred* Earl of *Northumberland*, with his People, the Inhabitants of *Lindfey*, with all the Countries Northward of *Watling-ftreet*, being a highway croffing from the Eaft to the Weft Sea, and gave their Oath and Hoftages to obey him. Whereupon, King *Swane* perceiving his Undertaking to prove fo fortunate beyond expectation, committed the care of his Fleet to his Son *Cnute*, and marched himfelf firft to *Oxford*, and then to *Winchefter*; which Cities, whether for fear of further Calamities, readily acknowledged him for their King. From thence he marched for *London*, where King *Edelred* then lay; and which was fo ftoutly defended by the Citizens, that he was like to effect nothing againft that Town; and therefore he directed his courfe to *Wallingford* and *Bath*, where the principal Men of *Weft-Saxon* yielded him Subjection. The *Londoners* too, at laft, fearing

fearing his Fury and Difpleafure, made their peace, and fent him Hoſtages; which City being received to mercy, *Swane*, from that time was accounted King of all *England*. King *Edelred* perceiving all his Affairs in *England* to go againſt him, and his Authority and Government reduced to ſo narrow a compaſs, having ſent his Queen, with his two Sons *Edward* and *Alfred*, to *Normandy*, he thought convenient within a while after to follow himſelf. Being honourably received by his Brother in Law *Richard*, he had not been there long but News arrived of the death of *Swane*, and that he was defired by the *Engliſh* to return to his Kingdom. Being animated and comforted with this furpriſing News, he ſet forward with a great Army for *England*, and landing at *Lyndſey*, he cruelly harraſſed that Province, by reafon that it had owned Subjection to *Cnute* the Son of *Swane*, whom the *Danes* had elected King in his Fathers ſtead. King *Cnute* being at *Ipſwich*, and certified of the arrival of King *Edelred*, and the Devaſtation of *Lyndſey*; fearing that his Authority was going down the wind, barbarouſly cut off the Hands and Noſes of all the Hoſtages he received from the *Engliſh*, and preſently ſtruck fail for *Denmark*. And whilſt *England* was in this general Confuſion, there fell out no leſs a ſtorm in *Ireland*; for *Brian* King of that Iſland, and his Son *Murcath*, with other Kings of the Countrey ſubject to *Brian*, joyned their Forces againſt *Sutric* the Son of *Abloic* King of *Dublin*, and *Mailmorda* King of *Lagenes*. *Sutric* being of himſelf too weak to encounter ſo numerous a Multitude, hired all the Pyrates and Rovers who cruiſed upon the Seas, and then gave *Brian* battel, who, with his Son *Murcath*, was ſlain; and on the other ſide, *Mailmorda*, and *Broderic* General of the Auxiliaries.

But *Cnute*, though he was in a manner forced to forſake *England* upon the recalling of King *Edelred*, yet he did not abandon all his pretence to the Kingdom; and therefore the next year he came to renew his Claim, and landed with a ſtrong Fleet in *Weſt-Sex*, where he exerciſed very great Hoſtility. To

A. D. 1013.

prevent

The *History of* WALES.

prevent his Incursions, *Edric* and *Edmund* Bastard-Son to *Edelred*, raised their Forces separately; but when both Armies were united, they durst not, whether for fear, or the Dissention of the two Generals, fight with the *Danes*. *Edmund* therefore passed to the North, and joyned with *Uthred* Duke of *Northumberland*, and both together descended and spoiled *Stafford, Leicester*, and *Shropshire*. On the other side, *Cnute* marched forcibly through *Buckingham, Bedford, Huntingtonshire*, and so by *Stafford* passed toward *York*, whither *Uthred* hastened, and finding no other remedy, submitted himself, with all the *Northumbrians*, to *Cnute*, giving Hostages for the performance of what they then agreed upon. But nevertheless this Submission, *Uthred* was treacherously slain, not without the permission of *Cnute*, and his Dukedom bestowed upon one *Egrick* a *Dane*; whereupon *Edmund* left them, and went to his Father, who lay sick at *London*. *Cnute* returning to his Ships presently followed, and sailed up the *Thames* towards *London*; but before he could draw nigh the City, King *Edelred* was dead; having prolonged a long and troublesom Reign for Thirty Seven Years. After his decease, the *English* Nobility chose his base Son *Edmund*, for his eminent strength and hardiness in War, surnamed *Ironside*, for their King. Upon this *Cnute* brought his whole Fleet up the River to *London*, and having cut a deep Trench round about the Town, invested it on all sides; but being valourously repulsed by the Defendants, he detached the best part of his Army to fight with *Edmund*, who was marching to raise the Siege; and both Armies coming to battel at *Proman* by *Gillingham*, *Cnute* with his *Danes* were put to flight. But as soon as time and opportunity would give him leave to increase his Forces, *Cnute* gave *Edmund* a second Battel at *Caerstane*; but *Edric, Almar*, and *Algar* under-hand siding with the *Danes*, *Edmund* was hard put to it, to maintain the fight obstinately, till Night and Weariness parted them. Both Armies having sufficiently suffered in this action, *Edmund* went to *West-Sex* to reinforce himself, and the

Danes

The History of WALES.

Danes returned to the fiege of *London*, where *Edmund* quickly followed, raifed the fiege, and forced *Cnute* and his *Danes* confufedly to betake themfelves to their Ships, and then entered triumphantly into the City. Two days after, paffing the *Thames* at *Brentford*, he fell upon the Enemies backs; by which lucky opportunity obtaining a confiderable Victory, he returned again to raife Recruits among the *Weft-Saxons*. *Cnute*, upon *Edmund*'s removal, appeared again before *London*, and invefted it by Land and Water; but all in vain; the befieged fo manfully and refolutely defending themfelves, that it was impracticable to mafter the Town before *Edmund* could come to the relief of it. And this they prefently experienced; for *Edmund*, after having augmented his Forces, crofied again the *Thames* at *Brentford*, and came to *Kent* in purfuit of *Cnute*, who upon engaging, was fo fhamefully defeated at firft, and his Men put to that terrible flight, that there wanted nothing of a full and abfolute Victory, but the true Loyalty of the Traytor *Edric*, who perceiving the Victory to incline to *Edmund*, and the *Danes* like to receive their mortal and final Blow, cryed aloud, *Fled Engle*, *Fled Engle*, *Edmund is dead*, and thereupon fled with that part of the Army under his command, leaving the King over-power'd with number. By this Defertion the *Englifh* were at the laft overthrown, and a great number flain; among whom were Duke *Edmund*, Duke *Alfric*, Duke *Godwyn*, and *Ulfkettel*, the valiant Duke of the *Eaft-Angles*, together with all the *Englifh* Cavalry, and a great part of the Nobility. After this Victory, *Cnute* marched triumphantly to *London*, and was crowned King; but *Edmund* preparing to try his Fortune in another Field, mufter'd together all the Forces he could, and meeting with *Cnute* in *Gloucefterfhire*, intended to give him battel; But confidering what cruel and unnatural Bloodfhed had already happen'd, both generally agreed to put an end to this tedious Quarrel by fingle Combat; and the place being appointed, *Edmund* and *Cnute* fell to it very vigouroufly, till at laft *Cnute* perceiving it impracticable to vanquifh a Man of Iron

Sides

Sides, laid down his Weapon, moving this Composition, to divide the Kingdom fairly betwixt them : *Edmund* was not displeased at the Offer, and therefore both Parties submitted to this Decision, that *Edmund* should rule the *West-Saxons* and the *South*; *Cnute* in *Mercia* and all the *North*; and so they parted Friends, *Cnute* moving to *London*, and *Edmund* to *Oxford*. But *Edric* was not pleased, that *Edmund* should have any share at all of the Government, and therefore he is resolved to conspire against his Life, and to deliver the whole Kingdom of *England* into the hands of *Cnute*; of whom he might reasonably expect for this, and other traiterous Services, a very ample and an answerable return. This he committed to one of his own Sons to put in execution, an Imp of the old stock, and one early versed in wicked and traiterous Designs; who perceiving the King to go to stool, thrust up a sharp Knife up his *Fundament*, of which Wound he presently dyed. *Edric* being quickly certified of the Fact, posted it up to *London*, and with great Joy and loud Acclamations came to *Cnute*, greeting him as sole King of *England*, and withal, telling him in what manner, and by whose means his old Enemy King *Edmund* was assassinated and killed at *Oxford*. *Cnute*, though pleased at the death of *Edmund*, was a Person of greater Honour than to commend so horrible a Deed, though done to an Enemy, and therefore told *Edric*, that he would without fail take care to reward him, as his Deserts required, and would advance him above all the Nobility of *England*, which was quickly performed, his Head being placed upon the highest Tower in *London*, for a Terrour to such villainous Traytors to their King. *Edric* being thus deservedly disappointed of the mighty Thoughts he entertained of Greatness, upon the Advancement of King *Cnute*; this generous *Dane* scorned his Baseness, and so having paid him a Traytors Reward, caused Execution to be done upon all *Edric*'s Complices, and those that consented to the base Murther of that brave Prince King *Edmund*.

About

About the same time there happen'd no small Disturbance and Commotions in *Wales*; *Lhewelyn ap Sytsylht* having for some Years sate still and quiet, began now to bestir himself; and having drawn all his Forces together, marched against *Aedan*, who forcibly and without any legal Pretence, had entred upon, and for all this time had kept himself in the Government of *North-Wales*. *Aedan* would not easily eject himself from what had been so long in his possession; to maintain which, he gave *Lhewelyn* Battel: But the day going against him, himself, with his four Sons, were slain upon the spot; upon which, *Lhewelyn*, without any regard had to *Iago* the Son of *Edwal* the right Heir, took upon himself the Title and Authority of Prince of all *Wales*. His pretence to *North-Wales* was, as being descended from *Trawst* Daughter to *Elis*, second Son to *Anarawd*, who was the eldest Son of *Roderic* the Great; and to *South Wales*, as having married *Angharad* the onely Daughter of *Meredith* Prince of *South-Wales*; by virtue of which Pretensions he assumed to himself the Government of all *Wales*.

A. D. 1015.

Lhewelyn ap Sitsylht.

L*Hewelyn* having, as is said, taken upon him the general Government of *Wales*, managed his Charge with such Prudence and Moderation, that the Countrey in a short time became very flourishing and prosperous; Peace and Tranquility being established produced plenty and increase of all things necessary to humane Subsistence: For there was none that could lay any Claim or Pretence to either of the Principalities, excepting *Iago* the Son of *Edwal*, who was indeed lawful Heir of *North-Wales*; but either too weak to withstand, or unwilling to disturb *Lhewelyn*'s Title, he lay quiet for a time, expecting a better opportunity

portunity to recover his Right. In the mean time, *Cnute* being crowned King of all *England*, married *Emma* the Widow of King *Edelred*; and for the better securing the *English* Crown to himself and his Heirs, he thought it expedient to dispatch *Edmund* and *Edward* the Sons of *Ironside* out of the way. But left such an execrable Fact should seem too black to be done in *England*, he sent the two Youths to *Solomon* King of *Hungary*, willing him to use some convenient opportunity to take away their Lives; which seemed to *Solomon* so very unnatural, that instead of complying with *Cnute*'s Request, he educated and brought them up as his own Children. But *Cnute* imagined now that his Fear was over, and his business effectually finished; so that he could the more boldly demand of his Subjects, what either his Necessity or Curiosity would prompt him to. And reflecting with himself, what excessive Expence he had been at in the Conquest of *England*, was resolved that the *English* should repay him; and therefore required a Subsidy of Seventy Two Thousand Pounds, besides Eleven Thousand, which the City of *London* contributed. The same time *Meyric* the Son of *Arthfael*, a Person of Quality in *Wales*, rebelled, and raised an Army against Prince *Lhewelyn*, who no sooner appeared in the Field to quell this male-contented General, but manfully slew him with his own hand, and easily discomfited his Followers. The same time *Cnute* sailed over into *Denmark*, and made War upon the *Vandals*, who, for all that they had a greater Army in the Field, were overcome by the incomparable Valour of Earl *Godwyn*; for which famous Action *Cnute* had the *English* in great esteem ever after.

A. D.
1020.

But *Lhewelyn* Prince of *Wales*, though he had lately quell'd the Rebels headed by *Meyric*, was now to encounter with another Difficulty, which seemed to threaten greater Disturbance and trouble to him: For a certain Person of a mean Quality in *Scotland*, coming to *South-Wales*, assumed the Name of *Run*, and put out that he was the Son of *Meredith* Prince of *South-Wales*; to whom joyned a great Number of the Nobility,

The History of WALES.

bility, who had no great Affection to *Lhewelyn*, and proclaimed *Run* Prince of *South-Wales*. *Lhewelyn* being then in *North Wales*, and certified of this famous Impostor, drawing his Army together, marched to meet him; who with the whole strength of *South-Wales* then lay at *Abergwili*, where he abode the arrival of *Lhewelyn*. When both Armies were ready to joyn battel, *Run* makes a vaunting Speech to his Soldiers, assuring them of Victory; and so persuading them couragiously to fall on, privately himself retired out of harms way; there one might have observed on the one side a valiant Army under a cowardly General, and on the other part a valiant and a noble Commander engaging with a slow and a faint-hearted Army; for *Lhewelyn*, like a bold and couragious Prince, ventur'd into the midst of his Enemies, whilst *Run* privately sneaked off out all danger; and the *South-Wales* Men were more fierce and eager in the Cause of a Pretender than the *North-Wales* Men, to maintain the Quarrel of a Prince of their own Blood. But after great slaughter on both sides, the *North Wales* Men calling to mind the several Victories they had obtained, and withal being in a very great measure animated by the incomparable Valour of their Prince, fell on so warmly, that they put their Enemies to flight, and pursu'd *Run* so close, that notwithstanding his several shifts, he was at last overtaken and slain. *Lhewelyn*, after this Victory, returned laden with Spoil into *North-Wales*, and for some time lived peaceably and without Disturbance: But the next Year *Howel* and *Meredith*, the Sons of *Edwyn*, conspired against him and slew him, leaving behind him a Son called *Gruffydh ap Lhewelyn*, who afterwards, though not immediately, ascended to the Principality of *North-Wales*.

Iago ap Edwal.

After the death of *Lhewelyn*, *Iago* the Son of *Edwal*, the true Heir to the Principality of *North-Wales*, who had been all his time wrongfully kept from it; thought this the best opportunity to enter upon his Right, by reason of the minority of *Gruffydh* the Son of *Lhewelyn*; upon which pretence likewise *Rytherch* the Son of *Iestyn* forcibly assumed the Principality of *South-Wales*. About the same time *Cnute* King of *England* sailed over to *Denmark* and *Sweden*, against *Ulf* and *Alaf*, who had moved the *Finlanders* against him; whom he subdued with the loss of a great part of his Army, as well *English* as *Danes*. Within a while after his return to *England*, he made a very pompous and magnificent Journey to *Rome*; more to satisfie his ambitious Temper, and to signifie to the World his Greatness and Might, which he express'd by his costly Presents and princely Behaviour, than any way to make atonement for the Oppression and Bloodshed by which he had established himself in his Kingdom: For what Holiness and Mortification he had learnt at *Rome*, presently appeared upon his return to *England*; for upon no provocation he marched with an Army into *Scotland*, and forced *Malcolm* the King thereof, together with *Molbeath* and *Jermare*, the Kings of the *Orkneys* and *Ewist*, to do him Homage.

A. D. 1031. But the Affairs of *Wales* were at this time very turbulent and uneasie; for *Hewel* and *Meredith*, after the Murther of Prince *Lhewelyn*, expected to enjoy some part of his Principality themselves; but finding *Iago* to have seized upon *North-Wales*, and *Rytherch* upon *South-Wales*, and withal perceiving their own Power too weak to oppose their Designs, they invited over the *Irish-Scots* to their aid against *Rytherch ap Iestyn*, Prince

Prince of *South-Wales*. By the help of thefe, *Howel* and *Meredith* prevailed over *Rytherch*, who being at length flain, they joyntly took upon them the Rule and Government of *South Wales* But this was not a fufficient title to eftablifh them fo firmly in it, that their Ufurpation would not be called in queftion; for the Sons of *Rytherch*, prefently after their Fathers death, gathered their Forces together to fight with the Brothers *Howel* and *Meredith*, who met at *Irathory*, where a cruel Batrel was fought, called *Gwaith Irathwy*; and at laft the Sons of *Rytherch* were put to flight. But though thefe Victories, the one over *Rytherch*, and the fecond over his Sons, feemed in a great meafure to favour *Howel* and *Meredith*'s pretence to, and eftablifhment in the Principality, yet, fo unpardonable a Crime, as the murther of *Lhewelyn*, a Prince of fo extraordinary Qualities, could not remain long unrevenged; for the Sons of *Conan* the Son of *Sitfylht*, Prince *Lhewelyn*'s Brother, were refolved to return their Uncles Murther upon the two Ufurpers, which in a fhort time they effected againft *Meredith*, who met with the fame end from the Sons of *Conan*, that he had formerly inflicted upon *Lhewelyn*. But thefe civil Difcords in *Wales* were quickly difcovered by the *Englifh*, who taking advantage of fo fair an opportunity, entered with a great Army into the Land of *Gwent*, where after they had committed confiderable Wafts for fome time, *Caradoc* the Son of *Rytherch ap Ieftyn*, gave them battel, but was in that Engagement unhappily flain. And fhortly afterwards dyed King *Cnute*, the moft famous and mightieft Prince then in the Weftern Parts of the World; whofe Dominions extended over all *Sweden*, from *Germany* almoft to the North-Pole; together with the Kingdoms of *Norway* and *Denmark*, and the noble Ifland of *Britain*. To him fucceeded his Son *Harold*, for his Swiftnefs furnamed *Harefoot*, begotten upon *Alwyn* the Daughter of Duke *Alfelyn*; though feveral ftickled firmly for *Hardycnute*, his other Son by *Emma*, who was then in *Denmark*. But *Harold* being once advanced into the Throne, took care to eftablifh himfelf as firmly as he could

A. D.
1032.

1033.

1034.

1035.

The History of WALES.

could in it; and to that end, thought it expedient to banish out of his Dominions his Mother in Law *Emma*, who was restless to promote the Interest of her own Son *Hardycnute*, and to bring him to the Crown of *England*.

A. D. 1037.

And whilst *Harold* was by these measures settled in his Throne, *Iago ap Edwal* was just upon the point of losing his Principality of *North Wales*: For *Gruffydh* the Son of *Lhewelyn ap Sitsylht*, sometime Prince of *North-Wales*, having once hinted a Rebellion against *Iago*, was so generally encouraged, and universally follow'd by all People, for the love they bore to his Father; that in a short time his Army mounted to an invincible number. However, *Iago* was not so throughly affrighted, that he would deliver up his Principality without drawing Sword for it; but providing for himself as well as he could, and drawing together what Forces he was able, he gave *Gruffydh* battel: But his number being far too weak to oppose so great an Army as sided with *Gruffydh*, was presently over-power'd and put to the rout, and himself slain, leaving after him a Son called *Conan*, by his Wife *Afandred*, Daughter to *Gweir* the Son of *Pylh*.

Gruffydh ap Lhewelyn.

Iago ap Edwal being killed, *Gruffydh ap Lhewelyn* was received with loud Acclamations, and joyfully saluted Prince of *North-Wales*; who treading in his Father's steps, behaved himself in his Government with that Prudence and Conduct, that he manfully defended his Country from the frequent Invasions of the *English* and *Danes*: For he was scarce settled in his Throne, when these inveterate Enemies of the *Welch* entered in an hostile manner into *Wales*, and advanced as far as *Crosford* upon the *Severn*, where *Gruffydh* met them, and forced them shamefully to fly,

and

The History of WALES.

and retire back to their own Country. From thence *Gruffydh* passed to *Lhanbadarn Vawr* in *Cardiganshire*, which he laid in Ashes; and afterwards marched through all the Country of *South-Wales*, receiving of the People Oaths of Fidelity and Subjection to him. In the mean time, *Howel ap Edwyn* Prince of *South-Wales* fled to *Edwyn* Brother to *Leofric* Earl of *Chester*, and prevailed with him to come with an Army consisting of *English* and *Danes*, to his aid against *Gruffydh*, who meeting his Enemies in the Field, easily overcame them, *Edwyn* being slain upon the spot, and *Howel* forced to preserve his Life by flight. After which Victory, *Gruffydh* having reduced all the Country of *Wales* to subjection, returned again to *North-Wales*. But *Howel* as soon as he could recover himself, and recruit his Army, entred again into *South-Wales*, intending the recovery of that Principality, which he was now so well assur'd of, that he brought his Wife with him to the Field, to let her see how easily he could conquer and overcome Prince *Gruffydh*. But too great an assurance of Victory seldom proves prosperous, which *Howel* presently experienced; for *Gruffydh* meeting with him at *Pencadair*, gave him so warm an Entertainment, that he was forced presently to take his Heels, which however could not so well secure him, but that he was narrowly pursued, and his Wife who was to be entertained with the Conquest of *Gruffydh*, on the contrary, saw her self taken Prisoner by him, and forced to comply so far to his humour, as to be his Concubine.

A. D.
1039.

The same time *Harold* King of *England* died, and was succeeded by his Brother *Hardycnute*, a Prince very famous for Hospitality, and a great lover of good Chear, having his Table covered four times a day, with great plenty and variety of Dishes, with other Superfluities for all Comers. But he likewise dying at *Lambeth* after two Years reign, the *English* agreed to send for *Alfred* the eldest Son of *Edelred* from *Normandy*, and to make him King. This Message by no means pleased Earl *Godwyn*, a Man of great sway now in *England*; who knowing *Alfred* to be a person of
greater

greater spirit than to permit him to domineer as he pleased, endeavoured all he could to dissuade the *English* from sending for *Alfred*. He shewed them how dangerous it was to permit a warlike Nation to take root in their Country, and how well *Alfred* was accompanied with *Normans*, to whom he had promised the chief Places and Rule of the Kingdom; by which and other like Insinuations he so disgusted the *English* Nobility against the *Normans*, that to diminish their number, they put every tenth Man to death. But seeing this was not sufficient, they acted the same part over again, and tythed them the second time; and being highly enraged against the *Normans*, they lead *Alfred*, who had brought them over, from *Gilford*, where this Execution was committed, to *Gillingham*, where having put out his Eyes, they removed him to *Ely*, and there at length pitifully murthered him. Then they sent for *Edward* out of *Normandy*, and made him King, who according to his promise to Earl *Godwyn*, married his Daughter *Edith*, a Lady much commended not only for Beauty, Modesty, and other feminine Qualifications, but also beyond what is requisite for a Woman, Learning. But King *Edward* did not deal so favourably with her Brother *Swane*, Son to Earl *Godwyn*, who upon some Distaste was banished *England*, and thereupon forced to betake himself to *Baldwyn* Earl of *Flanders*, by whom he was very honourably received.

A. D. 1041.
These Troubles and Revolutions in *England* were succeeded by others of no less consequence in *Wales*. For *Howel*, not brooking to be kept so shamefully out of his Kingdom, returns again the third time into *South Wales*, where he had not continued long, but a great number of Strangers landed in the West of *Wales*, and advancing farther into the Country, pillaged and destroyed all places they came to. *Howel*, tho desirous to reserve his Army to fight with Prince *Gruffydh*, yet could not behold his Country so miserably wasted and over-run by Strangers; and thinking moreover, that by so charitable an Action he should win the universal Love of the *South-Wales* Men, drew up his Forces against them, and overtaking them at

Pwll

Pwll Fynach, forced them with much lofs, to retire to their Ships; which Action was call'd in *Welch*, *Gwaith Pwll Fynach*. At the fame time *Conan*. the Son of *Iago ap Edwal*, who was forced for fear of Prince *Gruffydh* to flee to *Ireland*, with the Forces of *Alfred* King of *Dublin*, whofe Daughter named *Ranulph* he had married, landed in *North-Wales*; and having by fome treacherous Stratagem taken *Gruffydh*, triumphantly carried him Prifoner towards his Ships. This unhappy accident being difcovered, and publickly known, the *North Wales* Men did rife on a fudden, and fo unexpectedly overtook the *Irifh*, that they eafily recover'd their Prince, and drove his Enemies with great flaughter to their Ships; who, without any farther confultation, were glad to ftrike fail with *Conan* for *Ireland*. And now *Wales*, both North and South, is free from all foreign Invafion, and *Howel*, as yet too weak to difpute his Title with *Gruffydh*; fo that the next Year could be fubject to no great Action, in which nothing happen'd remarkable, faving the death of *Howel* the Son of *Owen* Lord of *Glamorgan*, a Man of great Quality and Efteem in *Wales*. But as foon as *Howel* could call in his *Danes*, to whom he added all the Forces he could raife in *South-Wales*; he intended prefently to march againft Prince *Gruffydh*. But he being aware aforehand to what end thofe Levies were defigned, prepared againft the enfuing ftorm; and to avert the War from his own Country, marched couragioufly to *South Wales*, not fearing to face an Enemy whom he had fhamefully vanquifhed twice already. Both Armies being joyned, *Gruffydh* eafily overcame, and purfued *Howel* as far as the Spring-Head of the River *Towy*, where after a long and a bloody Fight, *Howel* was at laft flain, and his Army fo univerfally routed, that few efcaped with their Lives. But though *Howel* was dead, yet there remained ftill more Pretenders to the Principality of *South-Wales*; fo that *Gruffydh* was in no great profpect to enjoy the fame peaceably: For as foon as it was publifhed that *Howel*'s Army was defeated, and himfelf flain; *Rytherch* and *Rhys* the Sons of *Rytherch ap Ieftyn*

A. D.
1042.

1043.

ap Iestyn put in their claim to *South-Wales* in right of their Father, who had once enjoyed the Sovereignty of that Country. And in order to the recovery of the same, they drew together a great Army, consisting partly of Strangers and partly of such as they could raise in *Gwentland* and *Glamorgan*, and marched to fight with *Gruffydh*. The Prince according to his usual manner detracted no time, but animating and solacing his Soldiers with the remembrance of their former Victories and Conquests, bid the Enemies battel, which proved so very bloody and terrible, that nothing could part them beside the darkness of the Night. This Battel so tired and tamed both Armies, that neither was very desirous of another Engagement, and so one being unwilling to set upon the other, they both agreed to return to their own Habitations. The same time *Joseph* Bishop of *Teilo* or *Llandaf* died at *Rome*. But both Armies being separated, Prince *Gruffydh* enjoyed a quiet and unmolested Possession of all *Wales* for about Two Years; after which, the Gentry of *Ystrad Towy* treacherously slew 140 of the choice of his Army, which he took in so high an indignation, that to revenge their death, he destroyed all *Dyfed* and *Ystrad Towy*.

About the same time, *Lethen* and *Hyrling* two *Danish* Pyrats, with a great number of *Danes*, landed at *Sandwich*, and having plundered the Town, returned again to their Ships, and sailed for *Holland*, where they sold the Booty they had taken, and then returned to their own Country. Shortly afterwards Earl *Swayn* came out of *Denmark* with Eight Ships, and returned to *England*, and coming to his Fathers House at *Pevenese*, humbly requested of him, and his Brothers *Harold* and *Tostie*, to endeavour his reconciliation with the King. Earl *Beorned* too promised to intercede for him, and going to *Swayn*'s Fleet to sail to *Sandwich*, where the King then lay, he was by the way most treacherously and ungratefully murthered, and his Body cast upon the shoar, which lay there exposed, till his Friends hearing of the Fact, came and carried it to *Winchester*, and buried it by the Body of King *Cnute*,

Beorned's

The History of WALES.

Beorned's Uncle. *Swayn* having committed this most detestable Murder, put himself again under the Protection of the Earl of *Flanders*, not daring to shew his Face in *England*, till his Father by earnest Mediation wrought his Peace with the King.

This Year *Conan* the Son of *Iago* raised again an Army of his Friends in *Ireland*, and sailed towards *Wales*, purposing to recover his Inheritance in that Country. But when he was come near the *Welch* Coast, there suddenly arose such a violent Storm, that his Fleet was presently scattered, and most of his Ships drowned, which rendered this Expedition ineffectual. About the same time, *Robert* Archbishop of *Canterbury* impeached Earl *Godwyn* and his Sons *Swayn* and *Harold* of Treason, and the Queen of Adultery, and upon the account of their non-appearance when cited before the Peers at *Glocester*, the Queen was divorced, and *Godwyn* and his Sons banished, who with his Son *Swayn* fled to *Flanders*, and *Harold* to *Ireland*. But these unlucky Clashings, and the many Troubles that ensued thereupon, happened upon this occasion. *Eustace* Earl of *Bologne* being Married to *Goda* the King's Sister, came over this Year to *England* to pay King *Edward* a Visit, and in his return to *Canterbury*, one of his Retinue forcibly demanding a Lodging, provoked the Master of the House so far, as by Chance or Anger to kill him. *Eustace* upon this Affront returns back to the King, and by the insinuations of the Archbishop, makes a loud Complaint against the *Kentish*-men; to repress whose Insolencies, Earl *Godwyn* is commanded to raise Forces, which he refusing to do, for the Kindness he bore to his Country-men of *Kent*, the King summons a Parliament at *Glocester*, and commands *Godwyn* to appear there. But he mistrusting either his own Cause, or the Malice of his Adversaries, gathered a powerful Army out of his own and his Sons Earldoms, and marched towards *Glocester*, giving out that their Forces were to go against the *Welch*, who intended to invade the *Marshes*. But King *Edward* being satisfied by the *Welch* that they had no such Design

Design in hand, commanded *Godwyn* to dismiss his Army, and to appear himself to answer to the Articles exhibited against him. *Godwyn* refusing to obey, the King by the Advice of Earl *Leofrick*, summoned an Assembly at *London*, whither a great Number of Forces arrived from *Mercia*, which *Godwyn* perceiving, and withal, finding himself unable to withstand the King's proceedings, privately retired with his Sons out of the Kingdom, and fled into *Flanders*. Whereupon the King issued out an Edict, proclaiming *Godwyn* and his Sons Out-Laws, and then confiscating their Estates, bestowed them upon others of his Nobility. And to pursue his Displeasure the farther, he Divorced his Queen *Edith*, Earl *Godwyn*'s Daughter, and committed her to a Cloyster, where in a mean Condition she spent some part of her Life. In the distribution of the forfeited Estates, *Adonan* obtained the Earldoms of *Devon* and *Dorset*, and *Algar* the Son of *Leofrick*, that of *Harold*. But *Godwyn* could not patiently behold his Estate bestowed upon another, and therefore having hired some Men and Ships in *Flanders*, he sailed to the Isle of *Wight*, where after that he had made a sufficient havock, he put in at *Portland*, which he treated after the same manner. The same time *Harold* having sailed from *Ireland*, at length met with his Father, and then with their united Navy, they burnt *Prevenefeny*, *Romney*, *Heath*, *Folkston*, *Dover* and *Sandwich*, and entering the *Thames*, they destroyed *Cheppey*, and burnt the King's House at *Middletown*. Then they sailed up the River towards *London*, where the King's Army being ready to oppose them, a Treaty of Peace was by the means of Bishop *Stigand* agreed upon, which proved so effectual of *Godwyn*'s side, that the King received him again to his Favour, restored him and Sons to all their Estates, re-called the Queen, and banished the Archbishop, with all the *French-men* who had been promoters of that unhappy Suspicion the King had entertained of them.

About this time, *Rhys* Brother to *Gruffydh* Prince of *Wales*, who by several Irruptions upon the Borders, had

had confiderably gauled and damaged the *Englifh*, was taken and put to Death at *Bulendun*, whofe Head being cut off, was prefented to the King, then at *Glocefter*. But he received better News fome time after from the *North*, for *Siward* Earl of *Northumberland* having fent his Son againft *Macbeth* King of *Scotland* vanquifhed the *Scots*, tho' not without the lofs of his Son, and many others both *Englifh* and *Danes*. But *Siward* was not caft down at his Son's Death, but enquiring whether he received his Death's Wound before or behind, and being affured that it was before, replied, *He was very glad of it, for he could not wifh his Son to die otherwife.* After this Victory, King *Edward* marched in Perfon to *Scotland*, and having again overcome *Macbeth* in Battel, he made the whole Kingdom of *Scotland* Tributary to the Crown of *England*. The next year, Earl *Godwyn* fitting with the King at Table, funk down dead of a fudden, being choak'd, as 'tis thought, in fwallowing a morfel of Bread; whofe Earldom the King beftowed upon his Son *Harold*, and his upon *Algar* Earl of *Chefter*.

To this time is referred the Original of the *Stewards* in *Scotland*, which being a remarkable paffage, and in a great meafure dependant upon the Affairs of the *Welch*, is requifite to be here recorded. *Macbeth* King of *Scotland* having caufed *Bancho* a Nobleman of that Kingdom to be inhumanly murdered; *Fleance Bancho*'s Son, to avoid the like Cruelty to himfelf, fled to *Gruffydh ap Lhewelyn* Prince of *Wales*, who taking a very great liking to his Perfon, and withal commiferating his Condition, fhewed him all the Refpect and Kindnefs poffible. But *Fleance* had not continued long with *Gruffydh* when he fell enamoured upon the Prince's Daughter, and having obtained her Good-Will, without any regard had to her Father's Civility towards him, abufed her fo far as to beget her with Child. *Gruffydh* being acquainted with the Matter of Fact, fo hainoufly refented the Affront, that he occafioned *Fleance* to be flain, and treated his Daughter moft fervilely; for

proftrating

proftrating her Chaftity, efpecially to a Stranger. However, fhe was in a fhort time delivered of a Son, whofe Name was Chriftened *Walter*; a Child, who in his Youth expreffed very great hopes, and in all probability like to make a very confiderable Man, which happened according to expectation. But the firft Original of his future Greatnefs happened upon a very accidental occafion; being reproached of Baftardifm by one of his Fellow Companions, he took it in fo unpardonable a dudgeon, that nothing could fatisfy his Revenge, but the Life of the Aggreffor. Being upon this Mifchance affraid to undergo the Punifhment of the Law, he thought it fafe to fly to *Scotland*, where falling in Company with certain *Englifh* Men who were come thither with Queen *Margaret* Sifter to *Edgar Edeling*, he behaved himfelf fo foberly and difcreetly, that he won the Favour and good Character of all that knew him. But his Fame daily increafing, he grew at length to that height of Reputation, as to be employed in the moft inward Affairs of the Commonwealth, and at laft was made Lord Steward of *Scotland*, from which Office his Pofterity retained the Surname of *Steward*, the Kings of *Scotland* of that Name, with feveral other Families of Quality in that Kingdom being defcended from him.

But to return to *England*, *Siward* the worthy Earl of *Northumberland* died about this time of the Bloody-Flux, a Man of a rough Demeanour, and a meer Soldierly Temper, as he plainly manifefted at the point of Death. For bewailing his Misfortune that had efcaped fo many dangerous Engagements, and withal difdaining to die fo effeminately in Bed, he caufed himfelf to be compleatly Armed, and as it were in Defiance of Death, prefently expired in a Martial Bravery. But his Son being too young, the King beftowed his Earldom upon *Tofty* the Son of Earl *Godwyn*.

1054. *Wales* had been now a long time quiet, and void of all troubles both abroad and at home, but it could not be expected that fuch a Life fhould prove durable,

The History of WALES.

ble, but something or other would create New Commotions and Disturbances. *Gruffydh* Son to *Rytherch ap Iestyn* having recruited and recovered himself after the last Blow he received from Prince *Gruffydh*, must needs venture another trial for the Principality of *South-Wales*. The Prince protracting no time, speedily marched against him, and both Armies being joined, *Gruffydh ap Rytherch* was easily vanquished, and in fine, slain. But the troubles of the *Welch* did not end with him, for *Algar* Earl of *Chester* being convicted of Treason, and thereupon banished the Kingdom, fled to *Gruffydh* Prince of *Wales*, requesting his Aid against King *Edward*, who repeating the frequent Wrongs he had received at the hands of the *English*, by upholding his Enemies against him, gladly embraced the Opportunity, and promised him all imaginable Support. And thereupon assembling his Forces, he entred with him into *Herefordshire*, and advancing into the Country, within two Miles of the City of *Hereford*, they were opposed by *Randulph* Earl of that Country, who boldly gave them Battel. The Fight continued very dreadful and dubious for some hours, till at last *Gruffydh* so encouraged his Soldiers with the remembrance of their former Victories over the *English*, that they fell on a main, and easily discomfited *Randulph*, and slew the best part of his Army. Afterwards they pursued their Chase to the Town, and having made all the waste and havock they were able, they laid the Town it self in ashes, and so returned home triumphantly, laden with rich Booty and Plunder. King *Edward* receiving notice of this Invasion, presently gathered a great Army at *Glocester* under the Conduct of *Harold* Earl *Godwyn*'s Son, who couragiously pursuing the Enemies, entred into *Wales*, and encamped beyond *Stradelwyd*. But *Gruffydh* and *Algar* dreading to oppose him, retired further into *South Wales*, of which *Harold* being certified, leaves one part of his Army behind with Orders to Fight, if occasion offered, and with the other passed to *Hereford*, which he fortified with a strong Wall round the Town. *Gruffydh* perceiving his undaunted

Industry,

Industry, after many Messages concluded a Peace with *Harold* at a place called *Biligelhag*, by which Articles *Algar* was pardoned by the King, and restored to his Earldom of *Chester*. But he did not continue long in the King's Favour, for about two years after, upon Conviction of Treason, he was again banished the Land, so that he was forced to betake himself to his old Friend *Gruffydh* Prince of *Wales*, by whose Aid, and a Fleet from *Norway*, in spight of the King he was restored to his Earldom. But King *Edward* was sore offended with the Prince of *Wales*, for harbouring Traytors, and therefore to be Revenged upon him, he dispatched *Harold* again with an Army to *North-Wales*, who coming to *Ruthlan*, burnt the Prince's Palace there, and his Fleet that lay in the Harbor, and then returned to the King at *Glocester*.

This year *Edward* the Son of *Edmund Ironside*, who was sent for out of *Hungary*, being designed Successor to the Crown came to *England*, but in a short time after his coming, died at *London*, leaving behind him a Son called *Edgar Edeling*, and a Daughter named *Margaret*, who was afterwards Queen of the *Scots*, and Mother to *Maud* the Wife of *Henry* the First.

1056. About two Years after, *Roderic* Son to *Harold* King of *Denmark* came with a considerable Army into *Wales*, and being kindly received by Prince *Gruffydh*, united his Power with the *Welch*, and so entred into *England*, which they cruelly harassed and destroyed. But before they could advance any considerable distance, *Roderic* was compelled to Sail for *Denmark*; and so *Gruffydh* returned laden with Spoils into *Wales*. The same time *Harold* Earl *Godwyn*'s Son sailing to *Flanders*, was driven by force of Weather to Land at *Poytiers*, where being seized upon, he was brought before *William* Bastard Duke of *Normandy*, to whom he declared the reason of his Voyage, that it was purposely to tender him his Service in the Affairs of *England*; and so taking an Oath, first to Marry the Duke's Daughter, and after the Death of *Edward* to secure the Kingdom of *England* for him, he

The History of WALES.

he was honourably difmiffed. Upon his return to *England*, by the perfuafions of *Caradoc* the Son of *Gruffydh ap Rytherch*, himfelf with his Brother *Tofty*, railed a great Army and entred into *South-Wales*, which they deftroyed after that manner, that the *Welch* were glad to deliver up Hoftages for the payment of the antient Tribute, which afore-time they were ufed to pay. *Gruffydh* hearing of the Infolencies of the *Englifh* in *South Wales*, made all poffible hafte and preparation to oppofe them, but all to no purpofe; *Harold* having already treacheroufly hired fome of *Gruffydh's* neareft Friends to Murder him, who watching their opportunity, executed their wicked Defign and brought his Head to *Harold*. *Gruffydh* being dead, *Harold* by King *Edward's* Orders, appointed *Meredith* Son of *Owen ap Edwyn* Prince of *South Wales*, and the Government of *North-Wales* to *Blethyn* and *Rywalhon* the Sons of *Confyn*, Brothers by the Mother fide to Prince *Gruffydh*, and who probably for the defire of Rule, were acceffary to the Murder of that Noble Prince. This *Gruffydh ap Lhewelyn* enjoyed the Principality of *Wales* for the fpace of thirty four years; a Prince of incomparable Vertues, both Wife and Valiant, Beloved of his Subjects and Formidable to his Enemies, in all his Actions he behaved himfelf Great and Princely; and having Defended his Country fo bravely againft all Foreign Oppofition; he was far unworthy of that treacherous and cruel Death, which his unkind Subjects and unnatural Friends beftowed upon him. He left Iffue but one Daughter called *Neft*, abufed firft by *Fleance* Son of *Bancho*, and afterwards married to *Trahaern ap Caradoc* Prince of *North-Wales*.

Blethyn

Blethyn and *Rywalhon*.

After the deplorable Murder of Prince *Gruffydh*, *Meredith* the Son of *Owen ap Edwyn*, who according to some, was Son to *Howel Dha*, did take upon him, as 'tis said, the Government of *South-Wales*, and *Blethyn* and *Rywalhon* the Sons of *Confyn*, half Brothers to *Gruffydh*, as descended from *Angharad* Daughter to *Meredith* sometime Prince of *Wales*, entered upon the Principality of *North-Wales*; *Conan* the Son *Iago ap Edwal* the right Heir to that Crown, being then with his Father-in-Law in *Ireland*. This partition of *Wales* fell much short of the expectation of *Caradoc ap Gruffydh ap Rytherch*, who being the chief promoter of *Harold's* making an Expedition against *Gruffydh ap Lhewelyn*, made no question to attain to the Government of *South-Wales*, in case *Gruffydh* got the worse. But it happened otherwise; *Harold* being sensible of *Caradoc*'s Subtilty and Knavery, and doubting whether if he was made Prince of *South-Wales*, he could obtain a certain Lordship nigh *Hereford*, which he had a longing mind to, made a Composition with *Meredith ap Owen* for the said Lordship, and created him Prince of *South-Wales*, and on the contrary banished *Caradoc* out of the Country. *Harold* having obtained his Request, built a very magnificent House at a place called *Portascyth* in *Monmouth-shire*, and storing it with great quantity of Provision, splendidly entertained the King, who honoured him with a Visit. This was by no means pleasing to *Tosty*, to see his younger Brother in greater Esteem and Favour with the King than himself, and having concealed his displeasure for a time, could not forbear at length but discover his grievance. For one day at *Windsor*, while *Harold* reached the Cup to King *Edward*, *Tosty* ready to burst

for

The History of WALES.

for Envy that his Brother was so much respected beyond himself, could not refrain to run furiously upon him, and pulling him by the Hair, dragged him to the Ground, for which unmannerly Action, the King forbad him the Court. But he with continued Rancour and Malice rides to *Hereford*, where *Harold* had many Servants preparing an Entertainment for the King, and setting upon them with his Followers, lopped off the Hands and Legs of some, the Arms and Heads of others, and threw them into the Butts of Wine and other Liquors, which were put in for the King's drinking, and at his departure charged the Servants to acquaint him, *That of other fresh Meats he might carry with him what he pleased, but for Sauce he should find plenty provided ready for him;* for which barbarous Offence, the King pronounced a Sentence of perpetual Banishment upon him. But *Caradoc ap Gruffydh* gave a finishing stroak to *Harold's* House, and the King's Entertainment at *Portascyth*; for coming thither shortly after *Tosty's* departure, to be revenged upon *Harold*, he killed all the Work-men and Labourers, with all the Servants he could find, and utterly defacing the Building, carried away all the Costly Materials which with great Charges and Expence had been brought thither to beautify and adorn the Structure. Soon after which, the *Northumbrians* (who could not endure the Insolencies of the two Brothers *Harold* and *Tosty*, who bearing an uncontroulable sway in the Kingdom, were used to practise most hellish Villanies to encompass any Man's Estate that displeased them,) in a Tumult at *York*, beset the Palace of *Tosty*, and having pillaged his Treasure, slew all his Family, as well *English-men* as *Danes*. Then adjoining to themselves the People of *Lincoln*, *Nottingham* and *Derby shire*, they elected *Marcher* the Son of Earl *Algar* their General, to whom came his Brother *Edwyn* with a considerable number of Forces, and a great party of *Welch men*. Then they marched in an hostile manner to *Northampton*, where *Harold* met them, being sent by the King to know their Demands; to whom they laid open their Grievances,

H and

and the Cruelty of *Tofty*'s Government, and at laft, with an abfolute refufal of admitting him again, defired that *Marcher* fhould be appointed Earl over them, which the King upon the reafonable Complaints of Injuries done by *Tofty*, eafily granted, and willingly confirmed *Marcher*'s Title. Whereupon they peaceably returned back to the *North*, and the *Welch* with feveral Prifoners and other Booties got in this Expedition, returned to *Wales*.

1066. The year following, King *Edward* died, and was buried at *Weftminfter*, being the laft King of the *Saxon* Blood before the Conqueft that Governed the Kingdom of *England*, which from *Cerdic* King of the *Weft-Saxons* had continued 544, and from *Egbert* the firft Monarch, 171 Years. *Edward* being dead, the next debate was about an Election of a Succeffor, *Edgar Edeling* being fet up by fome, as lawful Heir to the Crown, which *Harold* as being a Perfon of greater Power and Authority in the Kingdom, much wealthier and better befriended, prefently thwarted, and brought Matters fo cunningly about, that himfelf was chofen King, without any regard obferved to the Oath and Promife he had formerly made to *William* Duke of *Normandy*. Duke *William* upon notice of *Harold*'s advancement, how that he had accepted of the Crown of *England* contrary to the Articles between them, convened together his Nobles, and laid before them the feveral Wrongs and Affronts he had received at the Hands of *Harold*, as the Death of his Cofin *Alfred*, the Banifhment of Archbifhop *Robert*, Earl *Odam* and all the *Normans*, and laftly the Breach of his Oath and Promife. Then he declared to them the Pretence he had to Claim the Crown of *England*, that *Edward* had given him formerly an abfolute Promife in *Normandy* that if ever he enjoyed the *Englifh* Crown, *William* fhould be his Heir; which Title, tho' in it felf weak and infignificant ferved *William*'s purpofe well enough to make an Expedition againft an Intruder. Duke *William*'s Pretence feemed plaufible enough to the *Norman* Nobility, but the Difficulty of the Undertaking

taking and the Danger of this Expedition was something perplexive, and made them lefs inclinable to encourage fo precipitous an Undertaking; which they the more difliked upon the perfuafion of *William Fitzosbert* the Duke's Sewer, whom they pitched upon to deliver their thoughts as to the Expedition, unto the Duke. But he inftead of diffwading him from this Voyage, politickly declared that himfelf with all his Power were ready to live and die with him in this Expedition, which the reft hearing, could not but offer the Duke their Service in the fame manner; and fo all things were prepared for an Invafion of *England*. In the mean while *Tofty* full of Indignation at his Brother's advancement to the Crown, entered the River *Humber* with forty Sail, but meeting with Earl *Edwyn* who came to oppofe him, he was forced after a confiderable Encounter to bear off, and fecure himfelf by flight. But meeting with *Harold* King of *Norway* upon the Coaft of *Scotland*, coming for *England* with 300 Sail, he joined his Forces with *Harold*, and fo both together entring the *Humber*, they landed their Army and marched to *York*, where the Earls *Edwyn* and *Marcher* unfuccefsfully gave them Battel. Having pillaged and deftroyed that City, they paffed on to *Stamford*-Bridge, and there met with King *Harold*, who with a well difciplined Army was come to ftop their farther carreer. After a long and a terrible Fight, and much blood-fhed on both fides, the *Norwegians* began at laft to give back, which the *Englifh* perceiving, fell on fo manfully, that few or none efcaped with their Lives, *Harold* and *Tofty* being alfo flain upon the fpot. One of the *Norwegians* is defervedly recorded for his incomparable Exploits performed in this Battel, who with incredible Valour maintaining the Bridge againft the whole Strength of the *Englifh* Army for above an hour with his fingle Refiftance delayed their Victory, and having flain a great number of his Enemies, he feemed invincible, till in the end, no one daring to grapple with him fairly, he was run through with a Spear from under the Bridge, and fo by his fall, a Paffage

Passage was opened for pursuit to compleat the Victory. King *Harold* over-joyed with this Success, triumphantly entered into *York*, and whilst he was making merry with his Nobles at a sumptuous Feast, News came that Duke *William* of *Normandy* was safely landed at, and began to Fortify himself in *Hastings*, with which Tidings being no way dashed, as fearing nothing after his late Victory, he forthwith marched towards him, and as soon as he was arrived in *Sussex*, without any consideration of the Fatigue his Army had underwent in their March, bid *William* Battel. The Duke dividing his Army into five Battalions, made a long harangue to his Soldiers, wherein he repeated and commended the Noble Acts of their Ancestors the *Danes* and *Norwegians*, who had perpetually vanquished the *English* and *French*, and other Nations, as many as they had to do with; how that themselves being well Horsed and Armed, were now to engage with a People void of both, who had no other Defence to trust to than the nimbleness and swiftness of their Heels. Both Armies being joyned upon the 14th. of *October*, Duke *William* after some hours Engaging, ordered his Army so to retire, as if they seemed to fly, which the *English* perceiving, broke their Ranks in haste of pursuing the supposed Chase, which falling out according to the Duke's expectation, he sent in a fresh supply of *Normans*, who falling upon the confused Battalions of the *English*, easily overcame them, and *Harold* receiving first a Wound by an Arrow, was at length slain, and then both the Field and the Victory was left to the *Normans* The day being thus won, *William* from this time called the *Conqueror*, went strait to *London*, where he was received with all possible Formality, and upon *Christmas*-Day solemnly Crowned King of *England*. This change and Alteration in *England*, was afore prognosticated by a Comet which appeared in the Spring of this Year, upon which a certain Poet made the following Verses;

Anno milleno, sexageno quoque seno,
Anglorum metæ flammas censere Cometæ.

King

The History of WALES.

King *William* having established himself in the Crown of *England*, passed over the next Year to *Normandy*, so to settle Affairs there, as afterwards they might have no need of his presence. In the mean while *Edgar Edeling* taking Avantage of his absence, returned from *Scotland* to *York*, being declared King by the Inhabitants of that Country, who had already slain *Robert*, upon whom *William* had bestowed that Earldom with 900 of his Men. But the King upon his return from *Normandy*, presently marched to the *North*, and having sufficiently revenged himself upon the Inhabitants, by wasting and destroying their Country, chased *Edgar* to *Scotland* again. The like Advantage *Edric Sylvaticus* the Son of *Alfric* Earl of *Mercia* embraced, who refusing to own any Submission to the Conqueror, took the opportunity of his departure to *Normandy* to fall foul upon such as were appointed Vicegerents and Governours of the Kingdom in his absence. Whereupon *Richard Fitzscrope* Governor of the Castle of *Hereford*, with the Forces under his Command so bitterly gauled him, by wasting and consuming his Lands, and carrying off the Goods of his Tenants, that he was compelled to desire Aid of *Blethyn* and *Rywalhon* Princes of *Wales*, by whose help, to recompence the Loss he had received, he passed into *Hereford*, and after that he had over-run and pillaged the Country to *Wyebridge*, returned back with exceeding great Booty. But no sooner were *Blethyn* and *Rywalhon* arrived in *North-Wales*, but they received News of a Rebellion raised against them by *Meredith* and *Ithel* the Sons of *Gruffydh ap Lhewelyn*, who had drawn together a considerable number of Men, upon pretence of recovering the Principality of *North-Wales*, which they said was fraudulently detained from them. *Blethyn* and *Rywalhon* did not delay to march to find the Enemies, and meeting with them at a place called *Mechain*, without any farther Ceremonies set upon the Rebels, who behaved themselves so gallantly, that after a Fight of several hours, they wanted nothing but Number to compleat the Victory. There fell

1067.

in this Battel on the one side Prince *Rywalhon*, and on the other *Ithel*, who being slain, *Meredith* was forced to give Ground, and endeavour to save himself by flight, which could not secure him, he being narrowly pursued by *Blethyn*, that in fine, he was glad to escape to the Mountains, where for want of Victuals and other Necessaries, he quickly perished, leaving *Blethyn ap Confyn* sole Prince of *North-Wales* and *Powis*. During these *Welch* Disturbances, *Swane* King of *Denmark* and *Osburn* his Brother with 300 Sail came up the *Humber*, and being joyned by *Edgar Edeling* and Earl *Waltelfe*, marched to *York*, and taking the Castle, disposed of their Forces to Winter Quarters, betwixt the Rivers of *Ouse* and *Trent*. The King understanding the Matter, posted to the *North*; whose coming, so dashed the Confederates, that they quickly dispersed their Power, and the *Danes* escaped to their Ships, and the King having taken Vengeance upon the rebellious Inhabitants of the Country, and upon his submission, having pardoned Earl *Waltelfe*, returned back to *London*.

Blethyn ap Confyn.

1070. ABout the same time *Caradoc* Son to *Gruffydh ap Rytherch ap Iestyn* all this while being sorely dissatisfied that he could not attain to the Principality of *South Wales*, invited over a great Number of *Normans*, to whom he joined all the Forces he could raise out of *Gwentland*, and other Parts of *Wales*. Then setting upon Prince *Meredith* who was far too weak to Encounter so considerable an Army, gave him an easy over-throw near the River *Rymby*, where *Meredith* was slain, and so *Caradoc* obtained the Government of *South-Wales*, which for a long time he had endeavoured sinistrously to encompass. He had sometime afore procured *Harold* to make an Invasion upon

The History of WALES.

upon *Gruffydh ap Lhewelyn*, purposely that himself might arrive at the Principality of *South-Wales*; and failing then of his expectation, he now invites over the *Normans*, not being willing to trust the *English* any more, by reason that he had so ungratefully been balked by *Harold*: So that it seems he cared not by what course, or by whose means he should gain his point; though it were by the Ruin and Destruction of his Country, which hitherto he had earnestly promoted. Being at length advanced to his long expected Government of *South-Wales*, (which though not recorded, seems yet very probable, by reason that his Son *Rythe ch ap Caradoc* enjoyed the same very soon after) he did not enjoy this Honour long, but dying in a short time after his Advancement, left to succeed him, his Son *Rytherch ap Caradoc*. At the same time that *Caradoc* carried on this Rebellion in *Wales*, the Earls *Edwyn*, *Marcher*, and *Hereward* revolted from the King of *England*; but *Edwyn* suspecting the success of their Affairs, and determining to retire to *Malcolm* King of *Scotland*, in his Journey thither was betrayed, and slain by his own Followers. Then *Marcher* and *Hereward* betook themselves to the Isle of *Ely*, which though sufficiently fortified, was so warmly besieged by the King, that *Marcher* and his Accomplices were in a short time forced to surrender themselves up Prisoners; only *Hereward* made his escape to *Scotland*: But the King followed him close; and after he had received Homage of *Malcolm* King of *Scotland*, returned back to *England*; and after a short stay here, passed over to *Normandy*, where he received *Edgar Edeling* again to Mercy.

The next Year, the *Normans* having already tasted of the sweetness of wasting and plundering a Country, came over again to *Wales*; and having spoiled and destroyed *Dyfed* and the Country of *Cardigan*, returned home with very great Spoil; and the following Year sailed over again for more Booty. About the same time, *Bleythyd* Bishop of S. *Davids* died, and was succeeded by one *Sulien*. But this

1071.

this was not all the Misfortune that befel the *Welch*; for *Radulph* Earl of the *East-Angles*, together with *Roger* Earl of *Hereford* and Earl *Waltelpe*, entered into a Conspiracy against King *William*, appointing the day of Marriage between *Radulph* and *Roger*'s Sister, which was to be solemnized in *Essex*; to treat of and conclude their Design. *Radulph*'s Mother was come out of *Wales*, and upon that account, he invited over several of her Friends and Relations to the Wedding; meaning chiefly by this seeming Affection, by their help and procurement to bring over the Princes and People of *Wales*, to favour and assist his Undertaking. But King *William* being acquainted with the whole Plot, quickly ruined all their Intrigues; unexpectedly coming from *Normandy*, surprized the Conspirators; only *Radulph*, who either doubted of the success of their Affairs, or else had intimation given him of the King's landing, before hand took shipping at *Norwich*, and fled to *Denmark*. *Waltelpe* and *Roger* were executed, and all the other Adherents; more particularly the *Welch*, some of whom were hanged, others had their Eyes put out, and the rest were banished. Soon after, *Blethyn ap Confyn* Prince of *Wales* was basely and treacherously murthered by *Rhys ap Owen ap Edwyn* and the Gentlemen of *Ystrad Tywy*, after he had reigned 13 Years: A Prince of singular Qualifications and Virtues, and a great Observer of Justice and Equity towards his Subjects; he was very liberal and magnificent, being indeed very able, having a prodigious and almost an incredible Estate, as appears by these Verses made upon him;

Blethyn ap Confyn bôb Cwys
Ei him bioedh hên Bowys.

He had four Wives, by whom he had Issue, *Meredith* by *Haer* Daughter of *Gylhyn*, his first Wife; *Lhywarch* and *Cadogan* by the second; *Madoc* and *Riryd* by the third; and *Ioriwerth* by his last.

Trahaern

Trahaern ap Caradoc.

Blethyn being, as is said, traiterously Murdered, there was no regard had to his Issue, as to their right of Succession; but *Trahaern ap Caradoc* his Cousin-German being a Person of great Power and Sway in the Country, was unanimously elected Prince of *North-Wales*, and *Rhys ap Owen* with *Rytherch ap Caradoc* did joyntly govern *South-Wales*. *Trahaern* indeed had none of the least Pretence to that Principality, as having married *Nest* the only surviving Issue of that great Prince, *Gruffydh ap Lhewelyn*; his two Sons *Meredith* and *Ithel* being lately slain in their attempt against *Blethyn* and *Rywalhon*. But his Title could not secure him in his Government as much as his Possession, since there was one still living, tho' not much regarded, who without any Dispute, was true Heir and Proprietor of the Principality of *North-Wales*. And this was *Gruffydh* Son to *Conan*, Son to *Iago ap Edwal*, who being informed of the Death of *Blethyn ap Confyn*, and the Advancement of *Trahaern*, thought this a proper time to endeavour the Recovery of what was truly his Right, and out of which he had been all this time most wrongfully excluded. Wherefore having obtained help in *Ireland*, where he privately sojourned during the Reign of *Blethyn ap Confyn*, from *Encumalhon* King of *Ultonia*, *Ranalht* and *Mathawn* two other Kings of that Country, he sailed for *Wales*, and landed in the Isle of *Anglesey*, which he easily reduced and brought to subjection. At the same time *Cynwric ap Rywalhon*, a Noble-Man of *Maeler* or *Bromfield* was slain in *North-Wales*, but how, or upon what account, is not known. But whilst *Gruffydh ap Conan* endeavours to dispossess *Trahaern* out of *North-Wales*, *Gronow* and *Lhewelyn* the Sons of *Cadwgan ap Blethyn* having united their
Forces

Forces with *Caradoc ap Gruffydh ap Rytherch,* intended to revenge the Murther of their Grandfather *Blethyn ap Confyn,* upon *Rys ap Owen* and *Rytherch ap Caradoc,* the joynt Rulers of *South Wales.* And then marching confidently to find them, both Armies met together and fought at a place called *Camdhwr;* where after a fore Engagement, the Sons of *Cadwgan* at length obtained a glorious Victory. In *North Wales* the fame time, *Gruffydh ap Conan* having eftablifhed his Poffeffion of the Ifle of *Anglefey,* intended to proceed farther in the Continent of *Wales;* to which end, having tranfported his Forces over the River, incamped in the neighbouring Countrey of *Carnarvonfhire,* purpofing to reduce *North-Wales* by degrees: *Trahaern ap Caradoc* being informed of this Defcent of *Gruffydh's,* made all poffible fpeed to prevent his farther progrefs; and having made all neceffary Preparations that the fhortnefs of the Opportunity would permit, he drew up his Forces to *Bronyr Erw,* where he gave *Gruffydh* battel, and in fine put him to a fhameful flight; fo that he was glad to retire back fafe to *Anglefey.*

A. D. 1074.

The next Year *Rytherch ap Caradoc* Prince of *South-Wales* dyed, being murthered through the unnatural Villainy of his Cofin-German *Meyrchaon ap Rhys ap Rytherch;* after whom *Rhys ap Owen* obtained the fole Government of *South-Wales:* But his enjoyment of the whole Principality was not very lafting, and fcarce

1075. at all void of Trouble and Vexation of War. For fhortly after the death of *Caradoc,* the Sons of *Cadwgan* thinking they might eafily now foil and vanquifh one, feeing they had fometime ago victoriouſly overcome both Princes together, with all the Forces they could raife, fet upon *Rhys* again at a place called *Gwanyffyd;* who not being able to endure their Number, was routed and forced to flee; however the Blow was not fo mortal, but that *Rhys* gathered together new Levies, by the help of which he was embolden'd ftill to maintain himfelf in his Principality. But Fortune which had advanced him to the Crown, feemed now to frown at and crofs all his Endeavours and Undertakeings,

ings, and being reduced to a very weak condition in the late Battel, he was set upon by a fresh Enemy, before he could have sufficient time to recover and recruit himself. For *Trahaern ap Caradoc* Prince of *North-Wales*, perceiving the Weakness and Inability of *Rhys* to make opposition against any foreign Enemy that invaded his Territories, thought it now very feasible to obtain the Conquest of *South-Wales*, and then to annex it to his own Principality of *North-Wales*. Being egg'd on by these pleasant Imaginations, he dispatched his Army to *South-Wales*, to fight with *Rhys*, who with all the Forces he could possibly levie, as laying his whole Fortune upon the event of this Battel, boldly met him at *Pwlhgwttic*; where after a tedious Fight on both sides, *Rhys* having lost the best part of his Army, was put to flight, and so warmly pursu'd, that after long shifting from place to place, himself with his Brother *Howel* fell at length into the hands of *Caradoc ap Gruffydh*, who put them both to death, in revenge of the base Murther of *Blethyn ap Confyn*, by them formerly transacted. The Principality of *South-Wales* being thus vacant by the death of *Rhys ap Owen*; *Rhys* Son to *Theodor, ap Eineon, ap Owen, ap H.wel Dha*, as lawful Heir to that Government, put in his Claim, which being very plain and evident, so prevailed with the People of the Country, that they unanimously elected him for their Prince; much against the expectation of *Trahaern ap Caradoc* Prince of *North-Wales*. The next Year S. *Davids* suffer'd greatly by Strangers, who landing there in a considerable number, spoiled and destroyed the whole Town; shortly after which barbarous Action, *Abraham*, Bishop of that Sea, dyed; and then *Sulien*, who the Year before had relinquished and resigned up that Bishoprick, was compelled to resume it.

A. D. 1077.

The Government of all *Wales*, both *North* and *South*, had been now for a long time supply'd by Usurpers, and forcibly detained from the right and legal Inheritors; but Providence would suffer Injustice to reign no longer, and therefore restored the rightful Heirs to their Principalities. *Rhys ap Theodor* had actual

1079.

actual possession of *South-Wales*; and there wanted no more at this time, but to bring in *Gruffydh ap Conan* to the Principality of *North-Wales*; both these Princes being indisputably right and lawful Heirs to their respective Governments, as lineally descended from *Roderic* the Great, who was legal Proprietor of all *Wales*. *Gruffydh ap Conan* had already reduced the Isle of *Anglesey*; but not being able to levy a sufficient Army from thence to oppose *Trahaern*, he invited over a great Party of *Irish* and *Scots*, and then with his whole Army joyned with *Rhys ap Theodor* Prince of *South-Wales*. *Trahaern* in like manner associating to himself *Caradoc ap Gruffydh* and *Maslyr* the Sons of *Rywalhon ap Gwyn* his Cosin-Germans, the greatest and most powerful Men then in *Wales*, drew up his Forces together, with resolution to fight them. Both Armies meeting upon the Mountains of *Carno*, a terrible and a cruel Battel ensued presently thereupon; which proved the more fierce and bloody, by reason that both Parties resolutely referred their whole Fortune to the success of their Arms; and Life would prove vain if the Day was lost. But after a dismal Fight on both sides, the Victory fell at last to *Gruffydh* and *Rhys*, *Trahaern* with his Cosins being all slain in the Field; after whose death *Gruffydh* took possession of *North Wales*; and so the Rule of all *Wales*, after a tedious interval, was again restored to the right Line. About the same time, *Urgeney ap Sitsylht* a Person of noble Quality in *Wales*, was treacherously murthered by the Sons of *Rhys Sais*, or the *Englishman*; by which Name, the *Welch* were accustomed to denominate all Persons, as either had lived any considerable time in *England*, or could fluently and handsomly speak the *English* Tongue.

Gruffydh

Gruffydh ap Conan.

Gruffydh ap Conan being confirmed in the Principality of *North Wales*, and *Rhys ap Theodor* in that of *South-Wales*; there was no body that could create them any Molestation or Disturbance upon the account of Right, which was unquestionably just; so that they quietly enjoyed for some time their respective Dominions, without apprehension of any other Pretender. Indeed, it had seldom been known before, but that one of the Princes was an Usurper; and particularly in *North Wales*, where from the time of *Edwal Foel*, none had legally ascended to the Crown, excepting *Edwal* the Son of *Meyric*, eldest Son to *Edwal Foel*; in whose Line the undoubted Title of *North-Wales* lawfully descended. And the right Line being now restored in *Gruffydh ap Conan*, the same legally continued to *Lhewelyn ap Gruffydh*, the last Prince of the *British* Blood. But during these Revolutions in *Wales*, some things memorable were transacted in *England*; *Malcolm* King of the *Scots* descending into *Northumberland*, ravaged and destroyed the Country without Mercy, carrying away a great number of Prisoners; after which the *Northumbrians* fell upon *Walter* Bishop of *Durham*, whom they slew, together with a hundred Men, whilst he sate keeping of Court, not dreaming of any such treacherous Villainy. The same time *Robert Curthoys* the Bastards eldest Son, being for some reason disgusted against his Father, and set on by the instigation of the King of *France*, entered *Normandy* with an Army, and claimed it as his Right; which King *William* being acquainted with, passed over to *Normandy*, and meeting with his Son hand to hand in Battel, was by him overthrown. But being returned from *Normandy*, he entered with a great Army into *Wales*, and marching after the manner,

ner of a Pilgrimage as far as S. *Davids*, he offered and paid his Devotion to that Saint, and afterwards received Homage of the Kings and Princes of the Country. About the fame time the Tomb of *Walwey* King *Arthurs* Sister Son, a moſt valiant Perſon in his time, and Governour of that Country, from him called *Walwethcy*, was diſcovered in the Country of *Ros*, nigh the Sea-ſhoar, whoſe Body proved monſtrouſly prodigious, being in length about fourteen foot.

A. D. 1086. This year *Madawc*, *Cadwgan* and *Riryd*, the Sons of *Blethyn ap Confyn* ſometime Prince of *Wales*, raiſed a Rebellion againſt *Rhys ap Tewdor*; and having drawn together a great number of licentious and malecontented People, thought to eject him out of the Principality of *South-Wales*. *Rhys* had not Power and Forces enough to oppoſe them; the Rebels Army increaſing daily by the addition of the diſcontented Multitude, who always rejoyce at any new Commotion or Diſturbance; and therefore he was compell'd to retire to *Ireland*, where he obtained a very conſiderable party of *Iriſh* and *Scots*, upon promiſe of a ſufficient Reward, in caſe he was reſtored again to his Principality. Having by this meaſure got a very ſenſible increaſe to his former ſtrength, he landed in *South-Wales*; the News of whoſe arrival being blazed abroad, his Friends from all quarters preſently retired to him; ſo that in a ſhort time his Army became numerous, and able to confront the Enemy. The Rebels were ſenſible how the Princes Forces daily multiplyed, and therefore to prevent any farther addition, they made all poſſible haſte to force him to a Battel, which in a ſhort time after happened at *Lhech y Creu*, where the Rebels were vanquiſhed; *Madawc* and *Riryd* being ſlain, and *Cadwgan* glad to ſave his Life by flight. *Rhys* having won ſo ſignal a Victory, and fearing no farther Diſturbance, diſmiſſed the *Iriſh* and *Scots* with great Rewards, who honourably returned to their own

1087. Country. Within a while after, an unaccountable Sacriledg was committed at S. *Davids*; the Shrine belonging to the Cathedral, being felonioully convey'd out of the Church, all the Plate and other Utenſils

were

were stoln, and only the Shrine left empty behind. The same Year a Civil-War broke out in *England*, and several Armies in several parts of the Kingdom were up in Arms at the same time, and among the rest the *Welch*, who entering into *Glocester* and *Worcester Shires*, burnt and destroyed all before them, to the Gate of *Worcester*. The King having drawn his Army together, proceeded against his Enemies by degrees, and falling upon their seperate Parties, without any great difficulty, reduced all to Obedience. Within two Years after, Archbishop *Sulien*, the most pious and learned Person in *Wales*, dyed, in the Eightieth Year of his Age, and in the Sixteenth Year of his Bishoprick; presently after whose death the Town of S. *Davids* suffered a more sensible Calamity, being first plundered, and afterwards burnt by a company of Pyrats, who sorely infested the *British* Coasts. About the same time also dyed *Cadifer* the Son of *Calhoyn* Lord of *Dyfed*, whose Sons *Lhewelyn* and *Eineon* moved *Gruffydh ap Meredith* to take up Arms against his Sovereign Prince *Rhys ap Tewdor*, with whom they joyned all the Forces they couly levy among their Tenants and Dependants; then passing with their Army to *Lhandydoch*, boldly challenged *Rhys* to fight; who thereupon gave them battel, and after a resolute Engagement of both sides, the Rebels were at length worsted, and put flight, and then so narrowly pursued, that *Gruffydh ap Meredith* was taken Prisoner, and in fine executed as a Traitor: But *Eineon* made his escape, and not daring to trust himself with any of his own Kindred, he fled to *Iestyn ap Gurgant*, Lord of *Morgannwc*, who was then in actual Rebellion against Prince *Rhys*. And to ingratiate himself the more in *Iestyn's* favour, he promised, upon condition of the performance of certain Articles, one of which more especially was, That he should receive his Daughter in Matrimony; That he would bring over to his aid a considerable Body of *Normans*, with whom he was singularly acquainted, as having served a long time in *England*. These Articles being agreed to and recorded, *Eineon* posted to *England*, and in a little time

A. D. 1089.

A. D.
1090.

time brought matters fo about, that he prevailed with *Robert Fitzhamon* and Twelve more Knights, to levy a ſtrong Army of *Normans*, and to come to *Wales* to the protection and aid of *Ieſtyn*. The beginning of the following Year they landed in *Glamorganſhire*, and were honourably received by *Ieſtyn*, who joyning his Power to theirs, marched to Prince *Rhys* his Domininions, where, without the leaſt ſhew of Mercy to his own Countrymen, he encouraged the *Normans*, by his own Example, to ſpoil and deſtroy all that came before them. Prince *Rhys* was mightily grieved to find his Country fo unmercifully haraſſed; and though at this time very antient, being above 98 Years of age, he could not refrain but meet his Enemies; and having with all poſſible ſpeed raiſed a convenient Army; he met with them near *Brecnock*, where after a terrible Fight, and a great ſlaughter on both ſides, he was unhappily ſlain. With him fell the Glory and Grandeur of the Principality of *South-Wales*, being afterwards rent in pieces, and divided into ſeveral parts and piece-meals among theſe *Norman* Captains, as ſhall be by and by more particularly related. Prince *Rhys* left Iſſue behind him by the Daughter of *Rywalhon ap Confyn*, two Sons, *Gruffydh* and *Grono*, the latter of which was detained Priſoner by the King of *England*; thô the Author of the winning of the Lordſhip of *Glamorgan*, affirms, that he was ſlain, together with his Father, in this Battel againſt the *Normans*.

The *Normans* having received a ſufficient Reward from *Ieſtyn*, upon the account of their Service againſt Prince *Rhys*, returned to their Ships, in order to their Voyage homeward. But before they could looſe Anchor to ſail off, *Eineon* recalled them, being ungratefully affronted by *Ieſtyn*, who abſolutely refuſed to make good to him the Conditions which they had agreed upon, before the *Normans* were invited to *Wales*. Upon this account, *Eineon* was ſo irreconcilably incenſed againſt *Ieſtyn*, that to be revenged upon him, he was willing to ſacrifice his native Country into the hands of ſtrangers; and therefore endeavoured to perſuade the *Normans* concerning the Fatneſs and

Fertility

The History of WALES.

Fertility of the Country, and how easily they might conquer and make themselves Masters of it. But he needed not many Arguments to persuade a People that were willing of themselves, especially being encouraged thereto by a Person of some esteem in the Country; whereupon, without any more Questions, they presently fell to their business; and from Friends became unexpectedly Foes. *Iestyn* was much surprised to find the *Normans*, whom he had but lately honourably dismissed from his service, and as he thought, with Satisfaction, so soon become his Enemies; but perceiving a Serpent in the Hedg, and *Eineon* so amicably great among them, he quickly guessed at the reason, of which there was no other remedy left but to bewail the unnecessary Folly of his own Knavery. The *Normans* easily dispossessed *Iestyn* of the whole Lordship of *Glamorgan*; the most pleasant and fertile part of which they divided among themselves; leaving the more mountainous and craggy ground to the share of *Eineon*. The Knights who accompanied *Fitzhamon* in this Expedition were, *William de Londres* or *London*; *Richard de Grena villa*, or *Greenfield*; *Paganus de Turberville*; *Robert de S. Quintino*, or *Quintin*; *Richard de Syward*; *Gilbert de Humfrevile*; *Roger de Berkrolles*; *Reginald de Sully*; *Peter le Soore*; *John le Fleming*; *Oliver de S. John*; *William de Esterling*, or *Stradling*. These Persons having distributed that fair and pleasant Lordship among themselves, and considering that they were much better provided for here than they could be at home, settled in *Glamorgan*, where their Posterity have continued to this time. And here we may observe, what a Train of Circumstances concurr'd together, in favour of the *Normans*, having possession of this Lordship: For had not *Eineon*, being vanquished by Prince *Rhys*, fled to *Iestyn*, rather than to another; or had not *Iestyn* been so vain as to attempt the Conquest of *South-Wales*, and to that end consented to the Advice of *Eineon*; there had been no necessity of inviting the *Normans* at all to *Wales*. And then, the *Normans* being arrived, had not *Iestyn* ungenteely violated his Promise, and refused to perform

K the

the Articles agreed upon between him and *Eineon*; or, had not *Eineon* purſued ſo deſperate a Revenge, but ſatisfied his Paſſion upon *Ieſtyn*, without prejudice to his Country ; the *Normans* would have returned home with ſatisfaction, and conſequently could never have been Proprietors of that noble Country they then forcibly poſſeſſed. And now again the *Welch* experienced the dangerous Conſequence of calling in a foreign Nation to their aid ; the *Saxons* had already diſpoſſeſſed them of the beſt part of the Iſland of *Britain*, and now the *Normans* ſeized upon a great part of that ſmall Country, which had eſcaped the Sovereignty and Conqueſt of the *Eniiſh*. But here it will be neceſſary to lay down the ſtate and condition of this Lordſhip of *Morgannwc* or *Glamorgan*, and what ſhare each particular Knight obtained in the diſtribution of it.

The Lordſhip of *Glamorgan* reaches in length 27 Miles, even from *Rymny-Bridge* to the Eaſt, to *Pwlh Conan* Weſtward; and in breadth from *Aberthaw*, otherwiſe *Aberdaon* on the South-part, to the Confines of *Brecnockſhire* above *Morleys* Caſtle, 22 Miles. This being a Royal Lordſhip, the Lords thereof owing no other Subjection than Obedience only to the Crown, aſſumed to themſelves all the Priviledges of a regal Court, excepting only the pardoning of Criminals in caſe of Treaſon. And not only *Glamorgan*, but the ſeveral petty Lordſhips of which it conſiſted, namely, *Sengemyth*, *Myscyn*, *Ruthin*, *Lhanblethian*, *Tïr Iarlh*, *Glyn Rothney*, *Avan*, *Neth*, *Coyty*, *Talavan*, and *Lantuit* or *Boviartcn*; exerciſed the ſame Privelege of *Jura Regalia*, with this difference only, that in caſe of wrong Judgment in theſe Courts, appeal might be made in the County-Court of *Glamorgan*, which being ſuperiour to the reſt, had power to reverſe any Judgment given in them. Within this Lordſhip were 18 Caſtles, and 36 Knights Fees; beſides the Town and Caſtle of *Kynfig*, the Town of *Cowbridge* or *Pont Vaen*, and the Town and Caſtle of *Caerdiſ*; in the latter of which the Lord of *Glamorgan* chiefly reſided, wherein the County-Court was

The History of WALES.

was monthly kept. The annual Revenue of this Lordship amounted to a Thousand Marks; whereof Four Hundred was allowed for the Fees and Sallary of the several Officers belonging to the same. This Lordship of *Glamorgan Robert Fitzhamon* kept to himself, and the others he distributed between his several Followers; namely, to *William de Londres* he gave the Castle and Mannor of *Ogmore*; to *Richard Greenfield* the Lordship of *Neth*; to *Paine Turberville* that of *Coyty*; to *Robert S Quintine Lhan Blethyan*; to *Richard Syward Talavan*; to *Gilbert Humfrevile* the Castle and Mannor of *Penmarc*; to *Reginald Sully* the Castle and Mannor of *Sully*; to *Roger Berkrolles* that of *East Orchard*; to *Peter le Soor* that of *Peterton*; to *John Fleming* that of *S. George*; to *John S. John* that of *Fonmon* or *Fenvon*; and lastly, to *William le Esterling* or *Stradling* that of *S. Donats*. But that these Knights should have dependence upon, and might seem to hold their several Lordships and Estate from him; *Robert Fitzhamon* appointed them their several Apartments in his Castle of *Caerdâf*, where they were obliged to give their attendance at every Court-day, which was monthly kept upon *Monday*.

But about the same time that *Robert Fitzhamon* took the Lordship of *Glamorgan*, *Barnard Newmarch* a Nobleman likewise of *Normandy*, obtained by Conquest the Lordship of *Brecknock*; and *Henry de Newburgh* Son to *Roger de Bellemont*, by the Conquerour made Earl of *Warwick*, the Country of *Gower*. But *Barnard Newmarch* gave the People of *Wales* some small Satisfaction and Content, by marrying *Nest*, the Daughter also of *Nest*, Daughter to *Lhewelyn ap Gruffydh* Prince of *Wales*, by whom he had Issue, a Son called *Mahael*. This worthy Gentleman being legally to succeed his Father in the Lordship of *Brecknock*, was afterwards disinherited by the Malice and Baseness of his own unnatural Mother. The occasion was thus, *Nest* happening to fall in admiration of a certain Knight, with whom she had more than ordinary Familiarity, even beyond what she exprest to her own Husband; *Mahael* perceiving her dissolute and loose Behaviour, counselled her to take care of her Fame and Reputation, and to leave off that scandalous Liberty which she took; and afterwards meeting casually her Gallant coming from her, fought and grievously wounded him. Upon this, *Nest* to be revenged upon her Son, went to *Henry* the First King of *England*, and in his presence took her corporal Oath, that her Son *Mahael* was illegitimate, and not begot by *Barnard Newmarch* her Husband, but another Person; by virtue of which Oath, or rather Perjury, *Mahael* was disinherited, and his Sister, whom her Mother attested to be legitimate, was bestowed by the King upon *Milo*, the Son of *Walter Constable*, afterward Earl of *Hereford*, who in right of his Wife enjoyed the whole estate of *Barnard Newmarch* Lord of *Brecnock*. Of this *Milo* it is reported, that telling King *Henry* of a strange Accident which had occurred to him by *Lhyn Savathan* in *Wales*, where the Birds upon the Pond at the passing by of *Gruffydh* the Son of *Rhys ap Theodor*, seemed by their chirping to be in a manner overjoy'd; The King replyed, It was not so wonderful; for although, says he, we have violently and injuriously oppressed that Nation, yet it is manifestly known, that they are the lawful and original Inheritors of that Country.

But whilst the *Normans* were thus carving for themselves in *Glamorgan* and *Brecnock*, *Cadogan ap Blethyn ap Confyn* towards the end of *April*, entered into *Dyved*, and having ravaged and destroyed the Country, returned back. But within Eight Weeks after, there succeeded him a more fatal Enemy; for the *Normans* landing in *Dyved* and *Cardigan*, began to fortifie themselves in Castles and other strong places, and to inhabit the Country upon the Sea-shoar, which before was not in their possession. Indeed the *Normans* having by the connivance of the Conquerour already got into their hands all the best Estates in *England*, began now to spy out the Commodities of *Wales*; and perceiving moreover how bravely *Robert Fitzhamon* and *Barnard Newmarch* had sped there, thought

thought they might as well expect the like fortune. Wherefore having obtained a Grant from King *William* (who readily confented to their Requeft, becaufe by this means he killed two Birds with one Stone, procured to himfelf their utmoft Service upon occafion, and withal provided for them without any Charge to himfelf) they came to *Wales*, and fo entered upon the Eftates appointed them by the King, which they held of him by Knight-fervice, having firft done Homage and fworn Fealty for the fame. *Roger Montgomery* Earl of *Arundel* did Homage for the Lordfhips of *Powis* and *Cardigan*; *Hugh Lupus* Earl of *Chefter* for *Tegengl* and *Ryfonioc*, together with all the Land lying upon the Sea-fhoar to the River *Conwey*; *Arnulph* a younger Son of *Roger Montgomery* for *Dyved*; *Barnard Newmarch* for *Brecneck*; *Ralph Mortimer* for *Eluel*; *Hugh de Lacy* for the Land of *Ewyas*; *Euftace Omer* for *Mold* and *Hapredale*; and feveral others did the like Homage for other Lands. But *Roger Montgomery*, who by the Conquerour was created Earl of *Arundel* and *Shrewsbury*, entered in an hoftile manner into *Powys-land*, and having won the Caftle and Town of *Baldwyn*, fortified it in his own right, and called it *Montgomery* after his own Name. King *William* of *England* was now in *Normandy*, and bufily engaged in a War againft his Brother *Robert*; by the advantage of whofe abfence, *Gruffydh ap Conan* Prince of *North-Wales*, and *Cadogan ap Blethyn*, who now ruled in *South-Wales*, with joynt Forces entered into *Cardigan* and flew a great number of *Normans*, whofe Pride and exceffive Cruelties towards the *Welch*, were altogether intolerable. But after fufficient execution there, being returned home, the *Normans* fent for more Aid from *England*; which being arrived, they thought to make a private in-road into *North-Wales*, and fo to be revenged upon the *Welch*. But their Defign being happily difcovered to *Cadogan*, he drew up his Forces to meet them, and then unexpectedly fetting upon them in the Foreft of *Yfpys*, after a very warm Refiftment of the *Normans* fide, forced them to retire by flight, and then triumphantly marching

marching through *Cardigan* and *Dyved*, he deſtroyed all the Caſtles and Fortifications in the Country, beſides *Pembrock* and *Rydcors*, which proved too ſtrong, and impregnable.

A. D. 1093. The next Year the *Normans* who inhabited the Country of *Glamorgan*, fell upon and deſtroyed the Countries of *Gwyr*, *Kidwely*: and *Yſtrâd Tywy*, which they harraſſed in ſuch a cruel manner, that they left them bare of any People to inhabit. And to increaſe, as it was thought, the Miſeries of the *Welch*, King *William Rufus* being informed of the great ſlaughter which *Gruffydh ap Conan*, and the Sons of *Blethyn ap Confyn* had lately committed upon the *Engliſh*, as well within *Cheſhire*, *Shropſhire*, *Worceſterſhire*, and *Herefordſhire*, as within *Wales*; entered the Country at *Montgomery*, which place the *Welch* having ſometime ſince demoliſhed, King *William* lately rebuilt. But the *Welch* kept all the Paſſages through the Woods and Rivers, and all other Streights ſo cloſe, that the King could effect nothing conſiderable againſt them; and therefore when he perceived that his labour was but loſt, in continuing in thoſe Parts, he forthwith decamped, and returned with no great Honour back to *England*. But this retreat of King *William* was not altogether ſo favourable to the Intereſt of the *Welch*, as the death of *William Fitz-Baldwyn*, who

1094. was Owner of the Caſtle of *Rydcors*, and did the greateſt miſchief and hurt to the *South-Wales* Men of any other. He being dead, the Garriſon of *Rydcors* which was, wont to keep the *Welch* in continual awe, forſook that place, and by that means gave opportunity to the Inhabitants of *Gwyr*, *Brecnock*, *Gwent*, and *Gwentlhwc*, to ſhake off that intolerable Yoak the *Normans* forced upon them, who after they had rob'd them of their Lands, kept them in perpetual ſubjection. But now *William Fitz-Baldwyn* being dead, and the Garriſon of *Rydcors* ſcatter'd, they ventur'd to lay violent hands upon the *Normans*, who thought themſelves free from all fear; and prevailed ſo ſucceſsfully, that they drove them all out of the Country, and recover'd their own antient Eſtates. But the

The History of WALES.

the *Normans* liked that Country so well, that they were resolved not to be so easily befooled out of what they had with a great deal of Pains and Danger once possessed; and therefore having drawn a great number of *English* and *Normans* to their aid, they were desirous to venture another touch with the *Welch*, and to return, if possible, to their once acquir'd Habitations. But the *Welch* so abhorr'd their Pride and tyrannical Dominion over them when they were Masters, that they were resolved not to be subject to such Tyrants again; and therefore they boldly met them at a place called *Celly Iarfawc*, and set upon them so manfully, the very apprehension of Servitude whetting their Spirits, that they put them to flight with great slaughter, and drove them out of the Country. The *Normans* however were not so absolutely routed with this Overthrow, but like a Fly in the night which destroys it self in the Candle, they must needs covet their own Destruction; their greediness egging them on to venture with few what was not practicable to be effected by many. Therefore on they came as far as *Brecnock*, with this absolute Vow and Resolution, not to leave one living thing remaining in that Country. But they fell short of their Policy, the People of the Country being removed to a narrow Streight, to expect their passing through; whither the *Normans* being advanced, they fell upon them, and killed a great number of them. About the same time, *Roger Montgomery* Earl of *Salop* and *Arundel*, *William Fitzeuflace* Earl of *Gloucester*, *Arnold de Harecourt*, and *Neal le Vicount*, were slain by the *Welch* between *Caerdif* and *Brecnock*; and *Walter Eureux* Earl of *Sarum*, *Rofmer*, and *Mantilake*; *Hugh* Earl of *Gourney*, were wounded, who afterwards dyed in *Normandy*. The *Normans* finding that they continually lost ground, thought it not advisable to stay any longer; and therefore having placed sufficient Garrisons in those Castles which they had formerly built, they returned with what speed they could to *England*. But all the haste they did make, could not secure them from the Fury of

I 4   the

the *Welch*; for *Gruffydh* and *Ifor*, the Sons of *Ednerth ap Cadogan*, expected them privately at a place called *Aberlhech*, where falling unexpectedly upon them; they flew the greatest part of their number, the rest narrowly escaping safe to *England*. But the *Norman* Garrisons which were left behind, defended themselves with a great deal of Bravery, till at last, finding no prospect of Relief, they were forced for their own safety to deliver them up to the *Welch*, who, from that time, became again Proprietors of those Places which the *Normans* had dispossess'd them from. And this encouraged the *Welch* to undertake other things against the *English*; for immediately after this, certain of the Nobility of *North-Wales*, *Uchthed* the Son of *Edwyn ap Grono* by name, together with *Hewel ap Grono*, and the Sons of *Cadogan ap Blethyn* of *Powys-land*, passed by *Cardigan* into *Dyved* (which Country King *William* had given to *Arnulph* Son to *Roger Montgomery*, who had built thereon the Castle of *Fembrock*, and appointed *Gerald de Windsore* Governour of the same) and destroying all the Country with Fire and Sword, excepting *Pembrock* Castle, which was impregnable, they returned home with a great deal of Booty. In recompence of this, when the Lords of *North-Wales* were returned, *Gerald* issued out of the Castle, and spoiled all the Country about S. *Davids*; and after he had got sufficient Plunder, and taken divers Prisoners, returned back into the Castle.

A. D. 1095.

The Year following, King *William* being return'd from *Normandy*, and having heard how that the *Welch* had cut off a great number of his Subjects in *Wales*, gathered all his Power together, and with great Pomp and Ostentation entered the Marches, resolving utterly to eradicate the rebellious and implacable humour of the *Welch* Nation. But after all this Boast and seeming Resolution, he durst venture no farther than the Marches, where having built some few Castles, he returned with no greater Honour than he came. But the next Spring, *Hugh de Montgomery* Earl of *Arundel* and *Salop*, by the *Welch* named

1096.

The History of WALES.

named *Hugh Goch*, and *Hugh Fras*, or the fat, Earl of *Chester*, being invited by some disaffected *Welch* Lords, came into *North-Wales* with a very great Army. Prince *Gruffydh ap Conan*, and *Cadogan ap Blethyn*, perceiving themselves to be too weak to oppose so numerous an Army, and what was worse, being very suspicious of the Fidelity and Honesty of their own Forces, thought it their best way to take the Hills and Mountains for their safety, where they were like to remain most secure from the Enemy. Then the *English* Army marched towards *Anglesey*, and being come over against the Island, they built the Castle of *Aberlhiennawc*. But *Gruffydh* and *Cadogan* could no longer endure to see their Country over-run by the *English*, and therefore they descended from the Mountains, and came to *Anglesey*, thinking, with what Succours they should receive from *Ireland*, of which they were disappointed, to be able to defend the Island from any attempt that should be made upon it. And now the whole Treason, and the occasion of the *English* coming to *Wales* was discovered; for *Owen ap Edwyn*, the Prince his chiefest Counsellour, whose Daughter *Gruffydh* had married (having himself also married *Everyth* the Daughter of *Confyn*, Aunt to *Cadogan)* upon some private Grudge or other, called in the *English* into *Wales*, and at this time openly joyned his Forces with theirs, and led the whole Army over into *Anglesey*. *Gruffydh* and *Cadogan* finding how they were betrayed by their dearest Friend, as they thought; for fear of farther Treachery, judged it prudent to sail privately for *Ireland*; after whose departure, the *English* fell cruelly to work, destroying all they could come at, without any respect to either Age or Sex. And whilst the *English* continued in *Anglesey*, *Magnus* the Son of *Harold*, lately King of *England*, came over with a great Fleet, intending to lay faster hold upon that Kingdom, than his Father had done, and to recover the same to himself. But whilst he steered his Course thitherward, he was driven by contrary Winds to the Coasts of *Anglesey*, where he would

fain

fain have landed, had not the *English* Army kept him off. But in this Skirmish *Magnus* accidentally wounded *Hugh* Earl of *Salop* with an Arrow in the Face, whereof he dyed; and then of a sudden both Armies relinquished the Island, the *English* returning to *England*, appointing *Owen ap Edwyn*, who invited them over Prince of the Country. But *Owen* did not enjoy the Principality long; for in the beginning of the following Spring, *Gruffydh ap Conan* and *Cadogan ap Blethyn* returned from *Ireland*, and having concluded a Peace with the *Normans*, for some part of their Lands in *Wales*; *Gruffydh* remained in *Anglesey*, and *Cadogan* had *Cardigan*, with part of *Powys*. But though *Cadogan* recovered his Estate, yet in a little while after he lost his Son *Lhewelyn*, who was treacherously murthered by the Men of *Brecnock*: at which time also dyed *Rythmarch* Archbishop of S. *Davids*, the Son of *Sulien*, being in the 43 Year of his Age; a Man of the greatest Piety, Wisdom, and Learning, as had flourished a long time in *Wales*, excepting his Father, under whose Tutelage he was educated. The Year following, King *William Rufus*, as he was hunting in the new Forrest, was accidentally slain with an Arrow, which one *Walter Tyrrell* shot at a Stag; and his eldest Brother being then engaged in the Holy War, *Henry* his younger Brother, whom in his life-time he had nominated his Successor, was crowned in his stead. The same Year, *Hugh* Earl of *Chester*, *Grono ap Cadogan*, and *Gwyn ap Gruffydh* departed this life.

About two Years after, a Rebellion broke out in *England*; *Robert de Belesmo*, the Son of *Roger de Montgomery* Earl of *Salop*, and *Arnulph* his Brother Earl of *Pembrock*, took up Arms against King *Henry*; which he being informed of, sent them a very gracious Message to come before him, and declare their Grievances, and the reason of their rising up in Arms against his Majesty. But the Earls instead of appearing in Person, sent him slight and frivolous Excuses, and in the mean while made all necessary Preparations for the War, both by raising of Forces, and fortifying

The History of WALES.

fortifying their Castles and strong Holds. And to strengthen themselves the more, they sent rich Presents, and made large Promises to *Iorwerth*, *Cadogan*, and *Meredith*, the Sons of *Blethyn ap Confyn*; for to bring them to their side. *Robert* fortified four Castles, namely, *Arundel*, *Tekinhil*, *Shrewsbury*, and *Brugge*; which last, by reason that *Robert* built it without the consent of the King, was the chief occasion of this War; and *Arnulph* fortified his Castle at *Pembrock*. After this, they entered in an hostile manner into the Territories of the King of *England*, wasting and destroying all before them. And to augment their strength, *Arnulph* sent *Gerald* his Steward, to *Murkart* King of *Ireland*, desiring his Daughter in Wedlock; which was easily granted, with the Promise too of great Succours and large Supplies. King *Henry*, to put a stop to their bold Adventures, marched in person against them; and laying siege to the Castle of *Arundel*, wan it without any great Opposition; and quickly afterwards the Castle of *Tekinhill*; but that of *Brugge*, by reason of the situation of the place, and the depth of the Ditch about it, seemed to require longer time and harder service; and therefore King *Henry* was advised to send privately to *Iorwerth ap Blethyn*, promising him great Rewards if he forsook the Earl's part, and came over to him; urging to him, what Mischief *Roger*, Earl *Robert's* Father, and his Brother *Hugh*, had continually done to the *Welch-Men*. And to make him the more willing to accept of his Proposals, he promised to give him all such Lands as the Earl and his Brother had in *Wales*, without either Tribute or Homage; which was a part of *Powys*, *Cardigan*, and half *Dyfed*; the other part being in the possession of *William Fitz-Baldwyn*. *Iorwerth* receiving these Offers, accepted of them very gladly, and then coming to the King, he sent all his Forces to Earl *Robert's* Lands, who having received very strict Orders, destroyed without Mercy every thing they met with; and what made the Spoil the greater, Earl *Robert* upon his rebelling against King *Henry*, had caused his People to convey

vey all their Goods to *Wales*, for fear of the *English*; not thinking how his Father's Memory founded among the *Welch*. But when the News of *Iorwerth*'s Revolt reached the Ears of the Earl, *Cadogan* and *Meredith*, *Iorwerth*'s Brothers; their Spirits began to faint, as despairing any longer to oppose the King, since *Iorwerth*, who was the Person of greatest strength in *Wales*, had left and forsaken them. *Arnulph* was gone to *Ireland* to fetch home his Wife, and to bring over what succour his Father in Law, King *Murkart*, could afford to send him; but he not coming in time, some other Method was to be tryed, how to get some Aid against the *English*. A little before this Rebellion broke out, *Magnus*, *Harold*'s Son, landed the second time in the Isle of *Anglesey*, and being kindly received by *Gruffydh ap Conan*, he had leave to cut down what Timber he had need for; and so returning to the *Isle of Man*, which he had got by Conquest, he built there three Castles, and then sent to *Ireland* to have the Daughter of *Murkart* in marriage to his Son, which being obtained, he created him King of *Man*. Earl *Robert* hearing this, sent to *Magnus* for Aid against King *Henry*; but receiving none, he thought it now high time to look to his own Safety; and therefore he sent to the King, requesting that he might quietly depart the Kingdom, in case he should lay down his Arms; which the King having granted, he sail'd to *Normandy*. And then King *Henry* sent an Express to his Brother *Arnulph*, requiring him either to follow his Brother out of the Kingdom, or to deliver himself up to his Mercy; and so *Arnulph* went over also for *Normandy*. When the King was returned to *London*, *Iorwerth* took his Brother *Meredith* Prisoner, and committed him to the King's custody; his other Brother *Cadogan* having reconciled himself beforehand, to whom *Iorwerth* gave *Cardigan*, with a part of *Powys*. Then *Iorwerth* went to *London*, to put the King in mind of his Promise, and the Service he had done him against Earl *Robert*; but the King finding now all matters at quiet, was deaf

to

to all such Remembrances, and instead of promising what he had once voluntarily proposed, against all Rules of Equity and Gratitude, he took away *Dyfed* from *Iorwerth*, and gave it to a Knight of his own, called *Saer* ; and *Stratywy Cydwely*, and *Gwyr* he bestowed upon *Howel ap Grono*, and sent *Iorwerth* away more empty than he came : Nor was this sufficient Reward for his former Services ; but the next Year King *Henry* must send some of his Counsel to *Shrewsbury*, and cite *Iorwerth* to appear there, under pretence of consulting about the King's Business and Affairs in those Parts. But the Plot was laid deeper ; and when without any suspicion of Treachery he made his appearance, he was surprizedly attainted of High-Treason, and then contrary to all Right and Justice actually condemn'd to perpetual Imprisonment ; the true reason of this unparallel'd Severity being, the King feared his Strength, and was apprehensive that he would revenge the Wrong and Affront he received at his hands. And indeed, well had he reason to fear that, when he so ungratefully treated him, whose Service he had experienced to be so greatly advantagious to him. But the Policy of Princes is unaccountable; and whether to value an eminent Person for his Service, or to fear him for his Greatness, is a Subject that frequently disturbs their most settled Considerations. But the Noblemen that were at this time sent by the King to *Shrewsbury*, were *Richard de Belmersh*, who being chief Agent about *Roger Montgomery* Earl of *Salop*, was preferred to the Bishoprick of *London*, and afterwards appointed by this King, to be Warden of the Marches, and Governour of the County of *Salop*. With him were joyned in company, *Walter Constable*, the Father of *Milo*, Earl of *Hereford*, and *Rayner* the King's Lieutenant in the County of *Salop*. About this time, as *Bale* writes, the Church of *Menevia* or *S. Davids*, began to be subject to the See of *Canterbury*, being always afore the Metropolitan Church of all *Wales*.

A.D.
1101.

Shortly

A. D. Shortly after this, *Owen ap Edwyn*, who had been
1102. Author of no small Mischief and Disturbance to the *Welch*, in moving the *English* against his natural Prince, and Son in Law *Gruffydh ap Conan*, departed this Life, after a tedious and miserable Sickness; of which he was so much the less pityed, by how much he had proved an Enemy and a Traytor to his native Country. He was the Son of *Grono*, by his Wife *Edelflede* the Widow of *Edmund*, surnamed *Ironside*, King of *England*; and had the Title of *Tegengl*; though the *English*, when they had compelled *Gruffydh ap Conan* to flee to *Ireland* for safety, constituted him Prince of all *North-Wales*. After his death, *Richard Fitz-Baldwyn* laid siege to, and took the Castle of *Rydcors*, and forcibly drove *Howel ap Grono*, to whom King *Henry* had committed the custody of it, out of the Country. But *Howel* quickly returned, and with a high Spirit of Revenge, began to destroy and burn whatsoever he could meet with, and then meeting a Party of the *Normans* in their return homewards, he fell upon the flank of them with a very considerable slaughter; and so brought all the Country to his subjection, excepting some few Garrisons and Castles which would not surrender to him. The same time King *Henry* took away from *Saer* the Government of *Dyfed*, which formerly was *Iorwerth ap Blethyn*'s, and bestowed it upon *Gerald*, who had been some time Earl *Arnulph*'s Steward in those Parts; and therefore by reason of his knowledg of the Country, was in all probability best able to take upon him the Management of it. But the *Normans* in *Rydcors* Castle being sensible that they were not able to effect any thing against *Howel ap Grono* in open Field, after their accustomed manner, began to put that in execution by Treachery, which they could not compass by force of Arms. And how to make *Howel* a Sacrifice to those *Normans* he had lately slain, they could find no safer way than by corrupting one *Gwgan ap Meyric*, a Man in great Favour and Esteem with *Howel*, upon the account chiefly that one of his Children was nursed by *Gwgan*'s

Wife,

The History of WALES.

Wife. This ungrateful Villain, to carry on his wicked Intrigue the more unsuspected, gave Howel a very earnest invitation to his House to a Merriment, where, without any suspicion of Treachery, being come, he was welcomed with all the seeming Affection and Kindness imaginable. But no sooner was he settled, but *Gwgan* gave notice thereof to the *Norman* Garrisons; and therefore by break of day they entered the Town, and coming about the House where *Howel* lay in Bed, they presently gave a great shout. *Howel* hearing the noise, suspected something of Mischief, and therefore leaping in all haste out of Bed, he made to his Weapons, but could not find them, by reason that *Gwgan* had conveyed them away whilst he was asleep. And now being assured of Treachery in the case, and finding that his Men had fled for their Lives, he endeavour'd all he could to make his escape; but *Gwgan* and his Company were too quick for him; and so being secured, they strangled him, and deliver'd his Body to the *Normans*, who having cut off his Head, convey'd it to the Castle of *Rydcors*. This most villainous Murther, so barbarously committed upon the King's Lieutenant, was not in the least taken notice of; for King *Henry* was so unreasonably prejudiced in favour of the *Normans*, that whatever Misdemeanour, be it of never so high a nature, was by them committed, it was presently winked at, and let fall to the ground; whereas, if the *Welch* trespassed but against the least injunction of the King's Laws, they were most severely punished: which was the cause that they afterwards stood up against the King in their own defence, being by experience assured, that he minded nothing more than their utter Destruction.

A. D. 1103.

About this time *Anselm*, Archbishop of *Canterbury*, convened a Synod at *London*, wherein among other Injunctions then decreed, the Celibacy of the Clergy was enjoyned; Marriage being before ever allowed of in *Britain*, to them in Holy Orders. But this new Injunction created a great deal of Heat and Animosities among the Clergy, some approving of it as reasonable and orthodoxical; others condemning it, as an innovation, and contrary to the plain Letter of Scripture. But during thefe Difputes between the Clergy, King *Henry* being now in the Fifth Year of his Reign, failed over with a great Army into *Normandy*, where his Brother *Robert*, together with *Robert de Belefmo*, *Arnulph*, and *William* Earl of *Mortaign*, gave him battel; but the King having obtained the Victory, took the Duke his Brother, with *William* of *Mortaign*, Prifoners; and carrying them into *England*, he caufed firft his Brother *Robert*'s Eyes to be plucked out, and then condemned them both to perpetual imprifonment in the Caftle of *Cardyff*. About the fame time *Meyric* and *Gruffydh*, the Sons of *Trahaern ap Caradoc* were both flain by the means of *Owen ap Cadogan ap Blethyn*; whofe Uncle *Meredith ap Blethyn*, who had been Prifoner for a long time in *England*, now brake open the Prifon, wherein he was very narrowly confined; and returning to his own Country, had his Eftate reftored, which afterwards he quietly enjoyed.

A. D. 1104.

1105. The next Year a very difmal and calamitous Accident happening in the Low-Countries, proved very incommodious and prejudicial to the *Welch*; for a great part of *Flanders* being drowned by the overflowing of the Sea, the Inhabitants were compell'd to feek for fome other Country to dwell in, their own being now covered with Water. And therefore a great many being come over to *England*, they requefted of King *Henry* to affign them fome part of his Kingdom which was empty and void of Inhabitants, where they might fettle and plant themfelves. The King taking advantage of this charitable opportunity, and being in a manner affured, that thefe *Flemings* would be a confiderable Thorn in the fide of the *Welch*, beftowed upon them very liberally what was not juftly in his power to give; and appointed them the Country of *Ros*, in *Dyfed* or *Weft-Wales*, where they continue to this day. But *Gerald* the King's Lieutenant in thofe Parts, was refolved to be afore-hand with them, and rebuilt the Caftle of
Pembrock.

The History of WALES.

Pembrock, in a place called *Congarth Fechan*; whither he removed his Family and all his Goods. But here a very unfortunate accident happened to him; for *Cadwgan ap Blethyn* having prepared a sumptuous Feast in the *Christmas*, invited all the Lords to his Country-House in *Dyfed*, and among the rest his Son *Owen*, who lived in *Powys*. This young Gentleman being at his Father's House, and hearing *Nest* the Wife of *Gerald* universally praised for her incomparable Beauty, was so smitten with the rumour that went abroad of her, that by all means he must see the Lady, who was by all so much admired. And forasmuch as *Gwladys*, Wife to *Rhys ap Theodore*, and Mother to *Nest*, was the Daughter of *Rwalhon ap Confyn*, Cofin-German to *Cadwgan* his Father; under pretence of Friendship and Relation, he made bold to pay her a Visit. But finding the truth far to surpass the Fame that went of her, he returned home so inflam'd with her Charms, that not being able to keep the Mastery over himself, he went back again the very same night, and being attended by a company of wild, head-strong Youths, they privily entered into the Castle, and encompassing the Chamber about, where *Gerald* and his Wife lay, they set the House on fire. *Gerald* hearing a noise, would fain go out to know the meaning of such unseasonable Disturbance; but his Wife fearing some Treachery, persuaded him to make as private an Escape as he could; and then pulling up a Board in the Privy, let him go that way. Then returning to her Chamber, she would fain assure those notorious Youths, that there was no body besides her self and Children there; but this being not satisfactory, they forcibly broke in, and having searched every the most private Corner, and not finding *Gerald*, they took his Wife and two Sons, with a Son and a Daughter born by a Concubine, and carried them away to *Powys*; having first set fire to the Castle, and destroyed the Country as they went along. *Cadwgan*, *Owen*'s Father, hearing of what outragious Crime his Son had committed, was exceedingly concerned and sorry, chiefly because hereby he was like to incur King

A. D. 1106.

K   *Henry*'s

The History of WALES.

Henry's great Displeasure; and therefore he went with all speed to *Powys*, and desired his Son with all Intreaties, to send home to *Gerald* his Wife and Children, with whatever else he had taken away from him. But *Owen* was so amorously inexorable with respect to the Woman, that he would by no means part with her; however, upon her request he was willing to restore *Gerald* his Children back again, which forthwith he performed. But when *Richard* Bishop of *London*, whom King *Henry* had constituted Warden of the Marches, being now at *Shrewsbury*, heard of this, he sent for *Ithel* and *Madoc* the Sons of *Ryryd ap Blethyn*, Persons of great Power and Interest in *Wales*, promising them very considerable Reward, besides the Government of the whole Country, in case they could bring *Owen* and his Father *Cadwgan*, either dead or alive, to him, that he might revenge that hainous Affront which they had done to the King of *England*. With them he joyned *Lhywarch* the Son of *Trahaern ap Caradoc*, whose two Brethren *Owen* had slain, and *Uchtryd* the Son of *Edwyn*; which Four undertook to answer effectually the Bishop's Proposal to them. But when they had united their Forces, and began in an hostile manner to destroy the Country as they passed along; *Uchtryd* sent private notice before him, requiring all who were any way desirous of their own Safety, to come to him; because no Quarters was to be given to any that was found in the Country. The People being thus so opportunely forewarned, began to bethink with themselves how they might best avoid so eminent a danger; and thereupon some fled to *Arustly*, others to *Melienyth*, some to *Stradtywy*, and some to *Dyfed*; but in this latter place they met with very cold welcom; for *Gerald*, who was then very busie in exercising Revenge upon that Country, falling in among them, cut off a considerable number of them. The like fate befel them who escaped to *Arustly* and *Melienyth*; for *Walter* Bishop of *Hereford* having raised an Army in defence of the Town of *Caermyrdhyn*, before he could come thither, accidentally met with these stragling Fugitives, and

knowing

knowing what Country they belonged to, without any further Ceremony, he fell upon them, and put moſt of them to the Sword. But they who fled to *Stradtywy*, were gently received by *Meredith ap Rytherch*, and ſuch as reſorted to *Uchtryd*, were kindly entertained by him; and ſo he marched with the reſt of his Confederates to *Rydcors* Caſtle; it being the general opinion, that it was beſt to enter the Country by Night, and to take *Cadwgan* and *Owen* his Son by ſurprize. But *Uchtryd* reflecting upon the Difficulty of the Country, and how eaſily they might be entrapp'd by an Ambuſcade, diſſuaded them from any ſuch nocturnal Undertakings; and told them, that it was far more adviſable to enter the Country in good order, when the light gave the Soldiers opportunity to keep and obſerve their ranks. But whilſt they were thus conſidering of the moſt effectual way to carry on their purpoſe, *Owen* got a Ship at *Aberdyfi*, bound for *Ireland*; and eſcaping thither, avoided the narrow ſearch that was the following day made for them. But when neither Father nor Son could be found, all the fault was laid upon *Uchtryd*, who had diſſuaded them from falling upon the Caſtle unexpectedly; and therefore all they could do, ſince their eſcape, was to burn and deſtroy the Country; which they did effectually, excepting the two Sanctuaries of *Lhanpadarn* and *Lhandewi Brefi*; out of which however they took ſeveral Perſons who had eſcaped thither, and carried them away Priſoners to their ſeveral Countries. But *Owen*, with them, who were acceſſary to the burning of *Rydcors* Caſtle, being fled into *Ireland*, deſired the Umbrage and Protection of King *Murcart*; who received him very gladly, upon the account of their former acquaintance; for *Owen*, during the War betwixt the Earls of *Arundel* and *Cheſter*, and the *Welch*, had fled to King *Murcart*, and brought him very rich Preſents from *Wales*. *Cadwgan* all this while lay privately in *Powys*; but thinking it impoſſible to continue there long undiſcovered, he adjudged it his wiſer way to ſend to King *Henry*, and to declare his Innocency and Abhorrence of that Fact which his Son had

K 2 committed.

committed. The King was easily persuaded that the old Man was guiltless, and wholly ignorant of his Son's Crime; and therefore he gave him permission to remain in the Country, and to enjoy the Town and Lands he received by his Wife, who was the Daughter of a *Norman* Lord, called *Pygot de Say*. But his Lands in *Powys* were otherwise distributed; for his Nephews *Madoc* and *Ithel*, finding what Circumstances their Uncle *Cadwgan* lay under, upon the account of his Son *Owen*; they divided betwixt themselves such Lands as he and his Son possessed in *Powys*, though afterwards they could never agree about the equal distribution of it. To counter-ballance this, *Cadwgan* made such Friends to the King of *England*, that upon paying the Fine of 100 *l.* he had a grant of all his Lands in *Cardigan*, and a power to recall all the Inhabitants, who had rubb'd off upon the publication of the King's late Order, That no *Welchman* or *Norman* should dwell in *Cardigan*. Upon information of this grant to *Cadwgan*, several of them that retired to *Ireland* returned again privately to *Wales*, and lurkingly remained with their Friends; but *Owen* durst not appear in *Cardigan*, by reason that his Father had received that Country from King *Henry*, upon condition that he would never entertain or receive his Son, nor by any means succour him either with Men or Money. Nevertheless, *Owen* came to *Powys*, and would fain be reconciled to the King, and make an Attonement for his late Misdemeanour; but he could find no body that would venture to speak in his behalf, nor make the King acquainted with his desire and willingness to submit. And thus being hopeless and full of Despair, he could not possibly divine which way to turn himself; till at last, a very unexpected opportunity offered him means and occasion to oppose the *English*. The matter was this, there happened a Difference betwixt *Madoc ap Ryryd* and the Bishop of *London*, Lieutenant of the Marches of *Wales*, about certain *English* Felons; who being under the Protection of *Madoc*, he would not restore at the Bishop's request. The Bishop being much

offended

The History of WALES.

offended at *Madawc*'s denyal, threatned him very severely; and therefore to make all possible Preparations against an ensuing storm, *Madawc* sent to *Owen*, who heretofore was his greatest Enemy, desiring his help against the Bishop; and by this means being reconciled, they took their mutual Oaths not to betray each other, and that neither should make a separate Agreement with the *English*, without the Knowledg and Approbation of the other. And so uniting their Power, they spoiled and ravaged all the Country about them, destroying whatever they could meet with which belonged to those they had no kindness or affection for, without the least distinction of *English* or *Welch*.

Iorwerth ap Blethyn had been very unjustly detain'd in Prison all this time; and now King *Henry* calling to mind what Hardship he laboured under, and that he committed him to custody upon no pretence of Reason, sent to know of him, what he was willing to pay for his Liberty. *Iorwerth* being now almost ready to sink under a fatigue of so long Imprisonment, was glad to give any thing he was able, to obtain that which he had so long in vain hoped for; and therefore he promised either 300 *l.* in *specie*, or to the value of it in Cattel and Horses; for the payment of which, *Iorwerth* and *Ithel* the Sons of his Brother *Ryryd* were deliver'd for Pledges. Then the King released him out of Prison, and restored him all his Lands which were taken from him; and of the due for his Liberty, the King bestowed 10 *l.* upon *Henry*, *Cadwgan*'s Son by the Daughter of *Pygot de Say* the *Norman*. *Owen* and *Madawc* all this while committed all the waste and destruction possible, and cruelly annoyed both the *English* and *Normans*; and always withdrew and retired to *Iorwerth*'s Estate; which so troubled him, by reason of the King's strict Orders, not to permit *Owen* to come to his or *Cadwgan*'s Territories, that at length he sent to them this positive and peremptory Rebuke; " Since it hath pleas- " ed God to place us in the midst of our Enemies, " and to deliver us into their hands; and hath so far " weakened us, as that we are not able to do any thing

A. D.
1107.

" by

"by our own strength; and your Father *Cadwgan* and
"my self, are particularly commanded, under Penalty
"of forfeiting our Lands and Estates, not to afford you
"any Succour or Refuge during these your rebellious
"Practices; therefore as a Friend I intreat you, com-
"mand you as a Lord, and desire you as a Kinsman,
"that you come no more to mine or your Father *Ca-*
"*dwgan*'s Territories. *Owen* and *Madawc* receiving
such a presumptuous Message, were the more enraged,
and in the way of a malignant retribution, did more
frequently than heretofore, shelter themselves in *Ior-*
werth's Country; in so much, that at last, since that
they would neither by Threats nor Intreaties desist
from their wonted Courses, he was forced to gather
his Power, and to drive them out by force of Arms.
Being chased out hence, they made In-roads into
Uchtryd's Country in *Merionythshire*; but *Uchtryd*'s
Sons, being then in *Cyveilioc*, hearing of it, they sent
to the People of the Country, with positive Orders to
oppose and resist any offer they would make to enter
the Countrey. The People, tho wanting a skilful
Commander, were resolv'd to do as much as lay in
their power; and so meeting with them by the way,
they set upon them so furiously, that *Owen* and *Ma-*
dawe, tho after a brave Defence, were forced to bear
back; and to take the heels; *Owen* to *Cardigan* to his
Father *Cadwgan*, and *Madawc* to *Powys*. Yet all this
Misfortune could not suppress the restless Spirit of
Owen; for as soon as he could rally together his scatter'd Troops, he made divers In-roads into *Dyfed*, and
carrying away several Persons to the Ships, that they
came in from *Ireland*; he first ransom'd them, and
then listing them under his own Command, made
such addition to his Army, that he ventur'd to set
upon a Town in *Dyfed* belonging to the *Flemings*, and
having rased it to the ground, he returned to *Cardi-*
gan; having no regard to what Inconveniency might
befall his Father from the King of *England*, upon this
account; which a little afterwards unhappily fell out.
For it happen'd that some of *Owen*'s Men having had
intelligence, that a certain Bishop called *William de*
Brabant,

The History of WALES.

Brabant, was upon his Journey through that Country to the Court of *England*, laid wait for his coming; who without any apprehension of Treachery, passing through the Country, was unexpectedly slain, he and all his Retinue. *Iorwerth* and *Cadwgan* were then at Court, to speak with King *Henry*, concerning certain Business of their own; but whilst they discoursed the King, in comes a *Fleming*, that was a Brother to the deceased Bishop, and with a very loud Exclamation, complained how that *Owen*, *Cadwgan*'s Son, had slain his Brother and the rest of his Company; and that he was succour'd and entertained in *Cadwgan*'s Country. King *Henry* hearing this, was wrathfully displeased at such cruel Barbarity, that a Person of that Quality and Profession should be so treacherously murther'd; and therefore he asked *Cadwgan* what he could say to the matter; who answered, that what had so unhappily fell out, was done without the least of his knowledge or approbation, and therefore desired his Majesty to impute all the Blame and Guilt of that unfortunate Action to his Son *Owen*. But King *Henry* was so far from being satisfied with this Reply, that he told *Cadwgan* in a violent passion, That since he could not keep his Son so, but that he was aided and continually entertained in his Country, he would bestow it upon another Person, who was better able and more willing to keep him out; and would allow him a Maintenance upon his own proper Charges, upon these Conditions, That he should not enter into *Wales* any more, without his farther Orders; and so granting him Twenty Days for the ordering his Affairs, he gave him liberty to retire to any part of his Dominions, excepting *Wales*. When *Owen* and *Madawc* were informed how *Cadwgan* was treated by the King of *England*, and that *Cardigan*, which was their chiefest place of refuge, was to be given to another Person, they thought that their Condition by this time was desperate, and that they had not better stay any longer in *Britain*; and therefore with all speed they took shipping for *Ireland*, where they were sure to be honourably entertained by King *Murkart*. Then King

Henry sent for *Gilbert Strongbow*, Earl of *Strygill*, a Person of noted Worth and Valour, and one who had often sued to the King for to grant him some Lands in *Wales*, and bestowed upon him all the Lands and Inheritance of *Cadwgan ap Blethyn*, in case he could conquer and bring the Country under. *Gilbert* very thankfully accepted of the Proposal, and having drawn together all the Forces he was able to raise, he passed to *Wales*, and being come to *Cardigan*, without the least Trouble or Opposition, he reduced the whole Country to his Subjection. The first thing he did, was the best he could to secure himself in this new-purchased Inheritance; in order to which, he erected two Castles, one upon the Frontiers of *North-Wales*, upon the Mouth of the River *Yſtwyth*, a Mile distant from *Lhanbadarn*; the other towards *Dyfed*, upon the River *Teifi*, at a place called *Dyngerant*; where, as some think, *Roger Montgomery* had sometime before laid the Foundation of *Cilgarran* Castle. *Owen* and *Madawc* were all this while in *Ireland*; but this latter being at length tired with the Country, and not willing to endure the Manners and Customs of the *Irish*, came over for *Wales*, and passed to the Country of his Uncle *Iorwerth*. *Iorwerth* being acquainted with his arrival, was fearful to suffer the same Fate with his Brother *Cadwgan*, by winking at his being there; and therefore without any regard to Relation or Consanguinity, he presently issued out a Proclamation, forbidding any of his Subjects under a great Penalty to receive him, but that they should account him an open Enemy to their Country, and endeavour all they could to secure him, and to bring him Prisoner before him. When *Madawc* understood this, how that his Person was in continual danger whilst he remained there; having drawn to him all the Out-laws and Villains in the Country, he kept in the Rocks and Mountains, devising all the ways and means he could to be revenged upon *Iorwerth*; and so made a private League and Agreement with *Lhywarch ap Trahaern*, who for a long time had been a mortal Enemy of *Iorwerths*. These two Associates, having intelligence

that

The History of WALES.

that *Iorwerth* lay one night at *Caereineon*, gathered all their strength, and came and encompassed the House at Midnight; which when *Iorwerth*'s Servants perceived, they arose and defended the House with all the Might they could; but the Assailants at last putting the House on fire, they were glad, as many as could, to escape through the Flames; the greatest part being forced to yield, either to the Enemies Sword, or the more conquering Fire. *Iorwerth* seeing no remedy, but that he must undergo the same Fate as his Men had done, chose rather to dye in the presence of his Enemies, with his Sword in his Hand, than to commit his Life to the cowardly Flames; and therefore rushing out with great Violence, he was received upon the points of the Enemies Spears, and so being tossed into the Fire, he miserably perished by a double death. As soon as King *Henry* heard of his Death, he sent for *Cadwgan* to him, and gave him all his Brother's Estate, being *Powys-land*; and promising his Son *Owen* his Pardon, upon condition he would demean himself quietly and loyally hereafter, willed him to send for him back from *Ireland*. King *Henry* also about this time, married his natural Son *Robert* to *Mabil* Daughter and sole Heir to *Robert Fiz-hamon* Lord of *Glamorgan*, in whose Right this *Robert* became Lord of *Glamorgan*, being before by the King created E. of *Glocester*; by whom the Castle of *Cardaf* was built.

But *Madawc* finding the matter nothing mended, and that his other Uncle *Cadwgan*, who lay under the same Obligation to the King of *England*, ruled the Country, hid himself in the most private and inaccessible places, watching only an opportunity to commit the like Fact upon *Cadwgan*, and to murder him by one treacherous way or another. And this he effected in a little time; for *Cadwgan* having reduced the Country to some sort of Settlement and Quietness, and restored the Courts of Judicature, where he sate in person to administer Justice; came with the rest of the Elders of the Country to *Trallwng*, now *Pool*; and having begun to build a Castle, he thought to make that the constant Seat of his Habitation. *Madawc* understanding his Design, laid in ambush for him in his way to *Trallwng*; and as *Cadwgan* unconcernedly passed by, without the least suscicion of Treachery, he suddenly set upon him, and slew him, without allowing him any time either to fight or escape. Then he sent presently a message to *Shrewsbury*, to the Bishop of *London*, the King's Lieutenant in the Marches, to put him in mind of his former Promises to him, when he chased *Owen* out of the Country; because that the Bishop bearing an inveterate Enmity to *Cadwgan*, and his Son *Owen*, granted *Madawc* such Lands, as his Brother *Ithel* was possessed of. But *Meredith ap Blethyn*, being informed of the death of both his Brothers, went in all haste to the King, desiring of him the Lands of *Iorwerth* in *Powys*, which he had lately granted to *Cadwgan*; which the King granted him, till such time as *Owen* should return from *Ireland*. *Owen* did not stay long before he came over; and then going to King *Henry*, he was honourably received, and had all his Fathers Estate restored to him; whereupon, in gratitude of this signal Favour, he voluntarily promised to pay the King a considerable Fine, for the due payment of which, he gave very responsible Pledges. *Madawc* finding himself alone to be left in the lurch, and that he had no seeming Power to bear Head against the King, thought it also his wisest way to make what Reconciliation he could; and therefore he offered the King a very great Fine, if he should peaceably enjoy his former Estate, promising withal, never to molest or disturb any one that was subject to the Crown of *England*. King *Henry* willing to bring all matters to a settled condition, readily granted his Request, and conferred upon him all he could reasonably ask for; only with this Proviso, that upon his peril he should provide for the Relations of them whom he had so basely murthered.

A. D. 1109. And thus all matters being brought to a peaceable conclusion in *Wales*; the next Year, *Robert de Belesmo*, who had been one of the chief Instruments of these *Welch* Disturbances, in that great Rebellion, which himself, with *Roger de Montgomery*, Earl of *Salop*, and his

his Brother, *Arnulph* Earl of *Pembroke* had raised against the King; was taken Prisoner by King *Henry* in *Normandy*, and committed to perpetual Imprisonment in *Warham* Castle. The Year following, *Meredith ap Blethyn* detached a considerable Party of his Men, to make Incursions into the Country of *Lhywarch ap Trahaern ap Gwyn*, who was an inveterate Enemy of himself and *Owen*; by reason that by his Aid and Instigation, *Madawc* was encouraged to kill his Uncles *Iorwerth* and *Cadwgan*. These Men as they passed through *Madawc*'s Country, met a Person in the night-time who belonged to *Madawc*; who being asked where his Master was, after some pretence of ignorance, at last through fear confessed, that he was not far from that place. Therefore lying quietly there all Night, by break of day they arose to look out their Game; and unexpectedly surpizing *Madawc*, they slew a great number of his Men, and took himself Prisoner; and so carrying him to their Lord, they deliver'd him up, as the greatest Honour of their Expedition. *Meredith* was not a little proud of his Prisoner, and therefore to ingratiate himself the more with his Nephew *Owen*, he committed him to safe Custody, till he was sent for; who coming thither streight, *Meredith* delivered *Madawc* up to him. *Owen*, though he had the greatest reason for the most cruel Revenge, by reason that both his Father and Uncle were basely murthered by this *Madawc*, would not put him to death, remembring the intimate Friendship and Oaths that had passed betwixt them; but however, to secure him from any future Mischief he might practise, he pulled out his Eyes, and then set him at liberty. But least he should be capable of any Revenge, by reason of his Estate and Strength in the Country, *Meredith* and *Owen* thought fit to divide his Lands betwixt them; which were, *Caernarvon*, *Aberbiw*, with the third part of *Deuthwfyr*.

A. D. 1110.

These home-bread Disturbances being pretty well abated, a greater storm arose from abroad; for the next Year, King *Henry* prepared a mighty Army to enter into *Wales*, being provoked thereto by the request

1111.

of

of those who enjoyed a great part of the Welchmens Lands, but would not be satisfied till they got all. For *Gilbert Strongbow* Earl of *Strygill*, upon whom the King had bestowed *Cardigan*, made great Complaints of *Owen ap Cadwgan*, declaring how that he received and entertained such Persons as spoiled and robbed in his Country; and *Hugh* Earl of *Chester* made the like of *Gruffydh ap Conan* Prince of *North-Wales*, how that his Subjects and the Men of *Grono ap Owen ap Edwyn* Lord of *T'gengl*, unreproved, waited, and burnt the Country of *Cheshire*; and to aggravate the matter the more, he added farther, that *Gruffydh* neither owed any Service, nor paid any Tribute to the King. Upon these Complaints, King *Henry* was so cruelly enraged, that he swore he would not leave one living Creature remaining in *North-Wales* and *Powys-land*; but having extirpated utterly the present Race of People, he would plant a Colony of new Inhabitants. And then dividing his Army into three parts, he deliver'd one to the conduct of the Earl of *Strygill*, to go against *South-Wales*, which comprehended the whole Power of the fourth part of *England* and *Cornwal*: The next Battel was designed against *North-Wales*, in which was all the strength of *Scotland* and the North, and was commanded by *Alexander* King of the *Scots*, and *Hugh* Earl of *Chester*: the Third the King led himself against *Powys*, wherein was contained the whole strength of the middle part of *England*. *Meredith ap Blethyn* hearing of these mighty Preparations, and being informed that this vast Army was design'd against *Wales*, was quickly apprehensive that the *Welch* were not able to make any great Defence; and therefore thought it his safest way to provide for himself beforehand; and so coming to the King, yielded himself up to his Mercy. But *Owen* fearing to commit himself to those whom he knew so greedily to covet his Estate, and whom he was assured were far more desirous to dispossess the *Welch* of their Lands, than any other way to punish them for former Crimes and Miscarriages, fled to *Gruffydh ap Conan* to *North-Wales*. Upon that, King *Henry* converted his whole Force that

way,

way, and came himself as far as *Murcaftelh*, and the *Scotch* King to *Pennant Bachwy*; but the People flying to the Mountains, carried with them all the Cattel and Provision they had; so that the *English* could not follow them, and as many as attempted to come at them, were either slain or wounded in the streights. But *Alexander* King of the *Scots* finding that nothing could possibly be effected against the *Welch*, as long as they kept the Rocks and Mountains, sent to Prince *Gruffydh*, advising him to submit himself to the King, promising him all his Interest to obtain an honourable Peace. But the Prince was too well acquainted with *English* Promises, and therefore refused his Proposals; and so King *Henry* being very unwilling to return without doing something in this Expedition, sent to *Owen* to forsake the Prince, who was not able to defend himself, but was ready to strike a Peace with the *Scottish* King and the Earl of *Chester*. But this cunning Infinuation would not take effect; for *Owen* was for his life as distrustful of King *Henry* as Prince *Gruffydh*; and therefore he would hearken to no Intreaties for revolting from him, who had all this while afforded him Refuge, till at length his Uncle *Meredith*, an old infinuating Politician, persuaded him, with much ado, not to forsake the King of *England*'s Proposals, who offered him all his Lands without Tribute, in case he would come to his side; and therefore *Meredith* advised him instantly to accept of his offer, before Prince *Gruffydh* made a Peace with the King, which if it was once done, he would be glad upon any score to purchase the King's Mercy. *Owen* being prevailed upon by such Arguments, came to the King, who received him very gratiously, and told him, that because he believed his Promise, he would not only perform that, but likewise exalt him above any of his Kindred, and grant him his Lands free from any payment of Tribute. Prince *Gruffydh* perceiving how that *Owen* had submitted to the King, thought it also his wisest way to sue for Peace; and so promising the King a great Sum of Money, a Peace was then actually agreed upon, and confirmed; which the King of
England

England was the more ready to consent to, because he found it impossible to do him any hurt, whilst he continued encamped in that place. Some affirm, that the submission as well of Prince *Gruffydh* as *Owen*, was procured by the Policy of *Mered:th ap Blethyn* and the Earl of *Chester*; this last working with *Gruffydh*, and assuring him that *Owen* had made his Peace with the King before any such thing was in agitation, so that the Prince yielding somewhat to the Earl's Request, if *Owen* had gone contrary to his Oath, which they had mutually taken, not to make any Peace with the *English*, without one anothers Knowledge, seemed to incline to a Peace. On the other hand, *Meredith* going in Person to his Nephew *Owen*, affirmed for Truth, that the Prince and the Earl of *Chester* were actually agreed, and that the Prince was on his Journey to the King to make his Submission. And in the mean while *Meredith* took especial care that all Messengers betwixt the Prince and *Owen* should be intercepted, and by that means *Owen* willfully submitted himself to the King.

King *Henry* having thus finished and brought to an end all his Business in *Wales*, calling *Owen* to him, told him, that in case he would go over with him to *Normandy*, and there be faithful to him, he would upon his return confirm all his Promises upon him; and so *Owen* accepting of the King's Offer, went with him to *Normandy*, where he behaved himself so gallantly, that he was made a Knight; and after his return the Year following, he had all his Lands and Estate confirmed unto him. About the same time *Griffri* Bishop of St. *Davids* died, and King *Henry* appointed to succeed him one *Barnard* a *Norman*, much against the Good-will and Inclination of the *Welch*, who before this time were ever used to Elect their own Bishop. And this Year the rumour of *Gruffydh* Son to *Rhys ap Theodore* was spread throughout *South-Wales*, who, as the report went, for fear of the King had been from a Child brought up in *Ireland*, and having come over about two Years afore, past his time privately among his Relations, particularly with

The History of WALES.

with *Gerald* Steward of *Pembroke* his Brother-in-Law. And now the noise of a new Prince being spread abroad, it came at last to the Ears of the King of *England*, that a certain Person appeared in *Wales*, who pretended to be the Son of *Rhys ap Theodore* late Prince of *South Wales*, and laid Claim to that Principality, which was now in the King's Hands. King *Henry* being somewhat concerned with such a Report, and fearing lest that this new Starter should create him some greater trouble, he thought to nip him in the bud, and sent down Orders to apprehend him. But *Gruffydh ap Rhys* being aware of the Traps laid against him, sent to *Gruffydh ap Cenan* Prince of *North-Wales*, desiring his Assistance, and that he might have Liberty to remain safe in his Country, which *Gruffydh* for his Father's account, readily granted, and treated him honourably. A little after, his Brother *Howel* who was imprisoned by *Ardulph* Earl of *Pembroke* in the Castle of *Montgomery*, where he had remained for a great while, made his escape and fled to his Brother, then with *Gruffydh ap Conan* in *North-Wales*. But King *Henry* being informed that *Gruffydh ap Rhys* and his Brother *Howel* were entertained by the Prince of *North-Wales*, sent very smooth Letters to *Gruffydh ap Conan*, desiring to speak with him, who being come, he received him with all the Tokens of Honor and Friendship, and bestowed upon him very rich Presents, just after the *Norman* Policy, who usually make very much of those whom they design afterwards to be serviceable to them. After some time's general Discourse, King *Henry* came at length to the main Point, and promised the Prince even Mountains of Gold, in case he would send *Gruffydh ap Rhys* or his Head to him, which the Prince overcome by such fair Words and large Promises, promised to perform, and so returned joyfully home, big with the expectation of his future Reward. But some who wished better to *Gruffydh ap Rhys* and his Brother *Howel*, presently suspected the occasion of the King's Message, and therefore they advised them to withdraw themselves privately for some time, till

Prince

Prince *Gruffydh*'s mind be better underſtood, and whether he had made any agreement with the King of *England* to betray them to him. As ſoon as the Prince was returned to his Palace at *Aberffraw*, he preſently enquired for *Gruffydh ap Rhys*, and learning in a little time where he was, he ſent a Troop of Horſe to re-call him to his Court; but *Gruffydh* hearing of their approach, with all ſpeed made his eſcape to the Church of *Aberdaron*, and took Sanctuary there. But Prince *Gruffydh* was ſo reſolute to make his Promiſe good to the King of *England*, that without any reſpect to the Religious place he had eſcaped too, commanded the ſame Meſſengers to return, and to bring him away by Force, which the Clergy of the Country unanimouſly withſtood, proteſting that they would not ſee the Liberties of the Church in the leaſt infringed. And whilſt the Clergy and the Prince's Officers were thus at debate; that ſame night, ſome who had Compaſſion upon the young Prince, and ſeeing how greedily his Life was thirſted for, conveyed him away out of *North Wales* to *Straywy* in *South-Wales*. And ſo being delivered from the treacherous and more diſhonourable Practices of the Prince of *North Wales*, he was forced for the Defence of his own Life, to bid open Defiance to the King of *England*, and thereupon having raiſed all the Forces which the ſhortneſs of the opportunity would permit, he made War upon the *Flemings* and *Normans*.

1113. The next year, he laid Siege to the Caſtle which ſtood over-againſt *Arberth*, and winning the ſame, made it plain with the Ground, and from thence marched to *Lhanymdhyfiy* Caſtle, belonging to *Richard de Ptons*, upon whom the King had beſtowed *Cantref Bychan*, but the Garriſon commanded by *Meredith ap Rytherch ap Caradoc*, ſo manfully defended it, that *Gruffydh* after killing only ſome few of the Beſieged, and burning the Out-works, was forced to remove with no ſmall Loſs of his own Men. Finding this place impregnable, he came before *Abertawy*-Caſtle, which was built by *Henry Beaumont* Earl

Earl of *Warwick*, but this proving too strong to be quickly surrendered, after he had burnt some of the outward Buildings, he returned to *Stratywy*, burning and destroying all the Country as he went along. And now his Fame being spread abroad thro' all the Country, all the wild and head-strong Youth, and they whose Fortunes were desperate, resorted unto him from all Parts, by which means being waxed Strong and Numerous, he made in-Roads into *Ros* and *Dyfed* spoiling and destroying the Country before him. The *Normans* and *Flemings* were cruelly enraged with these continual Depredations, and how to remedy this Mischief, was not easily determined; but after long Consultation, they thought it the best way to call together such *Welch* Lords as were Friends to the King of *England*, such were *Owen ap Rhytherch*, and *Rhytherch ap Theodore*, with his Sons *Meredith* and *Owen* whose Mother was *Heynyth* the Daughter of *Blethyn ap Confyn*, and *Owen ap Caradoc* the Son of *Gwenlhian* another Daughter of *Blethyn*, and *Meredith ap Rhytherch*. These protesting their Loyalty and Fidelity to King *Henry* were desired to defend the King's Castle of *Carmardhyn*, and that by turns; *Owen ap Caradoc* the first Fortnight, and then by succession by *Rhytherch ap Theodore* and *Mered th ap Rhytherch*. *Owen* undertook the Defence of *Carmardhyn* Castle for the time required of him, and *Blethyn ap Gadifor* had committed to him the Government of *Abercomyn*, or *Abercorran*-Castle, which appertained to *Robert Courtmain*. But for all these Preparations, *Gruffydh ap R ys* had a wishful Eye upon *Carmardhyn*, and therefore he sent out some Spies to learn the Strength and Condition of the Town, who bringing him a very kind and hopeful Account, he decamped by Night, and rushing suddenly into the Town, ordered his Men to make a great shout, thereby to strike a great Terror into those within. *Owen ap Caradoc* the Governour, being surprized with such an unexpected uproar, made all possible haste to the place where he had heard the shouting, and thinking that his Men were at his

L   Heels,

Heels, fell in among the Enemy; but having none to support him, his Men being all fled, he was after a manful Defence cut in pieces, and so the Town being taken, *Gruffydh* burnt every thing to the ground, excepting the Castle, which was also sore defaced. And then returning with a great deal of Spoil and Booty to his usual residence at *Stratywy*; his Forces were considerably increased by the accession of many stout young Men, who came to him from all Quarters, and thought that Fortune so prospered his Arms, that no body was able to stand before him. After this he marched to *Gwyr*, but *William de Londres* thinking it impossible to stand before him, forsook the Castle with all his Men in all haste, so that when *Gruffydh* was come thither, he found a great deal of Cattel and Spoil, and none to own them, and therefore having burnt down the Castle, he carried away every thing of Value in the Country. When the *Cardigan-shire* Men heard how fortunately he succeeded in all his Attempts, and being extreamly fearful, lest his next Expedition should be against them, sent to him, desiring him, as being their near Relation and Country man, to take upon him the Rule and Government over them. *Gruffydh* willingly accepted of their Offer, and coming thither, was joyfully received by the Chief Men in the Country, who were *Cadifor ap Grono, Howel ap Dinerth,* and *Trahaern ap Ithel,* which three Persons had forsaken *Dyfed,* by reason that it was so thwacked with *Normans, Flemings* and *English* Men. Nor was *Cardigan* free from Strangers, who pretended to sway and rule the Country, but the People bearing in mind the continual Wrong and Oppression they received from them, bore an inveterate hatred to them, and were very glad to be delivered from their insolent and imperious Oppressours. For King *Henry* what by Force and Banishment of those that stood up stiff for their Liberty, and what by corrupting of those that were wavering, had brought all that Country to his subjection, and bestowed what Lands he thought fit upon his *English* or *Norman* Favourites. But notwithstanding

withstanding the Strength of the *English* in this Country, *Gruffydh* was not a whit cast down, but boldly coming on to *Cardigan Ifcoed*, he laid Siege to a Fort that Earl *Gilbert* and the *Flemings* had built at a place called *Blaen Porth Gwythan*. After divers Assaults, and the killing of several of the besieged, with the loss only of one of his Men, *Gruffydh* took the place, and rasing it to the ground, brought all the Country thereabouts to subjection. This Action proved very fatal to the *English*, for immediately upon this, they began to forsake their Houses and Habitations, as thinking it too hot for them to stay any longer in the Country, and so the *Welch* burnt and destroyed as far as *Penwedic* all the Houses of those Strangers whom Earl *Gilbert* had brought with him. Then *Gruffydh* besieged the Castle of *Stradpythylh* which belonged to *Ralph* Earl *Gilbert*'s Steward, and having made himself Master of it, he put all the Garrison to the Sword. Removing from thence, he incamped at *Glafgryg* a mile from *Lhanbadarn*, purposing to Besiege *Aberyftwith*-Castle next morning, but for want of Provision necessary for his Army, he was forced to make bold with some Cattel which grazed within the Limits of the Sanctuary. And here it may be observed, that not only Men enjoyed the Privilege of these Sanctuaries, but also Cattel and Horses, and whatever else lived within the Liberties of them. But the day following, *Gruffydh* marched disorderly towards the Castle, being apprehensive of no great opposition, by reason that he was ignorant of the number of the Garrison, and so encamping upon an opposite Hill, which was divided from the Castle by a River, with a Bridge over it, he called a Council to determin with what Engines they might with best Success play against it, and so make a general Assault. The *Normans* observing their Disorder, very cunningly sent out some of their Archers to skirmish with them, and so by little and little to entice them to the Bridge, where some of the best armed Horse-men were ready to issue out upon them. The *Welch* not thinking the Garrison to be

L 2 so

so strong, approached near the Bridg, still skirmishing with the *Normans*, who pretended to give ground; but when they came very near, out sallies one on horse back, who would fain pass the Bridg; but being received upon the points of their Spears, he began to flag, and as he endeavoured to return, he fell off his Horse, and so the *Welch* pursued him over the Bridg. The *Englishmen* seeing this, fled towards the Castle, and the *Welch* with all speed followed them to the top of the Hill; but whilst they thought that the day was their own, up rises a Party of Horse which lay in ambuscade under the Hill, and standing betwixt the *Welch* and the Bridg, prevented any Succour to come to them. And the *Welch* being thus hemm'd in betwixt both Parties, the former recoiling with greater strength, were so unmercifully cut off, that scarce one Man was left living. When the rest of the *Welch* Army, that staid on the other side of the River, saw what number the Garrison contained, and that they were strong beyond their expectation, presently decamped, and with all speed departed out of the Country.

When King *Henry* was informed of all the Mischief and Cruelties that *Gruffydh ap Rhys* had committed among his Subjects in *Wales*, he sent for *Owen ap Cadwgan*, desiring him and *Lhywarch ap Trahaern* to use all the effectual Method possible to take or kill the Arch-Rebel *Gruffydh*, promising very speedily to send his Son *Robert* with an Army to *Wales* for that purpose. *Owen* being very proud that the King put such Confidence in him, encouraged his Men to be now so industrious to merit the King's Favour, as they had been formerly to deserve his Displeasure; and so joyning his Forces with *Lhywarch*, they both marched to meet Prince *Robert* at *Stratymy*, where they supposed *Gruffydh ap Rhys* had hid himself in the Woods. When they were come to the Frontiers of the Country, they made a Vow, that they would let neither Man, Woman, or Child escape alive; which so affrighted the People of the Country, that all made what shift they could to save their Lives,

some

some by fleeing to the Woods and Mountains, and some by getting into the King's Castles, from whence they had come but a little before. Then *Owen* and *Lhywarch* separated with distinct Parties to scour the Woods, which about *Stratywy* are very desertous; and *Owen* having entred with an Hundred Men, presently discovered the tract of Men and Cattel, and follow'd their Foot-steps so close, that within a little while he overtook them; and having slain a great many of them, and put the rest to flight, he carried away all their Cattel back to his Army. But whilst *Owen* was busie in searching the Woods, *Gerald* Steward of *Pembrock*, who with a great Power of *Flemings* was upon his march to joyn the King's Son, met with them who fled from *Owen*; who desiring help of *Gerald*, declared how *Owen* had forcibly drove them out, slain a great many of their Companions, and spoiled them of all their Goods. *Gerald* and his *Flemings* understanding that *Owen* was so nigh with such a small number of Men, thought he had now very convenient opportunity to be revenged of him upon the account of his Wife; and therefore to make sure Work with him, he pursued him close into the Woods. *Owen* being fore-warned by his Men that a great number followed him, and advised to make all speed to get away, was deaf to all such Counsels, as thinking that they of whom his Men were so much afraid of, were the King's Friends, and therefore their Integrity need not be questioned, since they all had respect to the same common Cause. But he found, that a private Quarrel is sometime more regarded than the publick Good; and therefore when *Gerald* was advanced within bow-shot, he greeted him with a Volloy of Arrows, to shew how great a Friend he was; but *Owen*, tho persuaded to flee, was so little terrified at such an unwelcom Salutation, that tho' the Enemy were Seven to One, yet he told them, that they were but *Flemings*, and such as always trembled at the hearing of his Name. And then falling on with a great deal of Courage, he was at the first On-set struck with an Arrow into the Heart, of which Wound he presently

L 3 dyed;

dyed; which when his Men saw, they all fled, and brought word to *Lhywarch* and the rest of their Fellows of what had happen'd; and so suspecting the King's Army, seeing they could not be trusted in their Service, they all returned to their respective Countries. *Owen* being in this manner unhappily slain, his Brethren divided his Lands betwixt them; excepting *Caereneon*, which properly belonged to *Madawc ap Ryryd ap Blethyn*; and which he had forcibly taken away from his Uncle *Meredith*. His Father *Cadwgan* had several Children by different Women; and besides himself, he had Issue *Madawc* by *Gwenlbian* the Daughter of *Gruffydh ap Conan*; *Eineon* by *Sanna* the Daughter of *Dyfnwal*; *Morgan*, by *Efelhiw* or *Elhiw* the Daughter of *Cadifor ap Colhoyn* Lord of *Dyfed*; *Henry* and *Gruffydh* were by the Daughter of the Lord *Pigot* his wedded Wife; *Meredith* by *Eururon Hoedliw*; and himself by *Inerth* the Daughter of *Edwyn*. But a while afterwards, *Eineon ap Cadwgan* and *Gruffydh ap Meredith ap Blethyn*, besieged the Castle of *Cymmer* in *Merionythshire*, which was lately built by *Uchtryd ap Edwyn*; for *Cadwgan* had bestowed upon *Uchtryd* his Cosin-German *Merionyth* and *Cyfeilioc*, upon condition, that in all Cases he should appear his Friend, and his Sons after him; contrary to which Promise he bore no manner of regard to *Cadwgan*'s Children after *Owen*'s death; but to strengthen himself the better, he erected this Castle of *Cymmer*, which very much displeased many of *Cadwgan*'s Sons. And therefore *Eineon* and *Gruffydh*, to make *Uchtryd* sensible of his Error in despising of them, furiously set upon *Cymmer* Castle, and having slain divers of the Garrison, the rest surrender'd themselves; and so taking possession of it, they divided the Country betwixt them; *Mowdhwy Cyfycilioc* and half *Penlbyn* to *Gruffydh ap Meredith*; and the other half of *Penlhyn* with all *Merionyth* to *Eineon*.

The next Year King *Henry* sailed with a great Army into *Normandy*, against the *French* King, who with the Earl of *Flanders* and others, went about to make *William* the Son of *Robert Curthoise* Duke of
Normandy;

The History of WALES.

Normandy; but at the appearance of the King of England, they all scatter'd, and laid aside their intended Design. About the same time Gilbert Strongbow Earl of Strigill, to whom King Henry had given all Cardigan, departed this Life, after a long Fit of a Consumption; much to the Joy and Satisfaction of the Welch, who were in great measure displeased, that they should be deprived of their own natural Lord Cadwgan, from whom this Country was taken away, and be forced to serve and be subject to a Stranger, whose Kindness they had no great reason to expect. But the Year following, an irreconcilable Quarrel happen'd betwixt Howel ap Ithel Lord of Ros and Ryfonioc, now Denbigh-land, and Riryd and Lhywarch the Sons of Owen ap Edwyn. And when they could not otherwise agree, they broke out into open War; and thereupon Howel sent to Meredith ap Blethyn, and to Eineon and Madawc, Cadwgan's Sons; who came down from Merionyth with a Party of Four Hundred well-disciplin'd Men, and encamped in Dyffryn Clwyd. Riryd and Lhywarch on the other hand, desired the Assistance of their Cosins the Sons of Uchtryd; and so both Armies meeting in the Vale of Clwyd, they fell to Blows with a great deal of Spirit and Alacrity, and after a tedious and a bloody Fight, Lhywarch, Owen ap Edwyn's Son, was at last slain, and with him Iorwerth the Son of Nudh, a noble and a valorous Person; and Riryd was forced to make his Escape by flight. But though Howel obtained the Victory, yet he did not long survive his slain Enemies; for having received a desperate Wound in the Action, dyed of it within Fourty Days; and then Meredith ap Blethyn, and the Sons of Cadwgan finding it dangerous to stay longer there, for fear of some French, who lay garrisoned in Chester, returned home with all speed.

A. D.
1115.

King Henry was still in Normandy, and about this time, a very great Battel was fought betwixt him, and the French King, who was shamefully vanquished and overthrown, and had a great number of his Nobles taken Prisoners. But as King Henry returned the following Year for England, one of the Ships happened,

1116.

117.

by

by the negligence of the Pilot, to be cast away, wherein perished the King's two Sons, *William* who was legitimate, and Heir apparent to the Crown, and *Richard* his base Son; together with his Daughter and Neece, and several others of his Nobility, to the number in all of 150 Persons. This unparallel'd Loss of so many Kindred and Friends did not perplex his Mind so long, but that within a short time, he began to solace and raise his drooping Spirits with the thoughts of a new Wife; and having married *Adelice* the Daughter of the Duke of *Lovain*, he purposed to go against *Wales*, and having prepared his Forces, he led them in person to *Powys-land*. When *Meredith ap Blethyn* and *Eineon*, *Madawc* and *Morgan*, the Sons of *Cadwgan* and Lords of the Country heard of it, they sent to *Gruffydh ap Conan* Prince of *North Wales*, desiring some help at his hands; who flatly refused, assuring them, that because he was at peace with the King of *England*, he could neither with Honour nor Safety send them any Succour, nor permit them to come within his Dominions. The Lords of *Powys* receiving this unwelcom Answer, and having now no manner of hopes of any Aid, were resolved however to defend themselves as well as they could; and therefore they thought it the most effectual means to annoy the Enemy, and to keep them from entering into the Country, was to observe and defend the Streights, by which the Enemy must of necessity pass. Neither were they out in their Policy; for it happened that the King himself, with a small number, advanced to one of these narrow Passages, the rest of the Army, by reason of their Carriages, having taken some compass about; which the *Welch* perceiving, presently poured a Shower of Arrows upon them, and the advantage of the ground giving help to their Execution, they slew and wounded a great many of the *English*. The King himself was struck in the Breast, but for all that the Arrow could not hurt him, by reason of his Armour; yet he was so terrified with this unexpected Conflict, and considering with himself, that he must receive several such Brushes before he could advance to the plain Country;

A. D. 1118.

The History of WALES.   153

Country; and what was above all, being sensible that by such rash Misfortune he might lose all the Honour and Fame which he had before obtained, sent a Message to parly with them who kept the Passage, and with all assurance of Safety, to desire them to come to the King. The *Welch* being come, and question'd how they had such Confidence to oppose the King, and to put his Life in so much danger; made Answer, that they belonged to *Meredith ap Blethyn*, and according to their Master's Orders they were resolved to keep the Passage, or to dye upon the spot. The King finding them so resolute, desired them to go to *Meredith*, and propose to him an agreement of Peace, which he and his Cosins the Sons of *Cadwgan* accepted of; and promised to pay the King 10000 Head of Cattel, in Retribution for former Offences. And so King *Henry* leaving all things in a peaceable and quiet posture in *Wales*, and appointing the Lord *Fitz-Warren* Warden or Lieutenant of the Marches, returned to *England*.

But when a foreign Enemy was removed out of the Country, the *Welch* could never forbear quarrelling with each other; for *Gruffydh ap Rhys ap Theodore*, who had been now for some time quiet, fell upon *Gruffydh ap Sulhaern*, and for what reason not discovered, treacherously slew him. But the next Year there happened another occasion of Disturbances and falling out among the *Welch*; for *Eineon* the Son of *Cadwgan* dying, left all his share of *Powys* and *Merionyth* to his Brother *Meredith*. But his Uncle *Meredith ap Blethyn*, thinking that these Lands more properly belonged to him, ejected his Nephew *Meredith* to whom his Brother *Eineon* had left them, and took possession of them himself. And what augmented these Differences, King *Henry* set now at liberty *Ithel ap Riryd ap Blethyn*, *Meredith*'s Nephew, who had been for a long time detained in Prison; who coming to his own Country, was in expectation to enjoy his Estate, which, upon his being put in custody, his Relations had divided betwixt them; of which, the greatest share fell to his Uncle *Meredith*. But when
Gruffydh

A. D.
1120.

1121.

The History of WALES.

Gruffydh ap Conan was informed, how that *Meredith ap Blethyn*, contrary to all Justice, had taken away by force the Lands of his Nephew *Meredith ap Cadwgan*, he sent his Sons *Cadwalhon* and *Owen* with an Army into *Merionyth*, who conquering and bringing to subjection all the Country, carryed away the chief of the People, and all the Cattle to *Lhyn*. And at the same time the Sons of *Cadwgan* entered into the Lands of *Lhywarch ap Trahaern*, and cruelly wasted and destroyed it, by reason that he had countenanced the Doings of their Uncle *Meredith ap Blethyn*. But these inward Clashings and Animosities concerning Estates and Titles, were seconded by most unnatural Bloodshed and unparallell'd Cruelties; for *Meredith ap Blethyn*, when he found that his Nephew *Meredith ap Cadwgan* was assisted by the Prince of *North-Wales*, and that it was impracticable to keep *Merionyth* from him, he was resolved to practice that upon his Nephew, which he had failed to effect upon another. And therefore left his other Nephew *Ithel ap Riryd* should meet with the like Help and Encouragement to recover those Lands, which during his Imprisonment were taken away from him, of which his Uncle actually enjoyed a considerable share; *Meredith* thought it his wisest way to prevent all manner of Disputes, by sending *Ithel* out of the World, which upon mature Deliberation he treacherously effected. Nor was this the only Murther committed at this time; for *Cadwalhon* the Son of *Gruffydh ap Conan* exceeded him far, and slew his three Uncles, *Grono*, *Riryd*, and *Meilyr* the Sons of *Owen ap Edwyn*; but which was most unnatural of all, *Morgan ap Cadwgan* with his own hands killed his Brother *Meredith*; a Crime most execrable, tho he did afterwards repent of it.

A.D. 1122.

Not long after this, *Gruffyth ap Rhys*, by the false and invidious Accusations of the *Normans*, was dispossessed of all the Lands which King *Henry* had formerly granted him, and which he had for a considerable time peaceably enjoyed. And towards the end of the same Year dyed *Daniel ap Sulgien* Bishop of *S. Davids*, and Archdeacon of *Powys*, a Man of extraordinary

1124.

The History of WALES.

traordinary Piety and Learning, and one who made it his continual Employment to endeavour to work a Reconciliation betwixt *North-Wales* and *Powys*, which in his time were at perpetual Variance and Enmity with one another. The next Year dyed likewise *Gruffydh* the Son of *Meredith ap Blethyn*; and about the same time *Owen ap Cadwgan* having got into his hands *Meredith ap Lhywarch*, delivered him to *Pain Fitz-John*, to be kept safe Prisoner in the Castle of *Bridgnorth*. The reason of this was, because *Meredith* had slain *Meyric* his Cosin-German, and very barbarously had pulled out the Eyes of two more of his Cosins, the Sons of *Griffri*. This cruel and inhuman Custom of plucking out the Eyes of such as they hated or feared, was too frequently practised in *Wales*; for the following Year *Ievaf* the Son of *Owen* served two of his Brethren after this unnatural manner, and thinking that too little, passed a Sentence of perpetual Banishment upon them. A little after, his Brother *Lhewelyn ap Owen* flew *Iorwerth ap Lhywarch*; but all this Mischief practised by these two Brothers *Ievaf* and *Lhewelyn*, turned at last upon themselves; for their Uncle *Meredith ap Blethin* being apprehensive that his two Nephews were a considerable Rub in his way, and if they trooped off, that all their Estate would of right fall to him; flew *Ievaf* out-right, and having pluck'd out *Lhewelyn*'s Eyes, castrated him, for fear he should beget any Children to inherit his Lands after him. These no doubt were implacable Times, when for the least Offence, nay sometime Suspicion, Murther was so openly and incorrigibly committed; which must of necessity be attributed to this one Principle, That so many petty States having equal Power and Authority in their own Territories, and being subject to none but the King of *England*, still endeavoured to out-vie and over-top each other. And so, nearness of Relation giving way to Ambition, they never regarded those of the same Blood, so that themselves might add to their strength, and increase their Estate by their Fall; and for this reason *Meyric* flew *Lhywarch*, and his Son *Madawc* his own Cosins; but

A. D.
1125.

1126.

but before he could make any Advantage of their Death, he was himself served after the same manner. But the only Person who afterwards repented of such a foul Crime, was *Morgan ap Cadwgan*, who being severely troubled in mind for the Murther he had lately committed upon his Brother *Meredith*, took a Journey to *Jerusalem* to expiate for his Crime, and in his return from thence, dyed in the Isle of *Cyprus*. But this treacherous way of private murdering those by whom they were offended, could not be forgot among the *Welch*; for *Eineon* the Son of *Owen ap Edwyn* calling to mind how that *Cadwalhon* the Son of *Gruffydh ap Conan* had basely slain three of his Brothers, and taking the opportunity of his being at *Nanhewdwy*, assisted by *Cadwgan ap Grono ap Edwyn*, set upon him, and flew him. About the same time, that great Usurper *Meredith ap Blethyn ap Confyn*, who by most unnatural and most hellish Practices, had got the Lands of all his Brothers and Nephews, and by that means was become a Man of the greatest strength and sway in *Powys*, dyed of a severe Fit of Sickness, which reduced him to that apprehension of his former Miscarriages, that he endured Penance for the expiation of former Guilts.

A. D. 1129.

1134. In the Year 1134. till which time nothing of moment was transacted in *Wales*, *Henry* the first of that Name, King of *England*, dyed in *Normandy* in the Month of *October*; after whom *Stephen* Earl of *Buloign* Son to the Earl of *Bloys*, his Sisters Son, by the means of *Hugh Bygod*, was crowned King by the Archbishop of *Canterbury*, all the Nobility of *England* consenting thereunto; though contrary to a former Oath they had taken to *Maud* the Empress. The first thing that employed his Thoughts after his accession to the Government, was against *David* King of the *Scots*; who taking advantage of this new Revolution in *England*, by some treacherous means or other, got the Towns of *Carlisle* and *Newcastle* into his hands. But King *Stephen*, tho scarcely settled in his Throne, presently marched towards the North; of whose coming *David* being assured, and fearing

The History of WALES.

to meet him, voluntarily restored *Newcastle*, and compounded for *Carlisle*; but would not swear to him by reason of his Oath to *Maud*; which however his Son *Henry* did not stick at, and thereupon was by King *Stephen* created Earl of *Huntington*. This change and alteration of Affairs in *England*, made also the *Welch* bestir themselves; for *Morgan ap Owen*, a Man of considerable Quality and Estate in *Wales*, remembring the Wrong and Injury he had received at the hands of *Richard Fitz-Gilbert*, slew him, together with his Son *Gilbert*. And shortly after, *Cadwalader* and *Owen Gwyneth* the Sons of *Gruffydh ap Conan* Prince of *North-Wales*, having raised a mighty Army, marched against the *Normans* and *Flemmings*, and comming to *Cardigan*, committed very considerable Waste and Havock in the Country, and took two of the strongest Places, one belonging to *Walter Espec*, and the Castle of *Aberystwyth*. In this last place they were joyned by *Howel ap Meredith*, and *Rhys ap Madawc ap Ednerth*; who marching forward, took the Castle of *Richard de la Mare*, together with those of *Dinerth* and *Caerwedros*, and then returned with very valuable Booty. But having succeeded so well in this Expedition, they could not rest satisfied, till they had rid the whole Country from the intolerable Pride and Oppression of the *Normans* and *Flemings*; and therefore returning the same Year to *Cardigan* with 6000 Foot, and 2000 Horse, well disciplined and experienced Soldiers; and being joyned by *Gruffydh ap Rhys* and *Howel ap Meredith* of *Brecknock*, with his Sons, and *Madawc ap Ednerth*; they over-ran the Country, as far as *Aberteifi*, restoring all the former Inhabitants to their proper Inheritances, and discarding all such Strangers as the late Earl of *Strygil* had placed in the Country. But when *Stephen*, who was Governour of *Aberteifi*, saw that, he called to him *Robert Fitz-Martyn*, the Sons of *Gerald*, and *William Fitz-John*, with all the strength of the *Normans*, *Flemings*, and *English* in *Wales*, or the Marches; and meeting with the *Welch* betwixt *Aber Ned* and *Aber Dyfi*, gave
them

A. D.
1135.

them battel. But after a very fore and Bloody Encounter, the *English* began to give ground, and according to their ufual manner, trufting too much to the ftrength of their Towns and Fortifications, began to look how to fave themfelves that way. But the *Welch* preffed upon 'em fo hard, that they killed above 3000 Men, befides feveral that were drowned and taken Prifoners. This Victory being fo happily obtained, *Cadwalader* and *Owen* over-ran the whole Country, forcing all the *Normans* and *Flemings* to depart the Country with all fpeed, and placing in their room thofe miferable *Welch*, who had been fo long deprived and kept from their own Eftates; and after they had weeded the Country of thofe infatiable Caterpillars, they returned to *North-Wales*, laden with very rich Spoils and acceptable Plunder. The King of *England* was not in a condition to take notice to what Extremities his Subjects were reduced to in *Wales*, by reafon that his own Nobles of *England* were rifen in Arms againft him; the reafon of which Tumult among the Nobility was occafioned by a fallacious Report that went about of the King's Death, who lay then fick of a Lethargy. They that bore him no good Will, verified the Rumour as much as they could, and ftirred up the common People in behalf of the Emprefs; whereas on the other hand the King's Friends betook themfelves to Caftles and ftrong Holds for fear of the Emprefs, and among others *Hugh Bigod* fecured the Caftle of *Norwich*, and after that he was affured that the King was well again, he was loth to deliver the fame out of his poffeffion, unlefs it were to the King's own hands. But during thefe Commotions and Troubles in *England*, *Gruffydh ap Rhys*, Son to *Rhys ap Theodore*, the right Heir to the Principality of *South-Wales*, dyed, leaving Iffue behind him a Son called *Rhys*, commonly known by the Name of Lord *Rhys*, by *Gwenlhian* the Daughter of *Gruffydh ap Conan*, who by fome is faid to have poifoned her Husband. Towards the end of the fame Year dyed likewife *Gruffydh ap Conan* Prince of *North-Wales*, after he had reigned 57 Years; to

A. D.
1136.

the

The History of WALES.

the great Grief and Discontent of all his Subjects, as being a Prince of incomparable Qualities, and one who after divers Victories obtained over the *English*, had throughly purged *North-Wales* from all Strangers and Foreigners. He had Issue by *Angharad* the Daughter of *Owen ap Edwyn*, three Sons, namely, *Owen*, *Cadwalader*, and *Cadwalhon*, and five Daughters, *Marret*, *Susanna*, *Ranulht*, *Agnes*, and *Gwenlhian*: and by a Concubine *Iago*, *Afcain*, *Edwal* Abbot of *Penmon*, *Dolhing*, and *Elen*, who was married to *Hova ap Ithel Felyn* of *Yal*. There were several good and wholsom Laws and Statutes enacted in his time; and among the rest, he reformed the great Disorders of the *Welch* Minstrels, which were then grown to great Abuse. Of these there were three sorts in *Wales*; the first were called *Beirdh*, who composed several Songs and Odes of various Measures, wherein the Poet's Skill was not only required, but also a natural Endowment, or a Vein which the Latins term *furor Poeticus*. These likewise kept the Records of all Gentlemens Arms and Pedegrees, and were principally esteemed among all the Degrees of the *Welch* Poets. The next were such as plaid upon Musical Instruments, chiefly the Harp and the Crowd; which Musick *Gruffydh ap Conan* first brought over into *Wales*; who being born in *Ireland*, and descended by his Mothers side of *Irish* Parents, brought with him from thence several skilful Musicians, who invented almost all the Instruments as were afterwards plaid upon in *Wales*. The last sort were called *Atcaneaid*, whose Business it was to sing to the Instrument plaid upon by another. Each of these, by the same Statute, had their several Reward and Encouragement allotted to them; their Life and Behaviour was to be spotless and unblameable, otherwise their Punishment was very severe and rigid, every one having Authority to punish and correct them, even to the Deprivation of all they had. They were also interdicted and forbidden to enter any Man's House, or to compose any Song of any one, without the special leave and warrant of the Party concerned; with many other Ordinances relating to the like purpose.
Owen

Owen Gwynedh.

AFter the death of *Gruffydh ap Conan*, his eldest Son *Owen*, surnamed *Gwynedh*, succeeded in the Principality of *North Wales*; who no sooner had entered upon the Government, but together with the rest of his Brethren, he made an Expedition into *South-Wales*; and having demolished and overthrown the Castles of *Stradmeyric*, *Stephan*, and *Humffreys*, and laid in Ashes the Town of *Caermardhyn*, he returned home with no less Honor than Booty and Plunder. About the same time, *John*, Arch-Deacon of *Lhanbaran* departed this Life, a Man of singular Piety and strictness of Life, who for his rigid Zeal in Religion and Virtue, was thought worthy to be canonized, and to be counted among the number of the Saints. This Year likewise King *Stephen* passed over to *Normandy*, and having concluded a Peace with the *French* King, and the Duke of *Anjou*, returned back to *England* without any further delay. But the following Spring gave opportunity for greater Undertakings; *David*, King of *Scots*, upon the King of *England*'s going to *France* last Summer, had entered the Borders of *England*, and continued to make considerable Waste and Havock in that part of the Country. Whereupon King *Stephen*, to rid his Country and his Subjects from so dangerous an Enemy, marched with an Army towards the *North*, whose coming the King of *Scots* hearing of, he relinquished the Borders of *England*, and retired to his own Country. But that would not satisfie King *Stephen*, who desired to be further revenged for the unpardonable Hostilities committed by the *Scots* in his Country; and therefore pursuing the *Scots* to their own Country, he harassed and laid waste all the South part of the Kingdom of *Scotland*.

But

The History of WALES.

But the King's absence animated several of the *English* Nobility to rebel; to which purpose they fortified every one their Castles and strong Holds: *William* Earl of *Glocester* those of *Leeds* and *Bristol*; *Ralph Lunel*, *Cari*; *William Fitz-Allen*, *Shrewsbury*; *Paganellus*, *Ludlow*; *William de Moyun*, *Dunester*; *Robert de Nichol*, *Warham*; *Eustace Fitz-John*, *Merton*; and *Walklyn*, *Dover*. But for all these mighty Preparations, the King in a short time became Master of them all; some he won by assault, others upon fair Promises and advantageous Conditions were surrendred up, and some he got by treacherous and under-hand Contrivances. The *Scots* thought to make good advantage of these Commotions in *England*; and thereupon, as soon as they heard that some of the *English* Nobility were in actual Rebellion against the King, they entered into the Borders, and began, as they thought, without any apprehension of Opposition, to ravage and lay waste the Country before 'em. But *William*, Earl of *Albemarle*; *William Pyppell*, Earl of *Nottingham*; *Walter Espec* and *Gilbert Lacy*, gathered together all the Forces they could raise in the North; and being animated and encouraged by the eloquent and pressing Oration of *Ralph*, Bishop of *Orkneys*, which he delivered in the audience of the whole Army, they set upon the *Scots* at *Almerton* with such unanimous Courage, that after a very great slaughter of his Men, King *David* was glad to escape with his Life by flight. After this, King *Stephen* seized to his own use the Castles of *Ludlow* and *Leeds*, and pressed the Bishops of *Salisbury* and *Lincoln* so hard, that to prevent their perishing by Famine, they were constrained to surrender; the former the Castles of *Vises* and *Shirburn*; the latter those of *Newark upon Trent* and *Sleeford*. This did not a little augment the King's strength against the ensuing Storm; for in the Summer this Year, *Maud* the Empress, Daughter and Heir to King *Henry*, to whom King *Stephen*, with all the Nobility of *England*, had sworn Allegiance, landed at *Arundel*, with her Brother *Robert* Earl of *Glocester*,

The History of WALES.

and was there honourably received by *William de Albineto*, who was lately married to Queen *Adeliz*, King *Henry*'s Widow, with whom he received the Earldom of *Arundel* in Dowry. But as soon as King *Stephen* heard of her landing, he marched with all possible speed to *Arundel*, and laid siege to the Castle; but finding it upon tryal impregnable, he raised the siege, and by that means suffered the Empress and her Brother to escape to *Bristol*.

A. D. 1138.

The next Year an unlucky Accident fell out in *Wales*; *Cynric*, one of Prince *Owen*'s Sons, having by some means or other disgusted *Madawc ap Meredith ap Blethyn ap Confyn*, a Person of considerable Esteem and Estate in the Country, was, with his connivance set upon and slain by his Men. But the Affairs of *England* this Year, afforded greater rarity of action; King *Stephen* with a formidable Army laid siege to the City of *Lincoln*, to the relief of which, *Ranulph*, Earl of *Chester*, and *Robert* Earl of *Glocester*, marched with their Forces. But before they could arrive, the Town was taken; whereupon they drew up their Forces in order to give the King battel, who on the other side, was as ready to receive them. King *Stephen* drew up his Forces in three Battels, the first being led by the Earls of *Britain*, *Mellent*, *Norfolk*, *Hampton*, and *Warren*; the second by the Earl of *Albemarle*, and *William* of *Ypres*; and the third by the King himself, assisted by *Baldwyn Fitz-Gilbert*, with several others of his Nobility. Of the Enemies side, the disinherited Barons had the first place; the Earl of *Chester*, with a considerable Party of *Welchmen*, far better couraged than armed, led the second; and the Earl of *Glocester* the third Battel. After a hot and bloody Dispute of both sides, the Victory at length favoured the Barons, King *Stephen* being first taken Prisoner, and a little after the Queen, together with *William* of *Ypres*, and *Bryan Fitz-Count*. But within a while after *William Martell* and *Geffrey de Mandeville* gathered together some fresh Forces, and fought the Empress and her Brother at *Winchester*, and having put the Empress to flight, took Earl

Robert

The History of WALES.

Robert Prisoner, for exchange of whom the King was set at liberty. The next Year King Stephen would try the other Adventure, and received a second Overthrow at *Wilton*; which however did not so much discourage him, but that he laid so close a siege to the Empress at *Oxford*, that she was glad to make her escape to *Wallingford*. The same Year dyed *Madawc ap Ednerth*, a Person of great Quality and Note in *Wales*; and *Meredith ap Howel*, a Man of no mean Esteem, was slain by the Sons of *Blethyn ap Gwyn*.

For the two succeeding Years nothing remarkable passed in *Wales*; excepting that this Year *Howel ap Meredith ap Rhytherch* of *Cantref Bychan*, and *Rhys ap Howel* were cowardly slain by the Treachery and perfidious Practices of the *Flemings*; and the next Year *Howel ap Meredith ap Blethyn* was basely murthered by his own Men; at which time, *Howel* and *Cadwgan* the Sons of *Madawc ap Ednerth*, upon some unhappy Quarrel, did kill each other. But shortly after this, an irreconcilable Difference fell out betwixt *Anarawd* Son to *Gruffydh ap Rhys* Prince of *South-Wales*; and his Father in Law *Cadwalader* the Son of *Gruffydh ap Conan*, and Brother to Prince *Owen Gwynedh*; which from Words quickly proceeded to Blows. In this Scuffle *Anarawd* was unhappily slain; which so exasperated Prince *Owen* against his Brother *Cadwalader*, that together with his Son *Howel*, he marched with an army into his Brothers Country, and after a considerable Waste and Destruction, burnt to the ground the Castle of *Aberystwyth*. *Cadwalader*, upon the News of Prince *Owen*'s approach, withdrew himself and fled to *Ireland*; where having hired a great number of *Irish* and *Scots* for Two Thousand Marks, under the Command of *Octer*, and the Sons of *Turkel* and *Cherulf*, he struck sail for *Wales*, and landed at *Abermenay* in *Carnarvonshire*. The Prince, to protract no time, marched with all speed to prevent their farther progress into the Country; and both Armies being come in view of each other, a Peace was happily con-

A. D.
1139.

1140.

1141.

1142.

concluded betwixt the two Brothers. The *Irish* understanding this, and how that their coming over was like to prove but a Fool's Errant to them, they surprized and secured *Cadwalader*, till their Wages and Arrears were paid; who, to obtain his Liberty, deliver'd to them two thousand Heads of Cattel, besides many Prisoners, and other Booty, which they had taken in the Country. But as soon as the Prince was informed that his Brother *Cadwalader* was let loose, without any farther demur upon the case, he fell in upon the *Irish*, and having slain a very considerable number of them, recovered all the Booty they purposed to ship off, and forced as many as could escape, to return with great loss, and a greater shame back to *Ireland*.

But the *Normans* sped far better in *Wales*; *Hugh* Son to *Radulph* Earl of *Chester*, having fortified his Castle of *Cymaron*, set upon and won the Country of *Melienyth* a second time; and the Castle of *Clun* being fortified by another Lord, all *Eluel* became subject to the *Normans*. The same time King *Stephen* took *Geffry Mandeville* Prisoner at *S. Albans*, where the Earl of *Arundel* by the slip of his Horse was like to be drowned in the River. But the Earl of *Mandeville*, to obtain his liberty, delivered up to the King the Tower of *London*, with the Castles of *Walden* and *Plaffey*, which reduced him to that condition, that he was forced to live upon the Plunder and Spoil of Abbies and other religious Houses, till at length he was slain in a Skirmish against the King, and his Son banished the Kingdom.

1144. The next Year a Skirmish happened betwixt *Hugh de Mortimer* and *Rhys ap Howel*, wherein the latter was taken Prisoner, with many others of his Accomplices, who were all committed to Prison by the *English*. But it fared much better with *Howel* and *Conan* the Sons of Prince *Owen*, who having raised an Army against the *Flemings* and *Normans*, gain'd a considerable Victory at *Aberteifi*, and having placed a Garrison in the Town, returned home with great Honour, and much Booty. About the same time,

Sulien

The History of WALES.

Sulien ap Rhythmarch, one of the Colledg of *Lhanbadarn*, and a Person of great Reading and extensive Learning, departed this Life. Shortly after, *Gilbert* Earl of *Clare*, came with a great number of Forces to *Dyfed*, and built the Castle of *Caermardhyn*, and the Castle of the Sons of *Uchtryd*. *Hugh Mortimer* likewise slew *Meyric ap Madawc ap Riryd ap Bleddu*, and *Meredic ap Madawc ap Edrerth*. And so far it went of the side of the *English*; but now the *Welch* begin to gain ground; *Cadelh* the Son of *Gruffydh ap Rhys* Prince of *South Wales*, laid siege to the Castle of *Dynefowr*, belonging to Earl *Gilbert*, which being surrender'd up, *Cadelh*, assisted by his Brethren *Meredith* and *Rhys*, brought his Army before the Castle of *Caermardhyn*, which after a short siege yielded in like manner, reserving only this one Condition, that the Garison should not be put to the Sword. From thence he marched to *Lhanstephan*, and set before the Castle; to the Relief of which the *Normans* and *Flemings* coming with their Forces, were shamefully vanquished and overcome, and so the Castle was easily deliver'd up to the *Welch*. But the *Normans* were so cruelly nettled at this, that they muster'd up all the Forces they could possibly draw together out of the neighbouring Countries, and unexpectedly surrounded the Castle, intending by all possible means to recover the same. But the Governour, *Meredith ap Gruffydh*, a Man of great Years, and no less Experience, so animated and encouraged the besieged, that when the *Normans* and *Flemings* ventured to scale the Walls, they were bear back with such Vigour, and Loss of their side, that at length they were compell'd to raise the Siege, and leave the *Welch* in possession of the Castle.

Shortly after this, *Run* the Son of Prince *Owen* of *North-Wales*, a Youth of excellent hopes, and incomparable Qualifications, dyed, whose Death his Father took so much to heart, that for some time he seemed to be past all Comfort, being faln into such a melancholy Disposition, that he was diverted with nothing but Retirement. But an Accident fell

A. D.
1145.

out, which rouz'd him out of this lethargical Fit of Sorrow and Discontent; the Castle of *Mould* was so very strong and well garrison'd by the *English*, that it mightily annoyed the Country thereabouts, and had been frequently besieged, but could never be taken. Prince *Owen* at this time levied an Army and laid close siege to it; and the Garison for several assaults behaved it self so manfully, that the place seemed impregnable and invincible. But the Presence and Example of Prince *Owen* so encouraged his Men, that they fell on with all possible Vigour and Might, and at last forced their entrance into the Castle. Having put a great number of the Garrison to the Sword, and taken the rest Prisoners, the Castle was rased to the ground; and this fortunate Attempt so pleased the Prince, that he forgot all Sorrow for his Son, and returned to his usual Temper and accustomed Merriments. At the same time, King *Stephen* of *England* obtained a remarkable Victory over his Enemies at *Farendon*; and although the ensuing Year *Rondel* Earl of *Chester* and he were reconciled, yet he thought it more adviseable to detain him Prisoner, though contrary to his promise, until such time as the Earl would deliver up the Castle of *Lincoln*, with all the Forts and places of strength in his custody.

A. D.
1146.

The next Year, *Cadelh*, *Meredith*, and *Rhys*, the Sons of *Gruffydh ap Rhys ap Theodor*, brought an Army before the Castle of *Gwys*; but finding themselves too weak to master it, they desired *Howel*, Son to Prince *Owen Gwynedh*, a Person famously remarkable for martial Endowments, to come to their assistance. *Howel*, who was ever very desirous to signalize himself, and to evidence his Valour to the World, readily consented to their Request; and having drawn his Forces together, marched directly towards *Gwys*, where being arrived, he was joyfully received, and honourably entertain'd by such Lords as desired his help. Having viewed the Strength and Fortification of the Castle, he found it was impracticable to take the place, without the Walls could be destroyed; and therefore he gave orders, that certain battering

Engines

Engines should be provided, whilst the rest should gaul and moleft the besieged, by throwing of great Stones into the Castle. The Enemies perceiving what irresistible Preparations the Besiegers contrived, thought it to no purpose to withstand their Fury; and therefore to do that voluntarily which must be done by compulsion, they presently yielded up the Castle. Shortly after this a great Difference happen'd betwixt the Sons of Prince *Owen*, *Howel*, and *Conan*, and their Uncle *Cadwalader*; whereupon the former entered with an Army into the Country of *Merionyth*, and committed great Wastes and Hostilities there, insomuch that the Inhabitants flock'd into Sanctuaries to save their Lives. But the young Lords finding what fearful and unstable condition the People were in, and the better to draw them to their side, issued out their Proclamation, assuring that all who would favour their Country, should not only enjoy their Lives, but their former Liberty and accustomed Priviledges; upon the publication of which Edict, the People returned to their own Habitations. Having by this Stratagem brought all the Country under their own Pleasure and good Will, they lead their Army before the Castle of *Cynfael*, belonging to *Cadwalader*, which he had built and strongly fortified: The government of this Castle *Cadwalader* had committed to *Merfyn*, Abbot of *Tygwyn*, or the *White-House*; who being summoned to surrender, by the Brothers *Howel* and *Conan*, did not only refuse, but defied their utmost Efforts upon the place. The Lords finding they could do no good by Threats and Menaces, judged it more convenient to make use of the other Extream; and therefore promised the Abbot a very high Reward, if he would deliver the Castle into their hands. But all proved to no effect; the Abbot being a Person of more Honesty and greater Honour, than to be corrupted to betray his Trust; told them flatly, That he would not deceive his Masters expectation, and therefore would choose rather to dye with Honour, than to live with Shame. The Lords finding him inexorable, and withal being

being vexed, that a Church-man should put such a stop to their fortunate Proceedings, made such a vigorous Assault upon the Castle, that after they had pulled down some part of the Walls, they entred in by force, and ravaged so furiously, that they killed and wounded the whole Garrison, the *Abbot* only escaping, who by the help of some of his Friends in *Howel's* Army, got away safe. Towards the close of this Year, several Persons of Note departed this Life, among whom were *Robert* Earl of *Glocester*, and *Gilbert* Earl of *Clare*, as also *Uchtbryd* Bishop of *Llandaf*, a Man of great Piety and Learning, in whose See succeeded *Nickolas ab Gurgant*.

1147. The following Year also died *Bernard* Bishop of St. *Davids*, and was succeeded by *David Fitzgerald*,
1148. then Archdeacon of *Cardigan*. Sometime after Prince *Owen Gwynedh* built a Castle in *Yale*, called *Castelh y Rodwyth*; and his Brother *Cadwalader* built another at *Lhanrystid*, and bestowed his part of *Cardigan* upon his Son *Cadwgan*. Also *Madoc* the Son of *Meredith ap Blethyn* founded the Castle of *Ofwestry*, and gave his Nephews *Owen* and *Meyric* the Sons of *Gruffydh ap Meredith* his share of *Cyfeilioc*.

1149. The next Year, *Conan* Son to Prince *Owen Gwynedh*, for certain Faults and Miscarriages committed against his Father, tho' the particulars are not discovered, was put in Prison, where for some time he continued in Custody. But it fared better with his Brother *Howel*, who having made his Uncle *Cadwalader* his Prisoner, reduced all his Country, together with his Castle subject to himself. In *South-Wales*, some Business of moment happened this Year; *Cadelh* the Son of *Gruffydh ap Rhys* having fortified the Castle of *Carmardhyn*, marched with his Army towards *Cydwely*, wasted and destroyed the whole Country, and being returned home, joyned his Army with his Brothers *Meredith* and *Rhys*, who entring into the Country of *Cardigan*, won that part called *Is Aeron*. This was succeeded by an Action of greater Importance in *North-Wales*; some irreconcilable Difference arising betwixt Prince *Owen*, and *Rondel* Earl of *Chester*, quickly

The History of WALES.

quickly broke out into open War. The Earl made all the possible Preparations the opportunity would permit, and drew together a considerable Army from all parts of *England* and which strengthened and incouraged him the more, he was joyned by *Madoc ap Meredith* Prince of *Powys*, who disdaining to hold his Lands of Prince *Owen Gwynedh*, chose rather to side with, and abet his Enemies. The Prince on the other hand was not backward in his Preparations, and perceiving the Enemy to come upon him, thought it not advisable to suffer him to advance too far into the Country, but to stop and prevent his Carreer before he should take too firm a footing in his Dominions. To this end he marched with his whole Power as far as *Counsylht*, with full Resolution to give the Earl of *Chester* Battel, which the *English* were glad of, as thinking themselves far more numerous, and much better Armed and Disciplined than the *Welch*. But both Armies having joyned Battel, they quickly faltered in their expectation of undoubted Success, and finding the *Welch* to press so irresistibly severe upon them, they thought it wiser to retire, and endeavour to save themselves by flight. But the *Welch* pursued them so hard, that few escaped without being either slain or taken Prisoners, and they some of the Chief Commanders, who thro' the fleetness of their Horses, avoided the Fury of their pursuers.

The next Year, the Scene of Action removed to *South-Wales*, *Cadelh*, *Meredith* and *Rhys*, the Sons of *Gruffydh ap Rhys* Prince of *South-Wales*, being entred with an Army into *Cardigan*, wan all the Country from *Howel* the Prince of *North-Wales* Son, excepting the Castle of *Lhanfihangel* in *Pengwern*. The Siege of *Lhanrystyd* Castle proved so difficult and unmanagable, that the young Lords of *South-Wales* lost a great part of their bravest Souldiers before it, which so troubled and vexed them, that when they got possession of the Castle, they put all the Garrison to the Sword. From thence they marched to *Ystratmyric* Castle, which after they had won, manned and

1150.

and re-fortified, they disbanded their Forces, and returned home. But *Cadelh* the eldest of the Brothers, was upon the point of receiving his last Blow by treachery at home, which he had escaped from the Enemies abroad. For some of the Inhabitants of *Tenbigh* in *Pembrokeshire*, having conceived some displeasure and hatred against *Cadelh*, were resolved to revenge themselves, and to lay a Trap for his Life; and having observed what pleasure he took in Hunting, were resolved to execute their Plot, whilst he was hot and eager at his Sport. Observing therefore one day how he went a Hunting with only a few Companions, they placed themselves in an ambuscade, and when the Game came that way, they unexpectedly set upon the unarmed Sports-men, and having easily made all the rest fly away, they wounded *Cadelh* so cruelly, that he narrowly escaped their hands alive; who making shift to get home, lay for a long time dangerously ill, and with great difficulty at length recovered his Life. Upon this, his Brothers *Meredith* and *Rhys* passed with an Army into *Gwyr*, and having burnt and destroyed the Country thereabouts, they besieged and took the Castle of *Aberlhychwr*, but finding they could not keep it, they rased it to the Ground, and after that, returned home with great Booty to *Dynefawr*, and repaired the Fortifications of the Castle there. About the same time also, *Howel*, Prince *Owen Gwynedh*'s Son, fortified *Humphry*'s Castle in the Valley of *Caletwr*.

1151.

But the following Year, Prince *Owen* did a very barbarous Action to *Cunetha*, his Brother *Cadwalhon*'s Son, for fearing left that this young Man should lay claim to any part of his Estate as his Father's right, he first pulled out his Eyes, and afterwards castrated him, for fear he should beget any Children, who might some time or other renew their claim and right to *Cadwalhon*'s Estate. This inhuman severity was succeeded by another of no small remark; *Lhewelyn* Son to *Madoc ap Meredith* having watched a convenient Opportunity, set upon, and slew *Stephen* the Son of *Baldwin*. But *Cadwalader* Prince *Owen*'s

Brother

The History of WALES.

Brother after a tedious Imprisonment which he had sustained thro' the Malice and Rancour of his Nephew *Howel*, at length made his escape, and flying to the Isle of *Anglesey*, brought a considerable part of that Island under his subjection. But Prince *Owen* hearing how that his Brother had got loose from custody, and that he was in actual possession of a great part of *Anglesey*, he presently dispatched an Army over, which proving too formidable to *Cadwalader's* Party, he was constrained to escape to *England*, and to desire Succor from his Wife's Relations, who was the Daughter of *Gilbert* Earl of *Clare*. This Year *Galfrede Arthur*, commonly called *Geffrey* of *Monmouth*, was made Bishop of St. *Asaph*, and at the same time *Simon* Archdeacon of *Cyfeilioc*, a Man of great Worth and Esteem in his Country died.

But the Year following, *Meredith* and *Rhys* the Sons of *Gruffydh ap Rhys*, Prince of *South-Wales*, laid Siege to *Pentwedic* Castle, which belonged to *Howel* Prince *Owen's* Son, and after great pains and considerable loss of Men of their side, at last made themselves Masters of it. From thence they marched by Night to *Tenby*, and unexpectedly falling upon the Castle, of which one *William Fitzgerald* was Governor, they scaled the Walls before the Garrison were aware of any Danger, and so possessing themselves of the Castle, they fell foul upon the Garrison, in Revenge of the Mischief they had done, and further designed to their Brother *Cadelh*. For *Cadelh* at this time was gone upon a Pilgrimage, and during his absence had committed his whole Inheritance and all other concerns in *Wales*, to the Care of his Brethren *Meredith* and *Rhys*. But after the taking *Tenby*-Castle, they divided their Army into two Parties, with one of which, *Rhys* marched to *Ystratcongen*, and after great havock and waste committed there, he passed to *Cyfeilioc*. which fared in like manner with *Ystratcongen*. *Meredith* with the other Party sat before *Aberavan*-Castle, and after a short Siege won and got possession of it, and then returned home with very considerable Booty, and many rich Spoils. About the same time

1152.

time *Rondel* Earl of *Chester*, who had lived in continual Enmity and frequent Hostility with Prince *Owen* of *North-Wales*, departed this Life, leaving his Son *Hugh* to enjoy both his Titles and Estate in *England*, and to prosecute the Feuds and Hostilities against the *Welch*.

1153. And shortly after died *Meredith* Son to *Gruffydh ap Rhys* Prince of *South Wales*, who was Lord of *Cardigan Ystratywy* and *Dyfed*, being not passed the Twenty Fifth Year of his Age, a Person of incomparable Valor and Audacity, and in all his Warlike Attempts and Atchievements very Fortunate. He was presently followed by *Geoffrey* Bishop of *Llandaf*, a Man as Famous for Learning and a good Life, as the other was for Masculine Bravery and Martial Prowess. In *England* the face of things looked very lowring, *Henry* Surnamed *Shortmantel*, the Empress Son, landed in *England*, and in his progress thro' the Country took several Castles, among which were *Malmesbury*, *Wallingford* and *Shrewsbury*. But his Fury was quickly appeased by the Death of *Eustace* King *Stephen's* Son, so that the sole obstacle for his succeeding to the Crown, being now removed, he willingly concluded a Peace with King *Stephen*, permitting him to enjoy the Crown peaceably for his life, upon Condition that himself was declared his Successor. But King

1154. *Stephen* did not long survive this Treaty, and then *Henry Plantagenet*, the Empress Son, was Crowned in

1155. his stead. Towards the beginning of King *Henry's* reign, *Rhys Gruffydh ap Rhys*, King of *South Wales*, upon apprehension that *Owen Gwynedh* had raised an Army for the Conquest of *South Wales*, drew together all his Strength, and marched to *Aberdyfi* to face the Enemy upon their own Borders. But finding the Rumor to be false, and that the Prince of *North-Wales* had no such Design in hand, having built a Castle at *Aberdyfi*, which might defend the Frontiers from any future Design of his Country, he returned back without attempting any thing farther. At the same time, *Madoc ap Meredith* built a Castle at *Caereneon* near *Cymer*, and then *Eglwys Fair* in *Myfod*,

Was

The History of WALES.

was founded. About this time also, *Meyric* Nephew to Prince *Madoc ap Meredith* made his escape out of Prison, wherein he had been detained by his Uncle for a considerable time.

The same Year King *Henry* being displeased with the *Flemings* whom his Predecessor King *Stephen* had brought over into *England*, issued out a Proclamation, charging the greatest part of them to depart his Dominions, and to retire to their Country-men in *West-Wales*, where his Grandfather *Henry* the First the *Bastard*'s Son had planted them. And thus that part of *Wales* called *Pembroke-shire*, was over-run with these Strangers, who being better befriended by the Kings of *England*, than the *Welch* could well expect to be, made sure footing in that Country, where they have ever since continued firm. It was the *English* Policy of those times to accept of any opportunity to curb and keep under the *Welch*, whom they experienced to be none of the safest Neighbours, and therefore the Kings of *England* did grant any Lands and Priviledges in *Wales* to any that would accept of them, which honestly they had no Power to bestow.

But this was not enough in detriment to the *Welch*, 1156. for the Year following, King *Henry* raised a very great Army which he gathered from all parts of *England*, with purpose to subdue all *North-Wales*, being principally moved hereto, by the instigation of *Cadwalader* the Prince's Brother, whom *Owen Gwynedh*, for what Reasons not known, deprived of his Estate, and banished the Country. Also *Madoc ap Meredith* Prince of *Powis*, who maligned the Liberty and Priviledge of the Princes of *North-Wales*, who owned subjection to no other than the King of *England*, whereas those of *Powis* were obliged to do homage to the Prince of *North-Wales*, did joyntly consent to this Invitation. The King of *England* accepting of their Proposals, led his Army to *West-Chester*, and encamped upon the Marsh called *Saltney*, in *Welch*, *Morfa-Caer-Lleon*. Prince *Owen* all this while was not ignorant of this intended Invasion, and therefore having

having made all possible Preparations to confront the Enemy, he marched his Army to the Frontiers of *England*, and encamping at *Basingwerk*, resolved to give the *English* Battel. King *Henry* understanding of the Prince's Resolution, detached some of the chiefest Troops out of the Main-body, under the command of several Earls and other Lords, and sent them towards the Prince's Camp. But after they had advanced some little way, and were passing thro' a Wood, called *Coed-Eulo*, *David* and *Conan* Prince *Owen*'s Sons, unexpectedly set upon them, and what by the advantage of the Ground, and the suddeness of the Action, the *English* were born down with a great Slaughter, and those who survived, narrowly escaped to the King's Camp. This was a very unwelcome beginning to King *Henry*; but however, in order to prosper better hereafter, he thought it advisable to decamp from *Saltney*, and to rank his Troops along the Sea Coast, thinking thereby to get betwixt Prince *Owen* and his Country, which if he could effect, he was sure to reduce the *Welch* to a very great inconveniency. But the Prince foreseeing the Danger of this, retired with his Army to a place called *Cil Owen*, that is, *Owen*'s Retreat, which when King *Henry* perceived, he let fall his Design, and came to *Ruthlan*. *W. Parnus* writes, that in this Expedition against the *Welch*, King *Henry* was in great danger of his Life, in passing thro' a strait at *Counsylth* near *Flint*, where *Henry* Earl of *Essex*, who by inheritance enjoyed the Office of bearing the Standard of *England*, being over-charged by the Enemy, cast down the same and fled. This accident so incouraged the *Welch*, that they bore on so violently, that the King himself narrowly escaped, having of his Party *Eustace Fitz-John* and *Rob. Curcie*, two valiant Knights, together with several others of his Nobility and Gentry slain in the Action.

Lib. 2. *Cap.* 5.

After this Prince *Owen* decamped from *Cil Owen*, and intrenched himself upon *Bryn y Pin*, where little of moment passed betwixt the two Armies, only some slight Skirmishes happened frequently. King *Henry*

The History of WALES. 175

Henry in the mean time fortified the Castle of *Ruthlan*, and during his stay there, *Madoc ap Meredith* Prince of *Powis*, sailed with the *English* Fleet to *Anglesey*, and having put some Men on shoar, they burnt two Churches, and ravaged part of the Country about. But they paid very dear for it, for all the Strength of the Island being met together, they set upon them in their return to their Ships, and cut them off in such a manner, that not one remained to bring Tidings to the Fleet of what had befel them. But they on Board quickly perceived what had happened, and therefore thought it not very safe harbouring upon that Coast, but judging it more advisable to weigh Anchor, they presently set Sail for *Chester*; when they were arrived thither, they found that a Peace was actually concluded betwixt King *Henry* and Prince *Owen* upon these Articles; That *Cadwalader* should have all his Lands restored to him, and he received to the Favour and Friendship of his Brother. Then King *Henry* leaving the Castles of *Ruthlan* and *Basingwerk* well manned and fortified, and having near the latter founded a Publick Structure for the Order of Knights Templars, returned to *England*. But the troubles of *Wales* did not end with him, for *Iorwerdh Goch ap Meredith* who had taken part with the King of *England* during this War, laid Siege to the Castle of *Yale*, which was built by Prince *Owen*, and making himself Master of it, rased it to the ground.

The next Year commenced with a very unfortunate Action, *Ifor ap Meyric* having long before cast a very wishful Eye upon the Land and Estate of *Morgan ab Owen*, was now resolved to put in execution what he had before contrived; and as Covetousness seldom bears any regard to Vertue or Honor, he treacherously set upon him, and flew him; and with him fell *Gurgan ap Rhys*, the most Famous *British* Poet of his time. *Morgan*'s Estate *Ifor* bestowed upon his Brother *Iorwerth*, who about the same time got also possession of the Town of *Caer-Lheon*. But these inward and home-bread Disturbances

1157.

sturbances were quickly mitigated by a general Peace which was presently after this concluded betwixt the King of *England* and all the Princes and Lords of *Wales*, *Rhys ab Gruffydh ap Rhys* Prince of *South-Wales* only excepted. For this Prince *Rhys*, who probably would not rely too far upon the King of *England*'s Fidelity, refused to consent to a Peace; but however, to secure himself the best he could from the *English*, whom he had no small reason to be afraid of, he thought it his best Prudence to issue out his Orders, commanding his Subjects to remove their Cattel and other Effects to the Wilderness of *Tywy*, where they were like to remain securest from the Eyes and reach of the Enemies. But he had not continued there long, when he received a more positive Express from King *Henry*, commanding him to appear forthwith at his Court, and to accept of the Proposals of Peace, before the joynt Forces of *England* and *Wales* were sent to fetch him up. Prince *Rhys* having received such a threatning Message, thought it now high time to repent of what he had afore so rashly resolved upon, and therefore after long Consultation, he judged it his wisest way to accept of the King's Proposals and to appear at Court. There it was agreed upon, that *Rhys*, whose Lands heretofore lay scattered about, and were intermixed with other Person's Estate, should enjoy *Cantref Mawr*, and any other Cantref which the King should be pleased to bestow upon him. But contrary to this Article, the King assigned him several Lordships and other Lands far remote from each other, and particularly intermixed them with the Estates of *English-men*, whom he was sure would be a watch and a curb to all the motions of Prince *Rhys*. This was indeed a very politick Contrivance of King *Henry* to keep under the high and restless Spirit of *Rhys*; but the Justice of the Action does not so evidently appear in breaking one of the chiefest Articles of the Peace, and chopping and bestowing that which was not justly in his Power to give. But 'tis manifestly apparent that the *English* of these times were mainly concerned right

or

or wrong to oppress and keep under the *Welch* of whose mortal hatred to subjection they had so frequently and so cruelly felt. Prince *Rhys* was not at all ignorant of these wrongful and deceitful Dealings of King *Henry*, but knowing himself to be unable to redress these Grievances, he thought it more advisable for a time to live quietly with a little, than rashly to hazard all. But in a short time, he had opportunity either to demand redress from the King, or else to endeavour it himself by Force of Arms. For as soon as *Roger* Earl of *Clare* was informed of the distribution which the King of *England* had granted to Prince *Rhys*, he came to King *Henry*, requesting of his Majesty, that he would grant him such Lands in *Wales*, as he could win by force of Arms. The King readily complied with his Request, being always very forward to grant any thing which seemed to curb and discommode the *Welch*, and therefore the Earl of *Clare* marched with a great Army into *Cardigan*, and having fortified the Castles of *Yftrat-Meyric*, *Humphrey*, *Dyfi*, *Dynerth* and *Lhanrhyftyd*, he made several Incursions into the Country. In the same manner, *Walter Clyfford* who was Governour of *Lhanymdhyfri* Castle, made in-roads into the Territories of Prince *Rhys*, and after he had slain several of the *Welch*, and made great waste in the Country, returned with considerable Booty.

Prince *Rhys* as he was unable to bear these outrages, so he was resolved either to have immediate redress, or else to proclaim open War against the *English*, and therefore he sent an Express to King *Henry*, complaining of the Hostilities which his Subjects the Earl of *Clare* and *Walter Clifford* had committed in in his Country. But finding the King to put him still off with only smooth Words and fair Promises, and that he always winked at the Faults of the *English* and *Normans*, without any farther Consultation about the Matter, he laid Siege to the Castle of *Lhanymdhyfri*, and in short time made himself Master of it. Also *Eineon* the Son of *Anarawd*, *Rhys*'s Brother's Son, and a Person of great Valor, being desirous to

N free

free his Country from that miferable fervitude they now groaned under, and judging withal that his Uncle was now difcharged from the Oath he had lately fworn to the King of *England*, fat before the Caftle of *Humphrey*, and having forcibly made his entrance into it, he put all the Garrifon to the Sword, where he found a great number of Horfes and Armour, enough to arm a confiderable Body of Men And whilft *Eineon* was thus engaged at *Humphrey*'s Caftle, Prince *Rhys* perceiving that he could not enjoy any part of his Inheritance but what he afterwards got by the Sword, drew all his Power together and entred *Cardigan*, where like a moft violent Torrent, he over-run the Country, that he left not one Caftle ftanding of thofe which his Enemies had fortified, and fo brought all the Country to his fubjection. King *Henry* being fore offended at the progrefs which Prince *Rhys* fo fuddenly made againft him, returned with a great Army into *South-Wales*, but finding it to no purpofe to attempt any thing againft the Prince, he thought it more advifable to permit him to enjoy all that he had gotten, and only to take Hoftages for his obferving of Peace during his abfence out of the Kingdom, which Prince *Rhys* promifing to do, he forthwith returned to *England*, and foon after went for *Normandy*, where he concluded a Peace with the *French* King.

1158. But the Year following, Prince *Rhys* of *South-Wales* without any refpect to his promife to King *Henry* laft Year, led his Forces to *Dyfed*, and deftroyed all the Caftles that the *Normans* had fortified in that Country, and then laid Siege to *Caermardhyn*. But *Reynold* Earl of *Briftol*, the King's bafe Son, being informed of it, called together the Earl of *Clare*, his Brother-in-Law *Cadwalader*, Prince *Owen* of *North-Wales*'s Brother, *Howel* and *Conan Owen*'s Sons, with two Earls more, who with their joynt Forces marched to raife the Siege. But Prince *Rhys* was wifer than to abide their coming, and therefore upon the firft intimation of fuch great Oppofition, he retired to the Mountains called *Cefn Refter*, and there encamped.

The History of WALES.

camped, being sufficiently secure from any Enemy, by the natural Fortification of the place. The Confederate Army lay at *Dynwylhir*; and there built a Castle, but finding no news or tidings of Prince *Rhys*, they returned home without effecting any thing of Note. King *Henry* was still in *Normandy*, and there made War against the Earl of *St. Giles*, for the City and Earldom of *Tho'oufe*.

Towards the beginning of this Year, *Madoc ap Meredith ap Blethyn* Prince of *Powis* died at *Winchester*, whence his Body was honourably conveyed to *Powis*, and buried at *Myfod*. He was a Prince very much affected to Piety and Religion, very charitable to the necessitous, and good to the distressed; but his great Fault was, that he stickled too hard for the Interest of the *English*, and was always in Confederacy with King *Henry* against the good Success of his Native Country. He had Issue by his Wife *Sufanna*, the Daughter of *Gruffydh ap Conan* Prince of *North-Wales*, three Sons, *Gruffydh Maylor*, *Owen* and *Elis*, and a Daughter named *Marred*. He had also three natural Sons, *Owen Brogynton*, *Cynwric Efelh*, and *Eineon Efelh*, who tho' base born, yet according to the Custom of *Wales*, co-inherited with their Brethren who were legitimate.

And here it will not be amiss, once for all, to give a particular account of the Principality, afterwards the Lordships of *Powis*, how it came to be divided into many shares and portions, and by that means became so irrecoverably broken and weakened, that it was made subject to the *Normans* before the rest of *Wales*. For *Powis* before King *Offa*'s time, reached Eastward to the Rivers of *Severn* and *Dee*, in a right Line from the end of *Broxen* Hills to *Salop*, and comprehended all the Country between the *Wye* and *Severn*, which was antiently the Estate of *Brochwel Yscithroc*, of whom mention is made before. But after the making of *Offa*'s dike, *Powis* was contracted into a narrower compass, the plain Country toward *Salop* being inhabited by *Saxons* and *Normans*, so that the length of it reached North-East, from

N 2 *Pulford*

Pulford-Bridge to *Lhangiric*-Parish on the Confines of *Cardigan*-shire, to the South-West, and the breadth from the fartheſt part of *Cyfeilioc* Weſtward, to *Elſmere* on the Eaſt-ſide. This Principality, *Roderic* the Great gave to his youngeſt Son *Merfyn*, in whoſe Poſterity it remained intire, till the death of *Blethyn ap Confyn*, who tho' he had divided it betwixt his Sons *Meredith* and *Cadwgan*; yet it came again whole and intire to the poſſeſſion of *Meredith ap Blethyn*. But he again broke the Union, and left it between his two Sons *Madawc* and *Gruffydh*; the firſt of which was Married to *Sufanna* the Daughter of *Gruffydh ap Conan* Prince of *North-Wales*, and had with her that part, afterward called by his Name, *Powis Fadoc*. After his death, this Lordſhip was divided alſo betwixt his Sons *Gruffydh Maelor*, *Owen ap Madawc*, and *Owen Brogyntcn*, which laſt, tho' baſely born, had however, for his incomparable Valour and Courage, a ſhare of his Father's Eſtate, namely, *Edeyrneon* and *Dinmael*, which he left to his Sons *Gruffydh*, *Blethyn* and *Iorwerth*. *Owen Madawc* had to his Portion *Mechain-Is-Coed*, and had Iſſue *Lhewelyn* and *Owen Fychan*. But *Gruffydh Maelor* the eldeſt Son, Lord of *Bromfield*, had to his part, both the *Maelors* with *Mochnant-is-Raydar*, and married *Angharad* the Daughter of *Owen Gwynedh* Prince of *North-Wales*, by whom he had Iſſue one Son named *Madawc*, who held his Father's Inheritance intirely, and left it ſo to his only Son *Gruffydh*, who was called Lord of *Dinas Brân*, becauſe he lived in that Caſtle: He married *Emma* the Daughter *James* Lord *Audley*, by whom he had Iſſue *Madawc*, *Lhewelyn*, *Gruffydh* and *Owen*. This *Gruffydh ap Madawc* took part with King *Henry* the Third, and *Edward* the Firſt againſt the Prince of *North-Wales*; and therefore for fear of the ſaid Prince, he was forced to keep himſelf ſecure within his Caſtle of *Dinas Brân*, which being ſituated upon the ſummity of a very ſteep Hill, ſeemed impregnable to all the daring Efforts, that could be uſed againſt it. After his death, *Edward* the firſt dealt very unkindly with his Children who were of Age to manage their

The History of WALES.

their own Concerns ; and making two of them privately away, bestowed the Wardship of *Madoc* his eldest Son, who had by his Father's Will, the Lordships of *Bromfield* and *Yale*, with the reversion of *Maelor Saesnec*, *Hopesdale* and *Mouldsdale*, his Mother's Joynture, on *John* Earl *Warren* ; and the Wardship of *Lhewelyn*, to whose share fell the Lordships of *Chirke* and *Nanheudwy*, to *Roger Mortimer*, third Son to *Roger Mortimer* the Son of *Ralph Mortimer*, Lord Mortimer of *Wigmor*. But *Emma Gruffydh*'s Wife, having in her possession for her Dowry, *Maelor Saesnec*, *Hopesdale*, and *Moulsdale*, with the presentation of *Bangor* Rectory; and seeing two of her Sons disinherited and done away, and the fourth dead without Issue, and doubting left *Gruffydh* her only surviving Child could not long continue, she conveyed her Estate to the *Audley*'s, her own Kin, who getting possession of it took the same from the King, from whom it came to the House of *Derby*, where it continued for a long time; till at length it was sold to Sir *John Glynne*, Serjeant at Law, in whose Family it still remaineth. But Earl *Warren* and *Roger Mortimer*, forgetting what signal Service *Gruffydh ap Madoc* had performed for the King, guarded their new Possessions with such caution and strictness, that they took especial care they should never return to any of the Posterity of the legal Proprietor ; and therefore having obtained the King's Patent, they began to secure themselves in the said Lordships. *John* Earl *Warren* began to build *Holt*-Castle, which was finished by his Son *William*, and so the Lordships of *Bromfield* and *Yale* continued in the name of the Earls of *Warren* for three Descents, viz. *John*, *William* and *John*, who dying without Issue; the said Lordships, together with the Earldom of *Warren* descended to *Alice* Sister and Heir to the last *John* Earl *Warren*, who was married to *Edmond Fitz Alan* Earl of *Arundel*, in which House they remained for three Descents, namely *Edmund*, *Richard*, *Richard* his Son, and *Thomas* Earl of *Arundel*. But for want of Issue to this last, *Thomas* Earl of *Arundel* and *Warren*, the said Lordships fell

to

to two of his Sisters, whereof one named *Elizabeth*, was married to *Thomas Mowbray* Duke of *Norfolk*, and the other called *Joan*, to *William Beauchamp* Lord of *Abergavenny*: But since they came to the Hands of Sir *William Stanley* Knight, who being attainted of High Treason, they devolved by forfeiture to the Crown, and now are annexed to the Principality of *Wales*. But *Roger Mortimer* the other sharer in the Lands of *Gruffydh ap Madoc*, was made Justice of *North-Wales*, built the Castle of *Chirke*, and married *Lucia* the Daughter and Heir of Sir *Robert de Wafre* Knight, by whom he had Issue *Roger Mortimer*, who was married to *Joan Turbervill*, by whom he had *John Mortimer* Lord of *Chirke*. This *John* sold the Lordship of *Chirke* to *Richard Fitzalan* Earl of *Arundel*, *Edmund*'s Son, and so it was again annexed to *Bromfield* and *Yale*.

The third Son of *Gruffydh* Lord of *Dinas Bran*, named also *Gruffydh*, had for his part *Glyn Dwrdwy*, which *Gruffydh ap Gruffydh* had Issue *Madoc Crupl*, who was the Father of *Madoc Fychan*, the Father of *Gruffydh*, the Father of *Gruffydh Fychan*, who was the Father of *Owen Glyndwr*, who rebelling in the days of *Henry* the Fourth, *Glyndwrdwy* by confiscation came to the King, of whom it was afterwards purchased by *Robert Salisbury* of *Rug*, in whose Family it still remaineth. *Owen* the Fourth Son of *Gruffydh* Lord of *Dinas Bran*, had for his share *Cynlhaeth* with the Rights and Priviledges thereunto belonging. The other part of *Powys*, comprehending the Countries of *Arustly, Cyfeilioc, Lhannerch-hudol, Caereneon, Mochnach uwch Rayadr, Mechan uwch Coed, Moudhwy, Deudbwr, Ystrad Marchelh*, and *Teir Tref*, or the three Towns, rightfully descended to *Gruffydh ap Meredith ap Bletbyn*, by *Henry* the first created Lord *Powys* who married *Gweyryl* or *Weyryl* the Daughter of *Urgene ap Howel ap Jefaf ap Cadogan ap Athelstan Glodryth*, by whom he had Issue *Owen* Surnamed *Cyfeilioc*. This *Owen* enjoyed his Father's Estate intire, and married *Gwenlhiam* the Daughter of *Owen Gwynedh* Prince of *North-Wales*, who bore him one Son,

The History of WALES.

Son, named *Gwenwynwyn* or *Wenwynwyn*, from whom that part of *Powys* was afterwards called *Powys Wenwynwyn* He had moreover a base Brother, called *Cafwalhon*, upon whom he bestowed the Countries of *Swdh Lhannerch Hudol*, and *Braniarth*. *Gwenwynwyn* succeeded his Father in all his Estate, saving what *Cafwalhon* enjoyed, and married *Marga et* the Daughter of *Rhys ap Theodor* Prince of *South Wales*, by whom he had *Gruffydh ap Gwenwynwyn*, who succeeding his Father in all his Possessions, had Issue six Sons, by *Margaret* the Daughter of *Robert Corbet*, Brother to *Thomas* Lord *Corbet* of *Cous*; and so the intire Estate of *Gruffydh ap Meredith ap Blethyn* Lord of *Powys*, became shattered, and torn into divers Pieces. *Owen Gruffydh ap Gwenwynwyn*'s eldest Son, had for his part *Arustly, Cyfeilioc, Lhannerch Hudol*, and a part of *Caereneon*; *Lhewelyn* had *Mochnant uwch Rayadr* and *Mechain uwch Coed*; *John* the third Son, had the fourth part of *Caerenion*; *William* had *Moudhwy*; *Gruffydh Fychan* had *Deudh'ry Ystrat-Marchelh*, and *Teir Tref*; and *David* the sixth and youngest Son, had the other fourth part of *Caereneon*. *Owen ap Gruffydh* had Issue one only Daughter, named *Hawys Gadarn*, or the *Hardy*, whom he left his Heir; but her Uncles *Lhewelyn, John, Gruffydh Fychan*, and *David*, thinking it an easy matter to dispossess an Orphan, challenged the Lands of their Brother *Owen*, alledging for a Cloak to their Usurpation, that a Woman was not capable of holding any Lands in that Country. But *Hawys* made such Friends in *England*, that her Case was made known to King *Edward* the Second, who bestowed her in Marriage upon a Servant of his, named *John Charleton*, termed *Valectus Domini Regis*, who was born at *Appley* near *Wellington*; in the County of *Salop*, Anno One Thousand Two Hundred Sixty Eight, and in her Right, created him Lord *Powys*.

The History of WALES.

This *John Charleton* Lord *Powys*, being aided and supported by the King of *England*, quickly broke all their Measures; and having taken *Lhewelyn*, *John*, and *David*, his Wives Uncles, he put them in safe custody, in the Kings Castle of *Harlech*; and then obtained a Writ from the King to the Sheriff of *Shropshire*, and to Sir *Roger Mortimer*, Lord of *Chirkland*, and Justice of *North-Wales*, for the Apprehension of *Gruffydh Fychan*, with his Sons in Law, Sir *Roger Chamber* and *Hugh Montgomery*, who were then in actual Hostility against him and his Wife *Hawys*. But *Gruffydh Fychan* and his Accomplices suspecting their own Strength, and having lost *Thomas* Earl of *Lancaster*, their main support, thought it most advisable to submit themselves to the King's Pleasure, touching the Difference betwixt them and *Hawys*; who finding upon record, how that *Gruffydh ap Meredith*, Ancestor to the said *Hawys*, upon his Submission to King *Henry* the First, became Subject to the King of *England*, and thereupon was created Baron of *Powys*, which Barony he and his Posterity had ever since held *in capite* from the King; was of opinion, that *Hawys* had more Right to her Fathers Possessions now in their hands, than any pretence they could lay to her Estate. But to make a final determination of this matter, and to compose the Difference more amicably betwixt them; it was agreed, that *Hawys* should enjoy her Inheritance in Fee-Simple to her and her Heirs for ever, after the Tenure of *England*; and that her Uncles *Lhewelyn*, *John*, *David*, and *Gruffydh*, should quietly enjoy their Portion, and the same to descend to their Heir Males perpetually; but in default of such Heir Males, the same was to descend to *Hawys* and her Heirs. But *William* Lord of *Mowdhwy*, the Fourth Brother, called otherwise *Wilcock Mowdhwy*, because he did not joyn with the rest against *Hawys*, had all his Lands confirmed to him, and to all his Heirs, both Male and Female for ever. He married *Elianor*, the Sister of *Elen*, *Owen Glyndwr*'s Mother, who was lineally descended from *Rhys ap Theodore*, Prince of

South-

The History of WALES.

South-Wales, by whom he had Issue *John de Mowdhwy*; whose Daughter *Elizabeth*, being Heir to his whole Estate, was married to one Sir *Hugh Burgh*, Knight. His Son Sir *John Burgh*, Lord of *Mowdhwy*, married *Jane* the Daughter of Sir *William Clapton* of *Glocester-shire*, by whom he had four Daughters, *Elizabeth*, *Ancreda*, *Isabel*, and *Elianor*; the first of whom was married to *Thomas Newport*, the second to *John Leighton* of *Stretton*; the third to *John Lingen*; and the younger to *Tho. Mytton*; who by equal Distribution, had the Lordship of *Mowdhwy* divided betwixt them.

But *John Charleton* Lord of *Powys* had Issue by his Wife *Hawys*, a Son named *John*, who enjoyed the same Lordship for about Seven Years, and then left it to his Son, of the same Name, who was Lord of *Powys* Fourteen Years; and then it descended to his Son, called also *John Charleton*, who enjoyed his Fathers Estate Twenty Seven Years; but dying without Issue, the Lordship of *Powys* fell to his Brother *Edward Charleton*. This *Edward* had Issue by his Wife *Elianor*, the Daughter and one of the Heirs of *Thomas* Earl of *Kent*, and the Widow of *Roger Mortimer* Earl of *March*, two Daughters, *Jane* and *Joyce*; the first of which was married to Sir *John Gray*, Knight; and the second to *John* Lord *Tiptoft*; whose Son was by King *Henry* VI. created Earl of *Worcester*. But after the death of *Elianor*, this *Edward* Lord *Powys* marryed *Elizabeth* the Daughter of Sir *John Barkley*, Knight; and so after his death, which happened in the Year 1420. the Lordship of *Powys* was divided into three parts, whereof his Widow *Elizabeth* had for her Joynture *Lhannerch Hudol*, *Ystrad Marchelh*, *Deudhwr*, and *Teirtref*; and was afterwards married to Lord *Dudley*. *Jane* his eldest Daughter had *Caereneon*, *Mechain*, *Mochnant*, and *Plasdinas*; and *Joyce* had *Cyfeilioc*, and *Arustly*. But the Lordship of *Powys* continued in the Family of Sir *John Gray*, for five Descents, in right of his Wife *Jane*: the last of whom, *Edward Gray*, Lord *Powys*, married *Anne*, one of the Daughters and Co-Heirs of *Charles Brandon*, Duke of *Suffolk*, and dyed without

Dugdale out any lawful Iſſue. This *Edward* Lord *Powys*, in *Bar.Engl.* 15 *Henry* VIII. accompanied the Duke of *Suffolk* in Tom. II. the Expedition then made into *France*, and was at p. 284. the taking of *Bray*, and other places then won from the *French*. And in 36 *Henry* VIII. being again ready to march in the King's Service, he made his laſt Teſtament, whereby he ſetled the Succeſſion of his whole Barony and Lordſhip of *Powys*, his Caſtle and Mannor of *Pool*, with divers other Lordſhips in the County of *Montgomery*, and all the reſt of his Eſtate, in the County of *Salop*, upon the Heirs of his own Body lawfully begotten, or to be begotten; and in default of ſuch Iſſue, his Caſtle and Mannor of *Charlton* and *Pontisbury* in *Shropſhire* ; upon *Jane Orwell*, Daughter of Sir *Lewis Orwell*, Knight, and her Aſſigns, during her natural Life. And in caſe he ſhould dye without any Iſſue of his own Body lawfully begotten, that then *Edward Grey*, his illegitimate Son by the ſame *Jane Orwell*, ſhould have and enjoy his ſaid Barony and Mannor of *Powys*, his Caſtle and Mannor of *Pool*, and all other his Lordſhips in the County of *Montgomery*; with the Reverſion of the Caſtle and Mannor of *Charlton* and *Pontysbury*, to him and his Heirs lawfully begotten: and for lack of ſuch Iſſue, to remain to that Child, in caſe it ſhould be a Son, wherewith the ſame *Jane Orwell* was then great by him, and to the Heirs of his Body lawfully begotten. But if it ſhould not prove a Son, or if the Son dye without Iſſue, then that the whole Barony of *Powys* and all the Premiſes beforementioned, ſhould come to *Jane Grey* his Daughter, and to the Heirs of her Body lawfully begotten; and for lack of ſuch Iſſue, to *Anne Grey*, his other Daughter, and the Heirs of her Body lawfully begotten; and laſtly for default of ſuch Iſſue, to ſuch Woman-Child as ſhould be born of the Body of the ſaid *Jane Orwell*. But after *Edward Grey*, the Title of Lord of *Powys* lay extinct to the Fifth Year of K.*Charles* I. when Sir *William Herbert* Son of Sir *Edward Herbert* of *Redcaſtle* (antiently call'd *Pool*-Caſtle, now *Powys*-Caſtle) in the County of *Montgomery*, ſecond Son to

William

William Earl of *Pembrock*, was advanced to the Dignity of a Baron of the Realm, by the Title of Lord *Powys* of *Powys*, in the Marches of *Wales*; in whose Family it still continues, though the Title has been changed from a Baron to an Earl, and since to a Marquess.

About the same time that the Prince of *Powys* dyed, *Cadwathon ap Madawc ap Edwerth*, who had been for some considerable time at variance with his Brother *Eineon Clyd*, was taken Prisoner by him; who deliver'd him up to *Owen* Prince of *North-Wales*. But the Prince being willing to gratifie the King of *England*, whose Interest *Cadwalhon* has as much as in him lay opposed, sent him to the King's Officers to be imprisoned at *Winchester*; from whence he quickly found a way to escape: And by the advice of the rest of his Brethren, he returned home to his Country. King *Henry* continued all this while in *Normandy*, and during his stay there, a Match was concluded upon betwixt his Son *Henry* and *Margaret* Daughter to *Lewis* King of *France*. But this new alliance could not prevent these two Monarchs from falling at variance with each other, which happened the Year following; and thereupon King *Henry* marched with his Army to *Gascoyne*, to quell certain Rebels, who upon first notice of this Breach between both Kings, were up in Arms against the *English*. But the next Year, a Peace was again concluded, and so all things returned to their former state of Amity and Quietness. But it was not so in *Wales*; for *Howel* the Son of *Ievaf ap Cadwgan ap Athlestlan Glodryth*, having got to his hand the Castle of *Walwern* in *Cyfeilioc*, rased it to the ground, which so incensed Prince *Owen*, who was Owner of it, that nothing could lay his fury, till he had drawn his Forces together, and made an incursion into *Lhandhinam* in *Arustly*, *Howel*'s Country; which he cruelly harrassed, and carried away considerable Booty. The People of the Country perceiving these Devastations of the *North-Wales* Men, came together to the number of 300 Men, offering their Service to their natural

A. D.
1160.

1161.

tural Lord, *Howel ap Iefaf*; who upon this addition of strength, followed the Enemy to the Banks of *Severn*, where they were encamped. Prince *Owen* finding them to march after him, was glad of the opportunity to be further revenged upon *Howel*; and so turning suddenly upon them, he slew about Two Hundred Men; the rest narrowly escaping with *Howel* to the Woods and Rocks. *Owen* being more joyful for the Revenge he had taken of *Howel*, than for any Victory he had gained, rebuilt *Walwern* Castle, and having well fortified and mann'd it, returned home to *North-Wales*.

A. D. 1162.

The Year following, the like thing happened; *Owen* the Son of *Gruffydh ap Meredith*, commonly called *Owen Cyfeilioc o Wynedh*, together with *Owen ap Madawc ap Meredith*, and *Meredith ap Howel*, set upon *Carrechofa* Castle near *Ofweftry*, and having over-power'd the Garison, committed great Waste and Destruction therein. But about the same time, a pleasant passage happened in *England*; *Robert Mountford* and *Henry de Essex*, who had both fought against the *Welch* upon the Marches, and both run, began now to impeach each other, as being the first occasion of flying. The Dispute was to be tryed by Combat, in which being engaged, *Henry* was overcome; and for his false accusing of *Robert*, he was sentenced to have his Estate forfeited, and then having his Crown shorn, he was entered a Monk at *Redding*. Within a little after, King *Henry* calling to mind what Prince *Rhys* had committed during his absence out of the Kingdom, drew up a great Army against *South-Wales*, and having marched as far as *Pencadyr* near *Brecknock*, *Rhys* met him, and did his Homage; and having delivered up Hostages for his future Behaviour, stopp'd the King's farther progress, so that thence he returned to *England*. But after the King's departure, two very unlucky Accidents happened in *Wales*; *Eincon* the Son of *Anarawd ap Gruffydh*, Nephew to Prince *Rhys*, being villainously murthered in his Bed by his own Servant, called *Walter ap Lhywarch*; as also *Cadwgan ap Meredith* in

The History of WALES.   189

in like manner, by one *Walter ap Riccart*. But the loss of his Nephew, Prince *Rhys* made up, by possessing himself of that large Country called *Cantref Mawr*, and the Land of *Dynefowr*, which he afterwards enjoyed. Of men of Learning there dyed this Year, *Cadifor ap Daniel*, Archdeacon of *Cardigan*; and *Henry ap Arthen*, the greatest Scholar that had flourished in *Wales* for many Years.

The next Year, a total Rupture broke forth betwixt the *English* and *Welch*; Prince *Rhys*, a Man of an active and uncontroulable Spirit, being now experimentally sensible he could never carry on the Greatness and Grandeur of his Quality, with such Lands as the King of *England* had allotted him, made an Invasion into the Lordship of *Roger de Acre* Earl of *Glocester*; being moved thereto in a great measure, by reason that his Nephew *Anarawd ap Gruffydh* was murthered by his motive and instigation. Being advanced with a strong Army into the Earl of *Glocester*'s Estate, without any great opposition he took *Aberheidol* Castle, with those belonging to the Sons of *Wyhyaon*; all which he rased to the ground. Thence he marched to *Cardigan*, bringing all that Country under his subjection; and from thence he marched against the *Flemings*, whose Country he cruelly harassed with Fire and Sword. The rest of the Estates of *Wales*, perceiving Prince *Rhys* to prosper so successfully against the *English*, thought they might equally succeed, and shake off the *English* Yoke, which so unreasonably oppressed them. And therefore they unanimously agreed to cast off their Subjection to the *English*, whose Tyranny they could no longer bear, and to put over them Princes of their own Nation, whose Superiority they could better tolerate. And so this Year concluded with making suitable Preparations for the following Campaign.

A. D. 1163.

And therefore as soon as the time of year for action was advanced, *David* Son of *Owen* Prince of *North-Wales* fell upon *Flintshire*, which pertained to the King of *England*; and carrying off all the People and Cattel with him, brought them to *Dyffryn Clwyd*, otherwise

1164.

wife *Ruthyn* Land. King *Henry* underftanding this, gathered together his Forces, and with all fpeed marched to defend both his Subjects and Towns from the Incurfions and Depredations of the *Welch*. Being come to *Ruthlan*, and encamped there three days, he quickly perceived he could do no great matter, by reafon that his Army was not fufficiently numerous; and therefore he thought it more advifable to return back to *England*, and to augment his Forces, before he fhould attempt any thing againft the *Welch*. And accordingly he levied the moft chofen Men throughout all his Dominions of *England*, *Normandy*, *Anjou*, *Gafcoin* and *Gwien*; befides thofe Succours from *Flanders* and *Britain*; and then fet forward for *North-Wales*, purpofing to deftroy without Mercy every living thing he could poffibly meet with; and being advanced as far as *Croes-Ofwalt*, called *Ofweftry*, he incamped there. On the other fide, Prince *Own* and his Brother *Cadwalader*, with all the ftrength of *North-Wales*; Prince *Rhys* with thofe of *South-Wales*; *Owen Cyfeilioc* and *Madawc ap Meredith* with all the Power of *Powys*; the two Sons of *Madawc ap Ednerth* with the People living betwixt the Rivers of *Severn* and *Wye*, met together, and pitched their Camp at *Corwen* in *Edeyrneon*, intending unanimoufly to defend their Country againft the King of *England*. King *Henry* underftanding that they were fo near, was very defirous to come to Battel; and to that end he removed to the Banks of the River *Ceireoc*, caufing all the Woods thereabouts to be cut down, for fear of any Ambufhment lurking therein, and for a more clear profpect of the Enemy. But fome of the *Welch* took advantage of this opportunity, who being well acquainted with the Paffage, without the knowledg of their Officers, fell upon the King's Guard, where all the Pike-men were pofted; and after a hot Skirmifh, feveral were flain on both fides. But in fine, the King wan the paffage, and fo marched on to the Mountain of *Berwyn*, where he lay fometime without any Hoftility on either fide, both Armies ftanding in fear of each other. The *Englifh* kept the open Plains,
and

The History of WALES.

and were afraid to be entrapp'd in the Streights and narrow Paſſages; and the *Welch* on the other hand watched the Advantage of the place, and obſerved the *Engliſh* ſo narrowly, that neither Forage or Victuals could paſs to the King's Camp. And what augmented the miſery of the *Engliſh* Army, there happened to fall ſuch a Rain, that mightily diſturbed their Encampment, in ſo much that the Soldiers could ſcarcely ſtand, for the diſadvantage of thoſe ſlippery Hills. But in the end King *Henry* was forced to decamp, and after a very conſiderable loſs of Men and Ammunition, beſides the great Charges of this Expedition, was compell'd to return back to *England*. But to expreſs the great diſſatisfaction he entertained of this Enterprize, in a great fury he plucked out the Eyes of the Hoſtages, which he had ſome time afore received from the *Welch*; which were *Rhys* and *Cadwalhon* the Sons of *Owen* Prince of *North-Wales*, and *Cynric* and *Meredith* the Sons of *Rhys* of *South-Wales*. Some write, that in aſſailing of a Bridg, the King was in no ſmall danger of his Life; one of the *Welch* having aimed directly at him, was like to pierce him through the Body, had not *Hubert de Clare*, Conſtable of *Colcheſter*, who perceived the Arrow a coming, thruſt himſelf betwixt the King and it, though to the loſs of his own Life.

But though King *Henry* was ſhamefully forced to return to *England*, yet he did not give over the thoughts of ſubduing the *Welch*; and therefore after a long Conſultation, he made a third Expedition into *Wales*, conveying his Army by Sea, as far as *Cheſter*. There he ſtaid for ſome time, till all his Fleet, as well thoſe Ships that he had hired out of *Ireland*, as his own, were all arrived. But when they were all come together, and got ſafely to *Cheſter*, his mind was altered; and inſtead of a deſign againſt *Wales*, he unexpectedly diſmiſſed his whole Army. Prince *Rhys* was glad of this opportunity, and therefore withdrawing his Forces from the Confederate Army, he marched to the Siege of *Aberteifi* Caſtle, which being ſurrendred to him, he raſed to the ground. From thence he he got before *Cilgerran*, which he used after the same manner, and therein took Prisoner *Robert* the Son of *Stephen* his Cosin-German, who was the Son of *Nest* his Aunt, who after the death of *Gerald*, had married *Stephen* Constable. The joy of these happy Successes on the part of the *Welch*, was somewhat clouded by the death of *Lhewelyn*, Son of *Owen* Prince of *North-Wales*, a Person of great Worth, and exceedingly well beloved of all his Country.

A. D. 1165.

And now the *Welch* being something secure from any Invasion from the *English*; there rose up another Enemy to create them Disturbance; the *Flemings* and *Normans* finding the *English* to fail in their Attempt against the *Welch*, thought they might with better success quell and subdue them. And therefore they came to *West-Wales* with a great Army, and laid siege to the Castle of *Cilgerran*, which *Rhys* had lately fortified; but after two different Assaults, they were manfully beat back, and forced to depart home again. But what the *Flemings* could not effect against the *Welch* in *South-Wales*, the *Welch* easily brought about against the *English* in *North-Wales*; for Prince *Owen* having besieged *Basingwerk* Castle, then in the possession of the King of *England*, without much time spent, made himself Master of it. But it was always the misfortune of the *Welch*, that when they found themselves secure from any Enemy abroad, they were sure to quarrel and fall out at home; though indeed it could not be well otherwise expected, where so many petty States endeavoured still to surmount and out-vie one another. And now when all things went very successfully of their sides, in opposition to the *English*; two ambitious Persons began to kindle a Flame in their own bosoms; *Owen Cyfeilioc* the Son of *Gruffydh ap Meredith* Lord of *Powys*, and *Owen Fychan* second Son to *Madawc ap Meredith*, forcibly dispossessed *Iorwerth Goch* of his Estate in *Powys*, which they divided betwixt themselves; *Mochnant Uwch Rayadr* to *Owen Cyfeilioc*, and *Mochnant is Rayadr* to *Owen Fychan*.

But

The History of WALES.

But the rest of the Princes of *Wales* could not brook this Injury done to *Iorwerth Goch*; and therefore *Owen* Prince of *North-Wales*, with his Brother *Cadwalader*, and *Rhys* Prince of *South-Wales*, went with an Army into *Powys* against *Owen Cyfeilioc*, and having chased him out of the Country, they bestowed *Caereneon* upon *Owen Fychan*, to hold it of Prince *Owen*; and *Rhys* had *Walwern*, by reason that it lay near his own Territories. But within a while after, *Owen Cyfeilioc* returned with a numerous band of *Normans* and *English* along with him, and laid siege to the Castle of *Caereneon*, which he burnt to the ground. But the loss of this place was made up by the taking of *Ruthlan* Castle, which *Owen*, *Rhys*, and *Cadwalader* joyntly besieged; and which was so strongly fortified, and so manfully defended, that it cost them three Months before they could make themselves Masters of the place. Afterwards they won the Castle of *Prestatyn*, and reduced the whole Country of *Tegengl*, subject to Prince *Owen*; and then returned home to their respective Dominions. And from henceforward nothing of moment was transacted, during the remainder of Prince *Owen's* Reign, only his Son *Conan* most unmercifully slew *Urgeney* Abbot of *Lhwythlawr*, together with his Nephew *Lhawthen*. But a little after, Prince *Rhys* of *South-Wales* released out of Prison his Nephew *Robert*, Son to *Stephen Constable*, whom, as is said before, he had taken at the Siege of *Cilgarran* Castle, and sent him to *Ireland* to the aid of *Dermot* the Son of *Murchart* King of *Linster*, who was then in actual war with the King of *Leinster*. With him and his Brother *Morris Fitz-Gerald*, and their Nephews *Robert Meyler* and *Raymond*, went over a strong Detachment of *Welchmen*, under the command of *Richard Strongbow* Earl of *Strigule*, who were the chief motive of the Conquest of *Ireland*, when it was first brought in subjection to the Crown of *England*.

A. D.
1166.

1167.

1168,

But the next Year, *Owen Gwynedh* Son of *Gruffydh ap Conan* Prince of *North-Wales*, departed this Life, in the Two and Thirtieth Year of his Reign. He was a wife and a valourous Prince, ever fortunate and victorious in all his Undertakings, infomuch, as he never undertook any Defign but what he accomplifhed. He had by different Women feveral Iffues, who gat themfelves greater Efteem by their Valour, than by their Birth and Parentage. He had by *Gwladus* the Daughter of *Lhywarch ap Trahaern ap Càradoc*, *Iorwerth Drwyndwn*, or the broken Nofe, *Conan, Maelgon*, and *Gwenlhian*; by *Chriftian* the Daughter of *Grono ap Owen ap Edwyn*, he had *David, Roderic, Cadwalhon* Abbot of *Bardfey*, and *Angharad*, afterwards married to *Gruffydh Maylor*. He had by other Women feveral other Children, as *Conan, Lhewelyn, Meredith, Edwal, Rhun, Howel, Cadelh, Madawc, Eineon, Cynwric, Philip*, and *Ryrid* Lord of *Clochran* in *Ireland*. Of thefe, *Run, Lhewelyn*, and *Cynwric* died before their Father; and the reft will be mentioned in the Sequel of this Hiftory.

David ap Owen.

PRince *Owen Gwynedh* being dead, the Succeffion was of right to defcend to his eldeft legitimate Son, *Iorwerth Drwyndwn*, otherwife called *Edward* with the broken Nofe; but by reafon of that Blemifh upon his Face, he was laid afide as unfit to take upon him the Government of *North-Wales*. Therefore his younger Brothers began every one to afpire, in hopes of fucceeding their Father; but *Howel*, who was of all the eldeft, but bafe born, begotten of an *Irifh* Woman, finding they could not agree, ftept in himfelf, and took upon him the Government. But *David*, who was legitimately born, could not brook that a Baftard fhould afcend his Fathers

The History of WALES.

thers Throne; and therefore he made all the Preparations possible to pull him down. Howel on the other hand was as resolute to maintain his ground, and was not willing so quickly to deliver up, what he had not very long got possession of; and so both Brothers meeting together in the Field, were resolved to try their Title by the point of the Sword. The Battel had not lasted long, but *Howel* was slain; and then *David* was unanimously proclaimed and saluted Prince of *North-Wales*, which Principality he enjoyed without any Molestation, till *Lhewelyn, Iorwerth Drwyndwn's* Son came of age, as will hereafter appear. But *Madawc*, another of *Owen Gwynedh's* Sons, finding how his Brothers contended for the Principality, and that his native Country was like to be turmoil'd in a Civil War, did think it his better Prudence to try his Fortune abroad; and therefore leaving *North-Wales* in a very unsettled condition, sailed with a small Fleet of Ships which he had rigg'd and man'd for that purpose, to the Westward; and leaving *Ireland* upon the *North*, he came at length to an unknown Country, where most things appeared to him new and uncustomary, and the manner of the Natives far different from what he had seen in *Europe*. This Country, says the learned *H. Lhoyd*, must of necessity be some part of that vast tract of ground, of which the *Spaniards*, since *Hanno's* time, boast themselves to be the first Discoverers; and which by order of Cosmography, seems to be some part of *Nova Hispania* or *Florida*: whereby it is manifest, that this Country was discovered by the *Britains*, long before either *Columbus* or *Americus Vesputius* sailed thither. But concerning *Madawc's* Voyage to this Country, and afterwards his return from thence; there be many fabulous Stories and idle Tales invented by the Vulgar, who are sure never to diminish from what they hear, but will add to and increase any Fable as far as their Invention will prompt them. However says the same Author, it is certain that *Madawc* arrived in this Country, and after he had viewed the Fertility and Pleasantness of it, he thought it expedient to invite more of his Countrymen out of *Britain*; and therefore leaving most of those he had brought with him already behind, he returned for *Wales*. Being arrived there, he began to acquaint his Friends with what a fair and extensive Land he had met with, void of any Inhabitants, whilst they employed all their Skill to supplant one another, only for a ragged Portion of Rocks and Mountains; and therefore he would persuade them to change their present state of Danger and continual Clashings for a more quiet Being of Ease and Enjoyment. And so having got a considerable Number of *Welch* together, he bid his final adieu to his Native Country, and sailed with Ten Ships back to them he had left behind. It is therefore to be supposed, says our Authour, that *Madawc* and his People inhabited part of that Country, since called *Florida*, by reason that it appears from *Francis Loves*, an Author of no small Reputation, that in *Acufanus* and other places, the People honoured and worshipped the Cross; whence it may be naturally concluded, that Christians had been there before the coming of the *Spaniards*; and who these Christians might be, unless it were this Colony of *Maduwcs*, cannot be easily imagined. But by reason that the *Welch* who came over, were not many, they intermixt in a few Years with the Natives of the Country, and so following their Manners and using their Language, they became at length undistinguishable from the Barbarians. But the Country which *Madawc* landed in, is by the learned Dr. *Powel* supposed to be part of *Mexico*; for which Conjecture he lays down these following Reasons; First, as it is recorded in the *Spanish* Chronicles of the Conquest of the *West-Indies*, the Inhabitants and Natives of that Country affirm by Tradition, that their Rulers descended from a strange Nation, which came thither from a strange Country; as it was confessed by King *Montezeuma*, in a Speech at his Submission to the King of *Castile*, before *Hernando Cortez* the *Spanish* General. And then the *British* Words and Names of Places used in that Country, even at this day do

undoubtedly

The History of WALES.

undoubtedly argue the fame; as when they speak and confabulate together, they use this *British* Word *Gwrando*, which signifies to hearken or listen; and a certain Bird with a white Head, they call *Pengwyn*, which signifies the fame in *Welch*. But for a more complete confirmation of this, the Island of *Corroefo*, the Cape of *Bryton*, the River of *Gwyndor*, and the white Rock of *Pengwyn*, which are all *British* Words do manifestly shew, that it was that Country which *Madawc* and his People inhabited.

As soon as the Troubles of *North-Wales* were over, and Prince *David* securely settled in his Throne, the Storm fell presently upon *Powys*: For *Owen Cyfeilioc* the Lord of that Country, had always, as much as in him lay, opposed the Interest and Advantage of *Rhys* Prince of *South Wales*; upon which account Prince *Rhys* came with a great Army against *Powys*, and having subdued *Owen Cyfeilioc* his Enemy, he was for all that so favourable to him, that upon his delivering him Pledges for his future Behaviour, he presently departed out of *Powys*, and returned with much Honour to *South-Wales*. And now all the States of *Britain* being at perfect Rest and Amity with one another, the whole Tide and Scene of Action returned to *Ireland*; for *Henry* King of *England* having called together all his Nobility, began to consult about the *Irish* Expedition, which had already been determined to be taken in hand. To this Consultation there came some Messengers from *Richard Strongbow* Earl of *Strigule* Marshal of *England*, to deliver up to the Kings hands the City of *Dublyn*, the Town of *Waterford*, with all such Towns and Castles as he got in right of his Wife; whereupon the King restored to him all his Lands both in *England* and *Normandy*, and created him Lord Steward of *Ireland*. For this Earl of *Strigule* had lately, without the King's Permission, gone over to *Ireland*, and had married the Daughter of *Dermott* King of *Dublyn*; which King *Henry* took in such an indignation, that he presently seized upon all his Lands in *England* and *Normandy*. Therefore the King having now some footing in *Ireland*,

1171.

the Expedition was unanimously concluded upon; and so the King set upon his Journey, and coming towards *Wales*, he was received by Prince *Rhys*, whose Submission the King liked so well, that he presently confirmed to him all his Lands in *South-Wales*. To return the King's Favour, *Rhys* promised his Majesty 300 Horses and 4000 Oxen toward the Conquest of *Ireland*; for the sure payment of which, he delivered Fourteen Pledges. Then King *Henry* marching forward, came to *Caerlheon* upon *Uske*, and entering the Town, he dispossessed the right Owner *Iorwerth ap Owen ap Caradoc*, and kept it for his own proper use, placing a Garrison of his own Men therein. But *Iorwerth* was not so easie-mouth'd, as to be so unreasonably curb'd by the King; and therefore departing in a great fury from the King's presence, he called to him his two Sons *Owen* and *Howel*, whom he had by *Angharad* the Daughter of *Uchtryd* Bishop of *Llandaf*, and his Sisters Son *Morgan ap Sitsylht ap Dyfnwal*; and bringing together all the Forces they were able, upon the King's departure they entered the Country, and committing all the Waste and Destruction as they came along, they at last came before *Caerlheon*, which when they took, they used in the like manner, spoiling and destroying whatever they could meet with; so that nothing escaped their Fury, excepting the Castle, which they could not win. The King was in the mean time upon his Journey to *Pembroke*, where being accompanied by Prince *Rhys*, he gave him a grant of all *Cardigan*, *Ystratywy*, *Arustly*, and *Eluel*; in Recompence of all the Civilities and Honour he paid him. And so *Rhys* returned to *Aberteifi*, a Town he had lately won from the Earl of *Glocester*, and there having prepared his Present, about the beginning of *October* he returned again to *Pembrock*, having ordered Eighty Six Horses to follow him; which being presented to the King, he accepted of Thirty Six of the choicest, and returned the rest with great Thanks. The same day King *Henry* went to S. *Davids*, and after he had offered to the Memory of that Saint, he dined with the Bishop, who was the Son of *Gerald*, Cosin-German

to

to *Rhys* ; whither *Richard Strongbow* Earl of *Strygile* came from *Ireland* to confer with the King. Within a while after, King *Henry* being entertained by *Rhys* at the *White-House*, restored to him his Son *Howel*, who had been for a considerable time detained as a Pledg, and appointed him a certain day for payment of his Tribute , at which time, all the rest of the Pledges should be set at liberty. The day following, being the next after the Feast of *S. Luke*, the King went on board, and the Wind blowing very favourably, let sail for *Ireland* ; and being safely arrived upon those Coasts, he landed at *Dublyn* ; where he rested for that whole Winter, in order to make greater Preparations against the following Campaign.

But the change of the Air and Climate occasion'd such a raging Distemper and Infection among the Soldiers, that to prevent the perishing of his whole Army, the King was forced to return with what speed he could back for *England*; and so having shipp'd off all his Army and Effects, he loosed Anchor, and landed in *Wales* in the Passion Week next Year, and coming to *Pembrock*, he stayed there on *Easter-day*, and then proceeded upon his Journey towards *England*. *Rhys* hearing of the King's return, was very officious to pay him his Devotion, and would gladly feign to be one of the first who should welcome him over ; and so meeting with him at *Talacharn*, he expressed all the Ceremonies of Duty and Allegiance. Then the King passed on, and as he came from *Caerdyf* by the new Castle upon *Usk*, meaning to leave *Wales* in a peaceable condition , he sent for *Iorwerth ap Owen ap Caradoc*, who was the only Person in open Enmity against him, and that upon very just ground, willing him to come and treat about a Peace, and assuring him of a safe Conduct for himself, his Sons, and all the rest of his Associates. *Iorwerth* was willing to accept of the Proposal , and thereupon set forward to meet the King, having sent an Express to his Son *Owen*, a valourous young Gentleman, to meet him by the way. *Owen*, according to his Fathers Orders set forward on his Journey, with a small retinue, without any thing of

A. D.
1172.

Arms

Arms or Weapons of War, as thinking it Folly to clog himself with such needless Carriage, when the King had promised a safe Conduct. But he did not find it so safe; for as he passed the new Castle upon *Uske*, the Earl of *Bristol's* Men, who were garrison'd therein, laid in wait for him as he came along, and setting cowardly upon him, flew him, with most of his Company. But some few escaped to acquaint his Father *Iorwerth* of such a treacherous Action; who hearing that his Son was so basely murthered, contrary to the King's absolute promise of a safe Passage; without any farther consultation about the matter, presently returned home with *Howel* his Son, and all his Friends, and would no longer put any trust or confidence in any thing that the King of *England*, or any of his Subjects, promised to do. But on the other side, to avenge the Death of his Son, who was so cowardly cut off; he presently raised all the Forces that himself and the rest of his Friends were able to do; and so entering into *England*, he destroyed with Fire and Sword all the Country, to the Gates of *Hereford* and *Glocester*. But the King was so intent upon his return, that he seemed to take no great notice of what *Iorwerth* was doing; and therefore having by Commission constituted Lord *Rhys* Chief Justice of all *South-Wales*, he forthwith took his Journey to *Normandy*. About this time dyed *Cadwalader ap Gruffydh*; the Son of *Gruffydh ap Conan*, sometime Prince of *North-Wales*; who by his Wife, *Alice* the Daughter of *Richard Clare* Earl of *Glocester*, had Issue, *Cunetha*, *Radulph*, and *Richard*; and by other Women, *Cadfan*, *Cadwalader*, *Eineon*, *Meredith Goch*, and *Cadwalhon*. Towards the end of this Year *Sitsylht ap Dyfnwal* and *Iefan ap Sitsylht ap Riryd*, surprized the Castle of *Abergavenny*, which belonged to the King of *England*, and having made themselves Masters of it, they took the whole Garrison Prisoners.

A. D. 1175.

But the following Year, there happened a very great difference, and a falling out betwixt King *Henry* and his Son of the same Name; this latter being upholded by the Queen his Mother, his Brothers *Geffrey* and *Richard*,

The History of WALES.

Richard, the French King, the Earl of Flanders, together with the Earl of Chester, William Patrick, with several other valiant Knights and Gentlemen. But the old King having a stout and a faithful Army, consisting of *Almanes* and *Brabanters*, was not in the least dismay'd or discourag'd at such a seeming Storm; and which made him more bold and adventurous, he was joyned by a strong Party of *Welchmen*, which Lord *Rhys* had sent him, under the command of his Son *Howel*. King *Henry* overthrew his Enemies in divers Encounters, and having either killed or taken Prisoners most of them who were rose up against him, he easily dissipated the Cloud which at first seemed so black and threatning. *Iorwerth ap Owen* was not very sorry to see the *English* clash, and fall into civil Dissentions among themselves; and therefore taking advantage of such a seasonable opportunity, he drew his Army against *Caerlheon*, which stood out very stifly against him. But after many warm Disputes of both sides, *Iorwerth* at length prevailed, and entering the Town by force, he took most of the Inhabitants Prisoners; and then laying siege to the Castle, it was surrender'd up in exchange for the Prisoners he had taken in the Town. *Howel* his Son, at the same time was busie in *Gwent is Coed*; and having reduced all that Country, excepting the Castle, to subjection, he took Pledges of the Inhabitants, to be true and faithful to him, and to withdraw their Allegiance from the King of *England*. At the same time, something of action passed in *North-Wales*; for *David ap Owen Gwynedh* Prince of *North-Wales* bringing an Army over the River *Menai* into *Anglesey* against his Brother *Maelgon*, who kept that Island from him; forced him to make his escape to *Ireland*; in his return from whence the following Year, he was accidentally discovered and seized upon, and then by his Brothers orders committed to close Prison. Prince *David* having brought the Isle of *Anglesey* to its pristine state of subjection to him, was resolved to move all manner of Obstacles which might at any time for the future endanger its falling off from him; and these he judged to be his own next Relations,

1174. tions, and therefore he expell'd and banish'd all his Brethren and Cosins out of his Territories of *North-Wales*. But before this Sentence was put in execution, his Brother *Conan* dyed, and so escaped the Ignominy of being banished his native Country, for no other reason, but the Jealousie of an ambitious Brother.

About the same time, *Howel* the Son of *Iorwerth ap Owen* of *Caerlheon*, took Prisoner his Uncle *Owen Pencarn*, who was right Heir of *Caerlheon* and *Gwent*; and now having him secure, and to prevent his getting any Children to inherit those places which himself was next Heir to, he first pulled out his Eyes, and then very inhumanly cut off his Testicles. But Vengeance did not permit such a base Action to go unpunished; for upon the *Saturday* following, a great Army of *Normans* and *Englishmen* came unexpectedly before the Town, and wan both it and the Castle, notwithstanding all the Opposition which *Howel* and his Father *Iorwerth* made; though this last was not privy to his Sons Action. About the same time King *Henry* came over to *England*, a little after whose arrival, *William* King of *Scots*, and *Roger de Moubray* were taken Prisoners at *Alnewike* by the Barons of the North, as they came to destroy the Northern part of the Country in the Quarrel of the young King. But old King *Henry* having committed them to the safe custody of the Earl of *Leicester*, and received *Hugh Bygod* Earl of *Chester* to his Mercy, returned to *Normandy* with a very considerable Army of *Welchmen*, which *David* Prince of *North-Wales* had sent him; in return of which, he gave him his Sister *Emme* in Marriage. When he was arrived in *Normandy*, he sent a Detachment of the *Welch* to cut off some Provisions which were going to the Enemies Camp; but in the mean time, the *French* King came to a Treaty of Peace, which was shortly afterwards concluded upon; so that all the Brethren, who had all this time maintained such an unnatural Rebellion against their Father, were forced to beg the old King's Forgiveness and Pardon for all their former Misdemeanours. *David* Prince of

North-Wales began to grow very bold and aſſuming, by reaſon of his new Alliance with the King of *England*; and nothing would ſerve his turn, but he muſt put his Brother *Roderic* in Priſon, and ſecure him with Fetters, for no other account, than becauſe he demanded his ſhare of his Fathers Lands. It was the cuſtom of *Wales*, as is ſaid before, to make an equal diviſion of the Father's Inheritance between all the Children; and therefore *David* had no colour of Reaſon or Pretence to deal ſo ſeverely with his Brother; unleſs it were to verifie that Proverb; *Might overcomes Right.* But though Prince *David* might depend much upon his Affinity with the King of *England*; yet *Rhys* Prince of *South-Wales* gained his Favour and Countenance the more, by reaſon that he let ſlip no opportunity to further the King's Intereſt and Affairs in *Wales*, and by that means was a very neceſſary and uſeful Inſtrument to keep under the *Welch*, and to promote the ſurer Settlement of the *Engliſh* in the Country. Not that he bore any Love or Affection to either King *Henry* or his Subjects; but becauſe he was ſufficiently rewarded for former Services, and was ſtill in expectation of receiving more Favours at the King's hands, he was reſolved to play the Politician ſo far, as to have regard to his own Intereſt, more than the Good of his native Country. And what did ingratiate him to King *Henry* moſt of all, upon the Feaſt of S. *James* he brought all ſuch Lords of *South-Wales* as were at Enmity with the King, to do him Homage at *Gloceſter*; namely, *Cadwalhon ap Madawc* of *Melyenyth*, his Coſin-German; *Eineon Clyt* of *Eluel*, and *Eineon ap Rhys* of *Gwerthrynion*, his Sons in Law; *Morgan ap Caradoc ap Ieſtyn* of *Glamorgan*; *Gruffydh ap Iſor ap Meiric* of *Sengennyth*, and *Sitſylht ap Dyfnwal* of *Higher Gwent*, all three his Brothers in Law, who had married his Siſters; together with *Iorwerth ap Owen* of *Caerlheon*. King *Henry* was ſo well pleaſed with this Stratagem of *Rhys*, that notwithſtanding theſe Perſons had been his implacable Enemies, he readily granted them their Pardon, and received them to Favour; and reſtored to *Iorwerth ap Owen* the Town and Caſtle of *Caerlheon*, which he had unjuſtly taken from him. This

The History of WALES.

A. D. 1175.

This Reconciliation betwixt King *Henry* and these *Welch* Lords, some of the *English* in *Wales* took advantage of, and more particularly *William de Bruce* Lord of *Brecnock*, who having for a long time a great longing to *Gwentland*, could not bring about his Design, by reason that *Sitsylht ap Dyfnwal*, the Person of greatest sway and Power in the Country, was an inveterate Enemy to all the *English*. But being now reconciled to the King, *William de Bruce*, under pretence of congratulating this new Peace and Agreement betwixt the *English* and *Welch*, invited *Sitsylht* and *Geffrey* his Son, with several others of the Persons of chiefest note in *Gwentland*, to a Feast in his Castle of *Abergavenny*, which by composition he had lately received from them. *Sitsylht*, with the rest, came according to appointment, and without the least suspicion of any treasonable Designs; but after they had been civilly entertained for some time, *William Bruce* to move a Quarrel against them, began at last to propound certain Articles to them, to be by them kept and performed; and among other unreasonable Conditions, they were to swear, that none of them should at any time carry with them Bow or Sword. The *Welch* refusing to consent to and sign such improper Articles as these; *William Bruce* presently calls out his Men, who were ready for that purpose, and bidding them fall to their business, they most treacherously fell upon and slew the innocent and naked *Welch*; and as if it did not sufficiently express their Cruelty and Inhumanity, they immediately went to *Sitsylht*'s House, which stood not far from *Abergavenny*, and taking hold of *Gwladus* his Wife, they slew her Son *Cadwalader* before her face, and then setting fire to the House, they pack'd her away to the Castle. This execrable Murther being thus most barbarously, and which was worst of all, under pretence of Friendship and Kindness, committed; *William Bruce*, to cloak his Treason with some reasonable Excuse, and to make the World believe it was not for any private Interest or Expectation he had done such an Act, as he knew would be by all Men abhorred; caused it to be reported

The History of WALES.

ported abroad, that he had done such a thing in revenge of the death of his Uncle *Henry* of *Hereford*, whom the *Welch* on the *Easter-Even* before had slain. But whilst these things passed in *South-Wales*, *Roderic*, *David* Prince of *North-Wales*'s Brother, made his escape by some means or other out of Prison, and fleeing to *Anglesey*, he was receiv'd and acknowledg'd by all the Country t'other side the River *Conwey*, for their Lord and Prince; which they were the more willing to do, by reason that they conceived an utter Abhorrence of Prince *David*, who contrary to all Rules of Equity, and almost Nature, had disinherited all his Brethren and Cosins; as boldly relying upon his Affinity and Relation to the King of *England*. But *David* perceiving the Storm to grow very violent, and that the Country did numerously flock and adhere to his Brother *Cadwalader*, thought it his best way to stay a while, till the Storm was abated; and so retired over the River *Conwey*. Towards the end of this Year, *Cadelh* the Son of *Gruffydh ap Rhys*, and Brother to Lord *Rhys*, after a tedious fit of Sickness, and taken upon him the Monkish Order, departed this Life, whose Body was very honourably enterred at *Stratflur*.

In the Spring of the following Year, dyed also *David Fitz-Gerald* Bishop of *Menevia*, or S. *Davids*, whose See was supplyed by one *Piers*, being nominated thereunto by the King of *England*. But what happened most remarkable this Year; the Lord *Rhys* Prince of *South Wales* made a very great Feast at *Christmas* in his Castle of *Aberteifi*, which he caused to be proclaimed through all *Britain*, *Ireland*, and the Islands adjacent, some considerable time before; and according to their Invitation, many Hundreds of *English*, *Normans*, and others coming to *Aberteifi*, were very honourably received, and courteously entertained by Prince *Rhys*. But among other tokens of their Welcome and Entertainment, *Rhys* caused all the Bards or Poets throughout all *Wales* to come thither; and for a better Diversion to the Company, he provided Chairs to be set in the Hall, in which the Bards being seated, they were to answer each other in Rhyme; and those

1176.

that

that acquitted themselves most handsomly, and overcame the rest, were promised great Rewards and rich Presents. In this poetical Differtation, the *North-Wales* Bards obtained the Victory, with the Applause and Approbation of the whole Company; and among the Professors of Musick, between whom there was no small Strife, Prince *Rhys*'s own Servants were accounted the most expert. But for all this civil and obliging Treatment of Prince *Rhys*, the *Normans* upon the Marches fell to their accustomed manner of treacherous way-laying, and privately assaulting the harmless and undesigning *Welch*; and therefore *Eineon Clyt Rhys* his Son in Law, and *Morgan ap Meredith*, falling into the Net which the *Normans* had deceitfully laid for them, were treacherously murthered. Therefore to keep the *Normans* under greater fear and awe for the future, Prince *Rhys* built a Castle at *Rhayadr Gwy*, being a place where the River *Wye* falls with a very great Noise and Precipitation down a great Rock. But this Castle was like to stand him in a double stead; for it was not long after he had perfectly finished it, that the Sons of *Conan ap Owen Gwynedh* made War against him; but finding upon tryal that their Design against *Rhys* was impracticable, they thought it more advisable to retire back to *North-Wales*.

A. D. 1177.

1178.

1179. The next Year, *Cadwalhon*, Brother to *Owen Gwynedh*, and Uncle to *David* and *Roderic*, who for fear of his Brother had some time ago fled for Refuge to the King of *England*; as he was conveyed home by some of the King's Servants to enjoy his patrimonial Estate in *Wales*, was by those barbarous and treacherous Villains murthered in his Journey. This Year the Sepulchre of that famous and noble *British* King *Arthur*, with his Wife *Gwenhofar* (by the means of some *Welch* Bard, whom King *Henry* had heard at *Pembrock* relate in a Song the worthy and mighty Acts of that great Prince, and the place where he was buried) was found in the Isle of *Afalon*, without the Abbey of *Glastenbury*; their Bodies being laid in a hollow Elder Tree, buried Fifteen Foot in the Earth. The Bones of King *Arthur* were of marvelous and almost
incre-

incredible bigness, having ten Wounds in the Skull, whereof one being considerably larger than the rest, seemed to be his Death-Blow; and the Queens Hair seemed to the sight to be fair and yellow, but when touch'd, crumbled presently to Dust. Over the Bones was laid a Stone, with a Cross of Lead, upon the lower side of which Stone were engraven these words:

HIC JACET SEPULTUS INCLYTUS REX
ARTHURUS IN INSULA AVALONIA.

Here lies buried the famous King ARTHUR *in the Isle of Afalon.*

No Action of moment had passed in *Wales* this long time, and the *Welch* were in perfect Amity and Concord with the King of *England*; but some unlucky Accident fell out at last to dissolve this happy Union and Agreement. One *Ranulph de Poer*, who was Sheriff of *Glocesterſhire*, or rather as *Giraldus Cambrenſis* observes, of *Herefordſhire*, being a cruel and unreasonable Oppressor of the *Welch*, put the Lord of *Gwentland* to death; in revenge of whom, a certain young Person of that Country, set upon *Ranulph* with several other Gentlemen his Companions, and slew them to a Man. King *Henry* was implacably enrag'd at this News, and so cruelly incensed, that he presently raised and drew together all his Power, and came to *Worcester*, intending to march forward to *Wales*, and to invade the Enemies Country. But the Lord *Rhys ap Gruffydh*, a subtile and a politick Prince, thinking it impossible to withstand the *Engliſh* Army, and fearing the King's Puissance, which he perceived to be so implacably bent against the *Welch*, went in person to *Worcester*, and swearing Fealty to the King, became his perpetual Liege-Man; and for the due observance of this Contract, he promised to send his Sons and Nephews for Pledges. But when he would have persuaded them to answer his request, the young Men considering with themselves, how former Pledges had not been very genteely treated by the *Engliſh*,

1182.

refused

refused to go; and so the whole matter rested for that time. What became of the matter afterwards we know not; but probable it is, that King *Henry* returned to *England* satisfied with *Rhys*'s Submission; for we hear no more of his coming to *Wales*. And so the Country remained quiet and undisturbed for a long time; till at length the *Welch* began to fall to their wonted Method of killing and murdering one another.

A. D. 1186.   *Cadwalader* Prince *Rhys*'s Son was privately murdered in *West-Wales*, and buried in the *Ty Gwyn*. And the Year following, *Owen Fychan* the Son of *Madawc ap Meredith*, was slain by night in the Castle of *Carrergova* near *Osweftry*, by *Gwenwynwyn* and *Cadwalhon* the Sons of *Owen Cyfeilioc*. But what was most unnatural of all, *Lhewelyn*, whose Father *Cadwalhon ap Gruffydh ap Conan* was lately murdered by the *Englishmen*, was taken by his own Brothers, who very barbarously put out his Eyes. About the same time, *Baldwyn*, Archbishop of *Canterbury*, being attended by *Giraldus Cambrensis*, took a Progress into *Wales*, being the first Archbishop of *Canterbury* that visited that Country; whose Authority the Clergy of *Wales* in vain opposed, though they stifly alledged the Liberties and Priviledges of their Metropolitan Church of S. *Davids*. In this Visitation, described by *Giraldus* in his *Itinerarium Cambriæ*, he persuaded many of the Nobility of *Wales* to go to the *Holy Land* against those prevailing Enemies of Christianity, the *Saracens*; to whose prevailing Greatness, *Jerusalem* it self was now in great danger

1187.

1188.   to become subject. The Archbishop having left the Country, *Maelgon* the Son of Lord *Rhys* brought all his Power against *Tenbigh*, and having by force made himself Master of it, burnt the whole Town to the ground, and so carried away very confiderable Spoil. He was a Person of such civil Behaviour and easie Access, of so comly Personage, and Honesty in all his Actions, that he attracted the most earnest Love and Affection of all his Friends; by which means he became very terrible and formidable to his Enemies, especially the *Flemings*, of whom he obtained divers Victories and Conquests.

The

The History of WALES.

The next Year, being the Year of Christ 1189. *A. D.*
Henry the Second, furnamed *Courtmantel*, King of 1189.
England dyed, and was buried at *Fonteverard*; after
whom, his Son *Richard*, called *Curdelyon*, was by the
unanimous confent of all the Peers and Nobility of
England, crowned in his place. Prince *Rhys* being
thus deprived of his greateft Friend, thought it his
wifeft way to make the beft provifion he could for
himfelf, by enlarging his Dominions, and extending
the Bounds of his prefent Territories; and therefore
having raifed all the Strength he could, he wan the
Caftles of *Seynclere*, *Abercorran*, and *Lhanftephan*;
and having taken and committed to Prifon *Maelgwn*
his Son, who was the greateft Thorn in his Side, as
one that was moft paffionately beloved by the *South-Wales* Men, he brought the whole Country to his fubjection. Then he built the Caftle of *Cydwely*; but 1190.
what took away from him the Joy of all this good Fortune, he loft his Daughter *Gwenlhian*, a Woman of
fuch incomparable Beauty, and exceeding in all feminine Qualifications, that fhe was accounted the faireft
and beft accomplifhed Lady in all the Country. And
not long after her dyed *Gruffydh Maylor*, Lord of *Brom-* 1191.
field, a Man of great Prudence and Experience, and
one that excelled all the Nobility of his time in Hof-
pitality, and all other Acts of Generofity and Libera-
lity. His Corps were carried to *Myfod*, and honourably interr'd there, being attended by moft of the Perfons of Quality throughout the whole Country. He
had Iffue by his Wife *Angharad* Daughter of *Owen
Gwynedh* Prince of *North-Wales*, a Son called *Madawc*,
who fucceeded his Father in that part of *Powys*, called
from him *Powys Fadawc*. *Rhys*, Prince of *South-Wales*,
was growing very powerful, and had made himfelf
Mafter of the greateft part of *South-Wales*, only with
fome few places more, *Dynefowr* held out ftill; which
however, upon the firft Affault he made againft it, was
delivered up to him. But as he increafed in the number
of Towns and Caftles, he had the Misfortune to have
that of his Children diminifhed; for his Daughter
Gwenlhian was lately deceafed; and now he had no
longer

The History of WALES.

sooner got *Dynefowr* Castle into his possession, but his Son *Owen* dyed at *Strata Florida*, or *Ystratflur*. King *Richard* was gone to the *Holy Land* against the *Saracens*; but in his return to *England*, he wan the Kingdom of *Cyprus*, and gave it to *Gwido* King of *Jerusalem*, upon condition he would resign his former Title to him: During his stay in this Island, he marryed *Berengaria* the Daughter of the King of *Navarr*.

A. D. 1192.

Mae'gon, Prince *Rhys*'s Son had been now detain'd a long time in Prison, where his Father had shut him up; but being at last utterly weary of such a close Confinement, he found some means or other to get out, and to make his escape. His Father Prince *Rhys* was not so troubled at his being broke out, and that he had got his liberty, as to give over the Conquest, which all this while he had gone so furiously on with; but laying siege to *Lhanhayaden* Castle, he took it without any great Opposition, and brought all the Country about to his subjection. And what favoured him more in his Attempts against the *English*, King *Richard* having most bravely signalized himself against the Infidels, in his return home through *Austria*, was taken Prisoner by Duke *Leopold*, who presented him to the Emperour *Henry*, who demanded 200000 Marks for his Ransom; laying to his charge, that he had spoiled and plundered the Island of *Sicily* in his Voyage to the *Holy Land*. And as *Rhys* took the advantage of King *Richard*'s absence to subject *South-Wales*; so *Roderic* Brother to *David* Prince of *North Wales*, made use of *Gothrike*'s the King of *Man*'s help, to get the Principality of *North-Wales* to himself, and eject his Brother. And therefore entring into *Anglesey*, he quickly reduced the whole Island to his subjection. But he did not enjoy it long; for before the Year was over, the Sons of his Brother *Conan* came with an Army against him, and forcing him, together with the King of *Man* to fly the Island, they took present Possession of it themselves. And while these things were done in *North Wales*, *Maelgon*, Prince *Rhys* of *South-Wales* his Son, who was lately escaped from Prison, besieged *Ystratmeyric* Castle, and after some small Oppo-

1193.

sition

The History of WALES.

sition, got it into his own hands upon *Christmas* night; which encouraged him to farther Attempts. And at the same time, his Brother *Howel*, surnamed *Says*, or the *Englishman*, by reason that he had served for some time under the King of *England*, another Son of Prince *Rhys*, got by surprize the Castle of *Gwys*, and having secured *Philip de Gwys* the Owner, with his Wife and two Sons, he made them all Prisoners of War. Then the two Brothers *Howel* and *Maelgon* joyned their Forces; but fearing that they had more Castles than what they were able to defend, they thought it convenient to rase *Lhanhayaden* Castle; which the *Flemings* having notice of, they gathered all their Power together, and coming to *Lhanhayaden* at the day appointed, they unexpectedly set upon the *Welch*, and flew a great number of them. But notwithstanding this sudden and unhappy accident, they thought it necessary to destroy the Castle; and so coming to *Lhanhayaden* the second time, they rased it to the ground, without any Molestation from, or appearance of any Enemy to disturb them. But when *Anarawd*, another Son of Pr. *Rhys*, saw how prosperously his Brothers succeeded, he thought to make himself as rich as they, and by a shorter and an easier Method: And therefore having under a smooth pretence of Friendship and Love got his Brothers *Howel* and *Madawc* in private; being moved with Ambition and Covetousness to enjoy their Estates, he first made them Prisoners, and then very unnaturally pulled out their Eyes. But *Maelgon* escaped this Snare, and hearing what a foul Action was committed, he promised his Brother *Anarawd* the Castle of *Ystratmeyric*, for the Liberty and Releasment of his two Brothers, which *Anarawd* granted. But 'tis no wonder that those Brothers could be unnatural and cruel to one another, who could joyn and agree to rebel against their Father; and now Prince *Rhys* having rebuilt the Castle of *Rhayadr Gwy*, was laid wait for, and taken Prisoner by his own Sons, who were afraid, that in case their Father had them once in his power, he would severely revenge their cruel and unnatural Deeds. But *Howel* proved more kind and dutiful than

A. D. 1194,

P 2 the

The History of WALES.

the reſt ; who, though blind, found a way to let his Father eſcape out of *Maelgon*'s Priſon ; and ſo Prince *Rhys* being ſet at liberty, he took and deſtroyed the Caſtle of *Dynefcwr*, which belonged to his Son *Maelgon*. But though he ſucceeded in this Attempt, yet he loſt another caſtle elſewhere ; for the Sons of *Cadwalhon ap Madawc* of *Melyenydh* being informed that Prince *Rhys* was detained Priſoner by his Son *Maelgon*, they beſieged *Rhayadr Gwy* Caſtle, which being ſurrendred up to them, they fortified for their own uſe.

But whilſt theſe unhappy Differences, and unnatural Claſhings betwixt Prince *Rhys* and his Sons, continue and rage in *South-Wales*, a new revolution of Affairs happened in *North-Wales*. Prince *David* had now enjoyed the Sceptre of *North-Wales* for above Twenty Four Years ; and one would think, that ſo long a Poſſeſſion would ſecure him in his Throne, that it could not be very eaſie to pull him down. But Poſſeſſion is not always the ſureſt Card, which proved very true in Prince *David*'s caſe at this time ; for *Lhewelyn* the Son of *Iorwerth Drwyndwn*, who was the eldeſt Son of *Owen Gwynedh* Prince of *North-Wales*, being now arrived to Years of maturity, and having Senſe enough to underſtand what a juſt Title and Claim he had to the Principality of *North-Wales*, of which his Uncle *David* had ſo unjuſtly kept him out ; he thought it high time to endeavour to recover what was lawfully his own, which however he was well perſuaded his Uncle *David* would never eaſily part with. And therefore being well aſſured that the juſtneſs of his Title would never mount him up to the Throne, without he had an Army at his heels to help him on ; he called together all his Friends and Relations by his Mothers ſide, who was Married the Daughter of *Madawc ap Meredith* Prince of *Powys*, and having drawn to his ſide his Coſins the Sons of *Conan ap Owen Gwynedh*, and *Rhodri ap Owen*, he came into *North Wales*, proclaiming how againſt all Juſtice his Uncle *David* had firſt diſinherited his Father *Iorwerth*, and then had

had kept the Government from him who was the right Heir. And though his Father *Iorwerth* had been incapable of taking upon him the Government by reason of some Infirmity; yet there was no reason that his Fathers Weakness should exclude and turn him out; and therefore, being now sensible of what he was not capable to understand in his youth, he laid claim to the Principality, which was justly his own. But there was no great need of conjuring to understand his Claim, nor of much Rhetorick to persuade the People to own him for their Prince; whose Affection was cooled, and almost worn off from *David*, ever since he had dealt so unnaturally with his Brothers, whom after he had deprived of their Estates, he banished out of the Country. And therefore before *Lhewelyn* could expect to have any sure footing, the whole Country of *North-Wales* was at his devotion, excepting only Three Castles, which *David*, by the help of the *English*, in whom, by reason of his Affinity with the late King *Henry*, he depended much upon, kept to himself. And thus *David* being deprived of almost all that he formerly possessed; we shall reckon him no more among the Princes of *North-Wales*, but restore the Principality to the true Heir *Lhewelyn ap Iorwerth*.

Lhewelyn ap Iorwerth.

Lhewelyn ap Iorwerth the Son of *Owen Gwynedh*, having thus succesfully carried on his just Claim to the Dominion of *North-Wales*, and being quietly settled in the Government of it, *Roger Mortimer* marches with a strong Body to *Melyenith*, and built the Castle of *Cymaron*, whereby he reduced that Country to his subjection, and forced thence the two Sons of *Cadwalhen ap Madaine* that were Governours thereof. About this time *Rhys* and

A. D. 1195.

Meredith (two valiant but undutiful) Sons of Prince *Rhys*, having got together a Body of hot-headed daring Soldiers, came before *Dynefawr*, and took the Castle that was garrison'd by their Fathers Men: Hence they proceeded to *Cantre-Fychan*, where the Country civily received them, and surrender'd up the Castle to them. At this their Father was justly incensed, and therefore to put a stop to their farther Proceedings, he endeavoured by all means to take them, which not long after happened; for their Adherents now began to be touched with the Sense as well of their Treason against, as of their Allegiance due to their lawful Lord Prince *Rhys*; and therefore to attone for their past Faults, and to procure his future Favour, they betrayed their rebellious Leaders to their offended Father, who immediatly committed them to safe custody.

A. D. 1196.

The ensuing Year Prince *Rhys* levies a great Army, whose first Attempt was upon the Town and Castle of *Caermadthyn*, both which he took in a short time and destroyed, and then returned with considerable Booty. Not long after he led the said Army to the Marches, and invested the Castle of *Clun*, which was not so easily taken as the former; for this cost him a long Siege, and many a fierce Assault; and therefore to be revenged of it, when he took it he laid it in Ashes; thence he proceeded to the Castle of *Radnor*, which he likewise won; but immediately after it cost him a bloody Battel; for he was no sooner Master of the Castle, but *Roger Mortimer* and *Hugh de Say* came with a numerous and well-disciplin'd Army, consisting of *Normans* and *English*, to the relief of it. Whereupon Prince *Rhys* thinking it not his best course to confine his Men within the Walls, led 'em up into a Champion Ground hard by, and there, like a valiant Prince, resolved to give his Enemies Battel, though they had much the advantage of him; for his Men were neither so well armed, nor so much accustomed to Battel as the others were; however their Courage made amends for their Arms, and their Leaders Prudence

and

The History of WALES.

and Conduct supply'd the Defects of their Discipline; for they chose rather to die honourably in the Defence of their Country, than shamefully to survive the Loss of it; and therefore they attack'd their Enemies so valiantly, that they were not long able to withstand their Force, but quitted the Field in great Disorder, leaving a great number of their Men behind them slain upon the spot: and Prince *Rhys* pursued them so warmly, that they were glad of the shelter of the Night to protect them from his Fury. After this Victory, he besieged the Castle of *Payne* in *Elfel*, which he easily took, and kept in his own hands, till *William de Bruce*, the Owner thereof, came to him, and humbly desired Peace of him, which he granted him, and withal deliver'd him up his Castle again. Not long after, the Archbishop of *Canterbury* (whom King *Richard* had substituted his Lieutenant in *England*) marches with a powerful Army towards *Wales*, and besieges the Castle of *Gwenwynwyn*, at the Pool; but the Garrison made such a vigorous Defence, that he lost a great many of his Men, and all his Attempts proved ineffectual; therefore he sent for some Pyoneers, whom he ordered to undermine the Walls; which when the besieged understood, they bethought of securing themselves on the most honourable Terms they could; they were not willing to put themselves to the hazard of a Battel, for their Enemies were thrice their Number; therefore they proposed to surrender up the Castle, on condition they should carry off all their Arms along with them: Which Offer the Archbishop accepted of, and so permitted the Garrison to march out quietly. Then fortifying the Castle for the King's use, and putting a strong Garrison in it for its defence, he returned again to *England*. But *Gwenwynwyn* was not so willing to part from his Castle, as never to attempt the Recovery of it; therefore as soon as he understood that the Archbishop was gone back, he immediately besieged it, and shortly after received it on the same Terms that his Men had deliver'd it up; and afterwards kept it for his own use.

1197. The following Year there broke out a terrible Plague, which spread over all *Britain* and *France*, and carried off a great number of the Nobility, besides common People. This Year likewise dyed the valiant *Rhys*, Prince of *South-Wales*, the only Stay and Defence of that part of *Wales*; for he it was that got them their Liberty, and secured it to them. He often very readily exposed his own Life for the defence of theirs and their Country; generally he got the better of his Enemies, and at last either brought them entirely under his Subjection, or forced them to quit their Country. He was no less illustrious for his virtuous Endowments, than for his Valour and Extraction; so that it was with good reason that the *British* Bards and others wrote so honourably of him, and so mightily deplored his Death.

To this Prince were born many Sons and Daughters, whereof his eldest Son *Gruffydh* succeeded him; the others were *Cadwalhon*, *Maelgon*, *Meredith*, and *Rhys*. Of his Daughters, one called *Gwenlhian* was married to *Ednyfed Fychan*, Ancestor to *Owen Tudor* that married *Katharine* Queen-Dowager to King *Henry* the Fifth: And the rest were very well match'd with some of the Nobility of the Country. Prince *Gruffydh* being settled in the Government of his Country, did not long enjoy it peaceably; for his troublesome Brother *Maelgon* thought it now a fit time to endeavour the recovery of the Inheritance his Father had deprived him of. To this purpose he makes a League with *Gwenwynwyn*, the Son of *Owen Cyfeilioc*, Lord of *Powys*, and by their joynt-Interest got together a considerable Body of Men, wherewith they surprized Prince *Gruffydh* at *Aberystwyth*, whom, after they had slain a great many of his Men, they took Prisoner. Thus *Maelgon* effectually accomplished his Design in the recovery of the Castle, and the whole Country of *Cardigan*. His unfortunate Brother he committed to the custody of his spiteful Confederate *Gwenwynwyn*, who immediately out of Malice deliver'd him up to the Mercy of his inveterate

veterate Enemies the *English*. After this *Gwenwynwyn* having got together an Army entered *Aruftly*, and brought it to his subjection.

David ap Owen, whom Prince *Lhewelyn* had forced to quit his Usurpation of the Principality of *North-Wales*, had hitherto lived quietly and peaceably, not so much out of kindness to his Nephew, as because he knew not how to redress himself; but now having got a great Army of *English* and *Welch*, he used his utmost Efforts to recover his Principality. Whereupon Prince *Lhewelyn* who was the right Heir, and in possession of it, came on boldly to meet him, and gave him battel, wherein he shamefully routed his Army, and took his Uncle *David* Prisoner, whom he delivered into safe custody, whereby he secured to himself and his Country Peace and Quietness. Towards the close of this Year *Owen Cyfeilioc* Lord of the higher *Powys* departed this Life, and left his Estate to *Gwenwynwyn* his Son; after whom that part of *Powys* was called *Powys-Wenwynwyn*, to distinguish it from the other called *Powys Fadoc* the Inheritance of the Lords of *Bromfield*. Much about this time *Trahaern Fychan*, a Man of great Power and Authority in the County of *Brecknock*, was suddenly seized upon as he was going to *Llancors* to confer about some business with *William de Bruce* Lord thereof, and by an Order of the Lords, tyed to an Horse Tail and dragged through the Streets of *Brecknock* to the Gallows, where he was beheaded, and his Body hung up by the Feet for three Days. Which Barbarity inflicted upon him for no known just Cause, so frightned his Brothers Wife and Children, that they fled their Country for fear of the same Usage. The Year following *Maelgon*, who had before routed his Brother Prince *Gruffydh*'s Army, and taken him Prisoner, begins now to enlarge his Territories, and takes in his Brothers Castles of *Aberteifi* and *Yftratmeyric*. Also the youngest Son of Prince *Rhys* about this time recovered the Castle of *Dynefowr* from the *Normans*.

A. D. 1198.

The same Summer *Gwenwynwyn* took up a resolution of attempting to extend *Wales* to its antient Limits; and for this purpose he raises a powerful Army, with which he first designs to be avenged of *William de Bruce* for the inhuman Death of his Cosin *Trahaern Fychan*, and therefore he besiegeth his Castle of *Payn* in *Elfel*, where he makes a Protestation, that as soon as he had taken it, for a farther satisfaction to his Revenge, he would unmercifully ravage the whole Country as far as *Severn*. But these mighty Menaces were soon blown over; for he had neither Battering Engins nor Pioneers, so that he was forced to lay before the Castle for three Weeks without effecting any thing; whereby the Murtherers had time enough to apply themselves to *England* for Succours, which they obtained. For upon this *Geoffrey Fitz-Peter*, Lord Chief Justice of *England* levies a considerable Army, to which he joyns all the Lords Marchers, and comes in all hast to the Relief of the place, where he meets *Gwenwynwyn*; with whom, before he would hazard a Battel, he was desirous to have a Treaty of Peace, to which *Gwenwynwyn* and his Adherents would in no wise hearken or condescend, but returned in answer, that their business there was to be revenged of old Injuries done them. Hereupon the *English* Lords resolved to enlarge Prince *Gruffydh* of *South-Wales*, whom they knew to be an inveterate Enemy of *Gwenwynwyn*, as he that delivered him up to their hands; and likewise to be a Man of great Authority in his Country, therefore they rightly concluded he might be more serviceable to them when at liberty than under confinement; wherein they were not disappointed; for he immediately got together a strong Body of his Countrymen, and joyning with the *English*, advanced towards the Castle, where they furiously attack'd *Gwenwynwyn*, who made no less vigorous defence; hereupon there ensued a bloody Battel, with a great slaughter on both sides, but at length the *English* got the Victory, and *Gwenwynwyn* lost a great number of common Soldiers (if we believe *Matthew Paris* 3700 Men) besides a great many of his best
Com-

The History of WALES.

Commanders, among whom were *Anarawd*, Son of *Eineon*, *Owen ap Cadwalhon*, *Richard ap Iestyn*, and *Robert ap Howel*. *Meredith ap Conan* was likewise taken Prisoner, with many more. After this the *English* returned home triumphantly, and requited Prince *Gruffydh*'s Service with a perfect Liberty, who immediately, partly by his own Force, partly by the Affection of his People, repossessed himself of all his Dominions, save the Castles of *Aberteifi* and *Ystratmeyric*, which his usurping Brother *Maelgon*, by the Assistance of *Gwenwynwyn*, had, during his Confinement by the *English*, taken from him, and still unjustly detained. Hereupon, some of Prince *Gruffydh*'s prime Nobility and Clergy came to him, and offered him their Endeavours of reconciling him to his Brother, and made him so apprehensive of his just Displeasure at him, that he took a solemn Oath before them, that in case his Brother would give him Hostages for the security of his own Person, he would deliver him up his Castle of *Aberteifi* by a day appointed; which Proposals Prince *Gruffydh* accepted of, and accordingly sent him his Demands: But it was the least of *Maelgon*'s intention to make good his part, or else he was very unconstant in his resolution; for he had no sooner received the Hostages, but instead of delivering up the Castle, he fortifies it, and puts in a Garrison for his own use, and commits the Hostages to the custody of *Gwenwynwyn*, Prince *Gruffydh*'s mortal Enemy; but not long after, their Innocency procured them an opportunity of an Escape.

In the Year 1199. *Maelgon* still pursuing his Hatred of his Brother Prince *Gruffydh*, gets an Army, wherewith he besiegeth his Castle of *Dynerth*, which he was Master of in a short time, and then put all the Garrison to the Sword. But about the same time Prince *Gruffydh* in lieu of this, wan the Castle of *Cilgerran*, and strongly fortified it. This Year *Richard* the First of *England*, as he was besieging the Castle of *Chalons* in *France*, was shot from the Walls with an Arrow, whereof he not long after dyed, and left his Kingdom to his Brother *John*, who thereupon was

A. D.
1199.

with

The History of WALES.

with great Solemnity crown'd at *Westminster*. But he could not expect to enjoy this Kingdom peaceably; for his elder Brother *Geoffry Plantagenet* had left a Son behind him named *Arthur*, whose Right the Crown of *England* was by lineal descent; which now therefore he justly lays claim to, and by the assistance of King *Philip* of *France* (who espoused his Quarrel) endeavours to recover. But before Prince *Arthur* had made sufficient Preparations to carry on his Design, he was unexpectedly set upon by his Uncle, his Army routed, and he himself taken Prisoner, and committed to safe custody; not long after which, he dyed, and so King *John* was rid of his Competitor.

A. D. 1200.
The following Year *Gruffydh ap Conan ap Owen Gwynedh* dyed. and was buried in a Monk's Cawl in the Abby of *Conway*, which way of burying was very much practised (especially by the better sort) in those days; for the Monks and Friers had deluded the People into a strong Conceit of the Merits of it, and had firmly persuaded them it was highly conducing to their future Happiness to be thus interr'd. But this Superstition, together with the Propagators of it, they had lately received from *England*: For the first Abby or Monastery we read of in *Wales*, since the Destruction of that famous House of *Bangor*, which favour'd of *Romish* Dregs, was the *Ty-Gwyn* built in the Year 1146. after which they mightily increased and spread over all the Country; and now the Fountain Head began to be corrupted; for the Clergy maintained a Doctrin which their Ancestors abhorr'd, as may easily be gathered from the Writings of that worthy Divine *Ambrosius Telesinus*, who flourished in the Year 540. when the Christian Faith (which we suppose to be deliver'd at the Isle of *Afalon* by *Joseph* of *Arimathea*) flowed in this Land in a pure and uncorrupted Stream, before it was infected and polluted by that proud and blood-thirsty Monk *Augustine*. I say, he then wrote and left behind him as his own Opinion, and the Opinion of those days, these following Verses:

Gwae'r

The History of WALES.

Gwae'r offeiriad byd
Nys angreifftia gwyd
Ac ny phregetha:
Gwae ny cheidw ei gail
Ac ef yn figail

Ac nys areilia;
Gwae ni cheidw ei dhefaid
Rhae bleidhie Rhufeniaid
A'i ffon gnwppa.

From whence it is apparent, that the Church of *Rome* was then corrupt, and that the *British* Churches perfevered in the primitive and truly Apoftolical Profeffion of Chriftianity, as it was at firft planted in the Ifland ; and that no *Roman* Innovations had crept in among them, which afterwards mightily increafed, when they were once introduced by *Auguftin* the Monk.

This Year likewife we find the fpiteful and turbulent *Maelgon*, choofing rather to perfift ftill in his Rebellion, than to return to his Allegiance, and to prefer a fmall Lucre to the Love and Safety of his Country. For now finding that the Caftle of *Aberteifi* was not tenable by his own Power and Force, yet rather than deliver it up to his Brother Prince *Gruffydh*, and thereby procure his Favour, he chofe to fell it to his bitter Enemies the *Englifh*, for an inconfiderable Sum of Money, whereby he opened them a free paffage into all *Wales*; this being reckoned one of its chief Defences and Bulwarks. About this time *Madawc* Son of *Gruffydh Maylor* Lord of *Bromfield* built the Abby of *Lanegweft*, commonly known by the *Englifh* by the Name of *Vale Crucii*.

In the Year 1201. the valiant *Lhewelyn ap Iorwerth* Prince of *North-Wales* banifhed out of his Territories his Cofin *Meredith* the Son of *Conan ap Owen Gwynedh*, whom he fufpected of treafonable Practices, and therefore confifcated his Lands which were the *Cantref* of *Lhyn* and *Efyonyth*. Much about the fame time *Meredith* the Son of Prince *Rhys* was flain at *Carnwilhion* by Treafon, whereupon his elder Brother *Gruffydh* poffeffed himfelf of his Caftle in *Lhanymdhyfri* and all his Lands. This *Gruffydh* was a valiant and difcreet Prince, and one that was like to bring all *South-Wales*

1201.

Wales to good order and Obedience; for in all things he trod in his Fathers steps, and made it his business to succeed him as well in his Valour and vertuous Endowments, as in his Government. But the vast hopes conceived of him soon proved abortive; for in the ensuing Year, on S. *James's* day he dyed, to the great Grief and Loss of his Country, and shortly after was buried at *Ystratflur* with great Pomp and Solemnity. He left behind him for a Successor a Son called *Rhys*, which *Maud* the Daughter of *William de Bruce* had bore him. The following Year some of the *Welch* Nobility marched with an Army towards the Castle of *Gwerthrynion*, which belonged to *Roger Mortimer*, and after a short Siege, they took it and levell'd it with the ground.

A. D. 1202.

This Year *Lhewelyn ap Iorwerth* calling to mind his Estate and Title, and how all the *Welch* Princes were obliged both by the Laws of *Roderic* the Great, and those of *Howel Dha* to acknowledg the King or Prince of *North-Wales* for their Sovereign Lord, and to do Homage to him for their Dominions: Yet notwithstanding that they knew this to be their duty, and that they formerly had readily performed it; yet because of late Years his Predecessors had neglected to call them to their Duty, they now began to imagin themselves exempted from it; and some thought themselves accountable to no superiour Prince; others denyed Subjection to Prince *Lhewelyn*, and held their Dominions of the King of *England*. To put a stop therefore to the further growth of this Contempt, and to assert his own Right, Prince *Lhewelyn* summons all the *Welch* Lords, who for the most part appeared, and swore Allegiance to him. But *Gwenwynwyn* Lord of *Powys* neither came to this meeting, nor would own the Princes Supremacy: Which Stubborness and Disobedience the Prince acquainted his Lords with, whereupon they delivered their Opinion, that it was but reasonable, that *Gwenwynwyn* should be compell'd to his Duty, or else forfeit his Estate: This all the Lords consented to, but *Elis ap Madawc*, who was an intimate Friend of *Gwenwynwyn*, and therefore would

The History of WALES.

would not confent to the enacting any thing that might be prejudicial to him, but broke off from the Meeting much diffatisfied with their Proceedings. Notwithftanding which, Prince *Lhewelyn*, purfuant to the Advice of the reft of his Lords, raifes an Army, and marches towards *Powys*; but before he made any ufe of it, he was by the Mediation of fome learned and able Men reconciled to *Gwenwynwyn*, and fo *Gwenwynwyn* became his dutiful Subject, which he confirmed both by Oath and Writing; and indeed it was not without good reafon, that Prince *Lhewelyn* ufed all the caution imaginable to bind this Man; for he had fworn Allegiance before to the King of *England*. *Lhewelyn* having thus fubjected *Gwenwynwyn*, he thought it now convenient to fhew likewife fome Marks of his Refentments againft his Adherent *Elis ap Madawc*, and therefore he ftrips him of all his Lands; whereupon *Elis* fled the Country, but not long after, yielding himfelf to the Prince's Mercy, he received of him the Caftle of *Crogen*, and Seven Townfhips befides. And now having mentioned *Crogen*, it will not be improper to ftep a little out of the way, and here take notice of the reafon why the *Englifh* formerly, when they had a mind to reproach the *Welch*, called them *Crogens*. The firft occafion of it was this, King *Henry* the Second in his Expedition againft the *Welch* to the Mountains of *Berwin*, lay a while at *Ofweftre*, during which time he detached a number of his Men to try the Paffages into *Wales*, who as they would have paffed *Offa's* Ditch at the Caftle of *Crogen*, at which place there was a narrow way through the fame Ditch, which appears now very deep through all that Country, and bears its old Name; thefe Men, I fay, as they would have paffed this Streight, were met by a Party of *Welch*, and a great many of them flain and buried in that Ditch, as appears by their Graves there to be feen; and the Name of the Streight imports as much, being called in *Welch Adwy'r bedhaw*. The *Englifh* therefore bearing in mind this Slaughter, when ever they got any of the *Welch* into their Clutches, upbraided them with

the

the Name of *Crogen*, intimating thereby that they should expect no more Favour or Mercy at their hands, than they shew'd them in the Skirmish. But this word which at first was rather a Badg of Reputation than Disgrace to the *Welch*, came afterwards to be used in a bad Sense, and only then applyed when they designed to reproach and abuse them. But to return to Prince *Lhewelyn*, whom we find returning home after he had successfully asserted his Sovereignty over all *Wales*, and set all things in good order: And by the way he fortifies the Castle of *Bala* in *Penlhyn*. About this time *Rhys* the Son of *Gruffydh ap Rhys* the right Prince of *South-Wales* took the Castle of *Lhanymdhyfry* upon *Michaelmas*-day. This Year *Lhewelyn* Prince of *Wales* took to Wife *Joan* the Daughter of King *John*, which *Agatha* Daughter of *Robert Ferrers* Earl of *Derby* bore him, with whom he gave the Prince for a Dowry the Lordship of *Elsmere* in the Marches of *Wales*.

1203. Prince *Rhys* whom we mentioned the Year before to have taken the Castle of *Lhanymdhyfri*, wins likewise the Castle of *Llangadoc*, and puts a Garrison therein; but he enjoyed neither of them long; for shortly after, his Unkle *Maelgon*, with his Friend *Gwenwynwyn*, levied a powerful Army, and with it besieged and took the Castle of *Lhanymdhyfri*; thence they removed to *Lhangadoc*, and wan the Castle likewise, upon this Condition, that the Garrison be permitted to march out quietly. When they had taken these two Castles, they went to *Dinerth*, where *Maelgon* finished the Castle he had formerly begun there. This Year likewise Prince *Lhewelyn* set at liberty his Uncle *David ap Owen Gwynedh*, who made but a sorry return to this Kindness; for instead of living peaceably at home, and enjoying that Liberty that was granted him, he flees to *England*, and there gets an Army, wherewith he attempts to restore himself to his antient Estate of *North-Wales*; but he missed his Mark; for his prudent Nephew immediately met him on his March, and gave him a shameful Over-throw, wherewith *David* was so mightily disheartened, that he presently returned for *England*, and shortly after died for meer sorrow. The next Year *Howel*, a blind Son of Prince *Rhys* was slain at *Camaes* by his Brother *Maelgon*'s Men, and buried just by his Brother *Gruffydh* at *Yſtratflur*. But notwithstanding that, *Maelgon* in those days usurped all the Rule and Government of *South-Wales*; yet his Brother *Gruffydh*'s Sons, *Rhys* and his Brethren, wan from him the chief Defence of all that Country, to wit, the Castles of *Dynefowr* and *Lhanymdhyfri*. About this time *William Marſhal*, Earl of *Pembrock*, besieged the Castle of *Cilgerran*, and took it; and not long after, *Maelgon* hired an *Iriſhman* to kill *Gadifor ap Griffri*; after which horrid Fact, *Maelgon* seized upon his Four Sons, and put them to death; these were forward promising young Gentlemen, and descended from a Noble Stock; for their Mother *Suſanna* was a Daughter of the said *Howel ap Rhys*, by a Daughter of *Madawc ap Meredith* Prince of *Powys*. In the Year 1206. *Maelgon* built a Castle at *Aberenecn*. At which time there was such abundance of Fish seen at *Aberyſtwyth*, that the like number was never known to have come there in the memory of Man before.

A. D.
1204.

1205.

1206.

This Year the King of *England* banished the Realm *William de Bruce* and his Wife, on the account of a Grudg that he bore his Son, and then seized upon all his Lands; whereupon, *William* with his Wife and Son fled to *Ireland*, and there continued for some time. And this Hardship he now underwent was the less pitied, because he exercised the great Power he had in the Marches of *Wales* with extreme Cruelty and Injustice. The same Year *Gwenwynwyn* came to *Shrewsbury* to speak with the King's Council, where he was detained Prisoner: Whereupon Prince *Lhewelyn* conquered all his Country, took all his Towns and Castles, and garrison'd them for his own use. This Expedition of Prince *Lhewelyn* mightily alarm'd the usurping *Maelgon*, and the more, because he had intelligence that *Lhewelyn* was on his march towards *South-Wales*; therefore he now puts himself in the best posture he could to receive him; but finding

1207.

himself not able to abide the Prince's coming, and to withstand his Forces, he demolisheth his Castles of *Aberystwyth*, *Ystratmeyric*, and *Dinerth*, which before he had fortified. Notwithstanding which, the Prince comes to *Aberystwyth*, and rebuildeth the Castle and puts a Garrison therein; after this he seized upon the *Cantref* of *Penwedic* and the Land betwixt *Dyfi* and *Aeron* which he gave to *Maelgon*'s Nephews the Sons of *Gruffydh ap Rhys*, and then returned home with great Joy and Triumph. Not long after *Rhys Fychan*, Son to Prince *Rhys*, besieged the Castle of *Lhangadoc*, and took it, contrary to the Promise and League he had made with his Nephews, forgetting likewise how freely and readily they had administred to him in his necessity; therefore to be avenged of this Ingratitude and breach of promise, *Rhys* and *Owen* no sooner heard of it, but they furiously attack'd the Castle, and took it by assault, and put to the Sword, or took Prisoners all the Garrison, and then burnt the Castle to the ground.

1209. This Year King *John* levied a powerful Army with which he made a Voyage to *Ireland*; but as he was on the Borders of *Wales* on his Journey thitherwards, there was a Criminal brought before him who had murther'd a Priest. The Officer desired to know the King's Pleasure, how he would have the Delinquent punished; but the King, instead of ordering any Punishment to be inflicted upon him suitable to the heinousness of his Crime, discharged him with a *Well done* thou good Servant, thou hast slain mine Enemy; for such he reckon'd the Clergy of those days, who were very ill-affected to his usurped arbitrary Government, and therefore he slightly regarded any Injuries that were done them, nay, thought those did him good service who did them wrong. He had not been long in *Ireland*, but he got into his clutches the unfortunate *William de Bruce* the younger, and his Mother *Mawd de Saint Valerike*, whom we have mentioned afore to have quitted *England* for fear of him, and to have fled here for shelter. Upon his return to *England* he brought these in triumph along with him, and com-

mitted

The History of WALES.

mitted them to *Windsor*-Castle, where, by his Orders, not long after they were inhumanly famished. The reason of King *John*'s Displeasure against *William de Bruce* Lord of *Brecnock*, * *Matthew Paris* delivers, to be this; When the Pope had excommunicated the Realm of *England*, the King, to prevent any Inconveniences that might ensue thereupon, took Pledges of such of his Nobles as he thought were disaffected to him, and would be like, if occasion offered, to countenance and promote a Rebellion. Amongst others, he sends Messengers to *William de Bruce* to demand his Sons for Pledges, to whom *Mawd*, *de Bruce*'s Wife, being the readier speaker, answered, (though what she said was no less her Husband's Sentiment than her own) That the King, who had proved so base a Guardian to his Nephew Prince *Arthur*, whom instead of setting in, he deprived of his Right, should have none of her Children. This Answer the Messengers deliver'd to the King, whereat he was highly displeased, that he ordered some Soldiers should be sent to seize this Lord, but he having timely intelligence of this Order, fled into *Ireland* with his Wife and Children, where now his Wife *Mawd*, with her Son, were unfortunately taken by King *John*, but he himself escaped, and fled into *France*, where not long after he dyed.

* Pag. 303.

This Year the Earl of *Chester* rebuilt the Castle of *Dyganwy*, situate on the Sea-shore, East of the River *Conway*, which Prince *Lhewelyn* had before demolish'd. He likewise fortifies the Castle of *Treffynon* or S. *Wnefrid*. Upon this *Lhewelyn* enters into the Earl's Land, which when he had ravaged sufficiently, he returns home with considerable Booty. About this time *Rhys Fychan* Son to Prince *Rhys*, fearing lest Prince *Lhewelyn* should fall upon him for the wrong he had done to his Nephews, whom he, Prince *Lhewelyn*, stifly defended in their right; made his Application to the King of *England*, who readily granted him what Succours he desired; and with these he besieged the Castle of *Lhanymdhyfri*; the Garrison for some time made a vigorous defence, but having no hopes of any Relief, they thought it their wiſeſt courſe to Capitulate, and ſo they deſired they might march out with their Arms, Bag and Baggage, and all that belonged to them, which was granted them. About this time likewiſe *Gwenwynwyn* was ſet at Liberty, whom the King had hitherto detained Priſoner, and withal lends him ſome Forces to attempt the recovery of his Country which Prince *Lhewelyn* had ſeized upon during his Impriſonment; and tho' by his own Strength he was not able to cope with the Prince, yet by this Aſſiſtance granted him by the King, he ſoon re-poſſeſſ'd himſelf of his Dominions. This Succeſs of *Gwenwynwyn* encouraged *Maelgon* likewiſe to endeavour the recovery of that part of his Country which the Prince had taken from him in the ſame Expedition. Now he makes his application to the King of *England*, and ſwears Allegiance to him. Hereupon the King grants him a conſiderable Army as well *Engliſh* as *Normans*; to theſe he joyns what Forces he could raiſe in *Wales*, and then contrary to the Oath and Agreement he had made with his Nephews *Rhys* and *Owen*, he in a hoſtile manner enters their Country, when he was come to *Cantred Penwedic*, he encamped at *Cilcenny* where he ſtaid ſome time to take meaſures for the better accompliſhment of his Deſigns; by this time his Nephews had got together about 300 choſen well diſciplined Men, but with ſo ſmall a Number durſt not oppoſe their Uncle's numerous Army in open Field; therefore they were to endeavour to overthrow thoſe by a Stratagem which they could not do by main force. Herein they proved very ſucceſsful, for coming as near their Enemies as they could without being diſcovered, they ſent out their Spies that Night for Intelligence, who brought back the good News, that all was quiet in *Maelgon*'s Camp, and that they kept no ſtrict Watch, being not aware of an approaching Enemy. This Intelligence mightily encouraged the Brothers to proſecute their Deſigns, and now they march as ſilently as they can towards their Enemies Camp, where they met with no oppoſition, being not diſcovered

The History of WALES.

covered becaufe all were faft afleep. When they were advanced as they thought as far as *Maelgon*'s Tent, they furiously fell on, and flew a great number of his Men afore they awak'd; the reft being frightened with the noife and fhouts of their Enemies, and withal thinking their Numbers to be far greater than it was, were glad to make ufe of the darknefs of the Night to quit the Field, only *Maelgon*'s Guard valiantly kept their Poft, and defended their Lord till he had time and opportunity to efcape. But *Maelgon*'s Army fuffered very much in this Action, his Nephew *Conan ap Howel* with his Chief Counfellor *Gruffydh ap Cadwgan* were both taken Prifoners, and *Eineon ap Caradoc* with a great number more were flain upon the fpot. About the fame time *Gilbert* Earl of *Glocefter* fortified the Caftle of *Buelht*, where a little before he had loft a confiderable number of his Men, by reafon that the place was not very ftrong and tenable. And towards the conclufion of this year, *Mallt* or *Mawd de Bruce*, the Wife of *Gruffydh ap Rhys* departed this Life, and was interred by her Husband in a Monk's Coul in *Yftratflur*.

But the following Year a great Storm threatened 1210. *North-Wales*, by reafon that the *Marchers* made frequent and grievous Complaints to King *John*, how that Prince *Lhewelyn* perpetually molefted their Country, flew their Men, and committed all the wafte and deftruction poffible as he paffed along. The King hearing of fuch intolerable Depredations continually exercifed by the *North-Wales* Men, thought it high time to redrefs his Subjects, and therefore he raifed a mighty Army throughout all *England* and called to him all the Lords and Princes of *Wales* as held their Lands and Patents from him, as *Howel ap Gruffydh ap Conan ap Oven Gwynedh*, whom Prince *Lhewelyn* had banifhed out of *North-Wales*; *Madoc ap Gruffydh Maylor* Lord of *Bromfield*, *Chirke* and *Yale*, *Meredith ap Rotpert* Lord of *Cydewen*, *Gwenwynwyn* Lord of *Powys*, *Maelgon* and *Rhys* the Sons of Prince *Rhys* and Governours of *South-Wales*. With this formidable Army he came to *Chefter*, intending to enter

into

into *North Wales* by that way, and being fully resolved to execute the severest Vengeance upon the Inhabitants, and not to let one living Soul remain alive throughout the whole Country. But Matters of this nature are easier resolved upon, than accomplished; Prince *Lhewelyn* was no sooner informed of these mighty preparations against him, comprehending the whole Strength of the *English* Nation, and what was worst of all, being assisted by his own Country-men, but he issued forth his Orders, commanding all his Subjects of the In-land Counties of *Denbigh* and *Flint*, together with them of the Island of *Anglesey*, to remove for a time all their Cattel and other Effects to *Snowden*-Hills, where they were sure to remain securest from their Enemies. But King *John* marched his Army along the Sea-Coast to *Ruthlan*, and there passing the River *Clwyd*, he came to the Castle of *Teganwy*, where he encamped for some time to refresh and recreate his Army, which by reason of the long Marches they made, was in a great measure weary and fatigued. But what the more augmented their misery, *Lhewelyn* getting behind them, cut off all their hopes of Provision from *England*, and the *Welch* by the Advantage of being acquainted with the straits and narrow Passages, cut off all that straggled from the *English* Camp, so that in time, they were glad to take up with Horse-flesh, and any thing were it never so mean, which might fill up their greedy and empty Stomachs. At last King *John* finding no other Remedy, and perceiving it impossible to continue longer there so hungry and fainty, thought it his wisest way to march for *England* and leave the *Welch* to themselves, and so he decamped in a great fury, leaving *Lhewelyn* to bury that great number of Dead, which had starved in this successless Expedition. But to recover the Honour he had now lost, he was resolved to try another touch with the *Welch*, but possibly not with the same confidence and assurance of Victory. And therefore returning to *Wales* in the next *August*, he entred with such another terrible Army of *English*, and was as-

listed

The History of WALES.

sisted by the same *Welch* Lords, at *Blanchmonastery*, now *Oswestry*, being in the Lordship of *John* the Son of *William Fitzalan*. In this Expedition, King *John* passing the River *Conwey*, and encamping at the other side towards *Snowdon*-Hills, sent part of his Army conducted by Guides who were acquainted with the Country, to burn *Bangor*, which they effectually did; and taking *Rotpert* Bishop of that See out of Church, they carried him Prisoner to the *English* Camp, where he continued for some time, till he obtained his Ransom for a present of two hundred *Hawks*. But Prince *Lhewelyn* finding the whole Strength of *England*, and almost *Wales* to fight against him, and judging it impossible for himself alone, to withstand so great a multitude, thought it his best way to endeavour to find out some method or other, to reconcile himself to the King. And no better measures could possibly be thought of, than to send *Joan* his Wife, King *John*'s Daughter, to intreat with her Father about a Peace, and a cessation of all Hostilities; who being a prudent, sly Woman, so prevailed upon the King, that he granted Prince *Lhewelyn* her Husband, a safe Conduct to come to him, and to renew the former Peace and Amity that was betwixt them. And so *Lhewelyn* having done Homage, promised the King towards his Expences, in this Expedition, 20000 Head of Cattel and forty *Horses*, and what was more than all, he granted all the in-land Countries of *Wales*, with the Appurtenances, to him and his Heirs for ever. And then King *John* having received better Success in this, than the former Expedition, returned to *England* in great Triumph, having subdued all *Wales*, excepting that part which *Rhys* and *Owen* the Sons of *Gruffydh ap Rhys*, still kept and maintained against the *English*. But having no leisure to march against them himself at his departure out of the Country, he gave strict charge to *Foulke* Vicount of *Caerdyff*, Warden of the Marches, a cruel Tyrant, tho' well beloved and favoured by the King, to take an Army with him, and so joyning with *Maelgon* and *Rhys Fychan*, to compel the

Q 4   Sons

Sons of *Gruffydh ap Rhys* to acknowledge him for their Sovereign, and to do him Homage. *Foulke* having received so positive a Command, presently raised his Forces, and calling *Maelgon* and *Rhys*, came to the *Cantref* of *Penwedic*; which when the young Lords *Rhys* and *Owen* heard of, and being assured that this Blow was levelled against them, which they knew they were not able to bear, before the Stroak was struck, they sent to *Foulke* to sue for Peace, and a safe Conduct for them to pass to the Court of *England*. This being granted, they came to *London*, and making their submission to the King, and requesting his Pardon for all former Misdemeanors, they gave up all pretence to their Lands betwixt *Aeron* and *Dysi*; and so paying their Homage, they were dismissed very graciously. But *Foulke* before his departure out of the Country, fortified the Castle of *Aberystwyth*, and placing a strong Garrison therein, kept it to the King's use. But *Maelgon* and *Rhys Fychan*, a couple of head-strong, inconstant People, quickly repented them of the Peace they had made with the King of *England*, and thereupon, without the least reason or provocation, they laid Siege to *Aberystwyth* Castle, and with much ado having made themselves Masters of it they destroyed those Fortifications which *Foulke* had lately erected, and defaced the Castle to the ground. But they paid sawce for this another way, for as soon as *Rhys* and *Owen* had heard that their Uncles had broken and violated the King's Peace, they made in-roads into *Isaeron*, which was *Maelgon's* Country, and having slain a considerable number of his Men, among whom was one brave and lusty Youth called *Bachglâs*, they returned with very rich Booty.

1211. *Maelgon* and *Rhys Fychan* were quickly followed by the *North-Wales* Men in their revolt from the King of *England*, for Prince *Lhewelyn* being not able to endure any longer the tyranny and oppression which the King's Garrisons exercised in his Country; called together *Gwenwynwyn* from *Powys*, *Maelgon ap Rhys* from *South-Wales*, *Madoc ap Gruffydh Maylor* from Bromfield

The History of WALES.

Bromfield, and *Meredith ap Rotpert* from *Cydewen*, and plainly declared before them the Pride and insolency of the *English*, and how that they who were always used to have a Prince of their own Nation, were now by their own wilfulness and neglect become subject to Strangers. However, it was not too late to recover their antient Liberty, and if they did but unanimously agree among themselves, they might easily cast off that Yoke which was so intolerably burdersome to them. Then the Lords being sensible of the truth and reasonableness of what Prince *Lhewelyn* delivered, and being conscious to themselves that their present slavery and subjection to the *English*, was wholly owing to their own fear and cowardise, swore fealty to Prince *Lhewelyn*, and swore to be true and faithful to him, and to stick by each other to the utmost of their Lives and Fortunes. And so joyning their Forces together, they took all the Castles in *North-Wales* which were in the hands of the *English*, excepting *Ruthlan* and *Dyganwy*; and then going to *Powys*, they laid Siege to the Castle which *Robert Uspont* had built at *Mathrafal*. But King *John* being informed how the *Welch* had conspired against him, and that they had taken and sezied upon almost all his Castles in *North-Wales*, and how that they were now in actual besiegement of *Mathrafal*, presently drew up his Army, and coming to *Mathrafal*, quickly raised the Siege, and to prevent the *Welch* from coming any more against it, he burnt it to the ground and so returned to *England*, having no time to stay any longer in *Wales*, by reason of the Differences that happened betwixt him and his Nobility. But being afterwards at *Nottingham*, and hearing how that Prince *Lhewelyn* cruelly harrassed and destroyed the Marches, he caused all the *Welch* Pledges which he had received the last year to be hanged, among whom were *Howel* the Son of *Cadwalhon*, and *Madoc* the Son of *Maelgon*, with many others of the Nobilities Sons, to the number of Twenty Eight. And about the same time *Robert Vepont* caused *Rhys* the Son of *Maelgon* to be hanged at *Shrewsbury*, being a Youth of of about seventeen years of age, and so cruelly murdered the innocent Child to revenge the Crimes and Offences committed by his Father and others. But tho' King *John* was so severe to the *Welch*, yet the Princess of *North-Wales* was more dutiful and favourable to' him, for whilst he staid at *Nottingham*, she sent him an Express, declaring how that the Barons had entred into a Conspiracy with the *French* King against him, and that this latter was a preparing and raising an Army to come over to *England*, upon pretence that the King was a Rebel, and bid open Defiance to the Holy Church, in as much as he would not condescend nor yield to the Bishop of *Rome*'s Request. And in confirmation of all this, she told him that *Robert Fitzwalter*, *Eustace de Vescy* and *Stephen Redell*, were secretly fled into *France*, to promote and carry on this intrigue. And that this design against King *John* was no feigned surmise, the next year Pope *Innocent* the Third detached one of his Nuncio's to *Wales*, who absolved Prince *Lhewelyn*, *Gwenwynwyn* and *Maelgon* from their Oaths of Allegiance to King *John*, and withal gave them a strict command under the penalty of Excommunication, to molest and annoy him with all their Endeavours, as an open Enemy to the Church of God. Prince *Lhewelyn*, you may be sure, was not in the least troubled at this, for now he gained the fittest opportunity imaginable, to restore such Lands as he had formerly much against his mind delivered up to the King, being the in-land Country of *Denbigh* and *Flint*, which *Lhewelyn* at this time repossessed himself of. And well it was, he was so quick, for within a little while after, King *John* by the persuasions of *Pandulph* the Pope's Legate, granted his Holiness all his Request, and so obtained Absolution at *Pandulph*'s hands, and upon performance of his Promises, an assurance of a releasement from that Ecclesiastical Bull, which had so formidably roared against him.

1213. *South-Wales* had now been quiet for a considerable time, and they that used to be commonly very turbulent and contentious, were now pretty easy and amicable.

amicable. But it was impossible that such a peaceable Course of Life should hold long, where Injustice and Oppression had so much Liberty, and where People were wrongfully kept out of their just and rightful Inheritance. And this was the occasion of the breach of that quietness, which for the two or three years last past they had so satisfactorily enjoyed. For *Rhys* the Son of *Gruffydh ap Rhys*, who was right Heir to Prince *Rhys*, finding he could have no share of his Father's Estate, but that his Uncles forcibly kept all from him, thought it his best way to make his Case known to the King of *England*, and to desire a remedy and redress from him. King *John* in compassion of the young Man's hard Condition, sent to his Deputy *Foulke* Vicount of *Caerdyff* Warden of the Marches, and to the Steward of *Hereford*, commanding them to take away all *Ystratywy* from *Rhys Fychan*, by some called *Rhys Gryg*. unless he would permit his Nephews to enjoy *Lhanymdhyfry*-Castle, with all the Lands and Priviledges thereunto belonging. *Foulke* having received such Orders from his Master the King of *England*, sent to acquaint *Rhys* of the Proposals, and so demand of him whether or no he would deliver up *Lhanymdhyfry* to his Nephews, according to the King's Command; who returned answer, that he did not know of any such Obligation due from him to the King of *England*, as to part with his Lands at his Command, and therefore assured him peremptorily and in plain terms, that he would not willingly part with one foot of what he was in present possession of. *Foulke* therefore having received this resolute Answer, was likewise as resolute to get that by force which he could not obtain by fair means; and so having raised a great Army, he marched to *Talhwynelgain* to meet with young *Rhys*, who was to come thither with all the Forces he could raise in *Brecknock*; and from thence they marched in three Battles towards *Dynefawr*, the first being commanded by young *Rhys*, the second by *Foulke* and *Owen* Brother to *Rhys* led the third. *Rhys Fychan* was not in the least dismayed at their Number, but

thinking

thinking it more advisable to meet them in the Field, rather than suffer them to block him up at *Dynefawr*, came out very boldly, and gave them Battel, but after a warm Engagement on both sides, *Rhys Fychan* in the end got the worse, and after a loss of a great number of his Men, he was glad at last to make his escape by flight. And so retiring to *Dynefawr*, he doubled the Garrison of that place, but thinking the Town of *Lhandeilo-fawr* not to be Tenable, he burnt it to the Ground, and then kept himself private in the Woods and other desart places. But young *Rhys* and *Foulke* laid Siege to *Dynefawr*, and in the first Assault came on so fiercely, that they forced the Garrison to retire to the Castle, which for some time they defended very manfully. But the besiegers began to play so violently with their battering Engines, and to undermine the Wall in such a manner, that the Governour after a short defence began to Capitulate, giving three Pledges for security, that if they received no Relief by the morrow at Noon, the Castle should be surrendred up, conditionally that the Garrison should march out with all the Tokens of Honour, and carry their Arms and all other Implements of War along with them. No Relief being arrived, the Castle the next day was accordingly surrendred, and all the Articles of the Capitulation observed; and so young *Rhys* being possessed of *Dynefawr*, in a little time afterward, brought all *Cantref-fawr* to his subjection. When *Rhys Fychan* was sensible how the stream run violently against him, he thought it his wisest way to remove his Wife and Children, and all his other Effects, to his Brother *Maelgon*'s Country, and so leaving *Lhanymdhyfry* Castle well manned and fortified, he departed towards *Aberystwyth*. But as soon as *Foulke* was returned to the Marches, young *Rhys* came with an Army consisting of *Welch* and *Normans* before *Lhanymdhyfry*, intending to besiege that place, but before they were encamped before the Town, the Governour thought it his best way to surrender, upon Condition only, that the Garrison should depart away with their Lives. And shortly

The History of WALES.   237

ly afterwards, *Rhys Fychan* was taken at *Caermardhyn*, and committed to the King's Prison, and so all the Disturbances and Troubles of *South-Wales* came to a peaceable issue. But it was not so in *North-Wales*, for Prince *Lhewelyn* being desirous to rid his Country from the insupportable Tyranny and Oppression of the *English* Garrisons, laid Siege to the Castles of *Dygannwy* and *Ruthlan*, the only places now remaining in the hands of the *English*, which he took without any great opposition, and so freed his Country from any Title or Pretence the King of *England* might claim in *North-Wales*. King *John* indeed was engaged another way, and consequently in no good Condition to help himself, for having repented of all the indignities and stubborness he expressed against Pope *Innocent*; at this time he received Penance at the hands of the Archbishop of *Canterbury*, to attone for all the severities he had practised against the Church. And to restore himself the more to his Holiness Favour, he made the Kingdom of *England* Tributary to the Church of *Rome*, to be holden of the Pope, in paying him the summ of 1000 Marks yearly for ever; and withal recalled and restored to their former Preferments and Places all such as had been banished, or had voluntarily fled the Kingdom upon the account of their strict adherence and submission to the Pope of *Rome*.

   Nor was this all, for the next year King *John* with two of his Nobility, the Earls of *Chester* and *Derby*, was resolved upon a Voyage to the *Holy-Land*, but was unfortunately prevented of his Journey, by the Rebellion of his Barons, which now broke forth violently by reason that the King would not grant them some antient Laws and Priviledges, such as their fore-Fathers always enjoyed. Therefore the Barons entered into a Confederacy with Prince *Lhewelyn* of *North-Wales*, desiring him to make what Diversion he could on his part, which they were resolved to do on theirs; and so having raised an Army, they appointed *Robert Fitzwalter* their General. Coming to
Bedford,

1215.

Bedford, they were honourably received into the Castle by *William Beauchamp*, and from thence marching to *London*, they were entertained with all the Expressions and Tokens of Joy. King *John* perceiving how powerful they were like to prove, and how that the Country did in a great measure favour their Cause, thought it his wisest way to nip them in the bud, and to fall upon them before they grew too strong; and therefore having levied his Forces, he marched together with *William Marshall* Earl of *Pembroke*, towards the Castle of *Rochester*. Being arrived there, he laid close Siege to the Castle, but the Governour *William de Abbineto* so bravely defended it, that it could hardly be taken after three Months Siege, but at length the King's Men bore on so violently, that they took it by a Storm, where besides *William de Abbineto*, the King took several of the Barons Prisoners. This was an ill beginning to the Design of the Confederates, and what did not add a little to their Misfortune, the Pope presently issues out his Bull of Excommunication against *Lhewelyn* Prince of *Wales*, and all the *English* Barons as made War against King *John*, who was under the protection of the Church of *Rome*. But Prince *Lhewelyn* did not regard his threatning Anathemas, and therefore having raised an Army, he came to *Shrewsbury*, which was delivered up to him without any resistance. And whilst *Lhewelyn* remained there, *Giles de Bruce* Bishop of *Hereford*, one of the chief of this Conspiracy, sent his Brother *Reynold* to *Brecknock*, whom all the People readily owned for their Lord; and so without the least grumbling or opposition he received the Castles of *Abergefenny* and *Pencelhy*, the *Castelh Gwyn*, or the White Castle, together with *Grosmont* Castle and the Island of *Cynuric*. But when the Bishop came thither in Person, he had the Castles of *Aberhondhy, Hay, Buelht*, and *Blaenlhyfny*, delivered up to him; but thinking he had enough himself, and being rather desirous to secure his Interest, and to strengthen his Party in the Country, than to heap more upon his own shoulders than he was well able to

The History of WALES.

to support, he bestowed *Payn* Castle, *Clune* and all *Eluel* upon *Walter Fychan*, the Son of *Eineon Clyd*.

In the mean time, young *Rhys* the Son of *Gruffydh ap Rhys*, and his Uncle *Maelgon* were reconciled and made Friends, and so coming both to *Dyfed*, they destroyed *Arberth* and *Maenclochec* Castles, and recovered all such Lands as formerly belonged to them, excepting *Cemais*. But *Rhys's* Brothers *Maelgon* and *Owen* went to *North-Wales* and did Homage and Fealty to Prince *Lhewelyn*, whilst their Brother Prince *Rhys* marched forward to *Cydwely*, and having rased the Castles of *Carnwylheon* and *Lhychwr*, brought all the Country about under his subjection. But this was not enough to satisfy the ambitious humour of that young Prince, for having once tasted the pleasure of Victory, and the taking and demolishing of Towns, he was resolved to prosecute his Conquest whilst Fortune seemed to favour his Undertakings; and therefore he lead his Army against *Talybont* Castle, which belonged to *Hugh de Miles*, and forcing his entrance into the same, he put a great number of the Garrison to the Sword. The next day he marched to *Sengennyth* Castle, but the Garrison which kept it, thinking it fruitless and to no purpose to oppose him, burnt the place, and departed to *Ystymlhwynarth*. But he followed them at the Heels, and the next day took it, and rased it to the ground, and over-ran the Country in such a violent manner, that in three days time, he became Master of all the Castles and Fortresses in all *Gowerland* and *Morgannwc*, and so returned home with great Victory and Triumph. At the same time *Rhys Fychan*, otherwise *Rhys Gryg*, young Prince *Rhys's* Uncle, obtained his Liberty from the King of *England*, leaving his Son with two more for Pledges for his modest and peaceable Behaviour towards his Subjects, whom at other times he was wont to molest and oppress. About this time the Abbots of *Tal y Llecheu* and *Ty Gwyn*, were consecrated Bishops, the former of St. *Davids*, and the other of *Bangor*. But the Bishop of *Hereford* who seemed to be the most violently inclined against King *John*, and was otherwise wife unwilling to part with what he had got in *Wales*, could not for all that refuse the Injunction of the Pope, by whose express Command he was constrained to make Peace with the King, which being concluded, in his return homeward, he died at *Glocester*, leaving his Estate to his Brother *Reginald*, who had married the Daughter of Prince *Lhewelyn*.

But for all that, *Giles de Bruce* Bishop of *Hereford* was fallen off, and reconciled to King *John*, yet Prince *Lhewelyn* did not think it convenient to follow his Example, and therefore with his whole Army he marched against *Carmardhyn*, and took the Cattle in five days, having rased it to the ground, he successively laid Siege to the Castles of *Lhanstephan*, St. *Cleare*, and *Talacharn*, which he used after the same manner. From thence he went to *Cardigan*, and winning *Emlyn* Castle, he subdued *Cemaes*, and then laying Siege to *Trefdraeth* Castle, in *English* called *Newport*, he quickly took it, and afterwards rased it to the ground. His next Design was upon *Aberteifi* and *Cilgerran* Castles, but the Garrisons which defended them, finding it to no purpose to wait his coming, and so to withstand all his Attempts against those places voluntarily surrendred, and by that means prevented all the Mischief, which in opposing him, would in all probability unavoidably attend them. And so Prince *Lhewelyn* having successfully over-run and subdued all *Carmardhyn* and *Cardigan*, triumphantly returned to *North-Wales*, being attended by several of the *Welch* Nobility, such as *Hewel ap Gruffydh ap Conan*, *Lhewelyn ap Meredith*, *Gwenwynwyn* Lord of *Powys*, *Meredith ap Rotpert*, *Maelgon* and *Rhys Fychan* the Sons of Prince *Rhys* of *South Wales*, *Rhys* and *Owen* the Sons of *Gruffydh ap Rhys*, together with all the Power of *Madoc ap Gruffydh Maylor* Lord of *Bromfield*.

1216.   But the next year Prince *Lhewelyn* returned to *Aberteifi* to compose a Difference, which since his departure, had happened betwixt *Maelgon* and *Rhys Fychan*, Prince *Rhys*'s Sons on the one side, and *Rhys* and *Owen*, *Gruffydh ap Rhys*'s Sons on the other.

There-

The History of WALES.

Therefore to make up this Quarrel, and to reduce all Matters to a quiet and amicable issue, Prince *Lhewelyn* made an equal distribution of *South-Wales* betwixt them, allotting to *Maelgon*, three Cantrefs in *Dyfed*, viz. *Gwarthaf*, *Penlhwynoc*, *Cemaes*, and *Emlyn* with *Cilgerran* Castle; to young *Rhys*, two Castles in *Tstratywy*, *Hiruryn* and *Maelhaen*; *Maenor Bydfey*, with the Castle of *Lhanymdhyfry*, and two in *Cardigan Gwynionyth* and *Mabwyneon*. His Brother *Owen* had to his share the Castles of *Aberteifi* and *Nant yr Arian*, with three Cantrefs in *Cardigan*; and *Rhys Fychan*, otherwise called *Rhys Gryc*, had *Dynefawr* Castle, the *Cantref Mawr*, the *Cantref Bychan*, excepting *Hiruryn* and *Midhfey*, together with the Comotes of *Cydwely* and *Carnwylhion*. This Division being accomplished to every one's Satisfaction, and all the Lords of *South-Wales* being amicably reconciled, Prince *Lhewelyn* took his Journey for *North-Wales*; but he had not advanced very far, when News was brought him that *Gwenwynwyn* Lord of *Powys* was revolted, and was become again the King of *England*'s Subject. This unwelcome News struck very deep in the Prince's Mind, by reason that *Gwenwynwyn* was a Man of great Power and Strength in the Country, and went a great way to repel the Incursions of the *English* upon the Marches, which now he being gone off, could not, he feared, be so well effected. But however, to make the best of a bad Market, he endeavoured to take him off from the *English*, and to restore him to his former Allegiance due to himself as his Natural Prince; and to that end, he sent to him some Bishops and Abbots to put him in mind of his Oath and Promise, how that he with the rest of the Lords of *Wales*, had obliged himself to oppose the *English* to the utmost of his Power, and had delivered Pledges for the sure performance of what he had then by Oath engaged in; and lest he should have forgot what he had then promised, he was desired to read his own hand Writing, whereby it was apparent that he had very unjustly violated both his Oath and Promise. But all the Rhetorick the Bishops could make use of, was not of force enough to work *Gwenwynwyn* to reconciliation with the Prince, and an averſion to the King of *England*; and therefore ſeeing nothing would do, Prince *Lhewelyn* was reſolved to make him incapable of ſerving the *Engliſh*, and ſo entring *Powys* with a ſtrong Army, he ſubdued the whole Country to himſelf, *Gwenirynwyn* being forced to fly for Succor to the Earl of *Cheſter*.

Whilſt theſe things paſſed in *Wales*, *Lewis* the *Dauphin* of *France* being invited by the *Engliſh* Barons againſt King *John*, landed in the Iſland of *Thanet*, and marching forward to *London*, he there received Homage of all the Barons, that were in actual War againſt the King. And then ſetting forward to *Wincheſter*, where King *John* then lay, he took in his way the Caſtles of *Rygat*, *Guildford* and *Farnham*, and coming to *Wincheſter*, had the Town preſently ſurrendred to him. King *John* did not think fit to abide his coming, but removing to *Hereford*, in the Marches of *Wales*, he ſent to Prince *Lhewelyn* and *Reynoid Bruce*, deſiring their Friendſhip, and imploring their Aid and Aſſiſtance againſt the *French*. But they retuſing to hearken to his Propoſals, he deſtroyed *Radnor* and *Hay* Caſtles, and marching forward to *Oſweſtry*, which belonged to *John Fitzalan*, he burnt it to the ground, and then departed towards the *North*. But after that he had ſettled his Affairs there, and appointed Governours in all the Towns and Places of Strength; whilſt he was making all neceſſary Preparations at *Newark* to confront the Barons, he fell ſick, and in a ſhort time died, and was buried at *Worceſter*.

After his Death his Son *Henry* was by ſeveral of the *Engliſh* Nobility proclaimed King, and in a little while, moſt of the Barons, who upon their hatred to King *John*, had maintained an open War againſt him, came in, and owned their Allegiance to his Son *Henry*, tho' contrary to their Oath to *Lewis* the *Dauphine*. But what was moſt pernicious to the *Welch*, *Reynald de Bruce* who had all this while maintained a Confederacy with Prince *Lhewelyn* his Father-in-Law
againſt

The History of WALES.

against King *John*, underhand made his Peace with King *Henry*. But he suffered severely for his Treachery; for young *Rhys*, and *Owen* his Nephew by his Sister, seeing that he in whom they put their greatest Confidence, had deceitfully forsaken them, came upon him with all their Power, and took from him all *Buelht*, excepting only the Castle. Prince *Lhewelyn* was presently made acquainted with *Bruce*'s revolt, but as soon as he was informed that his Son-in-Law was gone over to the King of *England*, he went in great fury to *Brecknoc*, and laying Siege to the Town of *Aberhondhy*, he was with much ado prevailed upon by young *Rhys* to raise the Siege for the summ of a Hundred Marks ; and then crossing the Mountanous part of *Glamorgan*, called the *Black Mountains*, where his Carriages suffered very much, he came to *Gwyr*, and encamping at *Lhangruc*, *Reynald Bruce* with six Knights in his Company, came to meet him, desiring his Pardon for his passed Offence, assuring him that for the future, he would be true and faithful to him, and would to his endeavour assist him against the King of *England*. Prince *Lhewelyn* was too good natured to reject his submission, and so did not only receive him to his Favour, but bestowed upon him also the Castle of *Senghennyth*, which *Reynald* committed to the Custody of *Rhys Fychan*. Prince *Lhewelyn* having settled all things in good Order in *Gwyr*, marched to *Dyfed*, and being at *Cefn Cynwarchan*, the *Flemings* sent their Agents to him to desire Peace, which the Prince, by reason that they always adhered to the *English* Interest, would not grant them. And so young *Rhys* having the first Man passed the River *Cledeu* to Storm the Town, *Iorwerth* Bishop of St. *Davids*, with the rest of his Clergy came to the Prince to intreat for a Peace for the *Flemings*, which after a long debate, was granted, and concluded upon these Terms ; First, That all the Inhabitants of *Rhôs*, and the Country of *Pembroke* should from thence forward swear Allegiance to Prince *Lhewelyn*, and ever after acknowledge his Sovereignty. Secondly, That towards the defraying of his Charges in this Expedition, they should pay one Thousand Marks to be delivered to him before the ensuing Feast of St. *Michael.* Thirdly, That for the sure performance of these Articles they should deliver up Twenty Hostages, who were to be some of the most Principal Persons in their Country. Then Prince *Lhewelyn* having now brought all *Wales* subject to himself, and put Matters in a settled posture in *South Wales*, returned to *North-Wales*, having purchased very considerable Honour and Esteem for his Martial Achievements in this Expedition.

And now all Matters of Differences being adjusted, and the *Welch* in good hopes of a durable Freedom from all Troubles and Hostilities; another Accident unhappily fell out to cross their Expectation. *Lewis* the *Dauphin* perceiving the *English* Barons to slight and forsake him, concluded a Peace with King *Henry*, and returned to *France*; and then the Barons, the King promising to answer all their Request, and to redress their Grievances, made their submission, without including the *Welch* in their Articles. They had all this while gladly embraced the Friendship and Aid of the Prince of *Wales*; but now upon their Reconciliation to the King, thinking they had no farther need of him, they very basely forsook him, who had been the principal Support and Succour of their Cause. And not only so, but they conspired together to convert their Arms against *Wales*, thinking they could without any breach of Equity or Conscience, take away the Lands of the *Welch*, to make addition to what some of them had already unjustly possessed themselves of. *William Marshall* Earl of *Pembroke* opened the Scene, and coming unexpectedly upon the *Welch*, took the Town of *Caerlheon*. But he got nothing by this, for *Rhys Fychan* perceiving what he would fain be at, rased *Senghennyth* Castle, and all the rest in his Custody in that Country, and banishing the *English* with their Wives and Children, divided the Country betwixt the *Welch*, who kept sure possession of it. Prince
Lhewelyn

The History of WALES.

Lhewelyn also finding those to become his Foes, who had but lately courted his Friendship, and fearing lest that the *English* being now in Arms should make any Attempt upon his Castles, augmented the Garrisons of *Carmardhyn* and *Aberteifi*, to make them capable of withstanding the *English*, in case they should come against them. But tho' the *Welch* and *English* were at open Variance and in actual Hostility one against another, yet young *Rhys* with Prince *Lhewelyn*'s approbation and consent, thought it advisable to go and do Homage to the King of *England*, for his Lands in *Wales*. This might be thought a matter of Supererogation, to make courtship to one who was declared Enemy to all the *Welch*, and one that would not in all probability, suffer him to enjoy a quiet possession of his Estate, in case he had Ability and Opportunity to eject him. But the *Welch* Interest was 1219. in a great measure augmented by a new Alliance with some of the most powerful among the *English*; *Rhys Gryc*, Prince *Rhys*'s Son, being married to the Earl of *Clare*'s Daughter; and *Marret*, Prince *Lhewelyn*'s Daughter, to *John Bruce*.

The Prince of *Wales* had quickly an occasion to 1220. experience his Power, for the *Flemings* in *Dyfed*, who had lately sworn Allegiance to him, began now to repent of what they had but a little time ago gladly submitted to, and contrary to their Oaths, and the League they had sworn to observe, they fell upon *Aberteifi* Castle, which they took. Prince *Lhewelyn* being highly displeased with the treacherous practices of these perjured *Flemings*, marched with all speed to *Aberteifi*, and having recovered the Castle, which he afterwards rased, he put all the Garrison to the Sword. *Gwys* was served in the same manner, and the Town of *Haverford* was burnt to the ground, and over-running *Rhos* and *Daugledhau*, he committed a lamentable Destruction throughout the whole Country. This the *Flemings* received as the due reward of their sinistrous Dealing, which made them quickly apprehensive of their folly, and their imprudent Behaviour towards the Prince of *Wales*; and therefore being

The History of WALES.

being sorrowfully sensible how unable they were to put a stop to his farther progress by force of Arms, they made Overtures for Cessation of all Hostilities till the *May* following, which being granted them upon strict Conditions, Prince *Lhewelyn* returned to *North-Wales*. In the mean time some *Welch* Lords besieged *Buelbt* Castle, which was in the possession of *Reynald Bruce*, but before they could take it, King *Henry* brought an Army to the Marches and raised the Siege, and then marching forward to *Montgomery*, built a new Castle in that Town.

1221. The next year an unhappy dissention fell out betwixt Prince *Lhewelyn* and his Son *Gruffydh*, this latter having kept himself in possession of the Cantref of *Merionyth*, contrary to the Consent and well-liking of his Father. The Prince therefore having now no great matter of moment abroad, was resolved to curb the Insolency of his Son, and therefore sent to him to command his appearance, and to wish him to deliver up the Cantref quietly, lest he should be forced to take it violently out of his Hands. *Gruffydh* was not in the least dismayed at his threatnings, but being resolved to keep what at present he enjoyed, would neither go to his Father, nor deliver up the Cantref to him. The Prince being enraged that he should be so slighted by his Son, made a vehement Protestation, that he would be severely revenged both of him and all his accomplices; and therefore coming to *Merionyth* with a great Army, was resolved to drive his Son out of the Country. But *Gruffydh* made all possible preparations to oppose his Father, and drew up his Forces to give him Battel, but when both Armies were ready to joyn, the Differences betwixt them was happily composed, and *Gruffydh* prevailed upon to make his submission to his Father. But the Prince, tho' he forgave his Son his Offence, and received him to favour, would not however, permit him to enjoy *Merionyth* and *Ardydwy*; but taking them away from him, and building a Castle in the latter, returned home. But he had not continued long at his Palace at *Aberffraw,*

ffraw, when another occasion called him abroad; for young *Rhys* being disappointed of *Aberteifi*, which in the division of *South Wales* was allotted to his share, forsook the Prince, and put himself under the protection of *Willam Marshal* Earl of *Pembrock*. Prince *Lhewelyn* hearing this, marched in great haste to *Aberystwyth*, and being desirous to punish *Rhys* for his desertion from his Allegiance due to him, seized to his own use that Castle, together with all the Demain and Lands belonging to it. When *Rhys* understood what the Prince had done, he presently made his Complaint to the King of *England*, who coming to *Shrewsbury*, and sending for Prince *Lhewelyn*, adjusted matters so betwixt them, that the Prince promised to treat with *Rhys* for *Aberteifi*, after the same manner as he had done with *Maelgon* for *Caermardhyn*. And towards the close of the Year, *John Bruce*, Prince *Lhewelyn*'s Son in Law, obtained leave to fortifie *Senghenwyth* Castle, which in right to the Prince's grant to *Raynald Bruce*, belonged to him. But young *Rhys* did not long survive the Agreement betwixt him and Prince *Lhewelyn*; for he dyed the following Year, and was buried at *Ystratflur*; after whose death, the Prince divided his Estate betwixt his Brother *Owen* and his Uncle *Maelgon*.

A. D. 1222.

William Marshal Earl of *Pembrock* was now in *Ireland*, and very busie in prosecuting the War against the King of *England's* Enemies in that Kingdom; the opportunity of whose absence Prince *Lhewelyn* taking advantage of, won the Castles of *Aberteifi* and *Caermardhyn*, belonging to the Earl; and putting both the Garrisons to the Sword, placed in their room a strong Party of his own Men. But when the Earl was informed of what the Prince of *Wales* had done, he presently left *Ireland*, and landed at S. *Davids* with a great Army, and having recovered his Castles, he treated the *Welch* after the same manner, as Prince *Lhewelyn* had used his Garrisons, and passing forward into the Prince's Country, destroyed all before him as he went along. The Prince understanding how violently he came forward, sent his

Son *Gruffydh* with a considerable Body of Men to check his Fury; who coming to *Cydwely*, and receiving intelligence that the Magistrates of that place, had a private design to betray him to the Enemy, he put the whole Town in Flames, and burnt it to the ground, without sparing either Churches, or other Religious Houses. The Earl of *Pembrock* had passed the River *Tywy* at *Caermardhyn*, where *Gruffydh* met him, and gave him battel; but the Victory proved so uncertain, that the Night was forced to part them; and so the *English* retired over the River. *Matthew Paris* writes, that the Earl obtained a very signal Victory, and that of the *Welch* there were Nine Thousand slain and taken; though the *Welch* Account, which in this case is in all likelihood the best, makes the whole Army of the *Welch* to consist but of that number. But both Armies having layn for certain Days in that posture, and the River *Tywy* being betwixt them; *Gruffydh*, by reason that Provision began to grow scarce in his Camp, returned back; and then the Earl decamped, and marched to *Cilgerran*, where he began to build a very strong Castle. But before he could have time to finish it, he received an Express from the King, with orders to come to him; and so he went by Sea to *London*, leaving his Army at *Cilgerran*, to continue the Work which he had begun. Shortly after, the King, together with the Archbishop of *Canterbury*, came to *Ludlow*, and sending for Prince *Lhewelyn* thither, they had good hopes to adjust all Differences, and to make an amicable Composition betwixt him and the Earl. But when this could not be effected, both Parties sticking close to their private Interest; the Earl being assisted by the Earl of *Derby*, and *Henry Fyggot* Lord of *Emyas*, designed to pass by Land to *Pembrock*; but his purpose being discovered to the Prince, he detached his Son to secure the Passage of *Carnwylhion*, and came in person to *Mabedryd*; which when the Earl understood, finding it dangerous to prosecute his Design any further, he returned to *England*; and then the Prince marched to

North-

The History of WALES.

North-Wales. The next Action that passed in *Wales*, was somewhat rare, and not redounding much to the Credit and Esteem of the *Welch*; for *Rhys Fychan*, having by some sinistrous means or other, taken his Father *Rhys Gryc*, contrary to all filial Affection and Duty, detained him Prisoner, and would not let him at liberty, till he had delivered up *Lhanymdhyfri* Castle to him. About the same time, *Meredith*, Archdeacon of *Cardigan*, Prince *Rhys*'s Son, departed this Life, and was honourably interred at S. *Davids*, by his Father.

A. D. 1227.

But a while after, a great Storm threatned the *Welch*; King *Henry* having raised a great Army, was resolved to make a violent Prosecution of the Earl of *Pembrock*'s Quarrel, against the Prince of *Wales*, and if possible, to make all that Country, for ever subject to the Crown of *England*; and so being advanced into the Marches, he encamped at *Ceri*. Prince *Lhewelyn* on the other hand, being informed of these mighty Preparations in *England*, and understanding that they were intended against him, did use all the Endeavours possible, to make a vigorous Resistance; and having drawn together all the Forces he was able to levy, thought it his wisest way to meet the *English* upon the Marches, and not to permit the Enemy to enter his Country. Both Armies being come in sight of each other, frequent Skirmishes happened betwixt 'em; but one day, almost the whole Armies engaged, and after a vigorous Attack of both sides, the *English* at last got the worst, and were forced to retire, having a great many Men slain and taken Prisoners. Among the latter, was *William Bruce*, *Reynald*'s Son, who offered for his Ransom all *Buelht*, together with a considerable Sum of Money, which the Prince would not accept of. But King *Henry* finding that his Army was worsted in this Rencounter, thought it best to make Peace with the Prince of *Wales*, which being concluded, *Lhewelyn* came to the King, and having paid him all other Respects, besides that of Submission and Allegiance, he returned in great Honour to *North-Wales*. But this Action is somewhat otherwise laid down

1228.

down by *Matthew Paris*, who writes, that this Skirmish betwixt the *English* and *Welch* happened upon an other account; for the Garrison of *Montgomery* issuing out of the Castle, to enlarge a certain Passage leading through a Wood, where the *Welch* were wont to rob and kill all Passengers; began to fell the Timber, and cut down all the Bushes which lessened the Road, thereby to make the Passage more clear and secure. The *Welch* receiving intelligence of this, came presently upon him in great Numbers, and surprizing the Enemies, being busie at their Labour, forced as many as could escape, to betake themselves for refuge into the Castle, which afterwards, having first cast a deep Trench about it, they smartly invested. *Hubert de Burgh,* Lord Chief Justice of *England*, and Owner of the Castle, having notice of this, sent presently to King *Henry*, desiring his speedy help against the *Welch*, who thereupon came in Person with part of his Army, and raised the Siege. Then, the rest of his Forces being arrived, he marched into the Wood, which was Five Miles in length, and by reason of the thickness of the growth impassable; and for an easie passage through it, caused it to be burnt down. After that, he led his Army farther into the Country, and coming to an Abby called *Cridia*, which the *Welch* were wont to take for refuge, he caused it to be burnt down; but finding it a very convenient place for a Fortress, he granted leave to *Hubert de Burgh* to build a Castle there. But whilst the Work was going on, the *Welchmen* gauled the *English*, and skirmished with them frequently, so that many were slain on both sides; but at last *William Bruce*, with many others that went abroad to fetch Provision, was intercepted by the *Welch*, and taken Prisoner, and most of his Company were slain, among whom, one who was knighted a few days before, seeing some of his Fellows in great danger, rushed boldly into the midst of his Enemies, and after a manful defence, bravely lost his Life. Several of King *Henry's* Men were corrupted by Prince *Lhewelyn*, and upon that account took no great pains to repulse the Enemy; which when the King perceived,

The History of WALES.

ed, and finding withal the Provision was grown very scarce in his Camp, he was forced to conclude a dishonourable Peace with the *Welch*, consenting to demolish that Castle, which with so great an Expence both of Men and Mony was now almost finished, upon his own Charges, Prince *Lhewelyn* paying only Three Thousand Pounds towards it. Then both Armies separated, Prince *Lhewelyn* marching to *North-Wales*, and the King leaving *William Bruce* Prisoner with the *Welch*, returned to *England*, having purchased no small Discredit in this Expedition.

William Bruce was brought to *Wales*, and there had an honourable Confinement in the Prince his Palace; but he had not continued there very long, when he began to be suspected of being too familiar with the Princess, King *Henry*'s Sister; and as the report went, was taken in the very act of Adultery; for which the Prince caused him to be hanged forthwith. About the same time, *Lhewelyn*, *Maelgon*'s Son dyed in *North-Wales*, and was buried at *Conwey*; and *Maelgon*, Prince *Rhys* his Son in *South-Wales*, and was buried in *Ystratflur*; whose Estate descended to his Son *Maelgon*. And a little after, *William Marshall*, Earl of *Pembrock*, dyed, one that ever entertained an inveterate Enmity to the *Welch*, and upon whose account King *Henry* had chiefly brought his Army into *Wales*. He was succeeded both in his Title and Estate by his Brother *Richard*, who was much more favourably enclined towards the *Welch*, and never attempted any thing against them. But the King of *England* was resolved to retrieve the Honour he had lost in the late Expedition against the *Welch*; and therefore being returned from *France*, whither he had made a Descent, to recover what his Father had lost in that Kingdom, he came to *Wales*; and having remained some time in the Marches, he returned again to *England*, leaving his Army under the command of *Hubert Burgh*, Earl of *Kent*, to defend the Marches against any in-road which the *Welch* might attempt. And he had not remained there long, when he received Intelligence, that a Party of *Welch* had entered the Marches near

Mont-

A. D.
1230.

1231.

Montgomery, whom he forthwith purfued, and fetting upon them furprizedly, he put a great number of them to the Sword. Prince *Lhewylyn* hearing this, came in Perfon with a great Army to the Marches, and fitting before *Montgomery* Caftle, he forced *Hubert* to withdraw, and then making himfelf Mafter of the place, he burnt it to the ground, and put the Garrifon to the Sword; the like Fate attended the Caftles of *Radnor*, *Aberhondhy*, *Rhayadr Gwy*, *Caerlheon*, *Neth*, and *Cydwely*; though *Caerlheon* held out very ftubbornly, and the Prince had feveral of his Men deftroyed before the Place. King *Henry* being informed of what miferable Defolation the Prince of *Wales* fo fuccefsfully committed upon his Subjects in thefe Countries, had him prefently excommunicated; and then coming to *Hereford* with a mighty Army, he detached the greateft part of it, with a great number of his Nobility to *Wales*. Thefe by the direction of a Fryar of *Cymer*, unexpectedly as they thought, fell upon a Party of *Welch*; who at the firft Encounter feemed to fly, till they had allured the *Englifh* to purfue them to a place where a greater Party of *Welch* lay in ambufcade; who rufhing of a fudden upon the *Englifh*, put them in fuch a confufion, that the greateft part of them was cut off. The King being fenfible, that this was a treacherous Infinuation of the Friar, was refolved to be revenged, by burning the Abby of *Cymer*; but the Prior, for Three Hundred Marks, prevented it; and fo the King returned to *England*, having effected nothing in this Expedition, befides the building of *Mawd* Caftle. In the mean time, *Maelgon* Son of *Maelgon ap Rhys* laid fiege to *Aberteifi*, and having by force got entry into the Town, he put all the Inhabitants to the Sword, then deftroyed all before him to the Caftle Gates, which were fo ftrongly fortified, that it feemed almoft impracticable to take it in any fhort time. But *Maelgon*, being joyned by his Cofin *Owen*, *Gruffydh ap Rhys*'s Son, was refolved to try the utmoft that could be effected; and therefore taking with him fome of Prince *Lhewelyn*'s moft experienced Officers, he

The History of WALES.

he brake down the Bridg upon the River *Teifi*, and then investing the Castle more closely, he so batter'd and undermin'd it, that he became in a little time Master of it.

The Year following, Prince *Lhewelyn* made a Descent upon *England*, and having committed very considerable Waste and Destruction upon the Borders, he returned to *North Wales* with a rich Booty both of Men and Cattel. King *Henry*, to correct the *Welch* for these grievous Devastations, and to prevent their further Incursions into *England*, demanded a very great Subsidy of his Subjects to carry on the War against the *Welch*; which being granted him, he made all possible Preparations for his Expedition to *Wales*. In the mean time, *Randulph* Earl of *Chester* dyed, and was succeeded in that Honour by *John* his Sisters Son, who was afterwards married to Prince *Lhewelyn*'s Daughter. But the *English* in *Wales* being in expectation of King *Henry*'s coming thither, began to repair and fortifie their Castles; and particularly, *Richard* Earl of *Cornwal* rebuilt *Radnor* Castle, which the Prince had lately destroyed. Prince *Lhewelyn* was sufficiently sensible, that the King of *England* intended an Invasion, and therefore to be beforehand with him, he came with an Army to *Brecknock*, destroyed all the Towns and Castles throughout the Country, excepting *Brecknock* Castle, which held out so manfully, that after a Months sitting before it, he was at last constrained to raise the Siege. In his return to *North-Wales*, he burnt the Town of *Clun*, recovered all that Country called *Dyffryn Tefeidiat*, in the possession of *John Fitz-Alan*, destroyed *Red* Castle in *Powys*, and burnt *Ofwestry*. But what happened very fortunately to the *Welch*; *Richard Marshal* Earl of *Pembroke* being faln at variance with King *Henry*, took part with Prince *Lhewelyn*; with whom joyned *Hubert de Burgh*, who had lately made his escape out of the Castle of *Devizes*, where the King, upon some Articles of Information brought against him, had committed him to Prison. But the Earl of *Pembrock*, attended by *Owen ap Gruffydh ap Rhys*, came to *S. Davids*

A. D. 1232.

1233.

vids; and being very glad of an opportunity to revenge himself upon the King, flew every one that owned any Dependance upon the Crown of *England*. *Maelgon* and *Rhys Gryc*, with all the Forces of Prince *Lhewelyn*, quickly joyned the Earl; who in their march through the Country, took the Castles of *Cardyff*, *Abergevenny*, *Pencelhy*, *Blaenlhefyni*, and *Bwlch y Ddinas*, which all, excepting *Cardyff*, they burnt to the ground. The King receiving intelligence, that the Earl of *Pembrock* had entered into a Confederacy with the Prince of *Wales*, and that he was now in open Hostility against his Subjects in that Country, gathered a very formidable Army, consisting, besides *English*, of *Flemings*, *Normans*, and *Gascoigns*; and coming to *Wales*, he encamped at *Grofmont*, where the Earl, with the *Welch* Army met him. But when the *English* would have endeavoured to advance further into the Country, the *Welch* opposed them, and so a Battel ensued, wherein the *English* lost Five Hundred Horse, besides a far greater number of their Infantry. The *Welch* having gained a considerable Victory in this Action, the King was advised to withdraw his Forces, for fear lest that the *Welch* should again set upon them, and so sustain a greater Loss; which Counsel the King willingly hearkened unto, and so he returned for *England*. The *English* being withdrawn, the Earl likewise decamped, and marched to *Caermardhyn*, which he besieged; but after Three Months in vain Assault, the Garrison most bravely defending the place; and the *English* Fleet having thrown in new Provisions, he thought it most adviseable to raise the Siege. Shortly after, *Rhys Gryc*, Son to Prince *Rhys* dyed at *Lhandeilo Fawr*, and was honourably interr'd by his Father at S. *Davids*. About the same time, *Maelgon Fychan*, *Maelgon ap Rhys* his Son, finished *Trefilan* Castle, which was begun in his Fathers time.

A. D. 1234.
King *Henry* was not willing to hazard any more Campaigns in *Wales*, and therefore he appointed *John* of *Monmouth*, a great Soldier and General of the *English* Forces, Warden of the Marches of *Wales*, who

The History of WALES.

who thinking to get to himself an eternal Name in conquering the *Welch*, raised all the Power he could; and imagining that the *Welch* could not be privy to his purpose, he apprehended he could fall upon the Earl-Marshal unexpected. But in this, he was to his sorrow, most widely mistaken; for the Earl having received private intimation of his Design, hid himself in a certain Wood, by which the *English* were to march; and when they were come so far, the *Welch* of a sudden gave a great shout, and leaping out of the place they had absconded themselves in, they fell upon the *English*, being unprovided, and putting their whole Army to flight, they slew an infinite number both of the *English* and their Auxiliaries. *John* of *Monmouth* himself made his escape by flight; but the Earl-Marshal entering his Country, destroyed it with Fire and Sword. And what added to the Misery of the *English*, Prince *Lhewelyn* in the Week after *Epiphany*, joyning the Earl-Marshal, made an Incursion into the King's Territories, destroying all before them, from the Confines of *Wales* to *Shrewsbury*; a great part of which they laid in Ashes. King *Henry* was all this while with the Bishop of *Winchester* at *Glocester*, and for want of sufficient Power or Courage to confront the Enemy, durst not take the Field; of which being at length perfectly ashamed, he removed to *Winchester*, leaving the Marches naked to the mercy of the Enemy. And now, there being no apprehension of fear from the *English*, the Earl of *Pembrock*, by the Counsel of *Geoffrey de Marisco*, transported his Army into *Ireland*, thinking to obtain a Conquest in that Kingdom; but in the first Encounter with the *Irish*, he was unfortunately slain through the Treachery of his own Men: And so his Estate and Title descended to his Brother *Gilbert*.

But King *Henry* finding it impracticable to force the *Welch* to a Submission, and being in a great measure weary of continual Wars and incessant Hostilities, thought it his best Prudence to make some honourable Agreement with the Prince of *Wales*; and therefore he deputed *Edmund* Archbishop of *Canterbury*,

bury, the Bishops of *Rochester*, *Coventry* and *Lichfield*, and *Chester*, to treat with Prince *Lhewelyn* about a Peace. When the King came to meet with them in their return from this Negotiation, being at *Woodstock*, he was certified of the death of the Earl of *Pembrock*, which he took so much to heart, that he presently melted into Tears, being afflicted for the death of so great a Person, whom he openly declared had not left his Second in all his Kingdom. Going from thence to *Glocester*, he met with the Archbishop and Bishops, who delivered to him the * Form of the Treaty of Peace with Prince *Lhewelyn*, which he would not conclude, unless upon this condition; That all the *English* Nobility who were confederated with him, and by evil Counsel were exil'd, should be recalled, and restored to the King's Favour. The Archbishop further acquainted his Majesty, with what Difficulty he had brought the matter to this conclusion; being sometimes forced to add Threatnings on the King's behalf, with his Clergy; to which Menaces the Prince is said to have answered, That he bore more regard to the King's Charity and Piety, than he did fear his Arms, or dread his Clergy. But the King, who was very desirous of a Peace, readily consented to what the Prince required; and therefore he issued out his Letters, recalling all the Nobles who were out-law'd, or otherwise exil'd, requiring them to appear at *Glocester*, upon *Sunday* next before *Ascension day*, where they should receive their Pardons, and be restored to their Estates, which the King had taken into his own hands.

* See the Appendix.

The Peace being thus concluded betwixt the *English* and *Welch*, Prince *Lhewelyn* set his Son *Gruffydh* at liberty, whom for his disobedient and restless Humour he had detained in close Prison for the space of Six Years. About the same time, *Cadwalhon ap Maelgon* of *Melienydh*, departed this Life, who was quickly follow'd by *Owen*, *Gruffydh ap Rhys*'s Son, a Person of great Worth, and exceedingly beloved, and was buried at *Ystratflur*, by his Brother *Rhys*. And the Year following dyed *Owen ap Meredith ap Rotpert*

A. D. 1235.

of

The History of WALES.

of *Cydewen*; and not long after him, *Madawc*, the Son of *Gruffydh Mayelor*, Lord of *Bromfield*, *Chirk* and *Yale*, who was buried at the Abby of *Lhan Egwest*, or *Vale Crucis*, which he had built; leaving Issue behind him one Son, called *Gruffydh*, who succeeded into the Possession of all these Lordships. A little after *Gilbert*, Earl of *Pembrock*, got by Treachery *Marchen* Castle, which belonged to *Morgan ap Howel*, and fortified the same very strongly, for fear of Prince *Lhewelyn*. The next Spring *Joan*, King *John's* Daughter, and Princess of *Wales*, departed this Life, and was buried, according to her own desire, upon the Seashore, at a place called *Lhanfaes*, in the Isle of *Anglesey*; where the Prince, in memory of her, afterwards founded a religious House, for the Order of Mendicant-Friars. About the same time also dyed *John Scot*, Earl of *Chester*, without any Issue, upon which account the King seized that Earldom into his own hands. *Hugh Lupus* was the first that enjoyed this Honour, who coming over to *England* with the Conquerour, was by him created Earl of *Chester*, and Sword-bearer of *England*; *Habendum & tenendum dictum comitatum Cestriæ, sibi & hæredibus suis, ita liberè ad gladium, sicut ipse Rex totam tenebat Angliam ad coronam*: To have and to hold the said County of *Chester*, to him and his Heirs by right of the Sword, so freely and securely as the King held the Realm of *England* in the right of the Crown. After Five Descents, *Randulph Bohun* came to be Earl of *Chester*, who was Uncle to this *John*, the last Earl. This *Randulph* had several Encounters with Prince *Lhewelyn*, and was in continual agitation against him; but once more particularly, meeting with the Prince, and being sensible of his Inability to withstand him, he was obliged to retire for Refuge to the Castle of *Ruthlan*, which the Prince presently besieged. *Randulph* perceiving himself to be in danger, sent to *Roger Lacy*, Constable of *Chester*, requesting him to raise what strength he could possible, and come to succour him in this Extremity. Wherefore *Lacy* having received this Express, called to him presently all his

A. D. 1236.

1237.

Friends,

Friends, defiring them to make all the Endeavours imaginable to refcue the Earl from that imminent Danger which fo feverely threatned him: At whofe requeft, *Ralph Dutton*, his Son in Law, a valorous Youth, affembled together all the Players and Muficians, and fuch as then, being Fair-time, had met to make merry; and prefenting them to the Conftable, he forthwith marched to *Ruthlan*, raifed the Siege, and delivered the Earl from all his fear. In recompence of this Service, the Earl granted the Conftable feveral Freedoms and Priviledges; and to *Dutton* the ruling and ordering all Players and Muficians within the faid Country, to be enjoyed by his Heirs for ever.

A. D. In the Year 1238. Prince *Lhewelyn* being difcom-
1238. pofed in Body, called unto him all the Lords and Barons of *Wales* to *Tftratflur*, where each of them fwore to remain true and faithful Subjects, and did Homage to *David*, *Lhewelyn*'s Son, whom he had named to fucceed him. *Matthew Paris* writes, that Prince *Lhewelyn* being impotent by reafon of a Palfie, and fore difquieted by his Son *Gruffydh*, fent Embaffadours to the King of *England*, fignifying to him, that for as much as he could not expect to live long, by reafon of his Age, he was defirous to lead the remainder of his days in Peace and Tranquility; and therefore now purpofed to fubmit himfelf to the Government and Protection of the King, and would hold his Lands of him; promifing withal, that whenever the King fhould ftand in need of his help, he would ferve him both with Men and Money, to the utmoft of his power. The Bifhops of *Hereford* and *Chefter* were fent Mediators in this behalf, though fome of the Nobility of *Wales* openly and peremptorily withftood it, and upon no condition whatfoever would accept of fuch a Peace. But *David* being declared Succeffor to the Principality, began to plague his Brother *Gruffydh*, who though elder, was yet bafe-born; and took from him *Aruftly*, *Ceri*, *Cyfciliec*, *Mowdhwy*, *Mochnant*, and *Careneon*; and let him only enjoy the *Cantref* of *Lhyn*. But a little afterwards he difpoffeffed him of all, and contrary to his Oath to the Bifhop

of

of *Bangor*, in whofe protection *Gruffydh* then remained, took him Prifoner; having upon promife of no Violence, obtained to fpeak with him, and fent him to *Cricieth* Caftle. But whilft thefe two Brothers continued to entertain an irreconcilable Odium one to another, their Father, Prince *Lewelyn ap Iorwerth*, to the great Grief and Diffatisfaction of all the *Welch*, departed this Life, and was very honourably interred in the Abby of *Conwey*, after he had reigned Six and Fifty Years. He was a Prince of great Courage and Audacity, and had no lefs Prudence in contriving, than Boldnefs in executing any martial Adventure; he was a great Support to the *Welch*, and no lefs a Plague to the *Englifh*; he made very confiderable Conquefts upon the Borders, and extended the Frontiers of *Wales*, much beyond their former Limits. He had Iffue by his only Wife *Joan*, Daughter to King *John* of *England*, one Son called *David*, who afterwards fucceeded in the Principality of *Wales*; and a Daughter named *Gladys*, who was married to Sir *Ralph Mortimer*. He had alfo a bafe Son, named *Gruffydh*, whom his Brother *David* kept a clofe Prifoner to his dying day.

A. D.
1240.

David ap Lhewelyn.

PRince *Lhewelyn ap Iorwerth* being deceafed, his only legitimate Son *David*, whom all the Barons of *Wales* had, as is faid, in his Fathers Lifetime fworn to obey, legally fucceeded in the Goverment; wherein being actually confirmed, he went to the King of *England* to *Glocefter*, and there did him Homage * for his Principality. Then all the Barons, both *Englifh* and *Welch* who held any Lands in *Wales*, in like manner did Homage and Fealty for the fame. But the *Englifh* could not long refrain from their wonted Hoftilities towards the *Welch*; and thereupon

See *Appendix*.

upon *Gilbert Marſhal*, taking advantage of this Revolution, before Matters were throughly ſettled, brought an Army before the Caſtle of *Aberteifi*, which being delivered up to him, he fortified with a ſtrong Garriſon. Prince *David* was as yet too weak to appear in the Field; and indeed the more, by reaſon that ſeveral of his Nobility and others, could not affectionately love him, for that unnatural Spleen he ſhew'd to his Brother *Gruffydh*, whom, for no viſible reaſon, he detained in cloſe cuſtody. But above the reſt, *Richard*, Biſhop of *Bangor*, ſtormed at the Prince, and finding that he violated his Promiſe, in ſetting his Brother at liberty, whom, under pretence of an amicable Conſultation he had fraudulently ſeized upon in the Biſhop's preſence, without more ado excommunicated him; and then retiring to *England*, made a very querimonious relation of the whole matter to the King, deſiring him to releaſe *Gruffydh* out of Priſon, before the Rumour of ſo heinous a Fact ſhould reach the Court of *Rome*, and ſo reflect upon his Majeſty's Reputation. King *Henry* thereupon ſent to his Nephew, Prince *David*, blaming him highly for ſuch a treacherous Action, and dealing ſo ſeverely with his Brother; and then earneſtly requeſted him to deliver *Gruffydh* out of cuſtody, both to ſave himſelf from perpetual Defamation, and to deſerve an Abſolution from the ſevere Sentence pronounced againſt him. But *David* abſolutely refuſed to comply to the King's deſire, aſſuring him, that *Wales* could never enjoy a peaceable time, as long as his Brother *Gruffydh* had his liberty.

Gruffydh being acquainted with his Brothers Reſolution, and thinking that thereby he had unavoidably diſpleaſed the King of *England*, privately ſent to King *Henry*, aſſuring him, that if by Force he would deliver him out of Priſon, he would not only hold his Lands for ever from him, but alſo pay him the yearly Acknowledgment of Three Hundred Marks; offering both to give his corporal Oath, and to deliver up ſufficient Pledges for the performance of it; and withall to aſſiſt the King with all his Power in bringing in the

the rest of the *Welch* to his subjection. Moreover, *Gruffydh ap Madawc*, Lord of *Bromfield*, positively assured the King, that in case he would lead an Army into *Wales*, to revenge the Falsity and injurious Practices of *David*, he would give him all possible Aid and Assistance. Indeed, King *Henry*, besides this solemn Invitation, had no weak Pretence to come to *Wales*; for *Richard*, Bishop of *Bangor*, a fiery Man, had prosecuted the matter so warmly at *Rome*, that he obtained of the Pope also to excommunicate *David*, which Excommunication being denounced against him, his Lands were pretendedly forfeited. But the King being chiefly allured with the Promises of the *Welch* in the behalf of *Gruffydh*, levied a very formidable Army to lead to *Wales*; strictly commanding by Proclamation, all the *English*, who owed him any Martial-Service, to repair armed to *Glocester*, by the beginning of *Autumn*. This Rendezvouz being accordingly performed, the King came thither in person at the time appointed, and having regulated his Troops, and put all Matters in convenient order, he marched to *Shrewsbury*, where he remained Fifteen Days to refresh his Army. During his stay there several of the Nobility became Suitors unto him on behalf of *Gruffydh*, whose Condition they desired he would commiserate; among whom were, *Ralph* Lord *Mortimer* of *Wigmore*, *Walter Clifford*, *Roger de Monte Alto*, Steward of *Chester*, *Maelgn ap Maelgon*, *Meredith ap Rotpert* Lord of *Cydewen*, *Gruffydh ap Madawc* of *Bromfield*, *Howel* and *Meredith* the Sons of *Conan ap Owen Guynedh*, and *Gruffidh ap Gwenwynwyn* Lord of *Powys*. These Noblemen prevailed so far with King *Henry*, that a League was concluded between him and *Senena* the Wife of *Gruffydh*. For the performance of these Articles, the aforesaid Noblemen offered to be Securities, and bound themselves by their several Writings. But as if all things had conspired together against Prince *David*, several Persons that had been at continual variance and enmity among themselves to this time, were now, by reason that they equally favoured *Gruffydh*'s Cause, made

See *Appendix*.

See *Appendix*.

Friends

Friends among one another: *Morgan ap Howel* Lord of *Cery*, made his Reconciliation to Sir *Ralph Mortimer*, and his Submission to King *Henry*, in a very solemn manner: In the same form several others of the Nobility submitted to the King; as, *Owen ap Howel*, *Maelgon ap Maelgon*, *Meredith ap Meredith*, *Howel ap Cadwalhon*, and *Cadwalhon ap Howel*. *David* finding himself thus relinquished by the greatest part of his Nobility, and particularly by *Gruffydh ap Madawc*, Lord of *Bromfield*, whom he chiefly feared, by reason of his great Wisdom and Power, and that he was much esteemed by the King of *England*, could not easily conclude how to carry himself in this perplexity of Affairs. But in fine, considering with himself what a puissant Army King *Henry* brought against him, and how himself was considerably weakened by the defection of his Subjects, he thought it most adviseable to truckle to the King; and therefore with all speed sent him his Submission.

See Appendix.

Prince *David* having given a plenary Submission to the King, desired, that being his Nephew, and the lawful Heir and Successor of his Father Prince *Lhewelyn*, he should enjoy the Principality of *Wales*, rather than *Gruffydh*, who was illegitimate, and in no wise related to the King; assuring him further, that the War would never be at an end, if he was set at liberty. King *Henry* knowing well the truth of all this, and withal being assured that *Gruffydh* was not only valiant himself, but had likewise very powerful Abettors and Promoters of his Cause, was very inclinable to assent to *David*'s Request, and to prevent any farther Troubles, willingly granted it. Therefore *David* in a while after sent his Brother *Gruffydh* to the King, together with the Pledges promised for the performance of the Articles lately agreed upon; who were all sent to the Tower of *London* to be kept in safe custody; *Gruffydh* being allowed a Noble a day to provide himself with Necessaries. Shortly after, *David* came himself to *London*, and after he had done his Homage, and sworn Fealty to the King of *England*, returned to *Wales*, being honourably

nourably and peaceably difmiffed. But as foon as *Gruffydh* found out King *Henry*'s mind, and that it was the leaft part of his defign to fet him at liberty, having flatly denyed the Bifhop of *Bangor* his requeft therein; he began to fet his Brains a working, and to devife a means whereby he might make his efcape out of the Tower. Whereupon, having one night deceived his Keepers, he let himfelf down from the top of the Building, by a Line which he had compofed out of the Sheets and Hangings of the Room; which being too weak to bear his weight, being a heavy corpulent Perfon, let him down headlong to the ground; by the greatnefs of which Fall he was crufhed to pieces, and fo prefently expired. King *Henry* being informed of this unhappy Accident, feverely punifhed the Officers for their inexcufable Carelefnefs; and ordered that his Son, who was kept Prifoner with him in the Tower, fhould be more narrowly obferved.

After this King *Henry* fortified the Caftle of *Dyfcrth* in *Flintfhire*; and for their paffed Service, or rather to oblige them to the like after, granted to *Gruffydh ap Gwenwynwyn* all his Eftate in *Powys*, and to the Sons of *Conan ap Owen Gwynedh* their Lands in *Merionyth*. And the next Year *Maelgon Fychan* fortifyed the Caftle of *Garthgrugyn*, *John de Mynoc* the Caftle of *Buelht*, and *Roger Mortimer* that of *Melyenyth*. But all thefe Preparations were not to no purpofe; for the following Year early, King *Henry* came with an Army into *Wales*, and began very unreafonably to moleft the *Welch*, and without any juft pretence forcibly to feize upon their Lands and Eftates. Indeed, after the death of *Gruffydh*, he had a mind no longer to keep his Promife to *David*, and therefore entitled his eldeft Son *Edward* to the Principality of *Wales*, whom he thought to oblige the *Welch* to obey. But Prince *David* underftanding his defign, levyed all his Power for the defence of his juft Right; yet finding himfelf unable to withftand the Army of the *Englifh*, purpofed to effect that by Policy which he could not attain by Force. He fent therefore to the Pope,

A. D. 1242.

1243.

complain-

complaining how that King *Henry* of *England* compelled him unjustly to hold his Lands of him, and that upon no legal pretence he seized the Estates of the *Welch* at his pleasure; telling him moreover, that Prince *Lhewelyn* his Father had left him and the Principality of *Wales* to the Protection of the See of *Rome*, to which he was willing to pay the yearly Sum of Five Hundred Marks, obliging himself and his Successors by Oath, for the due performance of this Payment. The Pope (you may be sure) gladly accepted of the Offer, and thereupon gave commission to the two Abbots of *Aberconwey* and *Cymer*, to absolve *David* from his Oath of Allegiance to the King of *England*, and having enquired into the whole Estate of the Quarrel, to transmit an account of it to him. The Abbots, according to their Commission, directed a very positive *Mandat* to the King of *England*. King *Henry* admiring the strange Presumption and Confidence of these Abbots, or more the unsatiable Avarice and Greediness of the Pope, sent also to *Rome*; and with a greater Sum of Money, easily adjusted all matters; his Holyness being very desirous to make the best advantage of both Parties.

See *Append x*.

But Prince *David* finding that the Pope minded his own Gain, more than to justifie his Complaints against the King of *England*, thought it to no purpose to rely upon his Faith, but judged it more advisable to vindicate himself by force of Arms. Having therefore gathered his Forces together, (being now reconciled to, and followed by all the Nobility of *Wales*, excepting *Gruffydh' ap Gwenwynwyn* and *Morgan ap Howel*, who also shortly after submitted to him) he drew up his Army to the Marches, intending to be revenged upon the Earls of *Clare* and *Hereford*, *John de Monmouth*, *Roger de Monte Alto*, and others, who injured and oppressed his People; with whom he fought divers times, and with various success. But in the *Lent*-time next Year, the *Marchers* and the *Welch* met near *Montgomery*, between whom was fought a very severe Battel; the Governour of that Castle being General of the *English*, and having cunningly

1245.

cunningly placed an Ambuscade of Men, pretended, after some short Engagement, to flee, whom the *Welch* daringly pursued, not thinking of any Treachery. But as soon as they were past the Ambushment, up rises an unexpected Party of Men, who falling upon the backs of the *Welch*, put them to a very great disorder, and killed about Three Hundred Men, not without a considerable Loss of their own side, among whom was slain a valiant Knight called *Hubert Fitz-Matthew*. But King *Henry* being weary of these perpetual Skirmishes and daily Clashings between the *English* and *Welch*, thought to put an end to the whole with one stroak; and therefore raised a very great Army of *English* and *Gascoignes*, and entered into *North-Wales*, purposing to waste and destroy the Country. But before he could advance very far, Prince *David* intercepted him in a narrow Pass, and so violently set upon him, that a great number of his Nobility and bravest Soldiers, and in a manner all the *Gascoignes* were slain. The King finding he could effect nothing against the *Welch*, invited over the *Irish*, who landing in *Anglesey*, began to pillage and waste the Country; but the Inhabitants gathering themselves together in a Body, quickly forced them to their Ships; after which, King *Henry* having victualled and manned all his Castles, returned dissatisfied to *England*.

But concerning this Expedition to *Wales*, and the continuance of the *English* Army therein, a certain Person in the Camp, wrote to this effect to his Friends *Mat. Par.* in *England*: ' The King with his Army is encamped
' at *Gannock*, and is busie in fortifying that place, suf-
' ficiently strong already, about which we lay in our
' Tents, in watching, fasting, praying, and freezing.
' We watch for fear of the *Welch*, who were used
' to come suddenly upon us in the night-time: We
' fast for want of Provision, the Half-penny Loaf be-
' ing now risen and advanced to Five Pence: We
' pray that we may speedily return safe and Scot-free
' home: And we freez for want of Winter-Garments,
' having but a thin Linnen Shirt to keep us from the
                                           ' Wind,

'Wind. There is a small Arm of the Sea under the
'Castle where we lye, which the Tide reached, by
'the Conveniency of which, many Ships bring us
'Provision and Victuals from *Ireland* and *Chester*:
'This Arm lies betwixt us and *Snowden*, where the
'*Welch* are encamped, and is in breadth, when the
'Tide is in, about a Bow-shot. Now it happened,
'that upon the *Monday* before *Michaelmas*-day, an
'*Irish* Vessel came up to the Mouth of the Haven,
'with Provision to be sold to our Camp, which be-
'ing negligently lookt to by the Mariners, was upon
'low ebb stranded on the other side of the Castle,
'near the *Welch*. The Enemy perceiving this, de-
'scended from the Mountains, and laid siege to the
'Ship, which was fast upon the dry Sands; where-
'upon, we detached in Boats Three Hundred *Welch*
'of the Borders of *Cheshire* and *Shropshire*, with
'some Archers and armed Men, to rescue the Ship:
'But the *Welch*, upon the approach of our Men,
'withdrew themselves to their usual Retirements in
'the Rocks and Woods, and were pursued for about
'two Miles by our Men afoot, who slew a great
'number of them. But in their return back, our
'Soldiers being too covetous and greedy of Plunder,
'among other sacrilegious and profane Actions,
'spoiled the Abbey of *Aberconwey*, and burnt all the
'Books and other choice Utensils belonging to it.
'The *Welch* being distracted at these irreligious Pra-
'ctices, got together in great number, and in a de-
'sperate manner setting upon the *English*, killing a
'great number of them, and following the rest to
'the Water-side, forced as many as could not make
'their escape into the Boats, to commit themselves
'to the mercy of the Waves. Those they took Pri-
'soners they thought to reserve for exchange; but
'hearing how we put some of their captive Nobi-
'lity to death, they altered their minds, and in a
'revengeful manner scattered their dilacerated Car-
'casses along the surface of the Water. In this
'Conflict, we lost a considerable number of our
'Men, and chiefly those under the Command of

Richard

The History of WALES.

'Richard Earl of Cornwal; as Sir Alan Buscell, Sir
'Adam de Maio, Sir Geoffry Estueiny, and one Rai-
'mond a Gascoign, with about a Hundred common
'Soldiers. In the mean time Sir Walter Bisset stout-
'ly defended the Ship till Midnight, when the Tide
'returned; whereupon the Welch, who assailed us
'of all sides, were forced to withdraw, being much
'concerned that we had so happily escaped their
'hands. The Cargo of this Ship, were Three Hun-
'dred Hogsheads of Wine, with a plenty of other
'Provision for the Army, which at that time it stood
'in very great need of. But the next Morning,
'when the Sea was returned, the Welch came mer-
'rily down again to the Ship, thinking to surprize
'our Men; but as Luck would have it, they had at
'full Sea the Night before relinquished the Ship, and
'returned safe to the Camp. The Enemy missing of
'our Men, set upon the Cargo of the Ship, carryed
'away all the Wine and other Provisions; and then
'when the Sea began to flow, they put Fire to the
'Vessel, and returned to the rest of the Army. And
'thus we lay incamped in great Misery and Di-
'stress for want of Necessaries, exposed to great and
'frequent Dangers, and in great fear of the private
'Assaults and sudden Incursions of our Enemies.
'Oftentimes we set upon and assailed the Welch, and
'in one Conflict we carried away a Hundred Head
'of Cattel, which very triumphantly we convey-
'ed to our Camp. For the scarcity of Provision
'was then so great, that there remained but one
'Hogshead of Wine in the whole Army; a Bushel
'of Corn being sold for Twenty Shillings; a fed
'Ox for Three or Four Marks; and a Hen for Eight
'Pence; so that there happened a very lamentable
'Mortality both of Man and Horse, for want of
'necessary Sustenance of Life.

The English Army having undergone such Miseries as are here described, and King Henry, as is
said, perceiving it was in vain for him to continue
any longer in Wales, where he was sure to gain no
great Credit, he returned with his Army into England,
being

being not very desirous to make another Expedition into *Wales*. Then all the Nobility and Barons of *Wales*, and those that had favoured and maintained *Gruffydh*'s Cause, were made Friends and reconciled to Prince *David*, to whom they vowed true and perpetual Allegiance. But the Prince did not long survive this Amity and Agreement between him and his Subjects; for falling sick toward the beginning of this Year, he dyed in *March*, at his Palace in *Aber*, and was buryed at *Conwey*, leaving no Issue to succeed. The only thing unpardonable in this Prince, was his over Jealousie and Severity against his Brother *Gruffydh*, a Person so well-beloved of the *Welch*, that upon his account their Affection was much cooled, and in some entirely alienated from their Prince. Indeed thus much may be said for *David*, that *Gruffydh* was a valorous and an aspiring Man, and if set at liberty, would bid fair to eject him out of his Principality; which King *Henry* of *England* too (who thought he might bring over *David*, a milder Man, to what Terms he pleased) was sensible of, when he would by no persuasion dismiss him from custody in the Tower of *London*. But this occasioned all the Disturbances that happened in his time, the *Welch* themselves, for the Love they bore to G—*ffydh*, inviting the King of *England* to come to, invade their Country, and to correct the unnatural Enmity their Prince expressed to his Brother. But when all Differences were over, the King of *England* returned with his Army shamefully back, and the Prince and his Nobility reconciled; the *Welch* might have expected a very happy time of it, had not Death taken the Prince so unnaturally away, before he had well known what a peaceful Reign was.

A. D. 1246.

Lhewelyn

Lhewelyn ap Gruffydh.

PRince *David* being dead, the Principality of *North Wales* legally defcended to Sir *Ralph Mortimer*, in Right of his Wife *Gladys*, Daughter to *Lhewelyn ap Iorwerth*. But the *Welch* Nobility being affembled together for the electing and nominating a Succeffour, thought it by no means advifable to admit a Stranger to the Crown, though his Title was never fo lawful; and efpecially an *Englifhman*, by whofe Obligations to the Crown of *England*, they muft of neceffity expect to become Subjects, or rather Slaves to the *Englifh* Government. Wherefore they unanimoufly agreed to fet up *Lhewelyn* and *Owen Goch*, the Sons of *Gruffydh*, a bafe Son of *Lhewelyn ap Iorwerth*, and Brother to Prince *David*; who being fent for, and appearing before the Affembly, all the Nobles and Barons, then prefent, did them Homage, and received them for their Sovereigns. But as foon as the King of *England* underftood of the death of the Prince of *Wales*; he thought, the Country being in an unfettled and wavering condition, he might effect great matters there; and therefore he fent one *Nicholas de Miles* to *South-Wales*, with the Title of Juftice of that Country, with whom he joyned in Commiffion *Meredith ap Rhys Gryc*, and *Meredith ap Owen ap Gruffydh*; to eject and difinherit *Maelgon Fychan* of all his Lands and Eftate in *South-Wales*. The like injurious Practices were committed againft *Howel ap Meredith*, who was forcibly robb'd of all his Eftate in *Glamorgan* by the Earl of *Clare*. Thefe unreafonable Extortions being infupportable; *Maelgon* and *Howel* made known their Grievances to the Princes of *North-Wales*, defiring their Succour and Affiftance for the recovery of their lawful Inheritance from the Incroachments

of

The History of WALES.

of the *English*. But the King of *England* understanding their Design, led his Army into *Wales*; upon whose arrival, the *Welch* withdrew themselves to *Snowden*-Hills, where they so tired the *English* Army, that the King finding he could do no good, after some stay there returned back to *England*. Within a while after, *Ralph Mortimer*, the Husband of *Gladys Dhu* dyed; leaving his whole Estate, and with it, a lawful Title to the Principality of *North-Wales*, to his Son Sir *Roger Mortimer*.

A. D.
1247.
M.*Paris*,
p. 739.

The next Year nothing memorable passed between the *English* and the *Welch*, only the dismal Effects of the last Years Expedition, were not worn off; the ground being uncapable of Cultivation, and the Cattel being in great measure destroyed by the *English*, occasioned great Poverty and Want in the Country. But the greatest Calamity befel the Bishops; S. *Asaph* and *Bangor* being destroyed and burnt by the *English*, the Bishops thereof were reduced to that utmost Extremity, as to get their Subsistence by other Mens Charity; the Bishop also of S. *Davids* deceased, and he of *Landaff* had the Misfortune to fall blind. In the Bishoprick of S. *Davids* succeeded *Thomas*, surnamed *Wallensis*, by reason that he was born in *Wales*; who thinking himself obliged to benefit his own Country what lay in his power, desired to be advanced from the Archdeaconry of *Lincoln* to that Sea; which the King easily granted, and confirmed him in it.

1248. The next Summer proved somewhat more favourable to the *Welch*; *Rhys Fychan* Son to *Rhys Mechyl*, won from the *English* the Castle of *Carrec Cynnen*, which his unkind Mother, out of Malice, or some ill Opinion entertained of him, had some time afore privately delivered up to them. And about the same time the Body of *Gruffydh ap Lhewelyn* base Son to *Lhewelyn ap Iorwerth*, was recovered from the King of *England*, by the earnest sollicitations of the Abbots of *Conwey* and *Ystratflur*; who conveying it to *Conwey*, bestowed upon it a very pompous and honourable Enterment.

After

After this, the Affairs of the *Welch* proceeded peaceably for a long while, and the Country had sufficient opportunity to recover its former plenty; but at last, to make good the Proverb, that *Plenty begets War*; they began, for want of a foreign Enemy, to quarrel and fall out among themselves. *Owen* was too high and ambitious to be satisfied with half the Principality, and therefore must needs have a fling at the whole; wherein Fortune so far deceived him, that he lost his own Stake, as will afterwards appear. But the better to encompass his Design, by sly Insinuations he persuaded *David* his younger Brother, to second his Cause; and they with joynt Interest levied their Power, with intention to dethrone their elder Brother *Lhewelyn*. But that was no easie matter; for *Lhewelyn* was prepared to receive them, and with a puissant Army met them in the Field, and so was resolved to venture all upon the fortune of a Battel. It was strange and grievous to behold this unnatural Civil War; and the more grievous now, by reason that it so manifestly weakened the strength of the *Welch*, to withstand the Incursions of the *English*, who were extremely pleased with so fair an opportunity to fall upon them. But they were too far engaged, to consider of future Inconveniencies; and a tryal of War they must have, though the *English* were ready to fall upon both Armies. The Battel being joyned, the day proved bloody of both sides, and whether was like to conquer was not presently discovered; till at length, *Owen* began to give ground, and in fine was overthrown, himself and his Brother *David* being taken Prisoners. *Lhewelyn*, though he had sufficient reason, would not put his Brothers to death; but committing them into close Prison, seized all their Estates into his own hands, and so enjoyed the whole Principality of *Wales*.

The *English* seeing the *Welch* at this rate oppress and destroy one another, thought they had full liberty to deal with them as they pleased; and thereupon began to exercise all manner of Wrong and Injustice against them; insomuch that the next Year, all the

A. D.
1255.

1256.

the Lords of *Wales* came in a body to Prince *Lhewelyn*, and declared their Grievances, how unmercifully Prince *Edward* (whom his Father had sent to *Wales*) and others of the Nobility of *England* dealt with them, how without any colour of Justice they seized upon their Estates, without any room for Appeal; whereas if themselves offended in the least, they were punished to the utmost extremity. In fine, they solemnly declared, that they preferred to dye honourably in the Field, before to be so unmercifully enslaved to the Will and Pleasure of Strangers. Prince *Lhewelyn* was not a Stranger to all this; and now having happily discovered the Bent and Inclination of his Subjects, was resolved to prosecute, if possible, the Expulsion of the *English*, and to be revenged upon them for their most cruel, and almost inhuman Practices towards the *Welch*. Having therefore drawn all his Power together, being accompany'd by *Meredith ap Rhys Gryc*, in the space of one Week he recovered out of the hands of the *English* all the inland Country of *North Wales*, and then all *Merionyth* with such Lands as Prince *Edward* had usurped in *Cardigan*, which he bestowed upon *Meredith* the Son of *Owen ap Gruffydh*. Having also forced *Rhys Fychan* out of *Buelht*, he conferr'd it upon *Meredith ap Rhys*; and in like manner bestowed all the Lands which he recovered, between his Nobles; reserving nothing to his own use, besides *Gwerthryneon*, the

1257. Estate of Sir *Roger Mortimer*. The next Summer, he entered into *Powys*, and made War against *Gruffydh ap Gwenwynwyn*, who always had taken part with, and owned Subjection to the King of *England*, which he totally overcame, excepting the Castle of *Poole*, some small part of *Caerneon*, and the Country lying upon the bank of the *Severn*.

But *Rhys Fychan* was not satisfied with the loss of *Buelht*, and therefore was resolved to try to recover it; to which end, he went to the King of *England*, of whom he obtained a very strong Army, commanded by one *Stephen Bacon*, which being sent by Sea, landed at *Caermardhyn* in the *Whitsun*-Week.

From

The History of WALES.

From thence the *English* marched to *Dynefawr*, and laid Siege to the Castle, which valiantly held out, until *Lhewelyn's* Army came to its Relief. Upon the arrival of the *Welch*, the *English* decamped from before the Castle, and put themselves in posture of Battel, which the *Welch* perceiving, they made all haste to answer and oppose them. Whereupon there ensued a very terrible Engagement which lasted a very long while; this being for number of Men the greatest Battel that had been fought between the *English* and the *Welch*. But the Victory favoured the *Welch*, the *English-men* being at length forced to fly, having lost above Two Thousand Men, besides several Barons and Knights who were taken Prisoners. After this the Prince's Army passed to *Dyfed*, where having burnt all the Country, and destroyed the Castles of *Abercorran*, *Lhanstephan*, *Maenclochoc* and *Arberth*, with all the Towns thereunto belonging, returned to *North-Wales* with much Spoil. But as soon as he was arrived, great Complaints were exhibited to Prince *Lhewelyn* against *Jeffrey Langley* Lieutenant to *Edward* Earl of *Chester*, who without any regard to Equity and Conscience, most wrongfully oppressed the Inhabitants of *Wales* under his Jurisdiction. Whereupon the Prince to punish the Master for the Servant's Fault, entred with some part of his Army into the Earl's Estate, burnt and destroyed all his Country on both sides the River *Dee*, to the Gates of *Chester*. *Edward* had no power at present to oppose him, but being resolved to be revenged upon the *Welch* with the first opportunity, he desired Aid of his Uncle, then chose King of the *Romans*, who sent him a strong Detachment, with which he purposed to give Prince *Lhewelyn* Battel. But finding him too strong, he thought it more advisable to desist from Hostility, the Prince's Army consisting of Ten Thousand experienced Men, who were obliged by Oath, rather all to die in the Field, than suffer the *English* to gain any Advantage over the *Welch*. But *Gruffydh ap Madoc Maelor*, Lord of *Dinas Brân*, a Person of notorious Reputation for Injustice and Oppression, basely forT   sook took the *Welch* his Country-men, and with all his Forces went over to the Earl of *Chester.*

1258. The next Year Prince *Lhewelyn* passed to *South-Wales*, and seized into his Hands the Land of *Cemaes*, and having reconciled the Difference betwixt *Rhys Gryg* and *Rhys Fychan*, he won the Castle of *Trefdraeth*, with the whole Country of *Rhôs*, excepting *Haverford*. Thence he marched in an hostile manner toward *Glamorgan*, and rased to the ground the Castle of *Lhangynwch*, and then returning to *North-Wales*, he met by the way with *Edward* Earl of *Chester*, whom he forced precipitously to return back. But before he would put an end to this Expedition, he must needs be revenged upon that ungrateful fugitive *Gruffydh ap Madoc Maelor*, and thereupon passing thro' *Bromfield*, he miserably laid waste the whole Country. Upon this the Kings of *England* and *Scotland* sent to *Lhewelyn*, requiring him to cease from Hostility, and after that unmerciful manner to devour, and forcibly to take away other Mens Estates. The Prince was not over sollicitous to hearken to their Request, but finding the time of the year very seasonable for Action against the *English*, he divided his Army into two Battles, each of these consisting of 1500 Foot and 500 Horse, with which he purposed to enlarge his Conquest. *Edvard* Earl of *Chester*, to prevent the Blow which so desperately hung over his Head, sent over for Succors from *Ireland*, of whose coming Prince *Lhewelyn* being certified, manned out a Fleet to intercept them, which meeting with the *Irish* at Sea, after a sharp Dispute, forced them to return back with loss. King *Henry* being acquainted with the miscarriage of the *Irish*, resolved to come in Person against the *Welch*, and having drawn together the whole Strength of *England*, even from St. *Michael's* Mount in *Cornwul* to the River *Tweed*, marched with his Son *Edward* in a great Rage to *North-Wales*, and without any opposition advanced as far as *Teganny*. But the Prince had stopped his farther Progress, and prevented any long stay he could make in *Wales*, having before hand caused all
manner

manner of Provision and Forrage to be carried over the River, and then securing the ſtrait and narrow Paſſages whereby the *Engliſh* might get on farther into the Country, the Army was in a ſhort time ſo mortally fatigued, that the King for want of neceſſary Subſiſtance was forced to retire in haſte to *England* with conſiderable loſs.

The Prince after that ſending for all the Forces in *South-Wales*, came to the Marches, where *Gruffydh* Lord of *Bromfield* finding that the King of *England* was not able to defend his Eſtate yielded himſelf up, and then paſſing to *Powys*, he baniſhed *Gruffydh ap Gwenwynwyn*, and took all the Lands in the Country into his Hands. Proceeding farther, he was encountred with by *Gilbert de Clare* Earl of *Gloceſter*, who with a choice Party of *Engliſh* gave him Battel. But *Lhewelyn*'s Army exceeding both in Number and Courage, eaſily vanquiſhed and overcame the *Engliſh*, and ſo the Victory being quickly obtained, the Prince preſently reduced to his Power all the Cattles belonging to the Earl of *Gloceſter*. King *Henry* hearing of the Earl's overthrow, was much concerned at the loſs of ſo many brave Souldiers, in whoſe Valor and Experience he always put a very great Confidence, and therefore to revenge their Deaths, he was again reſolved to march againſt the *Welch*. Having called his Forces together, and received Supply from *Gaſcoign* and *Ireland*, he came to *Wales*, but not daring to venture far into the Country, for fear of being forced to make another ſhameful retreat, he only deſtroyed the Corn near the Borders, it being Harveſt time, and ſo returned to *England*. But Lord *James Audley*, whoſe Daughter was married to *Gruffydh* Lord of *Bromfield*, did more miſchief and hurt to the *Welch*, who having brought over a great Number of Horſemen from *Germany* to ſerve againſt the *Welch*. ſo terrified them with the unuſual largeneſs of the Horſes, and the unaccuſtomed manner of fighting, that in the firſt Encounter the *Welch* were eaſily overcome. But minding to revenge this Diſgrace, and withal being better acquainted with their method of Arms, the *Welch* in a little after made in-roads into the Lord *Audley*'s Lands, where the *Germans* presently set upon them, and pursued them to certain straits, which the *Welch* discovered for a politick retreat. The *Germans* thinking they had entirely drove the *Welch* away, returned carelesly back, but being set upon of the sudden, without any thought of an Enemy behind, they were all in a manner slain by the rallying *Welch*. This year a very great scarcity of Beefs and Horses happened in *England*, whereof several Thousands yearly were supplied out of *Wales*, by reason of which, the Marches were perfectly robbed of all their Breed, and not so much as a Beast to be seen in all the Borders.

1259. The next Spring all the Nobility of *Wales* convened together and took their mutual Oaths to defend their Country to Death, against the oppressing Invasions of the *English*, and not to relinquish and forsake one another upon pain of Perjury; tho' notwithstanding, *Meredith ap Rhys* of *South-Wales* violated this Agreement, and put himself in the Service of the King of *England*. King *Henry* was ready to fall upon the *Welch*, to which purpose he summoned a Parliament, wherein he proposed to raise a Subsidy towards the Conquest of *Wales*, being not able of himself to bear the Expences of this War, by reason of several Losses he had already received, the Country of *Pembroke* being lately destroyed and taken by the *Welch*, where they found plenty of Salt, which before they were in great necessity of. But *William de Valentia* accusing the Earls of *Leicester* and *Glocester* as the Authors of all this Mischief, quite broke all their measures, so the King was forced to prorogue the Parliament for a time without any grant of a Subsidy. But within a while after, it sat at *Oxford*, where King *Henry* and *Edward* his Son took a Solemn Oath to observe the Laws and Statutes of the Realm, and the same being tendred to *Guy* and *William* the King's Brothers, and to *Henry* Son to the King of *Almain*, and to Earl *Warren*, they refused to take it and so departed. In this Parliament

liament the Lords of *Wales* fairly proffered to be tryed by the Laws for any Offence they had unjuſtly committed againſt the King, which was mainly oppoſed by *Edward*, who cauſed one *Patrick de Canton* (to whom the Lordſhip of *Cydwely* was given, in caſe he could win and keep the ſame) to be ſent to *Caermardhyn* as Lieutenant for the King, with whom *Meredith ap Rhys* was joyned in Commiſſion. Being arrived at *Caermardhyn*, *Patrick* ſent to the Prince, to deſire him to appoint Commiſſioners to treat with him concerning a Peace, which he conſented to, and without any ſuſpicion of treachery, ſent *Meredith ap Owen*, and *Rhys ap Rhys* to *Emlyn*, if poſſible, to conclude the ſame. But *Patrick* meaning no ſuch thing, laid an ambuſcade for the *Welch*, who coming honeſtly forward, were by the way villanouſly ſet upon by the *Engliſh*, and a great many ſlain; but thoſe that happily eſcaped, calling up the Country, preſently gave chaſe to *Patrick* and his Accomplices, who being at length overtaken, were almoſt all put to the Sword. But Prince *Lhewelyn* was now altogether bent upon a Peace, and did not only deſire it, but was willing to purchaſe it for a ſumm of Money, to which purpoſe he offered to give the King 4000 Marks, to his Son 300, and 200 to the Queen, which the King utterly refuſed, replying, That it was not a ſufficient recompence for all the Damages he had ſuffered by the *Welch*. *Matthew* of *Weſtminſter* reporteth, that about *Michaelmas* this year, the Biſhop of *Bangor* was commiſſioned by the Prince and Nobility of *Wales* to treat with the King of *England* about a Peace, and to offer him 16000 Pound for the ſame, upon theſe Conditions, that according to their antient Cuſtom, the *Welch* ſhould have all Cauſes tryed and determined at *Cheſter*, and that they ſhould freely enjoy the Laws and Cuſtoms of their own Country; but what was the reſult of this Treaty, my Author does not mention.

There being no hopes of a Peace, Prince *Lhewelyn* 1260. early next year appeared in the Field, and paſſed to *South-Wales*, and firſt fell foul upon Sir *Roger Mortimer*,

timer, who contrary to his Oath, maintained the King of *England*'s Quarrel. Having forcibly dispossessed him of all *Buelht*, and without any opposition taken the Castle, where was found a plentiful Magazine, he marched thro' all *South-Wales*, confirming his Conquest, and afterwards returned to his Palace at *Aber*, betwixt *Bangor* and *Conwey*. The year following, *Owen ap Meredith* Lord of *Cydewen* died. But the next Summer was somewhat more noted for Action, a party of Prince *Lhewelyn*'s Men took by surprise the Castle of *Melienyth*, belonging to Sir *Roger Mortimer*, and having put the rest of the Garrison to the Sword, they took *Howel ap Meyric* the Governour, with his Wife and Children Prisoners; and after that, the Castle was demolished by the Prince's Order. Sir *Roger Mortimer* hearing of this, with a great Body of Lords and Knights came to *Melienyth*, where Prince *Lhewelyn* met him, but Sir *Roger* not daring to hazard a Battel, planted himself within the Ruins, and finding he could do no good, desired leave of the Prince to retire peaceably. The Prince upon the account of Relation and near Consanguinity betwixt them, and withal because he would not be so mean spirited as to fall upon an Enemy, who had no power to resist him, let him safely depart with his Forces; and then passing on himself to *Brecknock* at the request of the People of that Country, who swore Fidelity unto him; so passed on and returned to *North-Wales*. And now being Confederate with the Barons against King *Henry*, he was resolved to practise something in the prejudice of the *English*, and so set upon the Earldom of *Chester*, destroyed the Castles of *Tyganwy*, and *Diserth* belonging to *Edward*, who coming thither, was yet not able to prevent the Mischief done to him by the *Welch*. The next year *John Strange* Junior, Constable of *Montgomery* with a great Number of Marchers, came a little before *Easter* by night, thro' *Ceri* to *Cydewen*, intending to surprise the Castle, which when the People of the Country understood, they gathered together, and setting upon them, slew 200 of his Men, but *Strange* with a few got safely back. Within

1261.
1262.

1263.

Within a while after, the Marchers and the *Welch* met again near a place called *Clun*, where a hot Engagement happened between them, in which the *Welch* were worsted, and had a great Number of their Men slain. After this, nothing remarkable fell out for a considerable time, unless it were, that *David* being released out of Prison by Prince *Lhewelyn* his Brother, most ungratefully forsook him, and with all his might, sided with his Enemies the *English*; also *Gruffydh ap Gwenwynwyn* having taken the Castle of *Mold*, demolished it to the ground. During this quiet and unactive interval in *Wa'es*, *Meredith ap Owen*, the main Support and Defender of *South-Wales* died, to the great disadvantage of the Affairs of that Country. And now indeed, the *Welch* were like to be made sensible of the Loss of so considerable a Person; for King *Henry* was resolved once more to lead an Army into *Wales*, and to see if he could have better Success than he had hitherto against the *Welch*. But when he was prepared to undertake this Expedition, *Ottobonus* Pope *Clement*'s Legate in *England*, interposed and mediated a Peace, which was concluded upon at the Castle of *Montgomery*, wherein it was articled, that Prince *Lhewelyn* should give the King 30000 Marks, and the King was to grant the Prince a Charter, from thenceforth to receive Homage and Fealty of all the Nobility and Barons of *Wales*, besides one, so that they could hold their Lands of no other but himself, and from thence forward he was to be lawfully stiled Prince of *Wa'es*. This Charter being ratified and confirmed as well by the Authority of the Pope, as the King's Seal; Prince *Lhewelyn* desisted from any farther Acts of Hostility, and punctually observed all the Articles of Agreement betwixt him and King *Henry*, so that nothing more was outragiously transacted between the *English* and *Welch*, during the remainder of this King's reign. Within that space, died *Grono ap Ednyfed Fychan*, one of the Chief Lords of the Prince's Council, and shortly after him, *Gruffydh* Lord of *Bromfield*, who lies buried at *Vale-Crucis*.

1263.

1272.   But the Death of King *Henry* put an end to the observations of the Peace betwixt the *English* and *Welch*, who dying on the 16th. day of *November* this year, left this Kingdom to his Son *Edward*. Prince *Edward* was then in the *Holy-Land*, and very active against those Enemies of Christianity, the *Turks*, where he had already continued above a year; but understanding of his Father's Death, and that in his absence he was proclaimed King of *England*, he made all haste to return to receive the Solemnity of Coronation. But what by the tediousness of the Journey, and what by being honourably detained at Princes Courts in his way, it was two years before he could get into *England*, then upon the 15th. of *August*, and in the year 1274. he was Crowned at *Westminster*. Prince *Lhewelyn* was summoned to attend at his Coronation, but he flatly refused to appear, unless upon sure Terms of safe Conduct, for having offended several of the *English* Nobility, he could not in safety pass thro' their Country without the danger of exposing his Person to the inveterate Malice and acceptable Revenge of some of them. And therefore without the King's Brother, the Earl of *Glocester*, and *Robert Burnell* Lord Chief Justice of *England*, were delivered up as Pledges for his safe Conduct, he would not come up to do his Homage and Fealty at his Coronation, according to the Writ directed to him. And indeed, seeing King *Edward* had broke the Peace lately concluded upon before the Pope's Legate, and did receive, and honourably entertain such Noblemen of *Wales*, as for their disloyalty were banished by Prince *Lhewelyn*, by whom he feared some treachery; there was no reason that the Prince should pay him any subjection, but by the breach of Peace was exempted from all Homage. However, Prince *Lhewelyn* to shew that it was not out of any stubbornness or disrespect to the King of *England*, that he refused to come, sent up his Reasons by the Abbots of *Ystratflur* and *Conwey* to *Robert Kilwarby* Archbishop of *Canterbury*, and the rest of the Bishops then sitting

in

in Convocation in the *New-Temple* at *London*, which were to this effect.

To the moſt Reverend Fathers in God *Robert* Archbiſhop of *Canterbury*, and Metropolitan of all *England*, the Archbiſhop of *York*, and the reſt of the Biſhops in Convocation ; *Lhewelyn* Prince of *Wales* and Lord of *Snowden*, ſendeth Greeting.

WE *would have your Lordſhips to underſtand, that whereas formerly moſt terrible and inceſſant Wars were continually managed betwixt* Henry King *of* England *and our ſelf ; the ſame were at laſt compoſed, and all matters of Differences were adjuſted by the means of his Excellency Cardinal* Ottobonus *the Pope's Legate, who having drawn the Articles and Conditions of the Peace agreed upon, they were ſigned and ſwore to, not only by the* King, *but alſo the Prince his Son, now* King *of* England. *Among theſe Articles were comprehended, that we and our Succeſſors ſhould hold of the* King *and his Succeſſor the Principality of* Wales, *ſo that all the* Welch *Lords, one Baron excepted, ſhould hold their Baronies and Eſtates in* Capite *of us, and ſhould pay their Homage and Fealty for the ſame to us ; we in like manner doing Homage to the* King *of* England *and his Succeſſors. And beſides, that the* King *and his Succeſſors ſhould never offer to receive and entertain any of our Enemies, nor any ſuch of our own Subjects as were lawfully baniſhed and excluded our Dominions of* Wales, *nor by any means defend and uphold ſuch againſt us. Contrary to which Articles,* King Edward *has forcibly ſeized upon the Eſtates of certain Barons of* Wales, *of which they and their Anceſtors have been immemorably poſſeſſed of, and detains a Barony, which by the form of Peace ſhould have been delivered to us ; and moreover, has hitherto entertained* David ap Gruffydh our Brother, and Gruffydh ap Gwen-wynwyn, with several others of our Enemies who are Out-laws and Fugitives of our Country. And tho' we have often exhibited our Grievances and Complaints against them, for destroying and pillaging our Country, yet we could never obtain of the King any relief or redress for the several Wrongs and Injuries we received at their hands; but on the contrary, they still persist to commit wastes and other outrages in our Dominions. And for all this, he summons us to do him Homage at a place which is altogether dangerous to our Person, where our inveterate Enemies, and which is worse, our own unnatural Subjects, bear the greatest sway and respect with the King. And tho' we have alledged several Reasons to the King and his Council, why the place by him assigned, is not safe and indifferent for us to come, and desire him to appoint another, whereto we might with more safety resort, or else that he would send Commissioners to receive our Oath and Homage, till he could more opportunely receive them in Person; yet he would not assent to our just and reasonable Request, nor be satisfied with the Reasons we exhibited for our non-appearance. Therefore we desire your Lordships earnestly to weigh the dismal effects that will happen to the Subjects both of England and Wales upon the breach of the Articles of Peace; and that you would be pleased to inform the King of the sad Consequence of another War, which can no way be prevented, but by using us according to the Conditions of the former Peace, which for our part, we will in no measure transgress. But if the King will not hearken to your Counsel, we hope that you will hold us excused, if the Nation be disquieted and troubled thereupon, which as much as in us lieth we endeavour to prevent.

King *Edward* would admit of no Excuse, nor hearken to any manner of Reason in the case, but was unmercifully enraged, and conceived an unpardonable displeasure against Prince *Lhewelyn*, which yet he thought convenient to conceal and dissemble

The History of WALES.

for a time. Indeed, he could never abide *Lhewelyn*, since the time that he was vanquished and put to flight by him at the Marches, so that the chief Cause of King *Edward*'s anger, originally proceeded from a point of Honor, which this refusal of Homage served sufficiently to increase. But to prosecute his Revenge, which upon this score is in Princes very fierce and unforgetful, in a short time he came to *Chester*, meaning to recover by force what he could not obtain by fair means. From hence he sent to the Prince of *Wales*, requiring him to come over and do him Homage; which *Lhewelyn* either absolutely refusing, or willingly detracting to do, King *Edward* made ready his Army to force him to it. But there happened an Accident which took off a great part of Prince *Lhewelyn*'s stubborness; for at this time the Countess of *Leicester* the Widow of *Simon Montfort* who lived at *Montargis* a Nunnery in *France*, sent over for *Wales* her Daughter, the Lady *Eleanor* (whom *Lhewelyn* extreamly loved) with her Brother *Aemerike*, to be married to the Prince, according to the Agreement made in her Father, Earl *Montfort*'s time. But *Aemerike* fearing to touch upon the Coast of *England*, steered his course towards the Islands of *Scilly*, where by the way they were all taken by four *Bristol* Ships, and brought to King *Edward*, who received the Lady very honourably, but committed her Brother Prisoner to the Castle of *Coff*, whence he was afterward removed to the Castle of *Shirburne*. The King having obtained this unexpected Advantage over *Lhewelyn*, began boldly to fall upon him; and so dividing his Army into two Battalions, led one himself into *North-Wales*, and advanced as far as *Ruthlan*, where he strongly fortified the Castle. The other he committed to *Paganus de Camurtiis*, a great Souldier, who entring into *West-Wales*, burned and destroyed a great part of the Country. But the People of *South-Wales*, fearing that his next Expedition was levelled against them voluntarily submitted themselves to the King, and did him Homage, and then delivered up the Castle of *Ystratywy* to *Paganus*.

1277.

Prince

Prince *Lhewelyn* hearing of this, and finding his own Subjects to forsake him, but more especially being desirous to recover his espouse the Lady *Eleanor*, thought it likewise advisable to submit, and therefore sued to King *Edward* for a Peace, who granted it, but upon very severe Conditions upon *Lhewelyns* side. The Agreement consisted of ten Articles, which were; 1. That the Prince should set at liberty all manner of Prisoners, that upon the King's Account were detained in Custody. 2. That for the King's favour and good will, he should pay 50000 Marks, to be received at the King's pleasure. 3. That these four Cantreds or Hundreds, *viz*. *Cantref Ros* where the King's Castle of *Teganwy* stands; *Ryfonioc*, where *Denbigh*; *Tegengl*, where *Ruthlan*; *Dyffryn Clwyd*, where *Rhuthyn* stands, should remain in the King's hands. 4. That the Lords Marchers should quietly enjoy all the Lands they had conquered within *Wales*, excepting in the Isle of *Anglesey*, which was wholly granted to the Prince. 5. That in consideration of this Island, the Prince should pay 5000 Marks in hand, with the reserve of a 1000 Marks yearly to begin at *Michaelmas*; and in case the Prince died without Issue, the whole Island should return to the King. 6. That the Prince should come every year to *England* to pay his Homage to the King for all his Lands. 7. That all the Barons of *Wales*, excepting five in *Snowden*, should hold their Lands and Estates of the King, and no other. 8. That the Title of Prince should remain only for his Life, and not descend to his Successors, and after his Death, the five Lords of *Snowden* should hold their Lands only from the King. 9. That for the performance of these Articles, the Prince should deliver up for Hostages ten Persons of the best Quality in the Country, without imprisoning, disinheriting, and any time of redemption determined. And farther, that the King should chuse Twenty Persons within *North-Wales*, who besides the Prince, should take their Oaths for the due performance of these Articles, and in case the Prince should swerve and recede from them, and upon admonition thereof

The History of WALES.

thereof not repent, they should forsake him, and become his Enemies. 10. The Prince was obliged to suffer his Brethren quietly to enjoy their Lands in *Wales*, whereof *David* for his Service was dubbed Knight by the King, and had the Earl of *Derby*'s Widow given him in Matrimony, and with her as a Portion, the Castle of *Denbigh* in *North-Wales*, besides a 1000 Pounds in Lands. His other Brother *Roderic* was lately escaped out of Prison into *England*, and the younger called *Owen*, was upon his Composition delivered out of Prison.

King *Edward* having imposed these severe and unmerciful Conditions upon Prince *Lhewelyn*, and for a better security for the performance of them, built a Castle at *Aberystwyth*, returned very honourably into *England*; upon whose arrival, the People willingly granted him a Subsidy of the Twentieth part of their Estates towards his Charges in this War. But it seems very probable that Prince *Lhewelyn* submitted to these intolerable Conditions, more upon the account of his Amours, and to regain the Lady *Eleanora* out of the King of *England*'s hand, than that he was apprehensive of any considerable Danger he might receive by the *English* Troops. For it is hardly conceivable, that a Prince of such notorious Conduct and Valour, would so easily accept of such hard Terms, and in a measure deliver up his Principality, when there was no necessity so to do, without resisting an Enemy, whom he had frequently overcome, and forced to retire back with greater inequality than the *English* had at present over him. But the force of Love worked Wonders, and in this case, proved most irresistible, which to obtain, *Lhewelyn* did not think hard to forfeit his proper Right to his inveterate Enemies, and for ever to exclude his Posterity from succeeding in their lawful Inheritance. The next year 1278. therefore, he had his Wish accomplished, and was married to *Eleanora* at *Worcester*, the King and Queen, with all the Nobility and Persons of Quality in *England*, honouring the Wedding with their presence. But

The History of WALES.

But this specious Amity, and the Peace lately concluded betwixt them did not last long, the *English* Governours in the Marches and in-land-Countries of *Wales*, presuming upon the Prince's submission to the King, grievously oppressed the Inhabitants of the Country, with new and unheard of exactions, and with intolerable partiality openly encouraged the *English* to defraud and oppress the *Welch*. These insupportable practices moved the *Welch* to go in a Body to *David* Lord of *Denbigh*, to endeavour a reconciliation between him and his Brother the Prince, that they both being at Unity, might easily deliver themselves and their Country from the unmerciful Tyranny of the *English*.

1281. *David* was not ignorant of the miseries of his Country-men, and therefore gladly submitted to be reconciled to his Brother, with promise never to side again with the King of *England*, but to become his utter Enemy. This happy Union being thus effected, *David* was chose General of the Army, with which he presently marched to *Hawarden*, and surprizing the Castle, slew all that opposed him, and took *Roger Clifford* Prisoner, who had been sent by King *Edward*, *Justitiar* into those parts. From thence, being joyned by the Prince, he passed to *Ruthlan*, and laid Siege to the Castle; but upon notice given that the King was marching to raise the Siege, he thought convenient to withdraw, and to retire back. At the same time, *Rhys ap Maelgon* and *Gruffydh ap Meredith ap Owen*, with other Lords of *South-Wales*, took from the *English* the Castle of *Aberystwyth*, with divers others in that Country, and spoiled all the People thereabouts, who owned subjection to the Crown of *England*. In the mean while, *John Peckham* Archbishop of *Canterbury*, perceiving how matters were like to proceed between the King and the Prince, and how the Kingdom was effectually involved in a War, of his own proper motion came to Prince *Lhewelyn*, to endeavour a re-submission from him and his Brother *David* to King *Edward*, and so to put a stop to any farther Hostilities.

But

The History of WALES.

But he sent before-hand to the Prince and People of *Wales*; intimating to them, "That for the "Love he bore to the *Welch* Nation, he under- "took this Arbitration, without the knowledg, and "contrary to the King's liking; and therefore ear- "nestly desired, that they would submit to a Peace "with the *English*, which himself would endeavour "to bring to pass. And because he could make no "long continuance in those Parts, he wished them "to consider, how that if he should be forced to "depart before any thing was brought to a con- "clusion, they could hardly find another who would "so heartily espouse their Cause; and farther threat- "ned, that in case they contemned and derided his "Endeavours, he would not only instigate the *Eng-* "*lish* Army, now greatly strengthned and increased, "to fall upon them, but also signifie their Stubborn- "ness to the Court and Bishop of *Rome*, who e- "steemed and honoured *England*, beyond any other "Kingdom in the World. Moreover, he much la- "mented to hear of the excessive Cruelty of the "*Welch*, even beyond that of the *Saracens* and other "Infidels, who never refused to permit Slaves and "Captives to be ransomed; which the *Welch* were "so far from practising, that even some time they "slew those for whose Redemption they received "Money. And whereas they were wont to esteem "and reverence holy and ecclesiastical Persons, they "are now so far degenerated from Devotion and "Sanctity, that nothing is more acceptable to them "than War and Sedition, which they had now "great need to forsake and repent of. Lastly, he "proposed, that they would signifie to him, where- "in, and what Laws and Constitutions of theirs "was violated by the *English*, and by what means "a firm and a lasting Peace might be esta- "blished; which, if they rejected, they must ex- "pect to incur the Decree and Censure of the "Church, as well as endure the violent In-roads and "Depredations of a powerful Army. To these, partly Admonitions, and partly Threatnings of the

Arch-

Archbishop, Prince *Lhewelyn* returned an Answer;
"That he humbly thanked his Grace for the Pains
"and Trouble he undertook in his and his Subjects
"behalf; and more particularly, becaufe he would
"venture to come to *Wales*, contrary to the plea-
"fure and good liking of the King. And as for
"concluding a Peace with him, he would not have
"his Grace be ignorant, that with all readinefs he
"was willing to fubmit to it, upon condition that
"the King would duly and fincerely obferve the
"fame. And though he would be glad of his lon-
1201. "ger continuance in *Wales*, yet he hoped that no
"Obftructions would happen of his fide, why a
"Peace (which of all things he moft defired) might
"not be forthwith concluded, and rather by his
"Graces procuring than any others; fo that there
"would be no farther need of acquainting the Pope
"with his Obftinacy, nor moving the King of *Eng-
"land* to ufe any Force againft him. And though
"the Kingdom of *England* be under the immediate
"Protection of the See of *Rome*, yet, when his Ho-
"linefs comes to underftand of the great and unfuf-
"ferable Wrongs done to him by the *Englifh*; how
"the Articles of Peace were broken, Churches
"and all other religious Houfes in *Wales* were burn-
"ed down and deftroyed, and religious Perfons un-
"chriftianly murthered, he hoped he would rather
"pity and lament his Condition, than with addition
"of Punifhment increafe and augment his Sorrow.
"Neither fhall the Kingdom of *England* be any wife
"difquieted and molefted by his means, in cafe the
"Peace be religioufly obferved towards him and his
"Subjects. But who they are, that delight them-
"felves with War and Bloodfhed, manifeftly ap-
"pears by their Actions and Behaviour; the *Welch*
"being glad to live quietly upon their own, if they
"might be permitted by the *Englifh*, who coming
"to the Country, utterly deftroy whatever comes in
"their way, without regard either to Sex, Age, or
"religious places. But he was extreme forry that any
"one fhould be flain, having paid his Ranfom; the
"Author

"Author of which unworthy Action he did not
"pretend to maintain, but would inflict upon him
"his condign Punishment, in case he could be got
"out of the Woods and Desarts, where as an
"Outlaw, he lives undiscovered. But as to com-
"mencing a War in a Season inconvenient, he pro-
"tested he knew nothing of that till now; yet
"those that did so, do solemnly attest that to be
"the only measure they had to save themselves, and
"that they had no other security for their Lives
"and Fortunes, than to keep themselves in Arms.
"Concerning his Sins and Trespasses against God,
"with the assistance of his Grace, he would endea-
"vour to repent of; neither should the War be
"willingly continued by him, in case he might save
"himself harmless; but before he would be unjustly
"dispossessed of his legal Propriety, he thought it
"but reasonable, by all possible measures to defend
"himself. And he was very willing, upon due Exa-
"mination of the Trespasses committed, to make
"Satisfaction and Retribution of all Wrongs com-
"mitted by him and his Subjects; so that the *Eng-*
"*lish* would observe the same of their side; and like-
"wise was ready to conclude a Peace, which he
"thought was impossible to be established, as long
"as the *English* had no regard to Articles, and still
"oppress his People with new and unwarrantable
"Exactions. Therefore seeing his Subjects were un-
"christianly abused by the King's Officers, and all
"his Country most tyrannically harassed, he saw no
"reason why the *English*, upon any fault of his side,
"should threaten to bring a formidable Army to his
"Country, nor the Church pretend to censure him;
"seeing also, he was very willing upon the afore-
"said Conditions, to submit to a Peace. And lastly,
"he desired his Grace, that he would not give the
"more credit to his Enemies, because they were
"near his Person, and could deliver their Complaints
"frequently, and by word of mouth; for they who
"made no conscience of oppressing, would not in
"all probability, stick to defame, and make false Ac-
"cusations.;

The History of WALES.

"cusations; and therefore his Grace would make a
"better Estimation of the whole matter, by examin-
"ing their Actions, rather than believing their Words.

Prince *Llewelyn* having to this purpose replyed in general to the Archbishop's Articles, presented him with a Copy of the several Grievances, which himself and others of his Subjects had wrongfully and unjustly received at the hands of the *English*. And these, though somewhat tedious, are thought necessary to be particularly inserted in the Appendix, by reason that they demonstrably vindicate the *Welch* Nation, from the unreasonable Aspersions which the *English* of these times cast upon it. For, the breach of Peace, and the occasion of those dismal Disturbances in the Kingdom, are, by the *English* Writers of those times, wholly attributed to the restless and rebellious Humour and unconstant Temper of the *Welch*: Whereas, had they looked at home, they might have found the Original of all these Troubles, to have proceeded from the intolerable Extortions and insupportable Oppressions of their own Nation. For whoever considers these unmerciful Grievances, and the manifold Wrongs the *Welch* endured, it cannot in reason be expected, but that they would endeavour to vindicate themselves, and repel Force by Force. For, had the *English* the liberty of dispossessing them wrongfully of their proper Inheritance and Estates, and it was not lawful for the *Welch* to endeavour the defending and keeping their own? And must they be reckoned disobedient, and Promoters of Sedition, upon the account that they would not be trampled under, and enslaved by the *English*? These Measures were too hard and intolerable, and scarce allowable in an Infidel Nation; to oppress, (and what in them lay) eradicate a People, for no other reason, than because they were weaker and more helpless than themselves; and then, what is worse, to accuse them of being Authors of Sedition, because they would not suffer themselves to be peaceably enslaved, but endeavoured to vindicate their Right by main Force. But it is highly probable,

that

that King *Edward* had no inclination to obferve, what Articles of Agreement foever were concluded upon; and therefore encouraged his Deputies in the Marches and inland Country of *Wales*, in all their Oppreffions and finiftrous Dealings towards the *Welch*. This was the beft Method, and the moft expedient Means to reduce the Country of *Wales* to fubjection to the Crown of *England*, which the King had long ago intentionally effected: And to accufe the *Welch* of not obferving the Conditions of Peace, was a fpecious Pretence to bring that actually to pafs, and to lead an Army into the Country. But whaever the *Englifh* might pretend, 'tis evident the *Welch* had the greater occafion to complain, as appears from the Grievances committed as well againft the Prince himfelf, as others of his Subjects. *See the Appendix.*

The Archbifhop having read over thefe Grievances, and finding the *Welch* to be upon good reafon guiltlefs of that fevere Character, which by the malicious Infinuations of the *Englifh*, he had conceived of them, went to King *Edward*; requefting him to take into confideration the unjuft Wrongs and Injuries done to the *Welch*; which if he would not redrefs, at leaft he might excufe them from any breach of Obedience to him, feeing they had fo juft a reafon for what they did. The King replyed, That he willingly forgave them, and would make reafonable Satisfaction for any Wrong done; fo that they had free accefs to declare their Greivances before him; and then might fafely depart, in cafe it would appear juft and lawful they fhould. The Archbifhop upon this thought he had obtained his purpofe, and therefore, without any ftay, pofted it to *Snowden*, where the Prince and his Brother *David* refided; and having acquainted them with the King's mind, earneftly defired that they, and the reft of the Nobility of *Wales*, would fubmit themfelves, and by him be introduced to the King's prefence. Prince *Lhewelyn*, after fome times Conference and Debate, declared that he was ready to fubmit to the King, with the referve only of two particulars; namely, his Confci-
ence,

ence, whereby he was obliged to regard the Safety and Liberties of his People; and then the decency of his own State and Quality. But the King understanding by the Archbishop, how that the Prince stood upon Terms, positively refused to consent to any more Treaty of Peace, than that he should simply submit, without any farther Conditions. The Archbishop had experience enough, that the *Welch* would never agree to such Proposals; and therefore desired of his Majesty, that he would give him leave, with the rest of the *English* Nobility present, to confer and conclude upon the matter; which being granted, they unanimously resolved upon the following Articles, and sent them to the Prince by *John Wallensis*, Bishop of S. *Davids*.

I. *The King will have no Treaty of the four Cantreds, and other Lands which he has bestowed upon his Nobles; nor of the Isle of* Anglesey.

II. *In case the Tenants of the four Cantreds submit themselves, the King purposeth to deal kindly and honourably with them; which we are sufficiently satisfied of, and will, what in us lyes, endeavour to further.*

III. *We will do the like touching Prince* Lhewelyn, *concerning whom we can return no other Answer, than that he must barely submit himself to the King, without hopes of any other Conditions.*

These were the publick Articles agreed upon by the *English* Nobility, and sent to Prince *Lhewelyn*; besides which, they sent some private Measures of Agreement, relating both to him and his Brother *David*; promising, that in case he would submit, and put the King in quiet possession of *Snowden*, his Majesty would bestow an *English* County upon him, with the yearly Revenue of a Thousand Pound Sterling. And moreover, his Daughter should be provided for, suitable to her Birth and Quality, and all his

The History of WALES.

his Subjects according to their Estate and Condition; and in case he should have Male Issue by a second Wife, the aforesaid County and a Thousand Pound should remain to his Posterity for ever. As for *David* the Prince's Brother, if he would consent to go to the *Holy-Land*, upon condition not to return but upon the King's Pleasure, all things should be honourably prepared for his Journey with respect to his Quality; and his Child maintain'd and provided for by the King. To these the Archbishop added his Threats; That in case they did not comply, and submit themselves to the King's Mercy, there were very severe and imminent Dangers hanging over their Heads; a formidable Army was ready to make an inroad into their Country, which would not only gaul and opprefs them, but in all probability totally eradicate the whole Nation: Besides which, they were to expect the severest Censure and Punishment of the Church.

But all this could not force so unlimited a Submission from the Prince, but that he would stick upon some certain Conditions; and therefore by Letter he acquainted the Archbishop, "That he was " with all willingness desirous to submit himself to " the King; but withal, that he could not do it but " in such a manner as was safe and honest for him. " And because the Form of Submission contained in " the Articles sent to him, were by himself and his " Council thought pernicious and illegal for him to " consent to, as tending rather to the Destruction, than " the Security of himself and his Subjects, he could in " no wise agree to it; and in case himself should be " willing, the rest of his Nobility and People would " never admit of it, as knowing for certain the Mis- " chief and Inconveniency that would ensue thereby. " Therefore he desired his Lordship, that for a Con- " firmation of an honest and a durable Peace, which " he had all this while earnestly laboured for, he " would manage Matters circumspectly, and with " due regard to the following Articles. For it was " much more honourable for the King, and far more

" confo-

The History of WALES.

" confonant to Reafon, that he fhould hold his
" Lands in the Country where he was born and
" dwelt in, than that by difpoffeffing of him, his
" Eftate fhould be beftowed upon Strangers. With
this was fent the general Anfwer of the *Welch* to
the Archbifhop's Articles, *viz.*

1. Though the King would not confent to treat of
the four Cantreds, nor of the Ifle of *Anglefey*; yet
unlefs thefe be comprehended in the Treaty, the
Prince's Council will not conclude a Peace; by reafon that thefe Cantreds have ever, fince the time of
Camber the Son of *Brutus*, properly and legally belonged to the Princes of *Wales*; befides the Confirmation which the prefent Prince obtained by the
Confent of the King and his Father, at the Treaty
before Cardinal *Ottobonus* the Pope's Legate, whofe
Letters Patents do ftill appear. And more, the Juftice of the thing it felf is plainly evident, that it is
more reafonable for our Heirs to hold the faid Cantreds for Money, and other Services due to the King;
than that Strangers enjoy the fame, who will forcibly abufe and opprefs the People.

2. All the Tenants of the Cantreds of *Wales* do
unanimoufly declare, that they dare not fubmit themfelves to the King's Pleafure; by reafon that he never from the beginning took care to obferve either
Covenant, Oath, or any other Grant to the Prince
and his People; and becaufe his Subjects have no regard to Religion, but moft cruelly and unchriftianly
tyranize over Churches and religious Perfons; and
then, for that we do not underftand our felves any
way obliged thereunto, feeing we be the Prince's
Tenants, who is willing to pay the King all ufual and
accuftomed Services.

3. As to what is required, that the Prince fhould
fimply commit himfelf to the King's Will, we all declare, that for the aforefaid Reafons, none of us dare
come, neither will we permit our Prince to come to
him upon thofe Conditions.

4. That

4. That some of the *English* Nobility will endeavour to procure a provision of a Thousand Pounds a Year in *England*; we would let them know, that we can accept of no such Pension; because it is procured for no other end, than that the Prince being disinherited, themselves may obtain his Lands in *Wales*.

5. The Prince cannot in honesty resign his paternal Inheritance, which has for many Ages been enjoyed by his Predecessours, and accept of other Lands among the *English*, of whose Customs and Language he is ignorant; and upon that score, may at length be fraudulently deprived of all, by his malicious and inveterate Enemies.

6. Seeing the King intends to deprive him of his antient Inheritance in *Wales*, where the Land is more barren and untilled; it is not very probable that he will bestow upon him, a more fruitful and an arable Estate in *England*.

7. As to the Clause, that the Prince should give the King a perpetual Possession of *Snowden*; we only affirm, that seeing *Snowden* essentially belongs to the Principality of *Wales*, which the Prince and his Predecessors have enjoyed since *Brute*, the Prince's Council will not permit him to renounce it, and accept another Estate in *England*, to which he has not equal Right.

8. The People of *Snowden* declare, That though the Prince should give the King possession of it, they would never own, and pay Submission to Strangers; for in so doing, they would bring upon themselves the same Misery, that the People of the Four Cantreds have for a long time groaned under; being most rudely handled and unjustly oppressed by the King's Officers; as wofully appears by their several Grievances.

9. As for *David*, the Prince's Brother, we see no reason, why against his Will he should be compell'd to take a journey to the *Holy-Land*; which if he happens to undertake hereafter upon the account of Religion, it is no cause that his Issue should be disinherited, but rather encouraged. Now

Now seeing neither the Prince nor any of his Subjects upon any account whatsoever, have moved and begun this War, but only defended themselves, their Properties, Laws, and Liberties, from the Encroachments of other Persons; and since the *English*, for either Malice or Covetousness to obtain our Estates, have unjustly occasioned all these Troubles and Broils in the Kingdom, we are assured that our Defence is just and lawful, and therein depend upon the Aid and Assistance of Heaven; which will be most cruelly revenged upon our sacrilegious and inhumane Enemies, who have left no manner of Enormities, in relation to God and Man, uncommitted. Therefore your Grace would more justly threaten your Ecclesiastical Censures, against the Authors and Abettors of such unparallell'd Villanies, than the innocent Sufferers. And besides, we much admire, that you should advise us to part with our own Estates, and to live among our Enemies; as if, when we cannot peaceably enjoy what is our own unquestionable Right, we might expect to have quiet possession of another Mans: And though, as you say, it be hard to live in War and perpetual Danger; yet much harder it is, to be utterly destroyed and reduced to nothing; especially, when we seek but the Defence of our own Liberties from the insatiable Ambition of our Enemies. And seeing your Grace has promised to fulminate Sentence against all them that either for Malice or Profit would hinder and obstruct the Peace; it is evident who in this respect are Transgressors and Delinquents; the fear and apprehension of Imprisonment and Ejection out of our Estates, the sense of Oppression and tyrannical Government, haveing compell'd us to take up Arms for the security of our Lives and Fortunes. Therefore as the *English* are not dispossessed of their Estates, for their Offences against the King, so we are willing to be punished, or make other Satisfaction for our Crimes, without being disinherited; and as to the breach of the Peace, 'tis notorious that they were the Authors, who never regarded either Promise or Covenant, never

made

The History of WALES.

made Amends for Trespasses, nor Remedy for our Complaints.

When the Archbishop saw there was no likelihood of a Mediation, and that a Peace was impossible to be concluded as long as the *Welch* stuck upon Conditions; he presently relinquished his pretended Affection towards them, and denounced a Sentence of Excommunication against the Prince and all his Adherents. It was a subject of no little wonder, that a Person of so reputed a Sanctity, who esteemed the several Grievances done to the *Welch* to be intolerable, should now condemn them for refusal of unlimited Submission to the King of *England*; whereas he had already owned it to be unreasonable. But this ecclesiastical Censure was only a Prologue to a more melancholy Scene; King *Edward* immediately upon it, sending an Army by Sea to *Anglesey*, without any great Opposition, conquered the Island, and without any Mercy, put all that withstood him to the Sword. From thence designing to pass over to the Continent, he caused a Bridg of Boats covered with Planks to be built over the *Menay* (being an Arm of the Sea which parteth the Isle from the main Land) at a place called *Moel y don*, not far from *Bangor*, where the Water is narrowest. The Bridg being finished, which was so broad as that Threescore Men might pass in a breast, *William Latimer*, with a strong Party of the best experienced Soldiers, and Sir *Lucas Thany*, Commander of the *Gascoigns* and *Spaniards*, whereof a great number served the King, passed over, but could discover no sign, or any the least intimation of an Enemy. But as soon as the Tide began to appear, and the Sea had overflown beside the Bridg, down come the *Welch* fiercely out of the Mountains, and setting upon the disheartned *English*, killed or drowned their whole number, excepting *Latimer*, who by the swimming of his Horse got safe to the Bridg. In this Action, several worthy Soldiers of the *English* side were lost; among whom were Sir *Lucas Thany*, *Robert Clifford*, Sir *Walter Lyndsey*, two Brothers of *Robert Burnel* Bishop of *Bath*, with many others

others; in all to the number of Thirteen Knights, Seventeen young Gentlemen, and Two Hundred common Soldiers. A little after, or as some say afore, another Engagement passed between the *English* and the *Welch*, wherein the former lost Fourteen Colours, the Lords *Audley* and *Clifford* the younger being slain, and the King himself forced to retreat for safety to the Castle of *Hope*.

And while these things passed in *North-Wales*, the Earl of *Glocester* and Sir *Edmund Mortimer* acted vigorously with their Forces in *South-Wales*; and fighting the *Welch* at *Lhandeilo Fawr*, overthrew them, with the loss of no considerable Person, saving *William de Valence* the King's Cosin-German, and Four Knights besides. Prince *Lhewelyn* was all this while in *Cardigan*, a wasting and destroying all the Country, and principally the Lands of *Rhys ap Meredith*, who very unnaturally held with the King of *England* in all these Wars. But being at length tired with Action, with a few Men privately separated himself from his Army, and came to *Buelht*, thinking to ease and respit himself there undiscovered. But coming to the River *Wye*, he met with *Edmund Mortimer* and *John Gifford*, with a considerable Party of the People of that Country, which *Mortimer* was Lord of. But neither Party venturing to assail the other; Prince *Lhewelyn* with one only Servant retired to a private Grove in a neighbouring Valley, there to consult with certain Lords of the Country, who had appointed to meet him. In the mean time *Mortimer* descends from the Hill, with intention to fall upon *Lhewelyn*'s Men; which they perceiving, betook themselves to the Bridg called *Pont Orewryn*, and manfully defended the Passage he was to cross. *Mortimer* could effect nothing against them, till he had gained the Bridg, the River being unpassable; and to force them to quit it, seemed altogether impracticable. But at last, the River was discovered to be fordable a little below, and so *Helias Walwyn* was detached with a Party through the River, who unexpectedly falling upon the backs of the Defendants, easily forced them to leave the Bridg,

The History of WALES.

Bridg, and save themselves by flight. Prince *Lhewelyn* all this while in vain expected the Lords of *Buelht*, and in fine continued to wait so long, till *Mortimer* having passed over the Bridg, surrounded the Wood he was in with armed Men. The Prince perceiving himself to be betrayed, thought to make his escape to his Men; but the *English* so closely pursued him, that before he could come in, one *Adam Francton*, not knowing who he was, run him through with his Sword, being unarmed. The *Welch* still expected the arrival of their Prince, and though but a few in number, so gallantly maintained their ground, that in spight of the far greater number of the *English*, they were at length with much ado put to flight. The Battel being over, *Francton* returned to plunder his dead; but perceiving him to be the Prince of *Wales*, he thought himself to have obtained a sufficient Prize, and thereupon presently chopt off his Head, and sent it to King *Edward* at *Conivey*, who very joyfully caused it to be placed upon the highest Pinacle of the Tower of *London*. And thus fell this worthy Prince, the greatest, though the last of the *British* Blood, betrayed most basely by the Lords of *Buelht*, and being dead, most unworthily dealt with by the King of *England*; who contrary to all Presidents, treated a lawful Prince like a Traytor, and exposed his crowned Head to the Derision of the Multitude.

Not long after, *David* the Prince's Brother was delivered up by the *Welch* themselves, and in a Parliament for that purpose assembled at *Shrewsbury*, was condemned to dye; his Head to be sent to accompany his Brothers upon the Tower of *London*, and his four Quarters to the four Cities of *Bristol*, *Northampton*, *York*, and *Winchester*. Then the King for the easier keeping the *Welch* in due subjection, built Two strong Castles in *North Wales*; the one at *Conwey* and the other at *Caernarvon*. There was none that now stood out besides *Rhys Fychan* of *Tstratymy*; and he, finding *David* was gone, and himself like to do nothing to purpose, fairly yielded himself up to

the

the Earl of *Hereford*, who by the King's Orders committed him Prisoner to the Tower of *London*; and so all the Country of *Wales* became ever since subject to the Crown of *England*.

The PRINCES of WALES of English-*Blood*.

Anno 12.
Edw. I.

PRince *Lhewelyn* and his Brother *David* being so basely taken off, and leaving no body to lay any specious Claim to the Principality of *Wales*; King *Edward* by a Statute made at *Ruthlan*, incorporated and annexed it to the Crown of *England*; constituting several new and wholsom Laws; as concerning the Division of *Wales* into several Counties, the Form and Manner of Writs, and Proceedings in Tryals, with many others not very unlike the Laws and Constitutions of the *English* Nation. But all this could never win the Affection of the *Welch* toward him; who by no means would own him as their Sovereign, unless he would condescend and agree to live and reign among them. They had not forgot the cruel Oppressions and intolerable Insolencies of *English* Officers; and therefore they flatly told him, they would never yield Obedience to any other, than a Prince of their own Nation, of their own Language, and whose Life and Conversation was spotless and unblameable. King *Edward* perceiving the *Welch* to be resolute and inflexible, and absolutely bent against any other Prince, than one of their own Country, happily thought of this politick, though dangerous Expedient. Queen *Eleanor* was now quick with Child, and ready to be delivered; and though the Season was very severe, it being the depth of Winter, the King sent for her from *England*, and remov'd her to *Caernarvon* Castle, the place design'd for her to

lye

The History of WALES.

lye in. When the time of her Delivery was come, King *Edward* called to him all the Barons and chief Persons throughout all *Wales* to *Ruthlan*, there to consult about the publick Good and Safety of their Country. And being informed that his Queen was delivered of a Son, he told the *Welch* Nobility, that whereas they had oftentimes intreated him to appoint them a Prince, he having at this time occasion to depart out of the Country, would comply with their Request, upon condition they would allow of, and obey him whom he should name. The *Welch* readily agreed to the motion, only with the same Reserve, that he should appoint them a Prince of their own Nation. King *Edward* assured them, he would name such an one as was born in *Wales*, could speak no English, and whose Life and Conversation no body could stain; whom the *Welch* agreeing to own and obey, he named his own Son *Edward*, but little before born in *Caernarvon* Castle.

King *Edward* having by these means deluded the *Welch*, and reduced the whole Country of *Wales* to his own Devotion, began to reward his Followers with other Mens Proprieties, and bestowed whole Lordships and Towns in the midst of the Country upon *English* Lords, among whom *Henry Lacy* Earl of *Lincoln* obtained the Lordship of *Denbigh*; *Reginald Grey*, second Son to *John* Lord *Grey* of *Wilton*, the Lordship of *Ruthyn*. This *Henry Lacy* was Son to *Edmund Lacy*, the Son of *John Lacy*, Lord of *Halton Pomfret*, and Constable of *Chester*, who married *Margaret* the eldest Daughter, and one of the Heirs of *Robert Quincy* Earl of *Lincoln*. This *Henry Lacy* Lord of *Denbigh* married the Daughter and sole Heir of *William Longspear* Earl of *Salusbury*, by whom he had Issue two Sons, *Edmund* and *John*, who both dyed young, one by a Fall into a very deep Well within the Castle of *Denbigh*; and a Daughter named *Alicia*, who was married to *Thomas Plantagenet* Earl of *Lancaster*, who in right of his Wife was Earl of *Lincoln* and *Sarum*, Lord of *Denbigh*, *Halton Pomfret*, and Constable of *Chester*. After his Death, King *Edward* II.

bestowed

bestowed the said Lordship of *Denbigh* upon *Hugh* Lord *Spencer* Earl of *Winchester*, upon whose decease, King *Edward* III. gave it, together with many other Lordships in the Marches, to *Roger Mortimer* Earl of *March*, in performance of a Promise he had made, whilst he remained with his Mother in *France*, that as soon as he should come to the possession of the Crown of *England*, he would bestow upon the said Earl of *March*, to the value of a Thousand Pound yearly, in Lands. But within few Years after, *Mortimer* being attainted of High Treason, King *Edward* bestowed the said Lordship of *Denbigh* upon *Montague* Earl of *Salusbury*; but it was quickly restored again to the *Mortimers*, in which House it continued, till the whole Estate of the Earls of *March*, came with a Daughter to the House of *York*, and so to the Crown, *Richard* Duke of *York*, Grand-Father to *Edward* the Fourth, having married the sole Daughter and Heir of the House of the *Mortimers*. And so it continued in the Crown to Queen *Elizabeth's* time, who in the Sixth Year of her Reign, bestowed the said Lordship upon her great Favourite *Robert* Earl of *Leicester*, who was then created Baron of *Denbigh*. After him it returned again to the Crown, where it has continued to this present Year 1696. when his present Majesty granted a Patent under the great Seal to *William* Earl of *Portland*, for the Lordships of *Denbigh*, *Bromfield*, and *Yale*. Some of the *Welch* Representatives, perceiving how far such a Grant encroached upon the Properties and Priviledges of the Subject, disclosed their Grievances to the Honourable House of Commons, who after some consideration, resolved *(nemine contradicente)* that a Petition should be presented to his Majesty by the Body of the whole House, to request him to recall his Grant to the said Earl of *Portland*; which was accordingly done in the manner following:

May

The History of WALES.

May it please Your Most Excellent Majesty,

WE Your Majesty's most Dutiful and Loyal Subjects, the Knights, Citizens, and Burgesses in Parliament Assembled; Humbly lay before Your Majesty, That whereas there is a Grant passing to William Earl of Portland, and his Heirs, of the Mannors of Denbigh, Bromfield, and Yale, and divers other Lands in the Principality of Wales ; together with several Estates of Inheritance, enjoyed by many of Your Majesty's Subjects by Virtue of Antient Grants from the Crown:

That the said Mannors, with the large and extensive Royalties, Powers, and Jurisdictions to the same belonging, are of great Concern to Your Majesty and the Crown of this Realm: And that the same have been usually Annex'd to the Principality of Wales, and Settled on the Princes of Wales for their Support: And that a great number of Your Majesty's Subjects, in those Parts, hold their Estates by Royal Tenure, under great and valuable Compositions, Rents, Royal-Payments, and Services to the Crown and Princes of Wales; and have by such Tenure great Dependance on Your Majesty and the Crown of England; and have enjoyed great Privileges and Advantages with their Estates, under such Tenure.

We therefore most humbly beseech Your Majesty, to put a stop to the Passing this Grant to the Earl of Portland, of the said Mannors and Lands; and that the same may not be disposed from the Crown, but by Consent of Parliament: For that such Grant, is in Diminution of the Honour and Interest of the Crown, by placing in a Subject, such large and extensive Royalties, Powers, and Jurisdictions, which ought only to be in the Crown; and will Sever that Dependance, which so great a Number of Your Majesty's Subjects, in those Parts, have on Your Majesty and the Crown, by reason of their Tenure; and may be to their great Oppression in those Rights which they have purchased, and hitherto enjoyed with their Estates: And also, on Occasion of

great

great Vexation to many of Your Majesty's Subjects, who have long had the absolute Inheritance of several Lands (comprehended in the said Grant to the Earl of Portland) by Antient Grants from the Crown.

His MAJESTY's Answer.

Gentlemen,

I Have Kindness for my Lord Portland; which he has deserved of Me, by long and faithful Services; but I should not have given him these Lands, if I had imagined the House of Commons could have been concern'd; I will therefore Recal the Grant, and find some other way of shewing My Favour to him.

The Lordship of Ruthyn continued in the possession of the Grays, till the Reign of Henry VII. when George Grey Earl of Kent, and Lord of Ruthyn, upon some Bargain, passed the same over to the King, since which it has been in the possession of some of the Earls of Warwick, and afterwards came to the Middletons of Chirk Castle in the County of Denbigh, where it still continues; being now enjoyed by the Right Worshipful Sir Richard Middleton, Baronet.

But besides Henry Lacy and Reginald Grey, several other Gentlemen of Quality, came at this time with King Edward to North-Wales, who in some time became to be Men of great Possessions and Sway in the Country, whose Posterity enjoy the same to this time. But he that expected to fare best in the distribution of these Lordships and Estates in Wales, was one Rhys ap Meredith, a Welch Man, and one that, contrary to the Allegiance sworn to his Prince, and his Duty to his Native Country, had served the King of England in all these Wars, and done the greatest hurt of any Man to the Interest of Prince Lhewelyn. For these great Services done to King Edward, Rhys expected no less than to be promoted

to

to the highest Preferments; whom the King after the Prince of *Wales*'s Overthrow, first dubbed Knight, and afterwards fed him with fair Words and great Promises.

But when he, and all his Neighbours and Countrymen had submitted themselves to the Government of the King of *England*; it happened that the Lord *Pain Tiptoft*, Warden of the King's Castles which joyned to *Rhys*'s Country, and the Lord *Alan Plucknet*, the King's Steward in *Wales*, cited Sir *Rhys ap Meredith*, with all the rest of the Country, to the King's Court; which he refusing to do, alledging his antient Priviledges and Liberties, together with the King's Promises to him, the foresaid Officers proceeded against him according to Law. Whereupon Sir *Rhys* being greatly vexed to be thus served by those whose Interest he had all this while so warmly espoused, thought to be revenged of *Pain Tiptoft*, and the rest of the *English*. And to that end, having drawn together some of his Tenants and Countrymen, he fell upon the said *Pain Tiptoft*; between whom several Skirmishes afterwards happened, and several Men were slain on both sides. King *Edward* was now at *Arragon*, to compose the Difference betwixt the Kings of *Arragon* and *Naples*; but being informed of the Disturbances which had happened in *Wales*, betwixt his Ministers there, and Sir *Rhys ap Meredith*; he writ to this latter, requiring him to keep the Peace, till his return; at what time he would redress all Grievances, and reduce Matters to a good and reasonable Order. But Sir *Rhys* haveing already waited sufficiently upon the King's Promises, and being now in a good condition to offend his Enemies by force of Arms, would not give over the Enterprize he saw so promising, but marching with his Forces to his Enemies Lands, burnt and spoiled several Towns belonging to the *English*. Upon this, the King sent to the Earl of *Cornwal*, whom he had appointed his Deputy during his absence, to march with an Army into *Wales*, to repress the Insolencies, and to prevent any farther disorderly Attempts

A. D. 1289.

tempts of the *Welch*. The Earl accordingly prepared an Army and went againſt Sir *Rhys*'s, whoſe Army he quickly diſperſed, and overthrew his Caſtle of *Drefolan*, but not without the loſs of ſome of his Chief Men. For as they beſieged and undermined the ſaid Caſtle, the *Walls* unexpectedly fell down, by which unlucky Accident, ſeveral of the *Engliſh* were oppreſſed and bruiſed to Death, among whom were the Lord *Strafford*, and the Lord *William de Monchency*. But within a while after, *Robert Tiptoſt* Lord Deputy of *Wales*, raiſed a very powerful Army againſt Sir *Rhys*, and after a ſlaughter of 4000 of the *Welch*, took him Priſoner, who the *Michaelmas* following, at the King's going to *Scotland*, was condemned and executed at *York*.

1293. But the Death of Sir *Rhys* did not put a final period to all the Quarrels betwixt the *Engliſh* and *Welch*, for in a ſhort time after, there happened a new occaſion for the *Welch* to murmur againſt, and upbraid the Government of the *Engliſh* over them. King *Edward* was now in actual Enmity and War with the King of *France*, for the carrying on of which, he wanted a liberal Subſidy and Supply from his Subjects. This Tax was with a great deal of paſſion and reluctancy levied in divers places of the Kingdom, but more eſpecially in *Wales*, the *Welch* being never acquainted with ſuch large Contributions before, violently ſtormed and exclaimed againſt it. But

1294. not being ſatisfied with villifying the King's Command, they took their own Captain *Roger de Puelesdon*, who was appointed Collector of the ſaid Subſidy, and hanged him up, together with divers others who abetted the collecting of the Tax. Then *Weſt-Wales* Men choſe *Maelgon Fychan* for their Captain, and ſo entring into *Caermardhyn* and *Pembroke-ſhires*, they cruelly haraſſed all the Lands that belonged to the *Engliſh*, and then returned laden with conſiderable Booty. The *Glamorgan-ſhire* Men, and they towards the *South* Parts, choſe one *Morgan* for their Leader, and ſet upon the Earl of *Gloceſter*, whom they forced to make his eſcape out of the Country ; and ſo *Morgan*

The History of WALES.

gan was put in poffeffion of thofe Lands which the Anceftors of the Earl of *Glocefter* had forcibly taken away from *Morgan's* fore-Fathers. On the other fide, the *North-Wales* Men fet up one *Madoc*, related to the laft *Lhewelyn* flain at *Buelht*, who having drawn together a great Number of Men, came to *Caernarvon*, and fetting upon the *Englifh*, who in great multitudes had then reforted thither to a Fair, flew a great many, and afterwards fpoiled and ranfacked the whole Town. King *Edward* being acquainted with thefe different Infurrections and Rebellions in *Wales*, and defirous to quell the Pride and Stubbornefs of the *Welch*, but moft of all to revenge the Death of his great favourite *Roger de Pulefdon*, recalled his Brother *Edmund* Earl of *Lancafter*, and *Henry Lacy* Earl of *Lincoln*, and Lord of *Denbigh*, who with a confiderable Army were ready to embark for *Gafcoign*, and countermanded them into *Wales*. Being arrived there, they paffed quietly forward, till they came to *Denbigh*, and as foon as they drew near unto the Caftle, upon St. *Martin's* day the *Welch* with great Fury and Courage faced them, and joyning Battels, forced them back with a very confiderable lofs. *Polydore Virgil* fays, (but upon what Authority is not known) that the *Welch* obtained this Victory rather upon the account that the *Englifh* Army was hired with fuch Money as had been wrongfully taken out of the Abbies and other Religious places, fo that it was a Judgment from above, more than the Force of the *Welch*, that overcame the *Englifh* Army. But be the caufe of it what it will, 'tis certain the *Englifh* were vanquifhed, upon which account King *Edward* came in Perfon to *Wales*, and kept his *Chriftmas* at *Abcrconwey*, where *Robert Winchelfey* Archbifhop of *Canterbury* being returned from *Rome*, came to him, and having done Homage, returned honourably again to *England*. But as the King advanced farther into the Country, having but one part of his Army with him, the *Welch* fet upon and took moft of his Carriages, which contained a great quantity of Victuals and Provifion, fo that the King with all his followers were
conftrained

The History of WALES.

conſtrained to endure a great deal of hardſhips, in ſo much that at laſt Water mixed with Honey, and very courſe and ordinary Bread with the ſalteſt Meat, were accounted the greateſt Delicacies for his Majeſty's own Table. But their miſery was like to be greater, had not the other part of the Army come in time becauſe the *Welch* had encompaſſed the King round, in hopes to reduce him to the utmoſt diſtreſs, by reaſon that the Water was ſo riſen, that the reſt of the Army could not get to him. But the Water within ſome time after abating, the remainder of the Army came in, whereupon the *Welch* preſently retired, and made their eſcape. One thing is very remarkable of King *Edward* during his diſtreſs at *Snowden*, that when the Army was reduced to very great extremity, a ſmall quantity of Wine was found, which they thought to reſerve for the King's own uſe. But he to prevent any diſcontent, which might thereupon be raiſed in his Souldiers, abſolutely refuſed to taſte thereof, telling them, *That in time of Neceſſity all things ſhould be common, and as he was the Cauſe and Author of their Diſtreſs, he would not be preferred before them in his Diet.*

But whilſt the King remained in *Snowden*, the Earl of *Warwick* being informed that a great Number of *Welch* were aſſembled, and had lodged themſelves in a certain Valley betwixt two Woods, choſe out a Troop of Horſe, together with ſome Croſs-Bows and Archers, and ſet upon them in the Night time. The *Welch* being thus ſurpriſed, and unexpectedly encompaſſed about by their Enemies, made the beſt they could to oppoſe them, and ſo pitching their Spears in the ground, and directing the points towards their Enemies, endeavoured by ſuch means to keep off the Horſe. But the Earl of *Warwick* having ordered his Battel ſo, as that between every two Horſe there ſtood a Croſs-Bow, ſo gauled the *Welch* with the ſhot of the quarrels, that the Spear-men fell apace, and then the Horſe breaking eaſily in upon the reſt, bare them down with ſo great a ſlaughter, as the *Welch* had never received before. After this, King

Edward

Edward to prevent any more rebellious attempts of the *Welch*, cut down all the Woods in *Wales*, wherein, in any time of Danger, they were wont to hide and save themselves. And for a farther security, he repaired and fortified all the Castles and places of Strength in *Wales*, and built the Castle of *Bewmoris* in the Isle of *Anglesey*, and so having put all things in a settled posture, and punished those that had been the occasion of the Death of *Roger de Pulesdon*, he returned with his Army into *England*. But as soon as the King had left the *Welch*, *Madoc*, who, as it is said before, was chosen Captain by the *North-Wales* Men, gathered some Forces together, and came to *Ofweftry*, which presently yielded to him. And then meeting with the Lord *Strange* near *Knockine*, who with a Detachment of the *Marchers* came to oppose him, gave him Battel, vanquished his Forces, and miserably ravaged his Country. The like Success he obtained a second time against the *Marchers*, but at last they brought together a very great Number of Men, and met *Madoc* marching towards *Shrewsbury*, upon the Hills of *Cefn Digolh*, not far from *Camrs* Castle, where after a bloody Fight on both sides, *Madoc* was taken Prisoner, and his Army vanquished and put to flight. Then he was sent to *London*, and there sentenced to remain in perpetual Imprisonment in the *Tower*, tho' others affirm, that *Madoc* was never taken, but that after several Adventures and severe Conflicts, whereby the *Welch* were reduced to great extremities, he came in, and submitted himself to the King, who received him upon Condition he would not desist to pursue *Morgan* Captain of the *Glamorgan-shire* Men, till he brought him Prisoner before him. *Madoc* having performed this, and the whole Country being peaceable and undisturbed, several Hostages from the Chiefest Nobility of *Wales* for their orderly and quiet behaviour were delivered to the King, who disposed of them into divers Castles in *England*, where they continued in safe Custody till the end of the War, which was presently commenced with *Scotland*.

1301. In the 25th. year of King *Edward's* reign, the Prince of *Wales* came down to *Chester*, and received Homage of all the Free-holders in *Wales* as follows, *Henry* Earl of *Lancaster* for *Monmouth*; *Reginald Gray* for *Ruthyn* ; *Foulke Fitzwarren* for his Lands ; the Lord *William Martyn* for his Lands in *Cemaes* ; *Roger Mortimer* for his Lands in *Wales* ; *Henry Lacy* Earl of *Lincoln* for *Rhos* and *Rhyforeioc*; *Robert* Lord *Montalt*, for his Lands, and *Gruffydh* Lord of *Poole*, for the Lordship of *Powys*, at the same time paid their Homage *Tudor ap Grono* of *Anglesey*, *Madoc ap Tudor* Archdeacon of *Anglesey*, *Eineon ap Howel* of *Caernarvon*, *Tudor ap Gruffydh*, *Llewelyn ap Ednyfed*, *Gruffydh Fychan* Son of *Gruffydh ap Iorwerth*, *Madoc Fychan Denglfield*, *Llewelyn* Bishop of St. *Asaph*, and *Richard de Pulesdon*. This last in the Twelfth Year of King *Edward* was constituted Sheriff of *Caernarvon* for life, with the stipend of Forty Pounds *sterling* yearly. At the same place, *Gruffydh ap Tudor*, *Ithel Fychan*, *Ithel ap Blethyn*, with many more did their Homage. Then the Prince came to *Ruthlan*, where the Lord *Richard de Sutton* Baron of *Malpas*, paid Homage and Fealty for the said Barony of *Malpas*. Thence the Prince removed to *Conwey*, where *Eineon* Bishop of *Bangor*, and *David* Abbot of *Maynan* did their Homage ; as did *Lewis de Felton* Son of *Richard Felton*, for the Lands which his Father held of the Prince in *Maelor Saesneg*, or English *Maelor*. *John* Earl *Warren* swore Homage for the Lordships of *Bromfield* and *Yale*, and his Lands in *Hope-Dale*, at *London* in the Chappel of the Lord *John de Kirkby* sometime Bishop of *Ely* ; as also a while after, *Edmund Mortimer* for his Lands of *Cery* and *Cydewen*.

But besides all these, there paid Homage to the Prince of *Wales* at *Chester*, Sir *Gruffydh Llwyd* Son of *Rhys ap Gruffydh ap Ednyfed Fychan*, a stout and a valiant Gentleman, tho' not very fortunate, and as *Florus* says of *Sertorius*, he was *magnæ quidem, sed calamitosæ virtutis*. He was Knighted by King *Edward* the First, upon his bringing the first News of the Queen's safe delivery of a Son at *Caernarvon* Castle,

The History of WALES.

Castle, the King holding then a Parliament at *Ruthlan*. This Sir *Gruffydh* continued for some time very gratious with the King of *England*, but observing at length the intolerable Oppression and Tyranny exercised by the *English* Officers, especially by Sir *Roger Mortimer* Lord of *Chirke* and Justice of *North-Wales*, towards his Country-men the *Welch*, became so far concerned and discontented with such unwarrantable Practices, that he presently brake out into open Rebellion against the *English*. And the better to effect what he purposed, he treated with Sir *Edward Bruce* Brother to *Robert* then King of *Scotland*, who had conquered *Ireland*, to bring or send over some Forces to assist him in his Design against the *English*, upon which account he sent him the following Letter.

Nobili in Christo Conquestori Domino Edvardo, *Illustrissimo Regi* Hiberniæ, *suus, si placet,* Griffinus Llwyd *in* North-Wall: *reverentiam debitam in honore.*

Auditâ nobis vestri in terrarum conquisitione famâ egregiâ in partibus nostris, præcipuè debelland: æmulos nostros & vestros, qui tam vos quam nos ab Hæreditatibus vi injustè expellendo destruxerunt, & nomen nostrum memoriamque in terris delere conati fuerunt, ab initio supra modum applaudimus, ut meritâ debemus, omnes unanimiter in partibus nostris, unde vobis ex parte Wallensium Nobilium significo per præsentes, quod si ad Walliam cum hominibus vestris dignemini venire, vel si vos in propriâ personâ accedere illuc non poteritis, aliquem Nobilem Albanen. Comitem, Baronem vel Militem, cum paucis, si plurimi nequeant adesse, ad dictas partes nostras volueritis mandare. Parati erimus omnes unanimiter . . . . dicem eo quod nomen vestrum celebre ubique publicetur expugnat: si quid Saxonibus in Albaniâ, per illustrem Regem fratrem vestrum ultim. per vos in Hibernia, per vos & nos in Wallia statum vestrum pristinum per Brutum

*Brutum conquifitum recuperabimus, ipfifque fuppedita-
tis, confufis & difperfis, Britannia juxta difcretam
veftræ dominationis ordinationem inter Britones.&
Albaneos in pofterum divifa cohæreditabitur. Valeat
dominatio veftra Regia per cuncta Sæcula.*

To this Letter of Sir *Gruffydh Llwyd's,* Sir *Edward
Bruce* returned the following Anfwer.

*OMnibus defiderantibus à fervitute liberari falu-
tem in eo. Qui defiderant in fe relevat. &
liberat. ab anguftiis, temporibus opportunis, quia quilibet Chriftianus obligatur fuo proximo in omni angu-
ftia fubvenire, & præcipuè illis qui ex una radice
originis five parentela & patriæ primitus procefferunt,
ideo compatientes veftræ fervituti & anguftiæ, jam
. . . . Anglicana moleftia indigenti decrevimus
(auxiliante altiffimo) veftro gravamini occurrere, &
innaturalem & barbaricam totis viribus Anglicanam de
veftris finibus expellere fervitutem, ut fic ficut à principio Albanicus & Britannicus populus expulfis hoftibus
in perpetuum fiet unus. Et quia nullus inimicus faci-
liter relevatur libenter præcipimus, fi jugum Anglica-
num in tantum vos deprimit, quantum nuper depreffe-
rat populum Scotianum, ut fic ex veftro concordi cona-
mine, & noftro fuperveniente (juvamine difponente
femper divino) pofitis jura veftra & juftitiam recu-
perare & proprietatem . . . . hæreditatem pacificè poffidere. Veruntamen Dei cum omnia ferviunt in
ifto propofito filium invocamus, quod non ex præfum-
ptione & ambitione injufti dominii talia attemptamus,
fed ex mera compaffione effufionis innocentis veftri fanguinis & fubjectionis intollerabilis & fignant: ad hoc
quod vellemus inimicorum veftrorum & noftrorum vi-
res reprimere, qui nec pacem nec concordiam defiderant.
Imo veftram & noftram finalem deftructionem, ficut à
principio ingreffionis eorum in Britanniam inceffanter
diebus ac noctibus molientur, & quia nullo modo eft
noftræ confcientiæ quemquam decipere, nec etiam de-
cipi à quocunque, noftram intentionem & Propofit. fine
tergiverfatione aliqua declaramus quod libenter fcire-
mus*

The History of WALES.

mus vestram voluntatem, si rationem nostri laboris & conaminis intuitu relevationis vestræ acceptare decrement. nobis committere profecutionem querelæ vestræ & justitiæ nec non capitale dominium vestri prout alius hactenus Princeps vester liberius habere consuevit. Itá quod vos omnes & singuli cujufcunque extiteritis conditionis pristinis hæreditatibus, terris, libertatibus, possessionibus confuetis, & omnibus conditionibus ad vos expectantibus integré & finaliter gaudeatis. Vestram igitur voluntatem super his, & quibufcunque aliis in quibus vos confolari poterimus, si videatur expediens cauté & celeriter nobis remandetis. Valete Domini in Domino.

But for all that these Letters passed betwixt them, whether by reason that *Bruce's* Terms were conceived unreasonable, nothing however was concluded upon, and the whole Treaty came to nothing. But Sir *Gruffydh*, tho' without any hopes of assistance from the *Scots*, would not lay aside what he had once undertaken, and therefore having gathered all the Forces he could, desperately set upon, and almost in an instant over-ran all *North-Wales* and the *Marches*, seising upon all the Castles and Strong-holds thro' the Country. But all to no purpose, for as the most violent stream is quickly over, so Sir *Gruffydh*'s Army was presently spent, and then being met with by a strong Detachment of *English*, his Party was easily discomfited, and himself taken Prisoner.

The same Year being the 15th. of the reign of King *Edward* the Second, his eldest Son *Edward* born at *Windsor*, in a Parliament holden at *York*, was created Prince of *Wales*, Duke of *Aquitaine*, and Earl of *Chester*. This Prince succeeded his Father in the Kingdom of *England*, by the Name of *Edward* the Third, one of the greatest and most powerful Monarchs that ever sat upon the *English* Throne. 1322.

Edward born at *Woodstock*, eldest Son and Heir to King *Edward* the Third, was created Prince of *Wales*, upon the 12th. day of *May* in the 17th. year of his Father's reign, being then about fourteen years of age. 1343.

age. He was a Prince of incomparable Qualifications, but so signally Famous in Martial Affairs, that upon the account of the several Actions he was engaged in, he received the Name of *Black-Prince*. He took *John* the *French* King Prisoner at the Battel of *Poictiers*, and shamefully vanquished the *French* Army in the Battel of *Cressy*. He did not live to enjoy the Crown, but died one year before his Father, in the Forty Sixth Year of his Age; no Prince was in his life-time better beloved, and after his Death more lamented by the *English* Nation, who had he lived to sit upon the Helm, no one doubted but that he would have exceeded as to all Qualifications, the most glorious Renown of the greatest of his Ancestors.

In the time of *Edward* the Third, lived Sir *Tudor Vaughan ap Grono*, descended lineally from *Ednyfed Vaughan*, a Person as to Estate, Power and Interest, one of the Chiefest in *North Wales*. Upon some motive, either of Ambition or Fancy, he assumed to himself the Honor of Knighthood, requiring all People to call and stile him Sir *Tudor ap Grono*, as if he did prognosticate and fore-see, that out of his Loyns should arise those that should have Power to confer that Honor. King *Edward* being informed of such unparallell'd Presumption, sent for Sir *Tudor*, and asked him, *With what Confidence he durst invade his Prerogative, by assuming the degree of Knighthood, without his Authority.* Sir *Tudor* replied, *That by the Laws and Constitution of King* Arthur, *he had the Liberty of taking upon himself that Title, in regard he had those three Qualifications, which whosoever was endued with, could by those Laws claim the Honor of a Knight.* 1. *He was a Gentleman.* 2. *He had a sufficient Estate.* And 3. *He was Valiant and Adventurous*; adding this withal, *If my Valour and Hardiness be doubted of, loe here I throw down my Glove, and for due proof of my Courage, I am ready to Fight with any Man, whatever he be.* The King appproving and liking well the Man's forwardness and resolution, was easily persuaded to confirm the Honor of
Knighthood

The History of WALES.

Knighthood upon him. From this Sir *Tudor* lineally descended *Henry* the Seventh King of *England*, who was the Son of *Edmund* Earl of *Richmond*, the Son of Sir *Owen Tudor*, Son to *Meredith*, the Son of this Sir *Tudor ap Gono*.

After the Death of the *Black Prince*, his Son *Richard* born at *Bourdeaux* in *France*, being but Ten Years of age, was created Prince of *Wales* at *Havering* at *Bowre*, on the 20th. day of *November*, and in the 50th. Year of *Edward* the Third, his Grandfather's reign, whom he succeeded in the Crown of *England*. 1377.

Henry born at *Monmouth*, Son and Heir to *Henry* the Fourth King of *England*, upon the 15th. of *October*, in the 1st. Year of his Father's reign, was created Prince of *Wales* at *Westminster*, who succeeded his Father in the *English* Crown by the Name of *Henry* the Fifth.

Whilst *Richard* the Second reigned, one *Owen ap Gruffydh Fychan*, descended of a younger Son of *Gruffydh ap Madoc* Lord of *Bromfield* was not a little Famous. This *Owen* had his Education in one of the *Inns-of-Court*, where he became *Barister* at Law, and afterwards in very great Favour and Credit served King *Richard*, and continued with him at *Flint* Castle, till at length the King was taken by *Henry*, Duke of *Lancaster*. Betwixt this *Owen* and *Reginald* Lord *Gray* of *Rhuthyn*, there happened no small Difference touching a Common lying between the Lordship of *Rhuthyn*, whereof *Reginald* was Owner, and the Lordship of *Glyndowrdwy* in the possession of *Owen*, whence he borrowed the Name of *Glyndwr*. During the reign of *Richard* the Second, *Owen* as being a Courtier, and in no mean esteem with the King, did over-power *Reginald*, who was neither so well befriended at Court, nor beloved in the Country as *Owen* was. But after King *Richard's* deposal, the Scene was altered, and *Reginald*, as then better befriended than *Owen*, entred upon the Common, which occasioned *Owen* in the first Year of *Henry* the Fourth to make his Complaint in Parliament against him,

for

The History of WALES.

for thus divesting him of his Right. No redress being found, the Bishop of St. *Asaph* wished the Lords to take care, that by thus slighting his Complaint, they did not irritate and provoke the *Welch* to an Insurrection, to which some of the Lords replied, *That they did not fear those rascally bare-footed People*. *Glyndwr* therefore perceiving how his Petition was slighted in Parliament, and finding no other method to redress himself, having several Friends and Followers, put himself in Arms against *Reginald*, and meeting him in the Field, overcame and took him prisoner, and spoiled his Lordship of *Rhuthyn*. Upon this many resorted to him from all parts of *Wales*, some thinking him to be in as great Favour now, as in King *Richard*'s days, others putting in his head, that now the time was come when the *Britains* by his means might again recover the Honor and Liberties of their Ancestors. But *Reginald* being thus kept prisoner, and very severely handled by *Owen*, to terrify him into compliance with him in his rebellious Actings, and not permitted to have his Liberty, under Ten Thousand Marks for his Ransom, whereof Six Thousand to be paid upon the Feast of St. *Martyn*, in the 4th. Year of *Henry* the Fourth, and to deliver up his eldest Son with some other Persons of Quality as Hostages for the remainder; the King at the humble sute of *Reginald*, seeing no other way for his enlargement, gave way thereto, authorizing Sir *William de Roos*, Sir *Richard de Grey*, Sir *William de Willughby*, Sir *William le Zouche*, Sir *Hugh Huls*, as also, *John Harvey*, *William Vaus*, *John Lee*, *John Langford*, *Thomas Payne*, and *John Elneslow*, to treat with *Owen* and his Council, and to conclude in what they should conceive most expedient and necessary to be done for his redemption. Whereupon they consenting to give the sum demanded by *Glyndwr*. for his deliverance, the King gave Licenfe to *Robert Braybroke* Bishop of *London*, as also to Sir *Gerard Braybroke* the Father, and Sir *Gerard* the Son, then Feoffees of divers Lordships for this *Reginald*, to sell the Mannor of *Hertelegh* in the County of *Kent*, towards the raising of that Money.

The History of WALES.

Money. And for the better enabling him to pay so great a Fine, the King was pleased to grant, that whereas it was enacted, that such Persons who were owners of Lands in *Ireland*, and did not there reside, should for such their neglect, forfeit two parts of the Profits of them to the King; that notwithstanding this Act, he should forfeit nothing for non-residence there, during the term of six years next ensuing.

This good Success over the Lord *Gray*, together with the numerous resort of the *Welch* to him, and the favourable interpretations of the Prophecies of *Merdhyn*, which some construed very advantagiously, made the swelling mind of *Glyndwr* overflow its Banks, and gave him some hopes of restoring this Island back to the *Britains*. Wherefore he set upon the Earl of *March*, who met him with a numerous party of *Hereford-shire* Men, but when they came to close, the *Welch*-men proved too powerful, and having killed above a Thousand Men of the *English*, they took the Earl of *March* Prisoner. King *Henry* upon this was frequently requested to Ransom the Earl, but to no purpose; for whether by reason that *Mortimer* had a juster Title to the Crown than himself, he being the next Heir in Blood after King *Richard*, who was as yet living, or because of some other private *odium*, the King would never hearken to his Redemption, alledging that he wilfully threw himself into the hands of *Glyndwr*. But about the midst of *August*, to correct the presumptuous Attempts of the *Welch*, the King went in Person with a great Army into *Wales*; but by reason of extraordinary excess of weather, which some attributed to the Magic of *Glyndwr*, he was glad to return safe.

But the Earl of *March* perceiving that he was not like to obtain his Liberty by King *Henry*'s means, whether out of compliance, by reason of his tedious Captivity, or Affection to the young Lady, he agreed to take part with *Owen* against the King of *England*, and to marry his Daughter; with them joyned the Earl of *Worcester*, and his Brother the Earl of *Northumberland*, with his Son the valiant Lord *Percy*, who
conspiring

conspiring to depose the King of *England*, in the House of the Archdeacon of *Bangor*, by their Deputies divided the Realm amongst them, causing a tripartite Indenture to be made, and to be sealed with every one's Seal; by which Covenant all that Country lying betwixt the *Severn* and the *Trent*, *Southward*, was assigned to the Earl of *March*; all *Wales*, and the Lands beyoud the *Severn*, *Westward*, were appointed *Glyndwr*; and all from the *Trent*, *Northward*, to the Lord *Percy*. This was done (as some said) thro' a foolish Credit they gave to a vain Prophecy, as tho' King *Henry* was the execrable Moldwarp, and they three the Dragon, the Lion, and the Wolf which should pull him down, and distribute his Kingdom among themselves. After that they exhibited Articles of their Grievances to King *Henry*, and divulged their Reasons for taking up Arms; at length they marched with all their Power towards *Shrewsbury* to fight the King, depending mainly upon the arrival of *Glyndwr* and his *Welch-men*. But the matter was gone so far, that whether he came in or no, they must fight, and so both Armies being joyned, the King's Party prevailed, young *Percy* being slain upon the spot, and *Douglas*, besides most of the *English* of Quality, who with a Party of *Scotch* had come to the Aid of the Confederates, was taken Prisoner, but afterwards honourably set at Liberty by the Intercession of the Prince of *Wales*. In the mean time the Earl of *Northumberland* was a marching forward with a great Party from the *North*, but the King having settled Matters about *Shrewsbury*, coming to *York*, and sending to him to lay down his Arms, he voluntarily submitted and dismissed his Forces. Then the King returning from *York-shire*, determined to pass over to *North-Wales*, to chastise the presumptuous Practices of the immorigerous *Welch*, who after his departure from *Shrewsbury*, had made inRoads into the Marches, and done much hurt to his *English* Subjects. But other Business of greater Consequence intervening, he detached his Son the Prince of *Wales*, who took the Castle of *Aberystwyth*,

which

The History of WALES.

which was quickly again retaken by *Owen Glyndwr*, who thrust into it a strong Garrison of *Welch*. But in the Battel of *Huske* fought upon the fifteenth of *March*, the *Welch* received a very considerable Blow from the Prince's Men, *Glyndwr*'s Son being taken Prisoner, besides Fifteen Hundred more taken and slain. After this, we hear little of *Glyndwr*, excepting that he continued and persisted to vex and plague the *English* upon the Marches, to the tenth year of King *Henry*'s reign, when he miserably ended his life; being as *Holingshed* reporteth, towards his *Holinsf.* latter days driven to that extremity, that despairing of all comfort, he fled and lurked in Caves and other the most solitary places, fearing to shew his face to any Creature, till at length being starved for hunger and lack of sustenance, he miserably ended his life.

But these rebellious Practices of *Glyndwr*, highly exasperated King *Henry* against the *Welch*, insomuch that several rigorous and unmerciful Laws were enacted, relating to *Wales*, which in effect destroyed all the Liberties of the *Welch* Subject. They were made incapable of purchasing any Lands, or to be elected Members of any County or Burrough, and to undertake any Office, whether Civil or Military in any Town incorporated. If any Suit at Law happened betwixt an *English* Man and a *Welch* Man, the former could not be convicted, but by the Sentence of an *English* Judge, and the Verdict of an *English* Jury; besides, that any *English* Man who married a *Welch* Woman, was thereby forthwith disfranchised from all the Liberties of an *English* Subject. It was farther enacted, that no *Welch* Man should be in possession of any Castle, or other place of Strength, and that no Victuals or Armour should be brought into *Wales*, without a special Warrant from the King or his Council; and farther, that no *Welch* Man was capable of undertaking the Office of Justice, Chamberlain, Sheriff or any other place of Trust in any part of *Wales*, notwithstanding any Patent

or

or Licenſe heretofore given to the contrary. Theſe, with many others moſt rigorous and unjuſt Laws, particularly that forbidding any *Welch* Man to bring up his Children to Learning, or to bind them Apprentices to any Trade or Occupation, were enacted by the King againſt the *Welch*; ſo that nothing could cool his diſpleaſure, but that a whole Nation ſhould be wrongfully oppreſſed, for the fault and miſcarriage of one Perſon. But one might think, that this was no politick method to ſecure a Nation in its Allegiance, which upon lighter Affronts was uſed to defend its Priviledges; and therefore we may well attribute the quiet diſpoſition of the *Welch* towards this time, to the moderation of *Henry* the Fifth, who within a little time ſucceeded his Father in the Crown of *England*.

Co-temporary with *Glyndwr* was Sir *David Gam*, ſo called by reaſon he had but one Eye, the Son of *Lhewelyn ap Howel Vaughan* of *Brecknock*, by *Mawd* the Daughter of *Iefan ap Rhys ap Ifor* of *Eluel*. He was a great ſtickler for the Duke of *Lancaſter*, and for that reaſon became mortal Enemy to *Glyndwr*, who having his Education, as is ſaid before, at one of the Inns of Court, got to be preferred to the ſervice of King *Richard* the Second, who, as *Walſingham* ſays, made him his *Scutifer*, or Shield-bearer. But being informed that his Maſter *Richard* was depoſed and murdered, and withal being provoked by ſeveral Wrongs and Affronts done him by his Neighbour the Lord *Gray* of *Rhuthyn*, whom King *Henry* greatly countenanced, and looking upon *Henry* as an Uſurper, he cauſed himſelf to be proclaimed Prince of *Wales*. And for a better grace of the matter, he feigned himſelf to be deſcended by a Daughter from *Lhewelyn ap Gruffydh* the laſt Prince; whereas in truth, he came Paternally but from a younger Brother of the Houſe of *Powys*. But as Ambition has no moderation, ſo *Glyndwr* for a time acted the part of a Prince, and ſummoned a Parliament to meet at *Machynlleth*, whither the Nobility and Gentry of *Wales* appeared,

The History of WALES.

peared, and among the rest Sir *David Gam*, but not upon the same design with the rest, having an intention in this meeting to murder *Glyndyfwr*. But the Plot being discovered, and Sir *David* secured, he had liked to undergo present Execution, had not *Glyndyfwr's* best Friends, and the greatest Upholders of his Cause, pleaded in his behalf, by whose intercession he was prevailed with to grant Sir *David* both his Life and Liberty, upon condition he would ever after continue True and Loyal to him. Sir *David* promised very loudly, but with the reservation never to perform; for as soon as he came to his own Country, where he was a Person of very considerable Sway and Interest, he did exceedingly annoy and molest those that any way favoured or adhered to *Glyndyfwr*. While Sir *David* lay in Prison at *Machynlleth*, for his attempt against *Owen's* Life, this *Englyn* was made upon him.

Dafydd Gam dryglam dreigl, iti yn wan frwydr,
Fradwr Riffiart Bhrenin,
Llwyr y rhoes Diawl (hawn hwyl Flin
Y fath ystâd) ei fys ith Din.

But *Glyndyfwr* receiving information, how that Sir *David Gam*, contrary to the Promise he had made at his releasement, endeavoured all he could to destroy his Interest among the *Welch*, entred the Marches, and among other tokens of his Indignation, burned the House of Sir *David*, and as the report goes, calling to him one of Sir *David's* Tenants, spake to him thus merrily in Verse,

O Gweli di wr côch Cam
Yn ymofyn y Girnigwen
Dywed ei bôd hi Tan y Lan
A nôd y glo ar ei Phenn.

But Sir *David* had the luck to escape his reach, and was constrained to retire to *England*, where he lived for the moſt part at Court, till the Death of *Glyndyfwr*.

When King *Henry* the Fifth went with an Army to *France* againſt the *French* King, Sir *David Gam* brought into his ſervice a numerous Party of Stout and Valorous *Welch*-Men, who upon all occaſions expreſſed their Courage and Reſolution. In the Battel of *Agincourt*, News being brought to the King that the *French* Army was advancing towards him, and that they were exceeding numerous, he detached Captain *Gam* to obſerve their motion, and review their number. The Captain having narrowly eyed the *French* found them twice to exceed the *Engliſh*, but not being in the leaſt daunted at ſuch a multitude, he returned to the King, who enquiring of him what the Number of the *French* might be, he made anſwer, *An't pleaſe you my Liege, they are enough to be killed, enough to run away, and enough to be taken Priſoners*. King *Henry* was well pleaſed, and much encouraged with this reſolute and undaunted anſwer of Sir *David's*, whoſe Tongue did not expreſs more Valor than his Hands performed. For in the heat of Battel, the King's Perſon being in danger, Sir *David* charged the Enemy with that eagerneſs and maſculine Bravery, that they were glad to give ground, and ſo ſecured the King, tho' with the loſs of much Blood, and alſo his Life, himſelf and his Son-in-Law *Roger Vaughan*, and his Kinſman *Walter Llwyd* of *Brecknock*, having received their mortal Wounds in that encounter. When the King heard of their Condition, how that they were paſt all hopes of recovery, he came to them, and in recompence of their good Services, Knighted them all three in the Field where they ſoon after died; and ſo ended the Life, but not the Fame of the ſignally Valiant Sir *David Gam*.

Edward

Edward of *Westminster*, the sole Issue of that unfortunate Prince King *Henry* the Sixth, by *Margaret* the Daughter of *Rayner* Duke of *Anjou*, and titular King of *Jerusalem*, *Sicily*, and *Arragon*; was created Prince of *Wales*, in a Parliament held at *Westminster*, on the 15th day of *March*, in the Thirty Second Year of his Fathers Reign. When the Day was lost at *Tewksbury*, this young Prince thought to make his escape by flight, but being unfortunately taken, and brought to the presence of King *Edward* the Fourth, who then sat upon the Helm, made such resolute and unexpected Replies, that he put the King to such a passion, that he smote him on the Mouth with his Gauntlet; and then his Brother *Richard* the Crouch-back, ran him into the Heart with his Dagger.

Edward, born in the Sanctuary at *Westminster*, the eldest Son of King *Edward* the Fourth, was, after his Fathers Expulsion out of *England*, in the Fourty Ninth Year of King *Henry* the Sixth, created Prince of *Wales* and Earl of *Chester*, in the Eleventh Year of his Fathers Reign. Upon the death of *Edward* the Fourth, this young Prince being then at *Ludlow* in the *Marches* of *Wales*, was presently sent for to *London*, and proclaimed King of *England*, but never liv'd to be crowned; for his Uncle *Richard* Duke of *Glocester*, who was appointed his Protector, most vilainously made him away, together with his Brother the Duke of *York*; and afterwards was himself proclaimed and crowned King.

Edward the Fourth, in his Wars against *Henry* the Sixth, was very much assisted by the *Welch*; in recompence of which Service, he design'd to reform Matters so in *Wales*, as that intolerable Oppression which they had hitherto endured, should be regulated and taken off. And to that end, he meant to establish a Court within the said Principality; and constituted *John* Bishop of *Worcester* President of the Prince's Council in the *Marches*; who, together with *Anthony* Earl of *Rivers*, sat in the Town-Hall of *Shrewsbury*, and constituted certain Ordinances for

X x the

The History of WALES.

the publick Good and Tranquility of that place. But the matter proceeded no farther; for the Troubles and Disquietness of his Kingdom, coming heavy upon him, and the shortness of his Reign after his Establishment not permitting, he was forced to leave that to others, which himself thought once to bring about.

Edward, born at *Middleham* near *Richmond* in the County of *York*, the only Son of King *Richard* the Third, was at Ten Years of Age created by his Father Prince of *Wales*, and dyed soon after.

Arthur, the eldest Son of King *Henry* the Seventh, born at *Winchester*, was in the Seventh Year of his Fathers Reign created Prince of *Wales*. About the Fifteenth Year of his Age, being then newly married to *Katherine* the Infanta of *Spain*, he was sent by his Father into *Wales*, that by his presence he might keep that Country in better awe. With him King *Henry* sent Dr. *William Smith*, afterwards made Bishop of *Lincoln*, as President of his Council; together with Sir *Richard Pool*, his Chamberlain, Sir *Henry Vernon*, Sir *Richard Crofts*, Sir *David Philip*, Sir *William Udal*, Sir *Thomas Englefield*, Sir *Peter Newton*, and others, to be his Counsellors and Directors in his management of Affairs. But the Prince had not continu'd long there, but he fell sick at his Castle at *Ludlow*, of which Indisposition he shortly after dyed, and was buried with great Solemnity in the Cathedral Church of *Worcester*. But the creating of his Brother *Henry* Duke of *York* Prince of *Wales* in his stead, was deferred for about the space of a Month, to discover whether the Lady *Katherine* was got with Child by Prince *Arthur*. But when it appeared for certain, she had not conceived; on the 18th day of *February*, in the Nineteenth Year of his Father, King *Henry* the Seventh's Reign, *Henry* Duke of *York* was created Prince of *Wales*.

King *Henry* the Seventh, being by his Grandfather *Owen Tudor* descended out of *Wales*, and having sufficiently experienced the Affection of the *Welch* towards him; first, of those, who upon his first landing,

Wokins p. 789.

The History of WALES.

ing, opportunely joyned him under Sir *Rhys ap Thomas*; and then of those, who under the command of Sir *William Stanley*, Lord of *Bromfield, Yale,* and *Chirkland*, aided him in *Bosworth*-Field; could not in Honour and Equity, but bear some regard to the miserable state and condition of the *Welch*, under the *English* Government. And therefore this prudent Prince, finding the Calamities of the *Welch* to be insupportable, and seeing what grievous and unmerciful Laws were enacted against them by his Predecessours, he took occasion to redress and reform the same, and granted to the *Welch* a Charter of Liberty and Immunity, whereby they were released from the cruel Oppression, which since their Subjection to the *English* Government, they had most cruelly sustained. And seeing the Birth and Quality of his Grandfather *Owen Tudor* was called in question, and that he was by many upbraided of being of a mean and ignoble Parentage; King *Henry* directed a Commission to the Abbot of *Lhan Egwest*, Dr. *Owen Pool* Canon of *Hereford*, and *John King* Herald at Arms, to make inquisition concerning the Pedigree of the said *Owen*; who coming to *Wales*, made a diligent enquiry into this matter; and by the assistance of Sir *John Leyaf*, *Guttyn Owen Bardh*, *Gruffydh ap Lhewelyn ap Efan Fychan*, and others, in the consultation of the *British* Books of Pedigrees, they drew up an exact Genealogy of *Owen Tudor*, which upon their return, they presented to the King. *Vide Append.*

Edward, Son to *Henry* the Eighth, by the Lady *Jane Seymour*, his third Wife, was born at *Hampton-Court*, on the 12th of *October*; and upon the 18th. of the said Month, was created Prince of *Wales*, Duke of *Cornwal*, and Earl of *Chester*.

King *Henry* the Seventh, had already abrogated those unreasonable and intollerable Laws, which the former Kings of *England*, particularly *Henry* the Fourth, had made against the *Welch*; and now, King *Henry* the Eighth, willing to make a plenary Reformation of what his Father had wisely begun, thought it necessary towards the Good and Tranquility

lity of both Nations, to make the *Welch* subject to the same Laws, and the same Government with the *English*. He understood that the usual Hostilities and Depredations were still continued and kept up by both sides upon the Borders; and though his Father had eased the Yoak of the *Welch*, yet he perceived, that it did contribute but little towards the disannulling of that inveterate and implacable Envy and Animosity which raged in the Marches. Therefore to remedy this, otherwise unavoidable, Distemper, he concluded that it was the only effectual Method, to incorporate the *Welch* with the *English*; that they being subject to the same Laws, might equally fear the Violation of them. And accordingly, in the Twenty Seventh Year of his Reign, an Act of Parliament passed to that purpose, which together with another Act in the Thirty Fifth of his Reign, made a plenary Incorporation of the *Welch* with the *English*, which Union has had that blessed Effect, that it has dispelled all those unnatural Differences which heretofore were so rife and irreconcilable.

A. D.
1536.

When the Reformation was first established in *Wales*, it was a mighty Inconveniency to the vulgar People, such as were unacquainted with the *English* Tongue, that the Bible was not translated into their native Language. Queen *Elizabeth* was quickly apprehensive of the Inconveniency which the *Welch* incurred, for the want of such a Translation; and therefore, in the Eighth Year of her Reign, an Act of Parliament was passed, whereby the Bishops of *Hereford*, S. *Davids*, S. *Asaph*, *Bangor*, and *Landaff*, were ordered to take care that the Bible containing the Old and New Testament, with the Book of Common-Prayer, and Administration of the Sacraments, be truly and exactly translated into the *British* or *Welch* Tongue, and that the same so translated, being by them perused and approved, be printed to such a number at least; as that every Cathedral, Collegiate and Parish-Church and Chappel of ease within the said Diocess where that Tongue is vulgarly spoken, might be supplyed before the First of *March*, *Anno*

1566.

Anno 1566. And from that time forward, the *Welch* Divine Service should be used in the *British* Tongue, in all places throughout those Dioceses, where the *Welch* is commonly spoke, after the same manner as it was used in the *English* Tongue; and that the Charge of procuring the said Bible and Common-Prayer, should equally depend betwixt the Parson and the Parish; the former being obliged to pay one half of the Expence; and that the Price of the Book should be set by the foresaid Bishops, or by Three of them at the least. But this Act of Parliament was not punctually observed; for the Old Testament was wholly omitted, and only the New, with the Book of Common-Prayer and Administration of the Sacraments, then translated, which Translation was chiefly owing to Richard Bishop of S. *Davids*, who was assisted by *William Salusbury*, a Perfect Critick in the *Welch* Tongue, and one excellently conversant in all *British* Antiquities. But in the Year 1588. Dr. *William Morgan*, first Bishop of *Landaff*, and then of S. *Asaph*, undertook the Translation of the whole Bible; and by the help of the Bishops of S. *Asaph* and *Bangor*, *Gabriel Goodman* Dean of *Westminster*, *David Powell*, D.D. *Edmund Price* Archdeacon of *Merionyth*, and *Richard Vaughan*, he effectually finished it. This was of singular Profit and Advantage to the *Welch*, to have the whole Scripture read and perused in their own native Tongue; by which means they received a clearer demonstration of the Corruptions of the Church of *Rome*, when they saw many of their Principles apparently contradicting, and others not very firmly founded upon the Holy Scriptures. And on the other hand they perceived the Necessity and Advantage of the Reformation, they easily discovered that the whole Doctrine of the Church of *England* was found and orthodox, and that they were now happily delivered from that Popish Slavery which their Forefathers ignorantly adored; and therefore being convinced of the Truth of their Religion, they became, and continued generally, very strict Adherents and firm Observers of the Doctrine and Discipline of this Church.

The History of WALES.

And here by the bye, I cannot but observe what a reverend Writer has lately infinuated, relating to the Chriſtian Religion planted in *Wales*. For that Learned Perſon in his Funeral Sermon upon Mr. *Gouge*, would fain induce the World to believe, that Chriſtianity was very corrupt and imperfect among the *Welch*, before it was purifyed by that, whom he terms Apoſtolical Man. Whereas it is notoriouſly evident, that ſince the Reformation was ſetled in that Country, and the Bible, with the Book of Common-Prayer, tranſlated into the *Welch* Tongue, no place has been more exact, in keeping to the ſtrict Rubrick and Conſtitution of the Church of *England*, both as to the Subſtance and Form of Worſhip. But what may more truly be attributed to Mr. *Gouge*, is that ſince his Travels into *Wales*, and the propagating of his Doctrine among the ignorant of that Country, Presbytery, which before had ſcarce taken root, has daily increaſed, and grown to a Head.

Henry, eldeſt Son of King *James* the Firſt, being arrived to the Age of Seventeen Years, was created Prince of *Wales*, on the 30th. of *May, Anno* 1610. but he dying of a malignant Feaver, about Two Years after; his Brother *Charles* being Fifteen Years of Age, was created Prince of *Wales* in his room, *Anno* 1615. For joy of this new Creation, the Town of *Ludlow*, and City of *London*, performed very great Triumphs; and the more to honour this Solemnity, the King made Twenty Five Knights of the Bath, all Lords or Barons Sons; and the Inns of Court, to expreſs their Joy, elected out of their Body Forty choice Gentlemen, to perform ſolemn Juſts and Barryers.

Charles, eldeſt Son of King *Charles* the Firſt, by *Henrietta Maria*, Daughter to King *Henry* the Fourth of *France*, was born *May* 29. 1630. and afterwards created Prince of *Wales*.

Since the happy Incorporation of the *Welch* with the *Engliſh*, the Hiſtory of both Nations, as well as the People is united; and therefore I ſhall not repeat that which is ſo copiouſly and frequenty delivered

vered by the *English* Historians; but shall conclude with Dr. *Heylyn, That since the* Welch *have been incorporated with the* English, *they have shewed themselves most loyal, hearty, and affectionate Subjects of the State; cordially devoted to their King, and zealous in Defence of their Laws, Liberties, and Religion, as well as any of the best of their Fellow-Subjects.*

APPENDIX.

APPENDIX.

The return of a Commiſſion *ſent into* Wales *by* King Henry *the Seventh, to ſearch out the Pedigrees of* Owen Tudor.

HENRY the Seventh King of *England, &c.* Son of *Edmund* Earl of *Richmond,* Son of *Owen ap Meredith,* and of Queen *Catherine* his Wife, Daughter to *Charles* the Sixth, King of *France.* This *Owen* was Son of *Meredith ap Tudor ap Gronw ap Tudor, ap Gronw, ap Ednyfed Fychan,* Baron of *Brinfeingle* in *Denbigh* Land, Lord of *Kriceth,* Chief Juſtice and Chief of Council to *Llewelyn ap Iorwerth Drwyndwn* Prince of all *Wales.* And in the time of Prince *Llewelyn* grew a Variance between King *John* of *England* and the ſaid Prince ; whereupon *Ednyfed* came with the Prince's Hoſt, and Men of War, and alſo a number of his own People, and met theſe *Engliſh* Lords in a Morning, at what time theſe *Engliſh* Lords were hoſtied and ſlain ; and immediately brought their Heads, being yet bloody to the ſaid Prince *Llewelyn.* The Prince, ſeeing the ſame, cauſed *Ednyfed Fychan,*

Fychan, from thenceforth to bear in his Arms or Shield, three bloody Heads in token of his Victory, where he had born in his Arms before a *Saracen*'s Head; and so ever after this *Ednyfed* bore the said Arms, his Son, and his Son's Son, unto the time of *Tudor ap Gronw, ap Tudor ap Gronw, ap Ednyfed Fychan*. And after this *Ednyfed* wedded one *Gwenllian* Daughter to *Rhys* Prince of *South Wales*, and had Issue by her *Gronw*: which *Ednyfed Fychan* had in *Wales* divers goodly Houses, Royally adorn'd with Turrets and Garrets; some in *Anglesey*, some other in *Caernarvon-shire*, and and some in *Denbigh*-Land; but his chiefest Mannor-House was in the Commot of *Crythin* in *Caernarvon-shire*, which was a Royal Palace, now decay'd for want of Reparations. Also he builded there a Chappel in the Worship of our Lady, and had Licence of the Pope for evermore to sing Divine Service therein for his Soul, and his Ancestors and Progenitors Souls always; and had Authority to give his Tythes and Offerings to his Chaplain there * starving; which *Ednyfed Fychan* was Son to *Kyner ap Iers ap Gwgan, ap Marchudd*, which was one of the fifteen Tribes of *North-Wales*, and Son to *Kynan ap Elfyn, ap Mor, ap Mynan, ap Isbwis Newintyrche, ap Isbwis ap Cadrod Calch Efynydd*, Earl of *Dunstable* and Lord of *Northampton, ap Cywyd Cindion, ap Cynfelyn ap Arthuys, ap Morydd ap Cynnaw, ap Coel Godeboc* King of *Britain*, of whom King *Henry* the Seventh descended lineally by Issue-Male, and is Son to the said *Coel* in the thirty first Degree, as it is approved by old Chronicles in *Wales*. Which

Coel

* *Vid.* an serving.

APPENDIX. 333

Coel was Son of *Tegfan* ap *Debeufraint,* ap *Tudbwyl,* ap *Urban,* ap *Gradd,* ap *Rhyfedel,* ap *Rhydeirne,* ap *Endigant,* ap *Endeyrn,* ap *Enid,* ap *Endos,* ap *Enddolaw,* ap *Afalach,* ap *Afflech,* ap *Beli mawr* King of *Britain,* of whom King *Henry* the Seventh defcendeth by Iſſue-Male, and is Son to him in forty one Degree. Which *Beli* was Son to *Monnogon* King, ap King *Kaxor,* ap King *Pyr,* ap King *Sawl Beniſſel,* ap *Rhytherech* King, ap *Rydion* King, ap *Eidol* King, ap *Arthafel* King, ap *Seiſſilt* King, ap *Owen* King, ap *Caxhc* King, ap *Bleuddyd* King, ap *Meirion* King, ap *Gwrguſt* King, ap *Elydno* King, ap *Clydawc* King, ap *Ithel* King, ap *Urien* King, ap *Andrew* King, ap *Kereni* King, ap *Porrex* King, ap *Coel* King, ap *Cadell* King, ap *Geraint* King, ap *Elidr* King, ap *Morydd* King, ap *Dan* King, ap *Seiſſilt* King, ap *Cybelyn* King, ap *Gwrgan* King (alias) *Farfdrwch,* ap *Beli* King, ap *Dyfnwal* King, ap *Dodion* King, ap *Enyd,* ap *Kwrwyd,* ap *Cyrdon* ap *Dyfufarth Prydain,* ap *Aedd mawr,* ap *Antonius* ap *Seiſillt* King, ap *Rhegaw* Daughter and Heir of King *Lyr,* and Wife of *Henwin* Prince of *Cornwall.* This *Lyr* was Son of *Bleuddyd,* ab *Rhunbaladr brâs,* ap *Lleon,* ap *Brutus darian lâs,* ap *Effroc Cadarn,* ap *Mymbyr,* ap *Madoc,* ap *Locrine,* ap *Brutus* which inherited firſt this Land, and after his Name was called *Britain,* and had three Sons *Locrine Kamber,* and *Albanactus.* *Locrine* the eldeſt, parted the Iſle with his Brethren, and kept half the Land for himſelf, and called it *Loegria.* *Kamber* ſecond Son had the Land beyond *Severn,* and named it *Kambria,* in *Engliſh, Wales. Albanactus* had *Scotland,* which he then
called

called *Albania* after his own Name. Of which *Brute* King *Henry* the Seventh is lineally defcended by Iffue-Male, faving one Woman, and is Son to *Brute* in five fcore Degrees.

How Owen *Grandfire to King* Henry *the Seventh, cometh of* Beli mawr *by* Angharad, *Mother to* Ednyfed *by Iffue-Female, by* Gittin, Owen, *and Sir* John Leiaf's *Books*.

THE Mother of *Ednyfed* was *Angharad*, Daughter of *Hwfa, ap Cyner, ap Rhywallon, ap Dinged, ap Tudor Trefor, ap Mymbyr, ap Cadfarch, ap Gwrgenaw, ap Gwaethiawc, ap Bywyn, ap Biordderch, ap Gwriawn, ap Gwnnan, ap Gwnfiw frych, ap Cadell Deburnlluc, ap Pafgan, ap Rhydwf, ap Rhudd Fedel frych, ap Cyndeirn, ap Gwrtheirn Gwrthenau,* called in Englifh *Vortiger*, by whom King *Henry* the Seventh, by the forefaid *Angharad*, Mother to *Ednyfed Fychan*, and Wife to *Cyner ab Iers, ap Gwgon*, is Son to the faid *Vortiger* in thirty Degrees. Which *Vortiger* was Son to *Rhydeyrn ap Debeufraint, ap Eidigant, ap Endeirn, ap Enid, ap Endos, ap Enddolau, ap Afallach, ap Afflech, ap Beli mawr*, to whom King *Henry* the Seventh is Son by *Angharad*, Mother to *Ednyfed Fychan* in forty Degrees.

How King Henry *the Seventh cometh of* Beli mawr *by* Gwenllian *Wife to* Ednyfed Fychan, *and Daughter to the Lord* Rhys, *called* Arglwydd Rhys, *by Iffue-Female*.

Owen ap Meredith ap Tudor ap Gronw, ap Tudor, ap Gronw, ap Gwenllian, Daughter to
Rhys

APPENDIX.

Rhys Prince of *South Wales*, ap *Gruffydh* Prince, ap *Rhys* Prince, ap *Tudor mawr* Prince, ap *Cadell* Prince, ap *Rodri mawr* Prince of all *Wales*. This *Rodri* had three Sons, and divided the Principality of *Wales* between them in three Parts; to *Merfyn* his firſt Son, Prince of *North-Wales*, all *North-Wales*, which died without Iſſue; and *Anarawd* Prince of *Powys*, and *Cadell* Prince of *South-Wales*, of whom King *Henry* the Seventh deſcendeth, by *Gwenllian* Daughter to Prince *Rhys*, called Arglwydd *Rhys*, Wife to *Ednyfed Fychan*; and the ſaid King *Henry* the Seventh is Son to *Rodri mawr* in the ſeventeenth Degree; which *Rodri mawr* was Son to *Merfyn* firſt King of *Man*, which wedded *Eſſillt* Daughter and Heir to *Cynan Dyndaethwy*.

This *Merfyn frych* was Son to *Gwriad ap Elidur*, ap *Handdear Alcwn*, ap *Tegid*, ap *Gwiar*, ap *Dwywc*, ap *Llywarch hên*, ap *Elidur Lydanwin*, ap *Meirchion*, ap *Grwſt*, ap *Cenaw*, ap *Coel Godeboc* King of *Britain*, as before. This *Coel* was King of *Britain* and Earl of *Colcheſter*, a right worthy King, to whom King *Henry* the Seventh is Son, by the ſaid *Gwenllian* Wife to *Ednyfed Fychan*, in the thirty firſt Degree, by the ſaid *Gittin Owen*, and Sir *John Leia's* Books.

How Owen *Grandſire to King* Henry *the Seventh cometh of* Beli mawr, *by* Eſſillt *Daughter to* Cynan Dyndaethwy.

Owen ap *Meredith* ap *Tudor* ap *Gronw*, ap *Tudor* ap *Gronw*, ap *Gwenllian* Daughter of Prince *Rhys*, ap *Gruffydh* ap *Rhys*, ap *Tudor mawr*, ap *Engion*, ab *Owen*, ap *Howell Dda*,

ap

ap Cadell, ap Rodri mawr, ap Effillt Daughter of *Cynan Dyndaethwy* and Heir, Prince of *Wales, ap Rodri Moelwynoc, ap Idwal jwrch, ap Cadwalader Fendigaid* King of all *Britain*, to whom King *Henry* the Seventh is Son in the twenty fecond Degree. *Cadwalader* was Son to *Cadwallan* King, *ap Cadfan* King, *ap Iago, ap Beli, ap Rhun, ap Maelgwn Gwynedd* King, *ap Caffwallan Lawhir, ap Eineon irth, ap Cynedda weledig, ap Edeirn*, which wedded *Gwawl, Ferch Coel Godeboc* King, which *Edeirn* was Son to *Padarn Peifrydd, ap Tegid, ap Iago, ap Genedawc, ap Cain, ap Gwrgain, ap Doli, ap Gwrtholi, ap. Dufu, ap Gorddufu, ap Amwerid, ap Omwedd, ap Diwc Brichwain, ap Owen, ap Affallach, ap Afflech, ap Beli mawr*, to whom King *Henry* the Seventh is Son by the faid *Gwenllian* in the fiftieth Degree.

Owen ap Meredith ap Tudor ap Gronw, ap Tudor ap Gronw, ap Gwenllian, Daughter to *Arglwydd Rhys*, Son to *Gwenllian* Daughter of *Gruffydh* Prince, *ap Cynan* Prince of *North-Wales*, Son of *Iago* Prince, *ap Idwall* Prince, *ap Meuric* Prince, *ap Idwall Foel* Prince, *ap Anarawd* Prince, *ap Rodri mawr* Prince of all *Wales*, to whom King *Henry* the Seventh is Son by *Gwenllian* Mother to the *Arglwydd Rhys* in the feventeenth Degree.

Owen ap Meredith ap Tudor ap Gronw, ap Tudor, ap Gronw, ap Gwenllian, Ferch Arglwydd Rhys, ap Gwladis, Ferch Rhywallon ap Cynfyn Prince of *Powys*, and *Angharad* Wife to *Cynfyn*, Daughter and Heir to *Meredith* Prince of *Powys*, Son of *Owen* Prince of *Powys* and *South-Wales*, Son to *Cadell* Prince there. Which *Owen*

APPENDIX.

Owen ap Howell dda, had two Sons, *Meredith* and *Eineon*, and *Owen* their Father gave the Principality of *South-Wales* to *Eineon* his Son, and the Principality of *Powys* to *Meredith* his other Son. Which *Meredith* had Issue *Angharad*, that wedded *Cynfyn*, by whom he was Prince of *Powys*, which *Cadell* was Son to *Rodri mawr* Prince of all *Wales*, Son to *Merfyn frych*, &c. to *Beli mawr*, as above written by *Guttin Owen*'s Book.

Owen ap Meredith ap Tudor ap Gronw, ap Tudor, ap Gronw, ap Gwenllian, Ferch Arglwydd Rhys, ap Gruffydh, ap Rhys, ap Tudor, ap Eineon, ap Eineon, ap Howell Dda, ap Cadell, ap Angharad, Wife to *Rodri mawr*, Daughter to *Meyric ap Dyfnwal, ap Arthen, ap Seiffillt, ap Clydawc, ap Artholes, ap Arnothen, ap Brothan, ap Seirwell, ap Uffa, ap Caredic, ap Cwnedda weledic, ap Edeirn, ap Padarn Peifrydd*, which *Edeirn* wedded *Gwawl ferch Coel Godeboc*, Mother to *Cwnedda weledyc*, &c.

How Owen *cometh of* Meuryc *Lord of* Gwent, *by* Morfydd's *Daughter, Wife to* Gronw ap Ednyfed Fychan.

Owen ap Meredith ap Tudor ap Gronw, ap Tudor, ap Morfydd, Ferch Meuryc L. *of Gwent.*

How Owen *cometh of* Rodri mawr, *by* Angharad, *Daughter to* Ithel Fychan, ap Ithel Llwyd, *and Wife of* Tudor ap Gronw, ap Ednyfed Fychan.

Owen ap Meredith ap Tudor ap Gronw, ap Angharad, ferch Ithel Fychan, ap Ithel Llwyd, ap

APPENDIX.

Ithel Gam, ap *Meredith* ap *Vchdrud*, ap *Edwin* King of *Tegengle* in *Flintshire*.

How Owen *cometh of* Rodri mawr *by* Adleis, *Wife to* Ithel Fychan, Daughter *to* Ricart.

Owen ap Meredith ap Tudor ap Gronw, *ap Angharad Ferch Adleis* Wife to *Ithel Fychan*, Daughter to *Ricart, ap Cadwalader, ap Gruffydh, ap Kynan* Prince of *North-Wales*, *ap Iago*, *ap Idwal Foel, ap Anarawd, ap Rodri Mawr*, &c. All this by *Gyttin Owen's* Book.

How Owen *cometh of* Beli Mawr *by* Gwerfill Ferch Madawc, o'r hên dwr, *Wife to* Gronw ap Tudor, ap Gronw, ap Ednyfed Fychan.

Owen ap Meredith ap Tudor ap Gwerfill Ferch Madawc o'r hên dwr, ap Iers, ap Madawc, ap Meredith, ap Bleddyn, ap Kynfin Prince of *Powis*, &c. and so to *Beli Mawr*.

How Owen *cometh to* Beli Mawr *by the Mother of the said* Gwerfill Ferch Madawc.

Owen ap Meredith, ap Tudor, ap Gwerfill Ferch Madawc o'r hên dwr, ap Lleucu Ferch Angharad, Ferch Meredith, ap Madawc, ap Gruffudh Maelor Prince of *Powis*. This *Madawc ap Gruffudh Maelor*, builded the Abby of *Vala-crucis*, in *Welsh, Manachlog Llan Egwestl*, the Year of our Lord 1200. and lyeth there buried, and this *Gruffudh Maelor* was Son to *Madawc, ap Meredith, ap Bleddin, ap Cynfin, ap Gweristan, ap Gwalthfoed, ap Gwrydor, ap Cariadawc, ap Lles Llaw Ddeawc, ap Edwal, ap Gwyn-*

APPENDIX.

Gwnnan, *ap Gwnnawc Parf Sych*, *ap Keidic*, *ap Corf*, *ap Cadnawc*, *ap Tegonwy*, *ap Teon*, *ap Gwinaf Daufreuddwyd*, *ap Powyr lêw*, *ap Bywdec*, *ap Rhun rhudd baladr*, *ap Llary*, *ap Casfar Wledic*, *ap Lludd*, *ap Beli Mawr* King of all *England* and *Wales*, to whom King *Henry* the Seventh is Son this way by *Ludd* in 36 degrees.

How Owen *cometh to* Beli Mawr *by the Mothers side of* Gwerfill Ferch Madawc.

Owen *ap Meredith, ap Tudor, ap Gwerfill Ferch Eva, Ferch Llewelyn ap Gruffydh, ap Gwenwynwin, ap Owen Cyfeilioc, ap Gruff. ap Madawc, ap Meredith of Powis, ap Bleddyn, ap Cynfin,* &c. to *Beli Mawr.*

Owen *ap Meredith ap Tudor ap Gwerfill Ferch Eva, Ferch Margret, Ferch Meredith gôch, ap Meredith, ap Iers Fychan, ap Iers gôch, ap Meredith ap Bleddyn, ap Cynfin,* &c. to *Beli.*

Owen *ap Meredith ap Tudor, ap Gwerfyll, Ferch Eva, Ferch Margret, Ferch Meredith gôch, ap Chriftin, ap Bledrws, ap Edwal Owen Bendew* one of the fifteen Tribes of *North-Wales*, Son to *Cynan Feiniard ap Gwalthfoed, ap Gwlyddien, ap Gwridor, ap Caradawc, ap Lles Llaw ddeawc, ap Edwal, ap Gwnnan, ap Gwnnawc Farf fych, ap Ceidio, ap Corf, ap Cadnawc, ap Tegonwy, ap Teon, ap Gwinau dau Freuddwyd,* &c. and fo to *Beli.*

Owen *ap Meredith, ap Margret Ferch Tomas, ap Lhewelin, ap Owen ap Meredith* Lord *Ifcoed, ap Owen, ap Gruffydh, ap Rhys* Prince of *South Wales*, fo to *Rodri Mawr.*

APPENDIX.

Owen ap Meredith, ap Margret, Ferch Tomas ap Llywelin, ap Angharad, Ferch Arglwydd Sion, John of Haffon by William ap David ap Gruffydh. Dubium.

Owen ap Meredith, ap Margret, Ferch Tomas ap Llewelyn, ap Angharad Ferch Margret, Ferch Philip, ap Ifor Lord Ifcoed by William ap Gruffydh. Dubium.

Owen ap Meredith, ap Margret, Ferch Tomas ap Llewelyn, ap Angharad, Ferch Margret, Ferch Angharad, Ferch Llewelyn ap Iers drwyndwn Prince of all Wales. This Llewelyn wedded Inet Daughter of King John, which was Son to Henry the Second, Son to Mawd the Emprefs, Daughter to Henry the Firft; Son to William the Conquerour, Son to Robert Duke of Normandy.

Owen ap Meredith, ap Margret, Ferch Tomas ap Elinor Ferch . . . . . Lord Barre by Gyttin Owen, by information of Dr. Owen Pool, and Mr. Lingam's Wife by an old Pedigree.

Owen ap Meredith, ap Margret, Ferch Tomas ap Elinor, ferch Elinor, Ferch Edward Longfhanks King of England.

Owen ap Meredith, ap Margret, Ferch Tomas, ap Elinor Ferch Elinor Ferch Elinor fecond to King Edward abovefaid. Dubium.

Owen ap Meredith, ap Margret, Ferch Elinor Ferch Meredith, ap Owen, ap Gruffydh, ap Rhys Prince of South-Wales, by Madawc ap Llewelyn ap Howel his Books.

Owen ap Meredith, ap Margret, Ferch Elinor, Ferch Catrin, ferch Llewelyn ap Gruffydb laft Prnce of Wales.

Owen ap Meredith, ap Margret, Ferch Elinor, Ferch Llewelyn ap Gruffydh, ap Tangwiftl,
Ferch

APPENDIX.

Ferch Llywarch gôch, ap Lhowarch ap Pyll, ap Cynan, ap Einion ap Gwridor gôch, ap Helic, ap Glannawc, ap Gwgon Gleddyfrudd, ap Cariadawc Freichfras, ap Llir Merini, ap Einion irth, ap Cunedda wledic.

Owen ap Meredith|, ap Margret, Ferch Elinor, Ferch Caterin, Ferch Elinor ap Gruffydh, ap Tangwiftl, Ferch Tangwiftl, Ferch Llowarch, ap Bran, ap Dinàwal, ap Efnydd, ap Alawe Alfer, ap Tudwal, ap Rodri mawr: by Gyttin Owen.

Gwen ap Meredith, ap Margret, Ferch Elinor Fychan, Ferch Simon Montford Earl of Leicefter: by Gyttin Owen.

Owen ap Meredith, ap Margret, Ferch Elinor, Ferch Caterin, Ferch Elinor Fychan, Ferch Elenor, Ferch John King of England.

Hereafter followeth the antient Lineage of the faid Owen's Mother Margret Wife to Meredith ap Tudor.

Owen ap Margret, Ferch Dafydd Fychan, ap Dafydd Llwyd, ap Cyner, ap Gronw, ap Cyner, ap Iers, ap Hwfa, ap Cwmus, ap Cillin, ap Maeloc dda, ap Gredef, ap Kwmus du, ap Cillin Ynad, ap Predur Teirnoe, ap Meilir Eryr, gwyr gorfedd, ap Tiday, ap Tyfodde, ap Gwybfyw, ap Marchwin, ap Branap Pill, ap Cerfyr, ap Meilir Meilirion, ap Goron, ap Cunedda wledic, ap Gwawl Ferch Coel Godeboc as before.

Owen ap Margret, Ferch Dafydd Fychan, ap Dafydd Llwyd, ap Cyner, ap Gronw, ap Cyner, ap Iers, ap Hwfa, ap Generis Ferch Ednowain Bendew, ap Cynon Finiaid, ap Gwarthfoed, ap

APPENDIX.

Gwridr ap Cradoc, ap Lles llaw ddeuawc, ap Edwal, ap Gwynnan: and so to *Ludd, ap Beli mawr,* as before by *Gyttin Owen.*

Owen ap Margret, Ferch Dafydd Fychan, ap Dafydd Lhwyd ap Cyner, ap Llayfedd Daughter to Sir *William Twychet,* Knight, by *William.* Indub.

Owen ap Margret, Ferch Dafydd Fychan, ap Dafydd Lhwyd, ap Alis, Ferch Robert, ap Turstan Holland Capitain of *Harlech*: by *William.*

Owen ap Margret, Ferch Dafydd Fychan, ap Dafydd Lhwyd, ap Alis, Ferch Margret, Ferch Alan Norris, Knight, by *William.* Indub.

Owen ap Margret, Ferch Dafydd Fychan, ap Angharad, Ferch Howell ap Meredith, ap Iers, ap Cadwgan, ap Llywarch, ap Bran, as before, &c.

Owen ap Margret Ferch Dafydd Fychan, ap Angharad Ferch Howell ap Meredith, ap Iers, ap Gwenllian, Ferch Cynan ap Owen Gwynedd, ap Gruffydh ap Cynan, &c.

Owen ap Margret, Ferch Dafydd Fychan, ap Angharad, Ferch Owen ap Bleddin, ap Owen Brogennwn, ap Madawc, ap Meredith, ap Bleddin, ap Cynfin Prince of *Powis*; these 3 by *Gyttin Owen.*

Owen ap Margret, Ferch Dafydd Fychan, ap Angharad, Ferch Gwladis, Ferch Llewelin gethni, ap Edwal, ap Gruffydh, ap Meuric, ap Cadhayarn, ap Gwrydd, ap Rhys gôch one of the 15 Tribes of *North Wales*; which was Son to *Sandwr ap Iarddwr, ap Mor, ap Tegerin, ap Aclaw, ap Gredres, ap Cwmus du, ap Cillin Ynad,* &c. to *Coel Godeboc.*

Owen

APPENDIX.

Owen ap Margret, Ferch Dafydd Fychan, ap Angharad, Ferch Gwladus, Ferch Mali Llwyd, Ferch Iers ap Engion, ap Geraint, ap Tegwared, ap Cynfawr, ap Madawc diffaeth, which were Rulers and Great Men in *Pentraeth.*

Owen ap Margaret, Ferch Nest, Ferch Jermy, ap Gruffydh, ap Howell, ap Meredith, ap Engion, ap Gwgon, ap Merwydd, ap Golwyn, one of the 15 Tribes of *North-Wales,* Son to *Tangno, ap Cadfael, ap Lludd, ap Llen, ap Llaminod Angel, ap Pafgen, ap Urien Rheged, ap Meirchion, ap Grwst, ap Cennaf, ap Coel godeboc* King as before.

Owen ap Margret, Ferch Nest, Ferch Jermy, ap Gwerfill, ferch Gwladus, Ferch Edwal Fychan as before.

Owen ap Margret Ferch Nest, Ferch Angharad, Ferch Gruffydb, ap Dafydd gôch, ap Gruffydb, ap Llewelyn Prince of *Wales.*

Owen ap Margret Ferch Nest, Ferch Angharad, Ferch Gruffydb ap Dafydd gôch, ap Dafydd, ap Gruffydh, ap Tangwistl, Ferch Llowarch gôch, ap Llowarch Holbwrch, ap Pill, ap Cynan, ap Gwridor gôch, ap Helic, ap Glannoc as before.

Owen ap Margret Ferch Nest, Ferch Angharad, Ferch Gruffydb, ap Dafydd gôch, ap Rhanullt, Ferch Rheinallt King of *Man.*

Owen ap Margret Ferch Nest, Ferch Angharad, Ferch Gruffydb, ap Angharad, Ferch Heylyn, ap Tudor, ap Ednyfed Fychan.

Owen ap Margret Ferch Nest, Ferch Anghabad, Ferch Gruffydh, ap Angharad, Ferch Heylyn, ap Adleir, Ferch Ricart, ap Cadwalader, ap Gruffydh, ap Cynan Prince. Thefe 4 by *Gyttin Owen.*

Owen ap Margret Ferch Nest, Ferch Angharad, ferch Gruffydb, ap Angharad, ferch Heylyn, ap Adleis, Ferch

APPENDIX.

Ferch Ricart, ap Cadwalader, ap Gruffydh, ap Cynan, ap Afandrec Wife to *Iago*, Daughter to *Gwayr, ap Pill, ap Cynan, ap Cynddelw gam, ap Elgudi, ap Grwyfnad, ap Diwgludd, ap Tegawc, ap Cyfnerth, ap Madoc Medogion, ap Sauddl bryd Angel, ap Llylwarch hên, ap Elidor Ludanwin, ap Meirchion gûl, ap. Erwst galedlwm, ap Cenaw, ap Coel godeboc* King as before.

Owen ap Margret Ferch Nest, Ferch Angharad, Ferch Marret, Ferch Tudor, ap Iers, ap Ewrgwnon, ap Cyfnerth, ap Rhuon, ap Nefydd hardd, one of the 15 Tribes of *North Wales*.

Owen ap Margaret Ferch Nest, Ferch Angharad, Ferch Margaret, Ferch Tangwistl, Ferch Madawc, ap Cyfnerth, ap Cyhelyn, ap Llywarch Fychan, ap Llywarch gôch, ap Llowarch Holbwrch, ap Pill, ap Cynon, ap Gwrydr gôch, ap Helic ap Glannoc, ap Gwgon gleddyfrudd, ap Cariadoc freich frâs, ap Glir Meirini, ap Engion yrth, ap Cynedda wledic, by *Gyttin Owen.*

Abstracted out of the old Cronicles of Wales, *by Sir* John Leiaf, *Priest,* Guttin Owen, Gruffydh ap Llewelyn ap Jermy, Fychan, Madawc ap Llewelyn ap Howell, Robert ap Howell ap Thomas, John King, *with many others, at the King's Majesty's Costs and Charges. The Abbot of* Llanegwestle, *and Dr.* Owen Pool, *Canon of* Harf, *Overseers.*

APPENDIX.

Rex omnibus, &c.

SCiatis, quod cum Lewelinus Princeps de Aberffraw & Dominus Snawerden, nobis concefferit & firmiter promiferit, quod ftabit provifioni venerabilium Patrum Redulphi Ciceftrenfis Epifcopi & Cancellarii noftri, & Alexandri Conventrenfis & Lichfield Epifcopi, & dilectorum & fidelium noftrorum Richardi Marefchalli Comitis Pembroch, Johannis de Lafcy Comitis Lincolniæ & Conftabularii Ceftriæ, Stephani de Segrave Jufticiarii noftri Angliæ, & Radulphi filii Nicholai Senefchalli noftri, una cum Idnevet Senefchallo ipfius Lewelini & Werrenoc fratre ejus, Imano Vachan & David Clerico, quam ipfi facturi funt fuper congruis emendis nobis faciendis, de omnibus exceffibus nobis & noftris, ab eo & fuis factis & de reftitutione nobis & hominibus noftris facienda de omnibus terris & poffeffionibus noftris, & noftrorum per ipfum Lewelinum & Wallenfes occupatis, occafione Werræ inter nos & ipfum motæ; fimul etiam de recipienda reftitutione à nobis & noftris, de omnibus terris ipfius Lewelini & hominum fuorum per nos & noftros occupatis, occafione Werræ prædictæ, & de affignando David filio ipfius Lewelini & Yfabellæ uxori ejus primogenitæ filiæ & hæreredis. Willielmi de Breus, rationabili portione ipfam Yfabellam contingente, de terris quæ fuerunt prædicti Willielmi patris fui, & de refufione pecuniæ nobis, facienda, pro prædictis exceffibus congruè emendandis & portione prædicta affignanda; Provifa tamen

APPENDIX.

men super hoc ab eisdem sufficiente securitate de fideli seruitio nobis præstando & de tranquilitate nobis & regno nostro Angliæ, observanda. Ita quod dampnum vel periculum, nec nobis nec regno nostro inde possit evenire. Et si pendente provisione prædicta, aliquid de novo emerserit emendandum, idem Lewelinus voluerit & concesserit, quod per prædictos provisores emendetur. Nos provisionem eorundem quam facturi sunt super omnibus præmissis, gratam habemus & acceptam pro nobis, & nostris sicut præfatus Lewelinus pro se & suis & in hujus rei testimonium has literas patentes inde fieri fecimus. Teste me ipso apud Salop septimo die Decembris & decimo septimo anno Regni nostri.

Rex, &c.

LEWELINO Principi de Aberfraw salutem. Sciatis quod recepimus in gratiam nostram, Gilbertum Mareschallum & omnes qui fuerunt imprisii Richardi Mareschalli tam de Angliâ quam de Walliâ qui ad pacem nostram venire voluerunt & eis reddidimus omnes terras & tenementa sua quæ de nobis tenuerunt, & de quibus dissesiti fuerunt occasione guerræ motæ inter nos & prædictum comitem, & nobis remanent quieta quæcunque super nos & nostros per prædictum comitem, vel suos imprisios occupata fuerunt quæ vobis duximus significanda. Volentes quod vobis innotescant quæ penes nos acta sunt in hac parte, & quia per venerabilem patrem Edmundum Cantuariensem Archiepiscopum & Co-episcopos suos captæ sunt Treugæ inter nos & vos sub firma spe tractandi de pace inter nos & vos formanda & fortius firmanda. Mittimus propter hoc prædictum Archiepiscopum & venerabiles Patres Alexandrum Coventrensem & Lichfieldensem & Henricum Roffensem Co-episcopos suos ad partes Marchiæ ; ita quod erunt apud Salop die Lunæ in Crastino sanctæ Trinitatis : Et rogamus vos quatenus sicut nostram desideratis amicitiam non omittatis quin
in

APPENDIX.

in Craftino die Martis loco tuto & compesenti, quem prædictus Archiepifcopus vobis fignificabit ipfi Archiepifcopo & Coepifcopis fuis occuratis ad tractatum cum eis habendum fuper præmiffis. In quorum etiam ore quædam quæ non duximus fcripto commendanda pofuimus vobis plenius exponenda; rogantes quatinus ficut decet taliter ea quæ reformationem pacis refpiciunt & quæ ipfi plenius in hac parte vobis explicabunt audire cum effectu & eifdem adquiefcere velitis, quod non ftet per vos quin firmum & ftabile pacis vinculum inter nos & vos roboretur ad noftrum pariter & veftrum commodum & honorem.

Rex, &c.

Dilecto & fideli fuo Richardo Comiti Cornubiæ & Pictaviæ falutem. Sciatis quod treugæ captæ funt inter nos & Lewelinum Principem de Aberfraw per venerabilem patrem Edmundum Archiepifcopum Cantuarienfem & Epifcopos fecum adjuntos & quofdam alios fideles noftrofs propter hoc ad partes Walliæ deftinatos duraturæ à fefto Sancti Jacobi anno regni noftri decimo octavo ufque in duos annos fequentes in hac forma. Quod omnes injuriæ & damnæ hinc inde facta infra ultimam treugam capram per venerabilem Patrem Henricum Roffenfem Epifcopum in media quadrageffima proximo præterita per Dictatores ejufdem treugæ emendabuntur, quod omnes terræ hinc inde occupatæ per ultimam Guerram motam, reftituentur his quibus poftea fint oblatæ, homines etiam illi qui hinc inde recefferint à fidelitate dominorum fuorum & fe tenuerunt ex parte adverfa libere revertantur. Ita quidem quod durantibus treugis prædictis in nullo occafionabuntur nec aliquid dampni vel mali eis fiet occafione prædicta. Adjectum eft etiam in eadem provifione treugarum; quod fi vos & dilectus & fidelis nofter Radulphus

APPENDIX.

phus de Thorny nolueritis sub eisdem treugis comprehendi bene placebit eidem Lewelino. Sin autem nihilominus, quod ad nos & alios fideles nostros eas firmiter observabit. Et sub tali conditione quod si forte tenere non velletis contra vos se defendet. Ita quod contra ipsum & defensionem suam nullum vobis faciemus nec facere poterimus per nos vel per aliquem de Marchia vel alium interim consilium vel auxilium ad ipsum gravandum, & taliter sunt treugæ prædictæ ex parte ipsius Lewelini juratæ & assecuratæ & in adventu prædicti Archiepiscopi ad nos similiter ex parte nostra eas jurari faciemus & assecurari, & ideo vobis mandamus firmiter injungentes, quatinus prædictis treugis sine difficultate aliquâ adquiescentes eas teneatis & ex parte vestra eas teneri faciatis. Quia modis omnibus volumus quod eas teneatis & firmiter observetis. Quid autem inde facere proposueritis aperte responsum vestrum nobis sub festinatione scire faciatis. Teste Rege apud Westmonasterium tricesimo die Junii.

Radulphus Herefordensis Episcopus, Decanus Herefordiæ, Walterus de Clifford & Walterus de bello Campo iterum constituti sunt Dictatores emendarum, faciendarum & recipiendarum de interceptionibus factis, ut dicitur Lewelino Principi de Aberfraw, &c. & Morganô de Carleon quoad Castrum Carleon & eisdem dictatoribus associati sunt Prior de Wenloc & Johannes extraneus & debent convenire in crastino clausi Paschæ apud vadum de Montgomery ad consequendum quod priore die ad hoc constituto debuisset fuisse executum. Teste Rege apud Northamton sexto die Martii.

REX

REX omnibus ad quod præsentes literæ pervenerint. Sciatis quod concessimus bona fide & fine malo ingenio & ratas habemus & gratas treugas captas apud Theokesburiam die Veneris in Festo Sancti Benedicti, anno regni nostri vicesimo per venerabilem Patrem Edmundum Cantuariensem Archiepiscopum inter nos & omnes homines & imprisios nostros apertos ex una parte, & Lewelinum Principem de Aberfraw & Dominum de Snaudan & omnes homines & imprisios suos apertos tam Walenses quam alios ex alia parte duraturos à Festo Sancti Jacobi, anno eodem usque in unum annum completum. Ita scilicet quod tam nos & nostri quam prædictus Lewelinus & sui simus in eisdem terris & tenementis, hominibus & homagiis in quibus fuimus prædicto die captionis treugarum istarum. Salva Morgano de Carleon restitutione sua tam de terris quam de bonis & Mobilibus suis quæ comes Gilbertus Marefchallus occuparerat, super eum infra treugas alias inter nos & ipsum Lewelinum ultimo captas. Siquid autem interim fuerit foris factum per captionem terrarum vel castrorum vel bonorum mobilium & manifestum de captione terrarum vel castrorum illorum terræ; & castra statim reddantur non expectata aliqua correctione emendatorum treugæ, sed de bonis mobilibus ita captis per ipsos correctores fiant emendæ, treugis nihilominus durantibus in suâ firmitate in forma prædicta. Ita quod hinc inde nulla namia capiantur pro aliqua interceptione facta infra treugas istas de bonis mobilibus, nec pro aliqua contentione ante captionem hujus treugæ orta, sed per ipsos correctores fiant. Nullus etiam receptet in potestate suâ imprisios alterius inde emendæ sicut prædictum est durantibus treugis. Nullum etiam castrum novum firmetur in Marchia vel dirutum reficiatur durantibus treugis, & terræ sint communes secundum formam treugarum quæ ultimo captæ fuerunt inter nos & ipsum Lewelinum.

Juraverunt

Juraverunt autem in animam noftram ex parte noftra in hanc treugam bona fide, & fine malo ingenio fideliter obfervandam ufque ad prædictum terminum dilicti & fideles noftri Henricus de Aldithely, Johannes Leftrange & Henricus de Stafford, in cujus, &c. Tefte me ipfo apud Theokesburiam, undecimo die Julii, anno regni noftri vicefimo.

Sciant præfentes & futuri, quod ita convenit inter Dominum Henricum RegemAngliæ illuftrem ex una parte, & David filium Lewelini quondam Principis Norwalliæ & Dominum de Aberfraw ex altera, apud Glouceftriam die Martis proximo ante Feftum Sancti Dunftanni, anno regni ipfius regis vicefimo quarto, de Homagio ipfius David quod ipfe offerrebat eidem Domino Regi pro jure fuo Norwalliæ & de terris quas Barones ipfius Domini Regis fcilicet Griffinus filius Wennuwan & alii Barones Domini Regis petebant verfus ipfum David ut jura fua excepta de monte alto fecundum quod continetur in fcripto nuper confecto apud crucem Griffini per Senefchallos Domini Regis, quæ ad præfens excipitur ab arbitrio, falvo tamen in pofterium jure Senefchalli Ceftriæ in terra illa fi quod habent. Scilicet, quod prædictus Dominus Rex cepit homagium præfati David de prædicto jure fuo Norwalliæ, & quod tam idem Dominus Rex pro præfatis Baronibus fuis de confcenfu eorundem quam præfatus David pro fe & fuis & hæredibus eorum fuper omnibus terris prædictis fe fubmiferunt, arbitrio venerabilium Patrum Ottonis Sancti Nicolai in Carcere Tulliano Diaconi, Cardinalis Apoftolici fedis legati; Wigorniæ & Noriveci Epifcoporum, & nobilis viri Richardi Comitis Pictaviæ & Cornubiæ, fratris ipfius Domini Regis & Johannis de Monemue ex parte ipfius Domini Regis, & venerabilis Patris Epifcopi de Sancto Afaph Idnevet Vaghan, Eynguan Vaghan ex parte præfati David. Ita quod quomodo libet ab ipfis omnibus vel à majori parte eorundem, fuper præmiffis fuerit arbitratum, utraque pars ipforum ftabit Arbitrio & illud in perpetuum firmiter obfervabit; & ad hæc fideliter fine fraude fervanda Willielmus de Cantelupo

APPENDIX.

telupo de præcepto Regis juravit in animam ipsius Regis & idem David in propria persona sua corporate præstitit Sacramentum. Et insuper se submiserunt jurisdictioni & inordinationi præfati Domini legati quamdiu in Anglia legationis fungatur officio, ut partem contra præmissa venientem per censuram Ecclesiasticam modis omnibus quibus melius viderit expedire, tam ad prædictum arbitrium observandum quam ad transgressionem contra illud perpetratam emendandam valeat coercere, ordine juris observato. Dum tamen idem David vel sui, si forsitan contra prædicta venire præsumpserint prius coram dicto Domino legato vel aliquibus aliis ad hoc ab ipso deputandis & partibus merito non suspectis in confinio Marchiæ loco eidem David & suis tuto legitime communicantur, si ad hoc vocari venerint: Vel si legitime vocati non venerint pro contumacibus habeantur nisi rationabile & sufficiens habeant impedimentum, finito vero prædictæ legationis officio sub forma præscripta & cohercioni & jurisdictioni Domini Cantuariensi Archiepiscopi & successorum suorum & Ecclesiæ Cantuariensis se partes prædictæ submiserunt. Et sciendum quod per hanc pacem remanent Domino Regi & hæredibus suis omnia homagia Baronum Walliæ quieta, & remittuntur omnia incendia, homicidia, & alia mala tam ex parte Anglicorum quam Wallensium perpetrata; ita quod ad invicem plene reconcilientur. Salvo præfati David jure suo, si quod habet in aliis terris. Et si forte aliquis prædictorum arbitrorum ante hoc arbitrium completum in fata decesserit, vel per impedimentum rationabile prædicto arbitrio faciendo non possit interesse; alius loco suo substituetur qui neutri partium merito suspectus habeatur: Ad hoc præfati Episcopus de Sancto Asaph Idnevet & Ignan & Griffinus filius Rotherich præstiterunt Sacramentum, quod quantum in eis est, prædicta fideliter observabunt & ab ipso David & suis modis omnibus quibus poterunt, facient observari: Ad majorem autem hujus rei securitatem factum est hoc scriptum inter ipsos Regem & David in modo Chirographi. Ita quod parti remanenti penes ipsum Dominum Regem appositum est Sigillum

ipsius

APPENDIX.

ipsius una cum Sigillo prædictorum Episcopi de Sancto Asapho Idnevet, Ignan & Griffini, & parti penes ipsum David remanenti appositum est sigillum Domini Regis: His testibus venerabilibus Patribus Ottone Sancti Nicolai in carcere Tulliano Diacono, Cardinali apostolicæ Sedis legato; Waltero Eboracensi Archiepiscopo, Waltero Carleolensi, Waltero Wygornensi & Willielmo Norwicensi Episcopis; Richardo Comite Pictaviæ & Cornubiæ fratre Domini Regis, venerabili Patre Episcopo de Sancto Antando; Seneschallis nostris Joanne extraneo, Edenyset Watham, Griffino filio Rotherich, David Archidiacon de Sancto Asaph & aliis.

Rex.

DAVID filio Lewelini salutem. Bene recolimus qualiter nos vobis nuper in mandatis dedimus, quod coram nobis apud Wigorniam compareretis ad providendum arbitros qui loco eorum qui primo ad hoc electi fuerint & qui ad partes recesserunt transmarinas, justitiam secundum formam pacis inter & vos provise singulis conquerentibus exhiberent; & in arbitrio prædicto secundum formam debitam procederent & similiter ad justitiam recipiendam de portione uxorem vestram contingente de hæreditate suâ: Et similiter ad standum recto super his de quibus Senescallus de Monte alto & aliis de vobis sunt conquesti. Et quia ad diem & locum vobis præfixos non accessistis, sed literas vestras nobis misistis; continentes quod tres ex vestris ad nos loco vestro destinastis, ex quibus tantum unus ad nos accessit qui ad præmissa adimplenda nullam potestatem habuit; unde quibusdam ex nostris visum fuerat quod hoc malitiose & ut subterfugium quæreretis per vos factum fuit. Nos tamen hoc non credentes sed fidelitatem vestram adhuc magis probare volentes, vobis mandamus in fide qua nobis tenemini, præcipiendo quatinus omni occasione
postposita

APPENDIX.

poftpofita perfonaliter compareatis apnd Salop, die Dominica ante Dominicam Palmarum coram fidelibus noftris quos illuc duxerimus tranfmittendos ad confentiendum in perfonas certas, ad procedendum in arbitrio prædicto loco eorum qui ad partes tranfmarinas recefferunt & ad faciendum in eodem arbitrio id quod adhuc reftat faciendum; & ad recipiendam juftitiam de portione uxorem veftram de hæreditate fua contingente & ad ftandum recto Senefchallo Celtriæ & aliis de vobis conquerentibus. Quod fi perfonaliter ad hoc faciendum venire non poffitis tales loco veftro mittatis qui plenam poteftatem habeant hæc omnia nomine veftro faciendi Nos enim vobis & veftris per eos quos ibidem mittimus aut per nofmet ipfos falvum & fecurum provideri faciemus conductum. Tefte Rege apud Wudeftock decimo nono die Februarii.

Anno Domini millefimo ducentefimo quadragefimo primo, die Dominica proxima ante inventionem Sanctæ crucis affignata, David filio Lewelini quondam Principis Norwalliæ & Marchionibus ad confentiendum in arbitros fuftituendos loco abfentium & ad faciendam & recipiendam juftitiam fecundum formam pacis conventæ inter Dominum Regem & dictum David comparuit Thudius Senefchallus ipfius David, Cancellarius & Philippus filius Ibor Clericus ex parte David procuratores; oftendentes literas ipfius David, in quibus dictus David promittebat fe ratum habiturum quicquid per ipfos fieret fecundum formam pacis fupradictæ. Radulphus vero de mortuo mari & Rogerus Senefchallus Ceftriæ & Griffinus pro fe & aliis Marchionibus comparuerunt; petentes inftanter quod fecundum dicta teftium productorum coram Domino Stephano de Segrave, & conjudicibus fuis vicem Domini Regis gerentibus apud Salop eifdem exhiberetur juftitiæ complementum. Sed contra procuratores præfati David afferebant dictos teftes non effe receptos fecundum formam pacis. Quare fecundum dicta eorum non dicebat nec poterat judicari. Tandem continuata die & altercatione magna

A a   fuper

super hoc & aliis habitata inter partes, forma pacis prædictæ producta in medio vifaque & perfecta loco abfentium arbitrorum fcilicet Domini Ottonis Sancti Nicolai in carcere Tulliano Diaconi Cardinalis, Domini Papæ quondam legati in Anglia Wigornenfis & Norwicenfis Epifcoporum subrogati funt per Dominum Regem de confenfu dictorum procuratorum Epifcopus Coventrenfis, Johannes filius Galfridi & Herebertus filius Matthæi, & Walterus de Clifford: Quibus data est eadem potestas quam haberent abfentes fi præfentes effent fecundum formam pacis prædictæ & affignata est dies partibus à die Pentecoftes proximo in unum menfem apud pontem de Maneford ultra Salop ad probanda hinc inde five per productos teftes; non obftante productione jam facta per alios & quolibet probationis genere five per inftrumenta, five alio modo quæ voluerunt & fibi noverint expedienda; & illa die dabitur alia ad judicium audiendum fecundum probata coram eifdem arbitris juxta formam pacis fuperius prælibatæ.

Rex.

DAVID filio Lewelini quondam Principis Norwalliæ falutem. Ex certâ quorundam relatione didicimus quod vos contra juramentum nobis præftitum quofdam fratres Griffini filii Madoc & etiam quofdam homines noftros de Keri, qui homagia nobis fecerunt vobis confeoderatis & ab obfequio & fidelitate noftra fubtraxiftis & fratres prædicti Griffini contra nos in terra veftra receptatis. Tres quidem de Senefchallis veftris in fuccurfum eorum qui expugnant dilectum & fidelem noftrum Radulphum de Mortuo mari deftinaftis cædes & incendia per vos & veftros in terra fua & terris aliorum fidelium committendo, terras etiam quæ in curia noftra abjudicatæ fuerunt Oweno Vaghan & nepotibus fuis, eis contra juftitiam deforciatis, non permittentes quod executio

APPENDIX.

executio fiat de his quæ in curia noſtra ſunt conſiderata. Quandam etiam navem Ceſtriæ quæ in poteſtate veſtra applicuit Cartata blado & aliis victualibus arctari feciſtis per vos & gentem veſtram, in nullo his quorum bladum & victualia fuerunt inde ſatisfacientes ſuper quibus non modicum admiramur & movemur; & multo fortius quod cum nuper miſiſſemus nuntios veſtros ſolempnes uſque Salop, utpote venerabilem Patrem Henricum Coventrenſem & Lichfieldenſem Epiſcopum, & dilectos & fideles noſtros Johannem filium Galfridi, & Henricum de Aditheleg paratos ad emendas faciendas & recipiendas de interceptionibus factis, tam ex parte noſtra, quam ex parte veſtra, vos tanquam in contemptum noſtrum prædictis fidelibus noſtris non occurriſtis, nec per aliquos de veſtris in eorum occurſum mittere curâſtis, quod quidem ægre nos movet cum tot & tantas injurias quas longum eſſet enumerare contra nos & noſtros nullo modo attemptare debuiſtis: & ideo vobis mandamus quod prædictos fideles noſtros tam fratres prædicti Griffini quam homines noſtros de Keri quos à fidelitate noſtra ſubtruxiſtis ad fidem noſtram redire faciatis. Non impedientes quin prædictus Owenus Vaghan & nepotes ſui ſecundum abjudicatum eſt in curia noſtra terris ſuis gaudere poſſint & eas pacificè poſſidere. Id etiam quod contra dilectum & fidelem noſtrum Radulphum de mortuo mari & alios fideles noſtros & etiam quod de navi illa Ceſtrenſi attemptâſtis, ſic emendari faciatis; quod nobis non relinquatur materia injurias prædictas gravius ulciſcendi quod nollemus. Nec omitatis quin citra feſtum Sancti Petri ad vincula nobis ſignificetis qualiter dampna & injurias prædictas, quæ nullo modo diſſimulare poterimus nobis emendare volueritis. Teſte Rege apud Merlebergh, quarto decimo die Julii.

Sciant præſentes & futuri quod ita convenit inter Dominum Henricum Regem Angliæ illuſtrem ex una parte & Senanam uxorem Griffini filii Lewelini quondam Principis Norwalliæ, quem David frater ejus tenet carceri mancipatum cum Owen filio ſuo nomine
ejuſdem

APPENDIX.

ejufdem Griffini ex altera ; fcilicet quod prædicta Senana manucepit pro prædicto Griffino viro fuo quod dabit Domino Regi fexcentas Marcas, ut Rex eum & prædictum Owen filium fuum liberari faciat à carcere detineri. Et ut Rex poftea judicio Curiæ fuæ fecundum legem Walenfem ei & hæredibus fuis habere faciat fuper portione quæ eum continget de hæreditate quæ fuit prædicti Lewelini patris fui & quam prædictus David, ipfi Griffino deforciavit. Ita fi quod idem Griffinus vel hæredes fui per confiderationem curiæ Domini Regis reciperent portionem quam fe dicunt contingere de hæreditate prædicta, eadem Senana manucepit pro prædicto Griffino & hæredibus fuis quod ipfe & hæredes fui imperpetuum inde reddent Domino Regi & hæredibus fuis trecentas Marcas annuas. Scilicet tertiam partem in denariis & tertiam partem in bobus & vaccis, & tertiam partem in equis per æftimationem legalium hominum liberandas vicecomiti Salop, apud Salop, & per manum ipfius vicecomitis ad faccarium Regis deferendas & ibidem liberandas, fcilicet unam medietatem ad feftum Sancti Michaelis & aliam medietatem ad Pafcham. Eadem etiam Senana manucepit pro prædicto Griffino viro fuo & hæredibus fuis quod firmam Pacem tenebunt cum præfato David fuper portione quæ eidem David remanebit de hæreditate prædicta : Manucepit etiam Senana pro præfato Griffino & hæredibus fuis, quod fi aliquis Walenfis aliquo tempore Regi vel hæredibus fuis rebellis extiterit, præfatus Griffinus & hæredes fui ad cultum fuum proprium ipfum compellent ad fatisfaciendum Domino Regi & hæredibus fuis. Et de his omnibus fupradictis obfervandis, dicta Senana dabit Domino Regi David & Rothery filios fuos obfides : Ita tamen quod fi de præfato Griffino & Oweyno filio fuo qui cum eo eft in carcere humanitùs contingat antequam inde deliberentur ; alter prædictorum filiorum eidem Senanæ reddetur reliquo obfide remanente : Juravit infuper Senana tactis Sacro-Sanctis Evangeliis pro fe & præfato Griffino & hæredibus fuis quod hæc omnia firmiter obfervabunt. Et manucepit quod præfatus Griffinus

idem

APPENDIX.

idem jurabit cum à carcere liberatus fuerit, & super præmissis se submisit nomine dicti Griffini jurisdictioni Herefordensis & Conventrensis Episcoporum. Ita quod præfati Episcopi, vel alter eorum quem Dominus Rex elegerit ad requisitionem ipsius Regis per sententias excommunicationis in personas & interdicti in terras eorum coherceant ad omnia prædicta & singula observanda. Hæc omnia manucepit prædicta Senana & bona fide promisit se facturam & curaturam quod omnia impleantur, & quod præfatus Griffinus cum liberatus fuerit, & hæredes sui hæc omnia grata habebunt & complebunt & instrumentum suum inde dabunt Domino Regi in formâ prædicta. Ad majorem siquidem hujus rei securitatem factum est hoc scriptum inter ipsum Dominum Regem & præfatam Senanam nomine præfati Griffini viri sui. Ita quod parti remanenti penes ipsum Dominum Regem appositum est sigillum præfati Griffini per manum præfatæ Senanæ uxoris suæ una cum sigillo ipsius Senanæ; & parti remanenti penes ipsam Senanam nomine præfati Griffini appositum est sigillum ipsius Domini Regis; De supradictis etiam omnibus complendis & firmiter observandis dedit prædicta Senana nomine præfati Griffini Domino Regi plegios subscriptos, viz. Radulphum de Mortuo Mari, Walterum de Clifford, Rogerum de Monte alto Senescallum Celtriæ, Mailgun filium Mailgwn, Mereduc filium Roberti, Griffinum filium Maddoc de Baunfeld, Howel & Mereduc fratres ejus, Griffinum filium Wennwen, qui hæc omnia pro præfatâ Senana manuceperunt & Cartas suas ipsi Domino Regi inde fecerunt. Actum apud Salop die Lunæ proxima ante assumptionem beatæ Mariæ anno ipsius Regis vicesimo quinto.

OMnibus hoc scriptum visuris Rogerus de Monte alto Seneschallus Celtriæ salutem. Sciatis quod ego me constituti plegium Senanæ uxoris Griffini filii Leolini quondam Principis Norwalliæ, & manu cepi pro

pro ea erga Dominum meum Henricum Regem Angliæ illuſtrem, quod omnia quæ conventionavit eidem Domino meo nomine præfati viri ſui à carcere in quo David frater ejus eos detinet & pro portione quæ ipſum Griffinum contingit de hæreditate quæ fuit prædicti Leolini patris ſuis & quam præfatus David frater ejus ei deforciat, Domino Regi firmiter obſervabit. In cujus rei teſtimonium huic ſcripto ſigillum meum appoſui. Actum apud Salopesbury die Lunæ ante aſſumptionem Beatæ Mariæ, Anno regni ipſius viceſimo quinto.

Sub eadem forma fecerunt ſinguli plegii præſcripti.

Sciant præſentes & futuri quod ego Mereduçus filius Howel, tactis ſacroſanctis juravi quod ab iſto die in antea omnibus diebus vitæ meæ ero ad fidelitatem Domini Regis Angliæ, & ſerviam ei fideliter & devote cum omnibus viribus meis & toto poſſe meo quandocunque indiguerit ſervitio meo, & treugam inter Dominum Radulphum de mortuo mari & me initam uſque ad feſtum S. Michaelis anno Regni Regis Henrici vigeſimo quinto ex parte mea fideliter obſervabo: & tam ad fidelitatem Domino Regi in perpetuum obſervandum quam ad treugas prædictas obſervandas uſque ad terminum prædictum ſuppoſui me juriſdictioni Domini Herefordenſis Epiſcopi, & Domini Coventrenſis & Lichfieldenſis Epiſcopi, vel alterius eorum, quem Dominus Rex ad hoc elegerit, ut ſi in aliquo contra prædictam fidelitatem Domini Regis, vel contra obſervantiam prædictarum treugarum venerit, liceat eis vel eorum alteri quem Dominus Rex ad hoc elegerit perſonam meam & omnes meos excommunicare & terram meam interdicere, donec de tranſgreſſione ipſam ſatisfecero ad plenum. Et ſi forſitan infra prædictum Feſtum Sancti Michaeli inter prædictum Radulphum de mortuo mari & me nulla pax fuerit formata, licet poſt feſtum illud bellum moveant prædicto Radulpho, non obligabit me prædictum juramentum dum tamen erga Dominum Regem fidelitatem obſervam continuam, ſicut prædictum eſt.

Etſi

APPENDIX.

Etfi bellum poſt prædictum terminum inter nos moveatur, nihilominus Dominus Rex ſuſtinebit quod ego & mei receptemur in terra ſua ſicut alii fideles ſui. Ad prædicta autem obſervanda Domino Regi & hæredibus ſuis obligo me per juramentum prædictum, & per ſigilli mei appoſitionem quod huic ſcripto appoſui, ad majorem confirmationem prædictorum. Actum in craſtino aſſumptionis Beatæ Mariæ, anno regni Regis Henrici vigeſimo quinto.

Sub eiſdem verbis fecerunt Domino Regi chartas ſuas, Owen filius Howell. Mailgon filius Mailgun. Mereduc filius Mereduc. Howel filius Cadwachlan, & Cadwachlan filius Howel.

OMnibus Chriſti fidelibus ad quos præſentes literæ pervenerunt, David, filius Leolini, ſalutem. Sciatis quod conceſſi Domino meo Henrico Regi Angliæ illuſtri filio Domino Johannis Regis: quod deliberabo Griffinum fratrem meum quem teneo incarceratum una cum filio ſuo primogenito & aliis qui occaſione prædicti Griffini ſunt in parte mea incarcerati, & ipſos eidem domino meo Regi tradam. Et poſtea ſtabo juri Curiæ ipſius Domini Regis tam ſuper eo, utrum idem Griffinus debeat teneri captus quam ſuper portione terræ quæ fuit prædicti Leolini patris mei, ſi qua ipſum Griffinum contingere debeat, ſecundum conſuetudinem Walenſium. Ita quod pax ſervetur inter me & prædictum Griffinum fratrem meum quod caveatur de ipſa tenenda ſecundum conſiderationem curiæ ipſius Domini Regis, & quod tam ego quam prædictus Griffinus portiones noſtras quæ nos contingent de prædictis terris tenebimus in capite de prædicto domino Rege. Et quod reddam Rogero de monte alto Seneſchallo Ceſtriæ terram ſuam de Monthaut cum pertinentiis: & ſibi & aliis Baronibus & fidelibus domini Regis ſciſinas terrarum ſuarum occupatarum à tempore belli orti inter ipſum dominum Johannem Regem & prædictum Leolinum patrem

APPENDIX.

trem meum, salvo jure proprietatis cujuslibet pacti & instrumenti super quo stabitur juri hinc inde in curiâ ipsius domini Regis: & quod reddam ipsi domino regi omnes expensas quas ipse & sui fecerunt occasione exercitûs istius. Et quod satisfaciam de damnis & injuriis illatis sibi & suis secundum considerationem prædictæ curiæ vel malefactores ipsos, ipsi domino regi reddam omnia homagia quæ dominus Johannes rex pater ejus habuit, & quæ dominus Rex de jure habere debet; & specialiter omnium nobilium Wallensium. Et quod idem dominus rex non dimittit aliquem de suis captivis quin ipsi domino regi & suis remaneant seisinæ suæ. Et quod terra de Engusmere cum pertinentiis suis in perpetuum remanebit domino regi, vel hæredibus suis, & quod de cætero non receptabo vilagas vel foris banniatos ipsius domini regis, vel Baronum suorum de Marchia in terra mea, nec permittam receptari; & de omnibus articulis supradictis, & singulis firmiter & in perpetuum observandis, domino regi, & hæredibus suis, pro me & hæredibus meis cavebo per obsides & pignora & aliis modis quibus dominus rex dicere voluit vel dictare. Et in his & in omnibus aliis stabo voluntati, & mandatis ipsius domini regis & juri parebo omnibus in curia sua. In cujus rei testimonium, præsenti scripto sigillum meum appendi. Actum apud Atrietum juxta fluvium Elvey de S. Asapho in festo decollationis S. Johanni Babtistæ, anno prædicti domini regis Henrici vigesimo quinto.

Sciendum quod illi qui capti detinentur cum prædicto Griffino, eodem modo tradentur domino regi donec per curiam suam consideratum fuerit, utrum & quomodo debeant deliberari. Et ad omnia firmiter tenenda, ego David juravi super crucem sanctam quam coram me feci deportari. Venerabilis etiam pater Howelus episcopus de S. Asaph ad petitionem meam firmiter promisit in ordine suo, quod hæc omnia prædicta faciet, & procurabit modis quibus poterit, observari. Ednevet siquidem Waugam per præceptum meum, illud idem juravit super crucem prædictam,

APPENDIX.

ctam. Actum ut supra. Præterea concessi pro me & hæredibus meis quod si ego, vel hæredes mei contra pacem domini regis, vel hæredium suorum, vel contra articulos prædictos, aliquid attentaverimus tota hæreditas nostra domino regi, & hæredibus suis incurratur. De quibus omnibus & singulis supposui me, & hæredes meos, jurisdictioni Archiepiscopi Cantuariensis, & episcoporum Londinensis, Herefordensis, & Coventrensis, qui pro tempore præerunt, quod omnes, vel unus eorum, quem dominus rex ad hoc elegerit, possit nos excommunicare, & terram nostram interdicere, si aliquid contra prædicta attentaverimus. Et procuravi quod episcopi de Bangor & de S. Asaph chartas suas domino regi fecerunt per quas concesserunt, quod omnes sententias tam excommunicationis quam interdicti à prædictis Archiepiscopo, episcopis, vel aliquo eorum, ferendas, ad mandatum eorum exequentur.

Rex omnibus, &c.

DAVID filius Lewelini quondam principis Norwalliæ, Salutem. Noverint universitas vestra me spontanea voluntate mea pepegisse Domino meo Henrico Dei gratia Angliæ, quod ego & hæredes mei eidem domino regi, & hæredibus suis omnibus diebus vitæ nostræ constanter & fideliter serviemus, nec aliquo tempore contra eos erimus: Quod si forte eveneiit, quod à fideli servicio suo, vel hæredum suorum, quod absit, recesserimus, tota terra nostra erga ipsum dominum regem & hæredes suos incurratur, & in usus eorum perpetuis cedat temporibus. Hanc autem pactionem & concessionem sigilli mei appositione roboravi, & ad majorem hujus rei declarationem venerabiles patres Bangorensem, & de S. Asaph Episcopi, ad petitionem meam præsenti scripto sigilla sua apposuerunt. Actum apud Rothetan tricesimo primo die Augusti.

Illustri

APPENDIX.

Illuftri viro domino Henrico Dei gratia regi Anglorum, &c. Abbates Haberconwiæ, & de de Kemere Ciftercienfis ordinis inquifitores dati à domino Papâ, falutem in Domino. Mandatum domini Papæ recipimus in hæc verba, Innocentius Epifcopus, fervus fervorum Dei, dilectis filiis Abbatibus de Haberconwiæ, & de Kemere Ciftercienfis ordinis Kangorum diocefis falutem & apoftolicam benedictionem. Ex parte dilecti filii noftri nobilis viri David Principis Northwalliæ fuit propofitum coram nobis, quod cum inter ipfum, quem parentes ejus in alumnum Romanæ Ecclefiæ donaverunt, & chariffimum in Chrifto filium noftrum regem Anglorum illuftrem bellum longo tempore perduraffet, tandem poftquam fuit in venerabilem fratrem noftrum epifcopum de S. Afaph, & collegas ipfius de ftando hinc inde eorum arbitrio fuper omnibus querelis juramento à partibus præftito concorditer bonis viris mediantibus conpromiffum. Idem rex, non attendens quod pendente illorum arbitrio, fibi fuper hoc aliquid attentare non licebit in prædictum principem ex infperato hoftiliter irruit ad præftandum, quod fuper prædictis de quibus conpromiffum fuerit & juratum, ac aliis ipfius regis, mandare per vim computit, & metum qui cadere poterat in conftantem.

Cum igitur ea quæ vi & metu fiant, carere debeant robore firmitatis, difcretioni veftræ per apoftolica fcripta mandamus, quatenus inquifita fuper hoc diligentius veritate, fi rem inveneritis ita effe, auctoritate noftra prædictum principem ab obfervatione fic extorti juramenti penitus abfolventes, fententia, fi qua occafione ejufmodi in ejus perfonam, vel terram ab aliquo forfan tota fuerit; juxta formam ecclefiæ fine difficultate qualibet, ficut juftum fuerit relaxetis. Teftes vero, &c. Datum *Januæ* feptimo calendas Augufti Pontificatûs noftri anno fecundo. Hujus igitur autoritate muniti vobis mandamus quatenus in vigilia S. Agnetis Virginis, apud Keyrus in ecclefia Guftefend coram vobis compareatis, fuper contentis in Autentico dicto principi refponfuri, fi vobis videritis expedire.

Ifti

APPENDIX.

Isti sunt ARTICULI *intimati Domino* LEOLINO *Principi* Walliæ, *& populo ejusdem loci, ex parte Archiepiscopi supra dicti.*

PRimo, quod propter salutem eorum spiritualem, & temporalem ad partes istas venimus, quas semper dileximus, ut plures eorum noverunt.

Secundo, Quia venimus contra Domini regis voluntatem, cui etiam adventus noster dicitur plurimum displicere.

Tertio, Quia rogamus eos & supplicamus eis pro sanguine Jesu Christi, quatenus venire velint ad unitatem cum gente Anglorum, & ad pacem Domini regis, quam eis intendimus, quanto melius poterimus procurare.

Quarto, Volumus eos scire quod in his partibus Domini non poterimus remanere.

Quinto, Volumus eos attendere quod post recessum nostrum non invenient aliquem, qui ita velit sua amplecti negotia promovenda, qui vellemus, si placeret. Altissima vita nostra temporali corporum pacem honestam & stabilem perpetuo procurasse.

Sexto, Quia si nostras preces spreverint & labores, statim intendimus eorum pertinaciam scribere summo Pontifici & Curiæ Romanæ, propter peccata mortalia, quæ multiplicantur occasione discordiæ omni die.

Septimo, Noverint quod nisi citius ad pacem venerint aggravabitur eis bellum, quod non poterunt sustinere, quia crescit regia potentia omni die.

Octavo, Noverint quod regnum Angliæ est sub speciali protectione sedis Apostolicæ, & quod Romana Curia plus inter regna cætera diligere confuevit.

Nono, Quod eadem Curia nullo modo volet permittere ftatum regni Angliæ vacillare, quod fibi fpecialibus obfequiis eft devotum.

Decimo, Amariffimè plangimus hoc quod dicitur Wallenfes crudeliores exiftere Saracenis; quia cum Saraceni capiunt Chriftianos, eos fervant pecunia redimendos, quos Wallenfes captos dicuntur illico jugulare quafi folo fanguine delectentur; immo quod eft deterius, quos promittunt redimi, tradunt accepta pecunia jugulandos.

Undecimo, Quod cum confueverit Deum & perfonas Ecclefiafticas revereri, à devotione hominum videntur multipliciter receffiffe, qui in tempore fanctiffimo in redemptoris injuriam moverunt feditionem, homicidia & incendia perpetrantes, in quo eos nullus poterit excufare.

Duodecimo, Petimus ut tanquam veri Chriftiani ad cor redeant pœnitentes, quia cœptam difcordiam non poffent continuare etiam fi juraffent.

Tertiodecimo, Petimus ut nobis fignificent quibus modis velint & valeant turbationem pacis regiæ, læfionem reipublicæ, & mala alia emendare.

Quartodecimo, Ut fignificent nobis qualiter valeat ipfa concordia ftabiliri, fruftra enim pax firmari videbitur quæ tam affidue violatur.

Quintodecimo, Ut fi dicant leges fuas vel fœdera ex pacto inito non fervari, nobis fignificent quæ funt illa.

Sextodecimo, Noverint quod etiam pofito quod eis derogatum fuiffet, quod nefcimus, nullo modo licebit eis quafi effent judices in caufa fua taliter majeftatem regiam impugnare.

Septimodecimo, Quod nifi modo pax fiat, proceditur contra eos forfitan ex decreto militiæ, facerdoti, & populi convocati.

Reverendiffimo

APPENDIX.

Reverediffimo Patri in Chrifto Domino J. De gratia Cantuarienfi Archiepifcopo totius Angliæ Primati, fuus humilis & devotus filius Leolinus Princeps Walliæ, Dominus Snauden, falutem & filialem dilectionem cum omnimoda reverentia, fubjectione & honore, fanctæ paternitati veftræ pro labore vobis quafi intolerabile quem affumpfiftis ad præfens pro dilectione quam erga nos & noftram nationem geritis, omni qua poffumus devotione regratiantes vobis affurgimus; & eo amplius quod contra Domini regis voluntatem veniftis prout nobis intimaftis. Cæterum quod nos rogaftis ut ad pacem Domini regis veniamus, fcire debet veftra fanctitas quod ad hoc prompti fumus, dummodo idem dominus rex pacem debitam & veram nobis & noftris velit obfervare. Ad hoc licet gauderemus de mora veftra facienda in Wallia, tamen per nos non eritis impediti quin pax fiat, quantum in nobis eft, quam optamus per veftram induftriam magis quam alicujus alterius roborari. Et fperamus nec per Dei gratiam erit opportunum propter noftram pertinaciam aliquid fcribere Domino Papæ. Nec veftras paternas preces ac graves labores fpernemus, fed eas amplectimur omni cordis affectu ut tenemur. Nec erit opus quod Dominus Rex aggravet contra nos manum, cum prompti fumus fibi obedire juribus noftris & legibus nobis ut præmittatur refervatis.

· Et licet regnum Angliæ fit Curiæ Romanæ fpecialiter fubjectum & dilectum, tamen cum Dominus Papa, necnon & Curia Romana audiverint quanta nobis per Anglicos mala funt illata, videlicet quod pax prius formata non fuit nobis fervata nec pacta; deinde devaftationes, combuftiones, & Ecclefiafticarum perfonarum interfectiones, facerdotum videlicet & inclufourm, & aliarum religiofarum perfonarum paffim mulierum & infantium fuggentium ubera & in utero portantium, combuftiones etiam hofpitalium & aliarum domorum religiofarum, homicidiorum in cœmiteriis, Ecclefiis, & fuper Altaria, & aliorum facrilegiorum & flagiciorum auditu etiam horribilium, auditu Paganorum

rum ficut expreffius in aliis rotulis confcripta vobis tranfmittimus infpicienda.

Speramus imprimis, quod vestra pia & fancta paternitas clementer nobis compatietur, nec non & Curia fupra dicta, nec per nos regnum Angliæ vacillabit, dum, ut promiffum est, pax debita nobis fiat & fervetur. Qui vero fanguinis effufione delectantur manifestum est factis. Nam Anglici hactenus nulli fexui vel ætati feu languori pepercerunt, nulla Ecclefiæ vel loco facro detulerunt, qualia vel confimilia Wallenfes non fecerunt. Super eo autem quod unus redemptus fuit interfectus, multum dolemus, nec occiforem manu tenemus, fed in fylvis uti latro vagatur. De eo vero quod inceperunt guerram aliqui in tempore indebito, illud ignoravimus ufque poft factum, & tamen ipfi afferunt quod nifi eo tempore hoc feciffent mortes & captiones eis imminebunt, nec audebunt in domibus refidere, nec nifi armati incedere, & fic præ timore tali tempore id fecerunt. De eis vero quæ fecimus contra Dominum, ut veri Chriftiani per Dei gratiam pœnitebimus, nec erit ex parte noftra quod bellum continuetur, dum fumus indemnes ut debemus. Ne tamen exhæredemur & paffim occidemur, oportet nos defendere ut valemus. Cum vero injuria & damna hinc inde confiderentur & ponderentur parati fumus emendare pro viribus quæ ex parte noftra funt commiffa, dum de prædictis injuriis & damnis nobis factis & aliis emenda nobis fiat. Et ad pacem firmandam & ftabiliendam fimiliter fumus prompti debitis modis.

Quando tamen regales chartæ & pacta inita nobis non fervatur, ficut nec hucufque funt obfervata, non poteft pax ftabiliri, nec quando novæ exactiones & inauditæ contra nos & noftros omni die adveniunt. Vobis autem tranfmittimus in rotulis damna nobis illata & fœdera non fervata fecundum formam pacis prius factam. Quod vero guerravimus quafi neceffitas nos cogebat; Nam nos & omnes Wallenfes eramus adeo oppreffi & fuppeditati & fpoliati & in fervitutem redacti per regales Jufticianos & Ballivos contra formam pacis & omnem jufticiam amplius quam

fi

APPENDIX.

si Saraceni essemus vel Judæi, sicut credimus & sæpe denunciavimus Domino Regi, nec aliquam emendam habere potuimus. Sed semper mittebantur justiciarii & ballivi ferociores & crudeliores, & quando illi erant saturati per suas injustas exactiones, alii de novo mittebantur ad populum excoriandum in tantum quod populus mallebat mori quam vivere. Nec oportet militiam ampliorem convocare, vel contra nos moveri Sacerdotium dum nobis fiat pax & servetur modis debitis ut superius est expressum. Nec debitis sancte pater omnibus verbis credere nostrorum adversariorum; sicut enim nos factis oppresserunt & opprimunt, ita & vobis diffamant, nobis imponentes quæ volunt.

Ipsi enim vobis sunt præsentes & nos absentes, ipsi opprimentes & nos oppressi. Et ideo propter Deum fidem eis in omnibus non exhibeatis, sed facta potius examinetis. Valeat sanctitas vestra ad regimen Ecclesiæ per tempora longa.

Primus Articulus est talis, Cum in forma pacis sic contineatur ut sequitur. Si vero idem Leolinus jus vendicaverit in aliquibus terris quas alii præter dictum dominum Regem occupaverint extra quatuor Cantredos prædictos, pleniariam sibi justitiam exhibebit præfatus dominus Rex secundum leges & consuetudines partium illarum in quibus terræ illæ consistunt: qui Articulus non fuit observatus super terris Arwystley & inter Dyvy & ductus fluviorum, pro eo quod cum Dominus Leolinus dictas terras vendicasset coram Domino Rege apud Ruthlan, & Rex sibi concessisset causam examinare secundum leges & consuetudines Walliæ ac advocati pretium fuissent introducti coram Rege ut judicarent de dictis terris secundum leges Wallicanas; parte rea comparente & respondente adeo quod eo die deberet finaliter terminari ex præfixione Domini Regis qui apud Gloverniam existens diem prædictum partibus assignavit, licet sæpius in diversis locis coram justiciariis fuisset dicta causa examinata, & terræ ipsæ essent in pura Wallia. Nec unquam judicata fuit super eis nisi secundum leges Wallicanas; Nec Dominus Rex posset

vel

APPENDIX.

vel deberet prorogare nisi secundum leges Walliæ: Diem tamen ipsum motu proprio prorogavit & contra leges antedictas, & ad ultimo fuit vocatus ad loca varia ad quæ non debuit evocari, nec justitiam obtinere potuit, nisi secundum leges Angliæ contra illud quod in dicto Articulo continetur. Et idem factum fuit coram justiciariis apud Montgomery, cum partes essent in judicio constitutæ & firmatæ, & dies datus ad sententiam audiendam, diem prorogaverunt leges memoratas. Demum apud Londinum post multos labores & expensas varias Rex ipse justitiam sibi denegavit, nisi vellet secundum leges Angliæ subire judicium in causa memorata.

Secundus Articulus non servatus est talis. Et omnes transgressiones injuriæ & excessus hinc inde factæ pœnitus remittuntur usque in diem hodiernum. Iste Articulus non fuit observatus quia Dominus Reginaldus de Grey statim cum fuit factus Justiciarius, movit varias quæstiones & innumerabiles contra homines de Tegengl, & nos super transgressis quæ factæ fuerunt in tempore Domini Henrici Regis, & dicti Domini Leolini dum Dominum in partibus illis obtinebat unde dicti homines multum timentes non audebant in domibus suis permanere.

Tertius Articulus, Ubi dictus Rys Vachan filius Nesi filii Maelgon cum terra quam nunc tenet & cum post pacem initam fuit spoliatus de terra de Geneverglyn, quam tunc tenebat cum hominibus & Averiis eorundem.

Quartus Articulus, Item concedit Dominus Rex quod omnes terras tenentes in quatuor Cantredis, & in aliis terris quas Dominus Rex retinet in manu sua, teneant eas adeo libere & plenarie sicut ante guerram tenere consueverint, & eisdem libertatibus & consuetudinibus gaudeant quibus prius gaudere solebant, & cum contra istum Articulum dictus Reginaldus consuetudines varias de novo introduxit, & hoc contra pacis formam supradictam.

Item *Quintus Articulus*, Controversiæ & contentiones motæ vel movendæ inter Principem & quoscunque terminabantur & decidentur secundum leges

Marchiæ

APPENDIX.

Marchiæ de his quæ emergunt in Marchia, & fecundum leges Walliæ de rebus contentiofis quæ in Wallia orientur. Contra iftum Articulum venit Dominus Rex mittendo Jufticiarios ufque ad Montgomery, qui ibidem judicare præfumpferunt homines dicti Leolini, *vindictam* ponendo fuper illos contra leges Walliæ, cum hoc vel aliud fimile nunquam factum fuiffet ibidem temporibus retroactis, quofdam incarcerando, alios in exilium mittendo, cum ipfe idem Princeps paratus effet de eifdem hominibus fuis exhibere juftitiæ complementum omnibus quærelantibus de eifdem.

Item *Sextus Articulus*. Item cum fit contentum in dicta pacis forma, quod Griffinus Vachan homagium faceret Domino Regi, de terra, de Yâl, & principi de terra de Edeyrnahu Jufticiarii Domini introduxerunt in totam terram prædictam de Edeyrnahu cujus cognitio caufæ ad Principem pertinebat fimpliciter, & non ad illos Jufticiarios; & tamen pro bono pacis princeps hoc tolerabat cum ipfe Princeps paratus effet eidem Dominæ fuper hoc juftitiam exhibere.

Septimus Articulus, ubi dicitur & licet idem Princeps fe noftræ ut dictum eft fuppofuerit voluntati, nos tamen concedimus & volumus quod voluntas noftra . . . . . ultra dictos Articulos fe in aliquo non extendant. Contra iftum Articulum exigebatur Aurum ad opus Reginæ in qualibet folutione facta Regi cum . . . . . Aurum nunquam fuit exactum Wallenfibus, nec in tempore Domini Henrici, vel alicujus alterius Regis Angliæ; quod Aurum exfolvit pro bono pacis, cum tamen nihil de hoc tactum fuit in forma pacis vel excogitatum: & nunc infuper exigitur à Principe Aurum ad opus Reginæ fenioris matris videlicet Domini Edvardi nunc Regis Angliæ, pro pace facta in tempore Domini Henrici nunc Regis Angliæ, cum nihil de hoc tunc fuerat dictum vel quoquomodo excogitatum, videlicet duo millia Marcarum & dimidium, & nifi dictæ Marcæ folverentur, minabatur dicta Regina quod bona ejufdem Leolini occuparet quæ invenire poterat in Dominio Regis, &

APPENDIX.

homines fuos capere vel venundare quoufque dictam fummam haberet ad plenum. Item cum invitâffet Dominus Rex dictum Principem adfectum Wiggornienfem verbis blandiffimis promittendo ei quod daret tunc confanguineam fuam fibi in uxorem, & multis ditaret honoribus; Nihilominus cum illuc veniffet in die defponfationis, ante miffam petiit Dominus Rex unam literam confignari à Principe continentem inter cætera, quod idem Princeps nullum omnino honorem in terra fua teneret contra Regis voluntatem, vel manu teneret ex quo poffit contingere quod omnes fideles Principis ab eo commoverentur. Quam quidem literam fibi figillatam tradidit, computans per metum qui cadere poffet in conftantem virum, cum tamen in forma pacis, ut præmiffum eft, contineatur quod nihil ab eo deberet exigi, ultra quod in dicta forma continetur.

Item, Cum fecundum eandem pacis formam confuetudines eidem Principi confirmentur quibus ufus fuerat ab antiquo; ac idem Princeps & Antecefores fui, ex confuetudine diutina & obtenta bona de naufragiis in terris fuis provenientia confueverant recipere, & in fuos ufus convertere ad libitum: Jufticiarius Ceftrenfis *namium* recepit fuper Principem pro bonis quæ recepit de naufragiis ante guerram contra dictam pacis formam per quam hinc inde erant remiffa, & contra confuetudines ante dictas. Dato etiam quod hoc effet foris factum *namium* recepit tale, videlicet quindecem libratas mellis & plures equos ac homines fuos incarceravit, & hoc ex propriis bonis Principis antedicti. Preterea, accipit fcaphas de Banweys quæ venerant apud Liverpol cum mercandiis per mercatores, & eas numquam deliberavit donec pecuniam pro eis accepit quantum volebat.

Item, Cum quidam homines de Geneurglyn quædam bona abftuliffent ab aliis vicinis fuis de Geneurglyn, dum effent in Dominio Principis de Merpyreton homines Regis de Llanbadarn prædam fecerunt, & acceperunt de terra Principis de Merpyreton, & cum homines fui veniffent illuc ad quærendum quare dictam prædam receperant, unum de eis interfecerunt, &

alios

APPENDIX.

alios vulneraverunt, & quofdam incarceraverunt. Et cum in dicta pacis forma contineatur quod in Marchia deberent emendari quæ in Marchia committebantur, tamen dicti homines Regis homines Principis audire noluerunt alibi quam in Caftro de Llanbadarn, & hoc contra pacis formam antedictam, fuper quo hactenus nullam juftitiam habere potuerunt. In iftis Articulis injuriatus Dominus Rex Principi & fuis, & etiam in multis aliis : Et licet Princeps tam per fe quam per fuos petiviffet fæpius à Domino Rege quod pacis formam fupradictam erga fe & fuos faceret obfervari, in nullo tamen extitit obfervata fed omni die de novo Jufticiarii & Ballivi Domini Regis in partibus illis injurias injuriis, & varia gravamina cumulaverunt ; propter quod mirum non debet videri alicui fi Princeps præfatus affenfum præftitit illis qui guerrare cœperunt, cum in his fides quam in animam Domini Regis fibi Dominus Robertus Tibetot juraverat in nullo fervabatur, & maxima & principaliter cum Princeps fuiffet præmunitus à perfonis fide dignis quod Princeps foret à Rege capiendus in fuo primo acceffu apud Ruthlan, & etiam fuiffet captus fi Rex illuc acceffiffet poft Natale ficut propofuerat.

Nec gravamina & alia quafi innumerabilia, fancte Pater, confiderantes, nobis affectu paterno compaciamini, & pro falute animæ Domini Regis, & noftræ, & etiam multorum aliorum, ad pacem bonam utriufque populi laboretis fructuosè.

Cum Dominus David primo veniffet ad Dominum Edwardum tunc Comitem Ceftriæ, ac homagium fibi feciffet, idem Dominus Edwardus eidem Davidi duas Cantredas, videlicet de dyffryn-Clwyd & Cywonant cum omnibus fuis pertinentiis dedit plenarie, & literas fuas patentes fuper hoc fieri fecit, tandem etiam donationem eidem invocavit, poftquam creatus eft in Regem, & etiam illum Davidem in poffeffionem illarum Cantredarum induxit corporalem.

Denium Domina Gwenlhian de Lacy mortua, tres villas quas in dictis Cantredis tenuit quoad vitam quæ ad ipfum Davidem fpectabant ratione Donationis fuæ

B b 4 prædictæ

APPENDIX.

prædictæ Dominus Rex sibi abstulit minus justè contra tenorem Chartæ suæ.

Item, Cum dictus David ex donatione Domini Regis prædicti villas de Hope & Eston obtineret in Wallia, de quibus nulli respondere tenebatur nisi secundum leges Wallicanas; tandem Justiciarius Cestriensis fecit ipsum ad instantiam cujusdam Anglici Willh. de Vanabel nomine ad comitatum Cestriensem super dictis villulis ad judicium evocari. Et licet dictus Dominus David petivisset multoties quod injuriose contra eundem non procederetur in dicto comitatu, pro eo quod ibidem respondere nullatenus tenebatur super villis prædictis quæ sitæ erant in Wallia, sed potius tractaretur, hoc sibi plane denegavit.

Item, Idem Justiciarius Cestriensis in gravamen dicti Domini Davidis nemus suum de Lleweni & Sylvas suas de Hope fecit succidi tam per villanos de Ruthlan, quam per alios, cum idem Justiciarius in terris prædicti Domini Davidis nullam omnino haberet jurisdictionem, & non contenti quod *meremium* ibidem quærerent ad ædificia exigenda tam apud Rodelanum quam alibi in patria, sed nemus destruendô *meremium* ibidem sectum ad vendendum in Hyberniam transtulerunt.

Item. Cum idem Dominus David quosdam *Fortanicos* de *terra* Domini Regis qui in nemoribus latitabant cepisset, ac suspendio tradidisset, idem tamen Justiciarius ipsum Davidem penes Regem accusabat, ac si ipse dictos malefactores defenderet & manuteneret, quod verisimile non erat cum ipse David dictos latrones suspendi faceret & occidi.

Item, Cum esset cautum in forma pacis quod Wallenses deberent in causis suis tractari secundum leges Wallicanas, istud tamen circa dictum Davidem & suos homines in nullo extitit observatum.

De premissis vero gravaminibus & aliis petiit idem David aliquam emendationem vel secundum leges Walliæ, vel consuetudines, vel etiam ex gratia speciali; & hoc etiam petiit à Domino Rege, quorum neutrum potuit aliquatenus obtinere: Et cum hoc præmunitus fuit à quibusdam à Curia Domini Regis, quod

in

APPENDIX. 373

In primo regreſſu Domini Reginaldi de Gray de Curia idem David eſſet capiendus ut filii ſui capiendi pro obſedibus eſſet, inſuper ſpoliandus caſtro ſuo de Hope, & etiam ſylva ſua ibidem ſuccidenda. Ideo cum idem David multum laboraſſet pro Demino Rege prædicto in diverſis guerris tam in Anglia quam in Wallia, & expoſuiſſet ſe & ſuos variis periculis & injuriis, ac amiſiſſet nobiliores de ſuis & fortiores, ac multos nimis, nihilominus de dictis gravaminibus & aliis nullam omnino juſtitiam, emendationem, ſeu gratiam potuit obtinere. Propter quæ gravamina & pericula, timens mortem propriam aut filiorum ſuorum, vel incarcerationem perpetuam, vel ſaltem diutinam, quaſi coactus & invitus incepit prout potuit ſe & ſuos defenſare.

Hæc eſt forma quam Dominus Rex Angliæ promiſit hominibus de Ros, antequam ipſi fecerunt ſibi homagium, & illam formam eis promiſit inviolabiliter obſervare, videlicet,

Quod ipſe Dominus Rex concederet unicuique eorum jus ſuum, & juriſdictionem ſuam, & etiam Dominium, bonæ memoriæ Domini Henrici quondam Regis Angliæ, ſecundum quod prædicti homines de Ros referent ipſos haberent temporibus prædicti Henrici.

Item, Promiſit prædictus Dominus Rex ſupradictis hominibus quod non darentur nec ad firmam ponerentur; quibus articulis conceſſis præfatis hominibus homagium fecerunt Domino Regi, & ipſe eis promiſit ore proprio dictos articulos obſervare. Hoc non obſtante quidam Cementarii redeuntes ad villam de Ruthlan, de loco ubi ipſi operabantur, obviaverunt cuidam nobili tranſeunti cum uxore ſua per viam regiam ſuper pace Domini Regis, qui Cementarii per vim propoſuerunt auferre à prædicto nobili ſuam uxorem, & quia ipſe nobilis defendit ſuam uxorem ne ab ipſo auferetur, prædicti Cementarii prædictum nobilem interfecerunt. Ille autem cui plus opponebatur dictum homicidium perpetraſſe, cum quibuſdam ſociis ſuis capti fuerunt; Et cum parentela prædicti interfecti petierit juſtitiam à Domino Juſticiario Ceſtrienſi de morte conſanguinii eorum,

APPENDIX.

eorum, illi de parentela ipsius interfecti fuerunt incarcerati, & interfectores fuerunt à carcere liberati.

Item, Quidam homo interfecit quendam nobilem qui videlicet filium Goronu de Heylyn nutriverat, & interfector captus fuit: Et cum quidam de parentela prædicti interfecti peterent justiciam de eorum consanguineo à Domino Justiciario Cestriensi, quidam eorum capti fuerunt, & interfector fuit in Castello Domini Regis liberatus, & adhuc est ibi, denegata justicia prædictæ parentelæ.

Item, Quidam nobiles vindicaverunt jus in quibusdam terris, & de mobilibus suis obtulerunt Domino Regi magnam summam pecuniæ pro justicia habenda per rationem & veredictum proborum & legalium hominum de patria; quæ quidem terræ adjudicatæ fuerunt, prædictis vendicantibus totam terram prædictam cum omnibus ædificiis *biadis*, & aliis bonis in ipsis contentis, Dominus Reginaldus de Grey; & sic amiserunt primo pecuniam quam pro terra pacaverunt, & postea terram.

Item, Jurisdictionis nostræ est quod nullus extraneus extirparet sylvas nostras, nisi prius habita licentia nostra; hoc non obstante, proclamatum fuit apud Rodolanum quod liceret unicuique Anglicano extirpare sylvas nostras sine nostra licentia ad libitum eorum voluntatis, & quod nobis fuit prohibitum dictas sylvas nostras extirpare.

Item, Terras quas probi homines à Domino Davide filio Leolini bonæ memoriæ habuerunt per donationem prædicti Davidis abstulit prædictus Justiciarius à prædictis probis hominibus.

Item, Quando aliquis ad villam de Ruthlan veniret cum mercandiis suis, si refutaret illud quod Anglicus eidem offerret pro suis mercandiis, statim duceretur ille Wallensis ad castrum, & emptor ibidem haberet rem quam larginaverat, & Dominus Rex haberet pretium dictæ rei, tunc Castellam dictum Wallensem spoliatum & atrociter verberatum deliberabant, pacatis prius Portario Castri quatuor denariis. Si vero aliquis Wallensis emeret aliquam rem in villa de Ruthlan, Anglicus qualiscunque superveniret, & rem venditam

dicto

APPENDIX.

dicto Wallenfi auferet ab ipfo pro minori pretio quam dictus Wallenfis folverat pro eadem.

Item, Contra promiffionem Domini Regis prædictis hominibus de Ros, ipfe dedit territorium villæ de Maenam in Penmayn & Lhysfaen.

Item, Taurus cujufdam probi hominis deprehenfus fuit in pratis Domini Regis apud Ros, & captus, & Dominus ejus vocatus fuit ad placitum ufque Rodolanum, & fuit condemnatus in quinque libris occafione dicti tauri; bis adivit Londinium pro juftitia petenda, & nullam fuit affecutus, & in illis duabus vicibus expendidit prædictus homo tres libras.

Item, Quidam nobiles de Cantreda de Ros emerunt officia pro certa fumma pecuniæ; pacata pecunia, meritis fuis non exigentibus, Dominus Jufticiarius Ceftrenfis abftulit ab eis eorum officia.

Item, Quidam rufticus Goronow ab *Heylyn* condemratus fuit in 17 *l*. bonæ & legalis monetæ juris, ordine non fervato.

Item, Goronow filius *Heylyn* accipit ad firmam territorium de Pennmaen & Lhysfaen à Magiftro Godfrido M. pro certa pecuniæ fumma, ufque ad finem quatuor annorum, quo facto Dominus Robertus de C. cum equis & armis, & cum viginti quatuor equitibus venit ad inequitandum prædictum Goronow occafione dictæ terræ, ita quod fic non fuit fecurus tranfitus nec ufque Rodolanum, nec ufque ad Jufticiarios nifi cum f.. *'tranfitura* de fua parentela & etiam de fuis amic..

Item, In reformationem pacis *ultro* factæ & firmatæ inter Dominum Regem, & fuos ex una parte, & Dominum Principem & fuos ex altera exprefsè continebatur; quod omnes injuriæ & tranfgreffiones factæ ex utraque parte penitus remitterentur; hoc non obftante, oppofitum fuit contra quofdam nobiles quoddam fore factum tempore guerræ, & ftatim capti fuerunt, nec potuerunt à carcere liberari antequam ipfi pacarent fedecem Marcas,

Item, Cum Caufæ debent tractari & terminari fecundum legem & confuetudinem terræ noftræ, compelluntur homines Cantredæ noftræ ad jurandum in caufis

APPENDIX.

prædictis contra suam conscientiam, nec aliter jurare patiuntur.

Præterea nos *constavimus* trecentas Marcas eundo ad Dominum Regem pro justitia petenda in prædictis Articulis, ibidem morando, & ad propria redeundo; & cum nos credebamus habere plenam justitiam de singulis Articulis prædictis, Dominus Rex transmisit ad partes nostras Dominum Reginaldum de Grey, cui dictus Dominus Rex totam terram ad firmam concessit, ad tractandos homines prædictæ Cantredæ prout suæ placeret voluntati; qui compulsit nos jurare per manum suam cum deberemus jurare per manum Domini Regis, & ubi Crux Domini Regis levari deberet, quod Crux prædicti Reginaldi levaretur, in signum quod ipse erat verus Dominus. Dictus vero Reginaldus in suo adventu ad partes Walliæ vendidit quibusdam servientibus Domini Regis officia sua, quæ prædicti servientes prius emerant à Dom. Rege pro 23 Marcis, & illa officia non deberent vendi nisi cum dominium dominorum mutaretur.

Item, Dominus Rex dedit Mareduco filio Madoc Magisterium satellitum pro suo servitio, Dominus Reginaldus de Grey abstulit ab eo suum officium, nec à Domino Rege assequi potuit aliquam justitiam.

Item, Unus de consilio prædicti Reginaldi nobis dixit ore tenus, *scilicet* Cynwricus Fychan, quod in adventu prædicti Reginald ad partes Walliæ, viginti quatuor homines de probioribus hominibus cujuslibet Cantredæ caperet ad incarcerandos ipsos perpetuo vel decapitandos : Propter ista gravamina, & alia quæ dictus Reginaldus nobis fecit, & etiam propter minas quas ipse nobis intulit, videlicet quod si mitteremus aliquos nuntios ad Curiam Domini Regis pro justitia petenda decapitarentur. Multa alia damna nobis allata, & injuriæ factæ; & quando mittebamus ad Curiam Domini Regis, nuntii non permittebantur nec ausi fuerunt intrare, sed expendebant multa inutiliter; ob ista gravamina æstimabamus nos esse liberos à juramento facto Domino Regis coram Deo.

Item, Bledyn Seis & *Anjanus* filius Genaf de Ros quoddam malefactum fecerunt temporibus David filii Lewelini, & Henrici Regis, de homicidiis factis tunc
satis-

satisfactionem & emendam satisfacere monstraverunt; Et modo de novo Reginaldus de Grey vellet & cogeret illam emendam renovare, donec oportuit ipsos terras proprias relinquere.

Item, Census & obventiones quos solvimus de veteri moneta per medietatem unius anni ante adventum novæ monetæ, cogerunt nos reddere eis novas monetas pro veteri & hoc sub eodem numero.

Ista sunt gravamina per Dominum Regem & suos Justiciarios illata Rheso parvo de Ystrad Tywy.

Primum est, Postquam dictus Rhys dedit & concessit Domino Regi castrum suum apud Dynefowr post ultimam pacis formam; qui dictus Rhesus tunc temporis erat in *tentilio* Domini Payn de Gadfry, eodem tempore interfecti fuerunt sex nobiles viri Domini Rhys, de quibus satisfactionem nec justiciam umquam habuit quod fuit eis damnum & gravamen.

Item, Johannes Giffard calumniavit eum Rhesum super hæreditatem propriam apud Hirwryn, quicquid Rhesus inquisivit à Domino Rege legem patriæ suæ, aut legem comitatus Caermardden, in quo comitatu Antecessores dicti Rhys solebant habere leges, quando fierent in unitatem Anglicorum, & sub eorum dominiis; quod idem Rhys nullas leges habuit, & suam terram prædictam totaliter amisit; vellent ipsum instringere in Comitatu Heretordiensi, ubi numquam antecessores ejus responderunt.

Præterea in terris præfati Rhesi talia gravamina fuerunt per Anglicos facta, maxime pertinent ad Ecclesiasticos, videlicet in Ecclesia Sancti Davidis quæ vocatur *Llangadawc* fecerunt stabula, & meretrices collocaverunt, & omnia bona quæ in ea continebantur omnino asportaverunt atque totos domos combusserunt; & in eadem Ecclesia juxta aram percusserunt Capellanum cum gladio ad caput ejus & eum reliquerunt semivivum.

Item, In eadem patria Ecclesiam Dyngad & Ecclesiam Llantredaf spoliaverunt & combusserunt; cæterasque Ecclesias in partibus illis omnino spoliaverunt calicibus, & libris, ac omnibus aliis ornamentis & rebus.

Gravamina

Gravamina Lewelini filii Rhys, & Howeli fratris ejus per Dominum Regem illata sunt hæc.

Postquam in formam pacis inter Dominum Henricum tunc temporis Regem Angliæ & Dominum Principem apud *Rhydchwnna*, tunc præfatus Rex concessit, & per Cartas suas confirmavit præfato Principi *So long as* homagium prædictorum Nobibium *exos*. Prædicti Nobiles fuerunt fideles & constantes cum præfato Principe, juxta eorum donationem & Cartarum suarum confirmationem: Edwardus nunc Rex Angliæ prædictos Nobiles dehæreditavit, denegando eisdem omnes leges & consuetudines Walliæ; ita quod non habuerunt terras suas nec per legem, nec per gratiam.

Ista sunt gravamina, damna, seu molestiæ per Anglicos illata filiis Maredudi filii Oweni.

Primum est quamquam Dominus Rex concessit prædictis Nobilibus suas proprias hæreditates post pacis formam, videlicet Geneur'glyn & Creudhyn; præfatus vero Rex, contra suam donationem & pacis formam, terris supradictis antedictos Nobiles dehæriditavit, denegando eidem omnes leges & consuetudines Walliæ, & Angliæ, atque Comitatus Caermardhyn.

Secundum est quod præfatus Rex in suo comitatu de Cardigan, per suos Justiciarios antedictos Nobiles compellit, ut ipsi traderent judicium super ignobiles ac subditos Patriæ, & quod tales homines *è Comisso* judicium super ipsos opponerent, ubi numquam antecessores eorum ab Anglicis talia sustinuerunt.

Tertium est, quod Justicarii Domini Regis Curiam eorum Nobilium abstulerunt, compellendo homines suos proprios coram eis satisfacere, quia de jure coram prædictis Nobilibus deberent satisfacere.

Quartum est, quod quoddam Naufragium in terris antedictorum Nobilium fuit, qui quidem Nobiles bona Naufragii receperunt, sicut antecessores eorum fecerunt, & hoc non fuit eis prohibitum per aliquos ex parte Regis : Antedictus vero Rex contra eorum consuetudinem & legem, occasione illius Naufragii eosdem damnavit in octoginta Marcis sterlingorum; atque bona quæ in Naufragio continebantur omnino asportaverunt.

Quintum est, quod nullus nostrum in Comitatu Uffegd de Cardigan ausus esset venire inter Anglicos propter timorem carceris & nisi fuisset propter periculum Nobilibus Metrop[d]. nihil contra honorem Domini Regis moverent.

Significant vero quod omnes Christiani habent leges & consuetudines in eorum propriis terris; Judæi vero inter Anglicos habent leges, ipsi vero in terris suis, & eorum antecessores habuerunt leges immutabiles & consuetudines, donec Anglia post ultimam guerram ab eis leges suas abstulerunt.

Memorandum de querelis omnium Nobilium virorum de Ystradatuy eisdem latis ac factis per Rogerum de Clyfford, & Rogerum Croscil vicem Domini Rogeri de Clyfford gerentem contra privilegium, justitiam, & consuetudinem prædictorum virorum de Ystratuy, ut dicunt & probant.

Primus Articulus est quod cum dicti Rogeri cogerunt dictos homines de Ystradatuy reddere sibi pro consuetudinibus suis viginti Marcas sterlingorum, & post solutionem dictæ pecuniæ cito fregerunt in hunc modum, quod posuerunt super 17 viros judicantes secundum jus Angliæ; quod numquam fuit consuetudo nec privilegium dictæ patriæ.

Item. Madecus filius Bledyn condemnatus fuit in quatuor Marcio injustè.

Item. Lewelinus Rufus condemnatus fuit in quinque Marcis & 17 averiis contra privilegium & consuetudinem patriæ.

Item. Quod ipsi Rogeri fecerunt forestam super terram propriam virorum patriæ : Et propter pedem unius Cervi inventum in ore canis alicujus, tres homines fuerunt spoliati omnino.

APPENDIX.

Item. Michael ab Yguftyl condemnatus fuit in decem folidis pro facto patris fui, quadraginta annis elapfis.

Item. Cogerunt parentes Ennii à Strabonis ad reddendum fuum relevagum in vita fua.

Item. Quod ipfi pofuerunt fuper nos omnes fatellitos de Anglicis, quod numquam fuit noftra dimidietas.

Item. Dati fuimus Domino Mauritio de Crumy, & venditi fuimus Domino Rogero de Clyfford, quod numquam fuit fuper parentes noftros.

Item. Relicta Roberti de Monte alto petiit, à Domino Rege tertiam partem terræ de Monte alto in Ward, & dijudicata fuit coram Domino Rege quod numquam dicta terra fuit in Ward data.

Hi funt Articuli quæftionum illati ab hominibus de Penlhyn, injufte per Conftabularium Albi Monafterii & fuos cives.

Primo. Cynwric filius Madoci fuit fpoliatus ab eis tempore pacis octo libris, & quatuor bobus, & blado laboris unius aratri, per duos annos & valore trium librarum à tribus hominibus ejufdem; affirmat etiam quod folvit 16 libras per octo in valore, & majorem habuit injuriam imponendo manus in ipfum quam totum quod amifit, quia tunc erat Conftabularius Domini Principis apud Penllyn: Non fuit alia caufa dictæ fpoliationis nifi quia dicebatur invenire 24 garbas de decimis in domo cujufdam hominis dicti Cynwrici.

Item. Adam Preco condemnatus fuit in feptem folidis & octo denariis, & Equa valoris unius libræ, imponendo manus in ipfum & liberando latronem dictæ equæ, quia ipfe venerat ibidem cum dicto latrone capto.

Item. Ednevot ab Gruffydh condemnatus fuit in 27 s. nec fuit caufa nifi quia vendidit equam unam ad unum miliare citra villam, ficut folebant à tempore quo non extat memoria, quando veniebant ad nundinas.

Item. Adaf Ddu condemnatus fuit in 30 s. eo quod duo boves quos propofuerat vendere in foro Albi Monafterij

Monasterii exibant villam ipso connivente, & captus fuit & detentus usque ad solutionem 30 *s.* nec ipsi boves exierant nisi de Plateo qua stabant usque ad aliam Plateam.

Item. Biryt filius Gwyn, condemnatus fuit in quinque solidis, & in carcerem ductus; eo quod percussit unum bovem indomitum ipsum calcantem in foro.

Item. Yorwerch ab Gorgonon condemnatus fuit 70 *s.* eo quod evaserat quondam de carcere eorum tempore guerræ, & in tempore pacis inventus fuit in dicta villa, & hoc contra formam pacis initæ inter Dominum Regem, & Dominum Principem.

Item. Duo famuli Kenwric ap Gruffydh condemnati fuerunt in duabus Marcis, eo quod dicebant ipsos non solvisse toletum postquam solverant.

Item. Caducanus Niger famulus Constabularii de Penllyn captus fuit & condemnatus in 6 *s.* & 4 *d.* eo quod nolebat recipere veterem monetam pro nova.

Item. Gruffydh ap Goronow *tercinarius* Domini *A Servant* Principis spoliatus fuit uno bove valoris 11 *s.* & 8 *d.* & postquam arraveret Constabularius cum dicto bove per septem menses, solvit dictus Gruffynus pro dicto bove, 40 *d.*

Item. Howel ab David spoliatus fuit per satellites albi Monasterii duobus solidis extra villam, eo quod denegaverat prius munera ut solent satellites petere.

Item. David ab Gronow ab Eynion spoliatus fuit 30 *s.* eo quod quidam Cives albi Monasterii dixit, quod quidam de Penlhyn, qui mortuus fuerat, denegabatur ei in quibusdam rebus.

Item. Duo famuli Y bongam capti fuerunt & condemnati in duabus libris, eo quod posuerunt manum in quendam latronem qui spoliabat eos in villa per noctem, & liberaverunt latronem.

Item. Eneyon filius Ichael captus & verberatus fuit, & spoliatus duobus bobus valoris, 24 *s.* & 6 *d.* nulla alia de causa, nisi quod boves ipso connivente moverunt se de platea ad aliam plateam.

Item.

APPENDIX.

Item. Adaf ap Ychael condemnatus fuit in duabus libris pro una libra, & ipfe pofuerat in juramento cujufdam civis de albo Monafterio quod non tenebatur nifi in una libra pro Principe, nec voluit jurare, & ideo fpoliatus fuit una libra.

Item. Guyan Maeftran fpoliatus fuit 5 s. eo quod dicebat quod quidam Mercator de Ardydwy tenebatur eis in quibufdam rebus, cum ipfe nec erat de dicta Balliva: Item condemnatus fuit in 8 d. quia dicebant ipfum vendere quafdam oves extra villam cum ipfe non vendiderat.

Item. Famulus Lewelini ab Gwyn fpoliatus fuit feptem ovibus,& 5 s. & fuo pallio,eo quod dicebant ipfum effe de Domino Griffydh ab Gwyn cum ipfe non erat.

Item. Iorwerch ab Meylir captus fuit & condemnatus in 15 s. cum pallio, eo quod denegavit dare munus fatellitibus quod petebant, ipfi finxerunt eum in villa pernoctare.

Item. Cives albi Monafterii rapuerunt à Madoco Rufo filio Ychael unum bovem valoris, 11 s. & 6 d.

Ifta omnia facta fuerunt per Henricum Gamber dicti loci Conftabularium, cum aliis innumerabilibus Articulis.

Item. Ybicre captus fuit in negotio Domini Principis, & condemnatus in 5 s. abfque aliqua caufa.

Hæc funt gravamina Goronow filii Heylyn, viz.

Quod quidem Villanus dictus Coronon vocatus fuit ad Curiam Domini Regis occafione indebitæ caufæ. Tunc dictus Goronow venit ad fuum villanum defendendum, & petiit pro ipfo veritatem à Domino Jufticiario, aut Legem qua utuntur homines fuæ patriæ ; omnibus autem his eidem denegatis, dictus villanus condemnatus fuit in 27 libris, & tribus obolis : Tunc dictus Goronow adivit Londonium pro juftitia habenda, & expendit quinque Marcas & quatuor Solidos, & promiffa fuit fibi juftitia, & nullam fuit affecutus.

Item. Quidam Nobilis fuit interfectus, videlicet, qui nutriverat filium dicti Goronow, & ille interfector

APPENDIX.

fector captus fuit & deportatus fuit apud Castrum de Ruthlan: Tunc dictus Goronow & quidem de parentela interfecti petierunt justitiam de interfectore: Tunc denegata eis justitia, quidam fuerunt incarcerati, & ille interfector fuit in Castello liberatus. Tunc dictus Goronow iterum adivit Londonium propter supradicta gravamina ad justitiam petendam, & expendit, 20 Marcas, 3 s. 4 d. Et Dominus Rex promisit eidem plenariam justitiam, & nullam fuit adeptus cum pervenit ad patriam suam.

Item. Tertio ex defectu justitiæ oportuit dictum Goronow adire Londonium occasionibus supradictis pro justitia petenda, & expendit illa vice 18 Marcas, 6 s. 8 d bonæ & legalis Monetæ; & tunc simpliciter promisit Dominus Rex eidem justitiam perhibere; & quando credebat habere justitiam, tunc venit Reginaldus de Grey, & dixit aperte quod ipse deberit tractare totam patriam per chartas Domini Regis, & abstulit totam Ballivam à dicto Goronow; quam sibi Dominus Rex concessit, & vendidit illam Ballivam ad voluntatem suam, & tunc petiit dictus Goronow justitiam à Domino Reginaldo de gravaminibus supradictis, & nullam fuit adeptus.

Item. Dictus Goronow recepit terram, videlicet, Penmaen & Llysfaen ad firmam de Godfrido Merlyn, usque ad finem quatuor annorum pro certa pecuniæ summa. Tunc Robertus de Cruquer venit cum equis suis & armis ad quærendum dictam terram per vim, & quia dictus Goronow non permitteret auferre dictam terram ab eodem usque terminum præsignatum, tunc vocatus fuit ad Curiam dictus Goronow illa occasione; Tunc venit Reginaldus de Grey, cum viginti quatuor equitibus armatis ad proponendum capere dictum Goronow, vel ad eundem decapitandum; & quia viderunt quod non possent implere suum propositum illo die, vocaverunt dictum Goronow crastino die apud Ruthlan, & tunc dictus Goronow habuit consilium ita quod non deberent adire dictam Curiam: Iterum dictus Goronow vocatus fuit adplacitum apud Caerwys, & non ausus fuit adire dictum placitum nisi per conductum Domini Episcopi Asaphensis,

APPENDIX.

Afaphenfis, quia dictus Reginaldus & fui complures ibidem erant armati.

Item. Propter ista gravamina de quibus nullam habuit justitiam nisi laborare & expendere duas libr. quatuor Marcas, & 9 *d*; & quia non ausus fuit in propria persona adire Curiam, misit quendam nuncium deportantem duas literas, unam ad Dominum Regem, & aliam ad fratrem Lewelinum, ad signandum Domino Regi quod amitteret totam patriam, & dictum Goronow quia non observavit illud quod eisdem promisit; & quia nullam possent homines de Ros & Arglifeld assequi justitiam, & quia noluit corrigere sive emendare ista gravamina propter hoc amisit totam patriam.

Supplicant sanctitati vestræ, Domine Archiepiscope Cantuariensis totius Angliæ Primas, Nobiles viri de Tegengyl, & vobis demonstrant quod cum prædicti Nobiles fecerunt homagium Domino Edwardo Regi Angliæ, ipse Rex eisdem promisit quod eosdem immunes observaret & indemnes, tam in bonis, libertatibus, juribus, jurisdictionibus, privilegiis quibus usi fuerunt tempore Henrici Regis per suum obtentum privilegium; ex quibus privilegiis fuerunt postmodo spoliati.

Imprimis. Juribus & consuetudinibus patriæ fuerunt spoliati, viz. prædictus Edwardus compellendo quod ipsi procederent in causis secundum legem Anglicanam, cum secundum tenorem privilegii sui secundum legem Wallicanam procedere debuissent, viz. apud Trêf Edwyn, & apud Ruthlan, & apud Caerwys; & optimati de patria fuerunt manu capti quia ipsi provocabant quod ipsi procederent in causa apud Trêf Edwyn secundum legem & consuetudinem Wallicanam secundum tenorem privilegii.

Secundo. Quia unus Justiciarius duceret in causis peragendis, alius suus prædecessor in irritum revocaret, viz. in causa Davidis Reginaldus de Grey recitavit processum quem suus Antecessor ratum habuit, & etiam approbavit.

Tertio,

Tertio. Quod fi unus Nobilis de patria fuiffet propter calumniam fibi impofitam captus, quod non remitterent eundem pro *cautione fidevifforia* evadere, *Surety.* quod facere debuiffent.

Quarto. Quod tres unius Nobilis deducti ad Caftrum fuerunt de Flynt, propter parvam accufationem, una cum Averiis fuis, nec potuerunt de Caftro devenire, nec dilationem obtinere donec unufquifque dedit unum bovem Conftabulario de Flynt, & donec folverunt tres libras Kynwrico *Seis* pro dilatione habenda.

Quinto. Reginaldus de Grey terras virorum de Merton dedit & conceffit Abbati de Bafingwerk ordinis *Cifterciend.* contra legem Wallicanam, & patriæ confuetudinem; & contra formam pacis initæ inter Dominum Lewelinum Principem & Dominum Regem, viz. 16. *Catatatas terræ.*

Sexto. Mirantur Nobiles & optimati patriæ pro eo quod Dominus Rex fecit ædificare Caftrum fuper terram & poffeffionem magnatum, & mandavit Dominus Rex Jufticiario fuo quod ipfe folveret eque bonam terram illis fpoliatis & adhuc aliquam terram, nec fuæ terræ æftimationem funt confecuti in Flynt.

Septimo. Reginaldus de Grey non permitteret poffeffores fylvarum uti fylvis fuis, donec ab eifdem pretium & præmium fuiffet confecutus, & aliis rufticis gratis permitteret fylvam prædictorum abfcidere, cum non debuiffent fecundum patriæ confuetudinem & legem Wallicanam.

Octavo. Cum homines de Cyrchynan fecerunt pactum cum Domino Rege, quod cum ipfi concederent dimidietatem cujufdam prati, ad hoc quod Dominus Rex non permitteret fylvam prædictorum abfcidere Howelo filio Gruffydd præfente, & moft modum Reginaldus de Grey prædictum pratum infirmavit, viz. concedendo aliis quod abfciderent fylvam prædictorum, & eofdem dimidietate prati fui fpoliando.

Nono. Filius Kynwrici ab Goronow fuit captus apud Ruthlan culpa fua minime præcedente, nifi vellet pignus fuum *acquietare* à quadam muliere, & Con- *Redeem* ftabularius de Ruthlan fecit eundem detradi in car- *the Gage.*
cerem

cerem injuriose, nec potuit exinde deliberari donec prædictus fuit condemnatus ultra suorum bonorum hypotheca.

Decimo. Cum Ballivus de Ruthlan erat in convivio apud villam *Four Hutmus* de *Limayl* quendam virum Nobilem crudeliter vulneravit in præsentia Ballivi supradicti; cujus vulneris occasione prædictus Hutmus fuit in octo libris condemnatus; & quum ille cui injuria fuisset facta petere voluisset prædictas libras, eundem fecit detrudi in carcerem una.

Undecimo. Nuntii Reginaldi de Grey proposuerunt facere illud quod erat absurdum & dissonum juris secundum Canonicas sanctiones; videlicet petere ab eisdem quod ipsi ararent Reginaldo de Grey, & quod ipsi seminarent illam araturam; & illi fuerunt Nuntii, viz. Kynwricus Seis & *Hutmus* de Limayl, quod prædictus vero Kynwricus in præsentia omnium de patria juravit, nisi omnes de patria ararent quod ipsi infra tempus pœniterent, & ipsi multum timuerunt metu qui potuit cadere in constantem virum,

Duodecimo. Quod Præcones de Tegeyngl emerunt officium Præconiæ pro 30 Marcis à Domino Rege, & postmodum Reginaldus de Grey prædictos præcones tam pecunia quam præconia spoliavit contra legem & consuetudinem Anglicanam.

Tertiodecimo. Septem Nobiles fuerunt interfecti minus juste ab Anglicis, & adhuc parentes prædictorum aliquam satisfactionem non habuerunt, cum illi malefactores fuerunt capti; & postmodum prædictos malefactores remiserunt prædicti Constabularii impunitos.

Quartodecimo. Constabularius unus de Ruthlan detradit duos Satellites Domini Regis in carcere, pro eo quod ipsi tenuerunt aliquem Anglicum qui grave delictum commisit hominem alium vulnerando.

Isti omnes Articuli in præmissis nominati, fuerunt perpetrati contra prædictorum virorum libertatem, jurisdictionem, & privilegium & contra legem & consuetudinem Wallicanam; videlicet, quod non erant

Ausi

APPENDIX.

Ausi eorum quærelas Domino Regi per suos nuncios denuntiare, propter metum Reginaldi & timorem, qui metus potuit cadere in constantem virum: quia prædictus Reginaldus sua voce *Dilvada* fuit protesta- *Openly.* tus; quod sin inveniret nuntios prædictorum quod eosdem decapitaret prout nobis ex parte unius ex consilio suo fuit certive intimatum. In tantum quod lingua non potest proferre, nec penna scribere in quantum prædicti homines de Tegeyngl fuerunt aggravati.

Conqueritur vobis, Domine Archiepiscope Cantuariensis totius Angliæ Primas, Lewelinus filius Griffini filii Madoci de Constabulario de Cruce Uswaldi Regis, & de hominibus ejusdem Villæ qui prædictum Lewelinum tertia parte cujusdam Villæ quæ vocatur Ledrot, & Curia patris sui, sine observatione juris patriæ suæ vel consuetudine inequiter spoliarunt.

Præterea. Prædictus Constabularius & sui complures eundem Lewelinum communi pastura, qua prædictus Lewelinus usus fuit temporibus retroactis, ordine juris patriæ minime observato, spoliarunt, & in 70 libris occasione prædictæ pasturæ condemnaverint. Cæterum Dominus Rex Angliæ concessit quasdam literas cuidam Bastardo, scil. Griffino Fychan ab Cynlhaeth, ad litigandum contra eundem Lewelinum pro toto Dominio suo obtinendo, quarum literarum occasione idem Lewelinus expendit cc *l.* sterlingorum legalis usualisæ monetæ.

Iterum. Prædictus Constabularius compulsit prædictum Lewelinum ad mittendum duos suos Nobiles ad eos suspendendos ad prædictum Constabularium quicquid viri Nobiles suspendi minime debuissent, quam suspensionem nollent parentes prædictorum hominum sustinuisse pro ccc libris sterlingorum. Postmidum prædictus Constabularius incacerravit bis 60 homines prædicti Lewelini nulla præmissa ratione, nisi quod quidam garco emisit quandam vocem, nec potuerunt evadere suum carcerem donec quilibet eorum solvit decem solidos pro sua deliberatione.

Item.

APPENDIX.

Item. Quando homines prædicti Lewelini venirent ad forum ad suos boves vendendos, prædictus Constabularius faceret boves deduci ad Castrum, nec postmodum boves restitueret, nec pretium solveret venditori: Præsertim idem Constabularius & sui ceperunt jumenta prædicti Lewelini ad terram suam propriam, & de eisdem jumentis fecerunt suam voluntatem.

Præterea. Justiciarii Domini Regis compulserunt prædictum Lewelinum ad tradendum quandam villam filiis Eneoni filii Griffini; qui quidem prædictam villam, nec à se, nec à prædecessoribus fuerunt consecuti, ordine juris patriæ suæ in hac parte minime observato.

Idem. Prædictus Constabularius abstulit equum Ballivi prædicti Lewelini sine aliqua ratione, nec sibi aliquid debebatur; nec adhuc prædictus Ballivus satisfactionem aliquam est consecutus.

Cæterum. Quando prædictus Lewelinus volebat adire villam quæ vocatur Caerlleon cum literis Domini Regis ad comperiendum ibidem in die sibi assignata; filii Griffini filii Gwenynny & Armigeri Domini Rogeri Starainge ex consilio Rogeri eundem Lewelinum & suos incarcerarunt in sui injuriam & suorum non modicam læsionem; quam injuriam & læsionem nollet prædictus Lewelinus & sui sustinuisse pro ccc Marcis sterlingorum; nec ab eisdem potuit evadere donec invenit pro se sufficientem cautionem.

His & aliis receptis in scriptis accessit, Archiepiscopus ad Dominum Regem; supplicans ei humiliter ut gravamina suppradicta dignetur avertere, & ea correctione debita terminare: Et saltem pro tanto habere excessus Wallensium excusatos: Qui respondit Wallenses in injuriis sibi illatis esse excusabiles, quia omni tempore paratus extiterat omni facere justitiam conquerenti: Quo audito, Archiepiscopus Regi iterum supplicavit ut permitteret Wallenses pro suis gravaminibus exponendis & remediis afferendis ad ipsum habere accessum liberum & regressum: Qui respondit quod libere permitteret eos ad se accedere sed & redire; si secundum justitiam regressus eorum meritis responderet.

APPENDIX.

responderet. Quibus auditis accessit Archiepiscopus ad principem Walliæ in Snawdoniam ut tam ipsum quam Davidem fratrem suum & cæteros Wallenses ad aliquam humilitatis regulam ipsorum animos inclinaret; per quam posset qui ipsorum nuntius regiam clementiam ad ipsos admittendos in gratiam inclinare. Post varios autem tractatus respondit princeps; quod paratus erat voluntati regiæ se supponere duobus præsuppositis, salva scilicet conscientia sua qua populo suo assistere tenebatur; salva etiam condescentia status sui. Quæ cum Archiepiscopus retulisset Domino Regi, respondit Dominus Rex quod nullum alium de pace volebat cum Principe ac subditis suis habere tractatum, nisi quod ipsi supponerent se in omnibus regiæ voluntati : Et cum constaret Archiepiscopo Wallenses nullo modo velle se regiæ voluntati supponere, nisi præcite in forma eis tolerabili & accepta, tractatum habuit ex permissione Domini Regis cum magnatibus tunc præsentibus, qui omnes consenserunt in Articulos infra scriptos, quos per fratrem Johannem Wallensem inscriptos principi & suis Archiepiscopus destinavit.

Primo. Quod Dominus Rex de quatuor Cantredis & terris ab eo datis, Magnatibus suis nullum vult habere tractatum, nec etiam de Insula Anglesey.

Idem. De tenentibus eorum Cantredorum si ad suam pacem venerint, proponit facere prout condecet Regiam Majestatem, credimus tamen quod aget cum eis misericorditer si ad pacem venerint, & ad hoc proponimus una cum cæteris amicis efficaciter laborare, sperantes efficaciter exaudiri.

Item. De facto Domini Lewelini nullum potuimus aliud habere responsum nisi quod simpliciter & absolute conformet ad Domini Regis voluntatem; ut credimus firmiter quod Dominus Rex cum eo aget miserecorditer, & ad hoc intendimus cum totis viribus laborare cum cæteris amicis exaudiendis ut confidimus cum effectu.

Primo. Quod proceres hanc formam gratiæ regiæ conceperunt; ut videlicet Domino Lewelino se Regiæ gratiæ submittente, provideatur ei per Regem honorifice

APPENDIX.

rifice in mille libratis fterlingorum de aliquo honorifico comitatu, in aliquo loco Angliæ; ita tamen quod prædictus Lewelinus ponat Dominum Regem in *Seyſina* Snaudonum abſolute, perpetue & quiete. Et ipſe Rex filiæ Principis ſecundum condiceſtiam ſui proprii Sanguinis providebit, & ad hoc ſperant ſe poſſe Regis animum inclinare.

Item. Si contingat Lewelinum ducere uxorem & habere de ea puellam maſculam, intendunt impetrare Proceres à Domino Rege, ut proles illa ſuccedat perpetuo hæreditario Lewelini in terra maſculorum liberorum videlicet Comitatu.

Item. De populo Principi immediate ſubjecto tam in Snaudon quam alibi providebitur ſecundum Deum prout complete ſaluti ejuſdem populi & honori ; & ad hoc eſt Regia clementia ſatis prona, populo deſiderans conſolabiliter providere.

Primò. Quod ſi ad honorem Dei & ſuum juxta crucis aſſumptæ debitum velit in terræ ſanctæ ſubſidium proficiſci, providebitur ei honorifice ſecundum condeſcentiam Status ſui, ita tamen quod non redeat niſi per Regiam clementiam vocatus : Rogabimus etiam Dominum Regem, & ſperamus efficaciter exaudiri, ut provideat proli ſuæ.

His omnibus motu noſtro ſubjungimus Wallenſibus omnia pericula imminere longe gravius quam eis diximus oraculo vivæ vocis ; ſcribimus dura valde ſed longe durius eſt obrui vi & armis, & in fine totaliter extirpari, quoniam omni die pericula nobis imminentia aggravantur.

Item. Longe difficilius eſt omni tempore in guerra eſſe in anguſtia cordis & corporis vivere, & ſemper in inſidiis malignari, & cum hoc vivere & mori in peccato mortali continuo & rancore.

Item. De quo doleremus valde ſi ad pacem minime veniatis, indubitanter timemus contra vos debere ſententiam Eccleſiaſticam intolerabiliter aggravari pro exceſſibus veſtris; de quibus non poteritis vos aliquatenus excuſare in quibus invenietis miſericordiam, ſi ad pacem veniatis & de his nobis reſpondeatur in ſcriptis.

Reveren-

APPENDIX.

Reverendissimo in Christo Patri ac Domino J. *Dei gratia Archiepiscopo Cantuariensi ac totius Angliæ Prrimati suus in Christo devotus filius Lewelinus Princeps Walliæ, Dominus Snaudon, salutem cum desideriis benevolentiæ filialis ac reverentiis multimodis & honoribus.*

Sancte Pater, sicut vosmet consuluistis, ad gratiam Regiam parati sumus venire sub forma tamen nobis secura & honesta : Sed quia forma contenta in Articulis nobis missis minime secura est & honesta prout nobis & consilio nostro videtur ; & de qua multum admirantur omnes audientes, eo quod plus tendit ad destructionem & ruinam populi nostri ac nostram, quam ad nostram honestatem & securitatem, nullo modo permittet consilium nostrum nos in ea consentire si vellemus ; alii quoque Nobiles & populus nobis subjectus nullo modo consentirent in eandem ob indubitatam destructionem & dissipationem quæ inde eis possent evenire.

Tamen supplicamus vestræ sanctæ parternitati quatenus ad reformationem pacis debitæ, honestæ, & securæ, ob quam tot labores assumpsistis, proinde laboretis, collationem habentes ad Articulos quos vobis mittimus in scriptis : Honorabilius enim est & rationi magis consonum ut de Domino Rege teneamus terras in quibus jus habemus, quam nos exhæredare & eas tradere alienis. Datum apud Garthcelyn.

Primo. Quod licet Dominus Rex de quatuor Cantredis & aliis terris ab eo datis magnatibus suis, ac de Insula Anglesey nullum voluerit habere tractatum, tamen consilium Principis non permittit, si contingat aliquam pacem fieri, quin tractetur de premissis ; eo quod isti Cantredi sunt de puro Principis tenemento, in quibus merum jus habuerunt Principes & prædecessores sui à temporibus Cambri filii Bruti, tum quia sunt de principatu, cujus confirmationem Princeps

C c 4 obtinet

APPENDIX.

Pope. obtinet pro bonæ memoriæ Octobonum sedis *Apostolicæ* legatum in Anglia, consensu Domini Regis & sui Patris ad hoc intervenienti, sicut patet Chartas eorum inspicienti, tum quia etiam equius est quod veri hæredes teneant dictos Cantredos de Domino Rege pro pecunia & servitiis consuetis, quam eos dari extraneis & Advenis, qui & si fuerunt regere aliquam tamen per vim & potentiam.

Dicunt etiam comiter omnes tenentes de omnibus Cantredis Walliæ quod non sunt ausi venire ad voluntatem Regis, ut de eis disponat secundum Regiam Majestatem.

Primo. Quod Dominus Rex nec pacta, nec juramenta, nec Chartas servavit ab initio versus Dominum suum Principem & ipsos,

Secundo. Quia regales in Ecclesias & Ecclesiasticas personas inivit crudelissimam tyrannidem.

Tertio. Quod non tenentur ad prædicta, cum sint homines Principis qui etiam paratus est de dictis tenementis Domino Regi obedire per servitia consueta. Ad id quod dicit quod Princeps veniet simpliciter & absolute ad voluntatem Domini Regis: Respondetur quod cum nulli de dictis Cantredis ausi sint venire ad talem voluntatem propter causas prædictas, nec comitas eorum permittat Principem venire ad dictam voluntatem modo prædicto.

Item. Quod proceres regni procurent ut Domino Principi provideatur in mille libratis in aliquo loco Angliæ; dicatur quod illam provisionem non debet acceptare cum sit procurata per dictos proceres, qui nituntur ad exhæreditationem Principis, ut habeant terras suas in Wallia. Item idem princeps non tenetur dimittere hæreditatem suam & progenitorum suorum in Wallia à tempore Bruti, & etiam sibi confirmatam per Romanæ sedis Legatum, ut dictum est; & terram in Anglia acceptare, unde linguam, mores & leges ac consuetudines ignorat; ubi possent etiam sibi quædam malitiori imponi ex odio inveterato à vicinis Anglicis quibus terra illa privaretur in perpetuum.

Item.

APPENDIX.

Item. Ex quo Rex proponit privare Principem fua priftina hæreditate, non videtur probabile quod Rex permitteret ei habere terram in Anglia ubi nullum jus videtur habere. Et fi etiam non permitteretur Principi terra fterilis & inculta jure hæreditario ab antiquo & debita in Wallia; nullatenus permitteretur eidem in Anglia terra fertilis culta & habundans.

Item. Quod dictus Princeps ponat Dominum Regem in *Seyfino* Snawdon abfolute, perpetue & quiete: Dicatur quod cum Snawdon fit de appendiciis principatus Walliæ, quem ipfe & anteceffores fui tenuerunt à tempore Bruti, ut dictum eft; confilium fuum non permittit eum renuntiare dicto loco, & locum nimis fibi debitum in Anglia receptare.

Item. Populus Snawdon dicit, quod licet Princeps vellet dare Regi *Seyfinam* eorundem, ipfi tamen nollent homagium facere alicui extraneo, cujus linguam, mores, legefque penitus ignorant. Quia fic poffet contingere eos in perpetuum captivari, ac crudeliter tractari, ficut alii Cantredi circumquaque per Ballivos Regis ac alios regales alias tractati fuerunt, crudelius quam Saraceni; prout patet in rotulis quos vobis, miferunt fancte pater. Ifta funt dicenda pro Davide fratre Principis. Quod cum voluerit terram fanctam adire hoc faciet voluntarie & ex voto pro Deo non pro homine, unde invitus non peregrinabitur Deo dante; Qui coacta fervitia Deo novit difplicere. Et fi contingat ipfum in pofterum terram fanctam adire bona ductus voluntate, non propter hoc deberent ipfe & hæredes fui in perpetuum exhæreditari; immò potius præmium obtinere. Præterea quia Princeps, & fui caufa odii, ad aliquos concipiendi, vel lucri captandi non moverunt guerram alienas terras invadendo; fed fuam propriam hæreditatem jura libertatefque, necnon fuorum defendendo; Dominufque Rex & fui odio inveterato, & caufa lucrandi terras noftras guerram fecit: Credimus in hoc juftam guerram nos fovere, & fperamus in hac Deum nos velle juvare, ac in Ecclefiarum devaftatores divinam ultionem convertere, qui Ecclefias funditus deftruxerunt ac combufferunt, facra ex eis rapuerunt, Sacer-
dotes,

APPENDIX.

dotes, Clericos religiofos, claudos, furdos, mutos, infantes, ubera lactentes, ac debiles & miferabiles perfonas, ut ufque fexu occiderunt ; & alia enormia perpetrarunt, ficut in dictis rotulis vobis tranfmiffis contineatur : Unde abfit à fancta paternitate veftra fententiam aliquam fulminare in alios quam in illos qui prædicta perpetrârunt. Nos enim qui regalibus prædicta paffi fuimus, fperamus à vobis fuper præmiffis paternum folatium, & remedium obtinere ; & in prædictos facrilegos eorumque fautores, qui nullo fuper his privilegio defenduntur, animadvertere ; ne præ defectu dignæ correctionis feu ultionis in eos exercendo prædicta mala in perpetuum per alios trahantur in exemplum.

Mirantur etiam quamplures in terra noftra, quod confuluiftis nobis dimittere terram noftram propriam, & alienam adire inter hoftes noftros comerfando ; quia ex quo non poffumus pacem habere in terra quæ noftra eft ipfo jure noftro, minime poterimus in aliena terra inter hoftes noftros pacifice confervari : Et licet durum fit in guerra & infidiis vitam ducere; durius tamen eft funditus deftrui, & ad nihilum, nifi Deus avertat, deduci populum Chriftianum qui nihil aliud quærit nifi fua jura defendere; Unde neceffitas ad hoc nos cogit,& inimicorum cupiditas non offendit ; & vos, fancte pater, coram nobis dixiftis, quod vos fententiaftis in omnes qui impediunt pacem caufa odii vel lucri ; fed manifeftum eft qui funt illi qui guerrant iftis caufis.

Timor enim mortis, & incarcerationis, vel perpetuæ exhæreditationis, nulla obfervatio fœderum pactorum vel chartarum, tyrannica dominatio, vel multa alia confimilia cogunt nos effe in guerris ; & hoc Deo & vobis oftendimus, & petimus à vobis paternum adjutorium, ut patet in literis noftris.

Ad hoc multi alii in regno Angliæ offenderunt Regem & tamen nullos exhæredavit in perpetuum, ut dicitur ; unde fi aliqui ex noftris ipfum offenderunt injufte, dignum eft ut fatisfaciant prout poffint fine exhæredatione ; & ficut in vobis confidimus, fupplicamus quod ad hoc laboretis fancte pater: Nam etfi nobis imponatur quod fregimus pacem, tamen illi verius fregerunt qui nullum fœdus vel pactum nobis fervaverunt ;

APPENDIX.

vaverunt; qui nullam emendam de quærimoniis nobis fecerunt, ut patet in rotulis.

Primo auditis refcripfit Archiepifcopus Wallenfibus in hæc verba:

IN nomine Domini, *Amen*. Cum nos frater J. permiffione divina Cantuarienfis Ecclefiæ minifter humilis totius Angliæ primas, fcientes noftro incumbere officio, pro vobis Domine Leweline Princeps Walliæ ac fubditis veftris exponere nos & noftra fpretis viarum incommodis & periculis, veftram adjuverimus præfentiam oves erroneas reducturi; & fpeculatoris fungentis officio vobis myfteriæ vivæ vocis diximus pericula quæ genti veftræ videbamus luce clarius imminere, fubjunctis remediis eorundem; tefte optantes altiffimo *juxta* pontificale debitum cuilibet veftrum Ecclefiam minimo de corpore noftro pontem facere ad falutis littora reducendo. Tandem veftris auditis precibus & anguftiis eas ut neceffitatis veftræ nuntius præfentavimus regiæ majeftati, quem ab olim ad pœnitentes adverfarios introitum fcimus effe propitium; ut quidam de veftris & aliis ut nobis certis conftat indiciis ipfius clementia abutantur. Tractavimus infuper cum magnatibus & proceribus Angliæ præfentibus de modificatione gratiæ regiæ ipforum affiftentia noftris vobis fupplicationibus impetranda, cujus modificationis feriem per fervum Dei fratrem Johannem Wallenfem vobis mifimus in fcriptum, una cum confilio noftro quod vobis fecundum Deum falubrius videbatur; vos autem deliberationem veftram nobis in quadam remififtis cedula per eundem, cujus cedulæ pernitiofas latebras vobis paterno affectu præfentibus aperimus. Primò igitur dictis vos juri nolle cedere quatuor Cantredarum, quia progenitores veftri à temporibus Cambri filii Bruti in eifdem juris plenitudinem habuerunt; fed ne fimpliciores in vobis de fucceffu *hujufmodi* gloriantur, falva in omnibus pace veftra, vobis licet inviti ipfius radicem originis ex geftis Britonum & Anglorum ad memoriam revocamus. Difperfis enim olim Trojanis pro eo quod Paridis adulterium defenfarunt; fatemur

APPENDIX.

mur progenitores veſtræ multitudinis interpoſitis quibuſdam feditionibus fugæ ſibi præſidium aſſumpſiſſe; &
utinam non maneat in eis *hujuſmodi* contagii memoria
qui ſic *libera matrimonia* parvipendunt ut ſpurios &
inceſtu genitos à ſucceſſione hæreditaria ut dicitur non
repellunt, quin potius uxores legitimæ *Howeli da* patro-
ciniæ, contra Evangelium dato repudio fama teſte, vel
potius infamia repelluntur; qualiter demum Brutus
Dianæ præſagiis non ſine Diaboli præſtigiis per Ido-
latriam immolato Cervæ Venatitiæ obtentis, Inſulam Britannicam pervaſerit per famoſas hiſtorias de-
claratur; pervaſerit inquam inhabitatam Inſulam,
agentibus ſtatura proceris quarum peremit fortiſſimum
Corineus. Gentibus inquam de boreali *praſapia* quæ
non ſolum . . . . verum etiam *Scythiam* trans
Danubium ab occidente noſtro per Aquilonis latera uſque in Orientales terminos occupavit. Quam ergo
quæſumus fecerunt vobis injuriam Angli & Saxones e-
juſdem generis, ſi vos proceſſu temporis ab uſurpato
Dominio perturbarunt : Cum ſcriptum eſſe noveritis,
væ qui prædaris *in omne* prædaberis. Non oportet
autem ſimplices in radice adulterina proceſſu Idolola-
triæ, & uſurpationis ſpoliis gloriari. Progenitores inſuper veſtri moderniores, cum enervati deliciis ſibi
non ſufficerent defenſandis, obruentibus eos Scotis &
Pictis, denegato etiam eis Romani imperii præſidio
poſtulato, ad Germanorum refugium convolârunt, qui
venientes repudiarunt, hoſtes uſque in præſentem diem
ſuarum labores manuum manducantes. Ex his cauſis
quum ſedet ſola à vobis inſula olim populo plenâ, ve-
ſtro proſcribente Jeremia, quia Prophetæ tui viderunt
tibi vana & ſtulta; Item prædictorum juribus Cantredorum confirmationem legati frivole allegatis, cum
non fuerit intentionis ſuæ jura Regia, ſeu etiam jura
civilia & Canonica, ſicut nec potuit enervare : Pro
crimine enim leſæ majeſtatis, in quod vos incidiſſe
dicimini, juxta quod ſcribitur ſexta quæſtione. Se-
cunda paragrapho; *Si quis cum militibus,* & 22.
Quæſt. *ultima capitulo* de forma fidelitatis. Omne
perit jus hæreditarium & expirat : In Cantredis igitur prædictis in quibus ab olim Domino Regi jus dicitur adquiſitum, & in Snawdon ac cæteris quæ tenetis
jure

jure hæreditario, nihil poteftis ficut nec fubditi veftri, ut ex præallegatis videtur, nifi ex fola regia clementia præftolari. Dicitur demum quod populus non vult ad gratiam regiam convolare, quia Dominus Rex, nec pacta, nec juramenta, nec chartarum fœdera Principi confervavit. Et nos quærimus ex cujus vel quorum iftud fit judicio declaratum, nifi per vos qui in caufa propria judicium ufurpatis, & per fingulas luftrales periodos pacem infringitis, innocentes jugulatis, incendia facitis, munitiones regias pro viribus vaftatis; ac Domini Howellda quitalia injuriarum remedia in lege fua quam vidimus inftituit, autoritate quam ei Diabolus delegavit. Præterea in regem impungitis, dicentes, quod regales Ecclefias & perfonas Ecclefiafticas crudeli vaftavit tyrannide, & confumunt; Ad quod taliter refpondemus, quod Dominus Rex prædicta mala nec fieri mandavit, nec rata habuit, quin potius nobis obtulit ultronei, quod quam citò aderit oportunitas Ecclefiarum proponit difpendia refarcire; quod differt ufque ad fedatam guerræ tempeftatem, ne fi prius fieret deftruerentur iterum per latrones. Præterea timeris in Anglia honorem fufcipere, ne confequenter vobis occafionata malitia auferatur, cum tamen fateamini quod Dominus Rex nullum fuum exhæredaverit inimicum; quod fruftra vos timere credimus, fi legaliter vivere vos & veftri didiceritis, & non a pari cum domino veftro contendere vel certare. Mores vobis & populo veftro caufamini incognitos; & nos è contrario opinamur quod expediret vobis omnibus in modum alium & mores penitus transformari. Cum enim fitis ficut cæteri homines donis Dei gratuitis adornati, fed in veftro Anglo devoramini; ut nec Ecclefiam juvetis contra hoftes fidei militando; Nec Clerum ftudio fapientiæ, exceptis pauciffimis, decoretis; quin potius major pars veftrûm torpet otio & lafciviis, ut pene nefciat mundus vos effe populum, nifi per paucos ex vobis qui videntur ut plurimum in — mendicare. Deinde fcribitis quod creditis altiffimum vos juvare pro juftitia decertantes; utinam inquam altiffimus juvet vos falubriter & dirigat ad falutem. Sed ne ruinas aliquas Anglorum ex inconfideratione fua provenientes veftris

velitis

APPENDIX.

velitis meritis arrogare curetis advertere qualiter qui in coelis habitat fatuos fublimat & elevat ad modicum ut perpetuo allidat; fic certe olim populus Dei electus ante *harum* repertam civitatem pro unius Anathemate Confortis verfus in fugam quofdam fuorum perdidit bellatorum: Sic certe quater centena millia bellatorum duodecim tribuum *Ifrael* in fuo numero & fortitudine confidentes ab unius tribus modico populo, occifis ex 40 millibus bellatorum, per vices varias funt confufi: Cum tamen purgato unius Anathemate, prædicta Civitas finaliter deleta fuerit per illos, qui prius confufi fuerant, & per lacrymas placato Domino cum jejuniis, oblatis Sacrificiis, tribus illa quæ prævaluerat prius, per prius confufos quafi totaliter fit deleta; fic certe aliter flagellat Dominus filios quos recipit, & aliter quos decernit ut arbores fteriles extirpare. Ifta vobis fcribimus in cordis amaritudine ab his partibus recedentes, nec *prenidicare* intendimus falubriori confilio, fi vobis coelitus deftinetur, nec latere vos volumus quod nullum per vos invenimus excufationis fufficiens remedium, quo obftante minime debeatis in *excors Irnam* incidiffe pernuntiari: Dudum latet in Oxon confilio contra pacis regiæ turbatores, viam autem pacis aliam invenire non poffumus, nec adhuc in fpe fumus aliud obtinendi. Sed fi nobis aliquid confultius videatur agendum, vobis numquam claudemus gremium, nec auxilium denegabimus opportunum. Dat. apud Ruthelan 18 Calend. Decemb. Ann. Dom. 1282.

Lewelinus autem princeps Walliæ prædictus fpretis omnibus oblationibus & pacis formis poft fcriptis, invafit hoftiliter terram Domini Regis Angliæ deftruendo eam incendio & rapina, nec non homines terræ illius ad fe trahendo, & à bonitate pacis regiæ feparando. Qui tamen princeps infra menfem illum ignominofa morte primus de exercitu fuo occifus eft, per familiam Domini Cadmundi de mortuo mari, filii Domini Rogeri de mortuo mari; & totus exercitus fuus vel occifus, vel in fugam converfus in partibus Montis Gomerici die Veneris *proximo*, ante Feftum S. Lucæ, videlicet 3. Id. Decemb. fub Anno Dom. 1282. In —— decima litera dominicali D. currente.

A

A TABLE
OF THE
Moſt Remarkable Things in this BOOK.

A.

A Berffraw *deſtroyed by the* Iriſh, *page* 57.
Adelred *King of the* Weſt-Saxons *vanquiſhed by the* Britains, 15.
Adelred *married* Emma *Daughter of the Duke of* Normandy, *and the reaſons of it*, 70. *The conſequence of the Marriage,* 71. *Flies with his Wife and Children into* Normandy, 75. *Returns,* ibid. *His Death,* 78.
Aedan ap Blegorad *having ſlain his Competitor* Conan, *is proclaimed Prince of* North-Wales, 69. *Is ſlain with his four Sons in Battel,* 79.
Alan *the* 2d. *King of* Little Britain *aſſiſted* Cadwalader, 9. *Adviſed him to obey the Viſion,* 11.
Alfred *King, an Encourager of Learning, and Founder of the* Univerſiity *of* Oxford, 32. *Routs the* Danes, *ibid.* *Makes them forſwear the ſight of* Engliſh *Ground,* 33. *He cauſed the Laws of* Dyfnwal Moelmut *and Queen* Marſia *to be tranſlated into* Engliſh, &c. 43.

Alfred

The TABLE.

Alfred *proposed to be sent for to be King over the English*, 85. *Opposed by Earl* Goodwyn, 68. *Had his Eyes put out*, ibid.
Anarawd *Prince of* North-Wales *succeeds his Father* Rodri, 37. *Dyes, his Issue*, 45.
Anglesey *destroyed by the Men of* Dublin, 46. *Ravaged by* Madoc ap Meredith *Prince of* Powys, *but all his Men were cut off*, 175.
Arthur *King of* Britain, *his Sepulchre found in the Isle of* Afalon, 206. *The Inscription upon it*, 207.
Arthur *eldest Son to King* Henry *the Seventh, created Prince of* Wales, *and Dies at* Ludlow, 324.
Athelstane, *tho' a Bastard, the worthiest Prince of the* Saxon *Blood*, 48. *His Victory over the* Danes, Scots *and* Normans, *ibid. Removes the* Britains *to* Cornwal, *Dies*, 49.
Aulafe *and all his* Danes *received Baptism*, 49. *Swears never to molest* England, 66.

B.

Baldwin *Archbishop of* Canterbury, *the first that made his Visitation in* Wales, 208.
Bede *his Education and Writings*, 16.
Bible, *how, when, and by whom translated into* Welch, 326.
Blethyn *and* Rhywalhon *Princes of* North-Wales *assist* Edric *against the King of* England, 101. *A Rebellion formed against them by* Meredith, *and* Ithel ap Gruffydh, *ibid. Battel wherein* Rhywalhon *and* Ithel *were slain*, Blethyn *murdered* Rich. 104.
Britain, *how and when forsaken by the* Roman *Forces*, 1. *Invaded by the* Scots *and* Picts, *ibid*.
Britains, *their sad Complaints to* Ætius *thrice Consul*, 2. *The Reasons of their weakness*, 3 *and* 4. *Their Message to the* Saxons, 5. *The* Britains *of* Stratclwyd *and* Cumberland *settle in* North-Wales, 38.
Brochwel *once Prince of* Powys *a great Defender of the Monks of* Bangor, 23.
Bruce de William, *Lord of* Brecknock *under pretence of Friendship, barbarously murders* Sitfylht ap Dyfnwal, *his Son and followers*, 204.
Bruce *Sir* Edward, *his Letter to Sir* Griffydh Llwyd, 312, *and* 313.

Cadelh

The TABLE.

C.

Adelh *Prince of* South-Wales *dyes, his Iſſue,* 44.
Cadelh *takes* Caermardhyn, *and beats the* Normans *and* Flemings, 165. *Like to be murdered,* 170. *Gone upon Pilgrimage,* 171.
Cadwgan *murdered by* Madawc, 138.
Cadwalader *the laſt King of* Britain *of the* Britiſh *Race,* 8. *Retires to* Alan *King of* Little Britain, *ibid. Learned in a Viſion to go to* Rome, *and there ſhorn a Monk,* 10.
Cadwalader *with his Brother* Owen Gwynedh *from* North-Wales *in conjunction with ſeveral* South-Wales *Lords made an horrible ſlaughter of the* Normans *and* Flemings, *and drove them out of* South-Wales, 157, 158.
Cadwalader *forced to flee from his Brother* Owen *to* Ireland, 163. *Returns with* Iriſh *Forces, concludes a Peace with his Brother, made Priſoner by the* Iriſh, *reſcued by his Brother,* 164. *Eſcapes out of Priſon,* 171. *Flies to* England, *ibid. His Death and Iſſue,* 200.
Canterbury *redeemed by the Citizens from being burnt by the* Danes *for* 3000 *l.* 73. *Betrayed afterward to them and burnt,* 74.
Caradoc *King of* North-Wales *fights and is ſlain by the* Saxons, 21. *His Pedigree,* ibid.
Celibacy *enjoyned to the Clergy in a Synod held at* London, 127.
Chriſtian Faith *pure in the* Britiſh *Church,* 221.
Charles *Duke of* York *created Prince of* Wales, 328.
Charles *eldeſt Son of King* Charles *the Firſt created Prince of* Wales, 318.
Civil War in Wales, *and* Edwal *Son of* Meyric *the indiſputable Heir ſet up in* North-Wales, 67.
Clare, *Earl of; poſſeſſed himſelf of divers Strong-holds in* Cardigan, 177.
Clynnoc fawr *an Abby in* Arſon, 11. *When and by whom built,* 12. *Endowed by Prince* Anarawd, 39.
Cnute *the Dane choſen King, and his Cruelty to the* Engliſh *Hoſtages,* 75. *Returns to* England, *ibid. The* Northumbers *ſubmit to him,* 76. *Beſieges* London, *is Routed by* Edmund, *ibid. Combats* Edmund, *agree and divide* England *between them,* 78. *Generouſly puniſhes* Edmund Ironſide's *Murder,* ibid. *Marries* Emma Edelred's *Widdow,* 80. *Requires a Subſidy of the* Engliſh, *ibid. Made a pompous Journey to* Rome, 82.

Makes

The TABLE.

Makes the Scots *do him Homage,* ibid. *Dies, and is succeeded by his Son* Harold Harefoot, 83.
Conel *prognosticating the* Norman *Invasion, and Success,* 100.
Commotions in England, 158.
Conan, *War between him and his Brother* Howel, 22. *Dies,* 23. *His Pedigree,* ibid.
Conspiracy against William *the Conqueror by the* English *and the* Welch *detected, and the Conspirators executed,* 104.
Constable, Walter, *marries* Nest*'s Daughter, and has the Lordship of* Brecknock, 116. *A strange Passage related by him to* Henry *the First, concerning* Gruffydh ap Rhys, *ibid.*
Crogens, *used as a Term of reproach by the* English *to the* Welch, 223. *No reason for it,* 224.
Cynric *Prince* Owen*'s Son slain,* 162.

D.

Danes *begin to disturb* England, 20, 21. *They prevail and Winter in* England, 28. *They take and destroy* Winchester, 30. *Kill* Osbright *and* Elba *Kings of* Northumberland. 31. *Slew* Edmund *King of the* Angles, *ibid. Fought five Battles with* Ethelred, *ibid. They won* London *and* Redding, 33. *Routed by the* West-Saxons, 34. *Are defeated by* Alfred *and received the Christian Faith,* 37. *They harrass* North-Wales, 39. *Defeated by the* Armorican Britains, *ibid. Forced to rise from before* Exeter, *and spoil the Sea-Coast of* Wales, 41. *Receive a great overthrown,* 42. *They grow powerful, not only in* England *but also in* Ireland, 44. *Thrice overthrown by the* English, 45. *Cruelly overthrown by* Tottenhale, 46. *Routed by King* Edward, 48. *Driven out of the Kingdom by King* Edmund, 52. *Force the* English *to pay the* Dane-Gelt, 65. *Make a terrible Havock in* Wales, *and had Tribute paid them,* 66. *Make fresh devastations in* Wales *and* England, 70. *They are massacred by the* English, 71. *Force the* English *Nobility to buy their Peace for* 30000 l. 72. *They beat* Wolfkettel, 73. *Slew* Ethelstan *and ransack'd the Country,* 74.
Dafydh ab Owen *kill'd his Brother* Howel *in Battel, and gets to be Prince of* North-Wales, 195. *Secures his Brother* Maelgon, *reduces* Anglesey, *and banishes his*

Brethren,

The TABLE.

Brethren, 202. *Sends a Band of* Welch *to accompany King* Henry *into* Normandy, *ibid. Is dispossest by his eldest Brother's Son* Lhewelyn ap Iorwerth, 213. *Ungrateful to Prince* Lhewelyn *for his Liberty*, 124. Dafydh ap Lhewelyn *Prince of* Wales *did Homage at* Glocester *to the King of* England, 259. *Is excommunicated by the Bishop of* Bangor *for detaining his Brother* Gruffydh *in Prison, whom he refused to deliver at the King's Request*, 260. *Submits to the King of* England, 262. *Cajols the King to detain his Brother* Gruffydh *Prisoner*, ibid. *Engages the Pope on his side against the King, but he proves false,* 264. *Fights the* English *often with various Success,* ibid. *Dies without Issue,* 268.

Davids, St. *burnt by the* West-Saxons, 21. *Destroyed by the* Danes, 45. *Again by the* Danes, 69. *Destroyed by Strangers,* 107. *The Cathedral sacrilegiously robbed,* 111. *Made subject to the See of* Canterbury, 125. Dunstan, St. *Bishop of* Canterbury, *his Prediction and Death,* 61.

E.

EAster, *the* Britains *and* Saxons *quarrel about the Observation of it*, 18, 19.
Edgar, *advanced to the Kingdom in his Brother* Edwin's *room,* 56. *He wasts* North-Wales, *and agrees for a yearly Tribute of* 300 *Wolves,* ibid. *Regulates drinking Vessels because of the* Danes *excess*, 57. *Rowed in his Barge by six Kings on the River* Dee, 59.
Edgar Edeling *proclaimed King, forced into* Scotland, 101. *Received to King* William's *Mercy,* 103.
Edmund *King of* England's *Death, and the uncertain manner of it,* 53.
Edmund Ironside *slain by* Edric's *Son,* 78.
Edwal Foel *and his Brother* Elis *fight the* English, *and are slain,* 49. *Their Issue,* ibid.
Edward *sent for from* Normandy *and made King,* 86 *The* Confessor's *death,* 98.
Edward I. *King of* England *invades* Wales, *and prevails,* 283. *Insists upon Prince* Lhewelyn's *submission without reserve,* 292. *Sets Prince* Lhewelyn's *Head upon the Tower of* London, *and puts his Brother* David *to death,* 299. *Subdues all* Wales, *ibid. Kept his* Christmas *at* Aber-Conwey, 307. *In necessity, would taste no Wine*

The TABLE.

for the satisfaction of his Soldiers, 308. *Cuts down all the Woods in* Wales, *and builds* Beumaris-Castle, 309.
Edward *of* Caernarvon *first Prince of* Wales *of the* English *Blood,* 301. *Received Homage at* Chester *of all the Free-holders of* Wales, 310. *Goes farther into the Country to the same purpose,* ibid.
Edward *eldest Son to King* Edward II. *created Prince of* Wales, 313.
Edward *eldest Son to King* Edward III. *created Prince of* Wales, 313. *His Character and Death,* 314.
Edward *Son to* Henry VI. *created Prince of* Wales, 323. *Murdered,* ibid.
Edward *eldest Son to King* Edward VI. *created Prince of* Wales, *murdered,* 223.
Edward VI. *inclined to favour the* Welch, 323.
Edward *Son to* Richard III. *created Prince of* Wales, 324.
Edward *Son to* Henry VIII. *created Prince of* Wales. 325.
Edwyn *King of* England *vitious, dispossess'd and dies,* 56.
Egbert *sole Monarch in* Britain, 25. *Calls the Country* England, *ibid. He fights the* Danes, 26.
Eineon *invites the* Normans *into* Wales, *and persuades them to stay,* 112.
Elfleda, Mercian *Queen, her Valiant Acts both against the* Danes *and* Welch, 46. *Her death,* 47. *Left a Daughter* Alswyden *disinherited by King* Edward, *ibid.*
Ethelwulph *King of the* West-Saxons *paid* Peter-pence *to* Rome, 29. *Learned and devout,* ibid.
Eyes of several pluck'd out a barbarous Custom, 155.
Ethelbald *King of* Mercia *invades* Wales, 16. *In conjunction with* Adelred, *overthrow the* Britains, *ibid.*

F.

Flanders *a part of it drowned prejudicial to the* Welch, 128.
Flemings *settled in part of* VVales, 128.

G.

Gallio *routs the* Scots *and* Picts, 2. *Builds a Wall cross the Land,* ibid.
Gam, *Sir* David, *imprisoned by* Owen Glyndyfwr *and released* 321. *Revolts from* Owen, *ibid. His answer in* France *to* Henry V. *concerning the* French *Army, mortally wounded at* Agincourt, *Knighted and died,* 322.

Gavelkind,

The TABLE.

Gavelkind, *that Custom in* Wales, 22.
Geoffrey *of* Monmouth *made Bishop of St.* Davids, 171.
Glamorgan Lord*ship described*,314. *The best of it* Fitzhamon *the Chief of the Normans kept to himself*, 115.
Godwyn, *Earl, rebels against King* Edward, 89. *Invades the Land, and is reconciled to the King*, 90. *Dies suddenly sitting at the King's Table*, 91.
Gray, Reginald, *Lord of* Ruthyn *taken Prisoner by* Owen Glyndyfwr *and ransomed*, 316, 317.
Gruffydh ap Lhewelyn *declared Prince of* North-Wales,84. *His Country invaded by the* English *and* Danes, *and routed by him*, 85. *Reduced all* Wales *under his subjection*, ibid. *Routs* Howel *Prince of* South-Wales *at* Pencader, *ibid. Taken Prisoner by the* Irish *under the command of* Iago ap Edwal, *and recovered by his own Men*, 87. *Overcomes and slays* Gruffydh ap Rhyderch *and his Army,* &c. *ibid. Concludes a Peace with* Harold *King* Edward's *General*,94. *His Palace at* Ruthlan *burnt by the* English, *ibid. Prince* Gruffydh *murdered by* Harold's *Contrivance after he had reigned* 30 *years*, 95.
Gruffydh ap Conan *confirmed in the Principality of* Wales, 109. *Refused at first an accommodation with King* Henry, *at last sues and obtains Peace,* 141. *Caressed by the King, and promised to deliver up* Gruffydh ap Rhys, 143. *Dies* 158. *His Issue*, 159.
Gruffydh *the Son of* Rhys ap Tudor *laid claim to* South-VVales,143. *Flies to* North-VVales, 143. *Wished with his Brother* Howel *to withdraw into* South-VVales, 144. *Forced to bid open defyance to the King of* England, *ibid. The* Flemings *and* VVelch *Lords joyn together to oppose him*, 145. *He takes* Caermardhyn, 146. *Invited to the Government of* Cardigan-shire,*ibid. Succeeds*,147. *War at* Aberystwyth, 148. *Invidiously dispossess'd of his Estate*,154. *Dies*, 158.
Gruffydh *Son to the Lord* Rhys *succeeded his Father*, 116. *Plagued with his Brother* Maelgon, 219. *A hopeful Prince, dies*,222.
Gruffydh ap Conan ap Owen ap Gwynedh *buried in a Monk's Cowl, the Superstition of it*, 221.
Gruffydh *Prince* David's *Brother endeavouring to make his escape out of the* Tower *of* London, *breaks his Neck*, 263. *His Body recovered and conveyed to* Conwey *and honourably buried*, 270.

The TABLE.

Gruffydh Llwyd *Knighted by King* Edward I. *rebels*, 311. *Treats with Sir* Robert Bruce *for Succours against the* English, *with his Letter to him*, ibid. *Over-runs* North-Wales *and the Marches, and is taken Prisoner*, 313.
Gurmundus *a Norwegian from* Ireland, *invades* Britain, 7.
Gwenwynwyn *worsted by the* English, 218. *Refuses Homage to Prince* Lhewelyn, 222. *At last consents to it*, 223. *Detained Prisoner at* Shrewsbury, 225. *Set at Liberty, re-gains his Country*, 228. *Revolts from Prince* Lhewelyn *and is dispossest*, 242.

H.

Harold *succeeds* Canute *his Brother in* England, 83. *Dies, and is succeeded by* Hardi Canute *his Brother*, 85.
Harold's *favour with the King, envied by his Brother* Tosty, *who barbarously murder'd his Men at his House in* Hereford, *and his Saying*, 7. *Made King*, 98. *Slain*, 100.
Hasting *a Dane invades* France, 40. *His Policy to obtain* Limogis, 41. *His Cruelty*, ibid.
Henry I. *his partiality in favour of the* Normans, 127. *Makes his Brother* Robert *Prisoner, and puts out his Eyes*, 128. *Kind to* Cadwgan *the Father of* Owen, 132. *Invades* Wales *with three Armies* 140. *Overcomes the* French *King*, 151. *Lost his Children at Sea, and marries*, 152. *Invades* Wales, *in danger*, ibid. *Agrees with* Meredith ap Blethyn *and returns*, 153. *his Death and Successor*, 156.
Henry II. *sends the* Flemings *into* West-Wales, 173. *Invited to the Conquest of* Wales, *ibid. Repulsed, and in danger of his Life*, 174. *Concludes a Peace with Prince* Owen, 175. *Quarrels and concludes a Peace with* France, 187. *Invades* VVales *and brings Prince* Rhys *to do him Homage*, 188. *Invades* VVales *again with a most potent Army*, 190. *Returns without any thing memorable, and for Revenge puts out the Eyes of the Hostages*, 191. *Makes a third Expedition into* VVales *to as little purpose*, ibid. *Passes thro'* VVales, *receiving Homage of Prince* Rhys *in his way to the Conquest of* Ireland, 198, 199. *Returns thro'* VVales *and inclined to leave it in a peaceable Condition*, 199, 200. *Engaged in a Civil War against his Son* Henry, 201. *Makes a Peace with* France, *and his Children forced to submit*, 202. *Dies*, 209.

Henry

The TABLE.

Henry III. *King of* England *invades* Wales, *and is worsted* 251. *Invades* Wales *again* 254. *Makes* Henry *of* Monmouth *his General against the* Welch, *but with ill Success* 255. *Laments the death of the Earl of* Pembrock 256. *Invades* Wales, *and makes Prince* David *to submit* 261, 2'2 *Invades* Wales 263. *Fights the* Welch *with no success, and invites the* Irish *into* Anglesey 265. *Oppresses* Wales, *and returns dissatisfied* 269, 270. Item 274. *Wasts the Borders* 275. *Requires a Subsidy to subdue* Wales 276. *Dies* 280.

Henry, *eldest Son to* Henry IV. *created Prince of* W. 318.
Henry IV. *makes unmerciful Laws against the* Welch 319.
Henry *Duke of* York *created Prince of* VVales 324.
Henry VII. *grants the* VVelch *a Charter of Liberty, and directed a Commission to enquire into the Birth and Quality of his Grandfather* Owen Tudor 325.
Henry VIII. *incorporates the* VVelch *with the* English 326.
Henry *eldest Son to King* James *created Prince of* VVales 328.
Howel Dha *preferred to be Prince of all* VVales 50. *His Laws* ibid. *Goes to* Rome *to have them confirmed* 51. *His Death and Issue* 53.
Howel ap Ievan *expelled his Uncle* Iago, *and took the Government of* VVales *upon him* 59. *At last agree* 60. *Kills* Edwal Fychan, *and the Reasons of it* ibid. *Overthrows the* Danes 61: *Invades* England, *and is slain* 62. *He is succeeded by his Brother* Cadwalhan, *who was quickly slain* 63.
Howel *and* Meredith, *Prince* Lhewelyn's *Murderers invite the* Irish Scots *into* South-VVales 82. *Slew* Rhydderch, *and take the Government* 83. Meredith *slain by the Sons of* Conan ap Sitsylht *ibid.* Howel *attempts the recovery of* South-VVales, *is overcome and slain by Prince* Gruffydh *near* Tywy-Head 87.
Howel ap Grono *driven out of* Rydcors *Castle by the* Normans, 126. *Basely betrayed to them, and murthered,* 127.
Howel ap Owen Gwynedh *won the Castle of* Ewyas, 167. *with his Brether* Conan *quarrel with their Uncle* Cadwalader, *besiege and take the Castle of* Cynfael *from him,* 168. *makes* Cadwalader *his Prisoner, and possesses his Land,* ib. *he lost all his Country to* Cadelh, Meredith,

The TABLE.

and Rhys ap Gruffydh, *who put the Garison of* Llanrhyftyd *to the Sword*, 169.

I.

IAgo ap Edwal *recovers his Right to* North-Wales, 82. *Slain in Battle againſt* Gruffydh ap Lhewelyn, 84.
Ifor *ſent into Britain with an Army, by his Father* Alan, 13. *Routs the* Saxons, *ibid. Marries* Ethelburga, Kentwyn'*s Coſin, and ſucceeded him in the* Weſt-Saxon *Kingdom*, 14. *Founded* Glaſtenbury-Abby, *ib. Dyed at* Rome, 15.
John, *Arch-Deacon of* Llanbadarn *dies, and is canonized*, 160.
John K. *of* England *in his way to* Ireland *through* Wales, *diſcharged a Criminal that murther'd a Prieſt*, 226. *Famiſhed* Will. de Bruce, *and* Maud *his Aunt at* Windſor *after his return*, 227. *The reaſon of his Cruelty and Diſaffection to Prieſts*, ib. *Marches with a great Army into* VVales, *and returns without Succeſs*, 229, 230. *Makes a ſecond Expedition*, ib. *Orders* Foulk *Viſcount* Cardyff *to ſubdue thoſe that oppoſe in* South-VVales, *and they at laſt do him Homage, but quickly revolt*, 231, 232. *makes an Expedition into* VVales, 229. *Makes a ſecond and third, and hangs the Welch Pledges, reconciles himſelf to* Rome, *and engages in a Civil War with his Barons*, 237. *Dies, and is ſucceeded by his Son* Henry, 242.
Iorwerth ap Blethyn *revolts from the Earl of* Salop, 124. *Baſely uſed by* K. Henry *for it, the reaſon of it*, 125. *delivered out of Priſon* 133. *Forbids* Owen *and* Madawc *to retire to his Eſtate*, 134. *Beſet and ſlain by* Madawc *and* Llywarch ap Trahern 137.
Joſeph *Biſhop of* Llandaff *dies at* Rome 88.
Ireland *moleſted with Locuſts* 42.
Ithel *King of* Gwent *ſlain* 28.

L.

LHewelyn ap Sytſylht *makes himſelf Prince of all* VVales 79. *His good Government* ib. *Slays* Meuric *that rebelled againſt him with his own hand* 80. *ſuppreſſes another Rebellion* 81. *Baſely ſlain* ibid.
Lhewelyn P. *of* North-VVales *takes* David ap Owen *Priſoner* 217. *Receives Homage of moſt of the Welch Lords*

The TABLE.

Lords 222. *Conquers* Gwenwynwyn's *Country* 225. *Makes an Expedition into* South-VV. *and* Maelgon *flees* 225, 226. *Marries* Joan *King* John's *Daughter* 224. *Sues and obtains Peace of the King by the means of his wife* 231. *Animates the Lords of* North-Wales *to joyn with him in a Revolt against the King* 233. *Dispossesses the* English *of all their Holds in his Country* 237. *Takes* Shrewsbury, *though excommunicated by the Pope* 238. *Subdues* Cardigan *and* Carmarthen 240. *Reconciles the Lords in* South-Wales 241. *Subdues* Powis 242. *Refuses Assistance to King* John *against the Dauphine ibid. Makes* Rynald Bruce, *who had revolted, submit to him* 243. *Receives the Submission and Allegiance of the* Flemings *in* Dyfed *ibid. Subdues the revolted* Flemings *again* 246. *Makes his Son* Gruffydh *submit ibid. Complained of to the King of* England *by young* Rhys, *adjusts Matters with him* 247. *Seizes the Castle of* William Marshal *Earl of* Pembroke *in* Wales, *and occasions a War between them* 247, 248. *Worsts the* English *Army, pays Homage to* Henry III. 249. *Destroys the Marches* 252. *Makes a Descent upon* England 253. *Being joyned by the Earl of* Pembroke *against King* Henry, *routs his Army* 254. *Makes an Incursion into the King's Territories* 255. *Makes peace with the King* 256. *Sets his Son* Gruffydh *at liberty ibid. Buries his Princess* Joan 257. *Forced to quit the Siege of* Ruthlan 258. *Makes the* Welch *do Homage to his Son* David *ibid. Dies, his Character and Issue* 259.

Llewelyn ap Gruffydh, *and* Owen Gôch *his Brother, declared Princes of* North-Wales 269. *Quarrel, and* Owen *with his Brother* David, *made close Prisoners* 271. *Recovers the In-land Country of* North-Wales *from the* English 272. *Wastes* Cheshire *ibid. Beats the* Irish *by Sea* 273. *Desires peace with the King, but fails* 277. *Kind to Sir* Roger Mortimer 278. *Makes a Peace by the Popes Mediation with the King* 279. *Refuses to attend upon King* Edward's *Coronation* 280. *The Reasons for his refusal* 281. *An Accident made him pliable* 183. *Severe Conditions of Peace imposed upon him* 284. *Married to* Elianor *Earl* Montfords *Daughter at* Worcester 285. *Reconciled with his Brother* David *and joyn against*

the

The TABLE.

the English 286. *Offers to submit to the King conditionally* 292. *Sends a Letter to the Arch-Bishop of* Canterbury, *and the general Answer of the* Welch *to his Proposals* 293, 294, 295. *Betrayed in* Buellt *and killed* 297.
London *besieged by the* Danes 65.

M.

Mahael *dispossest of his Inheritance by his unnatural Mother* Nests *means, and how* 115.
Madoc ap Meredith *Prince of* Powis *sticks to the* English *Interest* 173.
Madawc *reconciled to* King Henry 138. *Taken Prisoner by* Meredith ap Blethin 139. *Has his Eyes pulled out by* Owen *ibid*.
Madawc ab Owen Gwynedh *sails into* America 196. *Plants a Colony there* ib.
Maelgon *disturbs* South-VVales 228. *Beaten by his Nephews* Rhys *and* Owen 229.
March, *Earl of, marries* Owen Glyndwr's *Daughter* 318. *Consented by indenture to divide* England *between* Owen, Piercy *and himself* 318.
Maud *the Empress lands in* England, *and is received at* Arundel 162.
Meredith ap Owen *possest of all* Wales 64. *Dispossest of* North-Wales 67. *And routed by* Edwal ap Meuric *their new Prince* 68. *Died without Issue Male* 69.
Meredith ap Owen *made Prince of* South-Wales 96. *Slain in Battel against* Caradoc ap Gruffydh 102.
Meredith *and* Rhys ap Gruffydh *prevail in* South-Wales 171. Meredith's *Death and Character* 172.
Merfyn frych *is made King of* Wales 24. *is slain* 27.
Merlyn, Ambrose, *and* Sylvester, *their Time, Country, and Prophesies* 10, 11.
Morgan Hen *dies, an Hundred Years old; his Marriage, Estate, and Issue* 58.
Morgan ap Owen *kills* Robert Fitz-Gilbert *and his Son* 157. *slain* 175.
Morgan ap Cadogan *repents of his Murder committed* 156.
Murders committed 156. Item 163.

Newmarch

The TABLE.

N.

Newmarch, *a Norman, obtains the Lordship of Breck-nock, and marries* Neft, *Daughter to* Llewelyn ap Gruffydh 115.
Normans *twice decimated and put to death in* England 86. *They wafte and plunder* Dyfed 103. *They seize upon the Lordship of* Glamorgan 113. *The Names of the Adventurers* ibid. *They poſſeſs themselves of several Lordships in* Wales 117. *Divers of them ſlain in* Cardigan *ibid. Routed again by* Cadwgan ap Blethyn *Prince of* South-Wales, *and their Caſtles deſtroyed* 118. *Slaughter'd divers times by the* Welch, *and forced to quit the Country* 119, 120.
Northumberland *invaded by the* Scots 109.

O.

Offa *King of* Mercia *makes a Ditch from Sea to Sea* 20. *his death* 21.
Owen ap Edwyn *a Traytor to his Country* 121. *Made Prince of* Wales *by the* English, *but ſoon left it* 122. *his Death and Pedigree* 126.
Owen *the Son of* Cadwgan *enamoured of* Neft *the Wife of* Gerald, *King* Henry's *Lieutenant in* Wales 129. *ſteals her away* ibid. *flies into* Ireland 135. *returns and waſts the Country, in conjunction with* Maradoc ap Riryd 133. *his Men ſlay an* Engliſh *Biſhop the cauſe of* Cadwgan *his Fathers being diſpoſſeſſed of his Eſtate* 135. *forced to flee into* Ireland *with* Madawc *ibid. returns, and is reconciled to the King* 138. *divides* Madawc's *Eſtate between himſelf and* Meredith ap Blethyn 139. *flees for fear of King* Henry *into* North-Wales 140. *reconciled to the King* 141. Owen *is brave and Knighted in* Normandy 142. *imployed by King* Henry *againſt* Gruffydh ap Rhys 148. *ſlain by* Gerald 149.
Owen Gwynedh *ſucceeds Prince of* North-Wales 160. *mightily concerned at the Death of his Son* Run 165. *takes and raſes the Caſtle of* Mould 166. *pulls out his Nephew* Cunedah's *Eyes, and caſtrates him* 170. *being provoked invades* Llandhinam 193. *dies, his Character and Iſſue* 194.
Owen Cyfeilioc *and* Owen Fychan *diſpoſſeſs* Iorwerth Gôch *of his Eſtate in* Powis 192. Cyfeilioc *dies, leaving his Eſtate to* Gwenwynwyn *his Son* 217. Owen

The TABLE.

Owen Glendwr *his Family, Education, and Employment* 315. *opposed by the Lord* Ruthyn *without Redress, takes up Arms, and makes him Prisoner* 316. *prevails, takes the Earl of* March *Prisoner* 317. *retakes* Aberyſtwyth *Caſtle* 319. *Summons a Parliament at* Machynlleth 320. *Secures* David Gam *upon a ſuſpicion of a deſign he had to murder him* 321. *burnt his Houſe, and his Verſe upon it* ibid.

P.

Patent *of Lands granted in* Wales *to the Earl of* Portland 302. *Commons addreſs upon it* 303. *King's Anſwer* 304.

Peekham, John, *Archbiſhop of* Canterbury *endeavours a Reconciliation of Prince* Llewelyn *and his Brother with the King* 286. *his Remonſtrance to the Prince and People* 287, 288, 289, 290. *Solicites the King on behalf of the* Welch 291. *Sends Articles to the* Welch 292. *Excommunicates the Prince of* Wales *and his Adherents* 297.

Peace *in general between* England *and* Wales, *except with Prince* Rhys, *who was forced to comply with the King* 176. *Unjuſtly dealt with* 177.

Powis, *Prince of, removes his Seat from* Pengwern *to* Ma:hraval 20. *An account of it while a Principality and a Lordſhip, with the ſeveral Diviſions and Poſſeſſors thereof, whether of* Britiſh *or* Engliſh *Blood,* 175, *to* 185.

R.

Rebellion *in the North, cauſed by Earl* Toſty's *Inſolence* 97. *Appeaſed* 98.

Rhydderch *ſeizes upon* South-Wales 82.

Rhydderch *and* Rhys *the Sons of* Rhydderch ap Ieſtyn *put in their Claim to* South-Wales 88.

Rhys *Brother to Prince* Gruffydh *taken by the* Engliſh, *and put to death at* Bulendun 91.

Rhys ap Owen *and* Rhyderch ap Caradoc *joyntly govern* South-Wales 105. *The latter dies* 106. *A Rebellion againſt the other* ibid. *Invaded alſo from* North-Wales, *flies, purſued, and ſlain* 187.

Rhys ap Theodor *allowed Prince of* South-Wales, *as lawful Heir* 107. *A Rebellion formed againſt him, flies into* Ireland, *returns and defeats his Enemy* 110.

Suppreſſes

The TABLE.

Suppresses another Rebellion 111. *Slain near* Brecknock *in a Fight against the invading* Normans *and his own rebellious Subjects* 112.

Rhys ap Gruffydh *Prince of* South-Wales *takes* Llanymddyfri *Castle* 177. *Subdues* Cardigan 178. *Gives* Henry II. *Hostages to observe the Peace made between them* ib. *Besieges* Carmarthen, *then forced to quit it* 179. *Possessed himself of divers Lands belonging to Foreigners in* Wales, *as did others according to his Example* 189. *Takes* Aberteifi *Castle and razes it* 191. *Subdues* Owen Cyfeilioc 197. *Brings the Lords of* South-Wales *at Enmity with* K. Henry *to do him Homage* 203. *Makes a great Feast at* Christmas *at* Aberteifi, *where the Bards of* North-Wales *and* South-Wales *strive for the Mastery* 205, 206. *Takes advantage upon King* Henry'*s death to enlarge his Country* 209. *His Family diminishes* 210. *Made Prisoner by his own Sons* 211. *Escapes* 212. *Takes two of his Sons Prisoners* 214. *Enlarges his Conquest, and defeats the* English *and* Normans 214, 215. *Dies, his Character and Issue* 216.

Rhys Fychan *takes* Lhanymdhyfri *Castle* 227.

Rhys ap Gruffydh ap Rhys *prevails in* South-Wales 239. *Does Homage to* Henry III. 145. *Dies* 147.

Rhys ap Meredith *unfaithful to his Country* 304. *Knighted by King* Edward; *revolts* 305. *Defeated, taken Prisoner, and executed* 306.

Rhythmarch *Archbishop of S.* David *dies* 122.

Richard *King of* England'*s feasts in the* Holy Land 210. *Taken Prisoner in* Austria *ibid. Died of his Wounds received at* Chalons *in* France 219.

Richard *of* Bourdeaux *created Prince of* Wales 315.

Robert Cyrthois *rebels against his Father in* Normandy 110.

Robert *Earl of* Salop *rebels against* Henry I. 122. *Engages the* Welch *in the Quarrel* 123. *Seeks Aid of* Magnus, Harold'*s Son, and fails; banished with his Brother* Arnulph *into* Normandy 124.

Robert de Belissimo *a great Disturber of the* Welch *committed to perpetual imprisonment by King* Henry 139.

Roderic Molwynoc *succeeded* Ifor, *Anno* 720. 15. *Driven by the* Saxons *out of the Western Countries to his Inheritance in* North-Wales 17. *dyed soon after* 18.

Roderic *the Great, Prince of* Wales 27. *Beats the*
Danes

The TABLE.

Danes *out of his Country* 33. *Fights the* English, *and with his Brother* Gwyriad *is slain* 34. *His Pedigree and Division of* Wales *between his three Sons* ibid. *his Imprudence herein* 36.

S.

Saxons, *their Answer to the* British *Message* 5. *They first repel the* Scots *and* Picts 6. *Enter into League with the* Scots *ib. They incroach upon the* Britains 19.
Scots *and* Picts *invade* Britain 1.
Siward, Earl, *his Saying upon his Sons being slain in Battel* 19. *His soldierly Temper at his death* 92.
South-Wales *invaded twice in one Year by* Ievaf *and* Iago *Princes of* North-Wales 55. *They quarrel, and the Consequence of it* 57. *Embroyled in War between* Rhys ap Gruffydh *and* Rhys Fychan, *and the former supported by the* English 235, 236.
Stephen King *of* England *agrees with the King of* Scots 157. *Ravages* Scotland 160. *Suppresses Insurrections at home, and routs the* Scots *by his Lieutenants* 161. *Besieges* Arundel *Castle in vain* 162. *Takes* Lincoln, *is defeated and taken Prisoner* ibid. *Exchanged for Earl* Robert, *and overthrown a second time at* Wilton 163. *Wins the Battel of* Farendon, *agrees with* Henry *the Empress's Son, and dies* 172.
Stewards, *the Family, and their Original* 91, 92.
Sulien *Archbishop of* S. Davids *dies* 111.
Sulien *a learned Man of* Llanbadarn *dies* 165.
Swane *the* Dane *wasts the Isle of* Man. *Lands in* North-Wales 68. *Kills* Edwal *Prince of the Country* ib. *His Success in* England, *and esteemed King hereof* 74, 75.
Swane *King of* Denmark *invades* England, *and takes* York 102. *forced to fly* ibid.

T.

Trahern Fychan *strangely hanged* 217.
Trahern ap Caradoc *made Prince of* North-Wales 105. *His Country invaded from* Ireland *by* Gruffydh ap Conan *the right Heir* ibid. *They fight, and* Trahern *with his Cosins worsted and all slain* 108.
Tribute, *paid by the Prince of* Wales *to the Kings of* England 48.
Tudor Vaughan ap Grono *his Family, would be stiled*
Knigh:

The TABLE.

Knight, and his Reasons for it to King Edward III. *who confirmed the Honour of it* 314.

V.

VOrtigern *invites the* Saxons *into* Britain 5. Vortimer *repels the* Saxons 7.

W.

WAles *wasted by the* Mercians 24. *by King* Egbert ibid. *Divided into three Provinces* 27. *Invaded by the* English 52. *Forcibly managed by* Ievaf *and* Iago *Princes of* North-Wales *only* 56. *Afflicted by the* Danes, *and a Murrain* 65. *Gives Hostages to pay the antient Tribute* 95. *Seldom governed by the right Heir* 109. *Wasted by the* English *as far as* Anglesey 121. *Embroiled with Civil Divisions* 151. *Item* 153, 154. *In great scarcity* 276. *annnext to the Crown of* England 300.

Walwey *King* Arthur's *Nephew his Tomb found, whose Body was of a prodigious length* 110.

Welch *quarrel amongst themselves* 22. Ibid. 23. *They defeat the* Mercians *at* Conwey, *and call it* Dial Rhodri 38. *Disable the* Danes *and* English *that invaded them, then fall out among themselves* 61. *Too late see the folly of foreign Aid* 114. *Miserably slaughter'd* 130, 131. *Being at peace from abroad, they fall to their wonted Method of destroying one another* 208. *Complain to their Prince of their Oppression from the* English 272. *Beaten by the* English 279. *Worst the* English 297, 298. *Beaten in* Buelht *ibid. Revolt because of an heavy Tax from* Edward I. *every where* 306. *Beat the* English 307. *Take the King's Carriages* ibid. *Routed by the Earl of* Warwick 308. *Beat the* Marchers, *but are at last overcome, and their Leader* Madoc *made Prisoner* 309.

Welch *Minstrels reformed, whereof were three sorts* 159.
William *Duke of* Normandy *claims the Crown of* England 98. *Lands at* Hastings, *and defeats the* English 100.

William I. *goes with an Army on Pilgrimage to S.* Davids 110.

William Rufus *invades the* Welch *without Success* 118. *Item* 120. *Killed* 122.

FINIS.

BOOKS Printed for and sold by ROBERT CLAVELL.

THE plausible Arguments of a *Roman* Catholick, answered by an *English* Protestant, in the *Welch* Tongue. Price 4 *d*.

The Church-History clear'd from the *Roman* Forgeries and Corruptions found in the Councils and *Baronius*, in Four Parts; from the beginning of Christianity, to the end of the Fifth General Council. By *Thomas Comber*, D. D. Dean of *Durham*. 4º.

An Historical Vindication of the Divine Right of Tythes, from Scripture, Reason, and the Opinion and Practice of Jews, Gentiles, and Christians in all Ages; to which is added a Discourse concerning Excommunication. By *Tho. Comber*, D. D. Dean of *Durham*. 4º.

www.ingramcontent.com/pod-product-compliance
Lightning Source LLC
Chambersburg PA
CBHW051850300426
44117CB00006B/343